Yamaha Trail Bikes Owners Workshop Manual

**by Mike Stubblefield,
Alan Ahlstrand
and John H Haynes**

Member of the Guild of Motoring Writers

Models covered:

PW50, 1981 through 2003
PW80, 1991 through 2003
RT100, 1990 through 2000
RT180, 1990 through 1998
TT-R90, 2000 through 2003
TT-R125, 1999 through 2003
TT-R225, 1999 through 2003
TT-R250, 1999 through 2003
XT225, 1992 through 2003
XT350, 1985 through 2000
Does not include 2003 TT-R90E models

(2350 - 5R3)

ABCDE
FGHIJ
K

Haynes Publishing
Sparkford Nr Yeovil
Somerset BA22 7JJ England

Haynes North America, Inc
861 Lawrence Drive
Newbury Park
California 91320 USA

Acknowledgments

Our thanks to G. P. Sports, Santa Clara, California, for providing the facilities used for these photographs; to Chris Campbell, service manager, for arranging the facilities and fitting the mechanical work into his shop's busy schedule; and to Craig Wardner, service technician, for doing the mechanical work and providing valuable technical information.

A book in the Haynes Owners Workshop Manual Series

Printed in the U.S.A.

ISBN: 978-1-62092-065-7

ISBN: 1-62092-065-4

Library of Congress Control Number: 2013941297

13-368

Contents

2000 TT-R225

About this manual

Its purpose

The purpose of this manual is to help you get the best value from your motorcycle. It can do so in several ways. It can help you decide what work must be done, even if you choose to have it done by a dealer service department or a repair shop; it provides information and procedures for routine maintenance and servicing; and it offers diagnostic and repair procedures to follow when trouble occurs.

We hope you use the manual to tackle the work yourself. For many simpler jobs, doing it yourself may be quicker than arranging an appointment to get the vehicle into a shop and making the trips to leave it and pick it up. More importantly, a lot of money can be saved by avoiding the expense the shop must pass on to you to cover its labor and overhead costs. An added benefit is the sense of satisfaction and accomplishment that you feel after doing the job yourself.

Using the manual

The manual is divided into Chapters, and each Chapter is divided into parts (A, B and C) covering different models. Each Chapter is divided into numbered Sections, which are headed in bold type between horizontal lines. Each Section consists of consecutively numbered paragraphs.

At the beginning of each numbered Section you will be referred to any illustrations which apply to the procedures in that Section. The reference numbers used in illustration captions pinpoint the pertinent Section and the Step within that Section. That is, illustration 3.2 means the illustration refers to Section 3 and Step (or paragraph) 2 within that Section.

Procedures, once described in the text, are not normally repeated. When it's necessary to refer to another Chapter, the reference will be given as Chapter and Section number. Cross references given without use of the word "Chapter" apply to Sections and/or paragraphs in the same Chapter. For example, "see Section 8" means in the same Chapter.

References to the left or right side of the vehicle assume you are sitting on the seat, facing forward.

Motorcycle manufacturers continually make changes to specifications and recommendations, and these, when notified, are incorporated into our manuals at the earliest opportunity.

Even though we have prepared this manual with extreme care, neither the publisher nor the author can accept responsibility for any errors in, or omissions from, the information given.

NOTE

A **Note** provides information necessary to properly complete a procedure or information which will make the procedure easier to understand.

CAUTION

A **Caution** provides a special procedure or special steps which must be taken while completing the procedure where the Caution is found. Not heeding a Caution can result in damage to the assembly being worked on.

WARNING

A **Warning** provides a special procedure or special steps which must be taken while completing the procedure where the Warning is found. Not heeding a Warning can result in personal injury.

Introduction to Yamaha Trail Bikes

This manual covers a range of the most popular trail bikes and dual-purpose bikes manufactured by Yamaha.

The PW50 is an entry-level play bike. Its small size and simple controls make it ideal for novice riders. The engine is a single-cylinder, air-cooled two-stroke design. Fuel is delivered to the cylinder by a single Mikuni piston-valve carburetor. Power is delivered to the rear wheel through a one-speed transmission, centrifugal clutch and shaft drive. The front suspension consists of two fork legs; the rear suspension uses twin coil-over shocks. Drum brakes are used at front and rear.

The PW80 is a a slightly larger play bike, well suited for beginning riders who have outgrown the PW50 in size and skill. The engine is a single-cylinder, air-cooled two-stroke design. Fuel is delivered to the cylinder by a single Mikuni carburetor. Power is delivered to the rear wheel through a three-speed transmission and chain drive. The front suspension consists of two fork legs; the rear suspension uses a single coil-over shock. Drum brakes are used at front and rear.

The RT100 and RT180 are lightweight trail bikes. Both use standard motorcycle controls for the clutch and brakes, and both use a single-cylinder, air-cooled two-stroke engine with a Mikuni carburetor. The RT100 has a five-speed transmission. The RT180 has six speeds.

The RT100 has drum brakes at front and rear, while the RT180 uses a front disc brake and rear drum brake.

The TT-R series (TT-R90, TT-R125, TT-R225 and TT-R250) are new-generation Yamaha trail bikes. All use air-cooled, overhead camshaft, four-stroke singles. The TT-R250 uses twin camshafts; the others all have a single overhead camshaft. The TT-R90 and TT-R125 use a single piston-valve Mikuni carburetor. The TT-R225 and TT-R 250 use a single Mikuni CV carburetor. The TT-R90 uses drum brakes at front and rear. The TT-R125 and TT-R225 use a disc brake at the front and a drum brake at the rear. The TT-R250 uses disc brakes at front and rear. All models have a conventional fork-type front suspension and a a monoshock rear suspension. Chain final drive is used on all TT-R models.

The XT225 and XT350 are dual-purpose bikes. Their design is similar to the TT-R series, but they include the necessary lights and emission controls to make them street legal. The XT225 uses a single overhead cam engine, while the XT350 uses a twin-cam design. Both motorcycles use a front disc brake, rear drum brake, fork-type front suspension, monoshock rear suspension and chain final drive.

Identification numbers

The frame serial number is stamped into the steering head **(see illustration)**. The engine number is stamped into a pad which is located on the crankcase **(see illustration)**. Both of these numbers should be recorded and kept in a safe place so they can be furnished to law enforcement officials in the event of a theft.

The frame serial number, engine serial number and carburetor identification number should also be kept in a handy place (such as with your driver's license) so they are always available when purchasing or ordering parts for your machine.

The models covered by this manual are as follows:

PW50, 1981 through 2003
PW80, 1991 through 2003
RT100, 1990 through 2000
RT180, 1990 through 1998
TT-R90, 2000 through 2003
TT-R125, 1999 through 2003
TT-R225, 1999 through 2003
XT225, 1992 through 2003
TT-R250, 1999 through 2003
XT350, 1985 through 2000

Identifying model years

The procedures in this manual identify the vehicles by model year. The model year is included in a decal on the frame, but in case the decal is missing or obscured, the following table identifies the initial frame number or production code of each model year. In some cases, the same production code is used for several years running, and the model year is identified by the initial frame number. In other cases, the production code is used for only one model and year.

PW50

Year	Initial frame number, VIN or production code
1981	4X4000101
1982	4X4200101
1983	4X4260101
1984	Not produced
1985	36E-000101
1986	36E-020101
1987	36E-040101
1988	Not produced
1989	Not produced
1990	3PT-000101
1991	3PT-027101
1992	3PT-015101
1993	3PT-070101
1994	3PT-099101
1995	3PT-138101
1996	Not available
1997	3PTM
1998	3PTR
1999	3PTU
2000	3PTW
2001	JYA3PT03*1A011478
2002	JYA3PT03*2A025570
2003	JYA3PT03*3YA035675

The engine serial number is located on the crankcase

The vehicle identification number is stamped on the steering head

PW80

Year	Initial frame number, VIN or production code
1991	3RV-000101
1992	3RV-010101
1993	3RV-020101
1994	3RV-032101
1995	Not available
1996	Not available
1997	3RVA
1998	3RVB
1999	3RVC
2000	3RVD
2001	JYA30VR3*1A009833
2002	JYA30VR3*2A022247
2003	JYA30VR3*3A030278

RT100

Year	Initial frame number, VIN or production code
1990	3UL-000101
1991	Not available
1992	3UL-038101
1993	3UL-043101
1994	3UL-050101
1995	3UL-057101
1996	Not available
1997	3UL-VA080907
1998	3UL9
1999	3ULA
2000	3ULB

RT180

Year	Initial frame number, VIN or production code
1990	3VA0-M0000101
1991	3VCA0-M00005596
1992	3VCA0-N1007696
1993	Not available
1994	Not available
1995	3VCA0-S0010096
1996	Not available
1997	3VCW0-VA012845
1998	Not available

TT-R90

Year	Initial frame number, VIN or production code
2000	JYACB03W-YA000014 (except California)
	JYACB03Y-YA000004 (California)
2001	JYACB03Y*1A000806
2002	JYACB03Y*2A010688
2003	JYACB03Y*3A020377

TT-R125

Year	Initial frame number, VIN or production code
1999	JYAC07Y-YA000239
2000	JYAC07W-YA000032 (except California)
	JYAC07Y-YA000019 (California)
2001	JYACE07Y*1A004634
2002	JYACE07Y*2A023525
2003	JYACE07Y*3A047527

TT-R225

Year	Initial frame number, VIN or production code
1999	5FG1 (except California)
	5FG2 (California)
2000	9C6CG043-YO000101 (except California)
	9C6CG04Y-YO001301 (California)
2001	9C6CG043*10002801 (except California)
	9C6CG04Y*10001601 (California)
2002	5FGA (except California)
	5FGB (California)
2003	5FGD (except California)
	5FGE (California)

TT-R250

Year	Initial frame number, VIN or production code
1999	5GF1 (except California)
	5GF2 (California)
2000	JYACG07W-YA002045
	JYACG07Y-YA000309
2001	JYACG073*1A000003 (except California)
	JYACG07Y*1A000509 (California)
2002	JYACG073*2A000638 (except California)
	JYACG07Y*2A000609 (California)
2003	JYACG073*3A001795 (except California)
	JYACG07Y*3A000919 (California)

XT225

Year	Initial frame number, VIN or production code
1992	4BE-000101 (except California)
	4BE-013001 (California)
1993	4BE-014101 (except California)
	4BE-020001 (California)
1994	4BE-024101
1995	4BE-029101 (except California)
	4BE-033001 (California)
1996	Not available
1997	JYA4BEEO-YA044681 (except California)
	JYA4BECO-YA044571 (California)
1998	Not available
1999	JYA4BEEO-XA049000 (except California)
	JYA4BECO-XA049073 (California)
2000	JYA4BEEO-YA051371 (except California)
	JYA4BECO-YA051537 (California)
2001	JYA4BEE0*1A054565 (except California)
	Initial frame number not available. 4BEW (California)
2002	4BEY (except California)
	5RK1 (California)
2003	JYA4BEE0*3A062627 (except California)
	JYA4BEC0*3A062951 (California)

XT350

Year	Initial frame number, VIN or production code
1985	57T-000101 (except California)
	56R-000101 (California)
1986	57T-000701 (except California)
	56R-010101 (California)
1987	2KJ-000101 (except California)
	2GK-000101 (California)
1988	2KJ-008101 (except California)
	2GK-002101 (California)
1989	3NV-000101 (except California)
	3NV-004101 (California)
1990	3NV-005101 (except California)
	3NV-008101 (California)
1991	3NV-010101
1992	3NV-013101 (except California)
	3NV-018101 (California)
1993	3Y1-021101 (except California)
	3Y1-023101 (California)
1994	3NV-026101 (except California)
	3NV-029101 (California)
1995	3NV-031101 (except California)
	3NV-033101 (California)
1996	Not available
1997	JYA3NVEO-VA041271 (except California)
	JYA3NVCO-VA041271 (California)
1998	JYA3NVEO-VA041371 (except California)
	JYA3NVCO-VA041371 (California)
1999	3NVV (except California)
	3NVW (California)
2000	JYA3NVEO-YA048150 (except California)
	JYA3NVCO-YA048494 (California)

General specifications

PW50

Wheelbase	855 mm (33.7 inches)
Overall length	1245 mm (49.0 inches)
Overall width	575 mm (22.6 inches)
Overall height	715 mm (28.1 inches)
Seat height	485 mm (19.1 inches)
Ground clearance	105 mm (4.1 inches)
Weight with oil and full fuel tank	39 kg (86 lbs)

PW80

Wheelbase	1055 mm (41.5 inches)
Overall length	1540 mm (60.6 inches)
Overall width	640 mm (25.2 inches)
Overall height	880 mm (34.6 inches)
Seat height	635 mm (25.0 inches)
Ground clearance	185 mm (7.3 inches)
Weight with oil and full fuel tank	61 kg (134 lbs)

RT100

Wheelbase	1190 mm (46.9 inches)
Overall length	1795 mm (70.7 inches)
Overall width	760 mm (29.9 inches)
Overall height	960 mm (37.8 inches)
Seat height	730 mm (28.7 inches)
Ground clearance	200 mm (7.9 inches)
Weight with oil and full fuel tank	79 kg (174 lbs)

RT180

Wheelbase	1345 mm (52.93 inches)
Overall length	2050 mm (80.71 inches)
Overall width	860 mm (33.86 inches)
Overall height	1175 mm (46.26 inches)
Seat height	860 mm (33.86 inches)
Ground clearance	290 mm (11.42 inches)
Weight with oil and full fuel tank	112 kg (247 lbs)

TT-R90

Wheelbase	1040 mm (40.9 inches)
Overall length	1525 mm (57.0 inches)
Overall width	605 mm (23.8 inches)
Overall height	865 mm (34.1 inches)
Seat height	625 mm (24.6 inches)
Ground clearance	100 mm (3.94 inches)
Weight with oil and full fuel tank	63.7 kg (140 lbs)

TT-R125

Wheelbase	1270 mm (50.0 inches)
Overall length	
Except Canada	1885 mm (74.2 inches)
Canada	1890 mm (74.4 inches)
Overall width	795 mm (31.3 inches)
Overall height	1085 mm (42.7 inches)
Seat height	805 mm (31.7 inches)
Ground clearance	295 mm (11.6 inches)
Weight with oil and full fuel tank	84 kg (185 lbs)

TT-R225

Wheelbase	1350 mm (53.1 inches)
Overall length	2070 mm (81.5 inches)
Overall width	820 mm (32.2 inches)
Overall height	1160 mm (45.7 inches)
Seat height	855 mm (33.6 inches)
Ground clearance	285 mm (11.2 inches)
Weight with oil and full fuel tank	126 kg (278 lbs)

TT-R250

Wheelbase	1405 mm (55.3 inches)
Overall length	2095 mm (82.5 inches)
Overall width	835 mm (32.9 inches)
Overall height	1260 mm (49.6 inches)
Seat height	915 mm (36.0 inches)
Ground clearance	305 mm (12.0 inches)
Weight with oil and full fuel tank	124 kg (273 lbs)

XT225

Wheelbase	1350 mm (53.1 inches)
Overall length	2070 mm (81.5 inches)
Overall width	800 mm (31.5 inches)
Overall height	1160 mm (45.7 inches)
Seat height	810 mm (31.9 inches)
Ground clearance	285 mm (11.2 inches)
Weight with oil and full fuel tank	121 kg (267 lbs)

XT350

Wheelbase	1420 mm (55.9 inches)
Overall length	2240 mm (88.2 inches)
Overall width	865 mm (34.1 inches)
Overall height	1210 mm (47.6 inches)
Seat height	855 mm (33.6 inches)
Ground clearance	275 mm (10.8 inches)
Weight with oil and full fuel tank	
Except California	130 kg (287 lbs)
California	131 kg (289 lbs)

Maintenance techniques, tools and working facilities

Basic maintenance techniques

There are a number of techniques involved in maintenance and repair that will be referred to throughout this manual. Application of these techniques will enable the amateur mechanic to be more efficient, better organized and capable of performing the various tasks properly, which will ensure that the repair job is thorough and complete.

Fastening systems

Fasteners, basically, are nuts, bolts and screws used to hold two or more parts together. There are a few things to keep in mind when working with fasteners. Almost all of them use a locking device of some type (either a lock washer, locknut, locking tab or thread adhesive). All threaded fasteners should be clean, straight, have undamaged threads and undamaged corners on the hex head where the wrench fits. Develop the habit of replacing all damaged nuts and bolts with new ones.

Rusted nuts and bolts should be treated with a penetrating oil to ease removal and prevent breakage. Some mechanics use turpentine in a spout type oil can, which works quite well. After applying the rust penetrant, let it -work for a few minutes before trying to loosen the nut or bolt. Badly rusted fasteners may have to be chiseled off or removed with a special nut breaker, available at tool stores.

If a bolt or stud breaks off in an assembly, it can be drilled out and removed with a special tool called an E-Z out (or screw extractor). Most dealer service departments and motorcycle repair shops can perform this task, as well as others (such as the repair of threaded holes that have been stripped out).

Flat washers and lock washers, when removed from an assembly, should always be replaced exactly as removed. Replace any damaged washers with new ones. Always use a flat washer between a lock washer and any soft metal surface (such as aluminum), thin sheet metal or plastic. Special locknuts can only be used once or twice before they lose their locking ability and must be replaced.

Tightening sequences and procedures

When threaded fasteners are tightened, they are often tightened to a specific torque value (torque is basically a twisting force). Overtightening the fastener can weaken it and cause it to break, while under-tightening can cause it to eventually come loose. Each bolt, depending on the material it's made of, the diameter of its shank and the material it is threaded into, has a specific torque value, which is noted in the Specifications. Be sure to follow the torque recommendations closely.

Fasteners laid out in a pattern (i.e. cylinder head bolts, engine case bolts, etc.) must be loosened or tightened in a sequence to avoid warping the component. Initially, the bolts/nuts should go on finger tight only. Next, they should be tightened one full turn each, in a crisscross or diagonal pattern. After each one has been tightened one full turn, return to the first one tightened and tighten them all one half turn, following the same pattern. Finally, tighten each of them one quarter turn at a time until each fastener has been tightened to the proper torque. To loosen and remove the fasteners the procedure would be reversed.

Disassembly sequence

Component disassembly should be done with care and purpose to help ensure that the parts go back together properly during reassembly. Always keep track of the sequence in which parts are removed. Take note of special characteristics or marks on parts that can be installed more than one way (such as a grooved thrust washer on a shaft). It's a good idea to lay the disassembled parts out on a clean surface in the order that they were removed. It may also be help-ful to make sketches or take instant photos of components before removal.

When removing fasteners from a component, keep track of their locations. Sometimes threading a bolt back in a part, or putting the washers and nut back on a stud, can prevent mix-ups later. If nuts and bolts can't be returned to their original locations, they should be kept in a compartmented box or a series of small boxes. A cupcake or muffin tin is ideal for this purpose, since each cavity can hold the bolts and nuts from a particular area (i.e. engine case bolts, valve cover bolts, engine mount bolts, etc.). A pan of this type is especially helpful when working on assemblies with very small parts (such as the carburetors and the valve train). The cavities can be marked with paint or tape to identify the contents.

Whenever wiring looms, harnesses or connectors are separated, it's a good idea to identify the two halves with numbered pieces of masking tape so they can be easily reconnected.

Gasket sealing surfaces

Throughout any motorcycle, gaskets are used to seal the mating surfaces between components and keep lubricants, fluids, vacuum or pressure contained in an assembly.

Many times these gaskets are coated with a liquid or paste type gasket sealing compound before assembly. Age, heat and pressure can sometimes cause the two parts to stick together so tightly that they are very difficult to separate. In most cases, the part can be loosened by striking it with a soft-faced hammer near the mating surfaces. A regular hammer can be used if a block of wood is placed between the hammer and the part. Do not hammer on cast parts or parts that could be easily damaged. With any particularly stubborn part, always recheck to make sure that every fastener has been removed.

Avoid using a screwdriver or bar to pry apart components, as they can easily mar the gasket sealing surfaces of the parts (which must remain smooth). If prying is absolutely necessary, use a piece of wood, but keep in mind that extra clean-up will be necessary if the wood splinters.

After the parts are separated, the old gasket must be carefully scraped off and the gasket surfaces cleaned. Stubborn gasket material can be soaked with a gasket remover (available in aerosol cans) to soften it so it can be easily scraped off. A scraper can be fashioned from a piece of copper tubing by flattening and sharpening one end. Copper is recommended because it is usually softer than the surfaces to be scraped, which reduces the chance of gouging the part. Some gaskets can be removed with a wire brush, but regardless of the method used, the mating surfaces must be left clean and smooth. If for some reason the gasket surface is gouged, then a gasket sealer thick enough to fill scratches will have to be used during reassembly of the components. For most applications, a non-drying (or semi-drying) gasket sealer is best.

Hose removal tips

Hose removal precautions closely parallel gasket removal precautions. Avoid scratching or gouging the surface that the hose mates against or the connection may leak. Because of various chemical reactions, the rubber in hoses can bond itself to the metal spigot that the hose fits over. To remove a hose, first loosen the hose clamps that secure it to the spigot. Then, with slip joint pliers, grab the hose at the clamp and rotate it around the spigot. Work it back and forth until it is completely free, then pull it off (silicone or other lubricants will ease removal if they can be applied between the hose and the outside of the spigot). Apply the same lubricant to the inside of the hose and the outside of the spigot to simplify installation.

If a hose clamp is broken or damaged, do not reuse it. Also, do not reuse hoses that are cracked, split or torn.

Spark plug gap adjusting tool

Feeler gauge set

Control cable pressure luber

Hand impact screwdriver and bits

Tools

A selection of good tools is a basic requirement for anyone who plans to maintain and repair a motorcycle. For the owner who has few tools, if any, the initial investment might seem high, but when compared to the spiraling costs of routine maintenance and repair, it is a wise one.

To help the owner decide which tools are needed to perform the tasks detailed in this manual, the following tool lists are offered: *Maintenance and minor repair*, *Repair and overhaul* and *Special*. The newcomer to practical mechanics should start off with the *Maintenance and minor repair* tool kit, which is adequate for the simpler jobs. Then, as confidence and experience grow, the owner can tackle more difficult tasks, buying additional tools as they are needed. Eventually the basic kit will be built into the *Repair and overhaul* tool set. Over a period of time, the experienced do-it-yourselfer will assemble a tool set complete enough for most repair and overhaul procedures and will add tools from the *Special* category when it is felt that the expense is justified by the frequency of use.

Maintenance and minor repair tool kit

The tools in this list should be considered the minimum required for performance of routine maintenance, servicing and minor repair work. We recommend the purchase of combination wrenches (box end and open end combined in one wrench); while more expensive than

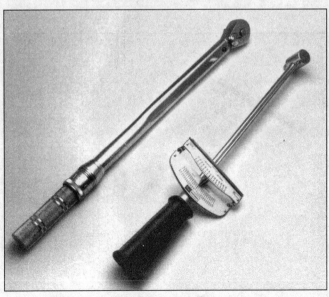

Torque wrenches (left - click; right - beam type)

Snap-ring pliers (top - external; bottom - internal)

Allen wrenches (left), and Allen head sockets (right)

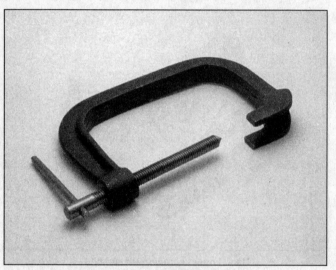

Valve spring compressor

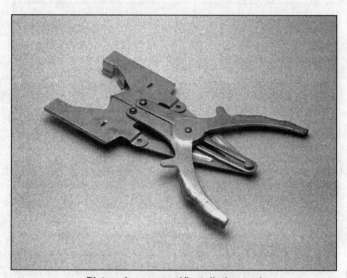

Piston ring removal/installation tool

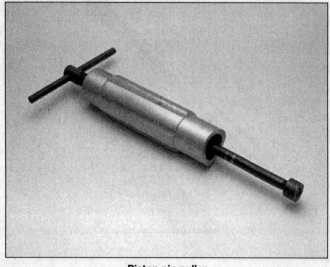

Piston pin puller

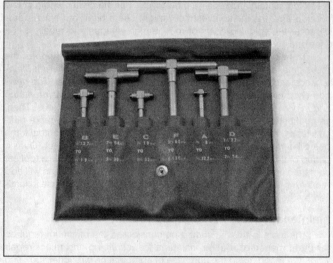

Telescoping gauges

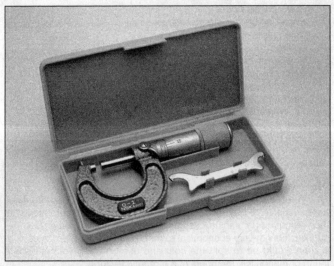

0-to-1 inch micrometer

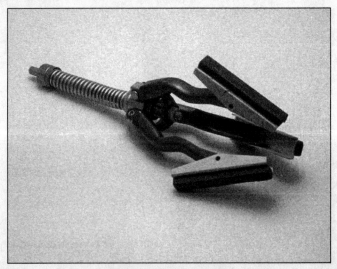

Cylinder surfacing hone

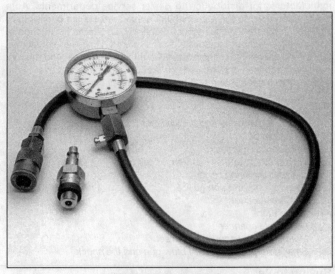

Cylinder compression gauge

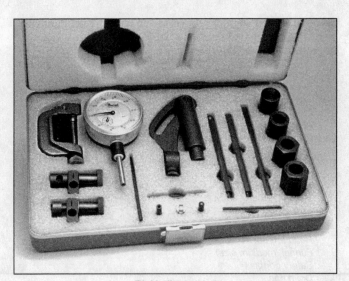

Dial indicator set

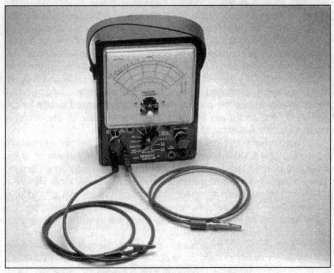

Multimeter (volt/ohm/ammeter)

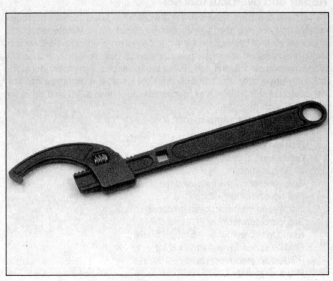

Adjustable spanner

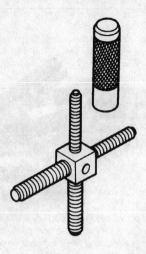

Alternator rotor puller

open-ended ones, they offer the advantages of both types of wrench.

> *Combination wrench set (6 mm to 22 mm)*
> *Adjustable wrench - 8 in*
> *Spark plug socket (with rubber insert)*
> *Spark plug gap adjusting tool*
> *Feeler gauge set*
> *Standard screwdriver (5/16 in x 6 in)*
> *Phillips screwdriver (No. 2 x 6 in)*
> *Allen (hex) wrench set (4 mm to 12 mm)*
> *Combination (slip-joint) pliers - 6 in*
> *Hacksaw and assortment of blades*
> *Tire pressure gauge*
> *Control cable pressure luber*
> *Grease gun*
> *Oil can*
> *Fine emery cloth*
> *Wire brush*
> *Hand impact screwdriver and bits*
> *Funnel (medium size)*
> *Safety goggles*
> *Drain pan*
> *Work light with extension cord*

Repair and overhaul tool set

These tools are essential for anyone who plans to perform major repairs and are intended to supplement those in the Maintenance and minor repair tool kit. Included is a comprehensive set of sockets which, though expensive, are invaluable because of their versatility (especially when various extensions and drives are available). We recommend the 3/8 inch drive over the 1/2 inch drive for general motorcycle maintenance and repair (ideally, the mechanic would have a 3/8 inch drive set and a 1/2 inch drive set).

> *Alternator rotor removal tool*
> *Socket set(s)*
> *Reversible ratchet*
> *Extension - 6 in*
> *Universal joint*
> *Torque wrench (same size drive as sockets)*
> *Ball pein hammer - 8 oz*
> *Soft-faced hammer (plastic/rubber)*
> *Standard screwdriver (1/4 in x 6 in)*
> *Standard screwdriver (stubby - 5/16 in)*
> *Phillips screwdriver (No. 3 x 8 in)*
> *Phillips screwdriver (stubby - No. 2)*
> *Pliers - locking*
> *Pliers - lineman's*

> *Pliers - needle nose*
> *Pliers - snap-ring (internal and external)*
> *Cold chisel - 1/2 in*
> *Scriber*
> *Scraper (made from flattened copper tubing)*
> *Center punch*
> *Pin punches (1/16, 1/8, 3/16 in)*
> *Steel rule/straightedge - 12 in*
> *Pin-type spanner wrench*
> *A selection of files*
> *Wire brush (large)*

Note: *Another tool which is often useful is an electric drill with a chuck capacity of 3/8 inch (and a set of good quality drill bits).*

Special tools

The tools in this list include those which are not used regularly, are expensive to buy, or which need to be used in accordance with their manufacturer's instructions. Unless these tools will be used frequently, it is not very economical to purchase many of them. A consideration would be to split the cost and use between yourself and a friend or friends (i.e. members of a motorcycle club).

This list primarily contains tools and instruments widely available to the public, as well as some special tools produced by the vehicle manufacturer for distribution to dealer service departments. As a result, references to the manufacturer's special tools are occasionally included in the text of this manual. Generally, an alternative method of doing the job without the special tool is offered. However, sometimes there is no alternative to their use. Where this is the case, and the tool can't be purchased or borrowed, the work should be turned over to the dealer service department or a motorcycle repair shop.

> *Paddock stand (for models not fitted with a centerstand)*
> *Valve spring compressor*
> *Piston ring removal and installation tool*
> *Piston pin puller*
> *Telescoping gauges*
> *Micrometer(s) and/or dial/Vernier calipers*
> *Cylinder surfacing hone*
> *Cylinder compression gauge*
> *Dial indicator set*
> *Multimeter*
> *Adjustable spanner*
> *Manometer or vacuum gauge set*
> *Small air compressor with blow gun and tire chuck*

Buying tools

For the do-it-yourselfer who is just starting to get involved in motorcycle maintenance and repair, there are a number of options available when purchasing tools. If maintenance and minor repair is the extent of the work to be done, the purchase of individual tools is satisfactory. If, on the other hand, extensive work is planned, it would be a good idea to purchase a modest tool set from one of the large retail chain stores. A set can usually be bought at a substantial savings over the individual tool prices (and they often come with a tool box). As additional tools are needed, add-on sets, individual tools and a larger tool box can be purchased to expand the tool selection. Building a tool set gradually allows the cost of the tools to be spread over a longer period of time and gives the mechanic the freedom to choose only those tools that will actually be used.

Tool stores and motorcycle dealers will often be the only source of some of the special tools that are needed, but regardless of where tools are bought, try to avoid cheap ones (especially when buying screwdrivers and sockets) because they won't last very long. There are plenty of tools around at reasonable prices, but always aim to purchase items which meet the relevant national safety standards. The expense involved in replacing cheap tools will eventually be greater than the initial cost of quality tools.

It is obviously not possible to cover the subject of tools fully here. For those who wish to learn more about tools and their use, there is a book entitled *Motorcycle Workshop Practice Manual* (Book no. 1454) available from the publishers of this manual. It also provides an introduction to basic workshop practice which will be of interest to a home mechanic working on any type of motorcycle.

Care and maintenance of tools

Good tools are expensive, so it makes sense to treat them with respect. Keep them clean and in usable condition and store them properly when not in use. Always wipe off any dirt, grease or metal chips before putting them away. Never leave tools lying around in the work area.

Some tools, such as screwdrivers, pliers, wrenches and sockets, can be hung on a panel mounted on the garage or workshop wall, while others should be kept in a tool box or tray. Measuring instruments, gauges, meters, etc. must be carefully stored where they can't be damaged by weather or impact from other tools.

When tools are used with care and stored properly, they will last a very long time. Even with the best of care, tools will wear out if used frequently. When a tool is damaged or worn out, replace it; subsequent jobs will be safer and more enjoyable if you do.

Working facilities

Not to be overlooked when discussing tools is the workshop. If anything more than routine maintenance is to be carried out, some sort of suitable work area is essential.

It is understood, and appreciated, that many home mechanics do not have a good workshop or garage available and end up removing an engine or doing major repairs outside (it is recommended, however, that the overhaul or repair be completed under the cover of a roof).

A clean, flat workbench or table of comfortable working height is an absolute necessity. The workbench should be equipped with a vise that has a jaw opening of at least four inches.

As mentioned previously, some clean, dry storage space is also required for tools, as well as the lubricants, fluids, cleaning solvents, etc. which soon become necessary.

Sometimes waste oil and fluids, drained from the engine or cooling system during normal maintenance or repairs, present a disposal problem. To avoid pouring them on the ground or into a sewage system, simply pour the used fluids into large containers, seal them with caps and take them to an authorized disposal site or service station. Plastic jugs (such as old antifreeze containers) are ideal for this purpose.

Always keep a supply of old newspapers and clean rags available. Old towels are excellent for mopping up spills. Many mechanics use rolls of paper towels for most work because they are readily available and disposable. To help keep the area under the motorcycle clean, a large cardboard box can be cut open and flattened to protect the garage or shop floor.

Whenever working over a painted surface (such as the fuel tank) cover it with an old blanket or bedspread to protect the finish.

Buying parts

Once you have found all the identification numbers, record them for reference when buying parts. Since the manufacturers change specifications, parts and vendors (companies that manufacture various components on the machine), providing the ID numbers is the only way to be reasonably sure that you are buying the correct parts.

Whenever possible, take the worn part to the dealer so direct comparison with the new component can be made. Along the trail from the manufacturer to the parts shelf, there are numerous places that the part can end up with the wrong number or be listed incorrectly.

The two places to purchase new parts for your motorcycle - the accessory store and the franchised dealer - differ in the type of parts they carry. While dealers can obtain virtually every part for your motorcycle, the accessory dealer is usually limited to normal high wear items such as shock absorbers, tune-up parts, various engine gaskets, cables, chains, brake parts, etc. Rarely will an accessory outlet have major suspension components, cylinders, transmission gears, or cases.

Used parts can be obtained for roughly half the price of new ones, but you can't always be sure of what you're getting. Once again, take your worn part to the wrecking yard (breaker) for direct comparison.

Whether buying new, used or rebuilt parts, the best course is to deal directly with someone who specializes in parts for your particular make.

Safety first!

Professional mechanics are trained in safe working procedures. However enthusiastic you may be about getting on with the job at hand, take the time to ensure that your safety is not put at risk. A moment's lack of attention can result in an accident, as can failure to observe simple precautions.

There will always be new ways of having accidents, and the following is not a comprehensive list of all dangers; it is intended rather to make you aware of the risks and to encourage a safe approach to all work you carry out on your bike.

Essential DOs and DON'Ts

DON'T start the engine without first ascertaining that the transmission is in neutral.

DON'T suddenly remove the pressure cap from a hot cooling system - cover it with a cloth and release the pressure gradually first, or you may get scalded by escaping coolant.

DON'T attempt to drain oil until you are sure it has cooled sufficiently to avoid scalding you.

DON'T grasp any part of the engine or exhaust system without first ascertaining that it is cool enough not to burn you.

DON'T allow brake fluid or antifreeze to contact the machine's paint work or plastic components.

DON'T siphon toxic liquids such as fuel, hydraulic fluid or antifreeze by mouth, or allow them to remain on your skin.

DON'T inhale dust - it may be injurious to health (see *Asbestos* heading).

DON'T allow any spilled oil or grease to remain on the floor - wipe it up right away, before someone slips on it.

DON'T use ill fitting wrenches or other tools which may slip and cause injury.

DON'T attempt to lift a heavy component which may be beyond your capability - get assistance.

DON'T rush to finish a job or take unverified short cuts.

DON'T allow children or animals in or around an unattended vehicle.

DON'T inflate a tire to a pressure above the recommended maximum. Apart from over stressing the carcase and wheel rim, in extreme cases the tire may blow off forcibly.

DO ensure that the machine is supported securely at all times. This is especially important when the machine is blocked up to aid wheel or fork removal.

DO take care when attempting to loosen a stubborn nut or bolt. It is generally better to pull on a wrench, rather than push, so that if you slip, you fall away from the machine rather than onto it.

DO wear eye protection when using power tools such as drill, sander, bench grinder etc.

DO use a barrier cream on your hands prior to undertaking dirty jobs - it will protect your skin from infection as well as making the dirt easier to remove afterwards; but make sure your hands aren't left slippery. Note that long-term contact with used engine oil can be a health hazard.

DO keep loose clothing (cuffs, ties etc. and long hair) well out of the way of moving mechanical parts.

DO remove rings, wristwatch etc., before working on the vehicle - especially the electrical system.

DO keep your work area tidy - it is only too easy to fall over articles left lying around.

DO exercise caution when compressing springs for removal or installation. Ensure that the tension is applied and released in a controlled manner, using suitable tools which preclude the possibility of the spring escaping violently.

DO ensure that any lifting tackle used has a safe working load rating adequate for the job.

DO get someone to check periodically that all is well, when working alone on the vehicle.

DO carry out work in a logical sequence and check that everything is correctly assembled and tightened afterwards.

DO remember that your vehicle's safety affects that of yourself and others. If in doubt on any point, get professional advice.

IF, in spite of following these precautions, you are unfortunate enough to injure yourself, seek medical attention as soon as possible.

Asbestos

Certain friction, insulating, sealing and other products - such as brake pads, clutch linings, gaskets, etc. - contain asbestos. *Extreme care must be taken to avoid inhalation of dust from such products since it is hazardous to health*. If in doubt, assume that they *do* contain asbestos.

Fire

Remember at all times that gasoline (petrol) is highly flammable. Never smoke or have any kind of naked flame around, when working on the vehicle. But the risk does not end there - a spark caused by an electrical short-circuit, by two metal surfaces contacting each other, by careless use of tools, or even by static electricity built up in your body under certain conditions, can ignite gasoline (petrol) vapor, which in a confined space is highly explosive. Never use gasoline (petrol) as a cleaning solvent. Use an approved safety solvent.

Always disconnect the battery ground (earth) terminal before working on any part of the fuel or electrical system, and never risk spilling fuel on to a hot engine or exhaust.

It is recommended that a fire extinguisher of a type suitable for fuel and electrical fires is kept handy in the garage or workplace at all times. Never try to extinguish a fuel or electrical fire with water.

Fumes

Certain fumes are highly toxic and can quickly cause unconsciousness and even death if inhaled to any extent. Gasoline (petrol) vapor comes into this category, as do the vapors from certain solvents such as trichloroethylene. Any draining or pouring of such volatile fluids should be done in a well ventilated area.

When using cleaning fluids and solvents, read the instructions carefully. Never use materials from unmarked containers - they may give off poisonous vapors.

Never run the engine of a motor vehicle in an enclosed space such as a garage. Exhaust fumes contain carbon monoxide which is extremely poisonous; if you need to run the engine, always do so in the open air or at least have the rear of the vehicle outside the workplace.

The battery

Never cause a spark, or allow a naked light near the vehicle's battery. It will normally be giving off a certain amount of hydrogen gas, which is highly explosive.

Always disconnect the battery ground (earth) terminal before working on the fuel or electrical systems (except where noted).

If possible, loosen the filler plugs or cover when charging the battery from an external source. Do not charge at an excessive rate or the battery may burst.

Take care when topping up, cleaning or carrying the battery. The acid electrolyte, even when diluted, is very corrosive and should not be allowed to contact the eyes or skin. Always wear rubber gloves and goggles or a face shield. If you ever need to prepare electrolyte yourself, always add the acid slowly to the water; never add the water to the acid.

Electricity

When using an electric power tool, inspection light etc., always ensure that the appliance is correctly connected to its plug and that, where necessary, it is properly grounded (earthed). Do not use such appliances in damp conditions and, again, beware of creating a spark or applying excessive heat in the vicinity of fuel or fuel vapor. Also ensure that the appliances meet national safety standards.

A severe electric shock can result from touching certain parts of the electrical system, such as the spark plug wires (HT leads), when the engine is running or being cranked, particularly if components are damp or the insulation is defective. Where an electronic ignition system is used, the secondary (HT) voltage is much higher and could prove fatal.

Motorcycle chemicals and lubricants

A number of chemicals and lubricants are available for use in vehicle maintenance and repair. They include a wide variety of products ranging from cleaning solvents and degreasers to lubricants and protective sprays for rubber, plastic and vinyl.

Contact point/spark plug cleaner is a solvent used to clean oily film and dirt from points, grime from electrical connectors and oil deposits from spark plugs. It is oil free and leaves no residue. It can also be used to remove gum and varnish from carburetor jets and other orifices.

Carburetor cleaner is similar to contact point/spark plug cleaner but it usually has a stronger solvent and may leave a slight oily residue. It is not recommended for cleaning electrical components or connections.

Brake system cleaner is used to remove grease or brake fluid from brake system components (where clean surfaces are absolutely necessary and petroleum-based solvents cannot be used); it also leaves no residue.

Silicone-based lubricants are used to protect rubber parts such as hoses and grommets, and are used as lubricants for hinges and locks.

Multi-purpose grease is an all purpose lubricant used wherever grease is more practical than a liquid lubricant such as oil. Some multi-purpose grease is colored white and specially formulated to be more resistant to water than ordinary grease.

Gear oil (sometimes called gear lube) is a specially designed oil used in transmissions and final drive units, as well as other areas where high friction, high temperature lubrication is required. It is available in a number of viscosities (weights) for various applications. The transmission on two-stroke models is lubricated by four-stroke motor oil.

Motor oil, of course, is the lubricant specially formulated for use in the engine. It normally contains a wide variety of additives to prevent corrosion and reduce foaming and wear. Motor oil comes in various weights (viscosity ratings) of from 5 to 80. The recommended weight of the oil depends on the seasonal temperature and the demands on the engine. Light oil is used in cold climates and under light load conditions; heavy oil is used in hot climates and where high loads are encountered. Multi-viscosity oils are designed to have characteristics of both light and heavy oils and are available in a number of weights from 5W-20 to 20W-50. On two-stroke models, the engine oil is injected into the fuel stream by a pump. On four-stroke models, the same oil supply is shared by the engine and transmission.

Gas additives perform several functions, depending on their chemical makeup. They usually contain solvents that help dissolve gum and varnish that build up on carburetor and intake parts. They also serve to break down carbon deposits that form on the inside surfaces of the combustion chambers. Some additives contain upper cylinder lubricants for valves and piston rings.

Brake fluid is a specially formulated hydraulic fluid that can withstand the heat and pressure encountered in brake systems. Care must be taken that this fluid does not come in contact with painted surfaces or plastics. An opened container should always be resealed to prevent contamination by water or dirt.

Chain lubricants are formulated especially for use on the final drive chains of vehicles so equipped. A good chain lube should adhere well and have good penetrating qualities to be effective as a lubricant inside the chain and on the side plates, pins and rollers. Most chain lubes are either the foaming type or quick drying type and are usually marketed as sprays.

Degreasers are heavy duty solvents used to remove grease and grime that may accumulate on engine and frame components. They can be sprayed or brushed on and, depending on the type, are rinsed with either water or solvent.

Solvents are used alone or in combination with degreasers to clean parts and assemblies during repair and overhaul. The home mechanic should use only solvents that are non-flammable and that do not produce irritating fumes.

Gasket sealing compounds may be used in conjunction with gaskets, to improve their sealing capabilities, or alone, to seal metal-to-metal joints. Many gasket sealers can withstand extreme heat, some are impervious to gasoline and lubricants, while others are capable of filling and sealing large cavities. Depending on the intended use, gasket sealers either dry hard or stay relatively soft and pliable. They are usually applied by hand, with a brush, or are sprayed on the gasket sealing surfaces.

Thread locking agent is an adhesive locking compound that prevents threaded fasteners from loosening because of vibration. It is available in a variety of types for different applications.

Moisture dispersants are usually sprays that can be used to dry out electrical components such as the fuse block and wiring connectors. Some types can also be used as treatment for rubber and as a lubricant for hinges, cables and locks.

Waxes and polishes are used to help protect painted and plated surfaces from the weather. Different types of paint may require the use of different types of wax polish. Some polishes utilize a chemical or abrasive cleaner to help remove the top layer of oxidized (dull) paint on older vehicles. In recent years, many non-wax polishes (that contain a wide variety of chemicals such as polymers and silicones) have been introduced. These non-wax polishes are usually easier to apply and last longer than conventional waxes and polishes.

Troubleshooting

Contents

Engine doesn't start or is difficult to start

1   Starter motor does not rotate (electric start models)

1   Engine kill switch Off.
2   Fuse blown. Check fuse (Chapter 4C).
3   Battery voltage low. Check and recharge battery (Chapter 4C).
4   Starter motor defective. Make sure the wiring to the starter is secure. Test starter relay (Chapter 4C). If the relay is good, then the fault is in the wiring or motor.
5   Starter relay faulty. Check it according to the procedure in Chapter 4C.
6   Starter switch not contacting. The contacts could be wet, corroded or dirty. Disassemble and clean the switch (Chapter 4C).
7   Wiring open or shorted. Check all wiring connections and harnesses to make sure that they are dry, tight and not corroded. Also check for broken or frayed wires that can cause a short to ground (see wiring diagrams,end of book).
8   Ignition (main) switch defective. Check the switch according to the procedure in Chapter 4C. Replace the switch with a new one if it is defective.
9   Engine kill switch defective. Check for wet, dirty or corroded contacts. Clean or replace the switch as necessary (Chapter 4C).
10   Starting circuit cut-off relay, neutral switch, reverse switch or front brake switch defective. Check the relay and switches according to the procedure in Chapter 4C. Replace the switch with a new one if it is defective.

2   Starter motor rotates but engine does not turn over (electric start models)

1   Starter motor clutch defective. Inspect and repair or replace (Chapter 4C).
2   Damaged starter idle or wheel gears. Inspect and replace the damaged parts (Chapter 4C).

3   Starter works but engine won't turn over (seized) (electric start models)

    Seized engine caused by one or more internally damaged components. Failure due to wear, abuse or lack of lubrication. Damage can include seized valves, rocker arms, camshaft, piston, crankshaft, connecting rod bearings, or transmission gears or bearings. Refer to Chapter 2 for engine disassembly.

4   No fuel flow

1   No fuel in tank.
2   Tank cap air vent obstructed. Usually caused by dirt or water. Remove it and clean the cap vent hole.
3   Clogged strainer in fuel tap. Remove and clean the strainer (Chapter 1).
4   Fuel line clogged. Pull the fuel line loose and carefully blow through it.
5   Inlet needle valve clogged. A very bad batch of fuel with an unusual additive may have been used, or some other foreign material has entered the tank. Many times after a machine has been stored for many months without running, the fuel turns to a varnish-like liquid and forms deposits on the inlet needle valve and jets. The carburetor should be removed and overhauled if draining the float chamber does not solve the problem.

5   Engine flooded

1   Float level too high. Check as described in Chapter 3 and replace the float if necessary.
2   Inlet needle valve worn or stuck open. A piece of dirt, rust or other debris can cause the inlet needle to seat improperly, causing excess fuel to be admitted to the float bowl. In this case, the float chamber should be cleaned and the needle and seat inspected. If the needle and seat are worn, then the leaking will persist and the parts should be replaced with new ones (Chapter 3).
3   Starting technique incorrect. Under normal circumstances (i.e., if all the carburetor functions are sound) the machine should start with little or no throttle. When the engine is cold, the choke should be operated and the engine started without opening the throttle. When the engine is at operating temperature, only a very slight amount of throttle should be necessary. If the engine is flooded, turn the fuel tap off and hold the throttle open while cranking the engine. This will allow additional air to reach the cylinder. Remember to turn the fuel tap back on after the engine starts.

6   No spark or weak spark

1   Ignition switch Off.
2   Engine kill switch turned to the Off position.
3   Spark plug dirty, defective or worn out. Locate reason for fouled plug using spark plug condition chart and follow the plug maintenance procedures in Chapter 1.
4   Spark plug cap or secondary wiring faulty. Check condition. Replace either or both components if cracks or deterioration are evident (Chapter 4).
5   Spark plug cap not making good contact. Make sure that the plug cap fits snugly over the plug end.
6   CDI magneto defective. Check the unit, referring to Chapter 4 for details.
7   CDI unit defective. Check the unit, referring to Chapter 4 for details.
8   Ignition coil defective. Check the coil, referring to Chapter 4.
9   Ignition or kill switch shorted. This is usually caused by water, corrosion, damage or excessive wear. The kill switch can be disassembled and cleaned with electrical contact cleaner. If cleaning does not help, replace the switches (Chapter 4).
10   Wiring shorted or broken between:
   a) *Ignition switch and engine kill switch (or blown fuse)*
   b) *CDI unit and engine kill switch*
   c) *CDI and ignition coil*
   d) *Ignition coil and plug*
   e) *CDI unit and CDI magneto*
    Make sure that all wiring connections are clean, dry and tight. Look for chafed and broken wires (Chapter 4 and Wiring diagrams).

7   Compression low

1   Spark plug loose. Remove the plug and inspect the threads. Reinstall and tighten to the specified torque (Chapter 1).
2   Cylinder head not sufficiently tightened down. If the cylinder head is suspected of being loose, then there's a chance that the gasket or head is damaged if the problem has persisted for any length of time. The head nuts and bolts should be tightened to the proper torque in the correct sequence (Chapter 2).
3   Incorrect valve clearance (four-stroke models). This means that the valve is not closing completely and compression pressure is leaking past the valve. Check and adjust the valve clearances (Chapter 1).
4   Cylinder and/or piston worn. Excessive wear will cause compression pressure to leak past the rings. This is usually accompanied by worn rings as well. A top end overhaul is necessary (Chapter 2).
5   Piston rings worn, weak, broken, or sticking. Broken or sticking piston rings usually indicate a lubrication or carburetion problem that causes excess carbon deposits or seizures to form on the pistons and rings. Top end overhaul is necessary (Chapter 2).
6   Piston ring-to-groove clearance excessive. This is caused by

excessive wear of the piston ring lands. Piston replacement is necessary (Chapter 2).

7 Cylinder head gasket damaged. If the head is allowed to become loose, or if excessive carbon build-up on a piston crown and combustion chamber causes extremely high compression, the head gasket may leak. Retorquing the head is not always sufficient to restore the seal, so gasket replacement is necessary (Chapter 2).

8 Cylinder head warped. This is caused by overheating or incorrectly tightened head nuts and bolts. Machine shop resurfacing or head replacement is necessary (Chapter 2).

9 Valve spring broken or weak (four-stroke models). Caused by component failure or wear; the spring(s) must be replaced (Chapter 2).

10 Valve not seating correctly (four-stroke models). This is caused by a bent valve (from over-revving or incorrect valve adjustment), burned valve or seat (incorrect carburetion) or an accumulation of carbon deposits on the seat (from carburetion or lubrication problems). The valves must be cleaned and/or replaced and the seats serviced if possible (Chapter 2).

8 Stalls after starting

1 Incorrect choke action. Make sure the choke knob or lever is getting a full stroke and staying in the out position.
2 Ignition malfunction (Chapter 4).
3 Carburetor malfunction (Chapter 3).
4 Fuel contaminated. The fuel can be contaminated with either dirt or water, or can change chemically if the machine is allowed to sit for several months or more. Drain the tank and float bowl and refill with fresh fuel (Chapter 3).
5 Intake air leak. Check for loose carburetor-to-intake joint connections or loose carburetor top (Chapter 3).
6 Engine idle speed incorrect. Turn throttle stop screw until the engine idles at the specified rpm (Chapter 1).

9 Rough idle

1 Ignition malfunction (Chapter 4).
2 Idle speed incorrect (Chapter 1).
3 Carburetor malfunction (Chapter 3).
4 Idle fuel/air mixture incorrect (Chapter 3).
5 Fuel contaminated. The fuel can be contaminated with either dirt or water, or can change chemically if the machine is allowed to sit for several months or more. Drain the tank and float bowl (Chapter 3).
6 Intake air leak. Check for loose carburetor-to-intake joint connections, loose or missing vacuum gauge access port cap or hose, or loose carburetor top (Chapter 3).
7 Air cleaner clogged. Service or replace air cleaner element (Chapter 1).

Poor running at low speed

10 Spark weak

1 Battery voltage low (if equipped). Check and recharge battery (Chapter 4C).
2 Spark plug fouled, defective or worn out. Refer to Chapter 1 for spark plug maintenance.
3 Spark plug cap or secondary (HT) wiring defective. Refer to Chapters 1 and 4 for details on the ignition system.
4 Spark plug cap not making contact.
5 Incorrect spark plug. Wrong type, heat range or cap configuration. Check and install correct plug listed in Chapter 1. A cold plug or one with a recessed firing electrode will not operate at low speeds without fouling.
6 CDI unit defective (Chapter 4).
7 CDI magneto defective (Chapter 4).
8 Ignition coil defective (Chapter 4).

11 Air/fuel mixture incorrect

1 Pilot screw out of adjustment (Chapter 3).
2 Pilot jet or air passage clogged. Remove and overhaul the carburetor (Chapter 3).
3 Air bleed holes clogged. Remove carburetor and blow out all passages (Chapter 3).
4 Air cleaner clogged, poorly sealed or missing.
5 Air cleaner-to-carburetor boot poorly sealed. Look for cracks, holes or loose clamps and replace or repair defective parts.
6 Float level too high or too low. Check and replace the float if necessary (Chapter 3).
7 Fuel tank air vent obstructed. Make sure that the air vent passage in the filler cap is open.
8 Carburetor intake joint loose. Check for cracks, breaks, tears or loose clamps or bolts. Repair or replace the rubber boot and its O-ring.

12 Compression low

1 Spark plug loose. Remove the plug and inspect the threads. Reinstall and tighten to the specified torque (Chapter 1).
2 Cylinder head not sufficiently tightened down. If the cylinder head is suspected of being loose, then there's a chance that the gasket and head are damaged if the problem has persisted for any length of time. The head nuts and bolts should be tightened to the proper torque in the correct sequence (Chapter 2).
3 Improper valve clearance (four-stroke models). This means that the valve is not closing completely and compression pressure is leaking past the valve. Check and adjust the valve clearances (Chapter 1).
4 Cylinder and/or piston worn. Excessive wear will cause compression pressure to leak past the rings. This is usually accompanied by worn rings as well. A top end overhaul is necessary (Chapter 2).
5 Piston rings worn, weak, broken, or sticking. Broken or sticking piston rings usually indicate a lubrication or carburetion problem that causes excess carbon deposits or seizures to form on the pistons and rings. Top end overhaul is necessary (Chapter 2).
6 Piston ring-to-groove clearance excessive. This is caused by excessive wear of the piston ring lands. Piston replacement is necessary (Chapter 2).
7 Cylinder head gasket damaged. If the head is allowed to become loose, or if excessive carbon build-up on the piston crown and combustion chamber causes extremely high compression, the head gasket may leak. Retorquing the head is not always sufficient to restore the seal, so gasket replacement is necessary (Chapter 2).
8 Cylinder head warped. This is caused by overheating or improperly tightened head nuts and bolts. Machine shop resurfacing or head replacement is necessary (Chapter 2).
9 Valve spring broken or weak (four-stroke models). Caused by component failure or wear; the spring(s) must be replaced (Chapter 2).
10 Valve not seating properly (four-stroke models). This is caused by a bent valve (from over-revving or improper valve adjustment), burned valve or seat (improper carburetion) or an accumulation of carbon deposits on the seat (from carburetion, lubrication problems). The valves must be cleaned and/or replaced and the seats serviced if possible (Chapter 2).

13 Poor acceleration

1 Carburetor leaking or dirty. Overhaul the carburetor (Chapter 3).
2 Timing not advancing. The CDI magneto or the CDI unit may be defective. If so, they must be replaced with new ones, as they can't be repaired.
3 Engine oil viscosity too high (four-stroke models). Using a heavier oil than that recommended in Chapter 1 can damage the oil pump or lubrication system and cause drag on the engine.
4 Brakes dragging. Usually caused by a sticking brake caliper piston, warped disc or bent spindle. Repair as necessary (Chapter 7).

Poor running or no power at high speed

14 Firing incorrect

1   Air cleaner restricted. Clean or replace element (Chapter 1).
2   Spark plug fouled, defective or worn out. See Chapter 1 for spark plug maintenance.
3   Spark plug cap or secondary wiring defective. See Chapters 1 and 4 for details of the ignition system.
4   Spark plug cap not in good contact (Chapter 4).
5   Incorrect spark plug. Wrong type, heat range or cap configuration. Check and install correct plugs listed in Chapter 1. A cold plug or one with a recessed firing electrode will not operate at low speeds without fouling.
6   CDI unit or CDI magneto defective (Chapter 4).
7   Ignition coil defective (Chapter 4).

15 Fuel/air mixture incorrect

1   Pilot screw out of adjustment. See Chapter 3 for adjustment procedures.
2   Main jet clogged. Dirt, water or other contaminants can clog the main jets. Clean the fuel tap strainer and in-tank strainer, the float bowl area, and the jets and carburetor orifices (Chapter 3).
3   Main jet wrong size (Chapter 3).
4   Throttle shaft-to-carburetor body clearance excessive. Refer to Chapter 3 for inspection and part replacement procedures.
5   Air bleed holes clogged. Remove and overhaul carburetor (Chapter 3).
6   Air cleaner clogged, poorly sealed, or missing.
7   Air cleaner-to-carburetor boot poorly sealed. Look for cracks, holes or loose clamps, and replace or repair defective parts.
8   Float level too high or too low. Check float level and replace the float if necessary (Chapter 3).
9   Fuel tank air vent obstructed. Make sure the air vent passage in the filler cap is open.
10   Carburetor intake joint loose. Check for cracks, breaks, tears or loose clamps or bolts. Repair or replace the rubber boots (Chapter 3).
11   Fuel tap clogged. Remove the tap and clean it (Chapter 1).
12   Fuel line clogged. Pull the fuel line loose and carefully blow through it.

16 Compression low

1   Spark plug loose. Remove the plug and inspect the threads. Reinstall and tighten to the specified torque (Chapter 1).
2   Cylinder head not sufficiently tightened down. If the cylinder head is suspected of being loose, then there's a chance that the gasket and head are damaged if the problem has persisted for any length of time. The head nuts and bolts should be tightened to the proper torque in the correct sequence (Chapter 2).
3   Improper valve clearance (four-stroke models). This means that the valve is not closing completely and compression pressure is leaking past the valve. Check and adjust the valve clearances (Chapter 1).
4   Cylinder and/or piston worn. Excessive wear will cause compression pressure to leak past the rings. This is usually accompanied by worn rings as well. A top end overhaul is necessary (Chapter 2).
5   Piston rings worn, weak, broken, or sticking. Broken or sticking piston rings usually indicate a lubrication or carburetion problem that causes excess carbon deposits or seizures to form on the pistons and rings. Top end overhaul is necessary (Chapter 2).
6   Piston ring-to-groove clearance excessive. This is caused by excessive wear of the piston ring lands. Piston replacement is necessary (Chapter 2).
7   Cylinder head gasket damaged. If a head is allowed to become loose, or if excessive carbon build-up on the piston crown and combustion chamber causes extremely high compression, the head gasket may leak. Retorquing the head is not always sufficient to restore the seal, so gasket replacement is necessary (Chapter 2).
8   Cylinder head warped. This is caused by overheating or improperly tightened head nuts and bolts. Machine shop resurfacing or head replacement is necessary (Chapter 2).
9   Valve spring broken or weak (four-stroke models). Caused by component failure or wear; the spring(s) must be replaced (Chapter 2).
10   Valve not seating properly (four-stroke models). This is caused by a bent valve (from over-revving or improper valve adjustment), burned valve or seat (improper carburetion) or an accumulation of carbon deposits on the seat (from carburetion or lubrication problems). The valves must be cleaned and/or replaced and the seats serviced if possible (Chapter 2).

17 Knocking or pinging

1   Carbon build-up in combustion chamber. Use of a fuel additive that will dissolve the adhesive bonding the carbon particles to the crown and chamber is the easiest way to remove the build-up. Otherwise, the cylinder head will have to be removed and decarbonized (Chapter 2).
2   Incorrect or poor quality fuel. Old or improper grades of fuel can cause detonation. This causes the piston to rattle, thus the knocking or pinging sound. Drain old fuel and always use the recommended fuel grade.
3   Spark plug heat range incorrect. Uncontrolled detonation indicates the plug heat range is too hot. The plug in effect becomes a glow plug, raising cylinder temperatures. Install the proper heat range plug (Chapter 1).
4   Improper air/fuel mixture. This will cause the cylinder to run hot, which leads to detonation. Clogged jets or an air leak can cause this imbalance (Chapter 4).

18 Miscellaneous causes

1   Throttle valve doesn't open fully. Adjust the cable slack (Chapter 1).
2   Clutch slipping. May be caused by improper adjustment or loose or worn clutch components. Refer to Chapter 1 for adjustment or Chapter 2 for clutch overhaul procedures.
3   Timing not advancing.
4   Engine oil viscosity too high (four-stroke models). Using a heavier oil than the one recommended in Chapter 1 can damage the oil pump or lubrication system and cause drag on the engine.
5   Brakes dragging. With mechanical (cable-operated) brakes, usually caused by a sticking brake cam, warped drum or bent axle. With hydraulic brakes, usually caused by a sticking caliper piston or warped disc. Repair as necessary.

Overheating

19 Engine overheats

1   Engine oil level low. Check and add oil (Chapter 1).
2   Wrong type of oil (four-stroke models). If you're not sure what type of oil is in the engine, drain it and fill with the correct type (Chapter 1).
3   Air leak at carburetor intake joint. Check and tighten or replace as necessary (Chapter 3).
4   Fuel level low. Check and adjust if necessary (Chapter 4).
5   Worn oil pump or clogged oil passages (four-stroke models). Replace pump or clean passages as necessary.
6   Clogged external oil line (four-stroke models). Remove and check for foreign material (see Chapter 2).

7   Lean fuel/oil mixture (two-stroke models). Check oil level in tank. Inspect Autolube pump adjustment (Chapter 1) and condition (Chapter 2). Adjust or replace as necessary.
8   Carbon build-up in combustion chambers. Use of a fuel additive that will dissolve the adhesive bonding the carbon particles to the piston crown and chambers is the easiest way to remove the build-up. Otherwise, the cylinder head will have to be removed and decarbonized (Chapter 2).
9   Operation in high ambient temperatures.

20 Firing incorrect

1   Spark plug fouled, defective or worn out. See Chapter 1 for spark plug maintenance.
2   Incorrect spark plug (Chapter 1).
3   Faulty ignition coil (Chapter 4).

21 Air/fuel mixture incorrect

1   Pilot screw out of adjustment (Chapter 3).
2   Main jet clogged. Dirt, water and other contaminants can clog the main jet. Clean the fuel tap strainer, the float bowl area and the jets and carburetor orifices (Chapter 3).
3   Main jet wrong size. The standard jetting is for sea level atmospheric pressure and oxygen content.
4   Air cleaner poorly sealed or missing.
5   Air cleaner-to-carburetor boot poorly sealed. Look for cracks, holes or loose clamps and replace or repair.
6   Fuel level too low. Check fuel level and float level and adjust or replace the float if necessary (Chapter 3).
7   Fuel tank air vent obstructed. Make sure that the air vent passage in the filler cap is open.
8   Carburetor intake manifold loose. Check for cracks or loose clamps or bolts. Check the carburetor-to-manifold gasket and the manifold-to-cylinder head O-ring (Chapter 3).

22 Compression too high

1   Carbon build-up in combustion chamber. Use of a fuel additive that will dissolve the adhesive bonding the carbon particles to the piston crown and chamber is the easiest way to remove the build-up. Otherwise, the cylinder head will have to be removed and decarbonized (Chapter 2).
2   Improperly machined head surface or installation of incorrect gasket during engine assembly.

23 Engine load excessive

1   Clutch slipping. Can be caused by damaged, loose or worn clutch components. Refer to Chapter 2 for overhaul procedures.
2   Engine oil level too high (four-stroke models). The addition of too much oil will cause pressurization of the crankcase and inefficient engine operation. Check Specifications and drain to proper level (Chapter 1).
3   Engine oil viscosity too high (four-stroke models). Using a heavier oil than the one recommended in Chapter 1 can damage the oil pump or lubrication system as well as cause drag on the engine.
4   Brakes dragging. Usually caused by a sticking brake caliper piston, warped disc or bent spindle. Repair as necessary (Chapter 7).

24 Lubrication inadequate

1   Engine oil level too low (four-stroke models) or fuel/oil ratio too lean (two-stroke models). Friction caused by intermittent lack of lubrication or from oil that is overworked can cause overheating. The oil provides a definite cooling function in the engine. Check the oil level (Chapter 1).
2   Poor quality engine oil or incorrect viscosity or type. Oil is rated not only according to viscosity but also according to type. Some oils are not rated high enough for use in these engines. Check the Chapter 1 Specifications and change to the correct oil.
3   Camshaft or journals worn (four-stroke models). Excessive wear causing drop in oil pressure. Replace cam or cylinder head. Abnormal wear could be caused by oil starvation at high rpm from low oil level or improper viscosity or type of oil (Chapter 1).
4   Crankshaft and/or bearings worn. Same problems as paragraph 3. Check and replace crankshaft assembly if necessary (Chapter 2).

Clutch problems

25 Clutch slipping

1   Clutch friction plates or shoes worn or warped. Overhaul the clutch assembly (Chapter 2).
2   Clutch metal plates worn or warped (Chapter 2).
3   Clutch spring(s) broken or weak. Old or heat-damaged spring(s) (from slipping clutch) should be replaced with new ones (Chapter 2).
4   Clutch release mechanism defective. Replace any defective parts (Chapter 2).
5   Clutch housing unevenly worn. This causes improper engagement of the plates. Replace the damaged or worn parts (Chapter 2).

26 Clutch not disengaging completely

1   Clutch cable incorrectly adjusted (except PW50) (see Chapter 1).
2   Clutch plates warped or damaged. This will cause clutch drag, which in turn will cause the machine to creep. Overhaul the clutch assembly (Chapter 2).
3   Sagged or broken clutch spring(s). Check and replace the spring(s) (Chapter 2).
4   Engine/transmission oil deteriorated. Old, thin, worn out oil will not provide proper lubrication for the discs, causing the secondary clutch to drag. Replace the oil and filter (Chapter 1).
5   Engine/transmission oil viscosity too high. Using a thicker oil than recommended in Chapter 1 can cause the clutch plates to stick together, putting a drag on the engine. Change to the correct viscosity oil (Chapter 1).
6   Clutch housing seized on shaft. Lack of lubrication, severe wear or damage can cause the housing to seize on the shaft. Overhaul of the clutch, and perhaps transmission, may be necessary to repair the damage (Chapter 2).
7   Clutch release mechanism defective. Worn or damaged release mechanism parts can stick and fail to apply force to the pressure plate. Overhaul the release mechanism (Chapter 2).
8   Loose clutch center nut. Causes housing and center misalignment putting a drag on the engine. Engagement adjustment continually varies. Overhaul the clutch assembly (Chapter 2).
9   Weak or broken clutch springs (Chapter 2).

Gear shifting problems

27 Doesn't go into gear or lever doesn't return

1   Clutch not disengaging. See Section 26.
2   Shift fork(s) bent or seized. May be caused by lack of lubrication. Overhaul the transmission (Chapter 2).
3   Gear(s) stuck on shaft. Most often caused by a lack of lubrication or excessive wear in transmission bearings and bushings. Overhaul the

transmission (Chapter 2).

4   Shift drum binding. Caused by lubrication failure or excessive wear. Replace the drum and bearing (Chapter 2).

5   Shift lever return spring weak or broken (Chapter 2).

6   Shift lever broken. Splines stripped out of lever or shaft, caused by allowing the lever to get loose. Replace necessary parts (Chapter 2).

7   Shift mechanism pawl broken or worn. Full engagement and rotary movement of shift drum results. Replace shaft assembly (Chapter 2).

8   Pawl spring broken. Allows pawl to float, causing sporadic shift operation. Replace spring (Chapter 2).

28 Jumps out of gear

1   Shift fork(s) worn. Overhaul the transmission (Chapter 2).

2   Gear groove(s) worn. Overhaul the transmission (Chapter 2).

3   Gear dogs or dog slots worn or damaged. The gears should be inspected and replaced. No attempt should be made to service the worn parts.

29 Overshifts

1   Pawl spring weak or broken (Chapter 2).

2   Shift cam stopper lever not functioning (Chapter 2).

Abnormal engine noise

30 Knocking or pinging

1   Carbon build-up in combustion chamber. Use of a fuel additive that will dissolve the adhesive bonding the carbon particles to the piston crown and chamber is the easiest way to remove the build-up. Otherwise, the cylinder head will have to be removed and decarbonized (Chapter 2).

2   Incorrect or poor quality fuel. Old or improper fuel can cause detonation. This causes the piston(s) to rattle, thus the knocking or pinging sound. Drain the old fuel (Chapter 3) and always use the recommended grade fuel (Chapter 1).

3   Spark plug heat range incorrect. Uncontrolled detonation indicates that the plug heat range is too hot. The plug in effect becomes a glow plug, raising cylinder temperatures. Install the proper heat range plug (Chapter 1).

4   Improper air/fuel mixture. This will cause the cylinder to run hot and lead to detonation. Clogged jets or an air leak can cause this imbalance. See Chapter 3.

31 Piston slap or rattling

1   Cylinder-to-piston clearance excessive. Caused by improper assembly. Inspect and overhaul top end parts (Chapter 2).

2   Connecting rod bent. Caused by over-revving, trying to start a badly flooded engine or from ingesting a foreign object into the combustion chamber. Replace the damaged parts (Chapter 2).

3   Piston pin or piston pin bore worn or seized from wear or lack of lubrication. Replace damaged parts (Chapter 2).

4   Piston ring(s) worn, broken or sticking. Overhaul the top end (Chapter 2).

5   Piston seizure damage. Usually from lack of lubrication or overheating. Replace the pistons and bore the cylinder, as necessary (Chapter 2).

6   Connecting rod upper or lower end clearance excessive. Caused by excessive wear or lack of lubrication. Replace worn parts.

32 Valve noise (four-stroke models)

1   Incorrect valve clearances. Adjust the clearances by referring to Chapter 1.

2   Valve spring broken or weak. Check and replace weak valve springs (Chapter 2).

3   Camshaft or cylinder head worn or damaged. Lack of lubrication at high rpm is usually the cause of damage. Insufficient oil or failure to change the oil at the recommended intervals are the chief causes.

33 Other noise

1   Cylinder head gasket leaking.

2   Exhaust pipe leaking at cylinder head connection. Caused by improper fit of pipe, damaged gasket or loose exhaust flange. All exhaust fasteners should be tightened evenly and carefully. Failure to do this will lead to a leak.

3   Crankshaft runout excessive. Caused by a bent crankshaft (from over-revving) or damage from an upper cylinder component failure.

4   Engine mounting bolts or nuts loose. Tighten all engine mounting bolts and nuts to the specified torque (Chapter 2).

5   Crankshaft bearings worn (Chapter 2).

6   Camshaft chain tensioner defective (four-stroke models). Replace according to the procedure in Chapter 2.

7   Camshaft chain, sprockets or guides worn (four-stroke models) (Chapter 2).

Abnormal driveline noise

34 Clutch noise

1   Clutch housing/friction plate clearance excessive (Chapter 2).

2   Loose or damaged clutch pressure plate and/or bolts (Chapter 2).

3   Broken clutch springs (Chapter 2).

35 Transmission noise

1   Bearings worn. Also includes the possibility that the shafts are worn. Overhaul the transmission (Chapter 2).

2   Gears worn or chipped (Chapter 2).

3   Metal chips jammed in gear teeth. Probably pieces from a broken gear or shift mechanism that were picked up by the gears. This will cause early bearing failure (Chapter 2).

4   Transmission oil level too low. Causes a howl from transmission. Also affects engine power and clutch operation (Chapter 1).

36 Chain noise (except PW50)

1   Dry or dirty chain. Inspect, clean and lubricate (see Chapter 1).

2   Chain out of adjustment. Adjust chain slack (see Chapter 1).

3   Chain and sprockets damaged or worn. Inspect the chain and sprockets and replace them as necessary (Chapter 5).

4   Sprockets loose (Chapter 5).

37 Final drive noise (PW50)

1   Lack of lubricant in final drive housing (see Chapter 5A).

2   Damaged final drive gears or shaft (see Chapter 5A).

Abnormal chassis noise

38 Suspension noise

1   Spring weak or broken. Makes a clicking or scraping sound.
2   Steering head bearings worn or damaged. Clicks when braking. Check and replace as necessary (Chapter 5).
3   Front fork oil level level incorrect. Check and correct oil level (see Chapter 5).
4   Front forks assembled incorrectly. Disassemble and check for correct assembly (see Chapter 5).
5   Defective rear shock absorber with internal damage. This is in the body of the shock and can't be remedied. The shock must be replaced with a new one (Chapter 5).
6   Bent or damaged shock body. Replace the shock with a new one (Chapter 5).

39 Brake noise

1   Squeal caused by dust on brake pads. Usually found in combination with glazed pads. Clean using brake cleaning solvent (Chapter 6).
2   Contamination of brake pads. Grease, water or dirt causing pads to chatter or squeal. Clean or replace pads (Chapter 6).
3   Pads glazed. Caused by excessive heat from prolonged use or from contamination. Do not use sandpaper, emery cloth or carborundum cloth or any other abrasives to roughen pad surface; abrasives will stay in the pad material and damage the disc. A very fine flat file can be used, but pad replacement is suggested as a cure (Chapter 6).
4   Disc warped. Can cause chattering, clicking or intermittent squeal. Usually accompanied by a pulsating lever and uneven braking. Replace the disc (Chapter 6).
5   Brake shoes worn or contaminated. Can cause scraping or squealing. Replace the shoes (see Chapter 6).
6   Brake shoes warped or worn unevenly. Can cause chattering. Replace the shoes (see Chapter 6).
7   Brake drum out of round. Can cause chattering. Replace the drum (see Chapter 6).
8   Loose or worn wheel bearings. Check and replace as necessary (Chapter 6).

Excessive exhaust smoke

40 White smoke

1   Piston oil ring worn (four-stroke models). The ring may be broken or damaged, causing oil from the crankcase to be pulled past the piston into the combustion chamber. Replace the rings with new ones (Chapter 2).
2   Cylinder worn, cracked, or scored. Caused by overheating or oil starvation. If worn or scored, the cylinder will have to be rebored and a new piston installed. If cracked, the cylinder will have to be replaced (see Chapter 2).
3   Valve oil seal damaged or worn (four-stroke models). Replace oil seals with new ones (Chapter 2).
4   Valve guide worn (four-stroke models). Perform a complete valve job (Chapter 2).
5   Engine oil level too high, which causes the oil to be forced past the rings (four-stroke models). Drain oil to the proper level (Chapter 1).
6   Head gasket broken between oil return and cylinder (four-stroke models). Causes oil to be pulled into the combustion chamber. Replace the head gasket and check the head for warpage (Chapter 2).
7   Abnormal crankcase pressurization, which forces oil past the rings. Clogged breather or hoses usually the cause (Chapter 2).

41 Black smoke

1   Air cleaner clogged. Clean or replace the element (Chapter 1).
2   Main jet too large or loose. Compare the jet size to the Specifications (Chapter 4).
3   Choke stuck, causing fuel to be pulled through choke circuit (Chapter 4).
4   Fuel level too high. Check the fuel level and float level and adjust if necessary (Chapter 3).
5   Inlet needle held off needle seat. Clean the float chamber and fuel line and replace the needle and seat if necessary (Chapter 3).

42 Brown smoke

1   Main jet too small or clogged. Lean condition caused by wrong size main jet or by a restricted orifice. Clean float chamber and jets and compare jet size to Specifications (Chapter 3).
2   Fuel flow insufficient. Fuel inlet needle valve stuck closed due to chemical reaction with old fuel. Float level incorrect; check and replace float if necessary. Restricted fuel line. Clean line and float chamber.
3   Carburetor intake tube loose (Chapter 3).
4   Air cleaner poorly sealed or not installed (Chapter 1).

Poor handling or stability

43 Handlebar hard to turn

1   Steering head ring nut(s) too tight (Chapter 1).
2   Steering stem bearings damaged. Roughness can be felt as the bars are turned from side-to-side. Replace bearings (Chapter 5).
3   Races dented or worn. Results from wear in only one position (e.g., straight ahead), striking an immovable object or hole or from dropping the machine. Replace races and bearing (see Chapter 5).
4   Steering stem bearing lubrication inadequate. Causes are grease getting hard from age or being washed out by high pressure car washes. Remove steering stem, clean and lubricate bearings (Chapter 5).
5   Steering stem bent. Caused by a collision, hitting a pothole or by rolling the machine. Replace damaged part. Don't try to straighten the steering stem (Chapter 5).
6   Front tire air pressure too low (Chapter 1).

44 Handlebar shakes or vibrates excessively

1   Tires worn or out of balance (Chapter 1 or 7).
2   Swingarm bearings worn. Replace worn bearings (Chapter 5).
3   Wheel rim(s) warped or damaged. Inspect wheels (Chapter 6).
4   Wheel bearings worn. Worn front or rear wheel bearings can cause poor tracking. Worn front bearings will cause wobble (Chapter 6).
5   Handlebar clamp bolts loose (Chapter 5).
6   Steering stem or triple clamps loose. Tighten them to the specified torque (Chapters 1 and 5).
7   Motor mount bolts loose. Will cause excessive vibration with increased engine rpm (Chapter 2).

45 Handlebar pulls to one side

1   Uneven tire pressures (Chapter 1).
2   Frame bent. Definitely suspect this if the machine has been rolled. May or may not be accompanied by cracking near the bend. Replace the frame.

3   Wheel out of alignment. Caused by incorrect toe-in adjustment (Chapter 1) or bent tie-rod (Chapter 6).
4   Swingarm bent or twisted. Caused by age (metal fatigue) or impact damage. Replace the swingarm (Chapter 6).
5   Steering stem bent. Caused by impact damage or by rolling the vehicle. Replace the steering stem (Chapter 6).

46 Poor shock absorbing qualities

1   Too hard:

a) *Fork oil level too high ((see Chapter 5).*
b) *Fork oil viscosity too high. Use a lighter oil (see the Specifications in Chapter 5).*
c) *Fork tube bent. Causes a harsh, sticking feeling (see Chapter 5).*
d) *Fork internal damage (see Chapter 5).*
e) *Shock internal damage.*
f) *Tire pressure too high (Chapters 1 and 6).*

2   Too soft:

a) *Fork or shock oil insufficient and/or leaking (Chapter 5).*
b) *Fork or shock springs weak or broken (Chapter 5).*

Braking problems

47 Brakes are spongy, don't hold

1   Disc brake pads worn (Chapters 1 and 6).
2   Disc brake pads contaminated by oil, grease, etc. Clean or replace pads (Chapter 6).
3   Disc warped. Replace disc (Chapter 6).
4   Shoe linings worn (see Chapter 6).
5   Contaminated shoes. Caused by contamination with oil, grease, etc. Clean or replace linings. Clean drum thoroughly with brake cleaner (see Chapter 5).
6   Drum warped. Replace drum (see Chapter 6).
7   Cable out of adjustment or stretched. Adjust or replace the cable (see Chapters 1 and 6).

48 Brake lever or pedal pulsates

1   Disc or drum warped. Replace disc or drum (Chapter 6).
2   Axle bent. Replace axle (Chapter 6).
3   Brake caliper bolts loose (see Chapter 6).
4   Brake caliper shafts damaged or sticking, causing caliper to bind. Lube the shafts or replace them if they're corroded or bent (Chapter 6).
5   Wheel warped or otherwise damaged (Chapter 6).
6   Wheel bearings damaged or worn (Chapter 6).
7   Drum out of round. Replace drum (see Chapter 6).

49 Brakes drag

1   Lever or pedal balky or stuck. Check pivot and lubricate (Chapter 6).
2   Brake caliper binds. Caused by inadequate lubrication or damage to caliper shafts (Chapter 6).
3   Caliper piston seized in bore. Caused by wear or ingestion of dirt getting past deteriorated seal (Chapter 6).
4   Brake pads or shoes damaged. Lining material separated from backing plate. Usually caused by faulty manufacturing process or contact with chemicals. Replace pads (Chapter 6).
5   Pads or shoes incorrectly installed (Chapter 6).
6   Cable sticking. Lubricate or replace cable (see Chapters 1 and 6).
7   Brake pedal or lever freeplay insufficient (Chapter 1).
8   Brake springs weak. Replace brake springs (see Chapter 6).

Chapter 1 Part A
Tune-up and routine maintenance (PW50 and PW80 models)

Contents

Engine

Spark plug type

PW50 .... NGK BP4HS or NIPPONDENSO W14FP-L

PW80 .... NGK BP6HS or NIPPONDENSO W20FP

Spark plug gap .... 0.6 to 0.7 mm (0.024 to 0.028 inch)

Pilot air screw setting

PW50 .... 1-3/8 turns out from seated position

PW80 .... 1-1/2 turns out from seated position

Engine idle speed .... 1,650 to 1,750 rpm

Cylinder compression .... Not specified

Miscellaneous

Front brake lever freeplay (between lever and lever bracket)

PW50 (both front brake levers) .... 3 to 5 mm (1/8 to 1/4 inch)

PW80 .... 5 to 8 mm (13/64 to 5/16 inch)

Rear brake pedal freeplay (PW80) .... 20 to 30 mm (51/64 to 1-13/64 inches)

Throttle cable freeplay

PW50

At twistgrip .... 1.5 to 3.5 mm (1/16 to 9/64 inch)

At carburetor .... 1.0 mm (3/64 inch)

PW80 (at twistgrip) .... 3 to 5 mm (1/8 to 1/4 inch)

Minimum tire tread depth .... 4.5 mm (11/64 inch)

Tire pressure (cold) .... 15 psi front and rear

Miscellaneous (continued)

Tire size	
PW50 (front and rear)	2.50-10-4PR
PW80	
Front	2.50-14-4PR
Rear	3.00-12-4PR
Drive chain slack (PW80)	15 to 20 mm (19/32 to 51/64 inches)
Autolube pump stroke	
PW50	
Minimum stroke	0.25 to 0.30 mm (0.010 to 0.012 inch)
Maximum stroke	1.00 to 1.15 mm (0.039 to 0.045 inch)
PW80	
Minimum stroke	0.40 to 0.45 mm (0.016 to 0.018 inch)
Maximum stroke	1.00 to 1.10 mm (0.039 to 0.043 inch)

Torque specifications

Transmission oil drain plug	
PW50	14 Nm (10 ft-lbs)
PW80	No specified torque
Spark plug	
PW50	20 Nm (168 in-lbs)
PW80	25 Nm (18 ft-lbs)
Steering stem bolt	
PW50	32 Nm (23 ft-lbs)
PW80	40 Nm (29 ft-lbs)
Steering stem ring nut	
PW50	
Initial	38 Nm (27 ft-lbs), then loosen
Final	1 Nm (8.4 in-lbs)
PW80	10 Nm (86.4 in-lbs)

Recommended lubricants and fluids

Fuel

Type	Regular unleaded gasoline
Capacity	
PW50	2.0 liters (0.53 gallon)
PW80	
Full tank	4.9 liters (1.29 gallons)
Reserve	1.0 liters (0.26 gallons)

Engine oil

Type	Yamalube "2-S" or air-cooled two-stroke engine oil
Oil tank capacity	
PW50	0.3 liter (0.32 qt)
PW80	0.95 liter (1.00 qt)

Transmission oil

Type	Yamalube "4" or SE multigrade four-stroke oil manufactured for use in motorcycles
Viscosity	10W30
Capacity	
PW50	
At oil change	0.3 liter (0.32 qt)
Overhaul	0.35 liter (0.37 qt)
PW80	
At oil change	0.65 liter (0.69 qt)
Overhaul	0.75 liter (0.79 qt)
Air cleaner element oil	Foam air filter oil, or engine oil
Drive chain lubricant	Chain lube

Miscellaneous

Wheel bearings	Medium weight, lithium-based multi-purpose grease
Swingarm pivot bushings	Molybdenum disulfide paste grease containing 40 percent or more molybdenum disulfide
Cables and lever pivots	Engine oil
Throttle grip, brake pedal/shift lever/throttle lever pivots	Medium weight, lithium-based multi-purpose grease

Use dipstick to determine exact amount (see text).

Yamaha PW50/PW80
Routine maintenance intervals

Note: *The pre-ride inspection outlined in the owner's manual covers checks and maintenance that should be carried out on a daily basis. It's condensed and included here to remind you of its importance. Always perform the pre-ride inspection at every maintenance interval (in addition to the procedures listed). The intervals listed below are the shortest intervals recommended by the manufacturer for each particular operation during the model years covered in this manual. Your owner's manual may have different intervals for your model.*

Before every ride

Check and, if necessary, adjust the brake cable(s)/brake rod

Check the oil level in the oil tank and, if necessary, add oil

Check and, if necessary, add or change transmission oil

Check the drive chain alignment and adjustment and, if necessary, lubricate the chain (PW80 models)

Inspect the condition of the spark plug

Verify that the throttle twist grip and throttle cable operate smoothly

Make sure that the foam air filter is clean and dampened with foam filter oil

Inspect the tires for wear and check the tire pressure and wheel runout

Make sure the bead stoppers/rim locks are in place

Make sure the wheel spokes are tight (PW80 models)

Check all fasteners, including the axle nuts, for tightness

Every six months

Decarbonize the cylinder head and exhaust system

Inspect, clean and gap - or replace - the spark plug

Inspect , wash and re-oil - or replace - the air filter element*

Inspect, clean and adjust the carburetor

Check and, if necessary, adjust and bleed the Autolube pump

Check and, if necessary, adjust the brakes

Inspect the tires for wear, and check the pressure, balance and runout

Inspect the suspension and repair or replace damaged or worn components as necessary

Flush and clean the fuel tank and fuel petcock

Check all fasteners, including axle nuts, for tightness

Lubricate the throttle cable and throttle twistgrip

Lubricate the brake pedal shaft (PW80 models)

Lubricate the brake lever pivot(s)

Lubricate the brake cam

Replace the oil in the transmission (PW80 models)

Lubricate the pivot bolt for the centerstand (PW50 models) or the sidestand (PW80 models)

Every 12 months

Replace the oil in the transmission (PW50 models)

Check, adjust and lubricate the brake and throttle cables**

Check the wheel bearings for looseness and damage and, if necessary, repack or replace them**

Change the fork oil

Every 24 months

Lubricate the steering head bearings**

Lubricate the middle driven pinion and final drive pinion (PW50 models)

* *More often in dusty conditions*

** *More often in wet conditions*

2   Introduction to tune-up and routine maintenance

Refer to illustration 2.1

This Chapter covers in detail the checks and procedures necessary for the tune-up and routine maintenance of your motorcycle. Section 1 includes the routine maintenance schedule, which is designed to keep the machine in proper running condition and prevent possible problems. The remaining Sections contain detailed procedures for carrying out the items listed on the maintenance schedule, as well as additional maintenance information designed to increase reliability. Maintenance and safety information is also printed on decals, which are mounted in various locations on the motorcycle **(see illustration)**. Where information on the decals differs from that presented in this Chapter, use the decal information.

Since routine maintenance plays such an important role in the safe and efficient operation of your motorcycle, it is presented here as a comprehensive check list. For the rider who does all his own maintenance, these lists outline the procedures and checks that should be done on a routine basis.

Deciding where to start or plug into the routine maintenance

2.1 Decals on the motorcycle include maintenance, safety and operation information

3.1 On PW50 models, the oil tank for the Autolube system is located in front of the steering head

3.2 On PW80 models, check the oil level through the window in the side cover . . .

schedule depends on several factors. If you have owned the bike for some time but have never performed any maintenance on it, then you may want to start at the nearest interval and include some additional procedures to ensure that nothing important is overlooked. If you have just had a major engine overhaul, then you may want to start the maintenance routine from the beginning. If you have a used machine and have no knowledge of its history or maintenance record, you may desire to combine all the checks into one large service initially and then settle into the maintenance schedule prescribed.

The Sections which outline the inspection and maintenance procedures are written as step-by-step comprehensive guides to the actual performance of the work. They explain in detail each of the routine inspections and maintenance procedures on the check list. References to additional information in applicable Chapters is also included and should not be overlooked.

Before beginning any actual maintenance or repair, the machine should be cleaned thoroughly, especially around the oil filler plug, radiator cap, engine covers, carburetor, etc. Cleaning will help ensure that dirt does not contaminate the engine and will allow you to detect wear and damage that could otherwise easily go unnoticed.

3   Fluid levels - check

Engine oil (Autolube system)

Refer to illustrations 3.1, 3.2 and 3.3

1   On PW50 models, the oil tank is located in front of the steering

head **(see illustration)**.

2   On PW80 models, there's a window in the side cover so you can check the oil level **(see illustration)**. Remove the seat (see Chapter 7A) to access the oil tank.

3   Look at the oil in the tank and verify that it is above the lower mark. If the level is below the lower mark on the tank, top up the tank. Remove the oil tank cap and pour in enough two-stroke oil (the recommended oil is listed in this Chapter's Specifications) to bring the level up to the upper mark **(see illustration)**. Install the cap. Make sure it's secure.

Transmission oil

Refer to illustrations 3.6a, 3.6b and 3.6c

4   Place the machine on level ground.

5   Start the engine and run it for several minutes. **Warning:** *Do not run the engine in an enclosed space such as a garage or shop.* Stop the engine and allow the bike to sit undisturbed in a level position for a few minutes.

6   With the engine off, unscrew the transmission oil filler cap **(see illustrations)**. On PW80 models, wipe off the dipstick and, with the bike in an upright position, insert it back into the hole (don't screw it in). Pull out the dipstick and note the oil level **(see illustration)**.

7   PW50 models don't have a dipstick, but you can make your own with a small piece of aluminum or steel rod that is cut to the appropriate length.

8   If the oil level is below the minimum mark, add enough four-stroke engine oil (the recommended oil is listed in this Chapter's Specifications) to bring the level up to the area between the two marks.

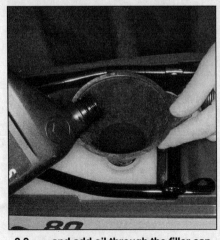

3.3 . . . and add oil through the filler cap under the seat

3.6a Here's the transmission filler cap for PW50 models

3.6b Here's the transmission filler cap for PW80 models

3.6c PW80 filler caps have a dipstick for checking the level of the transmission oil

5.1 Measure the front brake lever freeplay between the lever and the lever bracket

4 Brake system - general check

1   A routine general check of the brakes will ensure that any problems are discovered and remedied before the rider's safety is jeopardized.

2   Inspect the brake lever and pedal for loose connections, bends, and other damage. Replace any damaged parts with new ones (see Chapter 7). Check front brake lever and rear brake lever (PW50 models) or rear brake pedal (PW80 models) freeplay (see Section 5).

3   Make sure all brake fasteners are tight.

4   Operate the front brake lever. If it feels rough or sticky, lubricate the brake cable (see Section 9).

5   Operate the rear brake lever (PW50 models) or the rear brake pedal (PW80 models). If it feels rough or sticky, lubricate the brake cable (see Section 9).

6   Adjust the brake lever or rear brake pedal freeplay (see Section 5).

5 Brake lever and pedal freeplay - check and adjustment

Front brake lever

Refer to illustration 5.1

1   Apply the front brake lever to the point at which you feel initial resistance (the point at which the brake cable slack is taken up and the

cable begins to apply the brake shoes). With the lever applied to this point of initial resistance, measure the gap between the brake lever and the brake lever bracket **(see illustration)** and compare your measurement to the range of freeplay listed in this Chapter's Specifications. If the gap is outside the specified range, adjust the brake lever freeplay as follows.

PW50 models

Refer to illustration 5.2

2   Turn the adjuster in or out until the lever freeplay is within the specified range **(see illustration)**.

PW80 models

Refer to illustration 5.4

3   Loosen the locknut at the handlebar adjuster and turn the adjuster in or out until freeplay is correct.

4   If you can't achieve the correct freeplay range by turning the adjuster at the handlebar, use the adjuster at the front wheel **(see illustration)**. Loosen the locknut and turn the adjuster nut in or out until the lever freeplay is within the specified range.

5   Tighten the locknut securely.

Rear brake lever (PW50 models)

Refer to illustration 5.6

6   The procedure for checking rear brake lever freeplay is identical to the procedure for checking front brake lever freeplay (see Step 1). If the rear brake lever freeplay is outside the range of freeplay listed in

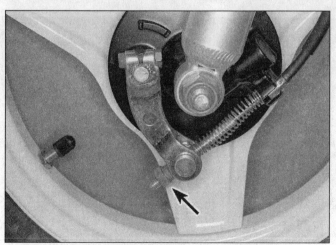

5.2 Turn the nut (arrow) to adjust the PW50 front brake

5.4 Loosen the locknut (A) and turn the adjuster (B) to adjust the PW80 front brake

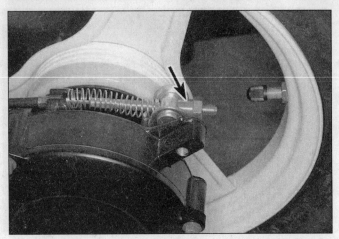

5.6 Turn the nut (arrow) to adjust the PW50 rear brake

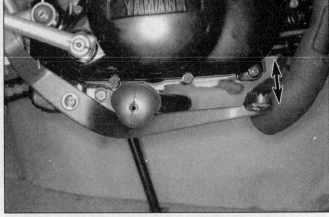

5.7 Measure PW80 brake pedal play at the pedal

this Chapter's Specifications, adjust the brake lever freeplay the same way you would adjust freeplay for the front brake lever (see Step 2). The adjuster is in the cable at the rear wheel **(see illustration)**.

Rear brake pedal (PW80 models)

Refer to illustrations 5.7 and 5.8

7   Apply the rear brake pedal and measure the distance that the end

5.8 Turn the adjuster wingnut (arrow) to adjust PW80 brake pedal play

of the pedal moves from its initial unapplied position to the point at which you feel initial resistance **(see illustration)**. This is the pedal freeplay. Compare your measurement to the pedal freeplay listed in this Chapter's Specifications. If the pedal freeplay is outside the specified range, adjust the brake pedal as follows.

8   Turn the adjuster nut at the rear end of the brake rod **(see illustration)** in or out to bring brake pedal freeplay within the specified range.

6   Throttle cable freeplay - check and adjustment

Check

Refer to illustration 6.2

1   Make sure the throttle twistgrip moves easily from fully closed to fully open with the front wheel turned at various angles. The grip should return automatically from fully open to fully closed when released. If the throttle sticks, check the throttle cable for cracks or kinks in the housings. Also, make sure the inner cable is clean and well-lubricated (see Section 10).

2   Measure the freeplay at the twistgrip flange **(see illustration)**. The freeplay is the distance that the twistgrip flange travels before you feel an initial resistance (the point at which the throttle cable begins to open the throttle plate) and compare your measurement to the range of freeplay listed in this Chapter's Specifications. If it's not within the specified range, adjust it as follows.

6.2 To measure throttle cable freeplay, measure how far the twistgrip rotates before you feel initial resistance

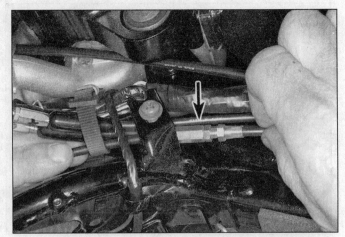

6.3 Pull on the oil pump cable near the adjuster (arrow) to check its freeplay (PW50)

6.4 On PW50s, loosen the locknut on the throttle cable adjuster (left arrow) and turn the adjuster – the right arrow shows the choke cable

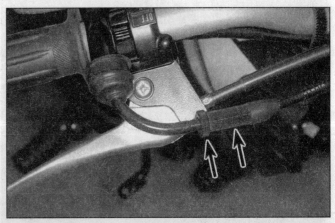

6.7 Loosen the locknut (left arrow) and turn the adjuster (right arrow) to adjust the throttle cable at the handlebar

Cable adjustment

PW50 models

Refer to illustrations 6.3, 6.4 and 6.7

3   Loosen the locknut on the oil pump cable adjuster, then back off the adjuster to create slack in the oil pump cable **(see illustration)**.

4   At the carburetor, pull pack the rubber cover from the throttle cable **(see illustration)**. Pull on the cable and measure freeplay at the gap between the end of the cable locknut and the end of the threaded barrel. Compare your measurement to the cable freeplay listed in this Chapter's Specifications. If the cable freeplay is incorrect, loosen the throttle cable adjuster locknut, turn the adjuster to obtain the correct freeplay, then tighten the locknut.

5   Once again, turn the throttle twist grip until you feel initial resistance and measure the freeplay **(see illustration 6.2)**.

7   If the throttle cable freeplay is now incorrect, loosen the cable adjuster locknut **(see illustration)** and turn the adjuster until the twist-grip freeplay is within the specified range. When the freeplay is correct, tighten the locknut.

8   Recheck the idle speed and readjust if necessary. Make sure idle speed does not increase when the handlebar is moved from full lock in one direction to full lock in the other direction.

PW80 models

14   Turn the throttle twist grip until you feel initial resistance. This is the throttle freeplay. Measure the freeplay **(see illustration 6.2)** and compare it to the throttle freeplay listed in this Chapter's Specifications.

15   If the throttle freeplay is incorrect, loosen the cable adjuster lock-

nut at the handlebar **(see illustration 6.7)** and turn the adjuster nut in or out to obtain the specified freeplay. Tighten the locknut.

Throttle limiter adjustment

Refer to illustration 6.16

16   PW50 models are equipped with a throttle limiter that can be used to restrict maximum throttle opening **(see illustration)**. Turning the screw all the way in reduces the maximum throttle opening; turning it out allows increased throttle opening. When the rider is skillful enough not to need the limiter, it can be removed completely and replaced with the plug supplied in the motorcycle's tool kit.

7   Idle speed - check and adjustment

Refer to illustrations 7.3a and 7.3b

1   Before adjusting the idle speed, make sure the spark plug gap is correct. Also, turn the handlebars back-and-forth and note whether the idle speed changes as the handlebars are moved. If it does, the throttle cable may not be adjusted correctly, or it may be worn out. Be sure to correct this problem before proceeding.

2   The engine should be at normal operating temperature, which is usually reached after 10 to 15 minutes of stop and go riding. Make sure the transmission is in Neutral, then connect an inductive tachometer.

3   Turn in the pilot air screw **(see illustrations)** until it bottoms lightly, then turn it back out the number of turns listed in this Chapter's Specifications.

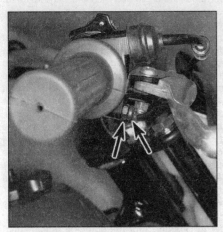

6.16 Loosen the locknut (left arrow) and turn the screw (right arrow) to adjust the throttle limiter

7.3a PW50 pilot air screw (right arrow) and throttle stop screw (left arrow)

7.3b PW50 pilot air screw (left arrow) and throttle stop screw (right arrow)

8.4 Check tire pressure with a tire gauge

8.5 Check the tension of the spokes periodically, but don't overtighten them

4   Turn the throttle stop screw until the idle speed listed in this Chapter's Specifications is obtained.
5   Turn the pilot air screw in or out in 1/8-turn increments to obtain the highest idle speed, then use the throttle stop screw to set the specified idle speed.
6   Snap the throttle open and shut a few times, then recheck the idle speed. If necessary, repeat the adjustment procedure.
7   If a smooth, steady idle can't be achieved, the air/fuel mixture might be incorrect (see Chapter 3).
8   After the idle speed has been adjusted, check and adjust the throttle cable freeplay (see Section 6).

8   Tires/wheels - general check

Refer to illustrations 8.4 and 8.5
1   Routine tire and wheel checks should be made with the realization that your safety depends to a great extent on their condition.
2   Check the tires carefully for cuts, tears, embedded nails or other sharp objects and excessive wear. Operation of the motorcycle with excessively worn tires is extremely hazardous, as traction and handling are directly affected. Check the tread depth at the center of the tire. Honda doesn't specify a minimum tread depth for these models, but as a general rule, tires should be replaced with new ones when the tread knobs are worn to 3 mm (1/8 inch) or less.
3   Repair or replace punctured tires as soon as damage is noted. Do not try to patch a torn tire, as wheel balance and tire reliability may be impaired.

9.3 Push up on the top run of the chain and measure the slack midway between the two sprockets

4   Check the tire pressures when the tires are cold and keep them properly inflated **(see illustration)**. Proper air pressure will increase tire life and provide maximum stability and ride comfort. Keep in mind that low tire pressures may cause the tire to slip on the rim or come off, while high tire pressures will cause abnormal tread wear and unsafe handling.
5   The wheels should be kept clean and checked periodically for cracks, bending, loose spokes (PW80 models) and rust. Never attempt to repair damaged wheels; they must be replaced with new ones. On PW80 models, loose spokes can be tightened with a spoke wrench **(see illustration)**, but be careful not to overtighten and distort the wheel rim.
6   Check the valve stem locknuts to make sure they're tight. Also, make sure the valve stem cap is in place and tight. If it is missing, install a new one made of metal or hard plastic.

9   Drive chain and sprockets (PW80 models) - check, adjustment and lubrication

Refer to illustration 9.3
1   A neglected drive chain won't last long and can quickly damage the sprockets. Routine chain adjustment isn't difficult and will ensure maximum chain and sprocket life.
2   To check the chain, support the bike securely with the rear wheel off the ground. Place the transmission in neutral.
3   Push up on the top run of the chain and measure the slack midway between the two sprockets **(see illustration)**, then compare the measurements to the value listed in this Chapter's Specifications. As wear occurs, the chain will actually stretch, which means adjustment by removing some slack from the chain. In some cases where lubrication has been neglected, corrosion and galling may cause the links to bind and kink, which effectively shortens the chain's length. If the chain is tight between the sprockets, rusty or kinked, it's time to replace it with a new one. **Note:** *Repeat the chain slack measurement along the length of the chain - ideally, every inch or so. If you find a tight area, mark it with felt pen or paint and repeat the measurement after the bike has been ridden. If the chain's still tight in the same areas, it may be damaged or worn. Because a tight or kinked chain can damage the transmission countershaft bearing, it's a good idea to replace it.*
4   Check the entire length of the chain for damaged rollers, loose links and loose pins.
5   Look behind the left engine cover and inspect the engine sprocket. Check the teeth on the engine sprocket and the rear sprocket for wear. Refer to Chapter 5 for the sprocket replacement procedure if the sprockets appear to be worn excessively.
6   Inspect the condition of the chain guide. If it's worn, replace it.

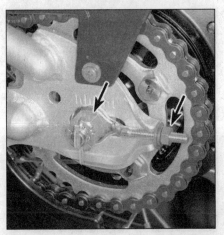

9.9 Remove the cotter pin and loosen the rear axle nut (left) , then turn the adjuster nuts (right arrow) *evenly* until the correct chain tension is obtained

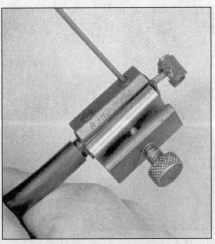

10.3 Lubricating a cable with a pressure lube adapter (make sure the tool seats around the inner cable)

11.4 Inspect each fork seal for leakage; if a seal is leaking, replace both fork seals

Adjustment

Refer to illustration 9.9

7   Loosen the rear brake rod adjuster nut **(see illustration 5.8)**.

8   Remove the rear axle nut cotter pin and loosen the rear axle nut.

9   Turn the chain puller adjusting nuts **(see illustration)** clockwise to tighten the chain, counterclockwise to loosen it. Be sure to turn the adjusting nuts *evenly* until the correct chain tension is obtained (get the adjusting nut on the chain side close, then set the adjusting nut on the opposite side). The adjusting nuts must be turned evenly to keep the rear wheel in alignment. If the chain pullers run out of travel, the chain is excessively worn and must be replaced (see Chapter 6). When the chain has the correct amount of slack, make sure the marks on the adjusters correspond to the same relative marks on each side of the swingarm.

10 ' Tighten the axle nut to the torque listed in this Chapter's Specifications, then install a new cotter pin through the axle nut and axle and bend it to secure the nut **(see illustration 9.9)**.

11   Tighten the chain puller adjusting nuts against the swingarm by turning each one about 1/4-turn.

Lubrication

Note: *If the chain is dirty, it should be removed and cleaned before it's lubricated* (see Chapter 6).

12   The best time to lubricate the chain is after the motorcycle has been ridden. When the chain is warm, the lubricant will penetrate the joints between the side plates, pins, bushings and rollers to provide lubrication of the internal bearing areas. Use a good quality chain lubricant and apply it to the area where the side plates overlap - not the middle of the rollers. Apply the lubricant along the top of the lower chain run, so that when the bike is ridden centrifugal force will move the lubricant into the chain, rather than throwing it off.

13   After applying the lubricant, let it soak in a few minutes before wiping off any excess.

10 Lubrication - general

Refer to illustration 10.3

1   Since the controls, cables and various other components of a motorcycle are exposed to the elements, they should be lubricated periodically to ensure safe and trouble-free operation.

2   The throttle twistgrip, brake lever, brake pedal, kickstarter pivot and sidestand pivot should be lubricated frequently. In order for the lubricant to be applied where it will do the most good, the component should be disassembled. However, if chain and cable lubricant is being used, it can be applied to the pivot joint gaps and will usually work its way into the areas where friction occurs. If motor oil or light grease is being used, apply it sparingly as it may attract dirt (which could cause the controls to bind or wear at an accelerated rate). **Note:** *One of the best lubricants for the control lever pivots is a dry-film lubricant (available from many sources by different names).*

3   The throttle and brake cables should be removed and treated with a commercially available cable lubricant which is specially formulated for use on motorcycle control cables. Small adapters for pressure lubricating the cables with spray can lubricants are available and ensure that the cable is lubricated along its entire length **(see illustration)**. When attaching the cable to the lever, be sure to lubricate the barrel-shaped fitting at the end with multi-purpose grease.

4   To lubricate the cables, disconnect them at the lower end, then lubricate the cable with a pressure lube adapter **(see illustration 10.3)**. See Chapter 3 (throttle cable) or Chapter 6 (brake cables).

5   Refer to Chapter 5 for the following lubrication procedures:

a) *Swingarm bearing and dust seals (PW80 models)*
b) *Steering head bearings*

6   Refer to Chapter 6 for the following lubrication procedures:

a) *Front and rear wheel bearings*
b) *Brake pedal pivot (PW80 models)*

11 Steering and suspension - check

1   The steering and suspension components must be maintained in top operating condition to ensure rider safety. Loose, worn or damaged suspension parts decrease the motorcycle's stability and control.

Steering and front suspension

Refer to illustrations 11.4, 11.7, 11.8 and 11.9

2   Check all steering and front suspension nuts and bolts for tightness. Make sure none of them have worked loose.

3   Inspect the fork tubes for scratches and scoring. If they're damaged, replace them (see Chapter 5).

4   Inspect the fork seals **(see illustration)** for leakage. If either fork seal is leaking, replace the fork seals (see Chapter 5).

5   Lock the front brake and push on the handlebars to compress the front forks several times. They should move up-and-down smoothly without binding. If the forks are binding, disassemble and inspect them (see Chapter 5).

6   Elevate the front wheel by placing a milk crate or some other suitable stand under the engine.

7   Grasp the bottom of the forks and try to move the fork assembly

11.7 Grasp the bottom of the forks and gently rock the fork assembly back and forth; if it's loose, adjust the steering head

11.8 Loosen the steering stem bolt

11.9 Tighten the ring nut (arrow) until you feel resistance

forward and backward **(see illustration)**. If it's loose, adjust the steering head.

8   Loosen the steering stem bolt **(see illustration)**.

9   If the ring nut is a cogged type, tighten it with a Yamaha ring nut wrench (YU-01268) or a suitable substitute **(see illustration)**. If it's a hex type, use a suitable open end wrench. On PW50 models, tighten the ring nut to the initial torque listed in this Chapter's Specifications, then loosen it and retighten it to the final torque listed in this Chapter's Specifications. On PW80 models, tighten the ring nut to the torque listed in this Chapter's Specifications.

10   Recheck the steering head by turning it from lock-to-lock. If it feels a little tight, loosen the ring nut a little bit and recheck. If it feels loose, tighten the ring nut a little.

11   When the steering head feels like all freeplay has been removed, but it's not binding or loose, tighten the steering stem bolt to the torque listed in this Chapter's Specifications.

12   Remove the bike from the milk crate or engine stand.

Rear suspension

13   Inspect the rear shock absorber(s) for fluid leakage and tightness of the mounting nuts and bolts. If a shock is leaking, replace it (on PW50 models, replace *both* shocks even if only one shock is leaking).

14   If you have a PW80 model, support the motorcycle securely upright with its rear wheel off the ground. Grab the swingarm on each side, just ahead of the axle. Rock the swingarm from side to side - there should be no discernible movement at the rear. If there's a little movement or a slight clicking can be heard, make sure the swingarm pivot shaft is tight. If the pivot shaft is tight but movement is still notice-

able, remove the swingarm and replace the swingarm bearings (see Chapter 5).

12   Sidestand - check

The sidestand should be checked to make sure it stays down when extended and up when retracted. Refer to Chapter 7 and check tightness of the sidestand mounting bolts. Check the spring for cracks or rust and replace it if any problems are found.

13   Clutch and transmission oil - change

Refer to illustrations 13.4a and 13.4b

1   The transmission and clutch share a common oil supply separate from the engine oil.

2   Park the vehicle in a level position, then start the engine and allow it to reach normal operating temperature. **Warning:** *Do not run the engine in an enclosed space such as a garage or shop.*

3   Remove the filler cap **(see illustration 3.6)**. Inspect the filler cap O-ring and replace it if it's cracked, cut or deteriorated.

4   Place a clean pan under the transmission drain plug **(see illustrations)**. Remove the plug. While the oil is draining, check the condition of the drain plug threads and the sealing washer.

5   After all the old oil has drained, install the drain plug with its sealing washer and tighten it to the torque listed in this Chapter's Specifications.

13.4a The transmission oil drain plug (arrow) (PW50 models)

13.4b The PW80 transmission oil drain plug is on the bottom

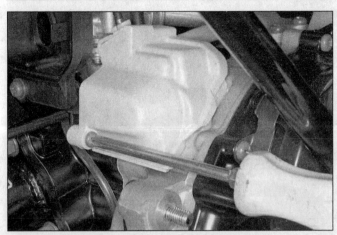

14.3 On PW50 models, remove the Autolube pump cover screw and the cover

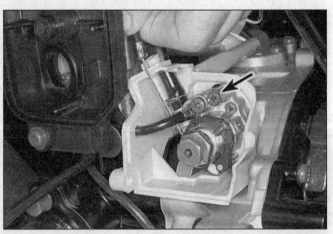

14.4 Remove the bleed screw (arrow), then run the engine with the cable pulled to bleed air from the oil

6   Before refilling the transmission, check the old oil carefully. If the oil was drained into a clean pan, small pieces of metal or other material can be easily detected. If the oil is very metallic colored, then the transmission is experiencing wear from break-in (new parts) or from insufficient lubrication. If there are flakes or chips of metal in the oil, then something is drastically wrong internally and the engine will have to be disassembled for inspection and repair.

7   If there are pieces of fiber-like material in the oil, the clutch is experiencing excessive wear and should be checked.

8   If the inspection of the oil turns up nothing unusual, refill the transmission to the proper level with the recommended oil and install the filler cap.

9   Start the engine and let it run for two or three minutes. Shut it off, wait a few minutes, and then check the oil level in the inspection window. If necessary, add more oil to bring the level up to the upper level mark on the window. Check around the drain plug for leaks.

14   Autolube pump - check and adjustment

1   Adjust throttle cable freeplay (see Section 6) and engine idle speed (see Section 7). Make sure the oil tank is full.

PW50 models

Refer to illustrations 14.3 and 14.4

Air bleeding

2   Remove the muffler and silencer (see Chapter 3).

3   Remove the Autolube pump cover **(see illustration)**.

4   Remove the bleed screw **(see illustration)**. Start the engine and let it idle, then pull the oil pump cable by hand as far as possible. If there's air in the oil, bubbles will flow from the bleed screw along with the oil. Let this continue until the bubbles stop appearing, then let go of the cable, shut off the engine and reinstall the bleed screw.

Cable adjustment

Refer to illustration 14.5

5   Run the engine, let it idle and operate the throttle. At the point where the throttle cable becomes tight and the engine speed increases, hold the throttle twistgrip steady and verify that the mark on the adjuster pulley is aligned with the Phillips screw **(see illustration)**. If it's not aligned, adjust the Autolube pump cable as follows.

6   Loosen the cable adjuster locknut **(see illustration 6.3)**, then turn the adjuster nut in or out until the mark on the pulley is aligned with the Phillips screw. Tighten the locknut securely.

Pump stroke adjustment

Refer to illustration 14.7

7   Set up a dial indicator with its pointer contacting the end of the pump plunger **(see illustration)**.

8   Have an assistant crank the engine over with the kickstarter. Watch the dial indicator and note the reading (pump stroke). If it's not within the range listed in this Chapter's Specifications, loosen the locknut. Turn the adjusting bolt counterclockwise to increase the stroke or clockwise to decrease it, then tighten the locknut.

9   Install the pump cover, muffler and silencer.

14.5 On PW50 models, verify that the mark on the adjuster pulley is aligned with the Phillips screw

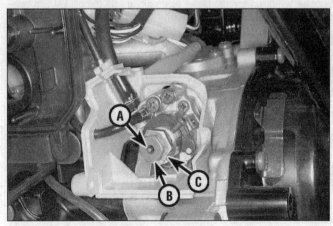

14.7 PW50 pump stroke adjustment points

A   Plunger   B   Adjusting bolt   C   Locknut

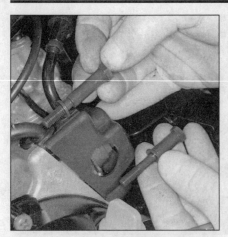

14.10 Remove the shouldered bolts and washers that secure the PW80 pump cover (note the different shoulder lengths) . . .

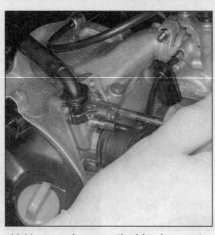

14.11 . . . and remove the bleed screw to bleed air from the oil

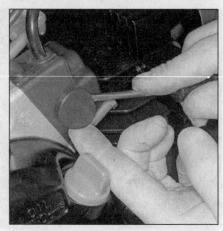

14.12 To check PW80 pump adjustment, pry the grommet out of the inspection hole . . .

14.13 . . . and check the position of the alignment marks (arrows)

14.14 Loosen the oil pump cable locknut (lower arrow) and turn the adjuster (upper arrow) (PW80)

15.2a On PW50 models, remove the air filter cover screw (arrow) . . .

PW80 models

Air bleeding

Refer to illustrations 14.10 and 14.11

10   Remove the oil pump cover **(see illustration)**.

11   Remove the bleed screw **(see illustration)**. If there's air in the oil, bubbles will flow from the bleed screw along with the oil. Let this continue until the bubbles stop appearing, then reinstall the bleed screw.

15.2b . . . lift off the cover . . .

Cable adjustment

Refer to illustrations 14.12, 14.13 and 14.14

12   Pry the grommet out of the inspection hole in the oil pump cover **(see illustration)**.

13   Run the engine, let it idle and operate the throttle. At the point where the throttle cable becomes tight and the engine speed increases, hold the throttle twistgrip steady and verify that the mark on the adjuster pulley is aligned with the Phillips screw **(see illustration)**. If it's not aligned, adjust the Autolube pump cable as follows.

14   Loosen the cable adjuster locknut **(see illustration)**, then turn the adjuster nut in or out until the mark on the pulley is aligned with the Phillips screw. Tighten the locknut securely.

Pump stroke

15   This is the same as for PW50 models (see Steps 7 and 8 above).

15 Air cleaner - filter element cleaning

Refer to illustrations 15.2a, 15.2b, 15,2c, 15.3a, 15.3b, 15.3c and 15.7

1   On PW50 models, remove the seat (see Chapter 7).

2   On PW50 models, remove the air filter cover screw, remove the filter cover and remove the filter element **(see illustrations)**.

3   On PW80 models, remove the air filter housing cover screws, and remove the cover, lift out the filter element and guide, and separate the filter from the guide **(see illustrations)**.

15.2c . . . and remove the filter element

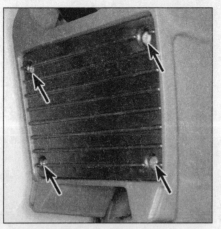

15.3a On PW80 models, remove the air filter housing cover screws (arrows) . . .

15.3b . . . note the different screw lengths . . .

15.3c . . . remove the cover, guide and filter element and separate the filter element from the guide

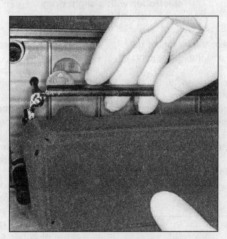

15.7 On installation, make sure the tab marked UP is upward

16.1a Inspect the PW50 fuel petcock lines (arrows) for leaks and evidence of damage

4   Clean the foam filter element in a high flash point solvent, squeeze the solvent out of the foam and let the element dry completely.

5   Soak the foam element in the foam filter oil listed in this Chapter's Specifications, then squeeze it firmly to remove the excess oil. Don't wring it out or the foam may be damaged. The element should be wet through with oil, but no oil should drip from it.

6   Reassemble the element and holder.

7   Installation is the reverse of removal. If you're working on a PW80, position the UP mark on the element upward (see illustration).

16   Fuel system - inspection

Refer to illustrations 16.1a and 16.1b

Warning: *Gasoline is extremely flammable, so take extra precautions when you work on any part of the fuel system. Don't smoke or allow open flames or bare light bulbs near the work area, and don't work in a garage where a natural gas-type appliance (such as a water heater or clothes dryer) is present. Since gasoline is carcinogenic, wear latex gloves when there's a possibility of being exposed to fuel, and if you spill any fuel on your skin, rinse it off immediately with soap and water. Mop up any fuel spills immediately and do not store fuel-soaked rags where they could ignite. When you perform any kind of work on the fuel system, wear safety glasses and have a fire extinguisher suitable for class B type fires (flammable liquids) on hand.*

1   Inspect the fuel tank, the fuel petcock and the fuel line for leaks and evidence of damage (see illustrations). If the fuel petcock is leaking on a PW80 model, tightening the screws may help. If leakage persists, remove, disassemble and repair, or replace, the petcock (see Chapter 3). If the fuel line is cracked or otherwise deteriorated, replace it.

16.1b The PW80 petcock is attached directly to the tank, with a single line to the carburetor (arrow)

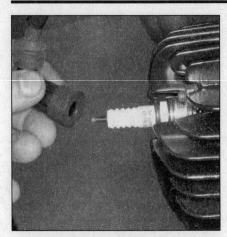

18.1 Twist the spark plug cap back and forth to free it, then pull it off the plug

18.5a Use a wire type gauge to check the gap; if the wire doesn't slide between the electrodes with a slight drag, adjust the gap

18.5b To change the gap, bend the side electrode (arrows); don't crack or chip the ceramic insulator around the center electrode

2   Inspect the hose clamp connections between the air intake duct and the carburetor and between the carburetor and the intake joint. If either hose clamp is loose, tighten it.

3   Inspect the carburetor for leaks. If the carburetor is leaking, remove, disassemble and rebuild it (see Chapter 3).

4   Remove the Autolube pump cover (see Section 14) and inspect the oil line from the pump to the engine. Replace the line if it's damaged or deteriorated.

5   Inspect the oil tank for cracks, melting or other damage. Replace it if you find any damage.

6   Place the fuel petcock lever in the Off position and disconnect the line that runs to the carburetor.

17 Exhaust system - inspection

1   Periodically check the exhaust system for leaks and loose fasteners. If tightening the holder nuts at the cylinder head fails to stop any leaks, replace the gasket with a new ones (a procedure which requires removal of the system).

2   The exhaust pipe flange screws at the cylinder head are especially prone to loosening, which could cause damage to the head (see Chapter 3). Check them frequently and keep them tight.

18 Spark plug - check and replacement

Refer to illustrations 18.1, 18.5a and 18.5b

1   Twist the spark plug cap to break it free from the plug, then pull it off **(see illustration)**. If available, use compressed air to blow any accumulated debris from around the spark plug. Remove the plug with a spark plug socket.

2   Inspect the electrodes for wear. Both the center and side electrodes should have square edges and the side electrode should be of uniform thickness. Look for excessive deposits and evidence of a cracked or chipped insulator around the center electrode. Compare your spark plugs to the color spark plug reading chart on the inside back cover. Check the threads, the washer and the ceramic insulator body for cracks and other damage.

3   If the electrodes are not excessively worn, and if the deposits can be easily removed with a wire brush, the plug can be regapped and reused (if no cracks or chips are visible in the insulator). If in doubt con-

cerning the condition of the plug, replace it with a new one, as the expense is minimal.

4   Cleaning the spark plug by sandblasting is permitted, provided you clean the plug with a high flash-point solvent afterwards.

5   Before installing a new plug, make sure it is the correct type and heat range. Check the gap between the electrodes, as it is not preset. For best results, use a wire-type gauge rather than a flat gauge to check the gap **(see illustration)**. If the gap must be adjusted, bend the side electrode only and be very careful not to chip or crack the insulator nose **(see illustration)**. Make sure the washer is in place before installing the plug.

6   Since the cylinder head is made of aluminum, which is soft and easily damaged, thread the plug into the head by hand. Slip a short length of hose over the end of the plug to use as a tool to thread it into place. The hose will grip the plug well enough to turn it, but will start to slip if the plug begins to cross-thread in the hole - this will prevent damaged threads and the accompanying repair costs.

7   Once the plug is finger tight, the job can be finished with a socket. If a torque wrench is available, tighten the spark plug to the torque listed in this Chapter's Specifications. If you do not have a torque wrench, tighten the plug finger tight (until the washer bottoms on the cylinder head) then use a spark plug socket to tighten it an additional 1/4 turn. Regardless of the method used, do not over-tighten it.

8   Reconnect the spark plug cap.

19 Fasteners - check

1   Since vibration of the machine tends to loosen fasteners, all nuts, bolts, screws, etc. should be periodically checked for proper tightness. Also make sure all cotter pins or other safety fasteners are correctly installed.

2   Pay particular attention to the following:

Spark plug
Transmission oil drain plug
Gearshift pedal
Brake pedal
Footpegs
Engine mounting nuts/bolts
Shock absorber nuts/bolts
Front axle nut
Rear axle nut
Skid plate bolts

Chapter 1 Part B
Tune-up and routine maintenance (RT100 and RT180 models)

Contents

Engine

Spark plug type	
RT100	NGK B7ES
RT180	NGK B8ES
Spark plug gap	
RT100	0.5 to 0.6 mm (0.020 to 0.024 inch)
RT180	0.6 to 0.7 mm (0.024 to 0.028 inch)
Pilot air screw setting	1-1/2 turns out from seated position
Engine idle speed	
RT100	1300 to 1450 rpm
RT180	1450 to 1550 rpm
Cylinder compression	Not specified

Miscellaneous

Front brake shoe lining limit (RT100)	2.0 mm (5/64-inch)
Front brake pad lining thickness limit (RT180)	0.8 mm (1/32-inch)
Rear brake shoe lining limit	2.0 mm (5/64-inch)
Front brake lever freeplay	
RT100 (between lever and lever bracket)	5 to 8 mm (13/64 to 5/16 inch)
RT180 (at tip of lever)	10 to 20 mm (7/64 to 13/64 inch)
Rear brake pedal freeplay	20 to 30 mm (51/64 to 1-13/64 inches)
Rear brake pedal height (RT180)	20 mm (51/64-inch) below top of footrest
Clutch lever freeplay	2 to 3 mm (5/64 to 1/8 inch)
Throttle cable freeplay at twistgrip	3 to 5 mm (1/8 to 1/4 inch)
Throttle cable freeplay at carburetor (RT180)	1.0 mm (3/64 inch)
Minimum tire tread depth	4.5 mm (11/64 inch)
Tire pressure (cold)	
RT100	18 psi front and rear
RT180	15 psi front and rear
Tire size	
RT100	
Front	2.50-18 4PR
Rear	3.00-16 4PR
RT180	
Front	80/100-21-4PA
Rear	100/100-18 59M
Drive chain slack	
RT100	20 to 30 mm (51/64 to 1-3/16 inches)
RT180	40 mm (1-38/64 inches)
Autolube pump minimum pump stroke	0.20 to 0.25 mm (0.008 to 0.010 inch)

Torque specifications

Transmission oil drain plug	20 Nm (168 in-lbs)
Spark plug	
RT100	25 Nm (18 ft-lbs)
RT180	20 Nm (168 in-lbs)
Valve stem locknut	1.5 Nm (13 in-lbs)
Steering stem ring (adjusting) nut	
RT100	
Initial torque	36 Nm (25 ft-lbs)
Final torque	6 Nm (52 in-lbs)
RT180	
Initial torque	38 Nm (27 ft-lbs)
Final torque	6 Nm (52 in-lbs)
Upper triple clamp pinch bolts	
RT100	Not specified
RT180	23 Nm (17 ft-lbs)
Steering stem flange bolt	
RT100	65 Nm (47 ft-lbs)
RT180	54 Nm (39 ft-lbs)
Autolube pump adjusting plate locknut	
RT100	7 Nm (60 in-lbs)
RT180	6 Nm (52 in-lbs)

Recommended lubricants and fluids

Fuel

Type	Regular unleaded gasoline
Capacity	
RT100	
Full tank	5.0 liters (1.32 gallons)
Reserve	1.5 liters (0.39 gallons)
RT180	
Full tank	13 liters (3.43 gallons)
Reserve	1.1 liters (0.29 gallons)

Engine oil

Type	Yamalube "2" or air-cooled two-stroke engine oil
Oil tank capacity	
RT100	1.0 liter (1.06 quarts)
RT180	0.75 liter (0.79 quart)

Transmission oil

Type	Yamalube "4" or SE multigrade four-stroke oil manufactured for use in motorcycles
Viscosity	10W30
Capacity at oil change*	
RT100	0.65 liter (0.69 qt)
RT180	0.55 liter (0.58 qt)
Air cleaner element oil	Foam filter oil or engine oil
Brake fluid (RT180)	DOT 4 (DOT 3 can be used if DOT 4 is not available)
Drive chain lubricant	Chain lube

Miscellaneous

Wheel bearings	Medium weight, lithium-based multi-purpose grease
Swingarm pivot bushings	Molybdenum disulfide paste grease containing 40 percent or more molybdenum disulfide
Cables and lever pivots	Engine oil
Throttle grip, brake pedal/shift lever/throttle lever pivots	Medium weight, lithium-based multi-purpose grease

Approximate capacity; use dipstick (RT180) to determine exact amount (see text).

Yamaha RT100/RT180
Routine maintenance intervals

Note: *The pre-ride inspection outlined in the owner's manual covers checks and maintenance that should be carried out on a daily basis. It's condensed and included here to remind you of its importance. Always perform the pre-ride inspection at every maintenance interval (in addition to the procedures listed). The intervals* *listed below are the shortest intervals recommended by the manufacturer for each particular operation during the model years covered in this manual. Your owner's manual may have different intervals for your model.*

Every month, or before every ride

Check the operation of both brakes - check the front brake lever and rear brake pedal for correct freeplay
Check brake fluid level in the front master cylinder (RT180 models)
Make sure the engine kill switch works properly
Check the throttle for smooth operation and correct freeplay
Check the oil level in the oil tank
Check the oil level in the transmission
Check and, if necessary, adjust the drive chain slack and the wheel alignment
Lubricate the drive chain
Inspect the condition of the drive chain sprockets and sliders
Check the tires for damage, the presence of foreign objects and correct air pressure
Check all fasteners, including axle nuts, for tightness

Check the front and rear brake shoes for wear
Check the front brake pads (RT180 models)
Check clutch operation and, if necessary, adjust freeplay
Check the swingarm pivot for looseness and tighten as necessary
Inspect the condition of the wheels and spokes
Check the wheel bearings for looseness and damage and, if necessary, replace them
Check the steering head bearings for looseness and, if necessary, adjust them
Check the front fork seals for leakage and, if necessary, replace the seals and change the fork oil
Check the rear shock absorber seal(s) for leakage and, if necessary, replace the shock(s)
Check all fittings and fasteners and tighten as necessary
Inspect the expansion chamber and muffler
Check the operation of the sidestand and lubricate as necessary
More often in dusty conditions.

Every six months

Check, clean and gap, or replace, the spark plug
Inspect and, if necessary, replace the air filter element*
Check and, if necessary, adjust the idle speed
Inspect and, if necessary, replace the fuel hose
Check the operation of the Autolube pump

Every 24 months

Change the brake fluid
Replace the transmission oil
Repack the swingarm pivot bearings
Repack the steering head bearings

2.1 Decals on the motorcycle include maintenance and safety information

2   Introduction to tune-up and routine maintenance

Refer to illustration 2.1

This Chapter covers in detail the checks and procedures necessary for the tune-up and routine maintenance of your motorcycle. Section 1 includes the routine maintenance schedule, which is designed to keep the machine in proper running condition and prevent possible problems. The remaining Sections contain detailed procedures for carrying out the items listed on the maintenance schedule, as well as additional maintenance information designed to increase reliability. Maintenance and safety information is also printed on decals, which are mounted in various locations on the motorcycle (**see illustration**). Where information on the decals differs from that presented in this Chapter, use the decal information.

Since routine maintenance plays such an important role in the safe and efficient operation of your motorcycle, it is presented here as a comprehensive check list. For the rider who does all his own maintenance, these lists outline the procedures and checks that should be done on a routine basis.

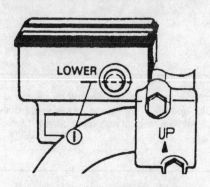

3.3 The front brake fluid level is visible in the window; make sure it's above the LOWER mark (1)

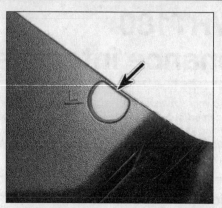

3.6 The Autolube system oil tank fluid level window (arrow)

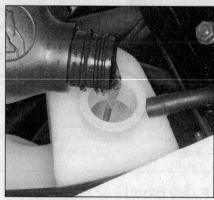

3.7 Remove the seat and oil tank cap, then pour oil into the tank

Deciding where to start or plug into the routine maintenance schedule depends on several factors. If you have owned the bike for some time but have never performed any maintenance on it, then you may want to start at the nearest interval and include some additional procedures to ensure that nothing important is overlooked. If you have just had a major engine overhaul, then you may want to start the maintenance routine from the beginning. If you have a used machine and have no knowledge of its history or maintenance record, you may desire to combine all the checks into one large service initially and then settle into the maintenance schedule prescribed.

The Sections which outline the inspection and maintenance procedures are written as step-by-step comprehensive guides to the actual performance of the work. They explain in detail each of the routine inspections and maintenance procedures on the check list. References to additional information in applicable Chapters is also included and should not be overlooked.

Before beginning any actual maintenance or repair, the machine should be cleaned thoroughly, especially around the oil filler plug, radiator cap, engine covers, carburetor, etc. Cleaning will help ensure that dirt does not contaminate the engine and will allow you to detect wear and damage that could otherwise easily go unnoticed.

3   Fluid levels - check

Front brake fluid (RT180 models)

Refer to illustration 3.3

1   To ensure proper operation of the hydraulic disc brakes, the fluid level in the master cylinder reservoirs must be maintained within a safe range.

2   With the motorcycle supported in an upright position, turn the handlebars until the top of the front brake master cylinder is as level as possible.

3   The fluid level is visible in the window on the reservoir **(see illustration)**. Make sure the fluid level is above the Lower mark cast on the master cylinder body next to the reservoir.

4   If the fluid level is low, clean the area around the reservoir cover. Remove the cover screws and take off the cover and diaphragm. Add new brake fluid of the type listed in this Chapter's Specifications until the fluid level is even with the line cast inside the reservoir.

5   Install the diaphragm and cover, then tighten the cover screws securely.

Engine oil (Autolube system)

Refer to illustrations 3.6 and 3.7

6   The oil tank fluid level is visible through a window in the tank **(see illustration)**. If the level is below the lower mark on the tank, top up the tank.

7   Remove the oil tank cap and pour in enough two-stroke oil (the recommended oil is listed in this Chapter's Specifications) to bring the level up to the upper mark **(see illustration)**. Install the cap. Make sure it's secure.

Transmission oil

Refer to illustrations 3.10a and 3.10b

8   Place the machine on level ground.

9   Start the engine and run it for several minutes. **Warning:** *Do not run the engine in an enclosed space such as a garage or shop.* Stop the engine and allow the bike to sit undisturbed in a level position for a few minutes.

3.10a The transmission oil filler cap is on the upper right side of the crankcase . . .

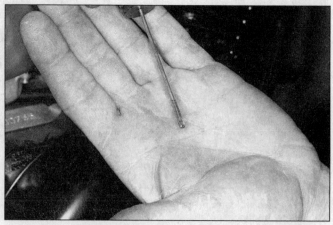

3.10b . . . remove it to check the oil level on the dipstick

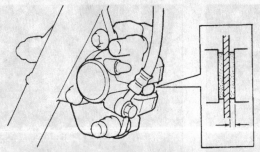

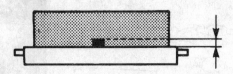

4.4a Remove the inspection plug to check the thickness of the RT180 brake pads . . .

4.4b . . . if either of the brake pads has worn enough to expose the wear slot, replace both of them

10   With the engine off, unscrew the transmission oil dipstick, wipe off the dipstick and, with the bike in an upright position, insert it back into the hole (don't screw it in). Pull out the dipstick and note the oil level **(see illustrations)**.

11   If the oil level is below the minimum mark, add enough four-stroke oil (the recommended oil is listed in this Chapter's Specifications) to bring the level up to the area between the two marks.

4   Brake system - general check

1   A routine general check of the brakes will ensure that any problems are discovered and remedied before the rider's safety is jeopardized.

2   Check the brake lever and pedal for loose connections, bends, and other damage. Replace any damaged parts with new ones (see Chapter 7). Check front brake lever and rear brake pedal freeplay (see Section 5).

3   Make sure all brake fasteners are tight. Check the brakes for wear as described below.

Wear check

Front disc brake (RT180 models)

Refer to illustrations 4.4a and 4.4b

4   Remove the rubber plug from the front brake caliper inspection hole and look at the brake pads **(see illustration)**. The pads should have wear indicator slots molded in the friction material next to the metal backing **(see illustration)**. If the friction material has been worn away to the point that that slots are exposed (or almost exposed), replace the pads as a set. Be sure to check both pads, since they tend to wear unevenly. If you can't see any wear indicator slots, measure the brake pad thickness and compare your measurements to the minimum thickness listed in this Chapter's Specifications. If the thickness

of either pad is below the minimum thickness, it's time to replace the pads (see Chapter 6B).

Rear drum brake

Refer to illustration 4.7

5   Operate the brake pedal. If operation is rough or sticky, lubricate the brake cable (see Section 10).

6   Adjust the rear brake pedal freeplay (see Section 5).

7   Apply the brake pedal and note whether the wear indicator on the brake arm points at the wear limit line on the brake panel **(see illustration)**. If the wear indicator lines up with the wear limit line when the pedal is applied, replace the brake shoes (see Chapter 6B).

5   Brake lever and pedal freeplay - check and adjustment

Front brake lever

RT100 models

Refer to illustrations 5.1a and 5.1b

1   Pull back the rubber cover from the brake lever and adjuster **(see illustration)**. Apply the front brake lever to the point at which you feel initial resistance (the point at which the brake cable slack is taken up and the cable begins to apply the brake shoes). With the lever applied to this point of initial resistance, measure the gap between the brake lever and the brake lever bracket **(see illustration)** and compare your measurement to the range of freeplay listed in this Chapter's Specifications. If the gap is outside the specified range, adjust the brake lever freeplay as follows.

2   Loosen the locknut and turn the adjuster in or out until the lever freeplay is within the specified range. Tighten the locknut and slide the rubber cover back into place over the adjuster and locknut.

4.7 If the wear indicator on the brake arm lines up with the wear limit line on the brake panel (arrows) with the brake applied, replace the shoes

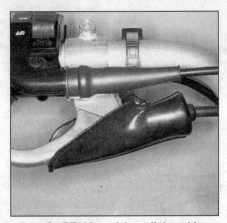

5.1a On RT100 models, pull the rubber cover back from the brake lever . . .

5.1b . . . measure front brake lever freeplay at the gap between the lever and the bracket (A); loosen the locknut (B) and turn the adjuster (C) to change it

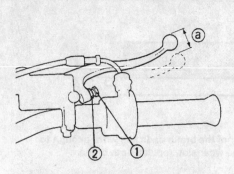

5.3 On RT180 models, measure the front brake lever freeplay at the tip (a); loosen the locknut (1) and turn the adjuster (2) to adjust it

5.5 On RT100 models, measure the distance the pedal travels from its released position to the point where you first feel resistance

5.6 To adjust rear brake pedal freeplay on RT100 models, turn the adjuster nut at the rear end of the brake rod (arrow)

RT180 models

Refer to illustration 5.3

3   Apply the front brake lever to the point at which you feel initial resistance (the point at which the lever adjuster screw begins to push against the piston inside the master cylinder). Measure the distance that the tip of the lever travels from its unapplied position to this point of initial resistance **(see illustration)**. If this measurement is outside the range of freeplay listed in this Chapter's Specifications, adjust the brake lever freeplay as follows.

4   Loosen the locknut **(see illustration 5.3)** and turn the adjuster in or out until lever freeplay is within the specified range. Tighten the locknut.

Rear brake

RT100 models

Refer to illustrations 5.5 and 5.6

5   Apply the rear brake pedal to the point at which you feel initial resistance (the point at which the brake cable slack is taken up and the cable begins to apply the brake shoes). Measure the distance that the pedal travels from its unapplied position to this point of initial resistance **(see illustration)** and compare your measurement to the range of freeplay listed in this Chapter's Specifications. If the freeplay is outside the specified range, adjust the brake pedal freeplay as follows.

6   Turn the adjuster nut at the rear end of the brake rod **(see illustration)** in or out to bring the brake pedal within the specified range of brake pedal freeplay.

RT180 models

Refer to illustrations 5.7 and 5.8

7   Measure the height of the rear brake pedal *below* the top of the footrest **(see illustration)** and compare your measurement to the rear

brake pedal height listed in this Chapter's Specifications. If the brake pedal height is incorrect, adjust it as follows.

8   Loosen the locknut **(see illustration)** and turn the adjuster in or out to bring the pedal to the correct height. Tighten the locknut securely.

9   After the pedal height has been checked and adjusted, check and adjust pedal freeplay as described in Steps 5 and 6.

6   Clutch cable - check and adjustment

Check

Refer to illustration 6.1

1   Squeeze the clutch lever and note the point at which you feel initial resistance (the point at which the clutch cable slack is taken up and the cable begins to release the pressure plate). With the clutch lever applied to this point of initial resistance, measure the gap between the clutch lever and the clutch lever bracket **(see illustration)** and compare your measurement to the range of freeplay listed in this Chapter's Specifications. If it's not within the specified range, adjust it as follows.

Adjustment

Freeplay adjustment

Refer to illustration 6.2

2   Pull back the rubber cover from the adjuster at the handlebar, loosen the locknut **(see illustration)** and turn the adjuster in or out to bring lever freeplay within the specified range. There is another freeplay adjuster several inches from the clutch lever bracket. To use this adjuster, simply loosen the locknut and turn the adjuster in or out to produce the correct freeplay.

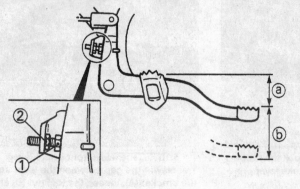

5.7 Adjust RT180 rear brake pedal height with the adjuster bolt . . .

a   *Pedal height*
b   *Pedal freeplay*
1   *Pedal height adjuster bolt*
2   *Locknut*

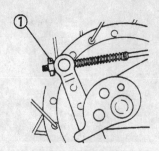

5.8 . . . and adjust pedal freeplay with the nut at the end of the brake rod (1)

6.1 Measure clutch freeplay at the gap between the clutch lever and its bracket (arrow) with the lever applied to the point of initial resistance . . .

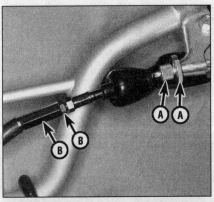

6.2 . . . to adjust it, loosen the locknut and turn the adjuster first at the handlebar adjuster (A), then at the mid-cable adjuster (B)

6.10a Loosen the locknut and turn the adjuster (arrow) with a screwdriver to adjust the clutch mechanism (RT180)

3   If freeplay can't be adjusted within the specified range, the clutch cable is probably stretched too much; replace the cable (see Chapter 2B).

Mechanism adjustment (RT180 models only)

Refer to illustrations 6.10a and 6.10b

4   Loosen the locknuts and the adjusters **(see illustration 6.2)**.

5   Disconnect the Autolube pump cover (Section 14).

6   Disconnect the Autolube pump cable and the pump hoses (Section 14).

7   Drain the transmission oil (see Section 13).

8   Loosen the rear brake adjuster (see Section 5).

9   Remove the kickstarter and the right crankcase cover (see Chapter 2B).

10   Loosen the clutch adjuster locknut **(see illustration)**. Move the push lever forward until it stops. With the push lever held at this forward position, turn the adjuster **(see illustration 6.10a)** to align the mark on the push lever with the projection on the crankcase **(see illustration)**. Tighten the adjuster locknut to the torque listed in this Chapter's Specifications.

11   Install the right crankcase cover and the kickstarter (see Chapter 2B).

12   Adjust the rear brake pedal freeplay (see Section 5).

13   Install the Autolube pump cover gasket.

14   Connect the Autolube pump hoses and cable (Section 14).

15   Adjust the clutch cable freeplay (see Steps 2 and 3).

16   Fill the transmission with the recommended four-stroke oil (see Section 13).

17   Bleed all air from the Autolube pump and install the Autolube pump cover (see Section 14).

7   Throttle cable freeplay - check and adjustment

Check

Refer to illustration 7.2

1   Make sure the throttle twistgrip moves easily from fully closed to fully open with the front wheel turned at various angles. The grip should return automatically from fully open to fully closed when released. If the throttle sticks, check the throttle cable for cracks or kinks in the housings. Also, make sure the inner cable is clean and well-lubricated (see Section 10).

2   Measure the freeplay at the twistgrip flange **(see illustration)**. The freeplay is the distance that the twistgrip flange travels before you feel an initial resistance (the point at which the throttle cable begins to open the throttle plate) and compare your measurement to the range of freeplay listed in this Chapter's Specifications. If it's not within the specified range, adjust it as follows.

Adjustment

At the handlebar

Refer to illustration 7.3

3   Pull back the rubber cover from the adjuster and loosen the locknut **(see illustration)**. Turn the adjuster until the twistgrip freeplay is within the specified range, and then tighten the locknut.

6.10b Align the pointer on the push lever arm with the cast mark on the crankcase (arrow)

7.2 Measure the freeplay at the twistgrip flange (the distance that the twistgrip flange travels before you feel an initial resistance)

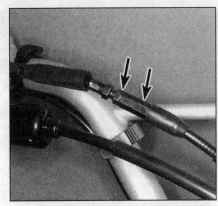

7.3 Loosen the locknut (left arrow) and turn the adjuster (right arrow) to adjust twistgrip freeplay

7.6 Loosen the locknut (right arrow) and turn the adjuster (left arrow) in or out to obtain the specified freeplay

8.4 Check tire pressure with a tire gauge

8.5 Check the tension of the spokes periodically, but don't over-tighten them

At the carburetor (RT180 models)

Refer to illustration 7.6

4   First, adjust freeplay at the twistgrip (see Step 3).

5   Pull up the rubber cover, measure freeplay at the gap between the end of the cable locknut and the end of the threaded barrel and compare your measurement to the freeplay listed in this Chapter's Specifications. If the freeplay is incorrect, adjust it as follows.

6   Loosen the locknut **(see illustration)** and turn the adjusting nut in or out to obtain the specified freeplay. Tighten the locknut securely.

8   Tires/wheels - general check

Refer to illustrations 8.4, 8.5 and 8.7

1   Routine tire and wheel checks should be made with the realization that your safety depends to a great extent on their condition.

2   Check the tires carefully for cuts, tears, embedded nails or other sharp objects and excessive wear. Operation of the motorcycle with excessively worn tires is extremely hazardous, as traction and handling are directly affected. Check the tread depth at the center of the tire. Yamaha doesn't specify a minimum tread depth for these models, but as a general rule, tires should be replaced with new ones when the tread knobs are worn to 3 mm (1/8 inch) or less.

3   Repair or replace punctured tires as soon as damage is noted. Do not try to patch a torn tire, as wheel balance and tire reliability may be impaired.

4   Check the tire pressures when the tires are cold and keep them properly inflated **(see illustration)**. Proper air pressure will increase tire life and provide maximum stability and ride comfort. Keep in mind that low tire pressures may cause the tire to slip on the rim or come off, while high tire pressures will cause abnormal tread wear and unsafe handling.

5   The wheels should be kept clean and checked periodically for cracks, bending, loose spokes and rust. Never attempt to repair damaged wheels; they must be replaced with new ones. Loose spokes can be tightened with a spoke wrench **(see illustration)**, but be careful not to overtighten and distort the wheel rim.

6   Check the valve stem locknuts to make sure they're tight. Also, make sure the valve stem cap is in place and tight. If it is missing, install a new one made of metal or hard plastic.

7   Check the tightness of the locknut on the rim lock **(see illustration)**. Tighten it if necessary to the torque listed in this Chapter's Specifications.

9   Drive chain and sprockets - check, adjustment and lubrication

Refer to illustration 9.3

1   A neglected drive chain won't last long and can quickly damage the sprockets. Routine chain adjustment isn't difficult and will ensure maximum chain and sprocket life.

2   To check the chain, support the bike securely with the rear wheel off the ground. Place the transmission in neutral. If you're working on an RT180, push the spring-loaded chain tensioner away from the chain while checking slack.

3   Push up on the bottom run of the chain and measure the slack midway between the two sprockets **(see illustration)**, then compare

8.7 Tighten the nut on the rim lock to the specified torque

9.3 Push up on the bottom run of the chain and measure the slack midway between the two sprockets

9.9 On RT100 models, loosen the chain adjuster bolt locknuts (left arrow), then turn the adjusting bolts (right arrow); turn both adjusters evenly

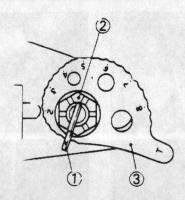

9.10 On RT180 models, rotate the chain pullers evenly in a clockwise or counterclockwise direction until the correct chain tension is obtained

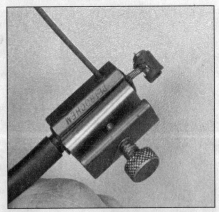

10.3 Lubricating a cable with a pressure lube adapter (make sure the tool seats around the inner cable)

the measurements to the value listed in this Chapter's Specifications. As wear occurs, the chain will actually stretch, which means adjustment by removing some slack from the chain. In some cases where lubrication has been neglected, corrosion and galling may cause the links to bind and kink, which effectively shortens the chain's length. If the chain is tight between the sprockets, rusty or kinked, it's time to replace it with a new one. **Note:** *Repeat the chain slack measurement along the length of the chain - ideally, every inch or so. If you find a tight area, mark it with felt pen or paint and repeat the measurement after the bike has been ridden. If the chain's still tight in the same areas, it may be damaged or worn. Because a tight or kinked chain can damage the transmission countershaft bearing, it's a good idea to replace it.*

4   Check the entire length of the chain for damaged rollers, loose links and loose pins.

5   Look through the slots in the left engine cover and inspect the engine sprocket. Check the teeth on the engine sprocket and the rear sprocket for wear. Refer to Chapter 5 for the sprocket replacement procedure if the sprockets appear to be worn excessively.

6   Inspect the condition of the chain guide. If it's worn, replace it.

Adjustment

Refer to illustrations 9.9 and 9.10

7   Rotate the rear wheel until the chain is positioned with the least amount of slack present.

8   Loosen the rear axle nut and the chain adjuster nut on the axle (see Chapter 6).

9   On RT100 models, loosen the chain adjuster bolt locknuts **(see illustration)**, then turn the adjusting bolts *evenly* until the correct chain tension is obtained (get the adjuster on the chain side close, then set the adjuster on the opposite side). Be sure to turn the adjusting bolts evenly to keep the rear wheel in alignment. If the adjusting nuts pull the adjusters to the end of their travel, the chain is excessively worn and must be replaced (see Chapter 6). When the chain has the correct amount of slack, make sure the marks on the adjusters correspond to the same relative marks on each side of the swingarm. Tighten the adjuster bolt locknuts securely.

10   On RT180 models, rotate the chain pullers **(see illustration)** *evenly* in a clockwise or counterclockwise direction until the correct chain tension is obtained (get the chain puller on the chain side close, then set the chain puller on the opposite side). Be sure to rotate the chain pullers evenly to keep the rear wheel in alignment. If you're unable to adjust the chain slack with the chain pullers, the chain is excessively worn and must be replaced (see Chapter 6). When the chain has the correct amount of slack, make sure the marks on the chain pullers correspond to the same relative marks on each side of the swingarm.

11   Tighten the axle nut to the torque listed in the Chapter 6 Specifications.

Lubrication

Note: *If the chain is dirty, it should be removed and cleaned before it's lubricated (see Chapter 6).*

12   The best time to lubricate the chain is after the motorcycle has been ridden. When the chain is warm, the lubricant will penetrate the joints between the side plates, pins, bushings and rollers to provide lubrication of the internal bearing areas. Use a good quality chain lubricant and apply it to the area where the side plates overlap - not the middle of the rollers. Apply the lubricant along the top of the lower chain run, so that when the bike is ridden centrifugal force will move the lubricant into the chain, rather than throwing it off.

13   After applying the lubricant, let it soak in a few minutes before wiping off any excess.

10 Lubrication - general

Refer to illustration 10.3

1   Since the controls, cables and various other components of a motorcycle are exposed to the elements, they should be lubricated periodically to ensure safe and trouble-free operation.

2   The throttle twistgrip, brake lever, brake pedal, kickstarter pivot and sidestand pivot should be lubricated frequently. In order for the lubricant to be applied where it will do the most good, the component should be disassembled. However, if chain and cable lubricant is being used, it can be applied to the pivot joint gaps and will usually work its way into the areas where friction occurs. If motor oil or light grease is being used, apply it sparingly as it may attract dirt (which could cause the controls to bind or wear at an accelerated rate). **Note:** *One of the best lubricants for the control lever pivots is a dry-film lubricant (available from many sources by different names).*

3   The throttle and brake cables should be removed and treated with a commercially available cable lubricant which is specially formulated for use on motorcycle control cables. Small adapters for pressure lubricating the cables with spray can lubricants are available and ensure that the cable is lubricated along its entire length **(see illustration)**. When attaching the cable to the lever, be sure to lubricate the barrel-shaped fitting at the end with multi-purpose grease.

4   To lubricate the cables, disconnect them at the lower end, then lubricate the cable with a pressure lube adapter **(see illustration 10.3)**. See Chapter 3 (throttle cable) or Chapter 6 (brake cables).

5   Refer to Chapter 5 for the following lubrication procedures:
   a) Swingarm bearing and dust seals
   b) Rear suspension linkage and dust seals
   c) Steering head bearings

6   Refer to Chapter 6 for the following lubrication procedures:
   a) Front and rear wheel bearings
   b) Brake pedal pivot

11.4 Inspect each fork seal for leakage; if a seal is leaking, replace both fork seals

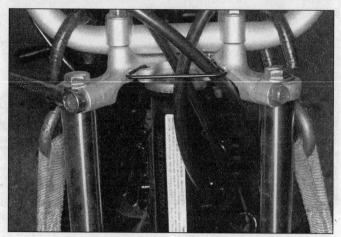

11.10a Loosen the upper triple clamp pinch bolts . . .

11   Steering and suspension - check

1   The steering and suspension components must be maintained in top operating condition to ensure rider safety. Loose, worn or damaged suspension parts decrease the motorcycle's stability and control.

Steering and front suspension

Refer to illustrations 11.4, 11.10a, 11.10b and 11.11

2   Check all steering and front suspension nuts and bolts for tightness. Make sure none of them have worked loose.

3   Inspect the fork tubes for scratches and scoring. If they're damaged, replace them (see Chapter 5).

4   Inspect the fork seals (see illustration) for leakage. If either fork seal is leaking, replace the fork seals (see Chapter 5).

5   Lock the front brake and push on the handlebars to compress the front forks several times. They should move up-and-down smoothly without binding. If the forks are binding, disassemble and inspect them (see Chapter 5).

6   Elevate the front wheel by placing a milk crate or some other suitable stand under the engine.

7   Grasp the bottom of the forks and gently rock the fork assembly back and forth (see illustration 11.7 in Chapter 1A). If it's loose, adjust the steering head.

8   Remove the seat and side covers (see Chapter 7) and the fuel tank (see Chapter 3).

9   Remove the front wheel (see Chapter 6).

10   Loosen the upper triple clamp pinch bolts (see illustration) and the steering stem bolt (see illustration).

11   Tighten the ring nut with a Yamaha ring nut wrench (YU-33975) or a suitable substitute (see illustration). Don't torque the nut; just tighten it until you feel resistance.

12   If you have the Yamaha special tool, attach a torque wrench to it so that they form a right angle. Tighten the ring nut to the initial torque listed in this Chapter's Specifications.

13   Loosen the ring nut one turn, then tighten it to the final torque listed in this Chapter's Specifications.

14   Recheck the steering head by turning it from lock-to-lock. If it feels a little tight, loosen the ring nut a little bit and recheck. If it feels loose, repeat the adjustment (Steps 11, 12 and 13).

15   When the steering head feels like all freeplay has been removed, but it's not binding or loose, tighten the steering stem bolt and the upper triple crown pinch bolts to the torque listed in this Chapter's Specifications.

16   Install the front wheel (see Chapter 5).

17   Install the tank (see Chapter 3), side covers and seat (see Chapter 7).

18   Remove the bike from the milk crate or engine stand.

Rear suspension

19   Inspect the rear shock absorber(s) for fluid leakage and tightness of the mounting nuts and bolts. If a shock is leaking, replace it (on RT100 models, replace *both* shocks even if only one is leaking).

20   Support the motorcycle securely upright with its rear wheel off the

11.10b . . . and the steering stem bolt

11.11 Tighten the ring nut with a Yamaha ring nut wrench (YU-33975) or a suitable substitute, such as this punch, until you feel resistance

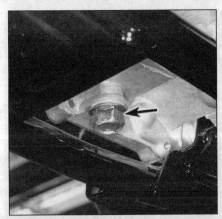

13.4 The transmission oil drain plug
(arrow) is on the bottom of
the crankcase

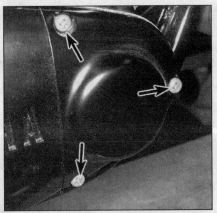

14.2 Remove the Autolube pump cover
screws (arrows) and remove
the cover

14.4 With the throttle closed, the
alignment mark should be aligned
with the pin (arrow) (RT100)

ground. Grab the swingarm on each side, just ahead of the axle. Rock the swingarm from side to side - there should be no discernible movement at the rear. If there's a little movement or a slight clicking can be heard, make sure the swingarm pivot shaft is tight. If the pivot shaft is tight but movement is still noticeable, remove the swingarm and replace the swingarm bearings (see Chapter 5).

12 Sidestand - check

The sidestand should be checked to make sure it stays down when extended and up when retracted. Refer to Chapter 7 and check tightness of the sidestand mounting bolts. Check the spring for cracks or rust and replace it if any problems are found.

13 Clutch and transmission oil - change

Refer to illustration 13.4

1   The transmission and clutch share a common oil supply separate from the engine oil.
2   Park the vehicle in a level position, then start the engine and allow it to reach normal operating temperature. **Warning:** *Do not run the engine in an enclosed space such as a garage or shop.*
3   Remove the filler cap/dipstick **(see illustration 3.10a)**. Inspect the filler cap O-ring and replace it if it's cracked, cut or deteriorated.
4   Place a clean pan under the transmission drain plug **(see illustration)**. Remove the plug. While the oil is draining, check the condition of the drain plug threads and the sealing washer.
5   After all the old oil has drained, install the drain plug with its sealing washer and tighten it to the torque listed in this Chapter's Specifications.
6   Before refilling the transmission, check the old oil carefully. If the oil was drained into a clean pan, small pieces of metal or other material can be easily detected. If the oil is very metallic colored, then the transmission is experiencing wear from break-in (new parts) or from insufficient lubrication. If there are flakes or chips of metal in the oil, then something is drastically wrong internally and the engine will have to be disassembled for inspection and repair.
7   If there are pieces of fiber-like material in the oil, the clutch is experiencing excessive wear and should be checked.
8   If the inspection of the oil turns up nothing unusual, refill the transmission to the proper level with the recommended oil and install the filler cap.
9   Start the engine and let it run for two or three minutes. Shut it off, wait a few minutes, and then check the oil level in the inspection window. If necessary, add more oil to bring the level up to the upper level mark on the window. Check around the drain plug for leaks.

14 Autolube pump - adjustment

Adjustment
Cable (RT100 models)
Refer to illustrations 14.2, 14.4 and 14.5

1   Adjust engine idle speed (see Section 19) and throttle cable freeplay (see Section 7).
2   Remove the Autolube pump cover bolts **(see illustration)** and remove the cover.
3   Make sure that the throttle is completely closed.
4   Note whether the alignment mark is aligned with the pin **(see illustration)**. If it's not aligned with the pin, adjust the Autolube pump cable.
5   Loosen the locknut **(see illustration)**, turn the adjuster in or out until the alignment mark is aligned with the pin. Tighten the locknut securely.
6   Install the Autolube pump cover and tighten the cover screws securely.

Pump stroke
Refer to illustration 14.9

7   Remove the Autolube pump cover **(see illustration 14.2)**.
8   Start the engine and allow it to warm up for a few minutes.

14.5 Loosen the locknut (right arrow) and turn the
adjuster (left arrow) in or out until the alignment
mark is aligned with the pin (RT100)

14.9 Measure the gap between the adjusting plate and the raised boss on the pump adjusting pulley (but don't force the feeler gauge into the gap)

9   With the engine running at idle, carefully observe the pump adjusting plate **(see illustration)**. As soon as the adjusting plate moves out to its limit, stop the engine.

10   Using a feeler gauge, measure the gap between the adjusting plate and the raised boss on the pump adjusting pulley. When you insert the feeler gauge between the adjusting plate and the adjusting pulley, make sure that neither the plate nor the pulley moves, *i.e.* do not *force* the feeler gauge into the gap. Compare your measurement to the minimum pump stroke range listed in this Chapter's Specifications. If the pump stroke is outside the specified range, adjust the pump stroke as follows.

11   Remove the locknut, spring washer and adjusting plate.

12   Adjust the pump stroke by adding or removing a shim. Adding a shim increases the pump stroke; removing a shim decreases the stroke.

13   Install the adjusting plate, spring washer and locknut. Tighten the locknut to the torque listed in this Chapter's Specifications.

14   Recheck the minimum pump stroke. If the stroke is still out of specification, repeat Steps 11 through 14.

15   When the pump stroke is correct, install the Autolube pump cover and tighten the cover screws securely.

---

15 Air cleaner - filter element and drain tube cleaning

Element cleaning

Refer to illustrations 15.2a, 15.2b and 15.3

1   Remove the seat and the left side cover (see Chapter 7).

2   Remove the air filter cover and lift out the filter element **(see illustrations)**.

3   Separate the filter element from the element guide **(see illustration)**.

4   Clean the foam filter element in a high flash point solvent, squeeze the solvent out of the foam and let the element dry completely.

5   Soak the foam element in the foam filter oil listed in this Chapter's Specifications, then squeeze it firmly to remove the excess oil. Don't wring it out or the foam may be damaged. The element should be wet through with oil, but no oil should drip from it.

6   Reassemble the element and holder.

7   Installation is otherwise the reverse of removal.

Drain tube cleaning

8   Check the drain tube for accumulated water and oil. If oil or water has built up in the tube, squeeze its clamp, remove the tube from the air cleaner housing and clean it out. Install the drain tube on the hous-

15.2a Remove the air filter cover screw (note the UP mark) . . .

15.2b . . . remove the cover and inspect its foam seal . . .

ing and secure it with the clamp. **Note:** *A drain tube that's full indicates the need to clean the filter element and the inside of the case.*

Crankcase ventilation hose

Refer to illustration 15.9

9   Inspect the crankcase ventilation hose **(see illustration)**. Make sure that it's in good condition and securely attached to the crankcase and to the air cleaner housing. If the hose is cracked, torn or deteriorated, replace it.

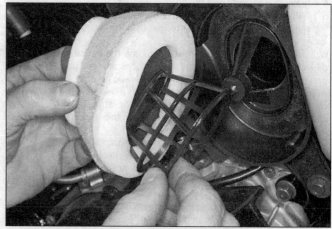

15.3 . . . then take out the filter element and separate the element from its guide

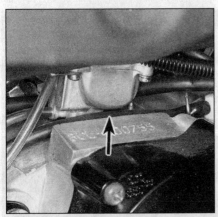

15.9 Inspect the condition of the crankcase ventilation hose (arrow) and make sure that it's securely attached to the crankcase and to the air cleaner housing

16.1 Inspect the fuel tank, the fuel tap and the fuel line for damage; look for leaks at the tap gasket and fuel line (arrows)

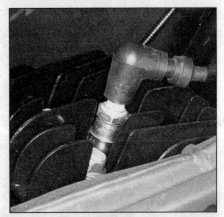

18.1 Twist the spark plug cap back and forth to free it, then pull it off the plug

16 Fuel system - inspection

Refer to illustration 16.1

Warning: *Gasoline is extremely flammable, so take extra precautions when you work on any part of the fuel system. Don't smoke or allow open flames or bare light bulbs near the work area, and don't work in a garage where a natural gas-type appliance (such as a water heater or clothes dryer) is present. Since gasoline is carcinogenic, wear latex gloves when there's a possibility of being exposed to fuel, and if you spill any fuel on your skin, rinse it off immediately with soap and water. Mop up any fuel spills immediately and do not store fuel-soaked rags where they could ignite. When you perform any kind of work on the fuel system, wear safety glasses and have a fire extinguisher suitable for class B type fires (flammable liquids) on hand.*

1   Inspect the fuel tank, the fuel tap and the fuel line for leaks and evidence of damage **(see illustration)**. If the fuel tap is leaking, tightening the screws may help. If leakage persists, remove, disassemble and repair, or replace, the tap (see Chapter 3B). If the fuel line is cracked or otherwise deteriorated, replace it.

2   Inspect the hose clamp connections between the air intake duct and the carburetor and between the carburetor and the intake joint. If either hose clamp is loose, tighten it.

3   Inspect the carburetor for leaks. If the carburetor is leaking, remove, disassemble and rebuild it (see Chapter 3).

4   On RT180 models, inspect the Yamaha Energy Induction System (Y.E.I.S.). The Y.E.I.S. system, which improves performance by

increasing the flow of the air/fuel mixture into the engine, is generally trouble free. It has no moving parts and requires no maintenance. Inspect the Y.E.I.S. hose and make sure it's not cracked, torn or disconnected. If the hose is damaged, replace it.

5   Remove the Autolube pump cover **(see illustration 14.2)** and inspect the oil line from the pump to the engine. Replace the line if it's damaged or deteriorated.

6   Check the oil tank for cracks, melting or other damage. Replace it if you find any damage.

17 Exhaust system - inspection

1   Periodically check the exhaust system for leaks and loose fasteners. If tightening the holder nuts at the cylinder head fails to stop any leaks, replace the gasket with a new ones (a procedure which requires removal of the system).

2   The exhaust pipe flange nuts at the cylinder head are especially prone to loosening, which could cause damage to the head (see Chapter 3). Check them frequently and keep them tight.

18 Spark plug - check and replacement

Refer to illustrations 18.1, 18.5a and 18.5b

1   Twist the spark plug cap to break it free from the plug, then pull it off **(see illustration)**. If available, use compressed air to blow any accumulated debris from around the spark plug. Remove the plug with a spark plug socket.

2   Inspect the electrodes for wear. Both the center and side electrodes should have square edges and the side electrode should be of uniform thickness. Look for excessive deposits and evidence of a cracked or chipped insulator around the center electrode. Compare your spark plugs to the color spark plug reading chart on the inside back cover. Check the threads, the washer and the ceramic insulator body for cracks and other damage.

3   If the electrodes are not excessively worn, and if the deposits can be easily removed with a wire brush, the plug can be regapped and reused (if no cracks or chips are visible in the insulator). If in doubt concerning the condition of the plug, replace it with a new one, as the expense is minimal.

4   Cleaning the spark plug by sandblasting is permitted, provided you clean the plug with a high flash-point solvent afterwards.

5   Before installing a new plug, make sure it is the correct type and heat range. Check the gap between the electrodes, as it is not preset. For best results, use a wire-type gauge rather than a flat gauge to check the gap **(see illustration)**. If the gap must be adjusted, bend the

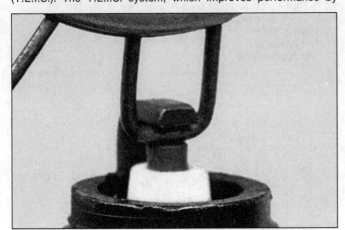

18.5a Spark plug manufacturers recommend using a wire type gauge when checking the gap - if the wire doesn't slide between the electrodes with a slight drag, adjustment is required

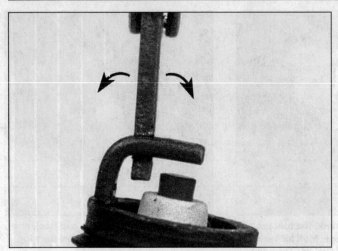

18.5b To change the gap, bend the side electrode only, as indicated by the arrows, and be very careful not to crack or chip the ceramic insulator surrounding the center electrode

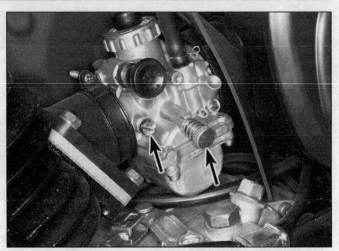

19.3 Seat the pilot screw (left arrow) lightly, then back it out the specified number of turns; turn the throttle stop screw (right arrow) to set idle speed

side electrode only and be very careful not to chip or crack the insulator nose **(see illustration)**. Make sure the washer is in place before installing the plug.

6   Since the cylinder head is made of aluminum, which is soft and easily damaged, thread the plug into the head by hand. Slip a short length of hose over the end of the plug to use as a tool to thread it into place. The hose will grip the plug well enough to turn it, but will start to slip if the plug begins to cross-thread in the hole - this will prevent damaged threads and the accompanying repair costs.

7   Once the plug is finger tight, the job can be finished with a socket. If a torque wrench is available, tighten the spark plug to the torque listed in this Chapter's Specifications. If you do not have a torque wrench, tighten the plug finger tight (until the washer bottoms on the cylinder head) then use a spark plug socket to tighten it an additional 1/4 turn. Regardless of the method used, do not over-tighten it.

8   Reconnect the spark plug cap.

19 Idle speed - check and adjustment

Refer to illustration 19.3

1   Before adjusting the idle speed, make sure the spark plug gap is correct. Also, turn the handlebars back-and-forth and note whether the idle speed changes as the handlebars are moved. If it does, the throttle cable may not be adjusted correctly, or it may be worn out. Be sure to correct this problem before proceeding.

2   The engine should be at normal operating temperature, which is usually reached after 10 to 15 minutes of stop and go riding. Make sure the transmission is in Neutral, then connect an inductive tachometer.

3   Turn in the pilot screw **(see illustration)** until it bottoms lightly, then turn it back out the number of turns listed in this Chapter's Specifications.

4   Turn the throttle stop screw **(see illustration 19.3)** until the idle speed listed in this Chapter's Specifications is obtained.

5   Turn the pilot screw in or out in 1/8-turn increments to obtain the highest idle speed, then use the throttle stop screw to set the specified idle speed.

6   Snap the throttle open and shut a few times, then recheck the idle speed. If necessary, repeat the adjustment procedure.

7   If a smooth, steady idle can't be achieved, the air/fuel mixture might be incorrect (see Chapter 3).

8   After the idle speed has been adjusted, check and adjust the throttle cable freeplay (see Section 7).

20 Fasteners - check

1   Since vibration of the machine tends to loosen fasteners, all nuts, bolts, screws, etc. should be periodically checked for proper tightness. Also make sure all cotter pins or other safety fasteners are correctly installed.

2   Pay particular attention to the following:

Spark plug
Transmission oil drain plug
Gearshift pedal
Brake pedal
Footpegs
Engine mounting nuts/bolts
Shock absorber nuts/bolts
Front axle nut
Rear axle nut
Skid plate bolts

Chapter 1 Part C
Tune-up and routine maintenance (TT-R and XT models)

Contents

Specifications

TT-R90 models

Engine

Compression pressure (at sea level)	1000 kPa (145 psi)
Spark plug	
Type	NGK CR6HSA or ND U20FSR-U
Gap	0.6 to 0.7 mm (0.024 to 0.028 in)
Engine idle speed	1450 to 1550 rpm
Valve clearance (COLD engine)	
Intake	0.05 to 0.09 mm (0.002 to 0.0035 inch)
Exhaust	0.08 to 0.12 mm (0.003 to 0.005 inch)

Miscellaneous

Front brake shoe lining thickness	
New	3 mm (1/8 inch)
Limit	1.5 mm (1/16 inch)
Rear brake shoe lining thickness	
New	4 mm (5/32 inch)
Limit	1.5 mm (1/16 inch)
Front brake lever freeplay	10 to 20 mm (25/64 to 25/32 inch)
Rear brake pedal freeplay	10 to 20 mm (25/64 to 25/32 inch)
Rear brake pedal height	15 mm (19/32 inch) below top of footpeg
Throttle grip freeplay	3 to 5 mm (1/8 to 13/64 inch)
Choke freeplay	Not adjustable
Minimum tire tread depth	Not specified
Tire pressures (cold, front and rear)	14.5 psi
Drive chain slack	40 to 53 mm (1.6 to 2.1 inches)

Torque specifications

Oil drain plug	20 Nm (14 ft-lbs)
Valve adjuster covers	18 Nm (13 ft-lbs)
Timing hole plug	7 Nm (61 inch-lbs)
Rotor bolt hole plug	7 Nm (61 inch-lbs)
Valve adjusting screw locknuts	7 Nm (61 inch-lbs)
Spark plug	13 Nm (113 inch-lbs)
Steering head ring nut	
Initial torque	38 Nm (27 ft-lbs)
Final torque	1 Nm (8 inch-lbs)

TT-R90 models (continued)

Recommended lubricants and fluids

Engine/transmission oil

Type	API grade SG or higher, meeting JASO standard MA (the MA standard is required to prevent clutch slippage)

Viscosity

40-degrees F (5-degrees C) or above	20W40
10-degrees F (-10-degrees C) or above	10W30

Capacity

After oil change	0.8 liters (0.85 US qt)
After engine overhaul	1.0 liter (1.06 US qt)
Wheel bearings	Medium weight, lithium-based multi-purpose grease (NLGI no. 3)
Swingarm pivot	Medium weight, lithium-based multi-purpose grease (NLGI no. 3)
Cables and lever pivots	Chain and cable lubricant or 10W30 motor oil
Brake pedal/shift pedal/throttle lever pivots	Chain and cable lubricant or 10W30 motor oil

TT-R125 models

Engine

Compression pressure (at sea level)	Not specified
Spark plug type	NGK CR7HSA or ND U22FSR-U
Spark plug gap	0.6 to 0.7 mm (0.024 to 0.028 in)
Engine idle speed	1300 to 1500 rpm
Intake valve clearance (COLD engine)	0.08 to 0.12 mm (0.003 to 0.005 inch)
Exhaust valve clearance (COLD engine)	0.10 to 0.14 mm (0.004 to 0.0055 inch)

Miscellaneous

Front brake pad lining thickness

New	4 mm (5/32 inch)
Limit	0.8 mm (1/32 inch)

Rear brake shoe lining thickness

New	4 mm (5/32 inch)
Limit	2 mm (5/64 inch)
Front brake lever freeplay	2 to 5 mm (5/64 to 3/16 inch)
Rear brake pedal freeplay	20 to 30 mm (25/32 to 37/32 inch)
Rear brake pedal height	1 mm (3/64 inch) below top of footpeg
Throttle grip freeplay	3 to 5 mm (1/8 to 13/64 inch)
Choke freeplay	Not adjustable
Minimum tire tread depth	Not specified
Tire pressures (cold, front and rear)	15 psi
Drive chain slack	35 to 60 mm (1.4 to 2.4 inches)

Torque specifications

Oil drain plug	20 Nm (14 ft-lbs)
Oil gallery bolt	7 Nm (61 inch-lbs)
Valve adjuster covers	18 Nm (13 ft-lbs)
Timing hole plug	7 Nm (61 inch-lbs)
Rotor bolt hole plug	7 Nm (61 inch-lbs)
Valve adjusting screw locknuts	8 Nm (70 inch-lbs)
Spark plug	13 Nm (113 inch-lbs)

Steering head ring nut

Initial torque	38 Nm (27 ft-lbs)
Final torque	20 Nm (14 ft-lbs)*

With Yamaha special tool at a right angle to the torque wrench.

Recommended lubricants and fluids

Engine/transmission oil

Type	API grade SG or higher, meeting JASO standard MA (the MA standard is required to prevent clutch slippage)

Viscosity

40-degrees F (5-degrees C) or above	20W40
10-degrees F (-10-degrees C) or above	10W30

Capacity

After oil change	1.0 liter (1.06 US qt)
After overhaul	1.2 liter (1.27 US qt)
Brake fluid	DOT 4
Wheel bearings	Medium weight, lithium-based multi-purpose grease (NLGI no. 3)
Swingarm pivot	Medium weight, lithium-based multi-purpose grease (NLGI no. 3)
Cables and lever pivots	Chain and cable lubricant or 10W30 motor oil
Brake pedal/shift pedal/throttle lever pivots	Chain and cable lubricant or 10W30 motor oil

TT-R225 models

Engine
Compression pressure (at sea level)... 1200 kPa (171 psi)
Spark plug type .... NGK DR8EA or ND X24ESR-U
Spark plug gap .... 0.6 to 0.7 mm (0.024 to 0.028 in)
Engine idle speed .... 1300 to 1500 rpm
Valve clearance (COLD engine)
    Intake .... 0.05 to 0.09 mm (0.002 to 0.004 inch)
    Exhaust .... 0.15 to 0.19 mm (0.007 to 0.007 inch)

Miscellaneous
Front brake pad lining thickness
    New .... 6 mm (19/32 inch)
    Limit.. 0.8 mm (1/32 inch)
Rear brake shoe lining thickness
    New .... 4 mm (5/32 inch)
    Limit.. 2 mm (5/64 inch)
Front brake lever freeplay .... 2 to 5 mm (5/64 to 3/16 inch)
Rear brake pedal freeplay .... 20 to 30 mm (25/32 to 37/32 inch)
Rear brake pedal height .... 10 mm (25/64 inch) below top of footpeg
Throttle grip freeplay... 3 to 5 mm (1/8 to 13/64 inch)
Clutch lever freeplay .... 10 to 15 mm (25/64 to 19/32)
Choke freeplay.. Not adjustable
Minimum tire tread depth .... Not specified
Tire pressures (cold, front and rear).. 15 psi
Battery specific gravity .... 1.260 at 20-degrees C (68-degrees F)
Drive chain slack... 35 to 45 mm (1.4 to 1.8 inches)

Torque specifications
Oil drain plug .... 43 Nm (31 ft-lbs)
Oil filter cover lower bolt .... 10 Nm (86 inch-lbs)
Oil gallery bolt .... 7 Nm (61 inch-lbs)
Valve adjuster cover bolts .... 10 Nm (86 inch-lbs)
Valve adjusting screw locknuts .... 13.5 Nm (162 inch-lbs)
Spark plug .... 17.5 Nm (150 inch-lbs)
Steering head ring nut
    Initial torque... 38 Nm (27 ft-lbs)
    Final torque .... 5.5 Nm (48 inch-lbs)*
With Yamaha special tool at a right angle to the torque wrench.

Recommended lubricants and fluids
Engine/transmission oil
    Type.. API grade SG or higher, meeting JASO standard MA (the MA standard is required to prevent clutch slippage)
    Viscosity
        40-degrees F (5-degrees C) or above... 20W40
        10-degrees F (-10-degrees C) or above 10W30
    Capacity
        After oil change... 1.0 liter (1.06 US qt)
        After oil and filter change... 1.1 liter (1.16 US qt)
        After engine overhaul... 1.3 liter (1.37 US qt)
Brake fluid.. DOT 4
Wheel bearings .... Medium weight, lithium-based multi-purpose grease (NLGI no. 3)
Swingarm pivot .... Medium weight, lithium-based multi-purpose grease (NLGI no. 3)
Cables and lever pivots .... Chain and cable lubricant or 10W30 motor oil
Brake pedal/shift pedal/throttle lever pivots................................. Chain and cable lubricant or 10W30 motor oil

XT225 models

Engine
Compression pressure (at sea level)... 1200 kPa (171 psi)
Spark plug
    Type .... NGK DR8EA or ND X24ESR-U
    Gap... 0.6 to 0.7 mm (0.024 to 0.028 in)
Engine idle speed .... 1300 to 1500 rpm
Valve clearance (COLD engine)
    Intake .... 0.05 to 0.09 mm (0.002 to 0.004 inch)
    Exhaust .... 0.15 to 0.19 mm (0.007 to 0.007 inch)

XT225 models (continued)

Miscellaneous

Front brake pad lining thickness	
New	6 mm (19/32 inch)
Limit	0.8 mm (1/32 inch)
Rear brake shoe lining thickness	
New	4 mm (5/32 inch)
Limit	2 mm (5/64 inch)
Front brake lever freeplay	2 to 5 mm (5/64 to 3/16 inch)
Rear brake pedal freeplay	20 to 30 mm (25/32 to 37/32 inch)
Rear brake pedal height	10 mm (25/64 inch) below top of footpeg
Throttle grip freeplay	3 to 5 mm (1/8 to 13/64 inch)
Clutch lever freeplay	10 to 15 mm (25/64 to 19/32)
Choke freeplay	Not adjustable
Minimum tire tread depth	0.8 mm (0.03 inch)
Tire pressures (cold)	
Up to 90 kg (198 lbs) load	
Front	18 psi
Rear	21 psi
90 kg (198 lbs) or higher load or high speed riding	
Front	21 psi
Rear	25 psi
Battery specific gravity (sealed battery)	1.320 at 20-degrees C (68-degrees F)
Drive chain slack	35 to 45 mm (1.4 to 1.8 inches)

Torque specifications

Oil drain plug	43 Nm (31 ft-lbs)
Oil filter cover lower bolt	10 Nm (86 inch-lbs)
Oil gallery bolt	7 Nm (61 inch-lbs)
Valve adjuster cover bolts	10 Nm (86 inch-lbs)
Valve adjusting screw locknuts	13.5 Nm (162 inch-lbs)
Spark plug	17.5 Nm (150 inch-lbs)
Steering head ring nut	
Initial torque	38 Nm (27 ft-lbs)
Final torque	5.5 Nm (48 inch-lbs)*

With Yamaha special tool at a right angle to the torque wrench.

Recommended lubricants and fluids

Engine/transmission oil	
Type	API grade SG or higher, meeting JASO standard MA (the MA standard is required to prevent clutch slippage)
Viscosity	
40-degrees F (5-degrees C) or above	20W40
10-degrees F (-10-degrees C) or above	10W30
Capacity	
After oil change	1.0 liter (1.06 US qt)
After oil and filter change	1.1 liter (1.16 US qt)
After engine overhaul	1.3 liter (1.37 US qt)
Brake fluid	DOT 3 or DOT 4
Wheel bearings	Medium weight, lithium-based multi-purpose grease (NLGI no. 3)
Swingarm pivot	Medium weight, lithium-based multi-purpose grease (NLGI no. 3)
Cables and lever pivots	Chain and cable lubricant or 10W30 motor oil
Brake pedal/shift pedal/throttle lever pivots	Chain and cable lubricant or 10W30 motor oil

TT-R250 models

Engine

Compression pressure (at sea level)	
Standard	1200 kPa (171 psi)
Minimum	1000 kPa (145 psi)
Maximum	1300 kPa (189 psi)
Spark plug type	NGK CR9E or ND U27ESR-N
Spark plug gap	0.7 to 0.8 mm (0.028 to 0.031 in)
Engine idle speed	1250 to 1350 rpm
Valve clearance (COLD engine)	
Intake	0.09 to 0.19 mm (0.004 to 0.007 inch)
Exhaust	0.19 to 0.27 mm (0.007 to 0.011 inch)

Miscellaneous

Front brake pad lining thickness
    New .... 4.2 mm (5/32 inch)
    Limit .... 1 mm (1/32 inch)
Rear brake pad lining thickness
    New .... 4 mm (5/32 inch)
    Limit .... 1 mm (1/32 inch)
Front brake lever freeplay .... 2 to 5 mm (5/64 to 3/16 inch)
Rear brake pedal freeplay .... Not measured
Rear brake pedal height .... 10 mm (25/64 inch) below top of footpeg
Throttle grip freeplay .... 3 to 5 mm (1/8 to 13/64 inch)
Clutch lever freeplay .... 10 to 15 mm (25/64 to 19/32)
Choke freeplay .... Not adjustable
Minimum tire tread depth .... 0.8 mm (0.03 inch)
Tire pressures (cold, front and rear) .... 14.5 psi
Battery specific gravity (sealed battery) .... Not specified
Drive chain slack .... 35 to 50 mm (1.4 to 2.0 inches)

Torque specifications

Oil drain plug .... 20 Nm (14 ft-lbs)
Oil filter cover bolts .... 10 Nm (86 inch-lbs)
Oil gallery bolt .... 7 Nm (61 inch-lbs)
Spark plug .... 13 Nm (113 inch-lbs)
Steering head ring nut
    Initial torque .... 38 Nm (27 ft-lbs)
    Final torque .... 5 Nm (43 inch-lbs)*
With Yamaha special tool at a right angle to the torque wrench.

Recommended lubricants and fluids

Engine/transmission oil
    Type .... API grade SG or higher, meeting JASO standard MA (the MA standard is required to prevent clutch slippage)
    Viscosity
        40-degrees F (5-degrees C) or above 20W40
        10-degrees F (-10-degrees C) or above 10W30
    Capacity
        After oil change .... 1.1 liter (1.16 US qt)
        After oil and filter change .... 1.2 liter (1.27 US qt)
        After engine overhaul .... 1.45 liter (1.53 US qt)
Brake fluid .... DOT 3 or DOT 4
Wheel bearings .... Medium weight, lithium-based multi-purpose grease (NLGI no. 3)
Swingarm pivot .... Medium weight, lithium-based multi-purpose grease (NLGI no. 3)
Cables and lever pivots .... Chain and cable lubricant or 10W30 motor oil
Brake pedal/shift pedal/throttle lever pivots .... Chain and cable lubricant or 10W30 motor oil

XT350 models

Engine

Compression pressure (at sea level)
    Standard .... 1100 kPa (156 psi)
    Minimum .... 900 kPa (128 psi)
    Maximum .... 1200 kPa (171 psi)
Spark plug
    Type .... NGK D8EA or ND X24ES-U
    Gap .... 0.7 to 0.8 mm (0.028 to 0.031 in)
Engine idle speed .... 1350 to 1450 rpm
Valve clearance (COLD engine)
    Intake .... 0.08 to 0.12 mm (0.003 to 0.005 inch)
    Exhaust .... 0.13 to 0.17 mm (0.005 to 0.007 inch)

Miscellaneous

Front brake pad lining thickness
    New .... 6.8 mm (17/64 inch)
    Limit .... 0.8 mm (1/32 inch)
Rear brake shoe lining thickness
    New .... 4 mm (5/32 inch)
    Limit .... 2 mm (5/64 inch)
Front brake lever freeplay .... 5 to 8 mm (3/16 to 5/16 inch)
Rear brake pedal freeplay .... 20 to 30 mm (25/32 to 37/32 inch)

XT350 models (continued)

Miscellaneous

Rear brake pedal height	15 mm (5/8 inch) below top of footpeg
Throttle grip freeplay	3 to 5 mm (1/8 to 13/64 inch)
Clutch lever freeplay	2 to 3 mm (3/32 to 1/8 inch)
Decompression lever freeplay	2 to 3 mm (3/32 to 1/8 inch)
Choke freeplay	Not adjustable
Minimum tire tread depth	1.0 mm (0.04 inch)
Tire pressures (cold)	
Up to 90 kg (198 lbs) load	
Front	18 psi
Rear	22 psi
90 kg (198 lbs) or higher load or high speed riding	
Front	22 psi
Rear	26 psi
Battery specific gravity	1.280 at 20-degrees C (68-degrees F)
Drive chain slack	30 tp 40 mm (1.2 to 1.6 inches)

Torque specifications

Oil drain plug	43 Nm (31 ft-lbs)
Oil filter cover bolt	10 Nm (86 inch-lbs)
Oil filter cover screws	7 Nm (61 inch-lbs)
Oil filter housing bleed bolt	7 Nm (61 inch-lbs)
Oil gallery bolt	7 Nm (61 inch-lbs)
Spark plug	17.5 Nm (150 inch-lbs)
Steering head ring nut	
Initial torque	38 Nm (27 ft-lbs)
Final torque	10 Nm (86 inch-lbs)*

*With Yamaha special tool at a right angle to the torque wrench.

Recommended lubricants and fluids

Engine/transmission oil	
Type	API grade SG or higher, meeting JASO standard MA (the MA standard is required to prevent clutch slippage)
Viscosity	
40-degrees F (5-degrees C) or above	20W40
60-degrees F (15-degrees C) or below	10W30
Capacity	
After oil change	1.1 liter (1.16 US qt)
After oil and filter change	1.2 liter (1.27 US qt)
After engine overhaul	1.45 liter (1.53 US qt)
Brake fluid	DOT 3 or DOT 4
Wheel bearings	Medium weight, lithium-based multi-purpose grease (NLGI no. 3)
Swingarm pivot	Medium weight, lithium-based multi-purpose grease (NLGI no. 3)
Cables and lever pivots	Chain and cable lubricant or 10W30 motor oil
Brake pedal/shift pedal/throttle lever pivots	Chain and cable lubricant or 10W30 motor oil

Yamaha TT-R and XT Routine maintenance intervals

Note: *The pre-ride inspection outlined in the owner's manual covers checks and maintenance that should be carried out on a daily basis. It's condensed and included here to remind you of its importance. Always perform the pre-ride inspection at every maintenance interval (in addition to the procedures listed). The intervals listed below are the shortest intervals recommended by the manufacturer for each particular operation during the model years covered in this manual. Your owner's manual may have different intervals for your model.*

Before every ride

Check the operation of both brakes - check the front brake lever and rear brake pedal for correct freeplay and pedal height
Check brake fluid level in the front or rear master cylinder (disc brake models)
Make sure the engine kill switch works properly
Check the throttle for smooth operation and correct freeplay
Check the engine oil level
Check and, if necessary, adjust the drive chain slack and the wheel alignment
Lubricate the drive chain
Inspect the condition of the drive chain sprockets and sliders
Check the tires for damage, the presence of foreign objects and correct air pressure
Check all fasteners, including axle nuts, for tightness

Off-road maintenance schedule

This schedule applies to strictly off-road models, as well as to dual-purpose models (XT225 and XT350) ridden extensively off-road.

Every 60 hours/600 miles/6 months

Check, clean and gap, or replace, the spark plug
Check and if necessary, adjust valve clearance
Inspect and, if necessary, replace the air filter element*
Check and, if necessary, adjust the idle speed
Check and, if necessary, adjust the idle speed
Inspect and, if necessary, replace the fuel tap and hose
Check the brake shoes for wear (drum brake models)
Check the brake pads for wear (disc brake models)
Check clutch operation and, if necessary, adjust freeplay
Check the swingarm pivot for looseness and tighten as necessary
Inspect the condition of the wheels and spokes
Check the wheel bearings for looseness and damage and, if necessary, replace them
Check the front fork seals for leakage and, if necessary, replace the seals and change the fork oil
Check the rear shock absorber seals for leakage and, if necessary, replace the shock

Repack the swingarm pivot bearings
Check all fittings and fasteners and tighten as necessary
Inspect the exhaust system

Every 120 hours/120 miles/12 months

Check the steering head bearings for looseness and, if necessary, adjust them
Clean the spark arrester (if equipped)
More often in dusty areas.

On-road maintenance schedule

This schedule applies to dual-purpose models (XT225 and XT350) ridden mostly on the highway.

Every 4000 miles/6 months

Check, clean and gap, or replace, the spark plug
Check and if necessary, adjust valve clearance
Inspect and, if necessary, replace the air filter element*
Check and, if necessary, adjust the idle speed
Check and, if necessary, adjust the idle speed
Inspect and, if necessary, replace the fuel tap and hose
Check the brake shoes for wear (drum brake models)
Check the brake pads for wear (disc brake models)
Check clutch operation and, if necessary, adjust freeplay
Check the swingarm pivot for looseness and tighten as necessary
Inspect the condition of the wheels and spokes
Check the wheel bearings for looseness and damage and, if necessary, replace them
Check the front fork seals for leakage and, if necessary, replace the seals and change the fork oil
Check the rear shock absorber seals for leakage and, if necessary, replace the shock
Repack the swingarm pivot bearings
Check all fittings and fasteners and tighten as necessary
Inspect the exhaust system

Every 8000 miles/12 months

Check the steering head bearings for looseness and, if necessary, adjust them

Every 16,000 miles/24 months

Repack the steering head bearings
More often in dusty areas.

2.1 Decals on the motorcycle include maintenance and safety information

3.3 The front brake fluid level is visible in the window; make sure it's above the LOWER mark

3.4 Lift off the cover and diaphragm

2   Introduction to tune-up and routine maintenance

Refer to illustration 2.1

This Chapter covers in detail the checks and procedures necessary for the tune-up and routine maintenance of your motorcycle. Section 1 includes the routine maintenance schedule, which is designed to keep the machine in proper running condition and prevent possible problems. The remaining Sections contain detailed procedures for carrying out the items listed on the maintenance schedule, as well as additional maintenance information designed to increase reliability. Maintenance and safety information is also printed on decals, which are mounted in various locations on the motorcycle **(see illustration)**. Where information on the decals differs from that presented in this Chapter, use the decal information.

Since routine maintenance plays such an important role in the safe and efficient operation of your motorcycle, it is presented here as a comprehensive check list. These lists outline the procedures and checks that should be done on a routine basis.

Deciding where to start or plug into the routine maintenance schedule depends on several factors. If you have owned the bike for some time but have never performed any maintenance on it, then you may want to start at the nearest interval and include some additional procedures to ensure that nothing important is overlooked. If you have just had a major engine overhaul, then you may want to start the maintenance routine from the beginning. If you have a used machine and

have no knowledge of its history or maintenance record, you may desire to combine all the checks into one large service initially and then settle into the maintenance schedule prescribed.

The Sections which outline the inspection and maintenance procedures are written as step-by-step comprehensive guides to the actual performance of the work. They explain in detail each of the routine inspections and maintenance procedures on the check list. References to additional information in applicable Chapters is also included and should not be overlooked.

Before beginning any actual maintenance or repair, the machine should be cleaned thoroughly, especially around the oil filler plug, radiator cap, engine covers, carburetor, etc. Cleaning will help ensure that dirt does not contaminate the engine and will allow you to detect wear and damage that could otherwise easily go unnoticed.

3   Fluid levels - check

Brake fluid (disc brake models)

Refer to illustrations 3.3, 3.4 and 3.6

1   To ensure proper operation of the hydraulic disc brakes, the fluid level in the master cylinder reservoirs must be maintained within a safe range.

2   With the motorcycle supported in an upright position, turn the handlebars until the top of the front brake master cylinder is as level as possible.

3   The fluid level is visible in the window on the reservoir **(see illustration)**. Make sure the fluid level is above the Lower mark cast on the master cylinder body next to the reservoir.

4   If the fluid level is low, clean the area around the reservoir cover. Remove the cover screws and take off the cover and diaphragm **(see illustration)**. Add new brake fluid of the type listed in this Chapter's Specifications until the fluid level is even with the line cast inside the reservoir. **Note:** *The fluid level drops as the pads wear. If the level is very low, inspect the pads and check the fluid line and caliper for leaks.*

5   Install the diaphragm and cover, then tighten the cover screws securely.

6   The rear brake master cylinder on TT-R250 models is located on the right side of the bike near the spring **(see illustration)**. The fluid level can be seen through the translucent reservoir body. If it's not between the upper and lower marks, unscrew the reservoir cap and add the specified fluid.

Engine oil

Refer to illustrations 3.9, 3.10 and 3.11

7   The engine, transmission and clutch on these models share a common oil supply.

3.6 The TT-R250 rear master cylinder fluid level is visible through the reservoir (arrow)

3.9 The engine oil level on some models is visible through a window in the crankcase cover

3.10 Unscrew the filler cap (arrow) . . .

3.11 . . . if the filler cap includes a dipstick, the oil level must be between the upper and lower marks

8 Warm up the engine, then shut it off and let it sit for five minutes. **Note:** *Hold the bike upright. Don't let it sit on the sidestand or the oil level reading will not be accurate.*
9 If there's an oil level window in the left crankcase cover, check the oil level through it **(see illustration)**. It should be between the upper and lower marks.
10 If there isn't an oil level window, unscrew the dipstick/filler cap from the right crankcase cover **(see illustration)**. Pull out the dipstick, wipe it clean and reinsert it (just let it sit on the threads, don't screw it in).
11 Pull the dipstick back out and check the oil level on the dipstick scale **(see illustration)**. It should be between the upper and lower marks.
12 If the oil level is low, add oil through the dipstick/filler cap hole (this includes models with an oil level window).
13 Reinstall the filler cap and tighten it securely.

4 Brake system - general check

1 A routine general check of the brakes will ensure that any problems are discovered and remedied before the rider's safety is jeopardized.
2 Check the brake lever and pedal for loose connections, bends, and other damage. Replace any damaged parts with new ones (see Chapter 6C). Check front brake lever and rear brake pedal freeplay (see Section 5).
3 Make sure all brake fasteners are tight. Check the brakes for wear as described below.

Wear check

Disc brakes

Refer to illustrations 4.4a, 4.4b and 4.5
4 Remove the rubber plug from the front brake caliper inspection hole and look at the brake pads **(see illustration)**. The pads should have wear indicator slots molded in the friction material next to the metal backing **(see illustration)**. If the friction material has been worn away to the point that that slots are exposed (or almost exposed), replace the pads as a set. Be sure to check both pads, since they tend to wear unevenly. If you can't see any wear indicator slots, measure the brake pad thickness and compare your measurements to the minimum thickness listed in this Chapter's Specifications. If the thickness of either pad is below the minimum thickness, it's time to replace the pads (see Chapter 6C).
5 Inspect the rear pads (TT-R250 models) in the same way as the front pads. Since the pads can be seen from the rear of the caliper, there's no inspection plug to remove **(see illustration)**.

Drum brakes

Refer to illustration 4.8
6 Operate the brake pedal. If operation is rough or sticky, lubricate the brake cable (see Section 00).
7 Adjust the rear brake pedal freeplay (see Section 5).
8 On all except XT350 models, apply the brake pedal and note whether the wear indicator on the brake arm points at the wear limit line on the brake panel **(see illustration)**. If the wear indicator lines up with the wear limit line when the pedal is applied, replace the brake shoes (see Chapter 6C).

4.4a Remove the inspection plug and look through the window (arrow) to check the thickness of the front brake pads . . .

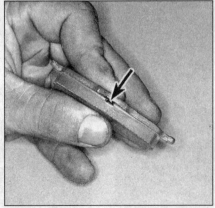

4.4b . . . if either of the brake pads has worn enough to expose the wear slot (arrow), replace both of them

4.5 The wear slots in TT-R250 brake pads (arrows) are visible from the rear of the caliper

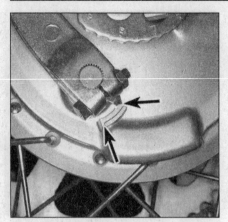

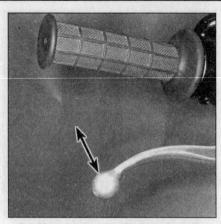

4.8 If the wear indicator on the brake arm (right arrow) lines up with the wear limit line on the brake panel (left arrow) with the brake applied, replace the shoes

5.4 Measure front brake lever freeplay at the lever tip . . .

5.5 Loosen the locknut (arrow) and turn the screw to change freeplay

9   On XT350 models, remove the inspection hole plug from the brake panel. Looking through the inspection hole, measure the thickness of the friction material on the shoes and replace them if they're worn.

5   Brake lever and pedal freeplay - check and adjustment

Front brake lever

TT-R90 models

1   Pull back the rubber cover from the brake lever and adjuster at the handlebar lever. Apply the front brake lever to the point at which you feel initial resistance (the point at which the brake cable slack is taken up and the cable begins to apply the brake shoes). With the lever applied to this point of initial resistance, measure the gap between the brake lever and the brake lever bracket and compare your measurement to the range of freeplay listed in this Chapter's Specifications. If the gap is outside the specified range, adjust the brake lever freeplay as follows.

2   Loosen the locknut and turn the adjuster in or out until the lever freeplay is within the specific range. Tighten the locknut and slide the rubber cover back into place over the adjuster and locknut.

3   If you can't obtain the specified freeplay with the handlebar adjuster, loosen the cable locknut at the front wheel. Turn the adjuster to obtain the correct freeplay, then tighten the locknut.

All models except TT-R90

Refer to illustrations 5.4 and 5.5

4   Apply the front brake lever to the point at which you feel initial resistance (the point at which the lever adjuster screw begins to push against the piston inside the master cylinder). Measure the distance that the tip of the lever travels from its unapplied position to this point of initial resistance **(see illustration)**. If this measurement is outside the range of freeplay listed in this Chapter's Specifications, adjust the brake lever freeplay as follows.

5   Loosen the locknut **(see illustration)** and turn the adjuster in or out until lever freeplay is within the specified range. Tighten the locknut.

Rear brake

Drum brake models

Refer to illustrations 5.6a, 5.6b and 5.8

6   Measure brake pedal height below the top of the footpeg **(see illustration)**. If it's not within the range listed in this Chapter's Specifications, loosen the adjuster locknut and turn the adjuster to correct it **(see illustration)**.

7   Apply the rear brake pedal to the point at which you feel initial resistance (the point at which the brake cable slack is taken up and the cable begins to apply the brake shoes). Measure the distance that the pedal travels from its unapplied position to this point of initial resistance and compare your measurement to the range of freeplay listed in this Chapter's Specifications. If the freeplay is outside the specified range, adjust the brake pedal freeplay as follows.

5.6a Measure pedal height below the top of the footpeg . . .

5.6b . . . loosen the locknut (arrow) and turn the adjuster bolt to change the setting

5.8 Adjust pedal freeplay with the nut at the end of the brake rod (arrow)

5.10 Loosen the locknut (lower arrow) and turn the adjuster (upper arrow) to adjust pedal height on TT-R250 models

8   Turn the adjuster at the rear end of the brake rod **(see illustration)** in or out to bring the brake pedal freeplay within the specified freeplay.

Disc brake models

Refer to illustration 5.10

9   Brake pedal height is not adjustable on disc brake models.

10 Measure brake pedal freeplay as described in Step 7 above. Adjust it if necessary by turning the nut on the master cylinder pushrod **(see illustration)**.

---

6   Clutch cable - check and adjustment

Check

Refer to illustrations 6.1 and 6.2

1   Operate the clutch lever and measure freeplay at the lever tip (all except XT350) or at the gap between the lever and bracket (XT350) **(see illustration)**. If it's not within the range listed in this Chapter's Specifications, adjust it as follows.

2   Pull back the rubber cover from the adjuster at the handlebar, loosen the locknut **(see illustration 6.1)** and turn the adjuster in or out to bring lever freeplay within the specified range. There's another freeplay adjuster several inches from the clutch lever bracket **(see illustration)**. To use this adjuster, simply loosen the locknut and turn

the adjuster in or out to produce the correct freeplay.

3   If freeplay can't be adjusted within the specified range, the clutch cable is probably stretched too much; replace the cable (see Chapter 2C).

---

7   Throttle cable freeplay - check and adjustment

1   All models except the TT-R250 and XT350 have a single throttle cable. TT-R250 and XT350 models have an accelerator cable and a decelerator cable.

Check

Refer to illustration 7.3

2   Make sure the throttle twist grip moves easily from fully closed to fully open with the front wheel turned at various angles. The grip should return automatically from fully open to fully closed when released. If the throttle sticks, check the throttle cable for cracks or kinks in the housing. Also, make sure the inner cable is clean and well-lubricated (see Section 10).

3   Measure the freeplay at the outer end of the twist grip **(see illustration)**. The freeplay is the distance that the twist grip flange travels before you feel an initial resistance (the point at which the throttle cable begins to open the throttle plate) and compare your measurement to the range of freeplay listed in this Chapter's Specifications. If it's not within the specified range, adjust it as follows.

6.1 On XT350 models, measure clutch freeplay at the gap (right arrow); on all models, loosen the locknut (center) and turn the adjuster (left) to set freeplay

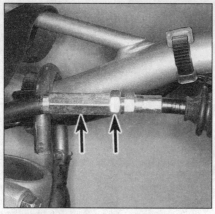

6.2 Loosen the locknut (right arrow) and turn the adjuster (left arrow) to use the in-line cable adjuster

7.3 Measure throttle freeplay at the grip

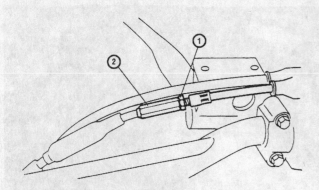

7.4 Loosen the in-line adjuster locknut (1) and turn the adjuster (2)

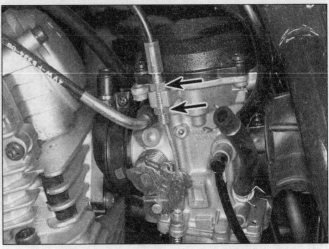

7.5 Loosen and reposition the locknuts to adjust the cable at the carburetor (TT-R225 shown)

Adjustment

All except TT-R250 and XT350 models

Refer to illustrations 7.4 and 7.5

4   Make the initial adjustment at the in-line cable adjuster **(see illustration)**. Loosen the locknut and turn the adjuster to set freeplay, then retighten the locknut.

5   If you can't set the freeplay with the in-line adjuster, loosen the locknuts at the carburetor **(see illustration)**. Turn the locknuts to reposition the cable in the bracket (this will change the freeplay setting). Once freeplay is set correctly, tighten the locknuts.

TT-R250 and XT350 models

Refer to illustration 7.6

6   These models use an accelerator cable and a decelerator cable **(see illustration)**.

7   Loosen the decelerator cable locknut and turn the adjuster to remove all slack from the decelerator cable. Once this is done, tighten the locknut.

8   Loosen the accelerator cable locknut and turn the adjuster to obtain the specified freeplay **(see illustration 7.6)**. Tighten the locknut after making the adjustment.

9   If you can't obtain the specified freeplay at the carburetor, try adjusting the in-line cable adjuster **(see illustration 7.5)**.

7.6 Dual throttle cable adjustment points (TT-R250 shown)

A   *Decelerator cable locknut*
B   *Decelerator cable adjuster*
C   *Accelerator cable locknut*
D   *Accelerator cable adjuster*
E   *Full throttle adjuster screw and locknut*

8   Tires/wheels - general check

1   Routine tire and wheel checks should be made with the realization that your safety depends to a great extent on their condition.

2   Check the tires carefully for cuts, tears, embedded nails or other sharp objects and excessive wear. Operation of the motorcycle with excessively worn tires is extremely hazardous, as traction and handling are directly affected. Check the tread depth at the center of the tire. Yamaha doesn't specify a minimum tread depth for these models, but as a general rule, tires should be replaced with new ones when the tread knobs are worn to 3 mm (1/8 inch) or less.

3   Repair or replace punctured tires as soon as damage is noted. Do not try to patch a torn tire, as wheel balance and tire reliability may be impaired.

4   Check the tire pressures when the tires are cold and keep them properly inflated **(see illustration 8.4 in Chapter 1B)**. Proper air pressure will increase tire life and provide maximum stability and ride comfort. Keep in mind that low tire pressures may cause the tire to slip on the rim or come off, while high tire pressures will cause abnormal tread wear and unsafe handling.

5   The wheels should be kept clean and checked periodically for cracks, bending, loose spokes and rust. Never attempt to repair damaged wheels; they must be replaced with new ones. Loose spokes can be tightened with a spoke wrench **(see illustration 8.5 in Chapter 1B)**, but be careful not to overtighten and distort the wheel rim.

6   Check the valve stem locknuts to make sure they're tight. Also, make sure the valve stem cap is in place and tight. If it is missing, install a new one made of metal or hard plastic.

7   Check the tightness of the locknut on the rim lock **(see illustration 8.7 in Chapter 1B)**. Tighten it if necessary to the torque listed in this Chapter's Specifications.

9   Drive chain and sprockets - check, adjustment and lubrication

Refer to illustration 9.3

1   A neglected drive chain won't last long and can quickly damage the sprockets. Routine chain adjustment isn't difficult and will ensure maximum chain and sprocket life.

2   To check the chain, support the bike securely with the rear wheel off the ground. Place the transmission in neutral.

3   Push up on the bottom run of the chain and measure the slack midway between the two sprockets **(see illustration)**, then compare

9.3 Push up on the bottom run of the chain and measure the slack midway between the two sprockets

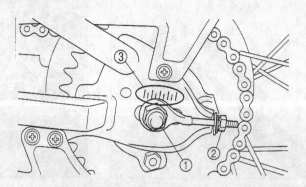

9.9 On TT-R90 models, loosen the axle nut (1), then turn the adjusting nuts (2) to align the scale marks (3) evenly

the measurements to the value listed in this Chapter's Specifications. As wear occurs, the chain will actually stretch, which means adjustment by removing some slack from the chain. In some cases where lubrication has been neglected, corrosion and galling may cause the links to bind and kink, which effectively shortens the chain's length. If the chain is tight between the sprockets, rusty or kinked, it's time to replace it with a new one. **Note:** *Repeat the chain slack measurement along the length of the chain - ideally, every inch or so. If you find a tight area, mark it with felt pen or paint and repeat the measurement after the bike has been ridden. If the chain's still tight in the same areas, it may be damaged or worn. Because a tight or kinked chain can damage the transmission countershaft bearing, it's a good idea to replace it.*

4   Check the entire length of the chain for damaged rollers, loose links and loose pins.

5   Look through the slots in the left engine cover and inspect the engine sprocket. Check the teeth on the engine sprocket and the rear sprocket for wear. Refer to Chapter 5 for the sprocket replacement procedure if the sprockets appear to be worn excessively.

6   Inspect the condition of the chain guide. If it's worn, replace it.

Adjustment

Refer to illustrations 9.9 and 9.10

7   Rotate the rear wheel until the chain is positioned with the least amount of slack present.

8   Loosen the rear axle nut (see Chapter 6).

9   On TT-R90 models, turn the chain adjuster bolt nuts **(see illustration)** *evenly* until the correct chain tension is obtained (get the adjuster on the chain side close, then set the adjuster on the opposite side). Be sure to turn the adjusting nuts evenly to keep the rear wheel in align-

ment. If the adjusting nuts pull the adjusters to the end of their travel, the chain is excessively worn and must be replaced (see Chapter 6). When the chain has the correct amount of slack, make sure the marks on the adjusters correspond to the same relative marks on each side of the swingarm. Tighten the adjuster bolt locknuts securely.

10   On all other models, rotate the chain adjusters **(see illustration)** *evenly* in a clockwise or counterclockwise direction until the correct chain tension is obtained (get the chain puller on the chain side close, then set the chain puller on the opposite side). Be sure to rotate the chain adjusters evenly to keep the rear wheel in alignment. If you're unable to adjust the chain slack with the chain adjusters, the chain is excessively worn and must be replaced (see Chapter 6). When the chain has the correct amount of slack, make sure the marks on the chain adjusters correspond to the same relative marks on each side of the swingarm.

11   Tighten the axle nut to the torque listed in the Chapter 6 Specifications.

Lubrication

Note: *If the chain is dirty, it should be removed and cleaned before it's lubricated* (see Chapter 6).

12   The best time to lubricate the chain is after the motorcycle has been ridden. When the chain is warm, the lubricant will penetrate the joints between the side plates, pins, bushings and rollers to provide lubrication of the internal bearing areas. Use a good quality chain lubricant and apply it to the area where the side plates overlap - not the middle of the rollers. Apply the lubricant along the top of the lower chain run, so that when the bike is ridden centrifugal force will move the lubricant into the chain, rather than throwing it off.

13   After applying the lubricant, let it soak in a few minutes before wiping off any excess.

9.10 On all except TT-R90 models, rotate the chain adjusters evenly to set chain tension

10 Lubrication - general

Refer to illustrations 10.3, 10.5a and 10.5b

1   Since the controls, cables and various other components of a motorcycle are exposed to the elements, they should be lubricated periodically to ensure safe and trouble-free operation.

2   The throttle twist grip, brake lever, brake pedal, kickstarter pivot and sidestand pivot should be lubricated frequently. In order for the lubricant to be applied where it will do the most good, the component should be disassembled. However, if chain and cable lubricant is being used, it can be applied to the pivot joint gaps and will usually work its way into the areas where friction occurs. If motor oil or light grease is being used, apply it sparingly as it may attract dirt (which could cause the controls to bind or wear at an accelerated rate). **Note:** *One of the best lubricants for the control lever pivots is a dry-film lubricant (available from many sources by different names).*

10.3 Lubricating a cable with a pressure lube adapter (make sure the tool seats around the inner cable)

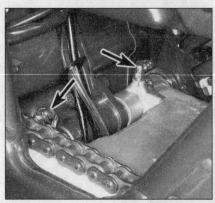

10.5a Look for grease fittings on the swingarm pivots (arrows) . . .

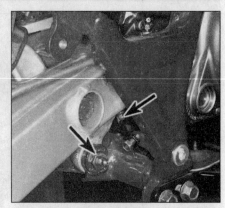

10.5b . . . and at the shock linkage pivot points (arrows)

3   The throttle and brake cables should be removed and treated with a commercially available cable lubricant which is specially formulated for use on motorcycle control cables. Small adapters for pressure lubricating the cables with spray can lubricants are available and ensure that the cable is lubricated along its entire length **(see illustration)**. When attaching the cable to the lever, be sure to lubricate the barrel-shaped fitting at the end with multi-purpose grease.

4   To lubricate the cables, disconnect them at the lower end, then lubricate the cable with a pressure lube adapter **(see illustration 10.3)**. See Chapter 3 (throttle cable) or Chapter 6 (brake cables).

5   Some models are equipped with grease fittings on the swingarm pivots and rear shock absorber linkage **(see illustrations)**. If so, lubricate the fittings with a grease gun. If there are no fittings, you'll need to remove the swingarm and shock linkage pivots to lubricate them (see Chapter 5).

6   The steering head bearings must be removed for cleaning and lubrication (see Chapter 5).

7   Refer to Chapter 6 for the following lubrication procedures:

a) Front and rear wheel bearings
b) Brake pedal pivot

11 Steering and suspension - check

1   The steering and suspension components must be maintained in top operating condition to ensure rider safety. Loose, worn or damaged suspension parts decrease the motorcycle's stability and control.

Steering and front suspension

Refer to illustration 11.4

2   Check all steering and front suspension nuts and bolts for tight-

ness. Make sure none of them have worked loose.

3   Inspect the fork tubes for scratches and scoring. If they're damaged, replace them (see Chapter 5).

4   Inspect the fork seals for leakage **(see illustration)**. On models with fork boots, the boot covers the seal. You'll need to remove the lower boot clamp and pull the boot away from the fork slightly to see if any fluid runs out. If either fork seal is leaking, replace both of them (see Chapter 5).

5   Lock the front brake and push on the handlebars to compress the front forks several times. They should move up-and-down smoothly without binding. If the forks are binding, disassemble and inspect them (see Chapter 5).

6   Elevate the front wheel by placing a milk crate or some other suitable stand under the engine.

7   Grasp the bottom of the forks and gently rock the fork assembly back and forth **(see illustration 11.7 in Chapter 1A)**. If it's loose, adjust the steering head as described below.

Steering head adjustment (TT-R90)

8   This is the same as for RT100 models. See Section 11 of Chapter 1B.

Steering head adjustment (all except TT-R90)

Refer to illustrations 11.11, 11.12 and 11.13

9   Support the bike with the front wheel off the ground (see Chapter 6).

10   Remove the handlebars and the upper triple clamp (see Chapter 5).

11   Remove the lockwasher, the upper ring nut and the damper washer **(see illustration)**.

12   Loosen the lower ring nut, then retighten it with a Yamaha ring nut wrench (YU-33975) or a suitable substitute **(see illustration)**. Don't torque the nut; just tighten it until you feel resistance.

11.4 If either fork seal is leaking, replace both fork seals

11.11 With the upper triple clamp removed, remove the lockwasher (left arrow), upper ring nut and damper ring (right arrows)

11.12 Loosen the ring nut with an adjustable spanner wrench such as this one, then tighten it slightly . . .

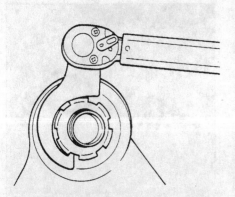

11.13 ... then tighten the ring nut with a Yamaha ring nut wrench to the correct torque (with the torque wrench at a right angle to the ring nut wrench)

12.1 Make sure the sidestand spring is securely attached and in good condition

13.4 Remove the bleed bolt (arrow) if equipped

13   If you have the Yamaha special tool, attach a torque wrench to it so that they form a right angle (see illustration). Tighten the ring nut to the initial torque listed in this Chapter's Specifications.

14   Loosen the ring nut one turn, then tighten it to the final torque listed in this Chapter's Specifications.

15   Recheck the steering head by turning it from lock-to-lock. If it feels a little tight, loosen the ring nut a little bit and recheck. If it feels loose, repeat the adjustment (Steps 12, 13 and 14).

16   When the steering head feels like all freeplay has been removed, but it's not binding or loose, reinstall the damper washer and upper ring nut. Tighten the upper ring nut with your fingers until the slots in the upper and lower nuts align, then install the lockwasher. Be sure the lockwasher fingers fit into the slots of both nuts.

17   Reinstall all parts removed for access and remove the bike from the support.

Rear suspension

18   Inspect the rear shock absorber(s) for fluid leakage and tightness of the mounting nuts and bolts. If a shock is leaking, replace it.

19   Support the motorcycle securely upright with its rear wheel off the ground. Grab the swingarm on each side, just ahead of the axle. Rock the swingarm from side to side - there should be no discernible movement at the rear. If there's a little movement or a slight clicking can be heard, make sure the swingarm pivot shaft is tight. If the pivot shaft is tight but movement is still noticeable, remove the swingarm and replace the swingarm bearings (see Chapter 5).

12   Sidestand - check

Refer to illustration 12.1

The sidestand should be checked to make sure it stays down

when extended and up when retracted. Refer to Chapter 7 and check tightness of the sidestand mounting bolts. Check the spring for cracks or rust and replace it if any problems are found (see illustration).

13   Engine oil and filter - change

Refer to illustrations 13.4 and 13.6a through 13.6e

1   The engine, transmission and clutch on these models share a common oil supply. TT-R90 and TT-R125 models do not have an oil filter. All other models have a replaceable-element filter mounted on the right side of the engine.

2   Consistent routine oil and filter changes are the single most important maintenance procedure you can perform on a vehicle. The oil not only lubricates the internal parts of the engine, transmission and clutch, but it also acts as a coolant, a cleaner, a sealant, and a protectant. Because of these demands, the oil takes a terrific amount of abuse and should be replaced often with new oil of the recommended grade and type. Saving a little money on the difference in cost between a good oil and a cheap oil won't pay off if the engine is damaged.

3   Before changing the oil and filter, warm up the engine so the oil will drain easily. Be careful when draining the oil, as the exhaust pipe, the engine and the oil itself can cause severe burns.

4   Park the motorcycle over a clean drain pan.

5   Remove the dipstick/oil filler cap to vent the crankcase and act as a reminder that there is no oil in the engine. If you're working on a TT-R250 or an XT350, remove the bleed bolt located above the oil filter housing (see illustration).

6   Remove the drain plug from the engine (see illustrations) and allow the oil to drain into the pan. The O-ring, spring and strainer used on XT225, TT-R225 and XT350 models will probably fall out as the plug is removed, so be careful not to lose them (see illustration).

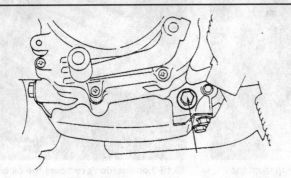

13.6a Here's the TT-R90 oil drain plug

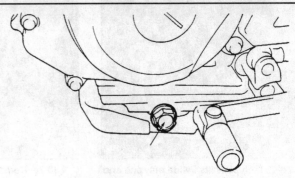

13.6b Here's the TT-R125 oil drain plug

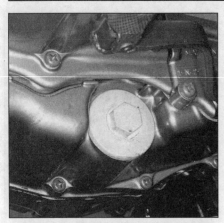

13.6c The XT225 and TT-R225 oil drain plug is located in the bottom of the crankcase on one side

13.6d The TT-R250 oil drain plug (shown) and the XT350 oil drain plug are in the bottom center of the crankcase

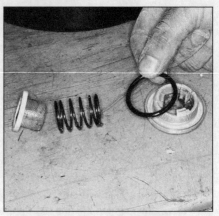

13.6e XT225, TT-R225 and XT250 models have an O-ring, spring and oil screen behind the drain plug

XT225, TT-R225, TT-R250 and XT350 models

Refer to illustrations 13.7a through 13.7e and 13.16

7   Remove the bottom bolt from the oil filter cover **(see illustration)**. Let the oil drain from the bolt hole for a few minutes, then remove the remaining screws or bolts and take off the cover, lower bolt O-ring and filter element **(see illustrations)**. If additional maintenance is planned for this time period, check or service another component while the oil is allowed to drain completely.

8   Wipe any remaining oil out of the filter housing area of the crankcase and make sure the oil passage is clear. Clean the oil strainer (if equipped) with solvent and let it dry completely.

9   Check the condition of the drain plug threads and the O-rings.

10   Install the filter element. **Caution:** *The filter must be installed facing the correct direction or oil starvation may cause severe engine damage.*

13.7a Unscrew the lower cover bolt first, then the upper bolts or screws . . .

13.7b . . . on some models, the screws are different lengths

13.7c Pull off the filter cover and O-ring (arrow) and note the flat post protruding from the cover . . .

13.7d . . . the post fits inside only one end of the element, to prevent it from being installed backwards

13.7e Remove the O-ring from the lower bolt hole

13.16 Loosen (don't remove) the oil check bolt or an oil line fitting; oil must seep out within one minute

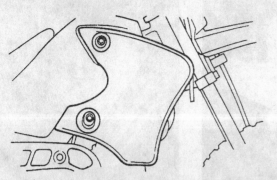

14.1 On TT-R90 models, remove the air scoop . . .

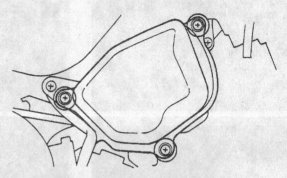

14.2 . . . and the filter housing cover

11 Install a new O-ring over the filter cover's bottom bolt hole **(see illustration 13.7e)**. Install the cover. Apply gasket sealant to the threads of the cover bolts, install them and tighten them to the torque listed in this Chapter's Specifications.

12 Install the engine drain plug (together with the strainer and spring if equipped), using a new O-ring if the old one is worn or damaged. Tighten the plug to the torque listed in this Chapter's Specifications. Avoid overtightening, as damage to the engine case will result. On models equipped with a bleed bolt, reinstall it, using a new washer, and tighten it to the torque listed in this Chapter's Specifications.

13 Before refilling the engine, check the old oil carefully. If the oil was drained into a clean pan, small pieces of metal or other material can be easily detected. If the oil is very metallic colored, then the engine is experiencing wear from break-in (new engine) or from insufficient lubrication. If there are flakes or chips of metal in the oil, then something is drastically wrong internally and the engine will have to be disassembled for inspection and repair.

14 If there are pieces of fiber-like material in the oil, the secondary clutch is experiencing excessive wear and should be checked.

15 If the inspection of the oil turns up nothing unusual, refill the crankcase to the proper level with the recommended oil and install the dipstick/filler cap. Start the engine and let it run for two or three minutes. Shut it off, wait a few minutes, then check the oil level. If necessary, add more oil to bring the level up to the upper level mark on the dipstick. Check around the drain plug(s) and filter cover for leaks.

16 Loosen the oil gallery plug on the cylinder head slightly **(see illustration)**, or loosen the union bolt that attaches the external oil line to the cylinder head. Start the engine and let it idle. Oil should seep from the plug or oil line fitting within one minute. If not, oil is not flowing properly. Shut the engine off and find out the problem before running it further.

17 The old oil drained from the engine cannot be reused in its present state and should be disposed of. Check with your local refuse disposal company, disposal facility or environmental agency to see whether they will accept the oil for recycling. Don't pour used oil into drains or onto the ground. After the oil has cooled, it can be drained into a suitable container (capped plastic jugs, topped bottles, milk cartons, etc.) for transport to one of these disposal sites.

14 Air cleaner - filter element and drain tube cleaning

Element cleaning

TT-R90 models
Refer to illustrations 14.1 and 14.2

1 Remove the right air scoop **(see illustration)**.

2 Remove the air filter cover and lift out the filter element **(see illustration)**.

3 Separate the filter element from the element guide.

TT-R125 models
Refer to illustrations 14.5 and 14.6

4 Remove the right side cover (see Chapter 7).

5 Unhook the retaining band and remove the air filter cover **(see illustration)**.

6 Pull the air filter out of the case, then remove the wing nut and washer and separate the foam filter element from the guide **(see illustration)**.

XT225, TT-R225 and XT350 models
Refer to illustrations 14.8a, 14.8b, 14.8c and 14.8d

7 Remove the left side cover (XT225 and TT-R225) or right side cover (XT350) (see Chapter 7).

8 Remove the filter case cover, take out the element and separate it from the guide **(see illustrations)**.

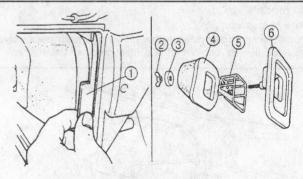

14.6 TT-R125 air filter details

1   *Filter assembly removal tab*
2   *Wing nut*
3   *Washer*
4   *Filter element*
5   *Element guide*
6   *Mounting plate*

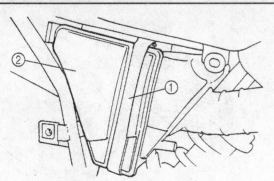

14.5 Unhook the retaining band (1) and remove the filter element (2)

14.8a On XT225, T-R225 and XT350 models, detach the side cover (TT-R225 shown) . . .

14.8b . . . and take it off the air cleaner housing . . .

14.8c . . . check the internal screen (if equipped) for clogging . . .

14.8d . . . and separate the foam element from the guide

TT-R250 models

Refer to illustrations 14.10a, 14.10b and 14.10c

9   Remove the left side cover (see Chapter 7).
10   Remove the air cleaner case cover **(see illustration)**. Unhook the retaining clip, take out the element and separate the element from the guide **(see illustrations)**.

All models

Refer to illustration 14.14

11   Clean the foam filter element in a high flash point solvent, squeeze the solvent out of the foam and let the element dry

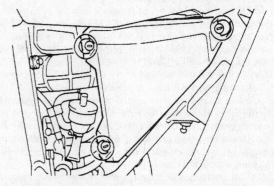

14.10a On TT-R250 models, twist the retainer at each corner of the cover and remove it from the housing . . .

completely.
12   Soak the foam element in the foam filter oil listed in this Chapter's Specifications, then squeeze it firmly to remove the excess oil. Don't wring it out or the foam may be damaged. The element should be wet through with oil, but no oil should drip from it.
13   Reassemble the element and guide.
14   Installation is the reverse of removal, with the following additions:

a) *If you're working on a TT-R90, align the pins on the case with the holes in the element* **(see illustration)**.

b) *If you're working on a TT-R125, apply a thin coat of multi-purpose grease to the mating surfaces of the element and its mounting plate* **(see illustration 14.6)**.

c) *If there's an UP mark on the filter, make sure it's upward when the filter is installed.*

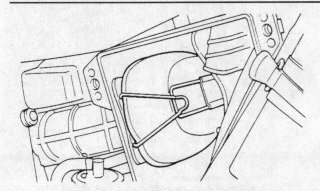

14.10b . . . release the clip and pull out the element . . .

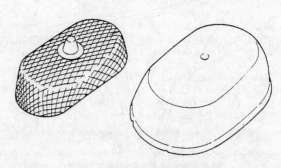

14.10c . . . and separate the element from the guide

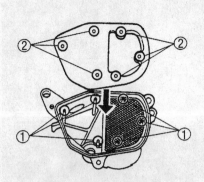

14.14 When installing a TT-R90 air cleaner, align the pins (1) with the holes (2)

14.15 Squeeze the clamp and take the drain tube off the air cleaner housing

14.16 Inspect the ventilation hose (arrow)

Drain tube cleaning

Refer to illustration 14.15

15   Check the drain tube for accumulated water and oil **(see illustration)**. If oil or water has built up in the tube, squeeze its clamp, remove the tube from the air cleaner housing and clean it out. Install the drain tube on the housing and secure it with the clamp. **Note:** *A drain tube that's full indicates the need to clean the filter element and the inside of the case.*

Crankcase ventilation hose

Refer to illustrations 14.16 and 14.17

16   Inspect the crankcase ventilation hose **(see illustration)**. Make sure that it's in good condition and securely attached to the crankcase and to the air cleaner housing. If the hose is cracked, torn or deteriorated, replace it.

17   If you're working on a TT-R250, inspect the ventillation valve **(see illustration)**. Make sure it's in good condition and securely fastened in the hose. Remove and empty the drain tube as described in Step 15 above.

14.17 On TT-R250 models, take the drain tube off the ventilation valve

---

15   Fuel system - inspection

Refer to illustration 15.1

Warning: *Gasoline is extremely flammable, so take extra precautions when you work on any part of the fuel system. Don't smoke or allow open flames or bare light bulbs near the work area, and don't work in a garage where a natural gas-type appliance (such as a water heater or clothes dryer) is present. Since gasoline is carcinogenic, wear latex gloves when there's a possibility of being exposed to fuel, and if you spill any fuel on your skin, rinse it off immediately with soap and water. Mop up any fuel spills immediately and do not store fuel-soaked rags where they could ignite. When you perform any kind of work on the fuel system, wear safety glasses and have a fire extinguisher suitable for class B type fires (flammable liquids) on hand.*

1   Inspect the fuel tank, the fuel tap and the fuel line for leaks and evidence of damage **(see illustration)**. If the fuel tap is leaking, tightening the screws may help. If leakage persists, remove and overhaul or replace the tap (see Chapter 3C). If the fuel line is cracked or otherwise deteriorated, replace it.

2   Remove the screws and lower the tap out of the fuel tank. Inspect the filter screen on the tap and clean it if necessary. If it's damaged or can't be cleaned, replace the tap. Install the tap in the tank, using a new gasket, and tighten the screws securely.

3   On early XT350 models, place the fuel tap lever in the OFF position. Place a wrench on the hex at the bottom of the fuel tank cup and remove the cup and O-ring. Clean the strainer if necessary and replace the tap if it's worn or damaged. Install the strainer and cup, using a new O-ring.

4   Inspect the hose clamp connections between the air intake duct and the carburetor and between the carburetor and the intake joint. If either hose clamp is loose, tighten it.

5   Inspect the carburetor for fuel leaks. If the carburetor is leaking, overhaul it (see Chapter 3C).

6   XT225 models first sold in California are equipped with an evaporative emission control system. Check the canister and hoses for leaks or other damage (see Chapter 3C).

15.1 Remove the screws (arrows) and take the tap off the tank (TT-R225 shown)

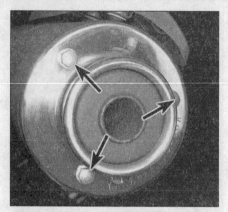

16.3 Remove the screws (arrows) and pull the spark arrester out of the muffler

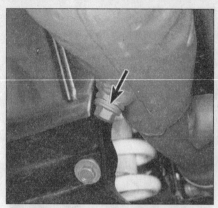

16.5 Unscrew the purging bolt (arrow) from the muffler

17.1 Twist the spark plug cap back and forth to free it, then pull it off the plug

16 Exhaust system - inspection and spark arrester cleaning

Refer to illustrations 16.3 and 16.5

1   Periodically check the exhaust system for leaks and loose fasteners. If tightening the holder nuts at the cylinder head fails to stop any leaks, replace the gasket with a new one (a procedure which requires removal of the exhaust system).

2   The exhaust pipe flange nuts at the cylinder head are especially prone to loosening, which could cause damage to the head (see Chapter 3). Check them frequently and keep them tight.

3   Some models have a removable spark arrester that should be cleaned periodically. If the muffler has screws in the end **(see illustration)**, it's equipped with a spark arrester.

4   **Warning:** *To avoid serious burns, make sure the exhaust system is cool before starting this procedure.* Remove the screws from the end of the muffler and pull out the spark arrester. Tap it on a workbench to remove carbon, then finish cleaning it with a wire brush. Reinstall the spark arrester and tighten the screws securely, but don't overtighten them and strip the threads.

5   If the muffler has a purging bolt **(see illustration)**, unscrew it. Start the engine and rev it about 20 times while holding a rag over the end of the muffler. Shut the engine off and reinstall the bolt.

17 Spark plug - check and replacement

Refer to illustrations 17.1, 17.5a and 17.5b

1   Twist the spark plug cap to break it free from the plug, then pull it off **(see illustration)**. If available, use compressed air to blow any accumulated debris from around the spark plug. Remove the plug with a spark plug socket.

2   Inspect the electrodes for wear. Both the center and side electrodes should have square edges and the side electrode should be of uniform thickness. Look for excessive deposits and evidence of a cracked or chipped insulator around the center electrode. Compare your spark plugs to the color spark plug reading chart on the inside back cover. Check the threads, the washer and the ceramic insulator body for cracks and other damage.

3   If the electrodes are not excessively worn, and if the deposits can be easily removed with a wire brush, the plug can be regapped and reused (if no cracks or chips are visible in the insulator). If in doubt concerning the condition of the plug, replace it with a new one, as the expense is minimal.

4   Cleaning the spark plug by sandblasting is permitted, provided you clean the plug with a high flash-point solvent afterwards.

5   Before installing a new plug, make sure it is the correct type and heat range. Check the gap between the electrodes, as it is not preset. For best results, use a wire-type gauge rather than a flat gauge to check the gap **(see illustration)**. If the gap must be adjusted, bend the

side electrode only and be very careful not to chip or crack the insulator nose **(see illustration)**. Make sure the washer is in place before installing the plug.

6   Since the cylinder head is made of aluminum, which is soft and easily damaged, thread the plug into the head by hand. Slip a short length of hose over the end of the plug to use as a tool to thread it into place. The hose will grip the plug well enough to turn it, but will start to slip if the plug begins to cross-thread in the hole - this will prevent damaged threads and the accompanying repair costs.

7   Once the plug is finger tight, the job can be finished with a socket. If a torque wrench is available, tighten the spark plug to the torque listed in this Chapter's Specifications. If you do not have a torque wrench, tighten the plug finger tight (until the washer bottoms on the cylinder head) then use a spark plug socket to tighten it an additional 1/4 turn. Regardless of the method used, do not over-tighten it.

8   Reconnect the spark plug cap.

18 Cylinder compression - check

Refer to illustration 18.5

1   Among other things, poor engine performance may be caused by leaking valves, incorrect valve clearances, a leaking head gasket, or a worn piston, rings and/or cylinder wall. A cylinder compression check will help pinpoint these conditions and can also indicate the presence of excessive carbon deposits in the cylinder head.

2   The only tools required are a compression gauge and a spark plug wrench. Depending on the outcome of the initial test, a squirt-type oil can may also be needed.

3   Check valve clearances and adjust if necessary (see Section 19). Start the engine and allow it to reach normal operating temperature, then remove the spark plug (see Section 17, if necessary). Work carefully - don't strip the spark plug hole threads and don't burn your hands.

4   Disable the ignition by disconnecting the primary (low tension) wire from the coil (see Chapter 4C).

5   Install the compression gauge in the spark plug hole **(see illustration)**. Hold or block the throttle wide open.

6   Crank the engine over a minimum of four or five revolutions (or until the gauge reading stops increasing) and observe the initial movement of the compression gauge needle as well as the final total gauge reading. Compare the results to the value listed in this Chapter's Specifications.

7   If the compression built up quickly and evenly to the specified amount, you can assume the engine upper end is in reasonably good mechanical condition. Worn or sticking piston rings and a worn cylinder will produce very little initial movement of the gauge needle, but compression will tend to build up gradually as the engine spins over. Valve and valve seat leakage, or head gasket leakage, is indicated by low initial compression which does not tend to build up.

8   To further confirm your findings, add a small amount of engine oil to the cylinder by inserting the nozzle of a squirt-type oil can through

17.5a Spark plug manufacturers recommend using a wire type gauge when checking the gap - if the wire doesn't slide between the electrodes with a slight drag, adjustment is required

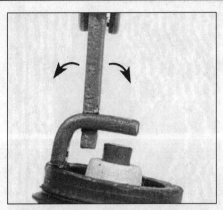

17.5b To change the gap, bend the side electrode only, as indicated by the arrows, and be very careful not to crack or chip the ceramic insulator surrounding the center electrode

18.5 A compression gauge with a threaded fitting for the spark plug hole is preferred over the type that requires hand pressure to maintain the seal

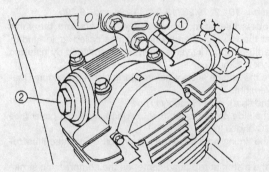

19.7a Unscrew the intake valve cover (1) and exhaust valve cover (2)

the spark plug hole. The oil will tend to seal the piston rings if they are leaking.

9   If the compression increases significantly after the addition of the oil, the piston rings and/or cylinder are definitely worn. If the compression does not increase, the pressure is leaking past the valves or the head gasket. Leakage past the valves may be due to insufficient valve clearances, burned, warped or cracked valves or valve seats or valves that are hanging up in the guides.

10   If compression readings are considerably higher than specified, the combustion chamber is probably coated with excessive carbon deposits. It is possible (but not very likely) for carbon deposits to raise the compression enough to compensate for the effects of leakage past

rings or valves. Refer to Chapter 2, remove the cylinder head and carefully decarbonize the combustion chamber.

19 Valve clearances - check and adjustment

TT-R90, TT-R125, XT225 and TT-R225 models

Refer to illustrations 19.7a, 19.7b, 19.8, 19.9a, 19.9b, 19.11, 19.12, 19.15a and 19.15b

1   The engine must be cool to the touch for this maintenance procedure, so if possible let the machine sit overnight before beginning.

2   If you're working on a TT-R90, remove the right air scoop and the air cleaner housing (see Chapter 3C).

3   If you're working on a TT-R125, remove the seat (see Chapter 7) and fuel tank (see Chapter 3C).

4   If you're working on an XT225 or a TT-R225, remove the side covers, air scoops, seat and fuel tank (see Chapters 7C and 3C).

5   If the motorcycle has an electric starter, disconnect the cable from the negative terminal of the battery (see Section 23, if necessary).

6   Refer to Section 17 and remove the spark plug. This will make it easier to turn the engine.

7   Remove the valve adjusting hole covers (there's one on each side of the cylinder head **(see illustrations)**.

8   Remove the timing hole plug and crankshaft bolt hole plug **(see illustration)**.

9   Position the piston at Top Dead Center (TDC) on the compression stroke. Do this by turning the crankshaft until the mark on the rotor is aligned with the timing notch on the crankcase **(see illustrations)**. You

19.7b Remove the Allen bolts (arrows) and take the cover off; the exhaust side (shown) has three bolts and the intake side has two

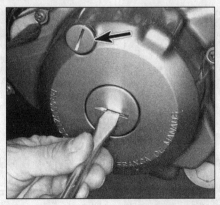

19.8 Unscrew the rotor bolt cover and the timing hole cover (arrow)

19.9a Turn the rotor bolt . . .

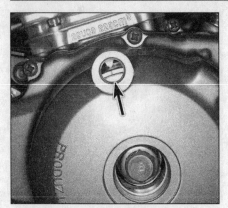

19.9b . . . to align the timing mark on the rotor with the indicator inside the hole (arrow)

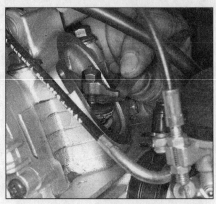

19.11 Measure the valve clearance with a feeler gauge . . .

19.12 . . . loosen the locknut, turn the adjuster screw to set the clearance and tighten the locknut

should be able to wiggle both rocker arms - if not (if the exhaust valve is open), the engine is positioned at TDC on the exhaust stroke. Turn the crankshaft one full turn and realign the marks.

10   With the engine in this position, both of the valves can be checked.

11   To check, insert a feeler gauge of the thickness listed in this Chapter's Specifications between the valve stem and rocker arm **(see illustration)**. Pull the feeler gauge out slowly - you should feel a slight drag. If there's no drag, the clearance is too loose. If there's a heavy drag, the clearance is too tight.

12   If the clearance is incorrect, loosen the adjuster locknut with a box-end wrench (ring spanner). **Note:** *You can hold the locknut during adjustment with an open-end wrench, but a box-end wrench should be used to loosen it.* While holding the locknut with the wrench, turn the adjusting screw with a small open-end wrench, needle-nosed pliers or a special valve adjusting tool until the correct clearance is achieved, then tighten the locknut **(see illustration)**.

13   After adjusting, recheck the clearance with the feeler gauge to make sure it wasn't changed when the locknut was tightened.

14   Now measure the other valve, following the same procedure you used for the first valve. Make sure to use a feeler gauge of the specified thickness.

15   With both of the clearances within the Specifications, install the valve adjusting hole covers, timing hole plug and rotor bolt plug. On XT225 and TT-R225 engines, make sure the UP mark on the cover with two bolt holes is upward **(see illustration)**. If there is no UP mark, make sure the ridge on the inside of the cover is upward when the cover is installed **(see illustration)**. Use new O-rings on the covers and plugs if the old ones are hardened, deteriorated or damaged.

16   Install all components removed for access.

TT-R250 models

Refer to illustrations 19.22, 19.23, 19.27, 19.29a and 19.29b

17   These models use shims between the tappets and the valve stems to adjust the valve clearances (sometimes called "shim-under-bucket" valve adjustment). The valve clearance is changed by installing shims of different thicknesses.

18   Make sure the engine is cool before starting this procedure. Ideally, let it sit overnight.

19   Remove the spark plug (Section 17).

20   Remove the side covers, seat, fuel tank and camshaft cover (see Chapters 7C, 3C and 2C).

21   Remove the timing hole cover and rotor bolt cover **(see illustration 19.8)**.

22   Position the piston at top dead center on the compression stroke as described in Step 9 above. To confirm that the piston is on the compression stroke and not the exhaust stroke, look at the cam lobe positions **(see illustration)**. If the lobes are positioned as shown, the piston is on the compression stroke. If not, it's on the exhaust stroke. Turn the crankshaft one full turn and realign the timing marks.

23   Measure the valve clearance between the cam lobe and tappet with a feeler gauge **(see illustration)**. If it's not within the range listed in this Chapter's Specifications, write it down.

24   Measure the other valve clearance in the same way and write it down if it's incorrect.

25   If either valve clearance needs to be adjusted, remove the exhaust system, cam chain tensioner and camshafts (see Chapters 3C and 2C).

26   Stuff clean shop rags into the cam chain cavity so the valve shims and other small parts or tools don't fall into it.

27   Remove the tappet and valve shim from the valve you're adjusting

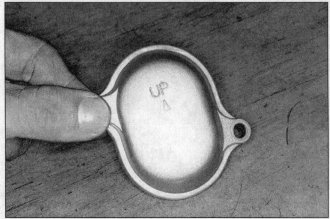

19.15a If there's an UP mark on the cover, make sure it's upright when the cover is installed . . .

19.15b . . . if there isn't an UP mark, install the cover with its internal ridge upright

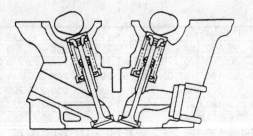

19.22 The cam lobes should be positioned like this (TT-R250)

19.23 Measure clearance between the cam lobe and tappet with a feeler gauge

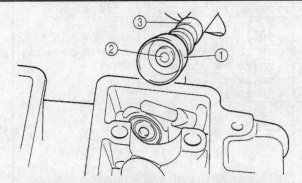

19.27 Pull out the tappet (1) and shim (2) with a magnet or suction cup (3)

with a magnet or suction cup (see illustration).

28 Determine the thickness of the removed shim. It should be marked on the bottom of the shim, but the ideal way is to measure it with a micrometer. **Note:** *If the number of the shim does not end in 0 or 5, round it off to the nearest zero or 5. For example, if the number on the shim is 258, round it off to 260. If it's 254, round it off to 255.*

29 If the clearance written down in Step 23 or 24 was too large, you'll need a thicker shim. If the clearance was too small, you'll need a thinner shim. Calculate the thickness of the replacement shim by referring to the accompanying charts (see illustrations).

30 Coat the new shim with moly-based grease and install it on its valve stem. Install the tappet, rotating it as you do so, taking care not to knock the shim out of position.

31 If you selected a new shim for the remaining valve, install it.

32 Install the camshafts (exhaust camshaft first). Rotate the engine several turns to settle the parts into position, then recheck the clearance. If it's within the Specifications, then the valves are properly adjusted.

33 Install all parts removed for access.

INTAKE

[B] MEASURED CLEARANCE	[A] INSTALLED PAD NUMBER																								
	120	125	130	135	140	145	150	155	160	165	170	175	180	185	190	195	200	205	210	215	220	225	230	235	240
0.00 ~ 0.04			120	125	130	135	140	145	150	155	160	165	170	175	180	185	190	195	200	205	210	215	220	225	
0.05 ~ 0.08		120	125	130	135	140	145	150	155	160	165	170	175	180	185	190	195	200	205	210	215	220	225	230	
0.09 ~ 0.17	RECOMMENDED CLEARANCE																								
0.18 ~ 0.20	120	125	130	135	140	145	150	155	160	165	170	175	180	185	190	195	200	205	210	215	220	225	230	235	240
0.21 ~ 0.25	125	130	135	140	145	150	155	160	165	170	175	180	185	190	195	200	205	210	215	220	225	230	235	240	
0.26 ~ 0.30	130	135	140	145	150	155	160	165	170	175	180	185	190	195	200	205	210	215	220	225	230	235	240		
0.31 ~ 0.35	135	140	145	150	155	160	165	170	175	180	185	190	195	200	205	210	215	220	225	230	235	240			
0.36 ~ 0.40	140	145	150	155	160	165	170	175	180	185	190	195	200	205	210	215	220	225	230	235	240				
0.41 ~ 0.45	145	150	155	160	165	170	175	180	185	190	195	200	205	210	215	220	225	230	235	240					
0.46 ~ 0.50	150	155	160	165	170	175	180	185	190	195	200	205	210	215	220	225	230	235	240						
0.51 ~ 0.55	155	160	165	170	175	180	185	190	195	200	205	210	215	220	225	230	235	240							
0.56 ~ 0.60	160	165	170	175	180	185	190	195	200	205	210	215	220	225	230	235	240								
0.61 ~ 0.65	165	170	175	180	185	190	195	200	205	210	215	220	225	230	235	240									
0.66 ~ 0.70	170	175	180	185	190	195	200	205	210	215	220	225	230	235	240										
0.71 ~ 0.75	175	180	185	190	195	200	205	210	215	220	225	230	235	240											
0.76 ~ 0.80	180	185	190	195	200	205	210	215	220	225	230	235	240												
0.81 ~ 0.85	185	190	195	200	205	210	215	220	225	230	235	240													
0.86 ~ 0.90	190	195	200	205	210	215	220	225	230	235	240														
0.91 ~ 0.95	195	200	205	210	215	220	225	230	235	240															
0.96 ~ 1.00	200	205	210	215	220	225	230	235	240																
1.01 ~ 1.05	205	210	215	220	225	230	235	240																	
1.06 ~ 1.10	210	215	220	225	230	235	240																		
1.11 ~ 1.15	215	220	225	230	235	240																			
1.16 ~ 1.20	220	225	230	235	240																				
1.21 ~ 1.25	225	230	235	240																					
1.26 ~ 1.30	230	235	240																						
1.31 ~ 1.35	235	240																							
1.36 ~ 1.40	240																								

VALVE CLEARANCE (cold):
  0.09 ~ 0.17 mm (0.004 ~ 0.007 in)
Example: Installed is: 170
  Measured clearance is:
  0.27 mm (0.011 in)
  Replace 170 pad with 180 pad

19.29a Intake valve shim selection chart (TT-R250 models)

EXHAUST

B MEASURED CLEARANCE	A INSTALLED PAD NUMBER 120	125	130	135	140	145	150	155	160	165	170	175	180	185	190	195	200	205	210	215	220	225	230	235	240
0.00 ~ 0.04						120	125	130	135	140	145	150	155	160	165	170	175	180	185	190	195	200	205	210	215
0.05 ~ 0.09					120	125	130	135	140	145	150	155	160	165	170	175	180	185	190	195	200	205	210	215	220
0.10 ~ 0.14				120	125	130	135	140	145	150	155	160	165	170	175	180	185	190	195	200	205	210	215	220	225
0.15 ~ 0.18			120	125	130	135	140	145	150	155	160	165	170	175	180	185	190	195	200	205	210	215	220	225	230
0.19 ~ 0.27	RECOMMENDED CLEARANCE																								
0.28 ~ 0.30	120	125	130	135	140	145	150	155	160	165	170	175	180	185	190	195	200	205	210	215	220	225	230	235	240
0.31 ~ 0.35	125	130	135	140	145	150	155	160	165	170	175	180	185	190	195	200	205	210	215	220	225	230	235	240	
0.36 ~ 0.40	130	135	140	145	150	155	160	165	170	175	180	185	190	195	200	205	210	215	220	225	230	235	240		
0.41 ~ 0.45	135	140	145	150	155	160	165	170	175	180	185	190	195	200	205	210	215	220	225	230	235	240			
0.46 ~ 0.50	140	145	150	155	160	165	170	175	180	185	190	195	200	205	210	215	220	225	230	235	240				
0.51 ~ 0.55	145	150	155	160	165	170	175	180	185	190	195	200	205	210	215	220	225	230	235	240					
0.56 ~ 0.60	150	155	160	165	170	175	180	185	190	195	200	205	210	215	220	225	230	235	240						
0.61 ~ 0.65	155	160	165	170	175	180	185	190	195	200	205	210	215	220	225	230	235	240							
0.66 ~ 0.70	160	165	170	175	180	185	190	195	200	205	210	215	220	225	230	235	240								
0.71 ~ 0.75	165	170	175	180	185	190	195	200	205	210	215	220	225	230	235	240									
0.76 ~ 0.80	170	175	180	185	190	195	200	205	210	215	220	225	230	235	240										
0.81 ~ 0.85	175	180	185	190	195	200	205	210	215	220	225	230	235	240											
0.86 ~ 0.90	180	185	190	195	200	205	210	215	220	225	230	235	240												
0.91 ~ 0.95	185	190	195	200	205	210	215	220	225	230	235	240													
0.96 ~ 1.00	190	195	200	205	210	215	220	225	230	235	240														
1.01 ~ 1.05	195	200	205	210	215	220	225	230	235	240															
1.06 ~ 1.10	200	205	210	215	220	225	230	235	240																
1.11 ~ 1.15	205	210	215	220	225	230	235	240																	
1.16 ~ 1.20	210	215	220	225	230	235	240																		
1.21 ~ 1.25	215	220	225	230	235	240																			
1.26 ~ 1.30	220	225	230	235	240																				
1.31 ~ 1.35	225	230	235	240																					
1.36 ~ 1.40	230	235	240																						
1.41 ~ 1.45	235	240																							
1.46 ~ 1.50	240																								

VALVE CLEARANCE (cold):
   0.19 ~ 0.27 mm (0.007 ~ 0.011 in)
Example: Installed is: 180
   Measured clearance is:
   0.34 mm (0.013 in)
   Replace 180 pad with 185 pad

19.29b Exhaust valve shim selection chart (TT-R250 models)

XT350 models

Refer to illustrations 19.39a, 19.39b, 19.43, 19.47a and 19.47b

34   These models use shims between the tappets and the cam lobes to adjust the valve clearances (sometimes called "shim-over-bucket" valve adjustment). The valve clearance is changed by installing shims of different thicknesses.

35   Make sure the engine is cool before starting this procedure. Ideally, let it sit overnight.

36   Remove the side cover, air scoop, seat and fuel tank (see Chapters 7C and 3C).

37   Remove the spark plug (Section 17).

38   Remove the shift pedal and left crankcase cover (see Chapters 2C and 4C).

39   Position the piston at top dead center on the compression stroke by using the alternator rotor bolt to turn the crankshaft. Align the T mark on the outside of the rotor with the indicator on the edge of the crankcase **(see illustration)**. To confirm that the piston is on the com-

19.39a Align the T mark on the rotor (right arrow) with the indicator on the crankcase (left arrow)

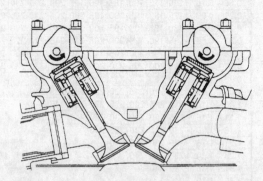

19.39b Be sure to turn the camshafts only in the indicated directions so the lobe won't drag across the holding tool

19.43 This holding tool is used for shim removal on XT350 models

pression stroke and not the exhaust stroke, look at the cam lobe positions **(see illustration)**. If the lobes are positioned as shown, the piston is on the compression stroke. If not, it's on the exhaust stroke. Turn the crankshaft one full turn and realign the timing marks.

40   Measure the valve clearance between the cam lobe and shim with a feeler gauge. If it's not within the range listed in this Chapter's Specifications, write it down.

41   Measure the other valve clearance in the same way and write it down if it's incorrect.

42   If either valve clearance needs to be adjusted, check the position of the notch in the upper edge of the valve tappet. Turn them with a screwdriver so the notches (one in each of the tappets) face each other.

43   Turn the camshaft until the valve to be adjusted is all the way open (the highest part of the cam lobe is pressing down on the valve shim). Install the Yamaha holding tool (YM-4106) on the valve tappet to hold it down **(see illustration)**. **Note:** *Be sure the tool bears against the tappet only, not against the shim.*

44   Turn the camshaft so the lobe points upward **(see illustration 19.39b)**. **Note:** *The camshafts must rotate only in the indicated directions (inward, toward the center of the engine) so they don't drag on the holding tool. The tool will hold the tappet down, forming a gap so the shim can be removed.*

45   Slip a small screwdriver into the lifter notch, under the shim, and pry it out of the tappet. Take the shim out with a magnet.

46   Determine the thickness of the removed shim. It should be marked on the bottom of the shim, but the ideal way is to measure it with a micrometer. **Note:** *If the number of the shim does not end in 0 or 5, round it off to the nearest zero or 5. For example, if the number on the shim is 258, round it off to 260. If it's 254, round it off to 255.*

47   If the clearance written down in Step 40 or 41 was too large, you'll need a thicker shim. If the clearance was too small, you'll need a thinner shim. Calculate the thickness of the replacement shim by referring to the accompanying charts **(see illustrations)**.

48   Coat the new shim with moly-based grease and install it on the tappet. Remove the holding tool.

49   If you selected a new shim for the remaining valve, install it.

50   Rotate the engine several turns to settle the parts into position, then recheck the clearance. If it's within the Specifications, then the valves are properly adjusted.

51   Install all parts removed for access.

20 Decompression lever freeplay (XT350 models) - check

Refer to illustration 20.2

1   Adjust the valves as described in Section 19. Leave the piston at Top Dead Center on its compression stroke.

INTAKE

[B] MEASURED CLEARANCE / [A] INSTALLED PAD NUMBER

MEASURED CLEARANCE	200	205	210	215	220	225	230	235	240	245	250	255	260	265	270	275	280	285	290	295	300	305	310	315	320
0.00 ~ 0.02			200	205	210	215	220	225	230	235	240	245	250	255	260	265	270	275	280	285	290	295	300	305	310
0.03 ~ 0.07		200	205	210	215	220	225	230	235	240	245	250	255	260	265	270	275	280	285	290	295	300	305	310	315
0.08 ~ 0.12																									
0.13 ~ 0.17	205	210	215	220	225	230	235	240	245	250	255	260	265	270	275	280	285	290	295	300	305	310	315	320	
0.18 ~ 0.22	210	215	220	225	230	235	240	245	250	255	260	265	270	275	280	285	290	295	300	305	310	315	320		
0.23 ~ 0.27	215	220	225	230	235	240	245	250	255	260	265	270	275	280	285	290	295	300	305	310	315	320			
0.28 ~ 0.32	220	225	230	235	240	245	250	255	260	265	270	275	280	285	290	295	300	305	310	315	320				
0.33 ~ 0.37	225	230	235	240	245	250	255	260	265	270	275	280	285	290	295	300	305	310	315	320					
0.38 ~ 0.42	230	235	240	245	250	255	260	265	270	275	280	285	290	295	300	305	310	315	320						
0.43 ~ 0.47	235	240	245	250	255	260	265	270	275	280	285	290	295	300	305	310	315	320							
0.48 ~ 0.52	240	245	250	255	260	265	270	275	280	285	290	295	300	305	310	315	320								
0.53 ~ 0.57	245	250	255	260	265	270	275	280	285	290	295	300	305	310	315	320									
0.58 ~ 0.62	250	255	260	265	270	275	280	285	290	295	300	305	310	315	320										
0.63 ~ 0.67	255	260	265	270	275	280	285	290	295	300	305	310	315	320											
0.68 ~ 0.72	260	265	270	275	280	285	290	295	300	305	310	315	320												
0.73 ~ 0.77	265	270	275	280	285	290	295	300	305	310	315	320													
0.78 ~ 0.82	270	275	280	285	290	295	300	305	310	315	320														
0.83 ~ 0.87	275	280	285	290	295	300	305	310	315	320															
0.88 ~ 0.92	280	285	290	295	300	305	310	315	320																
0.93 ~ 1.97	285	290	295	300	305	310	315	320																	
0.98 ~ 1.02	290	295	300	305	310	315	320																		
1.03 ~ 1.07	295	300	305	310	315	320																			
1.08 ~ 1.12	300	305	310	315	320																				
1.13 ~ 1.17	305	310	315	320																					
1.18 ~ 1.22	310	315	320																						
1.23 ~ 1.27	315	320																							
1.28 ~ 1.32	320																								

VALVE CLEARANCE (engine cold) 0.08~0.12 mm (0.031~0.048 in)
Example   Installed is 250
           Measured clearance is 0.32 mm (0.013 in)
           Replace 250 pad with 270
*Pad number: (example)   Pad No. 250 = 2.50 mm (0.098 in)
                               Pad No. 255 = 2.55 mm (0.100 in)
Always install pad with number down

19.47a Intake valve shim selection chart (XT350 models)

EXHAUST

MEASURED CLEARANCE (B)	200	205	210	215	220	225	230	235	240	245	250	255	260	265	270	275	280	285	290	295	300	305	310	315	320
0.00 ~ 0.02				200	205	210	215	220	225	230	235	240	245	250	255	260	265	270	275	280	285	290	295	300	305
0.03 ~ 0.07			200	205	210	215	220	225	230	235	240	245	250	255	260	265	270	275	280	285	290	295	300	305	310
0.08 ~ 0.12		200	205	210	215	220	225	230	235	240	245	250	255	260	265	270	275	280	285	290	295	300	305	310	315
0.13 ~ 0.17																									
0.18 ~ 0.22	205	210	215	220	225	230	235	240	245	250	255	260	265	270	275	280	285	290	295	300	305	310	315	320	
0.23 ~ 0.27	210	215	220	225	230	235	240	245	250	255	260	265	270	275	280	285	290	295	300	305	310	315	320		
0.28 ~ 0.32	215	220	225	230	235	240	245	250	255	260	265	270	275	280	285	290	295	300	305	310	315	320			
0.33 ~ 0.37	220	225	230	235	240	245	250	255	260	265	270	275	280	285	290	295	300	305	310	315	320				
0.38 ~ 0.42	225	230	235	240	245	250	255	260	265	270	275	280	285	290	295	300	305	310	315	320					
0.43 ~ 0.47	230	235	240	245	250	255	260	265	270	275	280	285	290	295	300	305	310	315	320						
0.48 ~ 0.52	235	240	245	250	255	260	265	270	275	280	285	290	295	300	305	310	315	320							
0.53 ~ 0.57	240	245	250	255	260	265	270	275	280	285	290	295	300	305	310	315	320								
0.58 ~ 0.62	245	250	255	260	265	270	275	280	285	290	295	300	305	310	315	320									
0.63 ~ 0.67	250	255	260	265	270	275	280	285	290	295	300	305	310	315	320										
0.68 ~ 0.72	255	260	265	270	275	280	285	290	295	300	305	310	315	320											
0.73 ~ 0.77	260	265	270	275	280	285	290	295	300	305	310	315	320												
0.78 ~ 0.82	265	270	275	280	285	290	295	300	305	310	315	320													
0.83 ~ 0.87	270	275	280	285	290	295	300	305	310	315	320														
0.88 ~ 0.92	275	280	285	290	295	300	305	310	315	320															
0.93 ~ 1.97	280	285	290	295	300	305	310	315	320																
0.98 ~ 1.02	285	290	295	300	305	310	315	320																	
1.03 ~ 1.07	290	295	300	305	310	315	320																		
1.08 ~ 1.12	295	300	305	310	315	320																			
1.13 ~ 1.17	300	305	310	315	320																				
1.18 ~ 1.22	305	310	315	320																					
1.23 ~ 1.27	310	315	320																						
1.28 ~ 1.32	315	320																							
1.33 ~ 1.37	320																								

(A) INSTALLED PAD NUMBER

VALVE CLEARANCE (engine cold) 0.13 ~ 0.17 mm (0.052 ~ 0.068 in)
Example   Installed is 250
          Measured clearance is 0.32 mm (0.013 in)
          Replace 250 pad with 265
*Pad number: (example)   Pad No. 250 = 2.50 mm (0.098 in)
                         Pad No. 255 = 2.55 mm (0.100 in)
Always install pad with number down

19.47b Exhaust valve shim selection chart (XT350 models)

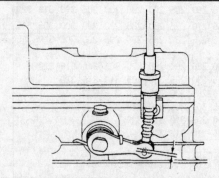

20.2 Measure decompression lever freeplay (XT350 models)

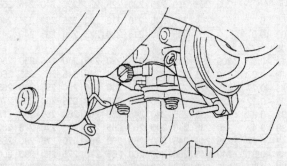

21.3a Throttle stop screw (left arrow) and pilot screw (right arrow) (TT-R90 models)

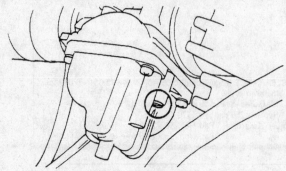

21.3b Here's the TT-R125 pilot screw . . .

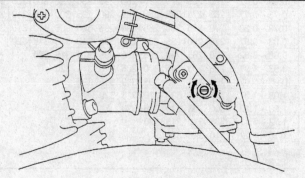

21.3c . . . and throttle stop screw

21.3d Throttle stop screw (right arrow) and pilot screw (left arrow) (TT-R225 models)

21.3e Throttle stop screw (right arrow) and pilot screw (left arrow) (TT-R250 models)

2   Check the freeplay of the decompression lever **(see illustration)**. If it's not within the range listed in this Chapter's Specifications, follow the cable up to the adjuster (it resembles the clutch cable adjuster). Loosen the adjuster locknut, turn the adjuster to set the freeplay, then tighten the locknut.

21 Idle speed - check and adjustment

Refer to illustrations 21.3a through 21.3e

1   Before adjusting the idle speed, make sure the valve clearances and spark plug gap are correct. Also, turn the handlebars back-and-forth and note whether the idle speed changes as the handlebars are moved. If it does, the throttle cable may not be adjusted correctly, or it may be worn out. Be sure to correct this problem before proceeding.

2   The engine should be at normal operating temperature, which is usually reached after 10 to 15 minutes of stop and go riding. Make sure the transmission is in Neutral, then connect an inductive tachometer.

3   On all except US-specification XT225 and XT350 models, turn in the pilot screw until it bottoms lightly, then turn it back out the number of turns listed in this Chapter's Specifications **(see illustrations)**. The pilot screw on US-spec XT225 and XT350 models is sealed and isn't adjusted as part of routine maintenance.

4   Turn the throttle stop screw **(see illustration 21.3a, 21.3c or 21.3d)** until the idle speed listed in this Chapter's Specifications is obtained.

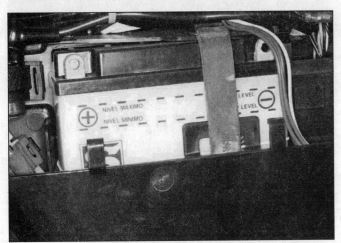

23.3 The + mark identifies the battery positive terminal and the - mark identifies the negative terminal

5   Snap the throttle open and shut a few times, then recheck the idle speed. If necessary, repeat the adjustment procedure.

6   If a smooth, steady idle can't be achieved, the air/fuel mixture might be incorrect (see Chapter 3).

7   After the idle speed has been adjusted, check and adjust the throttle cable freeplay (see Section 7).

22 Fasteners - check

1   Since vibration of the machine tends to loosen fasteners, all nuts, bolts, screws, etc. should be periodically checked for proper tightness. Also make sure all cotter pins or other safety fasteners are correctly installed.

2   Pay particular attention to the following:

Spark plug
Transmission oil drain plug
Gearshift pedal
Brake pedal
Footpegs
Engine mounting nuts/bolts
Shock absorber nuts/bolts
Front axle nut
Rear axle nut
Skid plate bolts

23 Battery electrolyte level/specific gravity - check

Refer to illustrations 23.3 and 23.7

Warning: *Be extremely careful when handling or working around the battery. The electrolyte is very caustic and an explosive gas (hydrogen) is given off when the battery is charging.*

1   This procedure applies to batteries that have removable filler caps, which can be removed to add water to the battery. If the original equipment battery has been replaced by a sealed maintenance-free battery, the electrolyte can't be topped up.

2   Remove the seat and side cover for access to the battery (see Chapter 7).

3   The electrolyte level is visible through the translucent battery case - it should be between the Upper and Lower level marks **(see illustration)**.

4   Disconnect the negative cable and remove the battery retaining strap**(see illustration 23.3)**. Disconnect the positive cable. **Warning:** *Always disconnect the negative cable first and reconnect it last to avoid sparks which could cause a battery explosion.*

5   If the electrolyte is low, remove the cell caps and fill each cell to the upper level mark with distilled water. Do not use tap water (except in an emergency) and do not overfill. The cell holes are quite small, so it may help to use a plastic squeeze bottle with a small spout to add the water. If the level is within the marks on the case, additional water is not necessary.

6   Next, check the specific gravity of the electrolyte in each cell with a small hydrometer made especially for motorcycle batteries. These are available from most dealer parts departments or motorcycle accessory stores.

7   Remove the caps, draw some electrolyte from the first cell into the hydrometer **(see illustration)**, then note the specific gravity. Compare the reading to the value listed in this Chapter's Specifications. **Note:** *Add 0.004 points to the reading for every 10-degrees F above 68-degrees F (20-degrees C) - subtract 0.004 points from the reading for every 10-degrees below 68-degrees F (20-degrees C).*

8   Return the electrolyte to the appropriate cell and repeat the check for the remaining cells. When the check is complete, rinse the hydrometer thoroughly with clean water.

9   If the specific gravity of the electrolyte in each cell is as specified, the battery is in good condition and is apparently being charged by the machine's charging system.

10   If the specific gravity is low, the battery is not fully charged. This may be due to corroded battery terminals, a dirty battery case, a malfunctioning charging system, or loose or corroded wiring connections. On the other hand, it may be that the battery is worn out, especially if the machine is old, or that infrequent use of the machine prevents normal charging from taking place.

11   Be sure to correct any problems and charge the battery if necessary. Refer to Chapter 8 for additional battery maintenance and charging procedures.

12   Install the battery cell caps, tightening them securely. Reconnect

23.7 Check the specific gravity with a hydrometer

the cables to the battery, attaching the positive cable first and the negative cable last. Make sure to install the insulating boots over the terminals.

13   Install all components removed for access and route the battery vent tube correctly. Be very careful not to pinch or otherwise restrict the tube, as the battery may build up enough internal pressure during normal charging system operation to explode.

14   If the vehicle will be stored for an extended time, fully charge the battery, then disconnect the negative cable before storage.

Chapter 2 Part A
Engine, clutch and transmission (PW50 and PW80 models)

Contents

Specifications

Cylinder head
Warpage limit.. 0.03 mm (0.0012 inch)

Reed valve
Thickness.. 0.2 mm (0.008 inch)
Reed valve stopper height
    PW50 .... 4.6 to 5.0 mm (0.181 to 0.197 inch)
    PW80 .... 7.4 to 7.8 mm (0.291 to 0.307 inch)
Reed valve bending limit
    PW50 .... 0.8 mm (0.03 inch)
    PW80 .... 0.2 mm (0.008 inch)

Cylinder
Bore
    PW50 .... 39.993 to 40.012 mm (1.5745 to 1.5753 inches)
    PW80 .... 47.000 to 47.018 mm (1.8504 to 1.8511 inches)
Taper limit.. 0.05 mm (0.0020 inch)
Out-of-round limit.. 0.01 mm (0.0004 inch)
Surface warpage limit.. Not specified

Piston and rings

Diameter	
PW50	39.952 to 39.972 mm (1.5729 to 1.5737 inches)
PW80	46.964 to 47.018 mm (1.8504 to 1.8511 inches
Piston diameter measuring point (above bottom of piston)	5 mm (0.2 inch)
Piston-to-cylinder clearance	
PW50	0.034 to 0.047 mm (0.0013 to 0.0019 inch)
PW80	0.033 0.038 mm (0.0013 to 0.0015 inch)
Piston offset	
PW50	0.2 mm (0.008 inch), on the exhaust side
PW80	0.2 mm (0.008 inch), on the intake side
Ring end gap (both rings)	
Standard	0.15 to 0.35 mm (0.006 to 0.014 inch)
Limit	0.5 mm (0.02 inch)
Ring side clearance (both rings)	0.020 to 0.060 mm (0.0008 to 0.0024 inch)

Autolube pump

Pump output (per 200 strokes)	
PW50	
Closed throttle	0.19 to 0.24 cc (0.006 to 0.008 ounces)
Wide open throttle	0.91 to 1.06 cc (0.031 to 0.036 ounces)
PW80	No specified output

Clutch

Spring free length	
PW50	34.5 mm (1.36 inches)
PW80	12.9 mm 0.51 inch)
OFF spring free length (PW80)	
Standard	30.5 mm (1.2 inch)
Minimum	28.5 mm (1.12 inch)
Clutch adjustment gap (PW80)	1.40 to 1.75 mm (0.055 to 0.069 inch)
Clutch shoe (PW50)	
Thickness	1.0 mm (0.040 inch)
Wear limit	0.7 mm (0.028 inch)
Friction plate (PW80)	
Thickness	2.9 to 3.1 mm (0.114 to 0.122 inch)
Wear limit	2.7 mm (0.106 inch)
Metal plate (PW80)	
Thickness	1.2 mm to 1.6 mm (0.047 to 0.063 inch)
Warpage limit	0.01 mm (0.004 inch)

Kickstarter

Kick clip friction force (PW80 models)	0.9 to 1.5 kg (2.0 to 3.3 lbs)

Mainshaft assembly (PW50 models)

Mainshaft bend limit	0.25 mm (0.010 inch)

Crankshaft

Connecting rod side clearance	
PW50	
Standard	0.35 to 0.55 mm (0.014 to 0.022 inch)
Limit	1.0 mm (0.04 inch)
PW80	0.30 to 0.80 mm (0.012 to 0.030 inch)
Connecting rod small end side play	
PW50	
Standard	0.4 to 0.8 mm (0.016 to 0.031 inch)
Limit	1.5 mm (0.059 inch)
PW80	1.0 mm (0.039 inch)
Crankshaft runout limit	0.05 mm (0.0020 inch)
Crankshaft assembly width	
PW50	37.90 to 37.95 mm (1.492 to 1.494 inch)
PW80	47.90 to 47.95 mm (1.886 to 1.888 inch)

Torque specifications

Engine mounts	
PW50	48 Nm (35 ft-lbs)
PW80	
Front	23 Nm (17 ft-lbs)

Under	26 Nm (19 ft-lbs)
Center	23 Nm (17 ft-lbs)
Cylinder head nuts	
PW50	10 Nm (86.4 ft-lbs)
PW80	14 Nm (120 in-lbs)
Reed valve mounting screws	9 Nm (78 in-lbs)
Reed valve/stopper retaining screws	1 Nm (0.5 in-lbs)*
Crankcase cover screws	
PW50	
Left cover	7 Nm (62 in-lbs)
Right cover	4 Nm (35 in-lbs)
PW80	No specified torque**
Clutch spring bolts (PW80)	No specified torque**
Clutch nut (PW80)	50 Nm (36 ft-lbs)
Autolube pump mounting screws	4 Nm (35 in-lbs)
Kickstarter-to-kickstarter shaft pinch bolt	
PW50	10 Nm (86 in-lbs)
PW80	12 Nm (104 in-lbs)
Primary drive gear nut	
PW50	30 Nm (22 ft-lbs)
PW80	50 Nm (36 ft-lbs)
Shift pedal pinch bolt	10 Nm (86 in-lbs)
Crankcase screws	
PW50	9 Nm (78 in-lbs)
PW80	No specified torque**
Bearing retainer-to-crankcase screws/bolts	No specified torque**

Apply non-permanent thread locking agent to the threads.
** *Fasteners without a factory-specified torque should be tightened in accordance with the following dimensions:*

Nuts	Bolts		Nm	Ft-lbs
10 mm....................	6 mm		6	52 in-lbs
12 mm....................	8mm		15	180 in-lbs
14 mm....................	10 mm		30	22
17 mm....................	12 mm		55	40
19 mm....................	14 mm		85	61
22 mm....................	16 mm		130	94

1   General information

The engine/transmission unit is an air-cooled, single-cylinder two-stroke design. The engine/transmission assembly is constructed from aluminum alloy. The crankcase is vertically divided.

The cylinder, piston, crankshaft bearings and connecting rod lower end bearings are lubricated by a mixture of gasoline and two-stroke oil which is circulated through the bottom end on its way to the combustion chamber. The two-stroke oil is injected into the carburetor by the Autolube system, which consists of an oil pump (mounted on the rear of the engine on PW50 models or on the right front of the engine on PW80 models), a control cable and connecting hoses. The transmission and the clutch are lubricated by four-stroke engine oil, which is contained in a sump within the crankcase. On PW50 models, power from the crankshaft is transmitted to a fully automatic one-speed transmission via a centrifugal clutch. On PW80 models, power is transmitted from the crankshaft to a fully automatic three-speed transmission via a wet, multi-plate type clutch.

2   Operations possible with the engine in the frame

The components and assemblies listed below can be removed without having to remove the engine from the frame. If, however, a number of areas require attention at the same time, removal of the engine is recommended.

Cylinder head
Cylinder
Piston and piston ring
External shift mechanism
Clutch (PW80 models)
Primary drive gear (PW80 models)
Kickstarter mechanism
Shift shaft
CDI magneto rotor
Stator
Autolube oil pump

3   Operations requiring engine removal

It is necessary to remove the engine/transmission assembly from the frame and separate the crankcase halves to gain access to the following components:

Crankshaft and connecting rod
Transmission shafts
Crankshaft and transmission bearings
Internal shift mechanism (shift drum and forks)

4   Major engine repair - general note

1   It is not always easy to determine when or if an engine should be completely overhauled, as a number of factors must be considered.

2   High mileage is not necessarily an indication that an overhaul is needed, while low mileage, on the other hand, does not preclude the need for an overhaul. Regular maintenance is probably the single most important factor. An engine that receives regular and frequent transmission oil changes, as well as other required maintenance, will most likely give many hours of reliable service. Conversely, a neglected engine, or one that has not been broken in properly, may require an overhaul very early in its service life.

3   Poor running that can't be accounted for by seemingly obvious causes (fouled spark plug, leaking head gasket or cylinder base gasket, worn piston rings, carburetor problems) may be due to leaking crankshaft seals. In two-stroke engines, the crankcase acts as a suction pump to draw in fuel mixture and as a compressor to force it into the cylinder. If the crankcase seals are leaking, the pressure drop will cause a loss of performance.

4   If the engine is making obvious knocking or rumbling noises, the connecting rod and/or main bearings are probably at fault. The upper connecting rod bearing should be replaced at the maintenance interval listed in Chapter 1.

5   A top-end overhaul consists of replacing the piston and rings and inspecting the cylinder bore. On these models, the cylinder cannot be bored for an oversize piston. If piston-to-cylinder clearance is excessive, the piston, the cylinder, or both, must be replaced.

6   A lower-end engine overhaul generally involves inspecting the crankshaft, transmission and crankcase bearings and seals. Unlike four-stroke engines equipped with plain main and connecting rod bearings, there isn't much in the way of machine work that can be done to refurbish existing parts. Worn bearings, gears, seals and shift mechanism parts should be replaced with new ones. The crankshaft and connecting rod components are available separately, but rebuilding a crankshaft is a specialized operation that should be done by a qualified shop. A rebuilt engine will provide as many trouble-free hours as a new motor.

7   Before beginning the engine overhaul, read through all of the related procedures to familiarize yourself with the scope and requirements of the job. Overhauling an engine is not all that difficult, but it is time consuming. Plan on the vehicle being tied up for a minimum of two weeks. Check on the availability of parts and be sure to obtain any necessary special tools, equipment and supplies in advance.

8   Most work can be done with typical shop hand tools, but some precision measuring tools are required for inspecting parts to determine if they must be replaced. Often a dealer service department or other repair shop will handle the inspection of parts and offer advice concerning reconditioning and replacement. As a general rule, time is the primary cost of an overhaul so it doesn't pay to install worn or substandard parts.

9   As a final note, to ensure maximum life and minimum trouble from a rebuilt engine, everything must be assembled with care in a spotlessly clean environment.

5   Crankcase pressure and vacuum - check

This test can pinpoint the cause of otherwise unexplained poor running. It can also prevent piston seizures by detecting air leaks that can cause a lean mixture. It requires special equipment, but can easily be done by a Yamaha dealer or other shop. If you regularly work on two-stroke engines, you might want to consider purchasing the tester for yourself (or with a group of other riders). You may also be able to fabricate the tester.

The test involves sealing off the intake and exhaust ports, then applying vacuum and pressure to the spark plug hole with a hand vacuum/pressure pump, similar to the type used for brake bleeding and automotive vacuum testing.

First, remove the carburetor and exhaust system. Block off the carburetor opening with a rubber plug, clamped securely in position. Place a rubber sheet (cut from a tire tube or similar material) over the exhaust port and secure it with a metal plate.

Apply air pressure to the spark plug hole with the vacuum/pressure pump. Check for leaks at the crankcase gasket, intake manifold, reed valve gasket, cylinder base gasket and head gasket. If the crankcase gasket leaks between the transmission sump and the crankcase (the area where the crankshaft spins), transmission oil will be sucked into the crankcase, causing the fuel mixture to be oil-rich. Also check the seal at the alternator end of the crankshaft. If the leaks are large, air will hiss as it passes through them. Small leaks can be detected by pouring soapy water over the suspected area and looking for bubbles.

After checking for air leaks, apply vacuum with the pump. If vacuum leaks down quickly, the crankshaft seals are leaking.

6   Engine - removal and installation

Note: *Engine removal and installation should be done with the aid of an assistant to avoid damage or injury that could occur if the engine is dropped.*

PW50 models

Refer to illustrations 6.14a, 6.14b and 6.15

1   Put the bike on its centerstand and drain the transmission oil (see Chapter 1).

2   Remove the seat (see Chapter 7).

3   Remove the fuel tank and exhaust system (see Chapter 3).

4   Disconnect the right shock absorber from the right arm (see Chapter 5).

5   Remove the rear axle nut (see Chapter 6).

6   Detach the right rear arm from the engine (see Chapter 5).

7   Disconnect the rear brake cable from the cam lever (see Chapter 6).

8   Remove the air cleaner housing (see Chapter 3).

9   Remove the Autolube pump cover and the pump (see Section 12). Do NOT disconnect the oil supply and delivery hoses. It's not necessary to do so (if you do disconnect the oil hoses, you will have to bleed the system after reassembly).

10   Remove the carburetor (see Chapter 3).

11   Label and disconnect the CDI magneto wires (see Chapter 4).

12   Disconnect the spark plug wire (see Chapter 1).

13   Disconnect the left shock absorber from the left arm (see Chapter 5).

14   Remove the pivot shaft nut **(see illustration)** and pull out the

6.14a Remove the pivot shaft nut and pull out the shaft (PW50)

6.14b While the pivot shaft is out, inspect the bushings

6.15 Separate the engine/final drive/rear wheel assembly from the frame (PW50 models)

pivot shaft. Check the pivot shaft bushings for wear and damage and replace them if necessary **(see illustration)**.

15   Separate the engine/final drive/rear wheel assembly from the frame **(see illustration)**.

16   Remove the rear wheel from the left arm (see Chapter 6).

17   Detach the left arm from the engine (see Chapter 5).

18   Before further disassembly, set the engine assembly on a suitable work surface.

19   For general information regarding engine disassembly, refer to the next Section.

20   Installation is the reverse of removal, with the following additions:

a)   *Use new gaskets at all exhaust pipe connections.*

b)   *Adjust the throttle cable and rear brake cable (see Chapter 1).*

c)   *Fill the engine oil tank and transmission with oil (see Chapter 1).*

d)   *Run the engine and check for oil or exhaust leaks.*

PW80 models

Refer to illustrations 6.31a and 6.31b

21   Drain the transmission oil (see Chapter 1).

22   Remove the seat and side covers (see Chapter 7).

23   Remove the fuel tank, exhaust system and carburetor (see Chapter 3).

24   Disconnect the spark plug wire (see Chapter 1).

25   Remove the Autolube pump cover. Detach and plug the supply

and outlet oil hoses, remove the pump cover gasket and disconnect the Autolube pump cable (see Section 12).

26   Disconnect the clutch cable from the clutch push lever (see Section 14).

27   Label and disconnect the CDI magneto wires (see Chapter 4).

28   Disconnect the crankcase ventilation hose.

29   Remove the drive chain and drive sprocket (see Chapter 5).

30   Support the engine with a jack, using a block of wood between the jack and the engine to protect the crankcase.

31   Remove the front and rear engine mounting bolts **(see illustration)**. **Note:** *Raise or lower the jack beneath the engine as necessary to relieve strain on the mounting bolts.* Inspect the engine mounting bushings and replace them if they're worn or damaged **(see illustration)**.

32   Have an assistant help you lift the engine out of the frame.

33   Set the engine on a suitable work surface.

34   Have an assistant help lift the engine into the frame so it rests on the jack and block of wood. Use the jack to align the mounting bolt holes, then install the bolts and nuts. Tighten them to the torques listed in this Chapter's Specifications.

35   The remainder of installation is the reverse of the removal steps, with the following additions:

a)   *Use new gaskets at all exhaust pipe connections.*

b)   *Adjust the throttle cable (see Chapter 1).*

c)   *Fill the transmission with oil (see Chapter 1).*

d)   *Run the engine and check for oil or exhaust leaks.*

6.31a Remove the three engine mounting bolts and nuts (two upper bolts shown) . . .

6.31b. . . and remove the bushings

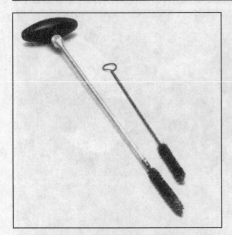

7.2 A selection of brushes is required for cleaning holes and passages in the engine components

7.3 An engine stand can be made from short lengths of lumber and lag bolts or nails

8.2 Loosen the cylinder head nuts gradually and evenly in a criss-cross pattern

7 Engine disassembly and reassembly - general information

Refer to illustrations 7.2 and 7.3

1   Before disassembling the engine, clean the exterior with a degreaser and rinse it with water. A clean engine will make the job easier and prevent the possibility of getting dirt into the internal areas of the engine.

2   In addition to the precision measuring tools mentioned earlier, you will need a torque wrench and oil gallery brushes **(see illustration)**. Some new, clean engine oil of the correct grade and type (two-stroke oil, four-stroke oil or both, depending on whether it's a top-end or bottom-end overhaul), some engine assembly lube (or moly-based grease) and a tube of RTV (silicone) sealant will also be required.

3   An engine support stand made from short lengths of 2 x 4's bolted together will facilitate the disassembly and reassembly procedures **(see illustration)**. If you have an automotive-type engine stand, an adapter plate can be made from a piece of plate, some angle iron and some nuts and bolts.

4   When disassembling the engine, keep "mated" parts together (including gears, shift forks and shafts, etc.) that have been in contact with each other during engine operation. These "mated" parts must be reused or replaced as an assembly.

5   Engine/transmission disassembly should be done in the following general order with reference to the appropriate Sections.

8.4 Pull the cylinder head off the studs and remove the gasket

Remove the cylinder head
Remove the reed valve
Remove the cylinder
Remove the piston
Remove the Autolube oil pump
Remove the clutch
Remove the primary drive gear
Remove the kickstarter
Remove the external shift mechanism
Remove the CDI magneto
Separate the crankcase halves
Remove the internal shift mechanism
Remove the mainshaft and the middle driven pinion gear
    (PW50 models)
Remove the transmission shafts and gears (PW80 models)
Remove the crankshaft and connecting rod

6   Reassembly is accomplished by reversing the general disassembly sequence.

8 Cylinder head - removal, inspection and installation

Caution: *The engine must be completely cool before beginning this procedure, or the cylinder head may become warped.*
Note: *This procedure is described with the engine in the frame. If the engine has been removed, ignore the steps that don't apply.*

Removal

Refer to illustrations 8.2 and 8.4

1   Disconnect the spark plug wire and remove the spark plug (see Chapter 1).

2   Loosen the cylinder head nuts in two or three stages, in a criss-cross pattern **(see illustration)**. Remove the nuts once they're all loose.

3   Lift the cylinder head off the cylinder. If the head is stuck, use a wooden dowel inserted into the spark plug hole to lever the head off. Don't attempt to pry the head off by inserting a screwdriver between the head and the cylinder - you'll damage the sealing surfaces.

4   Rotate the piston to the top of the cylinder or stuff a clean rag into the cylinder to prevent the entry of debris. Once this is done, remove the head gasket from the cylinder **(see illustration)**.

Inspection

Refer to illustrations 8.8a and 8.8b

5   Check the cylinder head gasket and the mating surfaces on the cylinder head and cylinder for leakage, which could indicate warpage.

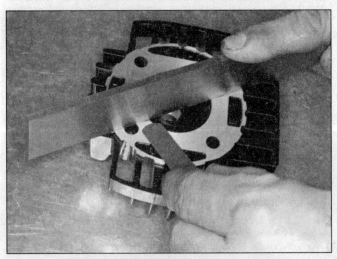

8.8a Check for head warpage with a straightedge
and feeler gauge . . .

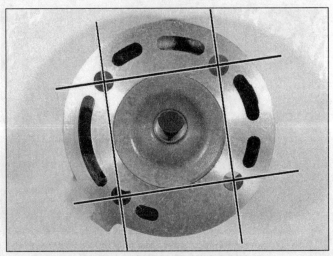

8.8b . . . in the directions shown

6   Clean all traces of old gasket material from the cylinder head and cylinder. Be careful not to let any of the gasket material fall into the cylinder or crankcase. Using a rounded scraper or a small wire brush, remove all carbon deposits from the combustion chamber. If you use a wire brush, make sure the bristles aren't too stiff. And make sure you don't damage the spark plug threads or scratch the metal surface of the chamber.

7   Inspect the head very carefully for cracks and other damage. If cracks are found, a new head will be required.

8   Using a precision straightedge and a feeler gauge, check the head gasket mating surface for warpage. Lay the straightedge across the head, intersecting the head bolt holes, and try to slip a feeler gauge under it, on either side of the combustion chamber (see illustrations). The feeler gauge thickness should be the same as the cylinder head warpage limit listed in this Chapter's Specifications. If the feeler gauge can be inserted between the head and the straightedge, the head is warped and must either be resurfaced or, if warpage is excessive, replaced with a new one.

9   To resurface the head, lay a piece of 400 to 600 grit emery paper on a perfectly flat surface, such as a piece of plate glass. Move the head in a figure-8 pattern over the sandpaper. Rotate the head 1/2 turn after each few figure-8 motions so you don't remove too much material from one side of the head. Don't remove any more material than necessary to correct the warpage.

Installation

10   Lay the new gasket in place on the cylinder (see illustration 8.4). Never reuse the old gasket and don't use any type of gasket sealant.

11   Carefully lower the cylinder head over the studs.

12   Install the cylinder head nuts and tighten them evenly, in a criss-cross pattern, to the torque listed in this Chapter's Specifications.

13   The remainder of installation is the reverse of the removal steps.

9   Reed valve - removal, inspection and installation

Removal

1   Remove the carburetor (see Chapter 3).

PW50 models

Refer to illustrations 9.2a, 9.2b and 9.2c

2   To remove the reed valve assembly from a PW50 model, unbolt the intake manifold from the cylinder, pull the reed valve assembly out of the cylinder and remove the gasket (see illustrations).

PW80 models

Refer to illustrations 9.3a, 9.3b and 9.3c

3   To remove the reed valve assembly from a PW80 model, unbolt

9.2a To remove the PW50 reed valve
assembly, remove the mounting
screws (arrows) . . .

9.2b . . . remove the housing . . .

9.2c . . . pull out the reed valve assembly
and remove the gasket

9.3a To remove the reed valve assembly from a PW80 model, remove the mounting screws (arrows) . . .

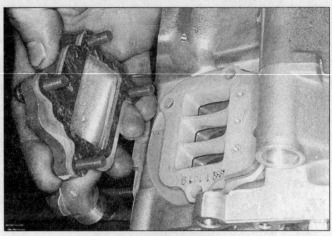

9.3b . . . remove the housing . . .

9.3c . . . pull out the reed valve assembly and remove the gasket

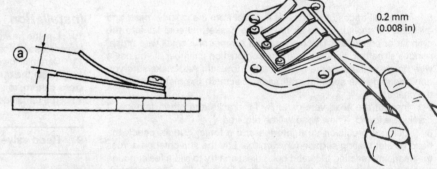

9.6a Measure the reed valve stopper height (a)

9.6b Measure the reed valve bending limit with a feeler gauge of the same thickness as the specified bending limit

the intake manifold from the cylinder, pull the reed valve assembly out of the cylinder and remove the gasket **(see illustrations)**.

Inspection

Refer to illustrations 9.6a, 9.6b, 9.7a and 9.7b

4   Inspect the reed valve for obvious damage, such as a cracked or broken reed or "stopper" (the stopper controls the "height," *i.e.* movement, of the reed). Also make sure there's no clearance between the edge of the reed and where it seats.

5   If inspection doesn't show any obvious damage, connect a vacuum pump to the carburetor side of the reed valve assembly and apply vacuum. There should be little or no leakage.

6   Measure the reed valve stopper height **(see illustration)**. The stopper controls the movement of the reed valve: If clearance (a) is excessive, the reed valve will break; if clearance (a) is too small, engine performance is impaired. If the stopper height is incorrect, replace the stopper. Measure any reed valve warp **(see illustration)**. If the reed is excessively warped, replace it.

7   To disassemble the reed valve assembly and replace the reed, remove the retaining screws and the stopper **(see illustrations)**. The screws have a thread-locking agent on the threads, so you may need to use an impact driver. Remove the reed and install a new one. Install the stopper, aligning the cutout in the stopper with the cutout in the reed. Coat the screw threads with a non-permanent thread-locking agent, then tighten them to the torque listed in this Chapter's Specifications. After reassembly, recheck the valve stopper height and any reed valve warp. Also, make sure that there's no gap between the end of the reed valve and the valve seat.

8   Using a straightedge and a feeler gauge, check the intake mani-

fold for warpage. If it's warped, resurface it with a piece of #600 grit sandpaper. To produce a uniform gasket surface on the manifold, lay the sandpaper on a flat surface, abrasive side up, and work the manifold back-and-forth and side-to-side.

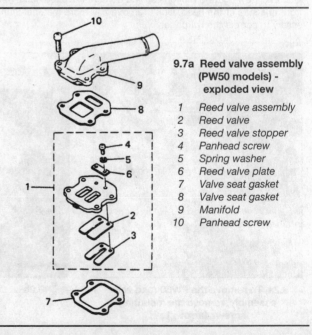

9.7a Reed valve assembly (PW50 models) - exploded view

1   *Reed valve assembly*
2   *Reed valve*
3   *Reed valve stopper*
4   *Panhead screw*
5   *Spring washer*
6   *Reed valve plate*
7   *Valve seat gasket*
8   *Valve seat gasket*
9   *Manifold*
10   *Panhead screw*

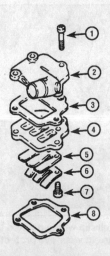

9.7b Reed valve assembly (PW80 models) - exploded view

1 Intake manifold screws (3)
2 Intake manifold
3 Valve seat gasket
4 Valve seat
5 Reed valve
6 Reed valve stopper
7 Stopper/reed valve screws (2)
8 Valve seat gasket

10.2 Pull the cylinder off the crankcase studs and remove the gasket (arrow)

10.4a Measure the head mating surface on the cylinder . . .

10.4b . . . in the directions shown

Installation

9   Installation is the reverse of removal, with the following additions:

a) *Use new gaskets between the reed valve assembly and the cylinder and between the reed valve assembly and the intake manifold.*

b) *Tighten the mounting screws in a criss-cross pattern to the torque listed in this Chapter's Specifications.*

10   Cylinder - removal, inspection and installation

Removal

Refer to illustration 10.2

1   Remove the cylinder head (see Section 8). Make sure the piston is positioned at top dead center (TDC).

2   Lift the cylinder straight up off the piston **(see illustration)**. If it's stuck, tap around its perimeter with a soft-faced hammer. Don't attempt to pry between the cylinder and the crankcase, as you'll ruin the sealing surfaces.

3   Stuff clean shop rags around the piston, then remove the gasket and all traces of old gasket material from the surfaces of the cylinder and the crankcase.

Inspection

Refer to illustrations 10.4a, 10.4b and 10.7

4   Inspect the top surface of the cylinder for warpage, using the same method as for the cylinder head (see Section 8). Make your measurements between the holes for the cylinder head studs and across the bore **(see illustrations)**.

5   If there's any warpage, resurface the cylinder the same way you would resurface the cylinder head (see Section 8).

6   Inspect the cylinder walls carefully for scratches and score marks. Check the port for built-up carbon.

7   Using the appropriate precision measuring tools, measure the cylinder diameter at the top, center and bottom of the cylinder bore, parallel to the crankshaft axis **(see illustration)**. Next, measure the cylinder's diameter at the same three locations across the crankshaft axis. Compare your measurements to the cylinder bore diameter listed in this Chapter's Specifications.

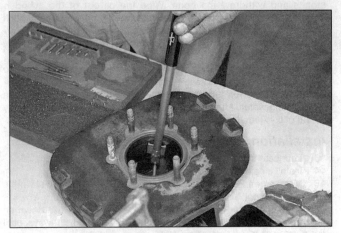

10.7 Measure the diameter of the cylinder bore with a bore gauge

11.3a The arrow mark on the piston points to the front of the engine

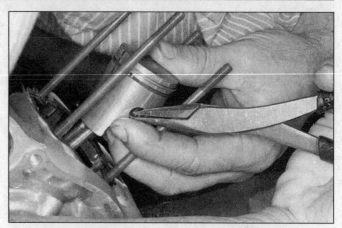

11.3b Remove the piston pin circlip with a pointed tool or needle-nosed pliers; be sure to wear eye protection

8   Differences between the top and bottom measurements indicate cylinder taper. Differences between your measurements parallel to and across the crankshaft axis indicate out-of-round. If the cylinder walls are tapered, out-of-round, worn beyond the specified limits, or badly scuffed or scored, have the cylinder honed or rebored by a dealer service department or a motorcycle repair shop. If the cylinder is rebored, over-size pistons and rings will be required. **Note:** *Consult with your local Yamaha dealer regarding the availability of oversize pistons and rings.*
9   If you don't have the measuring tools needed to do this job, ask a dealer service department or repair shop to measure the cylinder and ask for its advice about servicing the cylinder versus replacing it.
10   If the cylinder is in reasonably good condition and isn't yet worn to the outside limit, and if the piston-to-cylinder clearance is still within tolerance, then it's not necessary to rebore the cylinder; honing is all that is necessary.
11   To hone the cylinder, you will need a flexible hone with fine stones or a "bottle brush" type hone (see *Maintenance techniques, tools and working facilities* at the front of this book), plenty of light oil or honing oil, some shop towels and an electric drill motor. Hold the cylinder in a vise (cushioned with soft jaws or wood blocks) when performing the honing operation. Mount the hone in the drill motor, compress the stones and slip the hone into the cylinder. Lubricate the cylinder thoroughly, turn on the drill and move the hone up and down in the cylinder at a pace that will produce a fine crosshatch pattern on the cylinder wall with the crosshatch lines intersecting at approximately a 60-degree angle. Be sure to use plenty of lubricant and do not take off any more material than is absolutely necessary to produce the desired effect. Do not withdraw the hone from the cylinder while it is running. Instead, shut off the drill and continue moving the hone up and down in the cylinder until it comes to a complete stop, then compress the stones and withdraw the hone. Wipe the oil out of the cylinder. Remember not to remove too much material from the cylinder wall. If you do not have the tools, or do not desire to perform the honing operation, a dealer service department or vehicle repair shop will generally do it for a reasonable fee.
12   Next, wash the cylinder thoroughly with warm soapy water to remove all traces of the abrasive grit produced during the honing operation. Be sure to run a brush through the stud holes and flush them with running water. After rinsing, dry the cylinder thoroughly and apply a coat of light, rust-preventive oil to all machined surfaces.

Installation

13   Lubricate the piston with plenty of clean two-stroke engine oil.
14   Install a new cylinder base gasket **(see illustration 10.2)**.
15   Make sure the piston ring gaps are aligned with the dowels in the ring lands. Install the cylinder over the studs and carefully lower it down until the piston crown fits into the cylinder liner. Push down on the cylinder, making sure the piston doesn't get cocked sideways, until the bottom of the cylinder liner slides down past the piston rings. Be sure not to rotate the cylinder, as this may snag the piston rings on the

exhaust port. A wood or plastic hammer handle can be used to gently tap the cylinder down, but don't use too much force or the piston will be damaged.
16   The remainder of installation is the reverse of the removal steps.

11   Piston and rings - removal, inspection and installation

1   The piston is attached to the connecting rod with a piston pin that is a slip fit in the piston and connecting rod needle bearing.
2   Before removing the piston from the rod, stuff a clean shop towel into the crankcase hole, around the connecting rod. This will prevent the circlips from falling into the crankcase if they are inadvertently dropped.

Removal

Refer to illustrations 11.3a, 11.3b, 11.4a, 11.4b and 11.4c
3   The piston should have an arrow mark on its crown that goes toward the exhaust (front) side of the engine **(see illustration)**. If this mark is not visible due to carbon buildup, scribe an arrow into the piston crown before removal. Support the piston and pry the circlip out with a pointed tool or needle-nosed pliers **(see illustration)**.
4   Push the piston pin out from the opposite end to free the piston from the rod and the remove the needle roller bearing **(see illustrations)**. You may have to deburr the area around the groove to enable the pin to slide out (use a triangular file for this procedure). If the pin won't come out, you can fabricate a piston pin removal tool from a long bolt, a nut, a piece of tubing and washers **(see illustration)**.

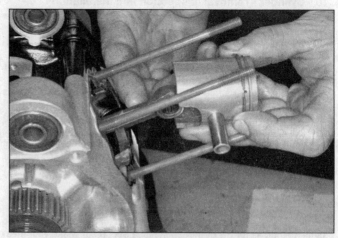

11.4a Push the piston pin partway out, then pull it the rest of the way . . .

11.4b . . . and remove the needle roller bearing from the connecting rod

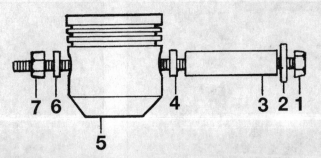

1	Bolt
2	Washer
3	Pipe (A)
4	Padding (A)
5	Piston
6	Washer (B)
7	Nut (B)
A	Large enough for piston pin to fit inside
B	Small enough to fit through piston pin bore

11.4c The piston pin should come out with hand pressure; if it doesn't, you can fabricate a removal tool from readily available parts

Inspection

Refer to illustrations 11.6, 11.11, 11.13, 11.14a, 11.14b, 11.14c, 11.15, 11.16 and 11.17

5   Before the inspection process can be carried out, the piston must be cleaned and the old piston ring removed.

6   Carefully remove the rings from the piston **(see illustration)**. Do not nick or gouge the piston in the process. A ring removal and installation tool will make this easier, but you can use your fingers if you don't have one - just be sure not to cut yourself.

7   Scrape all traces of carbon from the top of the piston. A hand-held wire brush or a piece of fine emery cloth can be used once most of the deposits have been scraped away. Do not, under any circumstances, use a wire brush mounted in a drill motor to remove deposits from the piston; the piston material is soft and will be eroded away by the wire brush.

8   Use a piston ring groove-cleaning tool to remove any carbon deposits from the ring groove. If a tool is not available, a piece broken off the old ring will do the job. Be very careful to remove only the carbon deposits. Do not remove any metal and do not nick or gouge the sides of the ring grooves.

9   Once the deposits have been removed, clean the piston with solvent and dry it thoroughly.

10   Normal piston wear appears as even, vertical wear on the thrust surfaces of the piston and slight looseness of the rings in their grooves.

11   Carefully inspect each piston for cracks around the skirt, at the pin bosses and at the ring lands. Make sure the ring locating dowels are secure in the ring lands **(see illustration)**.

12   Look for scoring and scuffing on the thrust faces of the skirt, holes in the piston crown and burned areas at the edge of the crown. If the skirt is scored or scuffed, the engine may have been suffering from oil starvation and/or abnormal combustion, which caused excessively high operating temperatures. A hole in the piston crown, an extreme to be sure, is an indication that abnormal combustion (pre-ignition) was occurring. Burned areas at the edge of the piston crown are usually a sign of spark knock (detonation). If any of the above problems exist, the causes must be corrected or the damage will occur again.

13   Measure the piston ring-to-groove clearance (side clearance) by laying a new piston ring in the ring groove and slipping a feeler gauge in beside it **(see illustration)**. Check the clearance at three or four locations around the groove. If the clearance is greater than specified, a new piston will have to be used when the engine is reassembled.

14   Measure the ring end gap. Push each piston ring into the cylinder

11.6 Remove the piston rings with a ring removal and installation tool, if you have one (or you can use your fingers, if you're careful)

11.11 There's a locating dowel in each ring land (arrow); center the ring gaps on these dowels

11.13 Measure side clearance between the rings and the piston with a feeler gauge

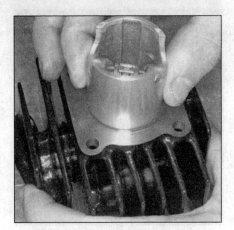

11.14a Use the piston to push the ring into the bore . . .

11.4b ... so it fits evenly like this ...

11.14c ... then measure the ring end gap with a feeler gauge

from the top, down to the bottom of the ring travel area inside the cylinder. Square the ring in the bore by tapping it with the piston crown **(see illustrations)**. Measure the gap between the ends of the ring with a feeler gauge **(see illustration)**. Measure both rings; if either has a gap greater than the value listed in this Chapter's Specifications, replace both rings with new ones.

15   Check the piston-to-bore clearance by measuring the bore (see Section 10) and the piston diameter **(see illustration)**. Measure the piston across the skirt on the thrust faces at a 90-degree angle to the piston pin, at the specified distance up from the bottom of the skirt.

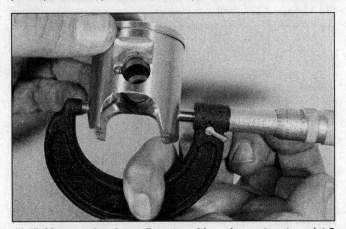

11.15 Measure the piston diameter with a micrometer at a point 5 mm (0.2 inch) above the bottom of the skirt

Subtract the piston diameter from the bore diameter to obtain the clearance. If it is greater than specified, the cylinder will have to be rebored and a new oversized piston and rings installed. If the appropriate precision measuring tools are not available, the piston-to-cylinder clearance can be obtained using feeler gauges (though not quite as accurately). Feeler gauge stock comes in 12-inch lengths and various thicknesses and is generally available at auto parts stores. To check the clearance, slip a piece of feeler gauge stock of the same thickness as the specified piston clearance into the cylinder along with appropriate piston. The cylinder should be upside down and the piston must be positioned exactly as it normally would be. Place the feeler gauge between the piston and cylinder on one of the thrust faces (90-degrees to the piston pin bore). The piston should slip through the cylinder (with the feeler gauge in place) with moderate pressure. If it falls through, or slides through easily, the clearance is excessive and a new piston will be required. If the piston binds at the lower end of the cylinder and is loose toward the top, the cylinder is tapered. If tight spots are encountered as the piston/feeler gauge is rotated in the cylinder, the cylinder is elongated (no longer round). Be sure to have the cylinder and piston checked by a dealer service department or a repair shop to confirm your findings before purchasing new parts.

16   Apply clean two-stroke oil to the pin, insert it into the piston and check for freeplay by rocking the pin side-to-side **(see illustration)**. If the pin is loose, a new piston and possibly a new pin must be installed. Check both for visible wear, replace whichever appears worn and repeat the freeplay check.

17   Repeat Step 16, this time inserting the piston pin into the connecting rod needle bearing **(see illustration)**. If it wobbles and the pin isn't worn, replace the needle bearing.

11.16 Slip the pin into the piston and try to wiggle it side-to-side; if it's loose, replace the piston and pin

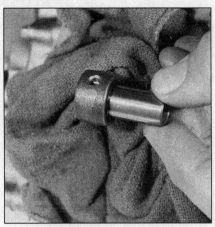

11.17 The needle bearing should be replaced if the pin wobbles inside it

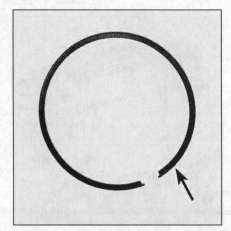

11.20 The manufacturer's mark (arrow) near the ring gap should be facing up when the ring is installed

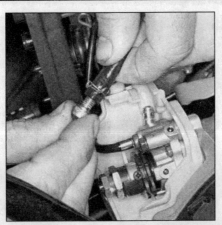

12.8a Disconnect the oil inlet hose from the Autolube pump (PW50) . . .

12.8b . . . and plug it so it won't drain the tank

12.10 Remove the pump mounting screws and take the pump off

Installation

Refer to illustration 11.20

18 Install the piston with its arrow mark toward the exhaust side (front) of the engine. Lubricate the pin and the connecting rod needle bearing with two-stroke oil of the type listed in the Chapter 1 Specifications.

19 Install a new circlip in the groove in one side of the piston (don't reuse the old circlips). Push the pin into position from the opposite side and install another new circlip. Compress the circlips only enough for them to fit in the piston. Make sure the clips are properly seated in the grooves.

20 Locate the manufacturer's mark on the piston rings near one of the ends **(see illustration)**. Turn the rings so this mark is upward, then carefully spread them and install them in the ring grooves. Make sure the end gaps are centered on the dowel pin in each ring groove **(see illustration 11.11)**.

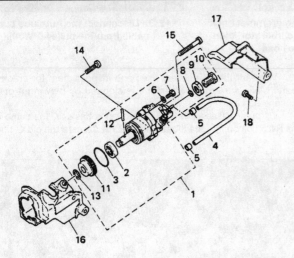

12.13 Autolube pump assembly (PW50) - exploded view

1	Oil pump assembly	*10*	Banjo bolt
2	Oil seal	*11*	Worm wheel gear
3	O-ring	*12*	Pin
4	Delivery pipe	*13*	Circlip
5	Clip	*14*	Panhead screw
6	Gasket	*15*	Panhead screw
7	Bind screw	*16*	Cover
8	Adjusting plate	*17*	Cover
9	Hexagon nut	*18*	Panhead tapping screw

12 Autolube pump - removal, inspection and installation

External inspection and output test

1 The Autolube pump is extremely reliable. It the pump's output has decreased, it's possible, but unlikely, that excessive wear or a malfunction inside the pump has occurred. If pump output is down, inspect the following things before removing the pump.

2 Make sure that neither the bleed screw nor any of the oil line fittings are loose. A loose bleed screw or oil line fitting will allow air to enter the system, which will decrease pump output.

3 Inspect the lines from the oil tank to the pump and from the pump to the carburetor. Make sure neither line is kinked or misrouted.

4 To check the pump output on PW50 models, disconnect the pump delivery line from the carburetor and place the open end of the line in a graduated container. Remove the spark plug. Open the throttle to its wide-open position, and then operate the kickstarter vigorously and continuously, counting the oil pump plunger strokes. When the pump plunger reaches 200 strokes, measure the amount of oil in the container and compare this volume to the pump output listed in this Chapter's Specifications. If the pump output is too low, replace the pump. (There is no specified pump output for PW80 models. If you're suspicious of the pump output on a PW80 model, have the pump checked out by a dealer service department, or replace it and see whether that solves the problem.)

5 If the pump checks out okay so far, but is still leaking, further inspection requires removal of the pump and some disassembly.

PW50 models

Removal

Refer to illustrations 12.8a, 12.8b and 12.10

6 Remove the muffler and silencer (see Chapter 3).

7 Remove the oil pump cover **(see illustration 14.3 in Chapter 1)**.

8 Disconnect the oil hoses **(see illustration)** and plug them to prevent contamination **(see illustration)**.

9 Disconnect the pump cable.

10 Remove the pump mounting screws and take off the pump **(see illustration)**.

Inspection

Refer to illustration 12.13

11 Wipe off the exterior of the pump and inspect it for oil leaks and obvious damage. If the pump is damaged, replace it. If it looks basically sound, proceed with the inspection.

12 Wipe off the oil delivery lines and inspect them for cracks and tears. Make sure that neither line is clogged by blowing it out with compressed air.

13 Disassemble the pump **(see illustration)**. Discard the old O-ring and seal.

12.19a Note how the PW80 hose grommet fits in the pump (arrow) . . .

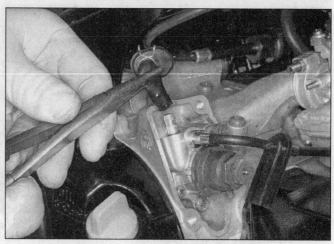

12.19b . . . then disconnect the hose

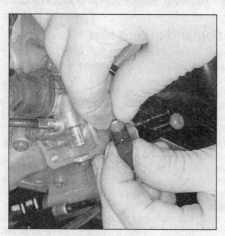

12.19c . . . and plug it so it won't drain the tank

12.19d . . . slide the fitting grommet back from the oil hose at the carburetor, then disconnect the hose

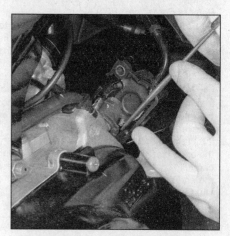

12.20 Disconnect the Autolube pump cable from the pulley (PW80)

14   After disassembling and cleaning all parts, inspect the worm wheel gear teeth for excessive wear and damage. If the teeth are worn or damaged, replace the gear.

15   Reassembly is the reverse of disassembly. Be sure to use a new O-ring and seal.

Installation

16   Installation is the reverse of removal. Be sure to tighten the oil pump mounting screws securely.

17   After installation, bleed air from the pump (see Chapter 1).

PW80 models

Removal

Refer to illustrations 12.19a, 12.19b, 12.19c, 12.19d, 12.20, 12.21a and 12.21b

18   Remove the oil pump cover **(see illustration 14.10 in Chapter 1)**.

19   Disconnect the oil hoses and plug them to prevent contamination **(see illustrations)**.

20   Disconnect the pump cable **(see illustration)**.

21   Remove the pump mounting screws **(see illustration)**, take off the pump and remove the O-ring **(see illustration)**.

Inspection

22   Wipe off the exterior of the pump and inspect it for oil leaks and obvious damage. If the pump is damaged, replace it. If it looks basically sound, proceed with the inspection.

23   Wipe off the oil delivery lines and inspect them for cracks and tears. Make sure that neither line is clogged by blowing it out with compressed air.

24   Oil pump disassembly for inspection is basically the same as for the PW50 oil pump **(see illustration 12.13)**. Discard the old O-ring and seal.

12.21a Remove the pump mounting screws (PW80) . . .

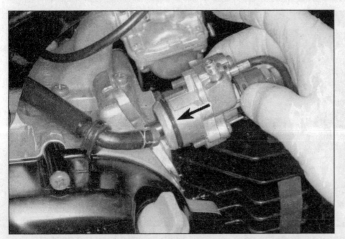

12.21b . . . pull the pump off the engine and remove the O-ring (arrow)

13.2a Remove the PW50 right crankcase cover screws (arrows) . . .

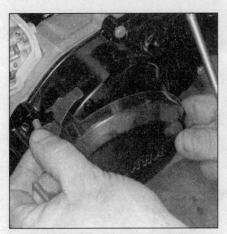

13.2b . . . and remove the outer cover, then the inner cover

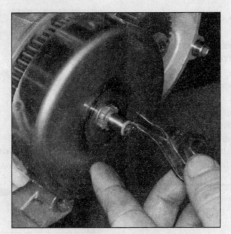

13.3a Remove the clutch housing snap-ring . . .

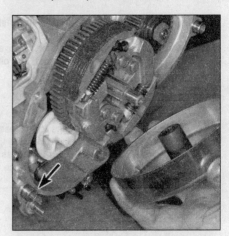

13.3b . . . and pull off the clutch housing; note the rear dowel location (arrow) . . .

25   After disassembling and cleaning all parts, inspect the worm wheel gear teeth for excessive wear and damage. If the teeth are worn or damaged, replace the gear.

26   Reassembly is the reverse of disassembly. Be sure to use a new O-ring and seal.

Installation

27   Installation is the reverse of removal. Be sure to tighten the oil pump mounting screws securely.

28   After installation, bleed air from the pump (see Chapter 1).

---

13 Clutch and oil pump drive gear (PW50 models) - removal, inspection and installation

---

Removal

Refer to illustrations 13.2a, 13.2b, 13.3a, 13.3b, 13.4, 13.5, 13.6a, 13.6b and 13.6c

1   Drain the transmission oil (see Chapter 1).

2   Remove the right crankcase cover screws, outer cover and main cover **(see illustrations)**. Remove and discard the old cover gasket. Locate and remove the dowel pins and store them in a plastic bag.

3   Remove the snap-ring and clutch housing **(see illustrations)**.

4   If you're planning to remove the primary drive gear, loosen the nut now while the clutch is still installed. The primary driven gear on the back of the clutch assembly is used to lock the primary drive gear, so

13.4 . . . and the front dowel location (A); wedge the gears at point B to loosen the primary drive gear nut (C)

its shaft won't just spin when you try to loosen the nut. Stuff a rolled-up shop rag or insert a penny between the teeth of the primary drive gear and the primary driven gear to lock the drive gear **(see illustration)**. Loosen the primary drive gear retaining nut. Remove the nut and gear and inspect the gear (see Section 15).

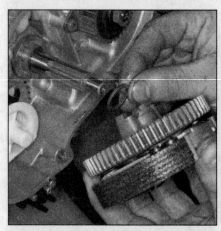

13.5 Remove the clutch carrier assembly and the O-ring

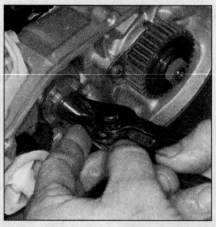

13.6a Remove the snap-ring from the oil pump drive gear . . .

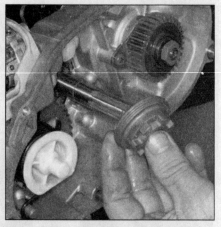

13.6b . . . and take the gear off its shaft . . .

5   Remove the clutch carrier and the flat washer behind it **(see illustration)**.

6   To remove the oil pump drive gear, remove its snap-ring and slide the gear off the shaft **(see illustrations)**. The oil pump driven gear can then be removed **(see illustration)**.

Inspection

Refer to illustration 13.7

7   Inspect the clutch shoe linings for excessive wear **(see illustration)**. If there are any signs of seizure, replace the clutch shoes.

8   Measure the clutch shoe lining thickness. If the lining is thinner than the minimum allowable thickness, replace the clutch shoes.

13.6c . . . the oil pump driven gear can then be removed

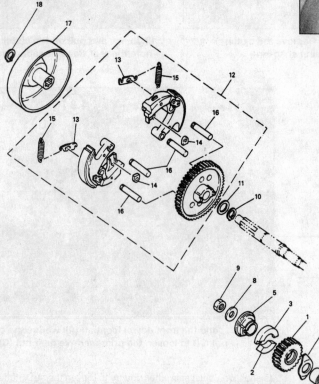

13.7 Clutch and primary drive gear (PW50) - exploded view

1   Primary drive gear
2   Absorber 1
3   Absorber 2
4   Thrust plate
5   Spacer
6   Collar
7   Straight key
8   Plate washer
9   Hexagon nut
10   Circlip
11   Plate washer
12   Clutch carrier assembly
13   Washer
14   Clutch weight damper
15   Spring
16   Clutch weight shaft
17   Clutch housing
18   Circlip

13.10a Center the snap-ring gap (arrow) between two of the ridges on the shaft, so the ridges support the ends of the snap-ring

13.10b Don't forget to install the clamp under this screw (arrow)

14.3a Right crankcase cover screws (PW80)

9   Measure the free length of the clutch shoe springs. If the free length of either spring is beyond the maximum allowable free length, replace both springs.

Installation

Refer to illustrations 13.10a and 13.10b

10   Installation is the reverse of removal, with the following additions:

a)   The machined side of the flat washer behind the clutch center faces out (away from the engine).

b)   The flat side of the clutch housing snap-ring faces out (away from the engine). Be sure the snap-ring is completely into its groove. Center the snap-ring gap between two of the ridges on the clutch shaft, so the ends of the snap-ring are under the ridges **(see illustration)**.

c)   If the clutch housing won't go far enough onto its shaft, the drive dogs on the back of the clutch center may not be engaged with the oil pump drive gear.

d)   Be sure to use a new cover gasket.

e)   Don't forget to install both cover dowels.

c)   Install the clamp on the outer cover **(see illustration)**.

d)   Tighten the cover screws to the torque listed in this Chapter's Specifications.

14   Clutch (PW80 models) - removal, inspection and installation

Removal

Refer to illustrations 14.3a, 14.3b, 14.3c, 14.4, 14.5a, 14.5b and 14.5c

1   Drain the transmission oil (see Chapter 1).

2   Remove the kickstarter (see Section 17).

3   Remove the right crankcase cover screws **(see illustration)** and pull the cover off the engine. Tap gently with a rubber mallet if necessary to break the gasket seal. Don't pry against the mating surfaces of

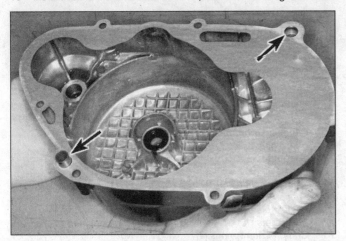

14.3b The cover dowels may come off with the cover (arrows) . . .

14.3c . . . or stay in the crankcase (arrows)

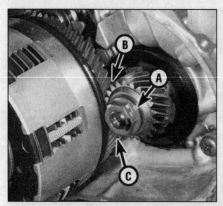

14.4 To loosen the primary drive gear nut (A), wedge the gears at point B; to loosen the clutch locknut, wedge the gears at point C

14.5a Bend back the lockwasher (arrow) . . .

14.5b . . . and unscrew the nut . . .

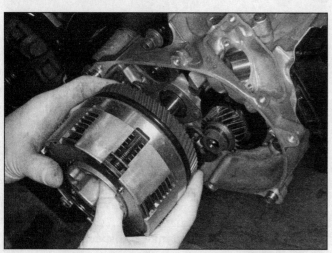

14.5c . . . then pull off the clutch assembly

the cover and crankcase. Once the cover is off, locate the dowels **(see illustrations)**; they may have stayed in the crankcase or come off with the cover. Remove the dowel pins and store them in a plastic bag. Remove and discard the old cover gasket.

4   If you're planning to remove the primary drive gear, loosen the primary drive gear nut now, before removing the clutch, by wedging a copper washer or penny between the primary drive and driven gears

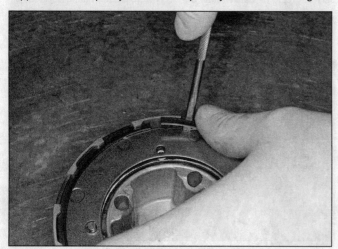

14.6b Pry out the retaining ring . . .

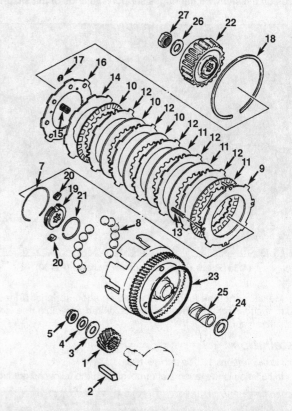

14.6a Clutch assembly and primary drive gear (PW80) - exploded view

1	Primary drive gear	15	Compression springs (6)
2	Key	16	Outer pressure plate
3	Washer	17	Circlips (2)
4	Conical spring washer	18	Retaining ring
5	Nut	19	One-way clutch mechanism
6	Clutch housing/primary driven gear assembly	20	Kick pawls (2)
7	Snap-ring	21	Pawl spring
8	Ball bearings	22	Clutch hub
9	Thrust weight plate (1)	23	O-ring
10	Friction plates (3)	24	Thrust washer
11	Friction plates (3)	25	Bushing
12	Metal plates (5)	26	Conical spring washer
13	Compression springs (4)	27	Nut
14	Inner pressure plate		

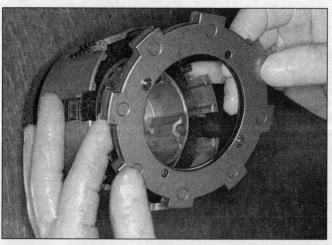

14.6c ... remove the pressure plate ...

14.6d ... the clutch springs ...

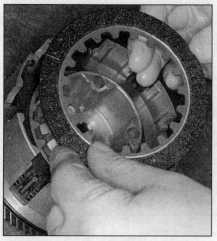

14.6e ... the first friction plate ...

14.6f ... followed by the first metal plate, then the remaining friction and metal plates ...

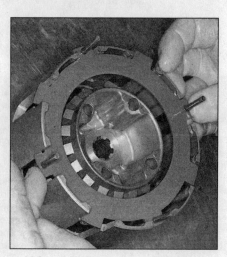

14.6g ... the inner pressure plate ...

(see illustration). Don't take the gear off yet, because you'll need it to be installed for the next step.
5   Lock the clutch so it won't turn (see Step 4), remove the nut and washer, then remove the clutch **(see illustrations).**

Disassembly

Refer to illustrations 14.6a through 14.6j
6   Pry out the retaining ring, then remove the components from the clutch assembly **(see illustrations).**

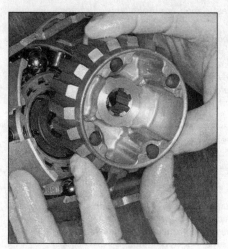

14.6h ... the clutch hub ...

14.6i ... the 12 balls (note how they're arranged in groups of three) ...

14.6j ... and the one-way clutch (note the direction of the two pawls)

14.7 Inspect the clutch housing for wear where the plate tabs contact the slots (arrow)

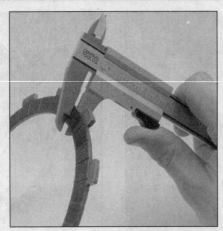

14.11 Measure the thickness of the friction plates

14.12 Check the metal plates for warpage

Inspection

Refer to illustrations 14.7, 14.11, 14.12 and 14.17

7   Check the edges of the slots in the clutch housing for indentations made by the friction plate tabs **(see illustration)**. If the indentations are deep they can prevent clutch release, so the housing should be replaced with a new one. If the indentations can be removed easily with a file, the life of the housing can be prolonged to an extent. Also, check the driven gear teeth for cracks, chips or excessive wear. If the gear is worn or damaged or the gear can be rotated separately from the clutch housing, replace the clutch housing.

8   Inspect the bushing surface in the center of the clutch housing; look for score marks, scratches and excessive wear. Replace the clutch housing if it's worn. If the bushing friction surface on the mainshaft is worn excessively, replace the mainshaft.

9   Inspect the clutch housing's friction surface and slots for scoring, wear and indentations. Also inspect the splines in the middle of the clutch housing. If there are any signs of excessive wear, replace the clutch housing.

10   Measure the free length of the clutch springs and compare the results to this Chapter's Specifications. If any of the springs have sagged, or cracked, replace the springs as a set.

11   If the lining material on the friction plates smells burnt, or if it's glazed, replace the friction plates. If the metal clutch plates are scored or discolored, replace them. Measure the thickness of the friction plates **(see illustration)** and replace any that are excessively worn.

12   Lay the metal plates, one at a time, on a perfectly flat surface (such as a piece of plate glass) and check for warpage by trying to slip a feeler gauge between the flat surface and the plate **(see illustration)**. The feeler gauge should be the same thickness as the maximum warpage listed in this Chapter's Specifications. Do this at several places around the plate's circumference. If the feeler gauge can be slipped under the plate, the plate is warped and must be replaced.

13   Inspect the tabs on the friction plates for excessive wear and mushroomed edges. They can be cleaned up with a file if the deformation is not severe. Check the friction plates for warpage as described in Step 10.

14   Measure the free length of each OFF spring. Compare your measurements to the OFF spring free length listed in this Chapter's Specifications. If any of the OFF springs have sagged, or cracked, replace the springs as a set.

15   Inspect the one-way clutch balls for excessive wear and damage. If any of the balls are worn or damaged, replace all of them as a set.

16   Inspect the ratcheting mechanism of the one-way clutch. Look for damage and excessive wear on each pawl and dog. Inspect the pawl springs for damage and tension. If a pawl or dog is excessively worn or damaged, or if a spring is sagged or damaged, replace the ratcheting mechanism.

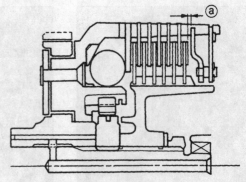

14.17 Using a feeler gauge, measure the clutch adjustment gap (a) between the outer pressure plate and the outer friction plate

17   Reassemble the one-way clutch mechanism, the friction plates, the steel plates, the hub and the pressure plate. Make sure that the outer friction disc is the special adjustment disc. Measure the gap between the outer friction plate and the pressure plate **(see illustration)**. Compare your measurement to the gap listed in this Chapter's Specifications. If the gap is incorrect, replace the outer friction plate with a thicker one. The outer friction plate is available in 1.2 mm (0.047 inch), 1.4 mm (0.055 inch) and 1.6 mm (0.063 inch).

Reassembly and installation

18   Reassembly and installation are the reverse of removal. Be sure to:

a) *Coat the friction plates with clean engine oil before you install them.*

b) *Install a friction plate, then alternate the remaining metal and friction plates until they're all installed. Friction plates go on first and last (the last, or outer, friction disc is the special adjustment disc described in the previous step).*

15 Primary drive gear - removal, inspection and installation

Removal

1   Remove the right crankcase cover (see Section 14).

2   Wedge a copper washer or penny between the teeth of the primary drive gear and the primary driven gear **(see illustration 13.4 or 14.4)**, then loosen the primary drive gear nut.

3   Remove the clutch (see Section 14).

4   Remove the primary drive nut and washer.

15.5a remove the primary drive gear nut and washer (PW50) . . .

15.5b . . . pull off the gear . . .

15.5c . . . and remove the spacer and dampers

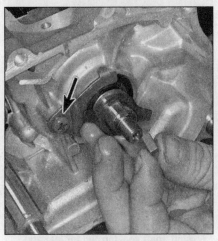

15.5d Remove the Woodruff key, then remove the screw (arrow) and bearing retainer

15.6a Remove the PW80 primary drive gear nut . . .

15.6b . . . the washer . . .

PW50 models

Refer to illustrations 15.5a, 15.5b, 15.5c and 15.5d

5   Remove the spacer, absorbers, primary gear, thrust plate, collar and Woodruff key (see illustrations).

PW80 models

Refer to illustrations 15.6a through 15.6i

6   Remove the plate washer, the primary drive gear and the Woodruff key (see illustrations).

15.6c . . . the spacer (note that its wider side faces the gear) . . .

15.6d . . . pull off the gear . . .

15.6e . . . and remove the O-ring . . .

15.6f . . . and the gear collar (note which side faces the engine)

15.6g . . . remove the Woodruff key . . .

15.6h . . . lift off the spacer, remove the retainer screw (arrow) and take the retainer off . . .

15.6i . . . and remove the seal collar

16.1 Look for the alignment marks on the shift pedal and the shift shaft; make your own if there aren't any

16.4 Remove the circlip and inspect the shift shaft seal (arrow) for leakage

Inspection

7   Inspect the primary drive gear for obvious damage such as chipped or broken teeth. Replace it if any of these problems are found.

Installation

8   Installation is the reverse of removal. Make sure the Woodruff key is in place. Wedge the gears using the same method used for removal (but insert the wedge from below, not from above), then tighten the primary drive gear nut to the torque listed in this Chapter's Specifications.

16   External shift mechanism (PW80 models) - removal, inspection and installation

Shift pedal

Removal

Refer to illustration 16.1

1   Look for alignment marks on the end of the shift pedal and shift shaft **(see illustration)**. If they aren't visible, make your own marks with a sharp punch.
2   Remove the shift pedal pinch bolt and slide the pedal off the shaft.

Inspection

Refer to illustration 16.4

3   Inspect the shift pedal for wear or damage such as bending.

Check the splines on the shift pedal and shift shaft for stripping or step wear. Replace the pedal or spindle if these problems are found.
4   Remove the alternator cover (see Chapter 4). Inspect the shift shaft seal for signs of oil leakage **(see illustration)**. If it has been leaking, remove the shift shaft as described below. Pry the seal out of the crankcase and install a new one. You may be able to push the seal in with your thumbs; if not, tap it in with a hammer and a socket the same diameter as the seal.

Installation

5   Line up the punch marks, install the shift pedal and tighten the pinch bolt.

External shift linkage

Removal

Refer to illustrations 16.10a, 16.10b, 16.11a, 16.11b and 16.11c

6   Remove the shift pedal as described above.
7   Remove the alternator cover (see Chapter 4).
8   Remove the right crankcase cover and the clutch (see Section 14).
9   On the alternator side of the engine, remove the C-clip from the shift shaft **(see illustration 16.4)**.
10   Working on the clutch side of the engine, disengage the shift lever pawls from the shift drum and slide the shift lever out of the crankcase **(see illustrations)**.
11   Unhook the stopper lever spring, disengage the lever from the shift drum and remove its mounting bolt **(see illustrations)**.

16.10a Pull the shift lever pawls in the direction shown so they clear the shift drum . . .

16.10b . . . and pull the shift shaft out of the case in the direction shown

16.11a Unhook the stopper lever spring . . .

16.11b . . . unscrew the pivot bolt (lower arrow) and pull the upper end of the stopper lever in the direction shown . . .

16.11c . . . then remove the pivot bolt and the stopper lever

Inspection

Refer to illustrations 16.13 and 16.15

12 Inspect the shift shaft for worn or damaged splines and make sure it's straight. If the shift shaft is damaged, excessively worn or bent, replace it.

13 Inspect the shift lever return spring, pawls and pawl spring for damage or excessive wear **(see illustration)**. If problems are found,

replace the shift lever.

14 Inspect the stopper lever for wear and a loose roller. If it's excessively worn, replace it.

15 Check the return spring post for wear or damage and make sure it's not loose **(see illustration)**. If it's worn or damaged, replace it. If it's loose, unscrew it, clean the threads and reinstall it, using a non-permanent thread locking agent.

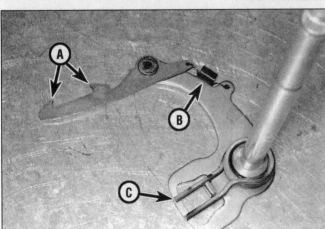

16.13 Check the shift pawls (A), pawl spring (B) and return spring (C) for wear or damage

16.15 Check the return spring post (arrow) for looseness or damage

16.16a If the stopper lever doesn't move freely in the directions shown, make sure its pivot bolt shoulder hasn't pinched the lever against the case

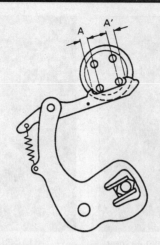

16.16b Make sure that the clearances (A and A') between the shift lever pawls and the shift drum pins are equal

17.3 Make an alignment mark on the end of the kick shaft next to the split in the kickstarter arm, then remove the pinch bolt

17.5a With the kickstarter shaft removed, pry out the seal (arrow) and push in a new one with a socket of the same diameter (PW50)

17.5b You'll need to remove the right crankcase cover to replace the PW80 kickstarter seal

Installation

Refer to illustrations 16.16a and 16.16b

16   Installation is the reverse of removal, with the following additions:

   a) *Grease the shift shaft oil seal before installing the shift shaft.*

   b) *Install the stopper lever first, using non-permanent thread locking agent on its bolt. Make sure the stopper lever pivots freely* **(see illustration)**. *Then install the shift shaft and engage its pawls with the shift drum.*

   c) *After installing the shift shaft, verify that the clearances between the prongs of the shift lever and the shift drum pins are equal* **(see illustration)**.

17 Kickstarter - removal, inspection and installation

1   The kickstarter pedal, arm and pivot can be removed and installed without disassembling the engine. For access to the kickstarter mechanism, remove the right crankcase cover (see Section 13 or 14).

Kickstarter pedal and seal

Refer to illustrations 17.3, 17.5a and 17.5b

2   If you're only replacing the kickstarter pedal rubber, simply pull the old rubber off the pedal (if it's stuck, cut it off) and push on a new one.

3   Before removing the kickstarter pedal from the kickstarter shaft,

look for a punch mark on the end of the shaft. The kickstarter mechanism will not operate correctly, nor will the pedal fold out of the way into its "riding" position, unless the pedal is installed on the kickstarter shaft in the correct position. If you don't see a punch mark, make your own (you can use a felt pen). Align your mark with the split in the pedal **(see illustration)**. Remove the pinch bolt and slide the pedal off the kickstarter shaft.

4   Inspect the kickstarter pedal for obvious wear and damage. Make sure it's not bent. Replace any worn or damaged parts.

5   Inspect the kickstarter shaft seal **(see illustrations)** for signs of oil leakage. If it's leaking, remove the kickstarter shaft on PW50 models (see below), or remove the right crankcase cover on PW80 models (see Section 14). Pry the seal out of the bore and tap in a new one with a socket the same diameter as the seal.

6   Installation is the reverse of removal.

Internal kickstarter mechanism

7   Remove the kickstarter pedal (see above).

8   Remove the right crankcase cover and the clutch (PW50 models, see Section 13; PW80 models, see Section 14).

PW50 models

Refer to illustrations 17.9a, 17.9b, 17.10 and 17.12

9   Note how the kick spring fits on its peg, then unhook it and release the tension **(see illustration)**. Remove the spring guide and spring and pull the kickstarter shaft out of the crankcase **(see illustration)**.

10   Remove the clip and slide the pinion gear off the transmission

17.9a Note the locations of the PW50 spring ends (arrows), then remove the kickstarter from the engine

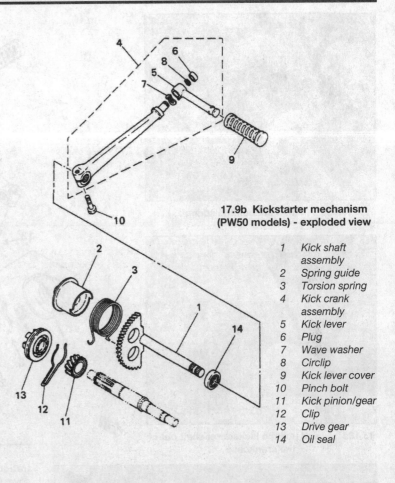

17.9b Kickstarter mechanism (PW50 models) - exploded view

1   *Kick shaft assembly*
2   *Spring guide*
3   *Torsion spring*
4   *Kick crank assembly*
5   *Kick lever*
6   *Plug*
7   *Wave washer*
8   *Circlip*
9   *Kick lever cover*
10 *Pinch bolt*
11 *Kick pinion/gear*
12 *Clip*
13 *Drive gear*
14 *Oil seal*

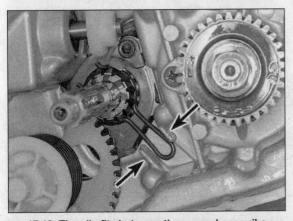

17.10 The clip fits between these crankcase ribs (arrows) when installed

shaft **(see illustration)**.

11   Inspect the teeth on the kickstarter gear and ratchet gear. The matching edges should fit flush against each other. If they're rounded off, replace the gears as a set.

12   Installation is the reverse of removal, with the following additions:

a) *Position the clip between the ribs on the crankcase* **(see illustration 17.10)**.

b) *Hook the inner end of the kick spring into the correct hole in the ratchet gear* **(see illustration)**.

PW80 models

Refer to illustrations 17.13a, 17.13b, 17.13c, 17.13d, 17.14a through 17.14e, 17.15a, 17.15b and 17.18

13   Slide the washer off the pedal end of the kickstarter **(see illustration)**. Unhook the kickstarter spring from its post in the crankcase **(see illustrations)**. Let it uncoil itself, turn the kickstarter shaft counterclockwise, then pull the kickstarter shaft assembly out of the engine **(see illustration)**.

14   Remove the snap-ring from the pedal end of the shaft **(see illus-**

17.12 The end of the spring fits in this hole in the ratchet (arrow)

17.13a Slide the washer off the kickstarter shaft (PW80)

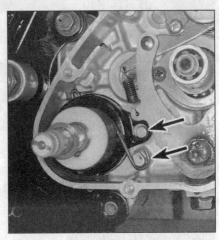

17.13b Note how the spring hook and the hole in the spring guide fit over posts on the crankcase (arrows) . . .

17.13c ... then unhook the spring ...

17.13d ... and pull the kickstarter shaft out of the crankcase

17.14b Remove the snap-ring ...

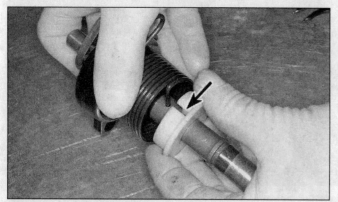

17.14c ... and the bushing; its slot fits over the spring end (arrow)

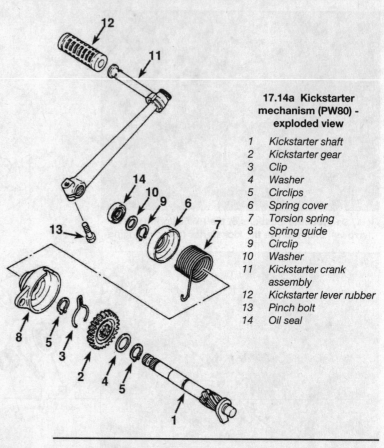

17.14a Kickstarter mechanism (PW80) - exploded view

1   *Kickstarter shaft*
2   *Kickstarter gear*
3   *Clip*
4   *Washer*
5   *Circlips*
6   *Spring cover*
7   *Torsion spring*
8   *Spring guide*
9   *Circlip*
10 *Washer*
11 *Kickstarter crank assembly*
12 *Kickstarter lever rubber*
13 *Pinch bolt*
14 *Oil seal*

trations). Remove the plastic bushing, kickstarter spring and gear cover **(see illustrations)**.

15   Remove the clip, then a second snap-ring **(see illustration)**. Remove the kickstarter gear, washer and third snap-ring **(see illustration)**.

16   Inspect the teeth on the kickstarter gear for excessive wear and damage. If they're worn or damaged, replace the gear.

17   Inspect the condition of the clip. If the clip is worn or damaged, replace it. Don't try to bend it.

18   Installation is the reverse of removal, with the following additions:

  a) *Position the dog on the kickstarter shaft in the crankcase notch* **(see illustration)**.
  b) *Engage the cover hole with the post on the crankcase.*
  c) *Hook the spring onto its post, then verify that the kickstarter mechanism operates correctly and returns to its normal position.*

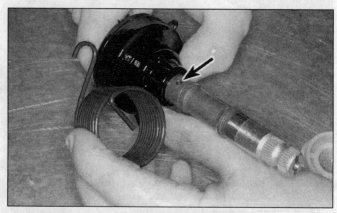

17.14d ... the other end of the spring fits into this hole in the shaft (arrow)

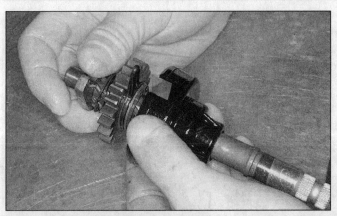

17.14e Remove the cover

17.15a Remove the snap-ring . . .

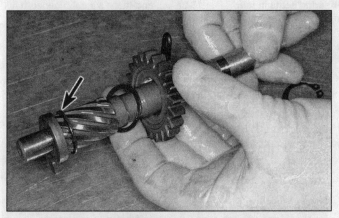

17.15b . . . the gear, washer and if necessary the
third snap-ring (arrow)

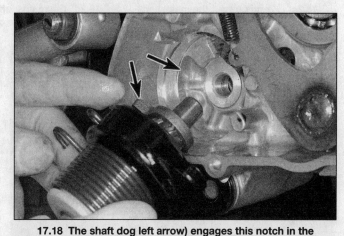

17.18 The shaft dog left arrow) engages this notch in the
crankshaft (right arrow)

18 Mainshaft assembly (PW50 models) - removal, inspection and installation

Removal

Refer to illustrations 18.2a through 18.2e

1   Remove the right crankcase cover and the clutch (see Section 13).

2   Remove the cover plate from the crankcase, pull out the mainshaft and remove the pinion shim **(see illustrations)**.

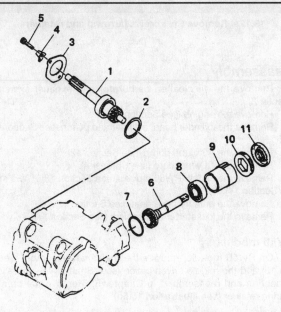

18.2a Mainshaft and middle driven pinion (PW50) - exploded view

1	Mainshaft and bearing assembly	6	Middle driven pinion
2	Pinion shim	7	Thrust shim
3	Cover plate	8	Bearing
4	Stopper	9	Spacer collar
5	Bolt	10	Screw
		11	Oil seal

18.2b Remove the bearing retainer bolts (arrows)
and the retainer . . .

18.2c . . . and pull out the mainshaft

18.2d The mainshaft bearing seats in this bore in the crankcase . . .

18.2e . . . and there's a shim beneath it

18.6 Don't forget to install this retainer under the bolt (arrow)

19.12a Remove the screws (arrows) and retainers . . .

Inspection

3   Inspect the mainshaft gear teeth. If the teeth are excessively worn or damaged, replace the mainshaft assembly and the middle driven pinion, which is part of the shaft drive assembly (see Chapter 5).

4   Inspect the mainshaft bearing. Make sure that it turns freely, quietly and smoothly. If the bearing is worn or damaged, have it pressed off the mainshaft at a dealer service department or motorcycle machine shop and have a new bearing pressed onto the mainshaft.

5   Place the mainshaft in V-blocks and measure any bend with a dial indicator. If the indicated bend exceeds the limit listed in this Chapter's Specifications, replace the mainshaft and the middle driven pinion of the shaft drive assembly (see Chapter 5).

Installation

Refer to illustration 18.6

6   Installation is the reverse of removal, with the following additions:

a) *Don't forget to install the pinion shim with the mainshaft.*

b) *Don't forget to install the retainer on the upper mainshaft bolt* **(see illustration)**.

c) *Tighten the retainer bolts to the torque listed in this Chapter's Specifications.*

19   Crankcase - disassembly and reassembly

1   To examine and repair or replace the crankshaft, connecting rod, bearings and transmission components, the crankcase must be split into two parts.

Disassembly

2   Remove the air cleaner, carburetor and exhaust system (see Chapter 3).

3   Remove the engine (see Section 6).

4   Remove the cylinder head, cylinder and piston (see Sections 8, 10 and 11).

5   Remove the Autolube pump (see Section 12).

6   Remove the CDI magneto (see Chapter 4).

7   Remove the clutch (PW50 models, see Section 13; PW80 models, see Section 14).

8   Remove the primary drive gear (see Section 15).

9   Remove the kickstarter mechanism (see Section 17).

PW50 models

10   On PW50 models, remove the mainshaft assembly (see Section 18) and the middle driven pinion (see "Shaft drive - disassembly, inspection and reassembly" in Chapter 5). Remove the crankshaft bearing retainer **(see illustration 15.5d)**.

PW80 models

Refer to illustrations 19.12a and 19.12b

11   On PW80 models, remove the external shift mechanism (see Section 16).

12   Remove the bearing retainers for the transmission mainshaft, shift drum and primary drive gear **(see illustration)**. If you haven't already done so, remove the seal collar from the crankshaft **(see illustration)**.

19.12b ... and lift out the seal collar

19.14a Loosen the crankcase screws (arrows) evenly in two or three stages, then remove them (PW50 models)

19.14b Loosen the crankcase screws (arrows) evenly in two or three stages, then remove them (PW80 models)

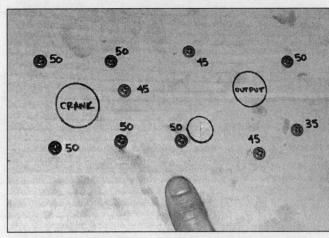

19.14c Place the screws in a cardboard holder and label them with their lengths for easy installation (PW80 shown)

All models

Refer to illustrations 19.14a, 19.14b, 19.14c, 19.15, 19.16a and 19.16b

13 Carefully inspect the crankcase for any other components that would prevent the separation of the case halves.

14 Loosen the crankcase screws **(see illustrations)** evenly in two or three stages, then remove them.

15 Place the crankcase with its left side down on a workbench. Care-

fully separate the right crankcase half by tapping it loose with a soft-face mallet. If necessary, attach a puller to the crankcase **(see illustration)**. As you slowly tighten the puller, carefully tap the crankcase halves apart. Don't pry against the mating surfaces or they'll develop leaks.

16 Locate the crankcase dowels **(see illustrations)**.

17 Refer to Sections 20 through 22 for information on the internal components of the crankcase.

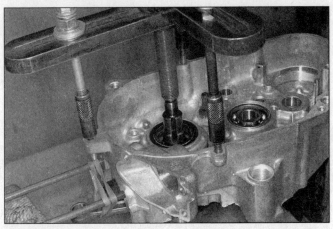

19.15 If necessary, separate the crankcase halves with a puller (PW80 models)

19.16a Crankcase dowels (arrows) (PW50 models)

19.16b Crankcase dowels (arrows) (PW80 models)

20.3a Crankcase bearings (PW80 models)

Reassembly

18   Remove all traces of old gasket and sealant from the crankcase mating surfaces with a sharpening stone or similar tool. Be careful not to let any fall into the case as this is done and be careful not to damage the mating surfaces.

19   Make sure the dowel pins are in place in their holes in the mating surface of the left crankcase half **(see illustration 19.16a or 19.16b)**.

20   On PW80 models, pour some four-stroke engine oil over the transmission gears. Don't get any oil in the crankshaft cavity or on the crankcase mating surface.

21   Apply a coat of Yamabond sealant or equivalent to the crankcase mating surface.

22   Carefully place the right crankcase half onto the left crankcase half. While doing this, make sure the transmission shafts and shift drum (PW80 models) and crankshaft fit into their bearings in the right crankcase half.

23   Install the crankcase screws and tighten them so they are just snug. Then tighten them evenly in two or three stages to the torque listed in this Chapter's Specifications.

24   On PW80 models, install the collar on the crankshaft **(see illustration 15.6i)**.

25   Make sure the crankshaft turns freely. On PW80 models, turn the transmission mainshaft to make sure it turns freely.

26   The remainder of assembly is the reverse of disassembly.

20 Crankcase components - inspection and servicing

Refer to illustrations 20.3a, 20.3b and 20.4

1   Separate the crankcase and remove the following:

 a) *Shift drum and forks (PW80 models)*

 b) *Transmission shafts and gears (PW80 models)*

 c) *Crankshaft*

2   Clean the crankcase halves thoroughly with new solvent and dry them with compressed air. All oil passages should be blown out with compressed air and all traces of old gasket should be removed from the mating surfaces. **Caution:** *Be very careful not to nick or gouge the crankcase mating surfaces or leaks will result. Check both crankcase halves very carefully for cracks and other damage.*

3   On PW80 models, check the bearings in the case halves **(see illustration 19.16b and the accompanying illustration)**. If the bearings don't turn smoothly, replace them. Drive the bearings out with a bearing driver or a socket having an outside diameter slightly smaller than that of the bearing outer race. You'll need a blind-hole puller **(see illustration)** to remove bearings that aren't accessible from the outside. The bearings are an interference fit, so heating the cases to about 200-degrees eases removal and installation. Before installing the bearings, allow them to sit in the freezer overnight, and then about fifteen minutes before installation, heat the cases to about 200-degrees F. **Warning:** *Before heating the cases, wash them thoroughly with soap and water so no explosive fumes are present. Also, don't use a flame to heat the case. Install the ball bearings with a socket or bearing driver that bears against the bearing outer race.*

4   Replace the crankshaft seals whenever the crankcase is disassembled **(see illustration)**. The crankshaft seals are critical to the performance of two-stroke engines, so they should be replaced even if they look perfectly all right.

5   If any damage is found that can't be repaired, replace the crankcase halves as a set.

6   Assemble the case halves (see Section 19) and check to make sure the crankshaft and the transmission shafts turn freely.

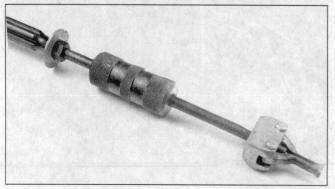

20.3b A blind hole puller like this one is needed to remove bearings which are only accessible from one side

20.4 The crankshaft seals (arrow) should be replaced whenever the crankcase is disassembled

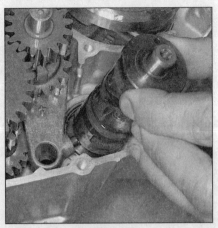

21.3a Pull out the shift fork shaft . . .

21.3b . . . and remove the countershaft shift fork; note the number on the fork, which faces upward

21.4 Lift out the shift drum

21 Transmission shafts and shift drum (PW80 models) - removal, inspection and installation

Note: *When disassembling the transmission shafts, place the parts on a long rod or thread a wire through them to keep them in order and facing the proper direction.*

Removal

Refer to illustrations 21.3a, 21.3b, 21.4, 21.5a and 21.5b

1   Remove the engine, then separate the case halves (see Sections 6 and 19).

2   The transmission components and shift drum remain in the left case half when the case is separated.

3   Pull out the shift fork shaft and the countershaft shift fork (**see illustrations**).

4   Lift the shift drum out of the case half (**see illustration**).

5   Lift the transmission shafts and the mainshaft shift fork out of the case (**see illustrations**).

Transmission shaft disassembly

Refer to illustrations 21.6a, 21.6b and 21.7a through 21.7f

6   The mainshaft is supplied by Yamaha only as a complete assembly (**see illustration**). Individual mainshaft parts are not available, and

21.5a Remove the transmission countershaft . . .

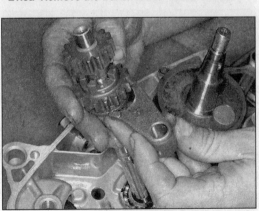

21.5b . . . and remove the mainshaft together with its shift fork; again, the number on the shift fork faces upward

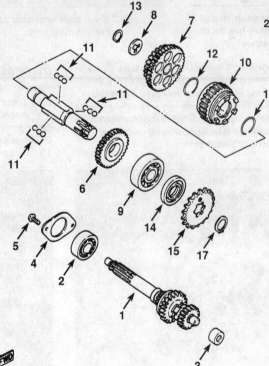

21.6a Transmission gears and shafts (PW80) - exploded view

1   Mainshaft (input shaft)
2   Right mainshaft bearing
3   Left mainshaft bearing
4   Bearing retainer
5   Bearing retainer screws (2)
6   Countershaft (output shaft)
7   First gear
8   Thrust washer
9   Second gear
10   Third gear
11   Ball bearings (9)
12   Circlip
13   Circlip
14   Bearing
15   Oil seal
16   Countershaft sprocket
17   Circlip

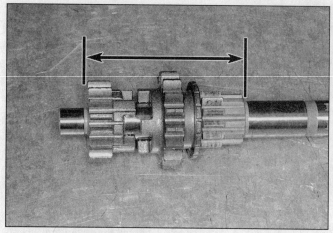

21.6b Measure the assembled length of the mainshaft

21.7a Remove the thrust washer from the end of
the countershaft . . .

21.7b . . . and remove the snap-ring (if
there's another thrust washer behind the
snap-ring, remove it as well) . . .

21.7c . . . slide first gear off
the countershaft . . .

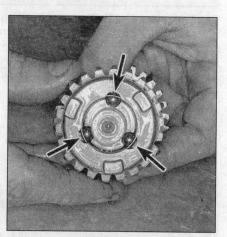

21.7d . . . note how the ball bearings fit in
the shaft grooves (arrows) . . .

the mainshaft is pressed together. If inspection shows wear or damage, replace the mainshaft as a complete unit. The mainshaft should also be replaced if its assembled length is incorrect **(see illustration)**.

7   Removal of the countershaft components requires only a pair of snap-ring pliers to remove the snap-rings. Slide the components off the shafts in the following sequence **(see illustrations)** and place them in order on a long rod or a piece of plastic pipe.

Inspection

Refer to illustrations 21.9, 21.10a, 21.10b and 21.13

8   Wash all of the components in clean solvent and dry them off.

9   Inspect the shift fork grooves in the gears. If a groove is worn or scored, replace the affected part and inspect its corresponding shift fork **(see illustration)**.

10   Inspect the shift forks for distortion and wear, especially at the

21.7e . . . then remove the ball bearings and third gear . . .

21.7f . . . and remove second gear from the countershaft

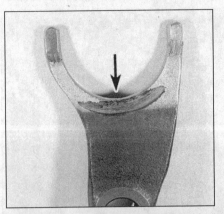

21.9 An arc-shaped burn mark like this means the fork was rubbing against a gear, probably due to bent or worn fork fingers

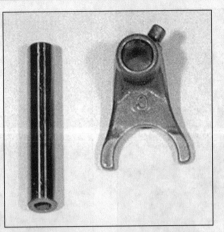

21.10a Inspect the shift fork pins and fingers and inspect the shift fork shaft

21.10b Check the shift drum grooves for wear, especially at the points

fork ears (see illustrations). If they are discolored or severely worn they are probably bent. Inspect the guide pins and shift drum grooves for excessive wear and distortion and replace any defective parts with new ones (see illustration).

11   Inspect the shift fork shaft for evidence of wear, galling and other damage. Make sure the shift forks move smoothly on the shaft. If the shaft is worn or bent, replace it.

12   Inspect the gear teeth for cracking and other obvious damage. Inspect the bushing surface in the inner diameter of the freewheeling gears for scoring or heat discoloration. Replace damaged parts.

13   Inspect the engagement dogs and dog holes on the gears for excessive wear or rounding off (see illustration). Replace the paired gears as a set if necessary.

14   Inspect the transmission shaft bearings in the crankcase for wear or heat discoloration and replace them if necessary (see Section 20).

Transmission shaft assembly

15   Assembly of the countershaft is the reverse of the disassembly procedure, with the following additions:

a) Refer to the illustrations in Step 7 to make sure all components face in the proper direction. Use new snap-rings. Install the outer snap-ring with its sharp side facing away from the thrust washer.

b) Once assembled, make sure the gears mesh correctly.

Installation

Refer to illustrations 21.16a and 21.16b

16   Installation is the reverse of the removal procedure, but take note of the following points:

21.13 Inspect the slots (left arrow) and dogs (right arrow) and replace the gears if the corners are rounded off

a) Lubricate the components with four-stroke engine oil before assembling them.

b) After assembly, check the gears to make sure they're installed correctly (see illustrations). Move the shift drum through the gear positions and rotate the gears to make sure they mesh and shift correctly. If they don't, stop and find the problem before you reassemble the case halves.

21.16a The assembled shafts and gears should look like this

21.16b Make sure the shift fork numbers are upward, the circlip is on the fork shaft and the fork pins are engaged with the shift drum (arrows)

22.2a The crankshaft may just lift out of the case . . .

22.2b . . . but if not, press it out . . .

22.2c . . . or use a puller

22 Crankshaft and connecting rod - removal, inspection and installation

Note: *The procedures in this section require special tools. If you don't have the necessary equipment or suitable substitutes, have the crankshaft removed and installed by a Yamaha dealer.*

Removal

Refer to illustrations 22.2a, 22.2b and 22.2c

1   Remove the engine (see Section 6) and separate the crankcase halves (see Section 19). (The transmission shafts need not be removed.)

2   You may be able to lift the crankshaft out of the crankcase **(see illustration)**. If it's stuck, place the case half on a press plate and press the crankshaft out **(see illustration)**. You can also use a puller **(see illustration)**.

Inspection

Refer to illustrations 22.3a, 22.3b, 22.4, 22.5a and 22.5b

3   Measure the side clearance and radial clearance between the connecting rod and the crankshaft with a feeler gauge **(see illustrations)**. If side clearance is more than the limit listed in this Chapter's Specifications, replace the crankshaft and connecting rod as an assembly. Radial clearance isn't specified, but if it's measurable, the big end bearing is probably worn.

4   Set up the crankshaft in V-blocks with a dial indicator contacting the small end of the connecting rod. Move the connecting rod side-to-side against the indicator pointer and compare the reading to the small-end side play value listed in this Chapter's Specifications **(see illustration)**. If it's beyond the limit, the crankshaft can be disassembled and the needle roller bearing replaced. However, this is a specialized job that should be done by a Yamaha dealer or other qualified machine shop.

5   Check the crankshaft threads, the ball bearing at the magneto

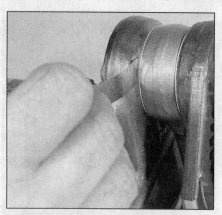

22.3a Check the connecting rod side clearance with a feeler gauge

22.3b Check the connecting rod radial clearance with a dial indicator

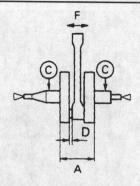

22.4 Crankshaft measurement points

A   *Crank assembly width*
C   *Runout measuring points*
D   *Connecting rod big end side clearance*
F   *Connecting rod small end side play*

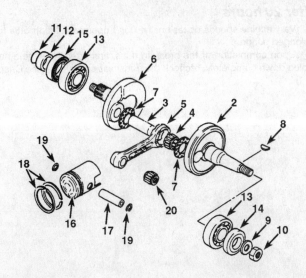

22.5b Use a bearing splitter and press to remove the ball bearings

22.5a Crankshaft and connecting rod - exploded view

1	Crankshaft assembly	12	Seal collar
2	Crankwheel	13	Ball bearing
3	Crank throw	14	Crankshaft seal
4	Big end needle roller bearing	15	Crankshaft seal
5	Connecting rod	16	Piston
6	Crankwheel	17	Piston pin
7	Thrust bearings (PW80 only)	18	Piston rings
8	Woodruff key	19	Circlips
9	Washer	20	Small end needle roller bearing
10	Nut		
11	O-ring		

end of the crankshaft and the bearing journals for visible wear or damage **(see illustration)**. The ball bearing can be pressed off the crankshaft, using a bearing splitter **(see illustration)**. Yamaha lists the crankshaft components (crankwheels, crankpin, PW80 crankpin thrust bearings, needle roller bearing and connecting rod) as separately available parts, but check with your dealer first; it may be more practical to replace the entire crankshaft if any parts are worn or damaged.

6   Set the crankshaft on a pair of V-blocks, with a dial indicator contacting each end **(see illustration 22.4)**. Rotate the crankshaft and note the runout. If the runout at either end is beyond the limit listed in this Chapter's Specifications, replace the crankshaft and connecting rod as an assembly.

7   Measure the assembly width of the crankshaft **(see illustration**

22.4). If it exceeds the limit listed in this Chapter's Specifications, replace the crankshaft.

Installation

Refer to illustrations 22.10a and 22.210b

8   Pry out the crankshaft seals, then install new ones with a seal driver or socket the same diameter as the seal.

9   Place the crankshaft in the left crankcase half and make sure the connecting rod is inside the cylinder opening.

10   Install the crankshaft with an installation puller **(see illustrations)**. Don't drive the crankshaft in with a hammer or you'll compress the crankwheels on the crankpin, ruining the crankshaft.

11   The remainder of installation is the reverse of the removal steps.

23 Recommended start-up and break-in procedure

Note: *Any rebuilt engine needs time to break in, even if parts have been installed in their original locations. Yamaha specifies a 20-hour break-in period for these models when new; you can use this as a guide for breaking in a rebuilt engine.*

First 10 hours

1   Don't operate continuously at more than half throttle.

2   Let the engine cool for five to ten minutes after each hour of operation.

22.10a Thread the adapter into the end of the crankshaft . . .

22.10b . . . and attach the puller to the adapter

3   Vary engine speeds; don't operate continuously at one throttle setting.

10 to 20 hours

4   Don't operate continuously at more than three-quarters throttle.
5   Rev the engine freely, but don't use full throttle.

After 20 hours

6   Vary engine speeds occasionally. Don't operate at full throttle for prolonged periods.
7   Upon completion of the break-in rides, and after the engine has cooled down completely, recheck the transmission oil level (see Chapter 1).

Chapter 2 Part B
Engine, clutch and transmission (RT100 and RT180 models)

Contents

Specifications

Cylinder head
Warpage limit
RT100 .... 0.02 mm (0.001 inch)
RT180 .... 0.03 mm (0.0012 inch)

Reed valve
Thickness
RT100 .... 0.2 mm (0.008 inch)
RT180 .... 0.18 to 0.22 mm (0.007 to 0.009 inch)
Reed valve stopper height
RT100 .... 6.7 to 7.3 mm (0.26 to 0.29 inch)
RT180 .... 8.7 to 9.3 mm (0.342 to 0.366 inch)
Reed valve bending limit
RT100 .... 0.3 mm (0.012 inch)
RT180 .... 0.9 mm (0.035 inch)

Cylinder
Bore
RT100 .... 52.00 to 52.02 mm (2.047 to 2.048 inches)
RT180 .... 64.50 to 64.52 mm (2.539 to 2.540 inches)
Taper limit .... 0.05 mm (0.002 inch)
Out-of-round limit .... 0.01 mm (0.0004 inch)
Surface warpage limit .... Not specified

Piston and rings
Diameter
RT100
Standard .... 51.94 to 52.00 mm (2.045 to 2.047 inches
First oversize .... 52.25 mm (2.057 inches)
Second oversize .... 52.50 mm (2.067 inches)
Third oversize .... 52.75 mm (2.077 inches)
Fourth oversize .... 53.00 mm (2.087 inches)

Piston and rings (continued)

Diameter (continued)

RT180

Standard	64.46 to 64.50 mm (2.538 to 2.539 inches)
First oversize	64.75 mm (2.549 inches)
Second oversize	65.00 mm (2.559 inches)
Piston diameter measuring point (above bottom of piston)	10 mm (0.39 inch)

Piston-to-cylinder clearance

RT100

Standard	0.050 to 0.055 mm (0.0020 to 0.0022 inch)
Limit	0.1 mm (0.004 inch)

RT180

Standard	0.035 to 0.040 mm (0.0014 to 0.0016 inch)
Limit	0.1 mm (0.004 inch)
Piston offset	0.5 mm (0.0020 inch)
Piston pin bore in piston	Not specified
Piston pin outer diameter	Not specified
Ring end gap (both rings)	0.3 to 0.5 mm (0.01 to 0.02 inch)
Ring side clearance (both rings)	0.03 to 0.05 mm (0.001 to 0.002 inch)

Clutch

Spring free length

RT100

Standard	31.5 mm (1.24 inches)
Limit	30.5 mm (1.20 inch)

RT180

Standard	33 mm (12.99 inches)
Limit	32 mm (1.260 inches)

Friction plate thickness

RT100

Standard	3.0 mm (0.120 inch)
Limit	2.7 mm (0.106 inch)

RT180

Standard	2.92 to 3.08 mm (0.115 to 0.121 inch)
Limit	2.7 mm (0.106 inch)

Metal plate

RT100

Thickness	1.2 mm (0.047 inch)
Warpage limit	0.05 mm (0.002 inch)

RT180

Thickness	1.1 to 1.3 mm (0.043 to 0.051 inch)
Warpage limit	0.05 mm (0.002 inch)

Clutch pushrod bending limit

RT100	0.15 mm (0.006 inch)
RT180	0.5 mm (0.02 inch)

Transmission

Shaft runout limit	0.08 mm (0.003 inch)

Crankshaft

Connecting rod side clearance

RT100

Standard	0.2 to 0.7 mm (0.008 to 0.028 inch)
Limit	1.0 mm (0.04 inch)

RT180

Standard	0.15 to 0.7 mm (0.006 to 0.0028 inch)
Limit	1.0 mm (0.04 inch)

Connecting rod small end side play

RT100

Standard	0.8 to 1.0 mm (0.032 to 0.039 inch)
Limit	2.0 mm (0.08 inch)

RT180

Standard	1.0 to 1.5 mm (0.039 to 0.059 inch)
Limit	Not specified
Runout limit	0.03 mm (0.0012 inch)

Crankshaft assembly width

RT100	49.90 to 49.95 mm (1.965 to 1.967 inches)
RT180	55.85 to 55.95 mm (2.19 to 2.20 inches)

Torque specifications

Engine mounts	
Front bolts/nuts and rear upper bolts/nuts	
RT100	26 Nm (19 ft-lbs)
RT180	25 Nm (18 ft-lbs)
Rear lower bolts/nuts	39 Nm (28 ft-lbs)
Cylinder head nuts	
RT100	22 Nm (16 ft-lbs)
RT180	25 Nm (18 ft-lbs)
Cylinder head studs	
RT100	Not specified
RT180	12 Nm (103 inch-lbs)
Cylinder base fasteners (RT180)	
Nuts	35 Nm (25 ft-lbs)
Studs	15 Nm (132 inch-lbs)
Carburetor intake joint bolts	
RT100	10 Nm (89 inch-lbs)
RT180	8 Nm (71 inch-lbs)
Reed valve screws	1 Nm (8 inch-lbs)*
Crankcase cover screws	
RT100	
Left	7 Nm (62 inch-lbs)
Right	10 Nm (86 inch-lbs)
RT180 (either side)	10 Nm (86 inch-lbs)
Clutch spring bolts	6 Nm (53 inch-lbs)
Clutch nut	
RT100	45 Nm (33 ft-lbs)
RT180	50 Nm (36 ft-lbs)
Autolube pump cover screws	8 Nm (71 inch-lbs)
Autolube pump mounting screws	
RT100	4 Nm (35 inch-lbs)
RT180	8 Nm (51 inch-lbs)
Kickstarter-to-kickstarter shaft pinch bolt	
RT100	16 Nm (132 inch-lbs)
RT180	23 Nm (17 ft-lbs)
Primary drive gear nut	60 Nm (43 ft-lbs)
Shift cam plate-to-shift drum Torx screw	Not specified*
Shift drum stopper arm bolt	10 Nm (89 inch-lbs)
Shift pedal pinch bolt	11 Nm (97 inch-lbs)
Crankcase screws	8 Nm (71 inch-lbs)
Crankshaft bearing retainer-to-crankcase screws	10 Nm (89 inch-lbs)*
Transmission bearing retainer-to-crankcase screws	10 Nm (89 inch-lbs)*

Apply non-permanent thread locking agent to the threads.

1 General information

The engine/transmission unit is an air-cooled, single-cylinder two-stroke design. The engine/transmission assembly is constructed from aluminum alloy. The crankcase is divided vertically.

The cylinder, piston, crankshaft bearings and connecting rod lower end bearings are lubricated by a mixture of gasoline and two-stroke oil which is circulated through the bottom end on its way to the combustion chamber. The two-stroke oil is injected into the carburetor by the Autolube system, which consists of an oil pump, mounted on the right side of the engine, a control cable and connecting hoses. The transmission and clutch are lubricated by four-stroke engine oil, which is contained in a sump within the crankcase. Power from the crankshaft is routed to the transmission via a wet, multi-plate type clutch. The transmission has five forward gears (RT100 models) or six forward gears (RT180 models).

2 Operations possible with the engine in the frame

The components and assemblies listed below can be removed without having to remove the engine from the frame. If, however, a number of areas require attention at the same time, removal of the engine is recommended.

Cylinder head
Cylinder
Piston and piston ring
External shift mechanism
Clutch
Primary drive gear
Kickstarter mechanism
Shift shaft
CDI magneto rotor
Stator
Autolube oil pump

3 Operations requiring engine removal

It is necessary to remove the engine/transmission assembly from the frame and separate the crankcase halves to gain access to the following components:

Crankshaft and connecting rod
Transmission shafts
Crankshaft and transmission bearings
Internal shift mechanism (shift drum and forks)

4   Major engine repair - general note

1   It is not always easy to determine when or if an engine should be completely overhauled, as a number of factors must be considered.

2   High mileage is not necessarily an indication that an overhaul is needed, while low mileage, on the other hand, does not preclude the need for an overhaul. Regular maintenance is probably the single most important consideration. An engine that has regular and frequent transmission oil changes, as well as other required maintenance, will most likely give many hours of reliable service. Conversely, a neglected engine, or one which has not been broken in properly, may require an overhaul very early in its life.

3   Poor running that can't be accounted for by seemingly obvious causes (fouled spark plug, leaking head gasket or cylinder base gasket, worn piston rings, carburetor problems) may be due to leaking crankshaft seals. In two-stroke engines, the crankcase acts as a suction pump to draw in fuel mixture and as a compressor to force it into the cylinder. If the crankcase seals are leaking, the pressure drop will cause a loss of performance.

4   If the engine is making obvious knocking or rumbling noises, the connecting rod and/or main bearings are probably at fault. The upper connecting rod bearing should be replaced at the maintenance interval listed in Chapter 1.

5   A top-end overhaul consists of replacing the piston and rings and inspecting the cylinder bore. The cylinder can be bored for an oversize piston if necessary.

6   A lower-end engine overhaul generally involves inspecting the crankshaft, transmission and crankcase bearings and seals. Unlike four-stroke engines equipped with plain main and connecting rod bearings, there isn't much in the way of machine work that can be done to refurbish existing parts. Worn bearings, gears, seals and shift mechanism parts should be replaced with new ones. The crankshaft and connecting rod components are available separately, but rebuilding a crankshaft is a specialized operation that should be done by a qualified shop. While the engine is being overhauled, other components such as the carburetor can be rebuilt also. The end result should be a like-new engine that will give as many trouble-free hours as the original.

7   Before beginning the engine overhaul, read through all of the related procedures to familiarize yourself with the scope and requirements of the job. Overhauling an engine is not all that difficult, but it is time consuming. Plan on the vehicle being tied up for a minimum of two (2) weeks. Check on the availability of parts and make sure that any necessary special tools, equipment and supplies are obtained in advance.

8   Most work can be done with typical shop hand tools, although a number of precision measuring tools are required for inspecting parts to determine if they must be replaced. Often a dealer service department or other repair shop will handle the inspection of parts and offer advice concerning reconditioning and replacement. As a general rule, time is the primary cost of an overhaul so it doesn't pay to install worn or substandard parts.

9   As a final note, to ensure maximum life and minimum trouble from a rebuilt engine, everything must be assembled with care in a spotlessly clean environment.

5   Crankcase pressure and vacuum - check

This test can pinpoint the cause of otherwise unexplained poor running. It can also prevent piston seizures by detecting air leaks that can cause a lean mixture. It requires special equipment, but can easily be done by a Yamaha dealer or other motorcycle shop. If you regularly work on two-stroke engines, you might want to consider purchasing the tester for yourself (or with a group of other riders). You may also be able to fabricate the tester.

The test involves sealing off the intake and exhaust ports, then applying vacuum and pressure to the spark plug hole with a hand vacuum/pressure pump, similar to the type used for brake bleeding and automotive vacuum testing.

6.11a Remove the upper and lower rear engine mounting bolts and nuts (arrows) . . .

First, remove the carburetor and exhaust system. Block off the carburetor opening with a rubber plug, clamped securely in position. Place a rubber sheet (cut from a tire tube or similar material) over the exhaust port and secure it with a metal plate.

Apply air pressure to the spark plug hole with the vacuum/pressure pump. Check for leaks at the crankcase gasket, intake manifold, reed valve gasket, cylinder base gasket and head gasket. If the crankcase gasket leaks between the transmission sump and the crankcase (the area where the crankshaft spins), transmission oil will be sucked into the crankcase, causing the fuel mixture to be oil-rich. Also check the seal at the alternator end of the crankshaft. If the leaks are large, air will hiss as it passes through them. Small leaks can be detected by pouring soapy water over the suspected area and looking for bubbles.

After checking for air leaks, apply vacuum with the pump. If vacuum leaks down quickly, the crankshaft seals are leaking.

6   Engine - removal and installation

Note: *Engine removal and installation should be done with the aid of an assistant to avoid damage or injury that could occur if the engine is dropped.*

Removal

Refer to illustrations 6.11a and 6.11b

1   Drain the transmission oil (see Chapter 1).

2   Remove the seat and side covers (see Chapter 7).

3   Remove the fuel tank, exhaust system and the carburetor (see Chapter 4).

4   Disconnect the spark plug wire (see Chapter 1).

5   Remove the Autolube pump cover. Detach and plug the supply and outlet oil hoses, remove the pump cover gasket and disconnect the Autolube pump cable (see Section 12).

6   Disconnect the clutch cable from the clutch push lever (see Section 14).

7   Label and disconnect the CDI magneto wires (see Chapter 4).

8   Remove the crankcase ventilation hose. On RT180 models, disconnect the hose from the Yamaha Energy Induction System (Y.E.I.S.) chamber and from the carburetor intake joint/reed valve body.

9   Remove the drive chain and sprocket (see Chapter 5).

10   Support the engine with a jack, using a block of wood between the jack and the engine to protect the crankcase.

11   Remove the front and rear engine mounting bolts **(see illustrations)**. **Note:** *Raise or lower the jack beneath the engine as necessary to relieve strain on the mounting bolts.*

12   Have an assistant help you lift the engine out of the frame from the right side (RT100 models) or the left side (RT180 models).

13   Set the engine on a suitable work surface.

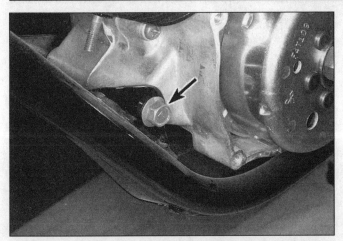

6.11b . . . and the front engine mounting bolt and nut (arrow)

6.14 On installation, be sure to place the bolts in the correct holes

Installation

Refer to illustration 6.14

14   Have an assistant help lift the engine into the frame so it rests on the jack and block of wood. Use the jack to align the mounting bolt holes, then install the bolts and nuts, making sure they're in the right locations **(see illustration)**. Tighten them to the torques listed in this Chapter's Specifications.

15   The remainder of installation is the reverse of the removal steps, with the following additions:

  a) *Use new gaskets at all exhaust pipe connections.*
  b) *Adjust the throttle cable and clutch cable following the procedures in Chapter 1.*
  c) *Fill the transmission with oil, also following the procedures in Chapter 1.*
  d) *Run the engine and check for oil or exhaust leaks.*

7   Engine disassembly and reassembly - general information

Refer to illustrations 7.2 and 7.3

1   Before disassembling the engine, clean the exterior with a degreaser and rinse it with water. A clean engine will make the job easier and prevent the possibility of getting dirt into the internal areas of the engine.

2   In addition to the precision measuring tools mentioned earlier, you will need a torque wrench and oil gallery brushes **(see illustration)**. Some new, clean engine oil of the correct grade and type (two-stroke oil, four-stroke oil or both, depending on whether it's a top-end or bottom-end overhaul), some engine assembly lube (or moly-based grease) and a tube of RTV (silicone) sealant will also be required.

3   An engine support stand made from short lengths of 2 x 4's bolted together will facilitate the disassembly and reassembly procedures **(see illustration)**. If you have an automotive-type engine stand, an adapter plate can be made from a piece of plate, some angle iron and some nuts and bolts.

4   When disassembling the engine, keep "mated" parts together (including gears, shift forks and shafts, etc.) that have been in contact with each other during engine operation. These "mated" parts must be reused or replaced as an assembly.

5   Engine/transmission disassembly should be done in the following general order with reference to the appropriate Sections.

  Remove the cylinder head
  Remove the reed valve
  Remove the cylinder
  Remove the piston
  Remove the Autolube oil pump
  Remove the clutch

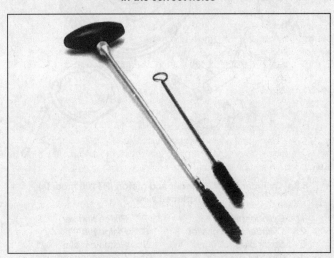

7.2 A selection of brushes is required for cleaning holes and passages in the engine components

7.3 An engine stand can be made from short lengths of lumber and lag bolts or nails

  Remove the primary drive gear
  Remove the kickstarter
  Remove the external shift mechanism
  Remove the CDI magneto
  Separate the crankcase halves
  Remove the internal shift mechanism
  Remove the transmission shafts and gears
  Remove the crankshaft and connecting rod

6   Reassembly is accomplished by reversing the general disassembly sequence.

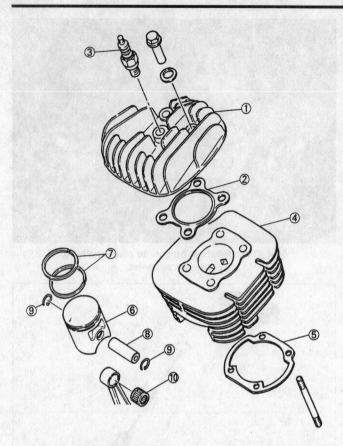

8.3a Cylinder head, cylinder and piston (RT100 models) - exploded view

1	Cylinder head	7	Piston ring set
2	Cylinder head gasket	8	Piston pin
3	Spark plug	9	Piston pin clip
4	Cylinder	10	Connecting rod small
5	Cylinder base gasket		end bearing
6	Piston		

8 Cylinder head - removal, inspection and installation

Caution: *The engine must be completely cool before beginning this procedure, or the cylinder head may become warped.*
Note: *This procedure is described with the engine in the frame. If the engine has been removed, ignore the steps that don't apply.*

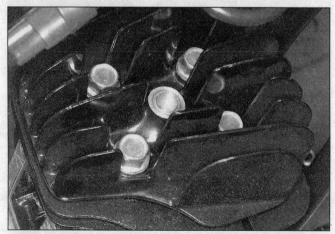

8.3c Loosen the hear bolts or nuts in a criss-cross pattern ...

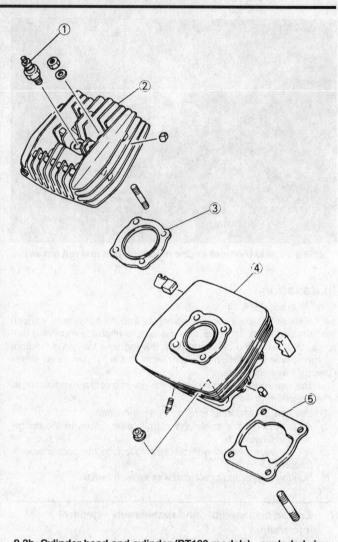

8.3b Cylinder head and cylinder (RT180 models) - exploded view

1	Spark plug	4	Cylinder
2	Cylinder head	5	Cylinder base gasket
3	Cylinder head gasket		

Removal

Refer to illustrations 8.3a, 8.3b, 8.3c, 8.3d and 8.5

1   Disconnect the spark plug wire (see Chapter 1).
2   Remove the seat (see Chapter 7), fuel tank and exhaust pipe (see Chapter 3).
3   Loosen the cylinder head nuts **(see illustrations)** in two or three stages, in a criss-cross pattern. Remove the nuts once they're all loose.
4   Lift the cylinder head off the cylinder. If the head is stuck, use a wooden dowel inserted into the spark plug hole to lever the head off. Don't attempt to pry the head off by inserting a screwdriver between the head and the cylinder - you'll damage the sealing surfaces.
5   Rotate the piston to the top of the cylinder or stuff a clean rag into the cylinder to prevent the entry of debris. Once this is done, remove the head gasket from the cylinder **(see illustration)**.

Inspection

Refer to illustration 8.9

6   Check the cylinder head gasket and the mating surfaces on the cylinder head and cylinder for leakage, which could indicate warpage.
7   Clean all traces of old gasket material from the cylinder head and cylinder. Be careful not to let any of the gasket material fall into the

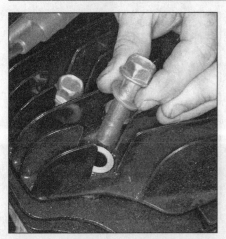

8.3d ... then remove the bolts or nuts and their washers

8.5 Remove and discard the old head gasket

8.9 Check for head warpage with a straightedge and feeler gauge

cylinder or crankcase. Using a rounded scraper or a small wire brush, remove all carbon deposits from the combustion chamber. If you use a wire brush, make sure the bristles aren't too stiff. And make sure you don't damage the spark plug threads or scratch the metal surface of the chamber.

8   Inspect the head very carefully for cracks and other damage. If cracks are found, a new head will be required.

9   Using a precision straightedge and a feeler gauge, check the head gasket mating surface for warpage. Lay the straightedge across the head, intersecting the head bolt holes, and try to slip a feeler gauge under it, on either side of the combustion chamber **(see illustration)**. Measure along the edges of the cylinder head between each pair of stud holes, and diagonally across the cylinder head, again between pairs of stud holes. The feeler gauge thickness should be the same as the cylinder head warpage limit listed in this Chapter's Specifications. If the feeler gauge can be inserted between the head and the straightedge, the head is warped and must either be resurfaced or, if warpage is excessive, replaced with a new one.

10   To resurface the head, lay a piece of 400 to 600 grit emery paper on a perfectly flat surface, such as a piece of plate glass. Move the head in a figure-8 pattern over the sandpaper. Rotate the head 1/2 turn after each few figure-8 motions so you don't remove too much material from one side of the head. Don't remove any more material than necessary to correct the warpage.

Installation

11   Lay the new gasket in place on the cylinder **(see illustration 8.5)**. Never reuse the old gasket and don't use any type of gasket sealant.

12   Carefully lower the cylinder head over the studs.
13   Install the cylinder head nuts and tighten them evenly, in a criss-cross pattern, to the torque listed in this Chapter's Specifications.
14   The remainder of installation is the reverse of the removal steps.

9   Reed valve - removal, inspection and installation

Removal

Refer to illustrations 9.2a, 9.2b and 9.3

1   Remove the carburetor (see Chapter 3).
2   Unbolt the carburetor intake joint from the cylinder **(see illustrations)**.
3   Pull the reed valve out of the cylinder and remove the gasket **(see illustration)**.

Inspection

Refer to illustrations 9.6a and 9.6b

4   Inspect the reed valve for obvious damage, such as a cracked or broken reed or "stopper" (the stopper controls the "height," *i.e.* the movement, of the reed). Also make sure there's no clearance between the edge of the reed and where it seats.

5   If inspection doesn't show any obvious damage, connect a vacuum pump to the carburetor side of the reed valve assembly and apply vacuum. There should be little or no leakage.

6   The reed valve can be disassembled and the reed replaced.

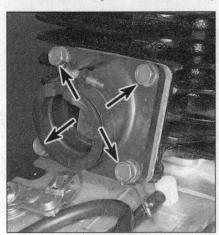

9.2a Unbolt the reed valve body ...

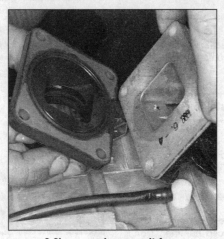

9.2b ... and remove it from the cylinder ...

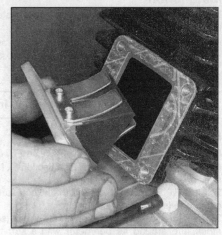

9.3 ... and then pull out the reed valve and remove the gasket

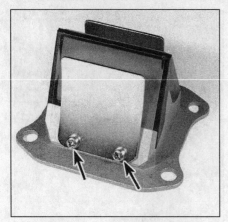

9.6a Remove the screws to detach the reed stoppers from the reed valve

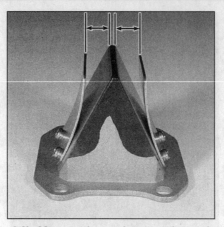

9.6b Measure the gap between the reed stoppers and reeds

10.2a On RT180 models, remove the two cylinder base nuts (arrows) on the left side . . .

10.2b . . . and the two (arrows) on the right side

10.3a Lift the cylinder off the piston (here's an RT100) . . .

10.3b . . . and here's an RT180

Remove the retaining screws and the stopper **(see illustration)**. The screws have a thread-locking agent on the threads, so you may need to use an impact driver. Remove the reed and install a new one. Install the stopper, aligning the cutout in the stopper with the cutout in the reed. Coat the screw threads with a non-permanent thread-locking agent, then tighten them to the torque listed in this Chapter's Specifications. After assembly, check the clearance between the reed and the stopper **(see illustration)**.

Installation

7   Installation is the reverse of the removal steps, with the following additions:

a) *Use a new gasket between the reed valve assembly and cylinder.*
b) *Tighten the intake joint bolts in a criss-cross pattern to the torque listed in this Chapter's Specifications.*

10 Cylinder - removal, inspection and installation

Removal

Refer to illustrations 10.2a, 10.2b, 10.3a and 10.3b

1   Remove the cylinder head (see Section 8). Make sure the piston is positioned at top dead center (TDC).
2   On RT180 models, remove the nuts securing the cylinder to the crankcase **(see illustrations)**.
3   Lift the cylinder straight up off the piston **(see illustrations)**. If it's stuck, tap around its perimeter with a soft-faced hammer. Don't attempt to pry between the cylinder and the crankcase, as you'll ruin the sealing surfaces.

4   Locate the dowel pins (RT180 models) - they may have come off with the cylinder or still be in the crankcase. Be careful not to let the dowels drop into the engine. Stuff clean shop rags around the piston and remove the gasket and all traces of old gasket material from the surfaces of the cylinder and the crankcase.

Inspection

Refer to illustrations 10.5a, 10.5b and 10.5c

5   Inspect the top and bottom surfaces of the cylinder for warpage, using the same method as for the cylinder head **(see illustration)**.

10.5a Check cylinder surface warpage with a straightedge and feeler gauge . . .

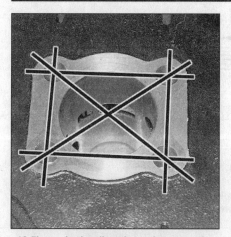

10.5b . . . in the directions shown on the upper surface . . .

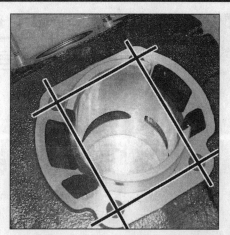

10.5c . . . and on the lower surface

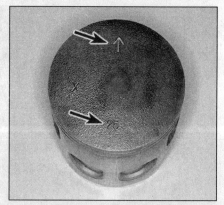

11.3a The arrow mark on the piston points to the front of the engine (the "25" mark on this piston indicates that it's a first oversize)

Make your measurements between the holes for the cylinder head studs and across the bore (see illustrations).

6   Inspect the cylinder walls carefully for scratches and score marks.

7   Using the appropriate precision measuring tools, measure the cylinder diameter at the top, center and bottom of the cylinder bore, parallel to the crankshaft axis. Next, measure the cylinder diameter at the same three locations across the crankshaft axis. Compare your measurements to the cylinder bore diameter listed in this Chapter's Specifications.

8   Differences between the top and bottom measurements indicate cylinder taper. Differences between the measurements parallel to and across the crankshaft axis indicate out-of-round. If the cylinder walls are tapered, out-of-round, worn beyond the specified limits, or badly scuffed or scored, have the cylinder rebored and honed by a dealer service department or a motorcycle repair shop. If the cylinder is rebored, oversize pistons and rings will be required as well. **Note:** Yamaha supplies pistons in two oversizes for these models.

9   If you don't have the measuring tools needed to do this job, ask a dealer service department or repair shop to measure the cylinder, and ask for its advice about servicing the cylinder versus replacing it.

10   If it's in reasonably good condition and isn't yet worn to the outside limit, and if the piston-to-cylinder clearance is still within tolerance, then it's not necessary to rebore the cylinder; honing is all that is necessary.

11   To hone the cylinder, you will need a flexible hone with fine stones or a "bottle brush" type hone (see Maintenance techniques, tools and working facilities at the front of this book), plenty of light oil or honing oil, some shop towels and an electric drill motor. Hold the cylinder in a vise (cushioned with soft jaws or wood blocks) when performing the honing operation. Mount the hone in the drill motor, compress the stones and slip the hone into the cylinder. Lubricate the cylinder thoroughly, turn on the drill and move the hone up and down in the cylinder at a pace that will produce a fine crosshatch pattern on the cylinder wall with the crosshatch lines intersecting at approximately a 60-degree angle. Be sure to use plenty of lubricant and do not take off any more material than is absolutely necessary to produce the desired effect. Do not withdraw the hone from the cylinder while it is running. Instead, shut off the drill and continue moving the hone up and down in the cylinder until it comes to a complete stop, then compress the stones and withdraw the hone. Wipe the oil out of the cylinder. Remember not to remove too much material from the cylinder wall. If you do not have the tools, or do not desire to perform the honing operation, a dealer service department or vehicle repair shop will generally do it for a reasonable fee.

12   Next, the cylinder must be thoroughly washed with warm soapy water to remove all traces of the abrasive grit produced during the honing operation. Be sure to run a brush through the stud holes and flush them with running water. After rinsing, dry the cylinder thoroughly and apply a coat of light, rust-preventive oil to all machined surfaces.

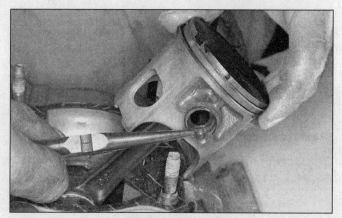

11.3b Wear eye protection and remove the circlip with a pointed tool or needle-nosed pliers

Installation

13   Lubricate the piston with plenty of clean two-stroke engine oil.

14   Install the dowel pins (RT180 models), then lower a new cylinder base gasket over them.

15   Make sure the piston ring gaps are aligned with the dowels in the ring lands. Install the cylinder over the studs and carefully lower it down until the piston crown fits into the cylinder liner. Push down on the cylinder, making sure the piston doesn't get cocked sideways, until the bottom of the cylinder liner slides down past the piston rings. Be sure not to rotate the cylinder, as this may snag the piston rings on the exhaust port. A wood or plastic hammer handle can be used to gently tap the cylinder down, but don't use too much force or the piston will be damaged.

16   The remainder of installation is the reverse of the removal steps.

11 Piston and rings - removal, inspection and installation

1   The piston is attached to the connecting rod with a piston pin that is a slip fit in the piston and connecting rod needle bearing.

2   Before removing the piston from the rod, stuff a clean shop towel into the crankcase hole, around the connecting rod. This will prevent the circlips from falling into the crankcase if they are inadvertently dropped.

Removal

Refer to illustrations 11.3a, 11.3b, 11.4a, 11.4b and 11.4c

3   The piston should have an arrow mark on its crown that goes toward the exhaust (front) side of the engine (see illustration). If this

11.4a Push the piston pin partway out, then pull it the rest of the way

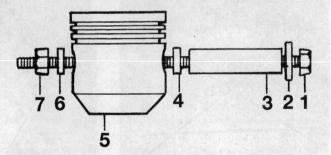

11.4b The piston pin should come out with hand pressure - if it doesn't, this removal tool can be fabricated from readily available parts

1	Bolt	7	Nut (B)
2	Washer	A	Large enough for piston pin to fit inside
3	Pipe (A)		
4	Padding (A)	B	Small enough to fit through piston pin bore
5	Piston		
6	Washer (B)		

mark is not visible due to carbon buildup, scribe an arrow into the piston crown before removal. Support the piston and pry the circlip out with a pointed tool or needle-nosed pliers **(see illustration)**.

4   Push the piston pin out from the opposite end to free the piston from the rod **(see illustration)**. You may have to deburr the area around the groove to enable the pin to slide out (use a triangular file for this procedure). If the pin won't come out, you can fabricate a piston pin removal tool from a long bolt, a nut, a piece of tubing and washers **(see illustration)**. Once you've removed the pin and piston, remove the needle bearing **(see illustration)**.

Inspection

Refer to illustrations 11.6, 11.11, 11.13, 11.14a, 11.14b, 11.15, 11.16 and 11.17

5   Before the inspection process can be carried out, the piston must be cleaned and the old piston ring removed.

6   Carefully remove the rings from the piston **(see illustration)**. Do not nick or gouge the piston in the process. A ring removal and installation tool will make this easier, but you can use your fingers if you don't have one - just be sure not to cut yourself.

7   Scrape all traces of carbon from the top of the piston. A handheld wire brush or a piece of fine emery cloth can be used once most of the deposits have been scraped away. Do not, under any circumstances, use a wire brush mounted in a drill motor to remove deposits from the piston; the piston material is soft and will be eroded away by the wire brush.

8   Use a piston ring groove cleaning tool to remove any carbon

deposits from the ring groove. If a tool is not available, a piece broken off the old ring will do the job. Be very careful to remove only the carbon deposits. Do not remove any metal and do not nick or gouge the sides of the ring grooves.

9   Once the deposits have been removed, clean the piston with solvent and dry it thoroughly.

10   Normal piston wear appears as even, vertical wear on the thrust surfaces of the piston and slight looseness of the rings in their grooves.

11   Carefully inspect each piston for cracks around the skirt, at the pin bosses and at the ring lands. Make sure the ring locating dowels are secure in the ring lands **(see illustration)**.

12   Look for scoring and scuffing on the thrust faces of the skirt, holes in the piston crown and burned areas at the edge of the crown. If the skirt is scored or scuffed, the engine may have been suffering from oil starvation and/or abnormal combustion, which caused excessively high operating temperatures. A hole in the piston crown, an extreme to be sure, is an indication that abnormal combustion (pre-ignition) was occurring. Burned areas at the edge of the piston crown are usually a sign of spark knock (detonation). If any of the above problems exist, the causes must be corrected or the damage will occur again.

13   Measure the piston ring-to-groove clearance (side clearance) by laying a new piston ring in the ring groove and slipping a feeler gauge in beside it **(see illustration)**. Check the clearance at three or four locations around the groove. If the clearance is greater than specified,

11.4c Slide the small end bearing out of the connecting rod

11.6 Remove the piston rings with a ring removal and installation tool if you have one; you can use your fingers instead if you're careful

11.11 There's a locating dowel in each ring land (arrow); center the ring gaps on these dowels

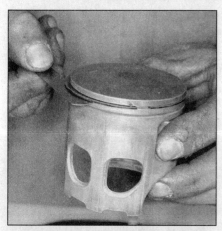

11.13 Measure side clearance between the rings and piston with a feeler gauge

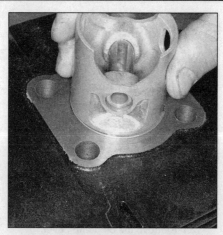

11.14a Use the piston to push the ring squarely into the bore . . .

11.14b . . . then measure the ring end gap with a feeler gauge

a new piston will have to be used when the engine is reassembled.

14   Measure the ring end gap. Push each piston ring into the cylinder from the top, down to the bottom of the ring travel area inside the cylinder. Square the ring in the bore by tapping it with the piston crown **(see illustration)**. Measure the gap between the ends of the ring with a feeler gauge **(see illustration)**. Measure both rings; if either has a gap greater than the value listed in this Chapter's Specifications, replace both rings with new ones.

15   Check the piston-to-bore clearance by measuring the bore (see Section 10) and the piston diameter **(see illustration)**. Measure the piston across the skirt on the thrust faces at a 90-degree angle to the piston pin, at the specified distance up from the bottom of the skirt. Subtract the piston diameter from the bore diameter to obtain the clearance. If it is greater than specified, the cylinder will have to be rebored and a new oversized piston and rings installed. If the appropriate precision measuring tools are not available, the piston-to-cylinder clearance can be obtained using feeler gauges (though not quite as accurately). Feeler gauge stock comes in 12-inch lengths and various thicknesses and is generally available at auto parts stores. To check the clearance, slip a piece of feeler gauge stock of the same thickness as the specified piston clearance into the cylinder along with appropriate piston. The cylinder should be upside down and the piston must be positioned exactly as it normally would be. Place the feeler gauge between the piston and cylinder on one of the thrust faces (90-degrees to the piston pin bore). The piston should slip through the cylinder (with the feeler gauge in place) with moderate pressure. If it falls through, or slides through easily, the clearance is excessive and a new piston will be required. If the piston binds at the lower end of the cylinder and is loose toward the top, the cylinder is tapered. If tight spots are encountered as the piston/feeler gauge is rotated in the cylinder, the cylinder

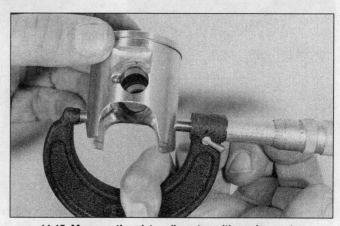

11.15 Measure the piston diameter with a micrometer

is elongated (no longer round). Be sure to have the cylinder and piston checked by a dealer service department or a repair shop to confirm your findings before purchasing new parts.

16   Apply clean two-stroke oil to the pin, insert it into the piston and check for freeplay by rocking the pin side-to-side **(see illustration)**. If the pin is loose, a new piston and possibly a new pin must be installed. Check both for visible wear, replace whichever appears worn and repeat the freeplay check.

17   Repeat Step 16, this time inserting the piston pin into the connecting rod needle bearing **(see illustration)**. If it wobbles and the pin isn't worn, replace the needle bearing.

11.16 Slip the pin into the piston and try to wiggle it side-to-side; if it's loose, replace the piston and pin

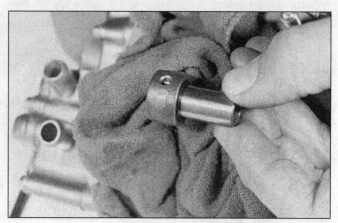

11.17 The needle bearing should be replaced if the pin wobbles inside it

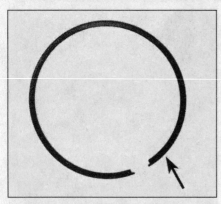

11.20 The manufacturer's mark (arrow) near the ring gap should be facing up when the ring is installed

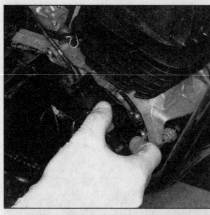

12.1 Remove the oil pump cover . . .

12.2a . . . disconnect the oil tank hose from the pump . . .

12.2b . . . and pass it through this grommet

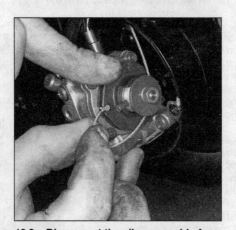

12.2c Disconnect the oil pump cable from the pulley . . .

12.2d . . . and unscrew the fitting nut from the engine

Installation

Refer to illustration 11.20

18   Install the piston with its arrow mark toward the exhaust side (front) of the engine. Lubricate the pin and the connecting rod needle bearing with two-stroke oil of the type listed in the Chapter 1 Specifications.

19   Install a new circlip in the groove in one side of the piston (don't reuse the old circlips). Push the pin into position from the opposite side and install another new circlip. Compress the circlips only enough for them to fit in the piston. Make sure the clips are properly seated in the grooves.

20   Locate the manufacturer's mark on the piston rings near one of the ends **(see illustration)**. Turn the rings so this mark is upward, then carefully spread them and install them in the ring grooves. Make sure the end gaps are centered on the dowel pin in each ring groove **(see illustration 11.11)**.

12   Oil pump - removal, inspection and installation

Removal

Refer to illustrations 12.1, 12.2a, 12.2b, 12.2c, 12.2d, 12.3a, 12.3b, 12.4a, 12.4b, 12.4c and 12.4d

1   Remove the oil pump cover **(see illustration).**

2   Disconnect and plug the oil hoses and disconnect the oil pump

12.3a Oil pump mounting screws

12.3b Remove the oil pump and clean away the old gasket

12.4a Pry the clip out of its groove . . .

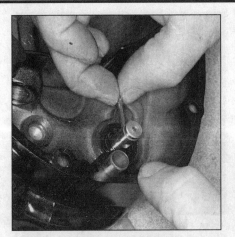

12.4b . . . lift the gear off the drive pin . . .

12.4c . . . slide out the drive pin and remove the second C-clip . . .

12.4d . . . and rotate the shaft to disengage it from the gear; don't lose the washer (arrow)

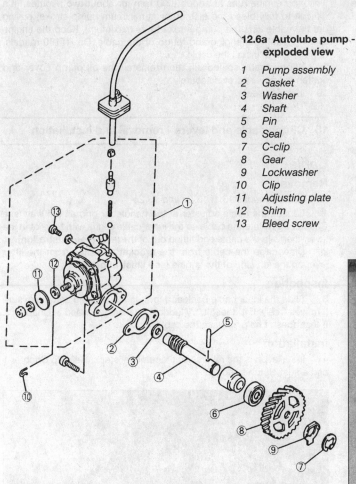

12.6a Autolube pump - exploded view

1   Pump assembly
2   Gasket
3   Washer
4   Shaft
5   Pin
6   Seal
7   C-clip
8   Gear
9   Lockwasher
10 Clip
11 Adjusting plate
12 Shim
13 Bleed screw

12.6b Inspect the gear inside the pump (arrow)

12.7 Inspect the oil seal and bushing in the crankcase cover (arrow)

cable **(see illustrations)**.

3   Remove the pump mounting screws, take the pump off and remove the gasket **(see illustrations)**.

4   For access to the oil pump gear, remove the right crankcase cover (see Section 14). Remove the C-clip, pump gear and drive pin, than take out the pump shaft and washer **(see illustrations)**.

Inspection

Refer to illustrations 12.6a, 12.6b, 12.6, 12.7 and 12.8

5   Check the exterior of the pump for damage or oil leaks at

the cover.

6   Check the disassembled components for wear or damage, such as broken teeth on the pump gear or a worn worm gear on the shaft **(see illustration)**. Look inside the pump and check the internal gear **(see illustration)**. Replace the pump if problems are found.

7   Check the oil seal and bushing in the right crankcase cover **(see illustration)**. If they're worn or damaged, pry out the oil seal, tap out

12.8 Make sure the C-clip is seated securely in its groove

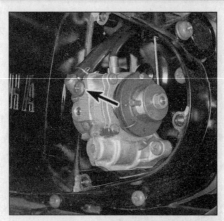

12.15 Use a new sealing washer on the oil pump drain screw (arrow)

12.16 The oil inlet hose attaches to this fitting on the carburetor

the bushing and install new ones.

8   Reassemble the pump, using new C-clips. Make sure they're securely seated in their grooves **(see illustration)**.

Installation

9   Installation is the reverse of removal. Be sure to use a new gasket.
10   After installation, bleed air from the pump.

Air bleeding the oil pump

Refer to illustrations 12.15 and 12.16

11   The oil pump must be bled of air whenever the oil tank has been run dry, any part of the lubrication system has been removed or disconnected or the machine has been rolled onto its side. The bleed screw sealing washer will need to be replaced if it's crushed or deteriorated, so you may want to buy a new sealing washer before you start.
12   Remove the seat (see Chapter 7). This isn't strictly necessary, but it's easy to do and will improve access.
13   Fill the oil tank with the recommended two-stroke oil (see Chapter 1).
14   Place a drain pan under the oil pump cover, then remove the pump cover screws and take off the cover **(see illustration 12.1)**.
15   Remove the oil pump bleed screw **(see illustration)**. Let oil run out of the screw hole into the pan until it's free of air bubbles, then install the bleed screw.
16   Disconnect the oil inlet hose from the carburetor **(see illustration)**. Using an oil can, pump two-stroke oil into the hose. When the hose is completely filled with oil, displacing any air in the hose, reconnect it to the carburetor.
17   To bleed the pump distributor and/or the delivery hose, start the engine. On RT180 models, remove the cable clip (there's no clip on

RT100 models). Pull out the pump cable all the way and hold it there while the engine runs at about 2000 rpm for about two minutes. (It's difficult to fully bleed the distributor at minimum pump stroke; pulling out the cable sets the pump stroke to its maximum). Keep the engine running. Stop the engine and let go of the cable. On RT180 models, don't forget to install the cable clip.
18   Wipe up any spilled oil, then reinstall the oil pump cover and tighten the cover screws securely.
19   Install the seat.

13 Clutch cable and levers - removal and installation

Cable

Removal

Refer to illustrations 13.1, 13.2a and 13.2b

1   Loosen the cable adjuster at the handlebar grip all the way (see Chapter 1). Rotate the cable so the inner cable aligns with the slot in the lever, then slip the cable end fitting out of the lever **(see illustration)**.
2   Disengage the cable from the bracket and then from the lifter lever on the left side of the engine **(see illustrations)**.

Inspection

3   Slide the inner cable back and forth in the housing and make sure it moves freely. If it doesn't, try lubricating it as described in Chapter 1. If that doesn't help, replace the cable.

Installation

4   Installation is the reverse of the removal steps. Refer to Chapter 1 and adjust clutch freeplay.

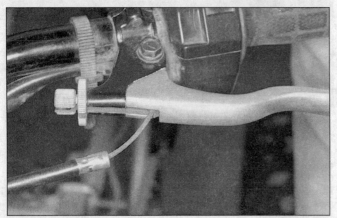

13.1 Rotate the cable and lower it away from the lever

13.2a Disengage the cable from the bracket

13.2b Slip the cable end out of the slot

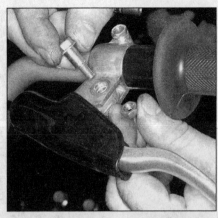

13.6 Remove the nut and shouldered bolt

13.7 Remove the bracket clamp bolts

13.9a Note the spring ends (upper arrows) and unscrew the locknut (RT100, shown) or hex-head screw (RT180) . . .

13.9b . . . RT100 models have an O-ring (arrow) under the locknut; RT180 models have a washer under the screw head

13.10 Unhook the spring from the crankcase, lift out the lever and its washer (upper arrow) and inspect the seal and bearing (lower arrow)

Handlebar lever

Refer to illustrations 13.6 and 13.7

5   Disconnect the cable from the lever **(see illustration 13.1)**.
6   To remove the lever, unscrew the locknut and remove the shouldered pivot bolt **(see illustration)**.
7   To remove the lever bracket, mark its position on the handlebar **(see illustration)**. Remove the bracket clamp bolt and take the bracket off.
8   Installation is the reverse of the removal steps.

Lifter lever

Refer to illustrations 13.9a, 13.9b, 13.10, 13.11, 13.13 and 13.14

9   Remove the lifter lever locating pin **(see illustrations)**. Note how

the lever spring is installed and unhook it from the crankcase.
10   Pull the lifter lever shaft out of the cover and remove the washer **(see illustration)**.
11   Look for visible wear or damage at the contact points of the lifter lever and pushrod **(see illustration)**. Replace any parts that show problems.
12   Pry the lifter shaft seal out of the cover. If the bearing is worn or damaged, drive it out with a shouldered drift the same diameter as the bearing, then use the same tool to drive in a new one. Pack the bearing with grease and press in a new seal.
13   Installation is the reverse of the removal steps. Engage the notch in the lever shaft with the lifter pin **(see illustration)** and hook the spring to the lever and cover.

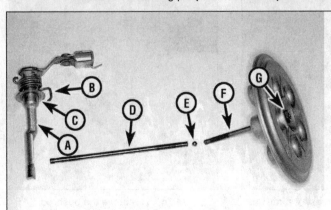

13.11 Release mechanism details

A   Lifter lever
B   Spring
C   Washer
D   Pushrod
E   Steel ball
F   Adjuster rod
G   Locknut

13.13 On installation, engage the pin with the groove in the lever shaft

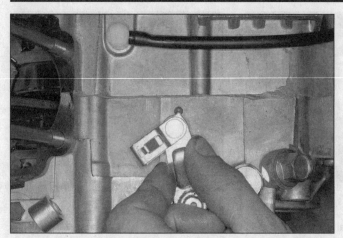

13.14 On RT100 models, align the lever pointer with the crankcase mark

14.3a Remove the cover screws (the two right screws are used on RT180 models only) . . .

14   If you're working on an RT100, turn the lifter pin to align the lever pointer with the mark on the crankcase **(see illustration)**, then secure the lifter pin with the locknut.

14   Clutch - removal, inspection and installation

Right crankcase cover

Removal

Refer to illustrations 14.3a and 14.3b

1   Drain the transmission oil (see Chapter 1).

2   Disconnect the oil pump cable and hoses from the Autolube oil pump (see Section 12). (The pump itself can remain attached to the right crankcase cover.) Remove the kickstarter (see Section 17). On RT180 models, remove the rear brake pedal (see Chapter 6).

3   Remove the right crankcase cover screws and pull the cover off the engine **(see illustration)**. Tap gently with a rubber mallet if necessary to break the gasket seal. Don't pry against the mating surfaces of the cover and crankcase. Once the cover is off, locate the dowels **(see illustration)**; they may have stayed in the crankcase or come off with the cover.

Installation

4   Installation is the reverse of removal. Use a new gasket, coated on both sides with gasket sealant. Don't forget to install the dowels.

5   Tighten the cover screws evenly to the torque listed in this Chapter's Specifications.

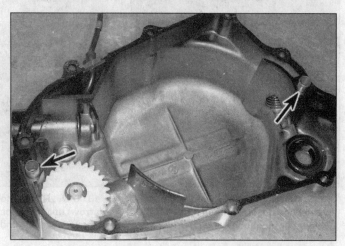

14.3b . . . and locate the cover dowels (arrows)

Clutch

Removal

6   Remove the right crankcase cover as described above.

Note: *If you're planning to remove the primary drive gear, loosen the primary drive gear nut now, before removing the clutch, by wedging a copper washer or penny between the primary drive and driven gears* **(see illustration 14.7a).**

14.7a Wedge a copper washer or penny between the clutch housing gear and primary drive gear and unscrew the clutch spring bolts . . .

14.7b . . . pull off the pressure plate . . .

14.7c . . . remove the pushrod

14.7d . . . wedge the gears again and remove the clutch locknut . . .

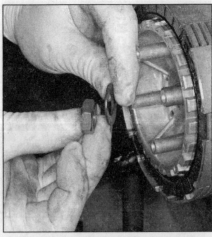

14.7e and conical washer; note the washer's direction . . .

14.7f . . . remove the clutch friction and metal plates and the thrust washer

14.7g . . . and pull off the clutch housing (you can leave the plates in the housing if you're not planning to replace them)

14.8a Wedge a copper washer or penny between the clutch housing gear and primary drive gear. . .

14.8b . . . and unscrew the clutch spring bolts

RT100 models

Refer to illustrations 14.7a through 14.7g

7   Refer to the accompanying illustrations to remove the clutch center, plates and housing **(see illustrations)**.

RT180 models

Refer to illustrations 14.8a through 14.8i

8   Refer to the accompanying illustrations to remove the clutch center, plates and housing **(see illustrations)**.

14.8c Remove the clutch springs . . .

14.8d . . . pull off the pressure plate . . .

14.8e . . . together with the adjuster rod

14.8f Bend the clutch nut's lockwasher tabs away from the nut . . .

14.8g . . . then unscrew the nut and slide the lockwasher off the mainshaft

14.8h Pull the clutch housing off the mainshaft . . .

14.8i . . . then pull off the splined spacer (arrow) and the clutch housing

14.9 Remove the bushing and thrust washer

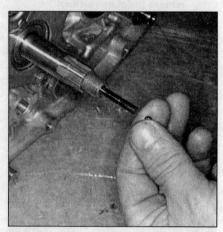

14.10 Remove the steel ball with a pencil magnet and remove the pushrod

All models

Refer to illustrations 14.9 and 14.10

9   Remove the collar and spacer from the mainshaft **(see illustration)**.

10   Remove the steel ball and pushrod from inside the mainshaft, using a pencil magnet **(see illustration)**.

Inspection

Refer to illustrations 14.11, 14.12, 14.15, 14.16 and 14.17

11   Check the friction surface on the pressure plate for scoring or wear **(see illustration)**. Replace the pressure plate if any defects are found.

12   Check the edges of the slots in the clutch housing for indenta-

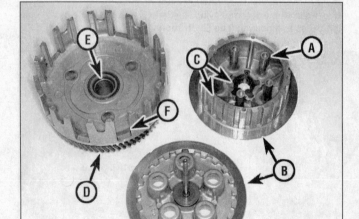

14.11 Clutch inspection points

A	Spring posts	D	Primary driven gear
B	Friction surfaces	E	Clutch housing bushing
C	Splines	F	Clutch housing slots

14.12 Hold the clutch housing so it won't turn and try to rotate the primary driven gear; if there's any play, replace the clutch housing

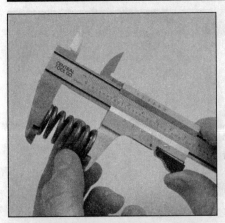
14.15 Measure the clutch spring free length

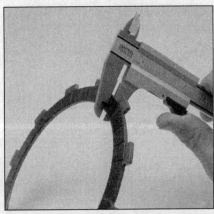
14.16 Measure the thickness of the friction plates

14.17 Check the metal plates for warpage

tions made by the friction plate tabs **(see illustration 14.11)**. If the indentations are deep they can prevent clutch release, so the housing should be replaced with a new one. If the indentations can be removed easily with a file, the life of the housing can be prolonged to an extent. Also, check the driven gear teeth for cracks, chips or excessive wear. If the gear is worn or damaged or the gear can be rotated separately from the clutch housing **(see illustration)**, replace the clutch housing.

13   Inspect the bushing surface in the center of the clutch housing for score marks, scratches and excessive wear **(see illustration 14.11)**. If the clutch housing is worn, replace it. If the mainshaft collar is excessively worn, replace the collar. If the collar's mounting surface on the mainshaft is worn, replace the mainshaft.

14   Inspect the clutch housing's friction surface and slots for scoring, wear and indentations **(see illustration 14.11)**. Also inspect the splines in the middle of the clutch housing. If there are any signs of excessive wear, replace the clutch housing.

15   Measure the free length of the clutch springs **(see illustration)** and compare the results to this Chapter's Specifications. If the springs have sagged, or if cracks are noted, replace the springs as a set.

16   If the lining material on the friction plates smells burnt, or if it's glazed, replace the friction plates. If the metal clutch plates are scored or discolored, replace them. Measure the thickness of the friction plates **(see illustration)** and replace any that are excessively worn.

17   Lay the metal plates, one at a time, on a perfectly flat surface (such as a piece of plate glass) and check for warpage by trying to slip a feeler gauge between the flat surface and the plate **(see illustration)**. The feeler gauge should be the same thickness as the maximum warpage listed in this Chapter's Specifications. Do this at several places around the plate's circumference. If you can slip the feeler gauge under the plate, the plate is warped and must be replaced.

18   Inspect the tabs on the friction plates for excessive wear and mushroomed edges. They can be cleaned up with a file if the deformation is not severe. Check the friction plates for warpage as described in Step 14.

Installation

Refer to illustrations 14.19a through 14.19e

19   Installation is the reverse of removal **(see illustrations)**, with the following additions:

   a) *On RT100 models, install the conical spring washer with its concave side facing toward the engine* **(see illustration 14.7e)**, *then install the clutch housing nut and tighten it to the torque listed in this Chapter's Specifications.*

   b) *On RT180 models, install a new lockwasher and position its tabs between the ribs of the clutch housing. Tighten the clutch housing nut to the torque listed in this Chapter's Specifications, and then bend the lockwasher tabs against two of the flats on the nut.*

   c) *Coat the friction plates with clean engine oil before you install them.*

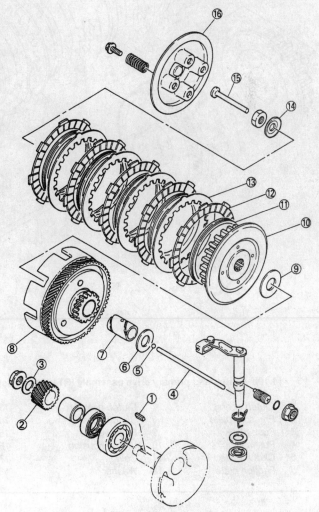

14.19a Clutch and primary drive assembly (RT100 models) - exploded view

1	*Straight key*	*9*	*Thrust washer*
2	*Primary drive gear*	*10*	*Clutch boss*
3	*Conical spring washer*	*11*	*Clutch damper*
4	*Pushrod no. 2*	*12*	*Friction discs (5)*
5	*Ball*	*13*	*Steel plates (4)*
6	*Thrust washer*	*14*	*Conical spring washer*
7	*Collar*	*15*	*Pushrod no. 1*
8	*Clutch housing*	*16*	*Pressure plate*

14.19c Install the damper over the splines . . .

14.19d . . . and set it against the metal plate . . .

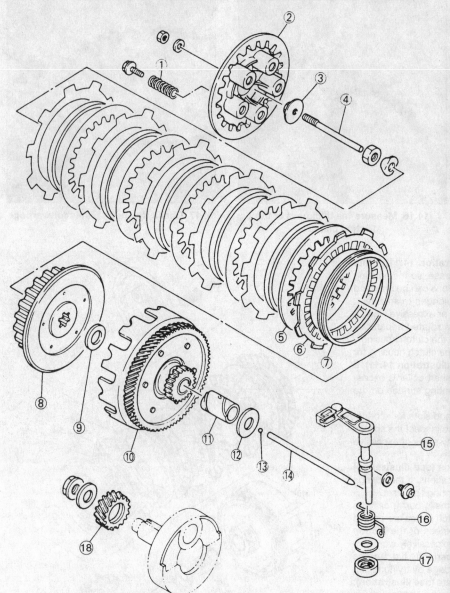

14.19b Clutch and primary drive assembly (RT180 models) - exploded view

1	Clutch spring	7	Clutch damper	13	Ball
2	Pressure plate	8	Clutch boss	14	Pushrod no. 2
3	Push plate	9	Plain washer	15	Push lever axle
4	Pushrod no. 1	10	Clutch housing	16	Return spring
5	Clutch plate	11	Collar	17	Oil seal
6	Friction plate	12	Washer	18	Primary drive gear

14.19e . . . then install the friction plate

d) Install a friction plate, then alternate the remaining metal and friction plates until they're all installed. Friction plates go on first and last, so the friction material contacts the metal surfaces of the clutch housing and the pressure plate. A damper fits inside each friction plate **(see illustrations)**. The tab on the outer circumference of the first metal plate installed goes straight up, then the remaining metal plate tabs are offset 90-degrees from the first tab (RT100) or 60-degrees from the first tab (RT180).

e) Apply grease to the ends of the clutch pushrod and the pushrod's steel ball **(see illustration 14.10)**.

15 Primary drive gear - removal, inspection and installation

Removal

Refer to illustrations 15.4a, 15.4b and 15.4c

1   Remove the right crankcase cover (see Section 14).

2   Wedge a copper washer or penny between the teeth of the primary drive gear and the primary driven gear **(see illustration 14.7a or 14.8a)**, then loosen the primary drive gear nut.

15.4a Remove the primary drive gear locknut and washer . . .

15.4b . . . slide off the primary drive gear and Woodruff key (arrow) (if it's not here, look on the floor) . . .

15.4c . . . and slide off the spacer collar

15.6 Remove the retainer for access to the seal

16.1 Look for alignment marks on the end of the shift pedal and shaft; if there are none, make your own

16.9a Remove the cover screws . . .

3   Remove the clutch (see Section 14).
4   Remove the primary drive nut and washer and slide the primary drive gear off the crankshaft **(see illustrations)**. Remove the Woodruff key from the crankshaft and store it so it won't be lost, then slide the spacer collar off the crankshaft **(see illustrations)**.

Inspection
Refer to illustration 15.6
5   Inspect the primary drive gear for obvious damage such as chipped or broken teeth. Replace it if any of these problems are found.
6   Check the seal for leaks. If it has been leaking, remove the seal retainer and carefully pry the seal out of the bore **(see illustration)**.

Installation
7   Installation is the reverse of removal. Make sure the Woodruff key is in place. Wedge the gears from below, using the same method used for removal, then tighten the primary drive gear nut to the torque listed in this Chapter's Specifications.

16 External shift mechanism - removal, inspection and installation

Shift pedal
Removal
Refer to illustration 16.1
1   Look for alignment marks on the end of the shift pedal and shift shaft **(see illustration)**. If they aren't visible, make your own marks.

2   Remove the shift pedal pinch bolt completely and slide the pedal off the shaft.

Inspection
3   Check the shift pedal for wear or damage such as bending. Check the splines on the shift pedal and shift shaft for stripping or step wear. Replace the pedal or spindle if these problems are found.
4   Check the shift shaft seal for signs of oil leakage **(see illustration 16.1)**. If it has been leaking, remove the shift shaft as described below. Pry the seal out of the cover and install a new one. You may be able to push the seal in with your thumbs; if not, tap it in with a hammer and block of wood or a socket the same diameter as the seal.

Installation
5   Line up the alignment marks, install the shift pedal and tighten the pinch bolt.

External shift linkage
Removal (RT100 models)
Refer to illustrations 16.9a through 16.9f, 16.11a, 16.11b, 16.12 and 16.13
6   Remove the shift pedal as described above.
7   If you're planning to remove the shift shaft, remove the clutch (Section 14). The linkage that connects the shift pedal to the shaft is beneath a cover on the opposite side of the engine from the clutch, so it can be removed with the clutch in place.
8   If the engine is still in the frame, remove the drive chain and the drive sprocket (see Chapter 5).
9   Remove the shift shaft cover screws **(see illustration)**. Remove

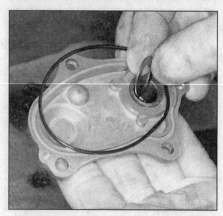

16.9b . . . and take off the cover and O-ring; the seal washer(s) may come off with the cover as shown or stay on the shift pedal shaft . . .

16.9c . . . remove the circlip (arrow) . . .

16.9d . . . the shift pedal lever . . .

16.9e . . . the shift pedal shaft collar . . .

16.9f . . . and the shift pedal shaft

16.11a Lift the pawls clear of the shift drum . . .

the cover and O-ring, then remove the shift linkage components **(see illustrations)**.

10   Remove the clutch (see Section 14).

11   Remove the shift shaft **(see illustrations)**.

12   Unhook the stopper lever spring, remove the pivot bolt and take the lever off **(see illustration)**.

13   If necessary, remove the shift drum stopper bolt, spring and detent ball **(see illustration)**.

Removal (RT180 models)
Refer to illustrations 16.15 and 16.16

14   Remove the shift pedal as described above.

15   Remove the circlip **(see illustration)**. Lift the pawls clear of the shift drum and remove the shift lever. Pull out the shift shaft.

16   Unhook the stopper lever spring, remove the pivot bolt and take the lever off **(see illustration)**.

16.11b . . . and pull the shift shaft out of the crankcase

16.12 Unhook the spring and unbolt the stopper arm from the crankcase

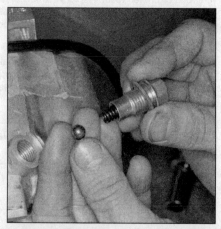

16.13 Unscrew the stopper plug and remove the washer, spring and detent ball

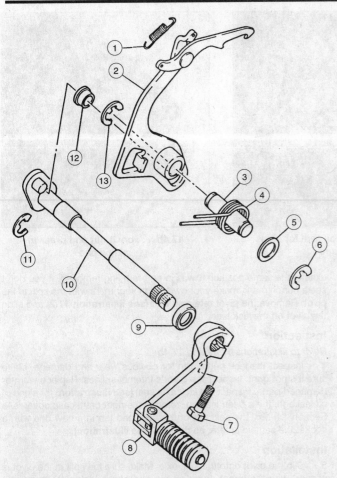

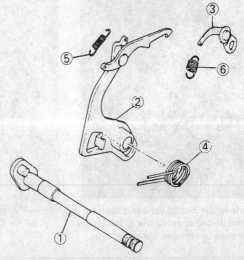

16.16 Stopper lever and related parts (RT180 models)

1	Shift shaft	4	Return	6	Stopper lever
2	Shift lever		spring		spring
3	Stopper lever	5	Pawl spring		

Inspect the shift lever for damage or excessive wear, especially on the points of the pawls **(see illustration)**. If the shift lever is damaged or excessively worn, replace it.

19   Inspect the shift pedal shaft, lever and collar for damage or excessive wear. If any of these parts are damaged or worn, replace them.

20   Inspect the return spring, pawl spring and stopper lever spring for bending or weakness. Replace the springs if their condition is in doubt.

21   Inspect the stopper lever. If the roller turns roughly or the stopper lever is bent or damaged, replace it.

Installation

Refer to illustrations 16.22a and 16.22b

22   Installation is the reverse of the removal steps, with the following additions:

a) *Make sure that the shift lever correctly engages the shift cam.*

b) *Make sure that the shift pedal shaft is correctly engaged with the splines on the shift lever.*

c) *If you're working on an RT180, make sure that the shift pawl is centered within the return spring ends* **(see illustration)** *so that clearances "a" and "b" are equal. If they're not equal, adjust them with the adjusting screw* **(see illustration)** *until they are equal.*

d) *Refill the transmission oil (see Chapter 1).*

16.15 External shift mechanism (RT180 models) - exploded view

1	Pawl spring	6	C-clip	10	Shift shaft
2	Shift lever	7	Shift pedal	11	C-clip
3	Shaft		pinch bolt	12	Collar
4	Return spring	8	Shift pedal	13	C-clip
5	Washer	9	Oil seal		

Inspection

Refer to illustration 16.18

17   Inspect the shafts for damage or excessive wear and make sure they're straight. Look for stripped splines.

18   If the shift shaft is damaged, excessively worn or bent, replace it.

16.18 Check the shift shaft, lever and springs for wear and damage; make sure the shaft is straight

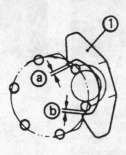

16.22a Make sure that the shift pawl is positioned as shown so that clearances "a" and "b" are equal . . .

16.22b . . . if they aren't, adjust them with the adjusting screw (arrow)

17.2 Remove the circlip (upper arrow) to remove the pedal; remove the pinch bolt (lower arrow) to remove the pedal arm

17.4a Check the oil seal for signs of leakage . . .

17.4b . . . pry it out and press in a new one

17 Kickstarter - removal, inspection and installation

1   The kickstarter pedal, arm and pivot can be removed and installed without disassembling the engine. The right crankcase cover must be removed to service the kickstarter mechanism (see Section 14).

Kick pedal/arm and pivot

Removal

Refer to illustration 17.2

2   If you're only removing the kick pedal/arm and the pivot in order to remove the right crankcase so that you can service the clutch, primary drive, kickstarter mechanism, etc., it's not necessary to disconnect the kick pedal/arm from the pivot. Skip this Step and proceed to Step 3. To replace the kick pedal rubber, simply pull the old rubber off the pedal (if it's stuck, cut it off) and push on a new one. To separate the kick pedal/arm from the pivot, remove the circlip and washer **(see illustration)** and pull the kick pedal/arm out of the pivot. Discard the old circlip. A detent in the kick pedal/arm and a spring-loaded ball inside the pivot lock the kick pedal/arm into its storage position when it's not being used. Make sure that you fish out the ball and spring from the pivot and put them in a plastic bag. If they fall out, and the kick pedal/arm is installed without them, the kick pedal/arm will not stay in its locked storage position; it will flop around during riding, which is both annoying and dangerous.

3   Before removing the pivot from the kick axle, look for a punch mark on the end of the kick axle. The kickstarter will not operate correctly, nor will the kick pedal/arm fold out of the way into its "riding" position, unless the kick pedal/arm pivot is installed on the kick axle at

exactly the same position it was in before being removed. If you don't see a punch mark, make your own. Align your mark with the split in the pivot. Remove the pivot retaining bolt **(see illustration 17.2)** and slide the pivot off the kick axle.

Inspection

Refer to illustrations 17.4a and 17.4b

4   Inspect the kick pedal/arm for obvious wear and damage. Make sure it's not bent. Inspect the pivot's internal splines. Replace worn or damaged parts. Inspect the kick axle seal **(see illustration)** for signs of oil leakage. If it's been leaking, remove the right crankcase cover (see Section 14). Pry the seal out of the bore and tap in a new one with a socket the same diameter as the seal **(see illustration)**.

Installation

5   Slip the pivot onto the kick axle. Make sure the split in the pivot is aligned with the punch mark on the end of the kick axle. Install the pivot retaining screw and tighten it to the torque listed in this Chapter's Specifications. If you disconnected the kick pedal/arm from the pivot, insert the arm through the pivot and secure it with the washer and a *new* circlip.

Kickstarter mechanism

Removal and disassembly (RT100 models)

Refer to illustrations 17.8a, 17.8b, 17.8c, 17.9a, 17.9b, 17.9c, 17.9d, 17.10a, 17.10b, 17.10c, 17.11a, 17.11b and 17.11c

6   Remove the kick pedal/arm and pivot (see above).

7   Remove the right crankcase cover and the clutch (see Section 14).

8   Unhook the spring from the crankcase **(see illustration)**. Turn the

17.8a Unhook the spring from the post . . .

17.8b . . . and slide the spring and kickstarter out . . .

17.8c . . . noting the positions of the clip (left arrow) and kick stopper (right arrow)

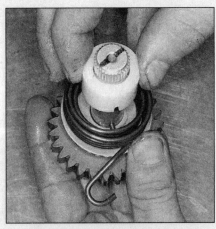

17.9a Note how the bushing notch fits over the spring and take off the bushing . . .

17.9b . . . and note how the spring end fits in the shaft and remove the spring

kickstarter mechanism counterclockwise, then pull the kickstarter out of the engine, noting the installed positions of the clip and kick stopper as you do so **(see illustrations)**.

9   Take off the bushing **(see illustration)**. Disengage the return spring from the hole in the shaft and slide off the return spring and thrust washer **(see illustrations)**.

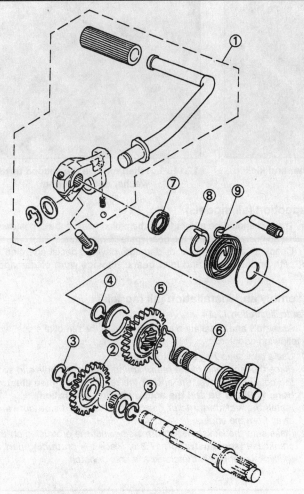

17.9c Kickstarter (RT100 models) - exploded view

1	Pedal and arm	4	Snap-ring	7	Oil seal
2	Kick idle gear	5	Kickstarter gear	8	Bushing
3	Snap-rings	6	Kick axle	9	Spring

17.9d Kickstarter (RT180 models) - exploded view

1	Pedal and arm	5	Washer	8	Kick axle
2	Oil seal	6	Kickstarter gear	9	Snap-rings
3	Bushing	7	Clip	10	Washers
4	Spring			11	Kick idle gear

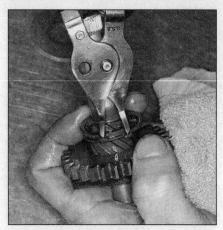

17.10a Remove the snap-ring (RT100) . . .

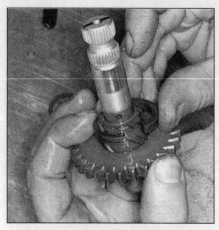

17.10b . . . and retainers (RT100) . . .

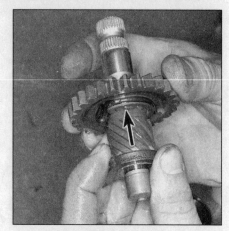

17.10c . . . and slide off the kickstarter gear and clip (arrow) (all models)

17.11a Remove the snap-ring . . .

17.11b . . . thrust washer and kick idle gear . . .

17.11c . . . then remove the second thrust washer and snap-ring

10   If you're working on an RT100, remove the snap-ring and retainers **(see illustrations)**. On all models, slide the kickstarter gear off together with the clip **(see illustration)**.

11   Remove the snap-ring and thrust washer and slip the idler gear off its shaft **(see illustrations)**. Remove the second thrust washer and snap-ring **(see illustration)**.

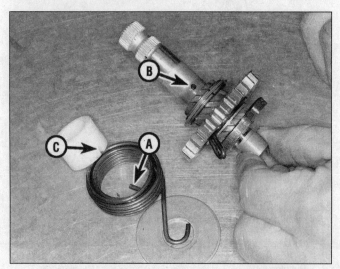

17.14 The end of the spring (A) fits in the shaft hole (B) and bushing notch (C)

Inspection (all models)

12   The clip should be a tight fit on the pinion gear. If the clip is damaged or spins easily around the gear, install a new one.

13   Check all parts for wear or damage, paying special attention to the teeth on the pinion and idler gears. Replace worn or damaged parts.

Assembly and installation (all models)

Refer to illustration 17.14

14   Assembly and installation is the reverse of the removal steps, with the following additions:

a) *Use a new snap-ring on RT100 models.*

b) *Place the inner end of the return spring in the shaft hole and slide the collar notch over the end of the return spring* **(see illustrations 17.9b, 17.9a and the accompanying illustration)**.

b) *Install the kickstarter idler gear with its beveled side outward, away from the engine.*

c) *Make sure the kickstarter stop rests against the protrusion on the crankcase* **(see illustration 17.8c)**. *Place the protruding part of the kickstarter clip in the crankcase hole or notch.*

---

18 Crankcase - disassembly and reassembly

---

1   To examine and repair or replace the crankshaft, connecting rod, bearings and transmission components, the crankcase must be split into two parts.

18.11a Crankcase screws (RT100 models shown; RT180 similar)

18.11b Use a cardboard holder to identify the screw lengths and locations

18.12 Use a puller like this one to push the crankshaft out of the right case half

18.13 Lift the left case half off the right half and locate the crankcase dowels (arrows)

19.3a Some case bearings are secured by retainers

Disassembly

Refer to illustrations 18.11a, 18.11b, 18.12 and 18.13

2   Remove the engine from the motorcycle (see Section 6).

3   Remove the carburetor (see Chapter 3).

4   Remove the cylinder head, cylinder and piston (see Sections 8, 10 and 11).

5   Remove the CDI magneto (see Chapter 4).

6   Remove the clutch (see Section 14).

7   Remove the primary drive gear (see Section 15).

8   Remove the external shift mechanism (see Section 16).

9   Remove the kickstarter (see Section 17).

10   Carefully check the crankcase for any other components that would prevent the separation of the case halves.

11   Loosen the crankcase screws **(see illustrations)** evenly in two or three stages, then remove them.

12   Place the crankcase with its left side down on a workbench. Attach a puller (Yamaha part no. YU-01135, or a similar tool) to the crankcase **(see illustration)**. As you slowly tighten the puller, carefully tap the crankcase apart and lift the left half off the right half. Don't pry against the mating surfaces or they'll develop leaks.

13   Locate the crankcase dowels **(see illustration)**.

14   Refer to Sections 19 through 21 for information on the internal components of the crankcase.

Reassembly

15   Remove all traces of old gasket and sealant from the crankcase mating surfaces with a sharpening stone or similar tool. Be careful not to let any fall into the case as this is done and be careful not to damage the mating surfaces.

16   Check to make sure the dowel pins are in place in their holes in the mating surface of the left crankcase half **(see illustration 18.13)**.

17   Pour some four-stroke engine oil over the transmission gears. Don't get any oil in the crankshaft cavity or on the crankcase mating surface.

18   Apply a coat of Yamabond sealant or equivalent to the crankcase mating surface.

19   Carefully place the right crankcase half onto the left crankcase half. While doing this, make sure the transmission shafts, shift drum and crankshaft fit into their bearings in the right crankcase half.

20   Install the crankcase screws and tighten them so they are just snug. Then tighten them evenly in two or three stages to the torque listed in this Chapter's Specifications.

21   Turn the transmission mainshaft to make sure it turns freely. Also make sure the crankshaft turns freely.

22   The remainder of assembly is the reverse of disassembly.

19   Crankcase components - inspection and servicing

Refer to illustrations 19.3a, 19.3b, 19.3c, 19.3d and 19.4

1   Separate the crankcase and remove the following:

a) *Shift drum and forks*

b) *Transmission shafts and gears*

c) *Crankshaft*

2   Clean the crankcase halves thoroughly with new solvent and dry them with compressed air. All oil passages should be blown out with compressed air and all traces of old gasket should be removed from the mating surfaces. **Caution:** *Be very careful not to nick or gouge the crankcase mating surfaces or leaks will result. Check both crankcase halves very carefully for cracks and other damage.*

3   Check the bearings in the case halves **(see illustrations)**. If the

19.3b Right case bearings
(RT100; RT180 similar)

19.3c Left case bearings
(RT100; RT180 similar)

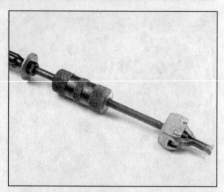

19.3d A blind hole puller like this one is
needed to remove bearings which are only
accessible from one side

19.4 The crankshaft seals have a major
effect on two-stroke engine performance

20.3a Lift out the single shift fork and
its shaft . . .

20.3b . . . then lift out the shift drum . . .

bearings don't turn smoothly, replace them. For bearings that aren't accessible from the outside, a blind hole puller will be needed for removal **(see illustration)**. Drive the remaining bearings out with a bearing driver or a socket having an outside diameter slightly smaller than that of the bearing outer race. Before installing the bearings, allow them to sit in the freezer overnight, and about fifteen minutes before installation, place the case half in an oven, set to about 200-degrees F, and allow it to heat up. The bearings are an interference fit, and this will ease installation. **Warning:** *Before heating the case, wash it thoroughly*

with soap and water so no explosive fumes are present. Also, don't use a flame to heat the case. Install the ball bearings with a socket or bearing driver that bears against the bearing outer race.

4   Replace the oil seals whenever the crankcase is disassembled **(see illustration)**. The crankshaft seals are critical to the performance of two-stroke engines, so they should be replaced even if they look perfectly all right.

5   If any damage is found that can't be repaired, replace the crankcase halves as a set.

6   Assemble the case halves (see Section 18) and check to make sure the crankshaft and the transmission shafts turn freely.

20   Transmission shafts and shift drum - removal, inspection and installation

Note: *When disassembling the transmission shafts, place the parts on a long rod or thread a wire through them to keep them in order and facing the proper direction.*

Removal

Refer to illustrations 20.3a, 20.3b and 20.5

1   Remove the engine, then separate the case halves (see Sections 6 and 18).

2   The transmission components and shift drum will remain in one case half when the case is separated.

3   Pull out the no. 2 shift fork and shaft and lift the shift drum out of the case half **(see illustrations)**.

4   If the transmission shafts have remained in the right case half,

20.5 . . . and lift out the transmission shafts together with the
remaining shift forks; note the clip on the end of the fork shaft

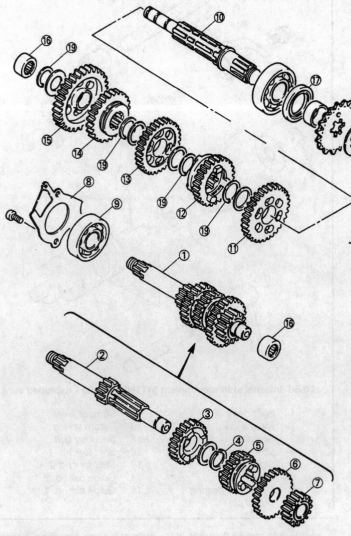

20.6a Transmission gears and shafts (RT100 models) - exploded view

1	Mainshaft assembly	11	2nd wheel gear
2	Mainshaft	12	5th wheel gear
3	4th pinion gear	13	3rd wheel gear
4	Circlip	14	4th wheel gear
5	3rd pinion gear	15	1st wheel gear
6	5th pinion gear	16	Bearing
7	2nd pinion gear	17	Oil seal
8	Bearing holder	18	Drive sprocket
9	Bearing	19	Circlip
10	Driveaxle		

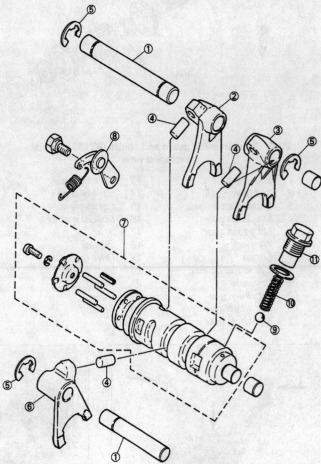

tape the exposed end of the countershaft (where the engine sprocket goes) to prevent damage to the seal.

5   Tap the countershaft out with a soft-faced hammer while you lift the transmission shafts and the two remaining shift forks and their shaft out of the case **(see illustration)**.

Transmission shaft disassembly

Refer to illustrations 20.6a, 20.6b, 20.6c and 20.6d

6   Removal of the shaft components on all except the RT100 mainshaft requires only a pair of snap-ring pliers to remove the snap-rings. Slide the components off the shafts and place them in order on a long rod or a piece of plastic pipe **(see illustrations)**. The RT100 third, fifth and second pinion gears are a press fit on the shaft. If you don't have a press, have them removed by a Yamaha dealer service department or a machine shop.

Inspection

Refer to illustrations 20.9a, 20.9b and 20.12

7   Wash all of the components in clean solvent, dry them off and lay them out for inspection.

8   Inspect the shift fork grooves in the gears. If a groove is worn or scored, replace the affected part and inspect its corresponding shift fork.

9   Inspect the shift forks for distortion and wear, especially in the

20.6b Internal shift mechanism (RT100 models) - exploded view

1	Shift fork guide bar	7	Shift drum assembly
2	Shift fork no. 3	8	Shift lever
3	Shift fork no. 1	9	Ball
4	Pin	10	Spring
5	Circlip	11	Bolt
6	Shift fork no. 2		

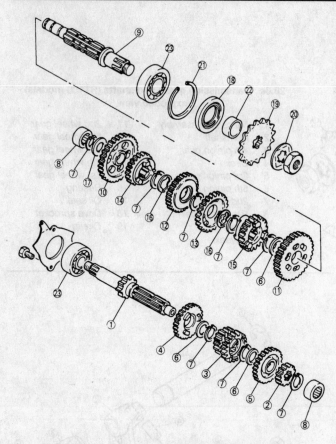

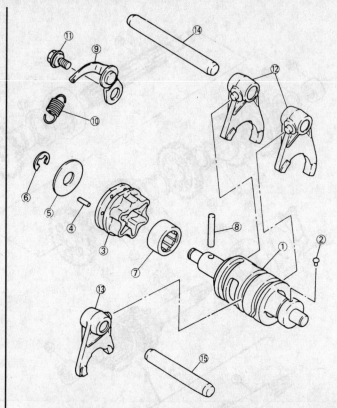

20.6c Transmission gears and shafts (RT180 models) - exploded view

1	Mainshaft	13	4th wheel gear
2	2nd pinion gear	14	5th wheel gear
3	3rd/4th pinion gear	15	6th wheel gear
4	5th pinion gear	16	Special washer
5	6th pinion gear	17	Shim
6	Washer	18	Oil seal
7	Circlip	19	Drive sprocket
8	Cylindrical bearing	20	Lock washer
9	Driveaxle	21	Circlip
10	1st wheel gear	22	Collar
11	2nd wheel gear	23	Bearing
12	3rd wheel gear		

20.6d Internal shift mechanism (RT180 models) - exploded view

1	Shift drum	9	Stopper lever
2	Neutral point	10	Return spring
3	Segment	11	Securing bolt
4	Dowel pin	12	Shift fork no. 1
5	Side plate	13	Shift fork no. 2
6	Circlip	14	Guide bar no. 2
7	Cylindrical bearing	15	Guide bar no. 1
8	Dowel pin		

saddle area and on the pads at the ends of the fork ears **(see illustration)**. If they are discolored or severely worn they're probably bent and must be replaced. Inspect the guide pins and shift drum grooves for excessive wear and damage **(see illustration)** and replace any defective parts.

10   Inspect the shift fork shafts (or guide bars) for evidence of wear,

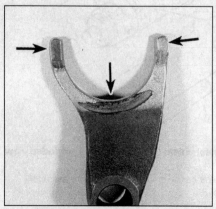

20.9a An arc-shaped burn mark like this means the fork was rubbing against a gear, probably due to bending or worn fork fingers

20.9b Unscrew the Torx screw (arrow) to remove the shift drum segment and bearing

20.12 Check the slots (left arrow) and dogs (right arrow) for wear, especially at the edges; rounded corners cause the transmission to jump out of gear - new gears (bottom) have sharp corners

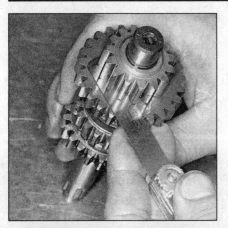

20.14a Check for clearance after the gears are assembled on the shaft

20.14b The assembled gears should mesh like this

20.15a Here's how the shift forks engage the gears (shafts installed in right case half) . . .

galling and other damage. Make sure the shift forks move smoothly on the shafts. If the bars are worn or bent, replace them with new ones.

11   Inspect the gear teeth for cracking and other obvious damage. Check the bushing surface in the inner diameter of the freewheeling gears for scoring or heat discoloration. Replace damaged parts.

12   Inspect the engagement dogs and dog holes on gears so equipped for excessive wear or rounding off **(see illustration)**. Replace the paired gears as a set if necessary.

13   Check the transmission shaft bearings in the crankcase for wear or heat discoloration and replace them if necessary (see Section 19).

Transmission shaft assembly

Refer to illustrations 20.14a and 20.14b

14   Assembly of the transmission shafts is the reverse of the disassembly procedure, with the following additions:

a) *Refer to the illustrations to make sure all components face in the proper direction* **(RT100 models, see illustrations 20.3a and 20.3b; RT180 models, see illustrations 20.3c and 20.3d)**. *Use new snap-rings, installed with their sharp sides facing away from the thrust washers.*

b) *Once assembled, make sure the gears mesh properly* **(see illustration)**.

c) *Make sure there is clearance between the gears on the RT100 mainshaft after pressing them on* **(see illustration)**.

Installation

Refer to illustrations 20.15a and 20.15b

15   Installation is the basically the reverse of the removal procedure, but take note of the following points:

a) *Lubricate the components with four-stroke engine oil before assembling them.*

b) *After assembly, check the gears and shift forks to make sure they're installed correctly* **(see illustrations)**. *Move the shift drum through the gear positions and rotate the gears to make sure they mesh and shift correctly. If they don't, stop and find the problem before you reassemble the case halves.*

21   Crankshaft and connecting rod - removal, inspection and installation

Note: *The procedures in this section require special tools. If you don't have the necessary equipment or suitable substitutes, have the crankshaft removed and installed by a Yamaha dealer.*

Removal

Refer to illustration 21.2

1   Remove the engine (see Section 6) and separate the crankcase halves (see Section 18). The transmission shafts need not be removed.

2   Place the case half on a press plate and press the crankshaft out of the case **(see illustration)**. You can also use a puller **(see illustration 18.12)**.

Inspection

Refer to illustrations 21.3, 21.4 and 21.6

3   Measure the side clearance between the connecting rod and the crankshaft with a feeler gauge **(see illustration)**. If it's more than the limit listed in this Chapter's Specifications, replace the crankshaft and

20.15b . . . the single shift fork engages its gear like this

21.2 Press the crankshaft out of the crankcase

21.3 Check the connecting rod side clearance with a feeler gauge

21.4 Check the connecting rod big-end radial clearance with a dial indicator

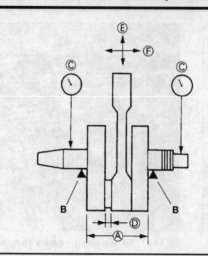

21.6 Crankshaft measurement points

A   *Assembly width*
B   *V-blocks*
C   *Runout measuring points*
D   *Connecting rod big end side clearance*
E   *Connecting rod big end radial clearance*
F   *Connecting rod small end side play*

connecting rod as an assembly.

4   Set up the crankshaft in V-blocks with a dial indicator contacting the small end of the connecting rod. Move the connecting rod side-to-side against the indicator pointer and compare the reading to the small-end side play value listed in this Chapter's Specifications **(see illustration)**. If it's beyond the limit, the crankshaft can be disassembled and the needle roller bearing replaced. However, this is a specialized job that should be done by a Yamaha dealer or other qualified machine shop.

5   Check the crankshaft threads, the ball bearing at the magneto end of the crankshaft and the bearing journals for visible wear or damage. Yamaha lists the crankshaft components (crankwheels, crankpin, crankpin thrust bearings and needle roller bearing, and connecting rod) as separately available parts, but check with your dealer first; it may be more practical to replace the entire crankshaft if the ball bearing is worn or damaged. Replace the crankshaft if any of the other conditions are found.

6   Set the crankshaft on a pair of V-blocks, with a dial indicator contacting each end **(see illustration)**. Rotate the crankshaft and note the runout. If the runout at either end is beyond the limit listed in this Chapter's Specifications, replace the crankshaft and connecting rod as an assembly.

7   Measure the assembly width of the crankshaft **(see illustration 21.6)**. If it exceeds the limit listed in this Chapter's Specifications, replace the crankshaft.

Installation

Refer to illustrations 21.9, 21.10a and 21.10b

8   Pry out the crankshaft seals, then install new ones with a seal driver or socket the same diameter as the seal.

9   Place the crankshaft in the left crankcase half and make sure the

connecting rod is inside the cylinder opening **(see illustration)**.

10   Install the crankshaft with an installation puller **(see illustrations)**. Don't drive the crankshaft in with a hammer or you'll compress the crank wheels on the crankpin, ruining the crankshaft.

11   The remainder of installation is the reverse of the removal steps.

22   Recommended start-up and break-in procedure

Note: *Any rebuilt engine needs time to break in, even if parts have been installed in their original locations. Yamaha specifies a 20-hour break-in period for these models when new; you can use this as a guide for breaking in a rebuilt engine.*

First 10 hours

1   Don't operate continuously at more than half throttle.

2   Let the engine cool for five to ten minutes after each hour of operation.

3   Vary engine speeds; don't operate continuously at one throttle setting.

10 to 20 hours

4   Don't operate continuously at more than three-quarters throttle.

5   Rev the engine freely, but don't use full throttle.

After 20 hours

6   Vary engine speeds occasionally. Don't operate at full throttle for prolonged periods.

7   Upon completion of the break-in rides, and after the engine has cooled down completely, recheck the transmission oil level (see Chapter 1).

21.9 Place the crankshaft in the case with the connecting rod in the cylinder opening

21.10a Thread the adapter into the end of the crankshaft . . .

21.10b . . . and attach the puller to the adapter

Chapter 2 Part C
Engine, clutch and transmission (TT-R and XT models)

Contents

Specifications

TT-R90 models

General
Bore...	47 mm (1.85 inches)
Stroke..	51.8 mm (2.04 inches)
Displacement...	89 cc

Rocker arms
Rocker arm inside diameter	
Standard	10.000 to 10.015 mm (0.3937 to 0.3943 inch)
Limit	10.03 mm (0.3949 inch)
Rocker shaft outside diameter	
Standard	9.981 to 9.991 mm (0.3930 to 0.3933 inch)
Limit	9.95 mm (0.3917 inch)
Shaft-to-arm clearance	Not specified

Camshaft
Lobe height	
Intake	
Standard	25.428 to 25.528 mm (1.0011 to 1.0050 inches)
Limit	25.4 mm (1.00 inch)
Exhaust	
Standard	25.286 to 25.386 mm (0.9955 to 0.994 inches)
Limit	25.26 mm (0.99 inch)
Camshaft runout limit	0.03 mm (0.012 inch)

TT-R90 models (continued)

Cylinder head, valves and valve springs

Cylinder head warpage limit..	0.03 mm 0.0012 inch)
Valve stem runout...	0.02 mm (0.0008 inch)
Valve stem diameter	
Intake	
Standard...	4.475 to 4.490 mm (0.1762 to 0.1768 inch)
Limit	4.45 mm (0.1752 inch)
Exhaust	
Standard...	4.460 to 4.475 mm (0.1756 to 0.1762 inch)
Limit	4.44 mm (0.1748 inch)
Valve guide inside diameter	
Standard...	4.500 to 4.512 mm (0.1772 to 0.1776 inch)
Limit	4.53 mm (0.1783 inch)
Stem-to-guide clearance	
Intake	
Standard...	0.010 to 0.037 mm (0.0004 to 0.0015 inch)
Limit	0.08 mm (0.0031 inch)
Exhaust	
Standard...	0.025 to 0.052 mm (0.0010 to 0.0020 inch)
Limit	0.10 mm (0.004 inch)
Valve seat width	
Standard...	0.9 to 1.1 mm (0.0354 to 0.0433 inch)
Limit	1.6 mm (0.063 inch)
Valve spring free length	
Standard...	28.32 mm (1.11 inch)
Limit	26.9 mm (1.06 inch)
Valve spring bend limit	1.2 mm (0.05 inch)

Cylinder

Bore diameter...	47.000 to 47.005 mm (1.8504 to 1.8506 inches)
Out-of-round and taper limits..	0.05 mm (0.002 inch)

Piston

Diameter	46.960 to 46.975 mm (1.8488 to 1.8494 inches)
Measuring point...	4.0 mm (0.16 inch) from bottom of skirt
Piston-to-cylinder clearance	0.025 to 0.045 mm (0.0010 to 0.0018 inches)
Piston pin bore	13.002 to 13.013 mm (0.5119 to 0.5123 inch)
Piston pin outer diameter	12.996 to 13.000 mm (0.5117 to 0.5118 inch)
Piston pin-to-piston clearance	Not specified
Ring side clearance	
Top ring	
Standard...	0.30 to 0.65 mm (0.0012 to 0.0026 inch)
Limit	0.12 mm (0.005 inch)
Second ring	
Standard...	0.20 to 0.55 mm (0.0008 to 0.0022 inch)
Limit	0.12 mm (0.005 inch)
Ring end gap	
Measuring point	0.5 mm (0.20 inch) from top of cylinder
Top and second rings	
Standard...	0.10 to 0.25 mm (0.004 to 0.010 inch)
Limit	0.4 mm (0.016 inch)
Oil ring	
Standard...	0.2 to 0.7 mm (0.01 to 0.03 inch)
Limit	Not specified

Primary (centrifugal) clutch

Weight lining thickness (groove depth)	
Standard...	1.0 to 1.3 mm (0.039 to 0.051 inch)
Limit	0.1 mm (0.004 inch)
Clutch drum inside diameter	
Standard...	105 mm (4.13 inches)
Limit	106 mm (4.17 inches)

Secondary clutch

Spring free length	
Standard...	26.2 mm (1.03 inches)
Limit	24.2 mm (0.95 inch)
Metal plate warp limit	0.2 mm (0.008 inch)

Friction plate thickness
  Standard .... 2.7 to 2.9 mm (0.106 to 0.114 inch)
  Limit .... 2.6 mm (0.102 inch)

Oil pump
Outer rotor-to-body clearance .... 0.06 to 0.10 mm (0.0024 to 0.0039 inch)
Inner-to-outer rotor clearance
  Standard .... 0.15 mm (0.006 inch) or less
  Limit .... 0.20 mm (0.008 inch)
Rotor side clearance (to straightedge)
  Standard .... 0.13 to 0.18 mm (0.005 to 0.007 inch)
  Limit .... 0.23 mm (0.009 inch)

Crankshaft and connecting rod
Runout limit .... 0.03 mm (0.0012 inch)
Assembly width .... 42.95 to 43.00 mm (1.691 to 1.693 inches)
Connecting rod big-end side clearance
  Standard .... 0.1 to 0.4 mm (0.0039 to 0.0157 inch)
  Limit .... 0.50 mm (0.02 inch)
Connecting rod big-end radial clearance
  Standard .... 0.010 to 0.025 mm (0.0004 to 0.0010 inch)
  Limit .... 0.05 mm (0.002 inch)

Torque specifications
Cylinder head Allen bolts.. 10 Nm (84 in-lbs) (1)
Cylinder head nuts .... 22 Nm (16 ft-lbs) (1)
Cam sprocket cover Allen bolts .... 7 Nm (61 in-lbs)
Camshaft bearing retainer bolts .... 8 Nm (70 inch-lbs)
Cam chain guide bolt .... 10 Nm (84 in-lbs) (2)
Camshaft sprocket bolt... 20 Nm (14 ft-lbs)
Cam chain tensioner body bolts .... 10 Nm (84 in-lbs)
Cam chain tensioner cap bolt .... 8 Nm (70 in-lbs)
Crankcase bolts .... 10 Nm (84 in-lbs)
Crankcase cover bolts.. 7 Nm (61 in-lbs)
Main axle bearing retainer screws... 10 Nm (84 in-lbs) (3)
Oil pump screws... 7 Nm (61 inch-lbs)
Clutch boss nut .... 60 Nm (43 ft-lbs) (3)
Clutch spring plate bolts .... 6 Nm (72 inch-lbs)
Primary clutch nut .... 50 Nm (36 ft-lbs)
Cylinder studs to crankshaft .... 13 (156 inch-lbs)
Engine mounting bolts/nuts
  Upper front.. 30 Nm (22 ft-lbs)
  Upper rear .... 26 Nm (19 ft-lbs)
  Lower rear .... 40 Nm (29 ft-lbs)

1 Apply engine oil to the threads.
2 Apply non-permanent thread locking agent to the threads.
3 Use a new lockwasher.

TT-R125 models

General
Bore.. 54 mm (2.126 inches)
Stroke .... 54 mm (2.126 inches)
Displacement.. 123.7 cc

Rocker arms
Rocker arm inside diameter
  Standard .... 10.000 to 10.015 mm (0.3937 to 0.3943 inch)
  Limit .... 10.03 mm (0.3949 inch)
Rocker shaft outside diameter
  Standard .... 9.981 to 9.991 mm (0.3930 to 0.3933 inch)
  Limit .... 9.95 mm (0.3917 inch)
Shaft-to-arm clearance .... Not specified

Camshaft
Lobe height
  Intake
    Standard .... 25.881 to 25.981 mm (1.0189 to 1.0229 inches)
    Limit... 25.851 mm (1.0178 inches)

TT-R125 models (continued)

Camshaft (continued)
Lobe height
   Exhaust
      Standard .... 25.841 to 25.941 mm (1.0174 to 1.0213 inches)
      Limit .... 25.811 mm (1.0162 inches)
Camshaft runout limit .... 0.03 mm (0.012 inch)

Cylinder head, valves and valve springs
Cylinder head warpage limit .... 0.03 mm 0.0012 inch)
Valve stem runout .... 0.01 mm (0.0004 inch)
Valve stem diameter
   Intake
      Standard .... 4.975 to 4.990 mm (0.1959 to 0.1965 inch)
      Limit .... 4.95 mm (0.1949 inch)
   Exhaust
      Standard .... 4.960 to 4.975 mm (0.1953 to 0.1959 inch)
      Limit .... 4.935mm (0.1943 inch)
Valve guide inside diameter
   Standard .... 5.000 to 5.012 mm (0.1969 to 0.1973 inch)
   Limit .... 5.042 mm (0.1985 inch)
Stem-to-guide clearance
   Intake
      Standard .... 0.010 to 0.037 mm (0.0004 to 0.0015 inch)
      Limit .... 0.08 mm (0.0031 inch)
   Exhaust
      Standard .... 0.025 to 0.052 mm (0.0010 to 0.0020 inch)
      Limit .... 0.10 mm (0.004 inch)
Valve seat width
   Standard .... 0.9 to 1.1 mm (0.0354 to 0.0433 inch)
   Limit .... 1.6 mm (0.063 inch)
Valve spring free length (intake and exhaust)
   Standard .... 32.55 mm (1.28 inch)
   Limit .... 31.2 mm (1.23 inch)
Valve spring bend limit .... 1.4 mm (0.06 inch)

Cylinder
Bore diameter .... 54.000 to 54.019 mm (2.1260 to 2.1267inches)
Out-of-round and taper limit .... 0.05 mm (0.002 inch)
Measuring point .... Not specified

Piston
Diameter .... 53.977 to 53.996 mm (2.1251 to 2.1258 inches)
Measuring point .... 5 mm (0.2 inch) from bottom of skirt
Piston-to-cylinder clearance .... 0.020 to 0.026 mm (0.0008 to 0.0010 inches)
Piston pin bore .... 15.002 to 15.013 mm (0.5906 to 0.5911 inch)
Piston pin outer diameter .... 14.991 to 15.000 mm (0.5902 to 0.5906 inch)
Piston pin-to-piston clearance .... Not specified
Ring side clearance
   Top ring
      Standard .... 0.035 to 0.090 mm (0.0014 to 0.0035 inch)
      Limit .... 0.12 mm (0.0047 inch)
   Second ring
      Standard .... 0.020 to 0.060 mm (0.0008 to 0.0024 inch)
      Limit .... 0.12 mm (0.0047 inch)
Ring end gap
   Top ring
      Standard .... 0.15 to 0.30 mm (0.006 to 0.012 inch)
      Limit .... 0.4 mm (0.16 inch)
   Second ring
      Standard .... 0.30 to 0.45 mm (0.012 to 0.018 inch)
      Limit .... 0.55 mm (0.022 inch)
   Oil ring
      Standard .... 0.2 to 0.7 mm (0.010 to 0.030 inch)
      Limit .... Not specified

Clutch
Spring free length
   Standard .... 33 mm (1.30 inches)
   Limit .... 31 mm (1.22 inches)

Metal plate thickness	1.05 to 1.35 mm (0.041 to 0.053 inch)
Friction plate thickness	
Standard	2.92 to 3.08 mm (0.115 to 0.121 inch)
Limit	2.8 mm (0.110 inch)
Friction and metal plate warpage limit	0.20 mm (0.008 inch)

Oil pump

Outer rotor-to-body clearance	
Standard	0.06 to 0.10 mm (0.0024 to 0.0039 inch)
Limit	0.15 mm (0.006 inch)
Inner-to-outer rotor clearance	
Standard	0.15 mm (0.006 inch) or less
Limit	0.20 mm (0.008 inch)
Rotor to straightedge clearance	
Standard	0.06 to 0.10 mm (0.0024 to 0.0039 inch)
Limit	0.15 mm (0.006 inch)

Transmission

Main axle and driveaxle runout limit	Not specified

Crankshaft and connecting rod

Runout limit	0.03 mm (0.0012 inch)
Assembly width	49.65 to 47.00 mm (1.848 to 1.850 inches)
Connecting rod big-end side clearance	
Standard	0.15 to 0.45 mm (0.006 to 0.012 inch)
Limit	0.5 mm (0.020 inch)

Torque specifications

Cylinder head Allen bolts	10 Nm (84 in-lbs) (1)
Cylinder head bolts	22 Nm (16 ft-lbs) (1)
Cam sprocket cover Allen bolts	10 Nm (84 in-lbs)
Oil check bolt	7 Nm (61 inch-lbs)
Camshaft bearing retainer bolt	10 Nm (84 inch-lbs)
Cam chain guide bolts	10 Nm (84 in-lbs) (2)
Camshaft sprocket bolt	20 Nm (14 ft-lbs)
Cam chain tensioner body bolts	10 Nm (84 in-lbs)
Cam chain tensioner cap bolt	8 Nm (70 in-lbs)
Crankcase screws	10 Nm (84 in-lbs)
Crankcase cover bolts	10 Nm (84 in-lbs)
Shift cam segment screw	12 Nm (108 in-lbs) (2)
Oil pump screws	7 Nm (61 inch-lbs)
Clutch locknut	60 Nm (43 ft-lbs) (1)
Clutch spring plate bolts	6 Nm (72 inch-lbs)
Engine mounting nuts/bolts	40 Nm (29 ft-lbs)

1 Apply engine oil to the threads.
2 Apply non-permanent thread locking agent to the threads.
3 Use a new lockwasher.

TT-R225 and XT225 models

General

Bore	70 mm (2.76 inches)
Stroke	58 mm (2.28 inches)
Displacement	223.21 cc

Rocker arms

Rocker arm inside diameter	12.000 to 12.018 mm (0.4724 to 0.4731 inch)
Rocker shaft outside diameter	11.981 to 11.991 mm (0.4717 to 0.4721 inch)
Shaft-to-arm clearance	0.009 to 0.037 mm (0.0004 to 0.0015 inch)

Camshaft

Lobe height	
Intake	36.51 to 36.61 mm (1.437 to 1.441 inches)
Exhaust	35.61 to 363.61 mm (1.437 to 1.441 inches)
Camshaft runout limit	0.03 mm (0.012 inch)

Cylinder head, valves and valve springs

Cylinder head warpage limit	0.03 mm 0.0012 inch)
Valve stem runout	0.01 mm (0.0004 inch)

TT-R225 and XT225 models (continued)

Cylinder head, valves and valve springs (continued)

Valve stem diameter

    Intake .... 5.975 to 5.990 mm (0.2352 to 0.2358 inch)

    Exhaust .... 5.960 to 5.975 mm (0.2346 to 0.2352 inch)

Valve guide inside diameter .... 6.000 to 6.012 mm (0.2362 to 0.2367 inch)

Stem-to-guide clearance

    Intake .... 0.010 to 0.037 mm (0.0004 to 0.0015 inch)

    Exhaust .... 0.025 to 0.052 mm (0.0010 to 0.0020 inch)

Valve seat width .... 0.9 to 1.1 mm (0.039 to 0.047 inch)

Valve spring free length

    Inner spring .... 36.17 mm (1.424 inch)

    Outer spring .... 36.63 mm (1.442inch)

Valve spring bend limit .... 1.6 mm (0.063 inch)

Cylinder

Bore diameter .... 69.970 to 70.020 mm (2.7547 to 2.7567 inches)

    Diameter limit .... 70.1 mm (2.76 inches)

Out-of-round limit .... Not specified

Taper limit .... Not specified

Measuring point .... 40 mm (1.57 inches) from top of bore

Piston

Diameter .... 69.925 to 69.975 mm (2.7530 to 2.7549 inches)

Measuring point .... 4.0 mm (0.16 inch) from bottom of skirt

Piston-to-cylinder clearance

    Standard .... 0.035 to 0.055 mm (0.0014 to 0.0022 inches)

    Limit .... 0.10 mm (0.004 inch)

Piston pin bore .... Not specified

Piston pin outer diameter .... Not specified

Piston pin-to-piston clearance .... Not specified

Ring side clearance

    Top rings .... 0.03 to 0.07 mm (0.001 to 0.003 inch)

    Second ring .... 0.02 to 0.06 mm (0.001 to 0.002 inch)

Ring end gap

    Top and second rings .... 0.15 to 0.30 mm (0.006 to 0.012 inch)

    Oil ring .... 0.3 to 0.9 mm (0.012 to 0.035 inch)

Clutch

Spring free length .... 37.3 mm (1.47 inches)

Metal plate thickness .... 1.50 to 1.70 mm (0.059 to 0.067 inch)

Friction and metal plate warpage limit .... 0.20 mm (0.008 inch)

Oil pump

Outer rotor-to-body clearance .... Not specified

Inner-to-outer rotor clearance .... 0.15 mm (0.006 inch) or less

Rotor to straightedge clearance .... 0.04 to 0.09 mm (0.002 to 0.004 inch)

Transmission

Main axle and driveaxle runout limit .... 0.08 mm (0.0031 inch)

Crankshaft and connecting rod

Runout limit .... 0.03 mm(0.0012 inch)

Assembly width .... 55.95 to 56.00 mm (2.203 to 2.205 inches)

Connecting rod big-end side clearance

    Standard .... 0.35 to 0.65 mm (0.013 to 0.026 inch)

Connecting rod small-end endplay limit .... 0.8 (0.031 inch)

Torque specifications

Cylinder head Allen bolts .... 20 Nm (168 in-lbs) (1)

Cylinder head bolts .... 22 Nm (17 ft-lbs) (1)

Cylinder base Allen bolts .... 10 Nm (84 in-lbs)

Cam sprocket cover Allen bolts .... 10 Nm (84 in-lbs)

Oil check bolt .... 7 Nm (61 inch-lbs)

Camshaft bearing retainer bolts .... 8 Nm (70 inch-lbs)

Cam chain guide bolts .... 10 Nm (84 in-lbs) (2)

Camshaft sprocket bolt .... 60 Nm (43 ft-lbs)

Cam chain tensioner body bolts .... 10 Nm (84 in-lbs)

Cam chain tensioner cap bolt .... 7 Nm (61 in-lbs)

Crankcase screws	7 Nm (61 in-lbs)
Crankcase cover screws	7 Nm (61 in-lbs)
Shift cam segment screw	12 Nm (108 in-lbs) (2)
Oil pump screws	Not specified
Clutch boss nut	70 Nm (51 ft-lbs) (1)
Clutch spring plate bolts	6 Nm (52 inch-lbs)
Balancer drive gear nut	50 Nm (36 ft-lbs) (1)
Balancer shaft and driven gear nut	50 Nm (36 ft-lbs) (1)
Engine mounting bolts/nuts	
Swingarm pivot shaft	80 Nm (58 ft-lbs)
Upper mount to frame	37.5 Nm (27 ft-lbs)
Upper front mount bolt	32.5 Nm (24 ft-lbs)
Lower front and lower rear	32.5 Nm (24 ft-lbs)

1   *Apply engine oil to the threads.*
2   *Apply non-permanent thread locking agent to the threads.*

TT-R250 models

General

Bore	73 mm (2.87 inches)
Stroke	59.6 mm (2.35 inches)
Displacement	249 cc

Camshaft

Lobe height (intake and exhaust)	
Standard	32.75 to 32.85 mm (1.2894 to 1.2933 inches)
Limit	32.7 mm (1.287 inches)
Camshaft runout limit	0.03 mm (0.012 inch)
Bearing oil clearance	
Standard	0.020 to 0.054 mm (0.0008 to 0.0021 inch)
Limit	0.08 mm (0.0031 inch)

Cylinder head, valves and valve springs

Cylinder head warpage limit	0.03 mm 0.0012 inch)
Valve stem runout	0.01 mm (0.0004 inch)
Valve stem diameter	
Intake	
Standard	4.975 to 4.990 mm (0.1959 to 0.1965 inch)
Limit	4.95 mm (0.195 inch)
Exhaust	
Standard	4.960 to 4.975 mm (0.1953 to 0.1959 inch)
Limit	4.94 mm (0.194 inch)
Valve guide inside diameter	
Standard	5.000 to 5.012 mm (0.1969 to 0.1973 inch)
Limit	5.03 mm (0.198 inch)
Stem-to-guide clearance	
Intake	
Standard	0.010 to 0.037 mm (0.0004 to 0.0015 inch)
Limit	0.08 mm (0.0031 inch)
Exhaust	
Standard	0.025 to 0.052 mm (0.0010 to 0.0020 inch)
Limit	0.1 mm (0.004 inch)
Valve seat width (intake and exhaust)	
Standard	0.9 to 1.1 mm (0.0354 to 0.0433 inch)
Limit	1.6 mm (0.063 inch)
Valve spring free length (intake and exhaust)	
Standard	35.59 mm (1.40 inch)
Limit	33.81 mm (1.33 inch)
Valve spring bend limit	1.6 mm (0.063 inch)

Cylinder

Bore diameter	
Standard	72.97 to 73.02 mm (2.8728 to 2.8748 inches)
Limit	73.1 mm (2.8779 inches)
Out-of-round limit	0.03 mm (0.0012 inch)
Taper limit	Not specified
Measuring point	40 mm (1.57 inches) from top of bore

TT-R250 models (continued)

Piston
Diameter	72.92 to 72.97 mm (2.8709 to 2.8728 inches)
Measuring point	1.0 mm (0.039 inch) from bottom of skirt

Piston-to-cylinder clearance
Standard	0.04 to 0.06 mm (0.0016 to 0.0024 inches)
Limit	0.15 mm (0.006 inch)

Piston pin bore
Standard	18.004 to 18.015 mm (0.7088 to 0.7093 inch)
Limit	18.045 mm (0.71 inch)

Piston pin outer diameter
Standard	17.991 to 18.000 mm (0.7083 to 0.7087 inch)
Limit	17.976 mm (0.71 inch)

Piston pin-to-piston clearance	Not specified

Ring side clearance

Top ring
Standard	0.04 to 0.08 mm (0.0016 to 0.0031 inch)
Limit	0.12 mm (0.0047 inch)

Second ring
Standard	0.03 to 0.07 mm (0.001 to 0.003 inch)
Limit	0.12 mm (0.0047 inch)

Oil ring
Standard	0.2 to 0.7 mm (0.008 to 0.028 inch)
Limit	Not specified

Ring end gap

Top ring
Standard	0.20 to 0.35 mm (0.008 to 0.014 inch)
Limit	0.4 mm (0.16 inch)

Second ring
Standard	0.20 to 0.35 mm (0.008 to 0.014 inch)
Limit	0.4 mm (0.16 inch)

Oil ring
Standard	0.2 to 0.7 mm (0.008 to 0.028 inch)
Limit	Not specified

Clutch

Spring free length
Standard	42.8 mm (1.69 inches)
Limit	40.8 mm (1.61 inches)
Metal plate thickness	1.5 to 1.7 mm (0.059 to 0.067 inch)

Friction plate thickness
Standard	2.9 to 3.1 mm (0.114 to 0.122 inch)
Limit	2.7 mm (0.11 inch)
Friction and metal plate warpage limit	0.05 mm (0.002 inch)

Oil pump
Outer rotor-to-body clearance	0.10 to 0.15 mm (0.004 to 0.006 inch)

Inner-to-outer rotor clearance
Standard	0.15 mm (0.006 inch) or less
Limit	0.20 mm (0.008 inch)

Rotor to straightedge clearance
Standard	0.04 to 0.09 mm (0.002 to 0.004 inch)
Limit	0.15 mm (0.006 inch)

Transmission
Main axle and driveaxle runout limit	0.08 mm (0.0031 inch)

Crankshaft and connecting rod
Runout limit	0.03 mm (0.0012 inch)
Assembly width	60.25 to 60.30 mm (2.372 to 2.374 inches)
Connecting rod big-end side clearance	0.35 to 0.85 mm (0.014 to 0.033 inch)
Connecting rod small-end endplay	0.8 mm (0.0315 inch)

Torque specifications
Cylinder head Allen bolts	10 Nm (86 in-lbs) (1)
Cylinder head bolts	40 Nm (29 ft-lbs) (1)
Cylinder cover bolts	10 Nm (84 in-lbs)
Oil check bolt	7 Nm (61 inch-lbs)
Camshaft bearing cap bolts	8 Nm (70 inch-lbs)

Cam chain guide bolts	8 Nm (70 in-lbs) (2)
Camshaft sprocket bolt	24 Nm (17 ft-lbs)
Cam chain tensioner body bolts	10 Nm (84 in-lbs)
Cam chain tensioner cap bolt	8 Nm (70 in-lbs)
Crankcase bolts	10 Nm (84 in-lbs)
Crankcase cover bolts	10 Nm (84 in-lbs)
Oil pump screws	6 Nm (52 inch-lbs)
Clutch boss nut	75 Nm (54 ft-lbs) (3)
Clutch spring plate bolts	8 Nm (70 inch-lbs)
Engine mounting bolts/nuts	
Upper rear bracket to frame	23 Nm (17 ft-lbs)
Upper rear bracket to engine	64 Nm (46 ft-lbs)
Cylinder head bracket to frame	30 Nm (22 ft-lbs)
Cylinder head bracket to engine	64 Nm (46 ft-lbs)
Front bracket to frame	30 Nm (22 ft-lbs)
Front bracket to engine	64 Nm (46 ft-lbs)

1 *Apply engine oil to the threads.*
2 *Apply non-permanent thread locking agent to the threads.*
3 *Use a new lockwasher.*

XT350 models

General

Bore	86.0 mm (3.39 inches)
Stroke	59.6 mm (2.35 inches)
Displacement	346 cc

Camshaft

Lobe height (intake and exhaust)	353.75 to 35.85 mm (1.407 to 1.411 inches)
Camshaft runout limit	0.03 mm (0.012 inch)

Cylinder head, valves and valve springs

Cylinder head warpage limit	0.03 mm 0.0012 inch)
Valve stem runout	0.01 mm (0.0004 inch)
Valve stem diameter	
Intake	5.475 to 5.490 mm (0.2156 to 0.2161 inch)
Exhaust	5.460 to 5.4765 mm (0.2150 to 0.21256 inch)
Valve guide inside diameter	
Standard	5.500 to 5.512 mm (0.2165 to 0.2170 inch)
Limit	5.6 mm (0.22 inch)
Stem-to-guide clearance	
Intake	0.010 to 0.037 mm (0.0004 to 0.0015 inch)
Exhaust	0.025 to 0.040 mm (0.0010 to 0.0016 inch)
Valve seat width	0.9 to 1.1 mm (0.035 to 0.044 inch)
Valve spring free length	
Inner spring	38.1 mm (1.500 inch)
Outer spring	41.2 mm (1.622 inch)
Valve spring bend limit	1.7 mm (0.067 inch)

Cylinder

Bore diameter	85.97 to 86.02 mm (3.385 to 3.387 inches)
Out-of-round limit	Not specified
Taper limit	0.08 mm (0.003 inch)
Measuring point	Top, center and bottom of bore

Piston

Diameter	85.92 to 85.97 mm (3.383 to 3.385 inches)
Measuring point	3 mm (0.12 inch) from bottom of skirt
Piston-to-cylinder clearance	0.04 to 0.06 mm (0.0016 to 0.0024 inches)
Piston pin bore	Not specified
Piston pin outer diameter	Not specified
Piston pin-to-piston clearance	Not specified
Ring side clearance	
Top ring	
Standard	0.04 to 0.08 mm (0.0016 to 0.0031 inch)
Limit	0.15 mm (0.006 inch)
Second ring	
Standard	0.03 to 0.07 mm (0.001 to 0.003 inch)
Limit	0.15 mm (0.006 inch)
Oil ring	0.02 to 0.06 mm (0.0008 to 0.0024 inch)

XT350 models (continued)

Piston (continued)

Ring end gap
  Top ring
    Standard .... 0.25 to 0.40 mm (0.010 to 0.016 inch)
    Limit .... 0.8 mm (0.032 inch)
  Second ring
    Standard .... 0.25 to 0.40 mm (0.010 to 0.016 inch)
    Limit .... 0.8 mm (0.032 inch)
  Oil ring
    Standard .... 0.2 to 0.7 mm (0.008 to 0.027 inch)
    Limit .... not specified

Clutch

Spring free length
  Standard .... 41.2 mm (1.622 inches)
  Limit .... 40.3 mm (1.587 inches)
Metal plate thickness
  One plate .... 2.0 mm (0.078 inch)
  Five plates .... 1.6 mm (0.063 inch)
Friction plate thickness
  Standard .... 2.90 to 3.10 mm (114 to 0.122 inch)
  Limit .... 2.5 mm (0.098 inch)
Friction and metal plate warpage limit .... 0.05 mm (0.002 inch)

Oil pump

Outer rotor-to-body clearance .... 0.03 to 0.09 mm (0.0012 to 0.0035 inch)
Inner-to-outer rotor clearance .... 0.15 mm (0.006 inch) or less
Rotor to straightedge clearance .... 0.03 to 0.09 mm (0.001 to 0.004 inch)

Crankshaft and connecting rod

Runout limit .... 0.03 mm (0.001 inch)
Assembly width .... 58.95 to 59.00 mm (2.321 to 2.323 inches)
Connecting rod big-end side clearance .... 0.35 to 0.85 mm (0.014 to 0.033 inch)
Connecting rod small-end endplay .... 2.0 mm (0.08 inch)

Torque specifications

Cylinder head Allen bolts .... 10 Nm (84 in-lbs) (1)
Cylinder head bolts .... 40 Nm (29 ft-lbs) (1)
Cam bearing cap bolts .... 10 Nm (84 in-lbs)
Oil check bolt .... 7 Nm (61 inch-lbs)
Cam chain guide bolts .... 8 Nm (70 in-lbs) (2)
Camshaft sprocket bolts .... 20 Nm (14 ft-lbs)
Cam chain tensioner body bolts .... 11 Nm (108 in-lbs)
Cam chain tensioner cap bolt .... 6 Nm (72 in-lbs)
Crankcase screws .... 7 Nm (61 in-lbs)
Crankcase cover screws .... 7 Nm (61 in-lbs)
Shift cam segment screw .... 12 Nm (108 in-lbs) (2)
Oil pump screws .... 7 Nm (61 inch-lbs)
Oil pipe banjo bolts .... 20 Nm (14 ft-lbs)
Clutch boss nut .... 60 Nm (43 ft-lbs) (3)
Clutch spring plate bolts .... 8 Nm (70 inch-lbs)
Engine mounting nuts/bolts
  Upper and front mounting bolts .... 33 Nm (24 ft-lbs)
  Rear mounting bolts .... 38 Nm (27 ft-lbs)
  Swingarm pivot shaft .... 85 Nm (61 ft-lbs)

1 *Apply engine oil to the threads.*
2 *Apply non-permanent thread locking agent to the threads.*
3 *Use a new lockwasher.*

1 General information

The engine/transmission unit is of the air-cooled, single-cylinder four-stroke design.

TT-R90, TT-R125, XT225 and TT-R225 models have two valves (one intake and one exhaust). The valves are operated by a single overhead camshaft, which is chain driven off the crankshaft.

TT-R250 and XT350 models have four valves (two intake and two exhaust). The valves are operated by dual overhead camshafts, which are chain driven off the crankshaft.

The engine/transmission assembly is constructed from aluminum alloy. The crankcase is divided vertically.

The crankcase incorporates a wet sump, pressure-fed lubrication system which uses a gear-driven rotor-type oil pump and an oil filter. All models have a separate strainer screen.

On TT-R90 models, power from the crankshaft is routed to the transmission via two clutches. The primary (centrifugal) clutch, which engages as engine speed is increased, connects the crankshaft to the secondary clutch, which is of the wet, multi-plate type. The secondary clutch transmits power to the transmission; it's engaged and disengaged automatically when the shift lever is moved from one gear position to another.

On all except TT-R90 models, a wet, multi-plate clutch connects the crankshaft to the transmission. Engagement and disengagement of the clutch is controlled by a lever on the left handlebar.

The transmission has three forward gears (TT-R90), five forward gears (TT-R125) and six forward gears (all others).

A kickstarter is used on TT-R90, TT-R125 and XT350 models. The XT350 is equipped with a decompression lever that makes it easier to crank the engine with the kickstarter. TT-R225, TT-R250 and XT350 models use electric starters.

2 Operations possible with the engine in the frame

The components and assemblies listed below can be removed without having to remove the engine from the frame. If, however, a number of areas require attention at the same time, removal of the engine is recommended.

Kickstarter (if equipped)
Starter motor (if equipped)
Starter reduction gears (if equipped)
Starter clutch (if equipped)
Magneto rotor and stator
Clutch(es)
External shift mechanism
Cam chain tensioner
Camshaft(s)
Rocker arms and shafts (if equipped)
Cylinder head
Cylinder and piston
Oil pump
Balancer gears (if equipped)

3 Operations requiring engine removal

It is necessary to remove the engine/transmission assembly from the frame and separate the crankcase halves to gain access to the following components:

Crankshaft and connecting rod
Transmission shafts
Shift drum and forks

4 Major engine repair - general note

1   It is not always easy to determine when or if an engine should be completely overhauled, as a number of factors must be considered.

2   High mileage is not necessarily an indication that an overhaul is needed, while low mileage, on the other hand, does not preclude the need for an overhaul. Frequency of servicing is probably the single most important consideration. An engine that has regular and frequent oil and filter changes, as well as other required maintenance, will most likely give many miles of reliable service. Conversely, a neglected engine, or one which has not been broken in properly, may require an overhaul very early in its life.

3   Exhaust smoke and excessive oil consumption are both indications that piston rings and/or valve guides are in need of attention. Make sure oil leaks are not responsible before deciding that the rings and guides are bad. Refer to Chapter 1 and perform a cylinder compression check to determine for certain the nature and extent of the work required.

4   If the engine is making obvious knocking or rumbling noises, the connecting rod and/or main bearings are probably at fault.

5   Loss of power, rough running, excessive valve train noise and high fuel consumption rates may also point to the need for an overhaul, especially if they are all present at the same time. If a complete tune-up does not remedy the situation, major mechanical work is the only solution.

6   An engine overhaul generally involves restoring the internal parts to the specifications of a new engine. During an overhaul the piston rings are replaced and the cylinder walls are bored and/or honed. If a rebore is done, then a new piston is also required. Generally the valves are serviced as well, since they are usually in less than perfect condition at this point. While the engine is being overhauled, other components such as the carburetor and the starter motor (if equipped) can be rebuilt also. The end result should be a like-new engine that will give as many trouble-free miles as the original.

7   Before beginning the engine overhaul, read through all of the related procedures to familiarize yourself with the scope and requirements of the job. Overhauling an engine is not all that difficult, but it is time consuming. Plan on the vehicle being tied up for a minimum of two (2) weeks. Check on the availability of parts and make sure that any necessary special tools, equipment and supplies are obtained in advance.

8   Most work can be done with typical shop hand tools, although a number of precision measuring tools are required for inspecting parts to determine if they must be replaced. Often a dealer service department or repair shop will handle the inspection of parts and offer advice concerning reconditioning and replacement. As a general rule, time is the primary cost of an overhaul so it doesn't pay to install worn or substandard parts.

9   As a final note, to ensure maximum life and minimum trouble from a rebuilt engine, everything must be assembled with care in a spotlessly clean environment.

5 Engine - removal and installation

Warning: *Engine removal and installation should be done with the aid of an assistant to avoid damage or injury that could occur if the engine is dropped.*

Removal

1   Drain the engine oil (see Chapter 1).

2   If the motorcycle has a battery, disconnect the ground cable from the engine and disconnect both battery cables.

3   Remove the seat. Remove the air scoops and side covers (if equipped). If the bike has guard bars or a skid plate, remove it (see Chapter 7).

4   Remove the fuel tank, carburetor and exhaust system (see Chapter 3).

5   On all except TT-R90 models, remove the clutch cable (see Section 16).

6   Disconnect the odometer/speedometer/tachometer cable if equipped).

7   Remove the starter motor (if equipped) (see Chapter 4).

8   If you're working on a TT-R250, detach the rear shock absorber gas reservoir from the frame and set it out of the way.

9 Disconnect the crankcase breather hose (see Chapter 1).

10 If you're working on a California XT225, remove the evaporative emission canister (see Chapter 3).

11 Disconnect the spark plug wire (see Chapter 1).

12 Label and disconnect the following wires (see Chapter 4 for component locations if necessary):

CDI magneto and alternator

Neutral switch

13 If you're working on an XT225, remove the horn (see Chapter 4).

14 Remove the shift pedal (see Section 21).

15 If you're working on a TT-R225, TT-R250, XT225 or XT350, remove the brake pedal (see Chapter 6C) and both footpegs (see Chapter 7).

16 Remove the drive sprocket from the engine (see Chapter 5C).

17 Support the engine securely from below.

18 Remove the engine mounting bolts, nuts and brackets at the front, lower front, lower rear and upper rear. **Note:** *On TT-R225, TT-R250, XT225 and XT350 models, the swingarm pivot bolt acts as an engine mounting bolt. Pull out the bolt just far enough to free the engine, but leave it in far enough to support one side of the swingarm.*

19 Have an assistant help you support the engine. Lower the engine out of the bike (TT-R90), remove it from the left side (TT-R125) or remove it from the right side (all others).

20 Slowly lower the engine to a suitable work surface.

Installation

21 Check the engine supports for wear or damage and replace them if necessary before installing the engine.

22 Make sure the motorcycle is securely supported so it can't be knocked over during the remainder of this procedure.

23 With the help of an assistant, lift the engine up into the frame. Install the mounting nuts and bolts at the rear, front and top. Finger-tighten the mounting bolts, but don't tighten them to the specified torque yet.

24 Tighten the engine mounting bolts and nuts evenly to the torques listed in this Chapter's Specifications.

25 The remainder of installation is the reverse of the removal steps, with the following additions:

a) Use new gaskets at all exhaust pipe connections.

b) Adjust the throttle cable and clutch cable (except TT-R90) following the procedures in Chapter 1.

c) Fill the engine with oil, also following the procedures in Chapter 1. Run the engine and check for oil and exhaust leaks.

6 Engine disassembly and reassembly - general information

1 Before disassembling the engine, clean the exterior with a degreaser and rinse it with water. A clean engine will make the job easier and prevent the possibility of getting dirt into the internal areas of the engine.

2 In addition to the precision measuring tools mentioned earlier, you will need a torque wrench, a valve spring compressor, oil gallery brushes **(see illustration 6.2 in Chapter 2A)**, a piston ring removal and installation tool, a piston ring compressor. Some new, clean engine oil of the correct grade and type, some engine assembly lube (or moly-based grease) and a tube of RTV (silicone) sealant will also be required.

3 An engine support stand made from short lengths of 2 x 4's bolted together will facilitate the disassembly and reassembly procedures **(see illustration 6.3 in Chapter 2A)**. If you have an automotive-type engine stand, an adapter plate can be made from a piece of plate, some angle iron and some nuts and bolts.

4 When disassembling the engine, keep "mated" parts together (including gears, rocker arms and shafts, etc.) that have been in contact with each other during engine operation. These "mated" parts must be reused or replaced as an assembly.

5 Engine/transmission disassembly should be done in the following general order with reference to the appropriate Sections.

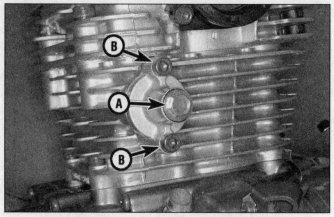

7.1 Loosen the tensioner cap bolt (A), then remove the tensioner bolts (B) and take the tensioner off

Remove the cam chain tensioner

Remove the cylinder head, rocker arms (single cam models) and camshaft(s)

Remove the cylinder

Remove the piston

Remove the clutch (primary and secondary clutches on TT-R90 models)

Remove the balancer gears (if equipped)

Remove the oil pump

Remove the external shift mechanism

Remove the alternator rotor

Remove the starter reduction gears (if equipped)

Separate the crankcase halves

Remove the shift drum and forks

Remove the transmission gears and shafts

Remove the balancer shaft (if equipped)

Remove the crankshaft and connecting rod

6 Reassembly is accomplished by reversing the general disassembly sequence.

7 Cam chain tensioner - removal and installation

Removal

TT-R90 models

Refer to illustrations 7.1 and 7.3

Caution: *Once you start to remove the tensioner bolts you must remove the tensioner all the way and reset it before tightening the bolts. The tensioner extends and locks in place, so if you loosen the bolts partway and then tighten them, the tensioner or cam chain will be damaged.*

1 Loosen the tensioner cap bolt **(see illustration)**.

2 Remove the tensioner mounting bolts and detach the tensioner form the cylinder.

3 If necessary, unscrew the tensioner cap bolt and remove the spring **(see illustration)**.

Installation

Refer to illustrations 7.6a and 7.6b

3 Clean all old gasket material from the tensioner body and engine.

4 Lubricate the friction surfaces of the components with moly-based grease.

5 Install a new tensioner gasket on the cylinder.

6 Lift the latch, compress the tensioner piston all the way into the body and release the latch **(see illustrations)**.

7 Position the tensioner on the cylinder and install the bolts, tightening them to the torque listed in this Chapter's Specifications.

8 Install the spring and cap bolt, using a new sealing washer, and tighten them to the torque listed in this Chapter's Specifications.

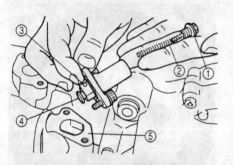

7.3 Cam chain tensioner details (TT-R-90 models)

1 Cap bolt	4 Piston
2 Spring	5 Gasket
3 Latch	

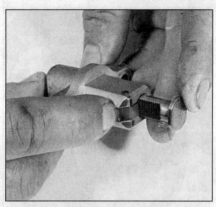

7.6a Lift the latch, press the piston into the tensioner and release the latch

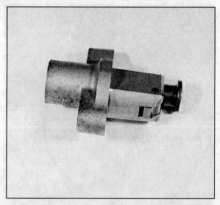

7.6b The piston should be retracted like this when the tensioner is installed

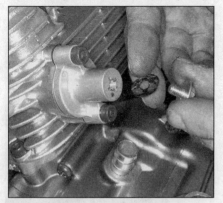

7.9 Remove the cap bolt and gasket

7.11 Place a new gasket on the tensioner body

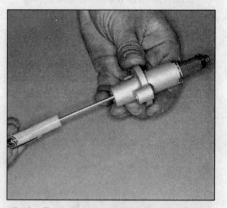

7.12a Turn the screwdriver clockwise to retract the piston . . .

All except TT-R90 models

Refer to illustrations 7.9, 7.11, 7.12a and 7.12b

9   Unscrew the tensioner cap bolt and remove the gasket **(see illustration)**. Remove the tensioner mounting bolts and take it off the engine.

10   Clean all old gasket material from the tensioner body and engine.

11   Place a new gasket on the tensioner body **(see illustration)**.

12   Insert a narrow-bladed screwdriver into the tensioner and rotate it clockwise to retract the tension piston **(see illustrations)**. Hold the screwdriver in position while installing the tensioner on the cylinder.

13   Position the tensioner body on the cylinder and install the bolts, tightening them to the torque listed in this Chapter's Specifications.

14   Remove the screwdriver so the tensioner piston can extend.

15   Install the cap bolt with a new sealing washer and tighten it to the torque listed in this Chapter's Specifications.

---

8   Cylinder head, camshaft and rocker arms (single cam models) - removal, inspection and installation

---

Removal

Camshaft

Refer to illustrations 8.2a, 8.2b, 8.3, 8.5a, 8.5b and 8.6

1   Remove the valve adjusting hole covers (see Chapter 1).

2   Remove the bolts and take the camshaft sprocket cover off **(see**

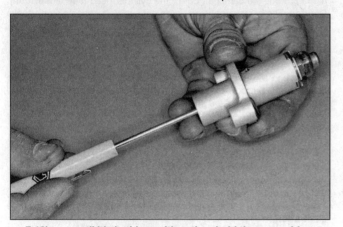

7.12b . . . until it's in this position, then hold the screwdriver

8.2a Camshaft cover styling differs from model to model, but all are secured by two screws (shown) or Allen bolts

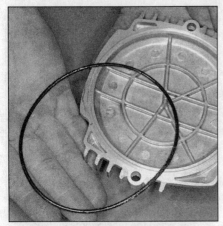

8.2b Remove the cover and O-ring

8.3 With the engine at TDC compression, the sprocket line should be even with the cast indicator in the cylinder head (arrows)

8.5a The camshaft dowel aligns with the sprocket line and the cast indicator

8.5b If there's a lockwasher, bend back its tabs, remove the bolt (TT-R90 and TT-R125) or two bolts (all others) and take off the lockwasher and retainer

8.6 Thread a 10 mm bolt into the camshaft and pull on it to remove the camshaft and outer bearing

8.7 Thread a bolt into each rocker shaft and pull it out

illustrations).

3   Refer to *Valve clearances - check and adjustment* in Chapter 1 and place the engine at top dead center on the compression stroke. The cam sprocket mark will align with the indicator cast into the cylinder head **(see illustration)** and the rocker arms will be loose when the cylinder is at TDC compression.

8.8 Remove the two Allen bolts

4   Use the socket on the alternator rotor bolt to keep the crankshaft from turning while you remove the cam sprocket bolt.

5   Unbolt the cam sprocket and take it off the camshaft **(see illustration)**. Disengage the sprocket from the chain and support the chain with wire so it doesn't fall down off the crankshaft sprocket. Unbolt the camshaft retainer from the head **(see illustration)**.

6   Thread a 10 mm bolt into the end of the camshaft and use it as a handle to pull the camshaft out of the cylinder head **(see illustration)**. **Caution:** *The camshaft should come out easily. If it seems stuck, make sure it isn't caught on the rocker arms.*

Rocker arms

Refer to illustration 8.7

7   Thread a 6 mm bolt into the end of each rocker arm shaft **(see illustration)**. Support the rocker and use the bolt as a handle to pull out the shaft. **Note:** *If the shaft is stuck, it may be necessary to use a slide hammer. These can be rented from equipment rental yards (some auto parts stores also rent tools).*

Cylinder head

Refer to illustrations 8.8, 8.9 and 8.10

8   Remove the cylinder head Allen bolts **(see illustration)**.

9   Loosen the main cylinder head nuts (TT-R90) or bolts (all others) in several stages, in the reverse order of the tightening sequence **(see illustration)**.

10   Lift the cylinder head off the cylinder **(see illustration)**. If it's stuck, don't attempt to pry it off - tap around the sides of it with a plas-

8.9 Cylinder head nut or bolt TIGHTENING sequence; washers are used on all models

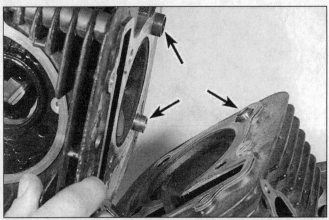

8.10 Lift the head off and locate the two dowels (TT-R90 and TT-R125) or three dowels and O-ring (TT-R225 and XT225)

8.12a Lift the front chain guide (arrow) . . .

8.12b . . . out of its cup (left arrow); to unbolt the rear chain guide (right arrows), you'll need to remove the CDI magneto

8.15a Check the cam lobes for wear - here's a good example of damage which will require replacement (or repair) of the camshaft

tic hammer to dislodge it. Be careful not to tap against the cooling fins; they're easily broken.

11 Locate the dowels. TT-R90 and TT-R125 models have two dowels, located on the side of the cylinder nearest the timing chain guides. All other models have three dowels, one with an O-ring **(see illustration 8.10)**. The dowels may be in the cylinder or they may have come off with the head.

Cam chain and guides

Refer to illustrations 8.12a and 8.12b

12 Lift the front cam chain guide out of the cylinder **(see illustrations)**. The rear guide is bolted at the bottom, so the alternator rotor and stator plate will have to be removed for access if the guide or the cam chain need to be removed.

13 Stuff clean rags into the cam chain openings so dirt, small parts or tools can't fall into them.

Inspection

Camshaft, chain and guides

Refer to illustrations 8.15a, 8.15b and 8.18

Note: *Before replacing camshafts or the cylinder head because of damage, check with local machine shops specializing in motorcycle engine work. In the case of the camshaft, it may be possible for cam lobes to be welded, reground and hardened, at a cost far lower than that of a new camshaft. If the bearing surfaces in the cylinder head are damaged, it may be possible for them to be bored out to accept bearing inserts. Due to the cost of a new cylinder head it is recommended that all options be explored before condemning it as trash!*

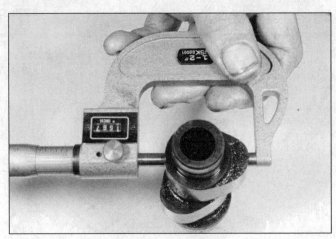

8.15b Measure the height of the cam lobes with a micrometer

14 Rotate the cam bearings and check for roughness, looseness or noise. Check the sealed side of the outer bearing for signs of leakage. Replace the bearing(s) if problems are found. On TT-R90 and TT-R125 models, the camshaft and bearings are supplied as an assembly.

15 Check the camshaft lobes for heat discoloration (blue appearance), score marks, chipped areas, flat spots and spalling **(see illustration)**. Measure the height of each lobe with a micrometer **(see illustration)** and compare the results to the minimum lobe height listed in

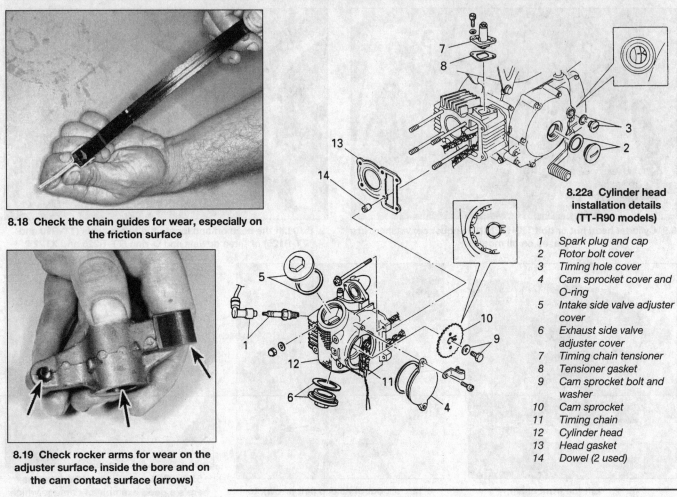

8.18 Check the chain guides for wear, especially on the friction surface

8.19 Check rocker arms for wear on the adjuster surface, inside the bore and on the cam contact surface (arrows)

8.22a Cylinder head installation details (TT-R90 models)

1   Spark plug and cap
2   Rotor bolt cover
3   Timing hole cover
4   Cam sprocket cover and O-ring
5   Intake side valve adjuster cover
6   Exhaust side valve adjuster cover
7   Timing chain tensioner
8   Tensioner gasket
9   Cam sprocket bolt and washer
10 Cam sprocket
11 Timing chain
12 Cylinder head
13 Head gasket
14 Dowel (2 used)

8.22b Cylinder head installation details (TT-R125 models)

1   Cam sprocket bolt
2   Timing chain tensioner cap bolt
3   Timing chain tensioner
4   Tensioner gasket
5   Cam sprocket
6   Cylinder head
7   Dowels (2 used)

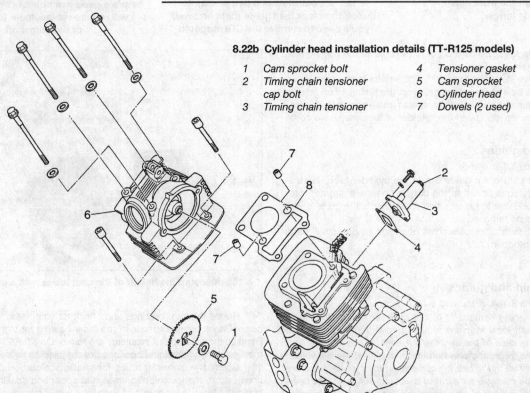

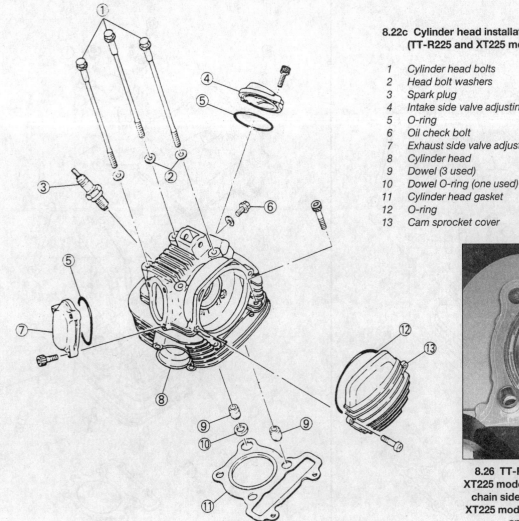

8.22c Cylinder head installation details
(TT-R225 and XT225 models)

1 *Cylinder head bolts*
2 *Head bolt washers*
3 *Spark plug*
4 *Intake side valve adjusting hole cover*
5 *O-ring*
6 *Oil check bolt*
7 *Exhaust side valve adjuster cover*
8 *Cylinder head*
9 *Dowel (3 used)*
10 *Dowel O-ring (one used)*
11 *Cylinder head gasket*
12 *O-ring*
13 *Cam sprocket cover*

**8.26 TT-R90, TT-R125, TTR-R225 and
XT225 models use two dowels on the cam
chain side (lower arrows); TT-R225 and
XT225 models also use a third dowel with
an O-ring (upper arrow)**

this Chapter's Specifications. If damage is noted or wear is excessive, the camshaft must be replaced. Check the bearing surfaces for scoring or wear. Also, be sure to check the condition of the rocker arms, as described below.

16   Except in cases of oil starvation, the camshaft chain wears very little. If the chain has stretched excessively, which makes it difficult to maintain proper tension, replace it with a new one. To remove the chain from the crankshaft sprocket, remove the clutch (see Section 16 or 17).

17   Check the sprocket for wear, cracks and other damage, replacing it if necessary. If the sprocket is worn, the chain is also worn, and possibly the sprocket on the crankshaft. If wear this severe is apparent, the entire engine should be disassembled for inspection.

18   Check the chain guides for wear or damage, especially along the friction surfaces **(see illustration)**. If they are worn or damaged, replace them.

Rocker arms and shafts

Refer to illustration 8.19

19   Check the rocker arms for wear at the cam contact surfaces, inside the shaft bores and at the tips of the valve adjusting screws **(see illustration)**. Try to twist the rocker arms from side-to-side on the shafts. If they're loose on the shafts or if there's visible wear, measure the rocker arm shaft diameter and bore diameter with a micrometer and hole gauge. If the parts are worn beyond the limits listed in this Chapter's Specifications, replace them. Replace the rocker arm and shaft as a set.

Cylinder head

20   Check the cylinder head gasket and the mating surfaces on the cylinder head and cylinder for leakage, which could indicate warpage. Refer to Section 11 and check the flatness of the cylinder head.

21   Clean all traces of old gasket material from the cylinder head and cylinder. Be careful not to let any of the gasket material fall into the crankcase, the cylinder bore or the bolt holes.

Installation

Refer to illustrations 8.22a, 8.22b, 8.22c and 8.26

22   Coat the rocker shafts and rocker arm bores with moly-based grease. Install the rocker shafts and rocker arms in the cylinder head **(see illustrations)**. Be sure to install the intake and exhaust rocker arms and shafts in the correct sides of the head.

23   Install the inner camshaft bearing in the cylinder head and the outer bearing on the camshaft (if they were removed). The sealed side of the outer bearing faces out (away from the cylinder head). Lubricate the camshaft bearings with engine oil.

24   Install the camshaft in the cylinder head with its lobes pointing down. On TT-R225 and XT225 models, the camshaft dowel should be up, so it aligns with the cast indicator in the cylinder head when the camshaft is installed **(see illustration 8.5a)**.

25   Install the bearing retainer and a new lockwasher (if equipped). Tighten the bearing retainer bolts to the torque listed in this Chapter's Specifications.

26   Install the two dowel pins (TT-R90 and TT-R125) or three dowel

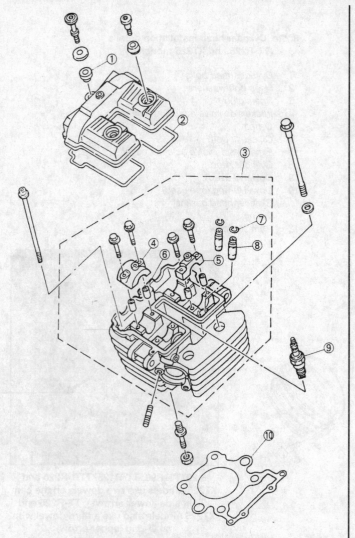

9.1a Cylinder head installation details (TT-R250 models)

1	Cover bolt grommet	6	Dowel
2	Cover gasket	7	Circlip
3	Cylinder head	8	Valve guide
4	Camshaft bearing cap	9	Spark plug
5	Camshaft bearing cap	10	Head gasket

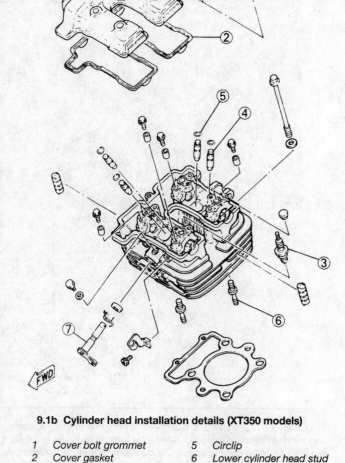

9.1b Cylinder head installation details (XT350 models)

1	Cover bolt grommet	5	Circlip
2	Cover gasket	6	Lower cylinder head stud
3	Spark plug	7	Decompression cam
4	Valve guide		

pins (TT-R225 and XT225). On TT-R225 and XT225 models, install the O-ring that surrounds one of the dowels, then place the new head gasket on the cylinder **(see illustration)**. Never reuse the old gasket and don't use any type of gasket sealant.

27   Install the exhaust side cam chain damper, fitting the lower end into its notch **(see illustration 8.12b)**.

28   Carefully lower the cylinder head over the dowels and O-ring, guiding the cam chain through the slot in the cylinder head. It's helpful to have an assistant support the cam chain with a piece of wire so it doesn't fall and become kinked or detached from the crankshaft. When the head is resting on the cylinder, wire the cam chain to another component to keep tension on it.

29   Lubricate the threads of the cylinder head bolts with engine oil, then install them finger-tight. Tighten the four main bolts or nuts in the correct sequence **(see illustration 8.9)**, in several stages, to the torque listed in this Chapter's Specifications. After the main nuts or bolts are tightened, tighten the two Allen bolts to the torque listed in this Chapter's Specifications.

30   Refer to the valve adjustment procedure in Chapter 1 and make sure the timing mark with the T next to it is aligned with the notch in the

timing hole. If it's necessary to turn the crankshaft, hold the cam chain up so it doesn't fall off the crankshaft sprocket and become jammed.

31   Engage the camshaft sprocket with the timing chain so its dowel hole aligns with the dowel **(see illustration 8.5a)**. Slip the sprocket onto the camshaft over the dowel, then install the sprocket bolt finger-tight. The line on the cam sprocket should be aligned with the cast indicator in the cylinder head **(see illustration 8.3)**.

32   Twist the cam sprocket in both directions to remove the slack from the cam chain. Insert a screwdriver in the cam chain tensioner hole and push against the cam chain guide. With the guide pushed in, the cam sprocket line and cast indicator should line up **(see illustration 8.3)**. If they don't, remove the cam sprocket from the chain, reposition it and try again. Don't continue with assembly until the marks are lined up correctly.

33   Tighten the cam sprocket bolt to the torque listed in this Chapter's Specifications.

34   Apply engine oil to a new O-ring for the cam sprocket cover. Install the O-ring and cover and tighten the screws or bolts to the torque listed in this Chapter's Specifications.

35   Install the cam chain tensioner (see Section 7).

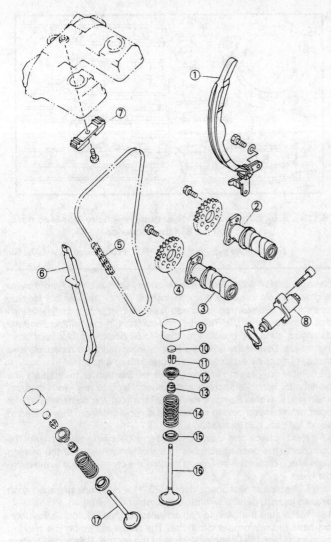

9.7a Camshaft and valve details (TT-R250 models)

1	Intake side timing chain guide	9	Tappets
2	Intake camshaft	10	Valve clearance adjusting shim
3	Exhaust camshaft	11	Valve keepers
4	Cam sprocket	12	Valve spring retainer
5	Timing chain	13	Valve stem seal
6	Exhaust side timing chain guide	14	Valve spring
7	Timing chain snubber	15	Valve spring seat
8	Timing chain tensioner	16	Intake valve
		17	Exhaust valve

36 Change the engine oil (see Chapter 1).
37 Adjust the valve clearances (see Chapter 1).
38 The remainder of installation is the reverse of removal.

9 Cylinder head, camshafts and tappets (twin-cam models) – removal and installation

Removal

Camshafts

Refer to illustrations 9.1a, 9.1b, 9.7a and 9.7b

1   Remove the Allen bolts, washer and grommets that secure the cylinder head cover **(see illustrations)**. Pull the cover off. If it won't

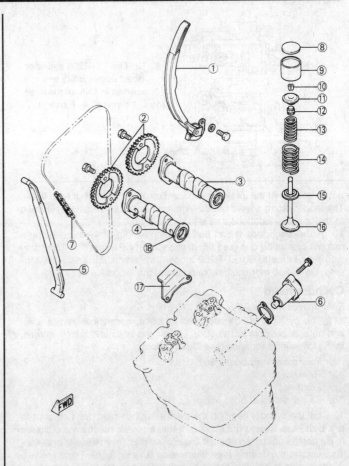

9.7b Camshaft and valve details (XT350 models)

1	Intake side timing chain guide	9	Tappet
2	Cam sprockets	10	Valve Keepers
3	Intake camshaft	11	Valve spring retainer
4	Exhaust camshaft	12	Valve stem seal
5	Exhaust side chain guide	13	Inner valve spring
6	Timing chain tensioner	14	Outer valve spring
7	Timing chain	15	Valve spring seat
8	Valve clearance adjusting shim	16	Valve
		17	Upper timing chain guide

come, tap gently with a rubber mallet to break the gasket seal.
2   Unscrew the spark plug (see Chapter 1).
3   Refer to *Valve clearances - check and adjustment* in Chapter 1 and place the engine at top dead center on the compression stroke.
4   Remove the cam chain tensioner (Section 7).
5   Tie the cam chain up with wire so it can't fall into the chain cavity. If you're working on an XT350, remove the upper chain guide, unbolt the sprockets from the camshafts and remove the union bolt that attaches the external oil line to the cylinder head.
6   Loosen the camshaft caps in several stages, working from the outer caps to the inner caps, then take off the caps and dowels **(see illustration 9.1)**.
7   Lift the intake camshaft out of its saddles and disengage the sprocket from the chain **(see illustrations)**. Remove the exhaust camshaft in the same way.

Tappets

8   Remove the camshafts following the procedure given above. Be sure to keep tension on the cam chain.
9   Make a holder for each tappet and its adjusting shim (an egg carton or box will work). Label the sections according to whether the tap-

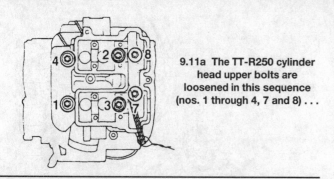

9.11a The TT-R250 cylinder head upper bolts are loosened in this sequence (nos. 1 through 4, 7 and 8) . . .

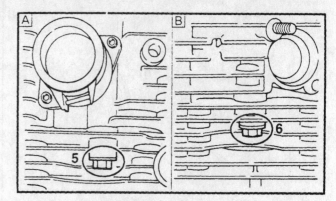

9.11b . . . together with the lower nuts, which are loosened no. 5 and no. 6 in the sequence

| A | Rear (intake side) nut | B | Front (exhaust side) nut |

pet belongs with the intake or exhaust camshaft, and left or right valve. The tappets form a wear pattern with their bores and must be returned to their original locations if reused.

10   Label each tappet and pull each tappet out of the bore, using a magnet or suction cup **(see illustration 9.7)**. Make sure the shims stay with their tappets. On TT-R250 models, the shims are inside the tappets; On XT350 models, they're on top of the tappets.

Cylinder head

Refer to illustrations 9.11a and 9.11b

11   The cylinder head is secured by bolts, accessible from above, and nuts, accessible from below. Loosen the bolts and nuts in stages, in the following sequence **(see illustrations)**:

a) *Four main head bolts (hex)*
b) *Rear nut*
c) *Front nut*
d) *Two small head bolts (Allen)*

12   Lift the cylinder head off the cylinder. If it's stuck, don't attempt to pry it off - tap around the sides of it with a plastic hammer to dislodge it. Be careful not to tap against the cooling fins; they're easily broken.

13   Locate the dowels **(see illustration 9.1a or 9.1b)**. There are two of them, one in each of the head bolt holes nearest the timing chain. The dowels may be in the cylinder or they may have come off with the head.

Timing chain and guides

14   Lift the front cam chain guide out of the cylinder **(see illustration 9.7a or 9.7b)**. The rear guide is bolted at the bottom, so the clutch will have to be removed for access if the guide or the cam chain need to be removed.

15   Stuff clean rags into the cam chain opening so dirt, small parts or tools can't fall into it.

Inspection

Camshaft, chain and guides

Refer to illustrations 9.21a and 9.21b

Note: *Before replacing camshafts or the cylinder head because of*

damage, check with local machine shops specializing in motorcycle engine work. In the case of the camshaft, it may be possible for cam lobes to be welded, reground and hardened, at a cost far lower than that of a new camshaft. If the bearing surfaces in the cylinder head are damaged, it may be possible for them to be bored out to accept bearing inserts. Due to the cost of a new cylinder head it is recommended that all options be explored before condemning it as trash!

16   Refer to Steps 15 through 18 of Section 8 to inspect the camshafts, sprockets, chain and guides. Replace any worn or damaged parts. **Note:** *Remove the sprockets from the camshafts at this point, whether you plan to replace the sprockets or not. They'll need to be off for camshaft installation later.*

17   Next, check the camshaft bearing oil clearances. Clean the camshafts, the bearing surfaces in the cylinder head and the bearing caps with a clean, lint-free cloth, then lay the cams in place in the cylinder head.

18   Cut strips of Plastigage (type HPG-1) and lay one piece on each bearing journal, parallel with the crankshaft centerline.

19   Make sure the bearing cap dowels are installed. Install the bearing caps in their proper positions. The arrow marks on the bearing caps must face the timing chain side of the engine. Tighten the bolts in three steps to the torque listed in this Chapter's Specifications, starting with the innermost bolts and working outward. **Note:** *Do not let the camshafts turn while the Plastigage is in place, or it will smear and give an inaccurate reading.*

20   Unscrew the cap bolts in stages, working from the outer bolts to the inner bolts, and carefully lift off the bearing caps.

21   To determine the oil clearance, compare the crushed Plastigage (at its widest point) on each journal to the scale printed on the Plastigage container **(see illustration)**. Compare the results to this Chap-

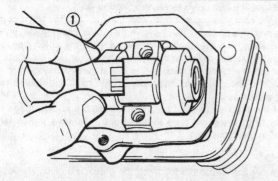

9.21a Compare the width of the crushed Plastigage to the scale on the Plastigage container to obtain the clearance

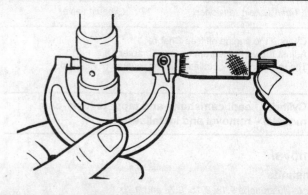

9.21b Measure the camshaft bearing journals with a micrometer

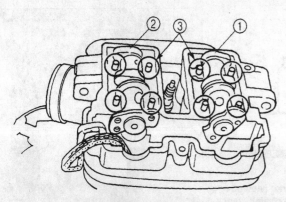

9.33 Remove the exhaust camshaft (1), intake camshaft (2) and dowels (3)

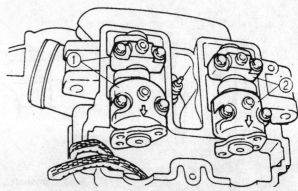

9.34 Install the intake camshaft (1) and exhaust camshaft (2) and their caps; position the sprocket flange holes as shown

ter's Specifications. If oil clearance is greater than specified, measure the diameter of the cam bearing journal with a micrometer **(see illustration)**. If the journal diameter is less than the specified limit, replace the camshaft with a new one and recheck the clearance. If the clearance is still too great, replace the cylinder head and bearing caps with new parts (see the Note that precedes Step 16).

Tappets

22   Check the tappets and their bores for wear, scuff marks, scratches and other damage. Check the camshaft contact surface, as well as the outer surface that rides in the bore. Replace the tappets if they're visibly worn or damaged.

23   Measure the outside diameter of each tappet with a micrometer or vernier caliper and compare to this Chapter's Specifications. If the diameter is less than the minimum, replace the tappet.

Cylinder head

24   Check the cylinder head gasket and the mating surfaces on the cylinder head and cylinder for leakage, which could indicate warpage. Refer to Section 11 and check the flatness of the cylinder head.

25   Clean all traces of old gasket material from the cylinder head and cylinder. Be careful not to let any of the gasket material fall into the crankcase, the cylinder bore or the bolt holes.

Installation

26   Install the exhaust side cam chain damper, fitting the lower end into its notch **(see illustration 8.12b)**.

27   Make sure the new head gasket and both dowels are installed, then carefully lower the cylinder head over the dowels, guiding the cam chain through the slot in the cylinder head. It's helpful to have an assistant support the cam chain with a piece of wire so it doesn't fall and become kinked or detached from the crankshaft. When the head is resting on the cylinder, wire the cam chain to another component to keep tension on it.

28   Lubricate the threads of the cylinder head bolts with engine oil, then install them finger-tight. Tighten the four main bolts, two nuts and two small bolts in the opposite of the loosening sequence **(see illustration 9.11a and 9.11b)**, in several stages, to the torque listed in this Chapter's Specifications.

29   Refer to the valve adjustment procedure in Chapter 1 and make sure the Top Dead Center mark is aligned with the notch in the timing hole. If it's necessary to turn the crankshaft, hold the cam chain up so it doesn't fall off the crankshaft sprocket and become jammed.

TT-R250 models

Refer to illustrations 9.33, 9.34 and 9.35

30   Coat the tappets and their bores with clean engine oil. Apply a small amount of moly-based grease to the shims and stick them to their respective valve stems.

31   Slide the tappets into their bores, taking care not to knock the valve shims out of position. When the tappets are correctly installed, it

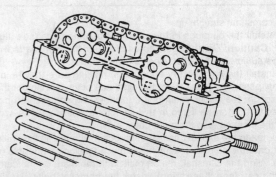

9.35 Install the exhaust cam sprocket (E) and intake cam sprocket (I) and align their marks with the cover gasket surface

should be possible to rotate them with a finger.

32   Coat the camshaft contact surfaces of the tappets and the bearing surfaces of the camshafts with moly-based grease.

33   Install the exhaust camshaft, then the intake camshaft in the cylinder head with their sprocket flanges aligned in the correct positions **(see illustration)**. Install the cap dowels in their holes (if they were removed).

34   Install the camshaft bearing caps, making sure they're in their original positions with their arrow marks pointing toward the timing chain end of the engine **(see illustration)**. Tighten the cap bolts in stages to the torque listed in this Chapter's Specifications, working from the inner caps to the outer caps.

35   Engage the exhaust camshaft sprocket with the timing chain and slip it onto the camshaft, keeping as much tension as possible on the chain. Align the sprocket match marks with the cover mating surface on the cylinder head **(see illustration)**. Install the sprocket bolts and tighten them to the torque listed in this Chapter's Specifications.

36   Install the intake camshaft in the same way as the exhaust camshaft, again aligning the match marks on the sprocket with the cover gasket surface on the cylinder head. Install the sprocket bolts and tighten them to the torque listed in this Chapter's Specifications.

XT350 models

Refer to illustrations 9.41 and 9.43

37   Coat the tappets and their bores with clean engine oil.

38   Slide the tappets into their bores. Apply a small amount of moly-based grease to the shims and stick them to their respective tappets. When the tappets are correctly installed, it should be possible to rotate them with a finger.

39   Coat the camshaft contact surfaces of the tappets and the bearing surfaces of the camshafts with moly-based grease.

40   Install the camshafts in the cylinder head with the alignment marks (punch marks on the flanges opposite the timing chain end of

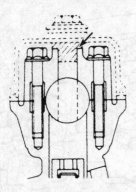

9.41 Be sure to reinstall the oil plugs (arrow) or the camshafts won't receive enough lubrication

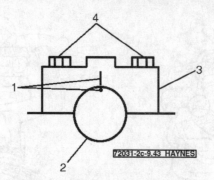

9.43 Camshaft alignment marks (viewed from end opposite timing chain)

1	Timing marks	3	Bearing cap
2	Camshaft	4	Cap bolt heads

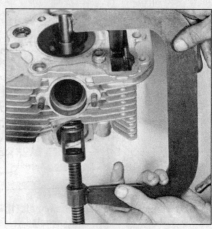

11.7a Compress the valve springs with a valve spring compressor

each camshaft) straight up.

41   Install the oil plugs in the camshaft bearing caps **(see illustration)**. **Caution:** *Don't forget the oil plugs or the camshafts will not receive sufficient lubrication when the engine runs.*

42   Install the camshaft bearing caps, making sure they're in their original positions. Install six of the eight cap bolts, leaving out the two that secure the upper chain guide for now. Tighten the cap bolts in stages to the torque listed in this Chapter's Specifications, working from the inner caps to the outer caps.

43   Engage the exhaust camshaft sprocket with the timing chain and slip it onto the camshaft, keeping as much tension as possible on the chain. Align the camshaft match mark with the mark on the camshaft bearing cap **(see illustration)**. Install the sprocket bolts and tighten them to the torque listed in this Chapter's Specifications.

44   Install the intake camshaft in the same way as the exhaust camshaft, again aligning the match marks on the camshaft and bearing cap. Install the sprocket bolts and tighten them to the torque listed in this Chapter's Specifications.

45   Install the upper timing chain guide and tighten its bolts to the torque listed in this Chapter's Specifications.

TT-R250 and XT350 models

46   Install the timing chain tensioner (Section 7). Release the tensioner so its piston presses against the chain.

47   Recheck the crankshaft timing mark in the timing hole cover and the match marks on both camshafts. If they are not still aligned, stop and find out why before continuing. **Caution:** *Don't run the engine with the marks misaligned or the valves may strike the pistons, bending the valves.*

48   Change the engine oil (see Chapter 1).

49   Adjust the valve clearances (see Chapter 1).

50   The remainder of installation is the reverse of removal.

10   Valves/valve seats/valve guides - servicing

1   Because of the complex nature of this job and the special tools and equipment required, servicing of the valves, the valve seats and the valve guides (commonly known as a valve job) is best left to a professional.

2   The home mechanic can, however, remove and disassemble the head, do the initial cleaning and inspection, then reassemble and deliver the head to a dealer service department or properly equipped vehicle repair shop for the actual valve servicing. Refer to Section 11 for those procedures.

3   The dealer service department will remove the valves and springs, recondition or replace the valves and valve seats, replace the valve guides, check and replace the valve springs, spring retainers and keepers (as necessary), replace the valve seals with new ones and

reassemble the valve components.

4   After the valve job has been performed, the head will be in like-new condition. When the head is returned, be sure to clean it again very thoroughly before installation on the engine to remove any metal particles or abrasive grit that may still be present from the valve service operations. Use compressed air, if available, to blow out all the holes and passages.

11   Cylinder head and valves - disassembly, inspection and reassembly

1   As mentioned in the previous Section, valve servicing and valve guide replacement should be left to a dealer service department or other repair shop. However, disassembly, cleaning and inspection of the valves and related components can be done (if the necessary special tools are available) by the home mechanic. This way no expense is incurred if the inspection reveals that service work is not required at this time.

2   To properly disassemble the valve components without the risk of damaging them, a valve spring compressor is absolutely necessary. If the special tool is not available, have a dealer service department or vehicle repair shop handle the entire process of disassembly, inspection, service or repair (if required) and reassembly of the valves.

Disassembly

Refer to illustrations 11.7a and 11.7b

3   Remove the carburetor intake tube from the cylinder head (see Chapter 3C).

4   Before the valves are removed, scrape away any traces of gasket material from the head gasket sealing surface. Work slowly and do not nick or gouge the soft aluminum of the head. Gasket removing solvents, which work very well, are available at most motorcycle shops and auto parts stores.

5   Carefully scrape all carbon deposits out of the combustion chamber area. A hand held wire brush or a piece of fine emery cloth can be used once most of the deposits have been scraped away. Do not use a wire brush mounted in a drill motor, or one with extremely stiff bristles, as the head material is soft and may be eroded away or scratched by the wire brush.

6   Before proceeding, arrange to label and store the valves along with their related components so they can be kept separate and reinstalled in the same valve guides they are removed from (again, plastic bags work well for this).

7   Compress the valve spring(s) on the first valve with a spring compressor, then remove the keepers and the retainer from the valve assembly **(see illustration)**. Do not compress the spring(s) any more than is absolutely necessary. Carefully release the valve spring com-

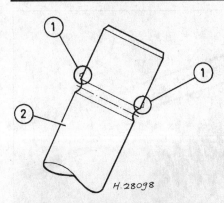

11.7b Check the area around the keeper groove for burrs and remove any that you find

1   Burrs (remove)   2   Valve stem

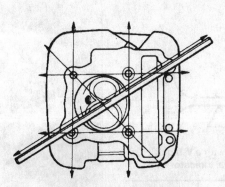

11.14 Check the gasket surface for flatness with a straightedge and feeler gauge in the directions shown

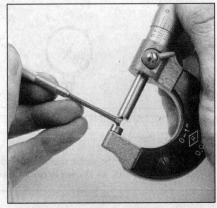

11.16 Measure the valve guide inside diameter with a hole gauge, then measure the gauge with a micrometer

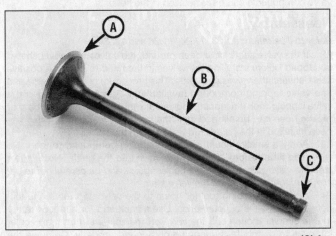

11.17 Check the valve face (A), stem (B) and keeper groove (C) for wear and damage

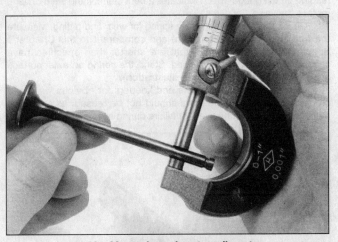

11.18a Measuring valve stem diameter

pressor and remove the spring(s), spring seat and valve from the head. If the valve binds in the guide (won't pull through), push it back into the head and deburr the area around the keeper groove with a very fine file or whetstone **(see illustration)**.

8   Repeat the procedure for the remaining valve. Remember to keep the parts for each valve together so they can be reinstalled in the same location.

9   Once the valves have been removed and labeled, pull off the valve stem seals with pliers and discard them (the old seals should never be reused).

10   Next, clean the cylinder head with solvent and dry it thoroughly. Compressed air will speed the drying process and ensure that all holes and recessed areas are clean.

11   Clean all of the valve springs, keepers, retainers and spring seats with solvent and dry them thoroughly. Do the parts from one valve at a time so that no mixing of parts between valves occurs.

12   Scrape off any deposits that may have formed on the valve, then use a motorized wire brush to remove deposits from the valve heads and stems. Again, make sure the valves do not get mixed up.

Inspection

Refer to illustrations 11.14, 11.16, 11.17, 11.18a, 11.18b, 11.19a and 11.19b

13   Inspect the head very carefully for cracks and other damage. If cracks are found, a new head will be required. Check the cam bearing surfaces for wear and evidence of seizure. Check the camshaft for wear as well (see Section 8).

14   Using a precision straightedge and a feeler gauge, check the head

gasket mating surface for warpage. Lay the straightedge lengthwise, across the head and diagonally (corner-to-corner), intersecting the head bolt holes, and try to slip a feeler gauge under it, on either side of each combustion chamber **(see illustration)**. The feeler gauge thickness should be the same as the cylinder head warpage limit listed in this Chapter's Specifications. If the feeler gauge can be inserted between the head and the straightedge, the head is warped and must either be machined or, if warpage is excessive, replaced with a new one.

15   Examine the valve seats in each of the combustion chambers. If they are pitted, cracked or burned, the head will require valve service that is beyond the scope of the home mechanic. Measure the valve seat width and compare it to this Chapter's Specifications. If it is not within the specified range, or if it varies around its circumference, valve service work is required.

16   Clean the valve guides to remove any carbon buildup, then measure the inside diameters of the guides (at both ends and the center of the guide) with a small hole gauge and a micrometer **(see illustration)**. Record the measurements for future reference. The guides are measured at the ends and at the center to determine if they are worn in a bell-mouth pattern (more wear at the ends). If they are, guide replacement is an absolute must.

17   Carefully inspect each valve face for cracks, pits and burned spots. Check the valve stem and the keeper groove area for cracks **(see illustration)**. Rotate the valve and check for any obvious indication that it is bent. Check the end of the stem for pitting and excessive wear and make sure the bevel is the specified width. The presence of any of the above conditions indicates the need for valve servicing.

18   Measure the valve stem diameter **(see illustration)**. If the diameter is less than listed in this Chapter's Specifications, the valves will

**11.18b Check the valve stem for bends with a V-block
(or V-blocks, as shown here) and a dial indicator**

have to be replaced with new ones. Also check the valve stem for bending. Set the valve in a V-block with a dial indicator touching the middle of the stem (see illustration). Rotate the valve and look for a reading on the gauge (which indicates a bent stem). If the stem is bent, replace the valve.

19   Check the end of each valve spring for wear and pitting. Measure the free length (see illustration) and compare it to this Chapter's Specifications. Any springs that are shorter than specified have sagged and should not be reused. Stand the spring on a flat surface and check it for squareness (see illustration).

20   Check the spring retainers and keepers for obvious wear and cracks. Any questionable parts should not be reused, as extensive damage will occur in the event of failure during engine operation.

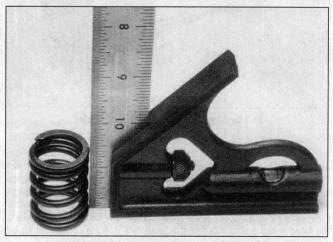

11.19b Checking the valve springs for squareness

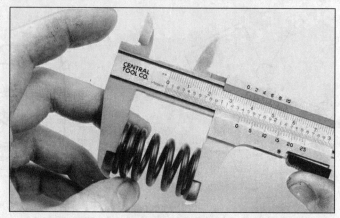

11.19a Measuring the free length of the valve springs

21   If the inspection indicates that no service work is required, the valve components can be reinstalled in the head.

Reassembly

Refer to illustrations 11.23, 11.24, 11.26 and 11.27

22   If the valve seats have been ground, the valves and seats should be lapped before installing the valves in the head to ensure a positive seal between the valves and seats. This procedure requires coarse and fine valve lapping compound (available at auto parts stores) and a valve lapping tool. If a lapping tool is not available, a piece of rubber or plastic hose can be slipped over the valve stem (after the valve has been installed in the guide) and used to turn the valve.

23   Apply a small amount of coarse lapping compound to the valve face (see illustration), then slip the valve into the guide. **Note:** *Make sure the valve is installed in the correct guide and be careful not to get any lapping compound on the valve stem.*

24   Attach the lapping tool (or hose) to the valve and rotate the tool between the palms of your hands. Use a back-and-forth motion rather than a circular motion. Lift the valve off the seat and turn it at regular intervals to distribute the lapping compound properly. Continue the lapping procedure until the valve face and seat contact area is of uniform width and unbroken around the entire circumference of the valve face and seat (see illustration). Once this is accomplished, lap the valves again with fine lapping compound.

25   Carefully remove the valve from the guide and wipe off all traces of lapping compound. Use solvent to clean the valve and wipe the seat area thoroughly with a solvent soaked cloth. Repeat the procedure for the remaining valves.

26   Lay the spring seat in place in the cylinder head, then install new valve stem seals on both of the guides (see illustration). Use an appropriate size deep socket to push the seals into place until they are

**11.23 Apply the lapping compound very
sparingly, in small dabs, to the valve
face only**

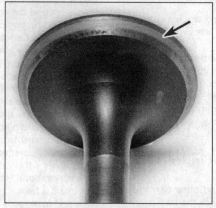

**11.24 After lapping, the valve face should
exhibit a uniform, unbroken contact
pattern (arrow)**

**11.26 Push the oil seal onto the valve
guide (arrow)**

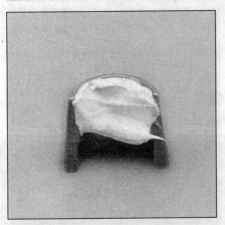

11.27 A small dab of grease will help hold the keepers in place on the valve while the spring compressor is released

12.3 On TT-R225 and XT225 models, remove the Allen bolts that attach the cylinder to the crankcase (arrows)

12.4 Lift the cylinder off the piston (and off the studs on TT-R90 models)

properly seated. Don't twist or cock them, or they will not seal properly against the valve stems. Also, don't remove them again or they will be damaged.

27 Coat the valve stems with assembly lube or moly-based grease, then install one of them into its guide. Next, install the spring seat, springs and retainers, compress the springs and install the keepers. **Note:** *Install the springs with the tightly wound coils at the bottom (next to the spring seat).* When compressing the springs with the valve spring compressor, depress them only as far as is absolutely necessary to slip the keepers into place. Apply a small amount of grease to the keepers **(see illustration)** to help hold them in place as the pressure is released from the springs. Make certain that the keepers are securely locked in their retaining grooves.

28 Support the cylinder head on blocks so the valves can't contact the workbench top, then very gently tap each of the valve stems with a soft-faced hammer. This will help seat the keepers in their grooves.

29 Once all of the valves have been installed in the head, check for proper valve sealing by pouring a small amount of solvent into each of the valve ports. If the solvent leaks past the valve(s) into the combustion chamber area, disassemble the valve(s) and repeat the lapping procedure, then reinstall the valve(s) and repeat the check. Repeat the procedure until a satisfactory seal is obtained.

12 Cylinder - removal, inspection and installation

Removal

Refer to illustrations 12.3, 12.4 and 12.5

1 Following the procedure given in Section 8 or Section 9, remove the cylinder head. Make sure the crankshaft is positioned at Top Dead Center (TDC).

2 Lift out the cam chain front guide **(see illustration 8.12a)**.

3 If you're working on a TT-R225 or XT225, remove the Allen bolts securing the base of the cylinder to the crankcase **(see illustration)**.

4 Lift the cylinder straight up to remove it **(see illustration)**. If you're working on a TT-R90, slide it off the studs; on all others, pull the cylinder sleeve out of the crankcase. If it's stuck, tap around its perimeter with a soft-faced hammer (but don't tap on the cooling fins or they may break). Don't attempt to pry between the cylinder and the crankcase, as you'll ruin the sealing surfaces.

5 Locate the dowel pins (they may have come off with the cylinder or still be in the crankcase) **(see illustration)**. All models have two dowels, located next to the timing chain cavity. TT-R225 and XT225 models also have an O-ring, which fits around one of the remaining bolt holes. Be careful not to let these drop into the engine. Stuff rags around the piston and remove the gasket and all traces of old gasket material from the surfaces of the cylinder and the crankcase.

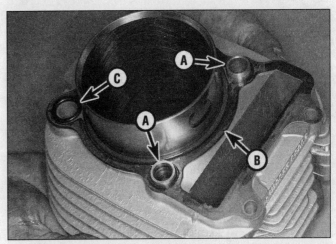

12.5 All models have two dowels (A); all except TT-R90 models have a base O-ring (B); TT-R225 and XT225 models have a bolt hole O-ring (C)

Inspection

Refer to illustration 12.8

6 Don't attempt to separate the liner from the cylinder.

7 Check the cylinder walls carefully for scratches and score marks.

8 Using the appropriate precision measuring tools, check the cylinder's diameter. Measure parallel to the crankshaft axis and across the crankshaft axis, at the depth from the top of the cylinder listed in this Chapter's Specifications **(see illustration)**. Average the two measurements and compare the results to this Chapter's Specifications. If the

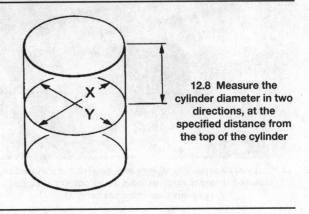

12.8 Measure the cylinder diameter in two directions, at the specified distance from the top of the cylinder

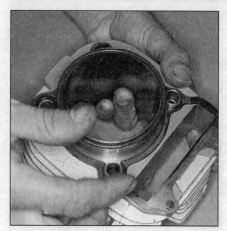

12.14 On all except TT-R90 models, install the base O-ring all the way onto the cylinder sleeve

12.15 On TT-R225 and XT225 models, install the O-ring on the intake side bolt hole farthest from the timing chain cavity

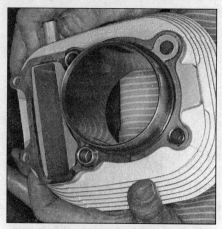

12.16 Install the dowels and base gasket

cylinder walls are tapered, out-of-round, worn beyond the specified limits, or badly scuffed or scored, have the cylinder rebored and honed by a dealer service department or a motorcycle repair shop. If a rebore is done, an oversize piston and rings will be required as well. Check with your dealer service department about available oversizes.

9   As an alternative, if the precision measuring tools are not available, a dealer service department or repair shop will make the measurements and offer advice concerning servicing of the cylinder.

10   If it's in reasonably good condition and not worn to the outside of the limits, and if the piston-to-cylinder clearance can be maintained properly, then the cylinder does not have to be rebored; honing is all that is necessary.

11   To perform the honing operation you will need the proper size flexible hone with fine stones as shown in Maintenance techniques, tools and working facilities at the front of this book, or a "bottle brush" type hone, plenty of light oil or honing oil, some shop towels and an electric drill motor. Hold the cylinder block in a vise (cushioned with soft jaws or wood blocks) when performing the honing operation. Mount the hone in the drill motor, compress the stones and slip the hone into the cylinder. Lubricate the cylinder thoroughly, turn on the drill and move the hone up and down in the cylinder at a pace which will produce a fine crosshatch pattern on the cylinder wall with the crosshatch lines intersecting at approximately a 60-degree angle. Be sure to use plenty of lubricant and do not take off any more material than is absolutely necessary to produce the desired effect. Do not withdraw the hone from the cylinder while it is running. Instead, shut

off the drill and continue moving the hone up and down in the cylinder until it comes to a complete stop, then compress the stones and withdraw the hone. Wipe the oil out of the cylinder and repeat the procedure on the remaining cylinder. Remember, do not remove too much material from the cylinder wall. If you do not have the tools, or do not desire to perform the honing operation, a dealer service department or vehicle repair shop will generally do it for a reasonable fee.

12   Next, the cylinder must be thoroughly washed with warm soapy water to remove all traces of the abrasive grit produced during the honing operation. Be sure to run a brush through the bolt holes and flush them with running water. After rinsing, dry the cylinder thoroughly and apply a coat of light, rust-preventative oil to all machined surfaces.

Installation

Refer to illustrations 12.14, 12.15, 12.16 and 12.18

13   Lubricate the cylinder bore with plenty of clean engine oil. Apply a thin film of moly-based grease to the piston skirt.

14   On all except TT-R90 models, install a new O-ring around the cylinder base **(see illustration)**.

15   On TT-R225 and XT225 models, install a new O-ring on the rearward bolt hole farthest from the timing chain cavity **(see illustration)**.

16   Install the dowel pins, then slip a new cylinder base gasket over them **(see illustration)**.

17   Attach a piston ring compressor to the piston and compress the piston rings. A large hose clamp can be used instead - just make sure it doesn't scratch the piston, and don't tighten it too much.

18   Install the cylinder and carefully lower it down until the piston crown fits into the cylinder liner **(see illustration)**. While doing this, pull the camshaft chain up, using a hooked tool or a piece of stiff wire. Push down on the cylinder, making sure the piston doesn't get cocked sideways, until the bottom of the cylinder liner slides down past the piston rings. A wood or plastic hammer handle can be used to gently tap the cylinder down, but don't use too much force or the piston will be damaged.

19   Remove the piston ring compressor or hose clamp, being careful not to scratch the piston.

20   The remainder of installation is the reverse of the removal steps.

13 Piston - removal, inspection and installation

1   The piston is attached to the connecting rod with a piston pin that's a slip fit in the piston and rod.

2   Before removing the piston from the rod, stuff a clean shop towel into the crankcase hole, around the connecting rod. This will prevent the snap-rings from falling into the crankcase if they are inadvertently dropped.

12.18 If you're experienced and very careful, the cylinder can be installed over the rings without a ring compressor, but a compressor is recommended

13.3a The arrow mark on top of the piston faces the exhaust (front) side of the engine

13.3b Wear eye protection and pry the snap-ring out of its groove with a pointed tool

13.4a Cylinder and piston details

1   Cylinder
2   Clutch cable bracket (TT-R/XT225 shown)
3   Base O-ring
4   Base gasket
5   Dowels
6   O-ring (TT-R/XT225 only)
7   Piston rings
8   Circlips
9   Piston

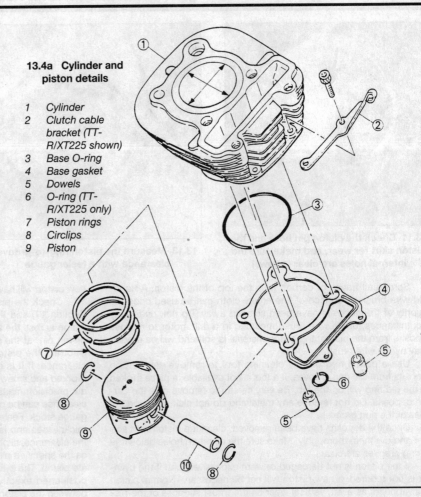

Removal

Refer to illustrations 13.3a, 13.3b, 13.4a and 13.4b

3   The piston should have an arrow mark on its crown that points toward the exhaust (front) side of the engine **(see illustration)**. If this mark is not visible due to carbon buildup, scribe an arrow into the piston crown before removal. Support the piston and pry the snap-ring out with a pointed tool **(see illustration)**.

4   Push the piston pin out from the opposite end to free the piston

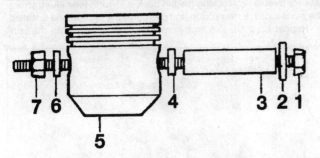

13.4b The piston pin should come out with hand pressure - if it doesn't, this removal tool can be fabricated from readily available parts

1   Bolt
2   Washer
3   Pipe (A)
4   Padding (A)
5   Piston
6   Washer (B)
7   Nut (B)
A   Large enough for piston pin to fit inside
B   Small enough to fit through piston pin bore

from the rod **(see illustration)**. You may have to deburr the area around the groove to enable the pin to slide out (use a triangular file for this procedure). If the pin won't come out, you can fabricate a piston pin removal tool from a long bolt, a nut, a piece of tubing and washers **(see illustration)**.

Inspection

Refer to illustrations 13.6, 13.11, 13.13, 13.14, 13.15 and 13.16

5   Before the inspection process can be carried out, the piston must be cleaned and the old piston rings removed.

6   Using a piston ring removal and installation tool, carefully remove the rings from the piston **(see illustration)**. Do not nick or gouge the piston in the process.

13.6 Remove the piston rings with a ring removal and installation tool

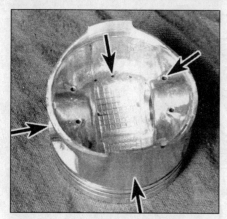

13.11 Check the piston pin bore and the piston skirt for wear, and make sure the internal holes are clear (arrows)

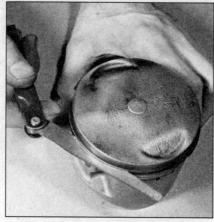

13.13 Measure the piston ring-to-groove clearance with a feeler gauge

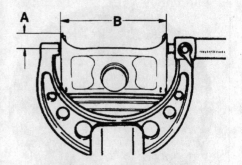

13.14 Measure the piston diameter with a micrometer

A Specified distance from bottom of piston
B Piston diameter

7   Scrape all traces of carbon from the top of the piston. A hand-held wire brush or a piece of fine emery cloth can be used once the majority of the deposits have been scraped away. Do not, under any circumstances, use a wire brush mounted in a drill motor to remove deposits from the piston; the piston material is soft and will be eroded away by the wire brush.

8   Use a piston ring groove cleaning tool to remove any carbon deposits from the ring grooves. If a tool is not available, a piece broken off the old ring will do the job. Be very careful to remove only the carbon deposits. Do not remove any metal and do not nick or gouge the sides of the ring grooves.

9   Once the deposits have been removed, clean the piston with solvent and dry them thoroughly. Make sure the oil return holes below the oil ring grooves are clear.

10   If the piston is not damaged or worn excessively and if the cylinder is not rebored, a new piston will not be necessary. Normal piston wear appears as even, vertical wear on the thrust surfaces of the piston and slight looseness of the top ring in its groove. New piston rings, on the other hand, should always be used when an engine is rebuilt.

11   Carefully inspect each piston for cracks around the skirt, at the pin bosses and at the ring lands **(see illustration)**.

12   Look for scoring and scuffing on the thrust faces of the skirt, holes in the piston crown and burned areas at the edge of the crown. If the skirt is scored or scuffed, the engine may have been suffering from overheating and/or abnormal combustion, which caused excessively high operating temperatures. The oil pump should be checked thoroughly. A hole in the piston crown, an extreme to be sure, is an indication that abnormal combustion (pre-ignition) was occurring. Burned areas at the edge of the piston crown are usually evidence of spark knock (detonation). If any of the above problems exist, the causes must be corrected or the damage will occur again.

13   Measure the piston ring-to-groove clearance (side clearance) by laying a new piston ring in the ring groove and slipping a feeler gauge in beside it **(see illustration)**. Check the clearance at three or four locations around the groove. Be sure to use the correct ring for each groove; they are different. If the clearance is greater then specified, a

new piston will have to be used when the engine is reassembled.

14   Check the piston-to-bore clearance by measuring the bore (see Section 11) and the piston diameter **(see illustration)**. Measure the piston across the skirt on the thrust faces at a 90-degree angle to the piston pin, at the specified distance up from the bottom of the skirt. Subtract the piston diameter from the bore diameter to obtain the clearance. If it is greater than specified, the cylinder will have to be rebored and a new oversized piston and rings installed. If the appropriate precision measuring tools are not available, the piston-to-cylinder clearance can be obtained, though not quite as accurately, using feeler gauge stock. Feeler gauge stock comes in 12-inch lengths and various thicknesses and is generally available at auto parts stores. To check the clearance, slip a piece of feeler gauge stock of the same thickness as the specified piston clearance into the cylinder along with appropriate piston. The cylinder should be upside down and the piston must be positioned exactly as it normally would be. Place the feeler gauge between the piston and cylinder on one of the thrust faces (90-degrees to the piston pin bore). The piston should slip through the cylinder (with the feeler gauge in place) with moderate pressure. If it falls through, or slides through easily, the clearance is excessive and a new piston will be required. If the piston binds at the lower end of the cylinder and is loose toward the top, the cylinder is tapered, and if tight spots are encountered as the piston/feeler gauge is rotated in the cylinder, the cylinder is out-of-round. Be sure to have the cylinder and piston checked by a dealer service department or a repair shop to confirm your findings before purchasing new parts.

15   Apply clean engine oil to the pin, insert it into the piston and check for freeplay by rocking the pin back-and-forth **(see illustration)**. If the pin is loose, a new piston and possibly new pin must be installed.

16   Repeat Step 15, this time inserting the piston pin into the con-

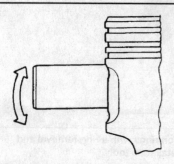

13.15 Slip the pin into the piston and try to wiggle it back-and-forth to check for looseness

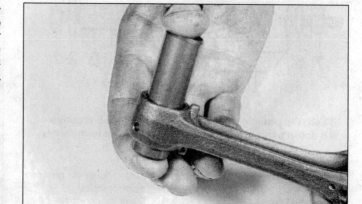

13.16 Slip the piston pin into the rod and try to rock it back-and-forth to check for looseness

13.18 Make sure both piston pin snap-rings are securely seated in the piston grooves

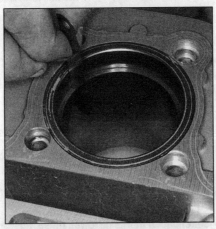

14.2 Check the piston ring end gap with a feeler gauge at the bottom of the cylinder

14.4 If the end gap is too small, clamp a file in a vise and file the ring ends (from the outside in only) to enlarge the gap slightly

necting rod **(see illustration)**. If the pin is loose, measure the pin diameter and the pin bore in the rod (or have this done by a dealer or repair shop). A worn pin can be replaced separately; if the rod bore is worn, the rod and crankshaft must be replaced as an assembly.

17   Refer to Section 14 and install the rings on the piston.

Installation

Refer to illustration 13.18

18   Install the piston with its arrow mark toward the exhaust side (front) of the engine. Lubricate the pin and the rod bore with moly-based grease. Install a new snap-rings in the groove in one side of the piston (don't reuse the old snap-rings). Push the pin into position from the opposite side and install another new snap-ring. Compress the snap-rings only enough for them to fit in the piston. Make sure the clips are properly seated in the grooves **(see illustration)**.

14   Piston rings - installation

Refer to illustrations 14.2, 14.4, 14.7a, 14.7b, 14.9a, 14.9b, 14.10 and 14.12

1   Before installing the new piston rings, the ring end gaps must be checked.

2   Insert the top (No. 1) ring into the bottom of the first cylinder and square it up with the cylinder walls by pushing it in with the top of the piston. The ring should be about one-half inch above the bottom edge of the cylinder. To measure the end gap, slip a feeler gauge between

the ends of the ring **(see illustration)** and compare the measurement to the Specifications.

3   If the gap is larger or smaller than specified, double check to make sure that you have the correct rings before proceeding.

4   If the gap is too small, it must be enlarged or the ring ends may come in contact with each other during engine operation, which can cause serious damage. The end gap can be increased by filing the ring ends very carefully with a fine file **(see illustration)**. When performing this operation, file only from the outside in.

5   Repeat the procedure for the second compression ring (ring gap is not specified for the oil ring rails or spacer).

6   Once the ring end gaps have been checked/corrected, the rings can be installed on the piston.

7   The oil control ring (lowest on the piston) is installed first. It is composed of three separate components. Slip the spacer into the groove, then install the upper side rail **(see illustrations)**. Do not use a piston ring installation tool on the oil ring side rails as they may be damaged. Instead, place one end of the side rail into the groove between the spacer expander and the ring land. Hold it firmly in place and slide a finger around the piston while pushing the rail into the groove (taking care not to cut your fingers on the sharp edges). Next, install the lower side rail in the same manner.

8   After the three oil ring components have been installed, check to make sure that both the upper and lower side rails can be turned smoothly in the ring groove.

9   Install the no. 2 (middle) ring next with its identification mark facing up **(see illustration)**. Do not mix the top and middle rings; they can

14.7a Installing the oil ring expander - make sure the ends don't overlap

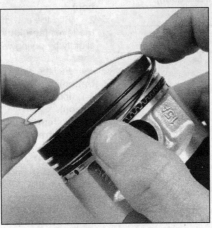

14.7b Installing an oil ring side rail - don't use a ring installation tool to do this

14.9a Install the middle ring with its identification mark up

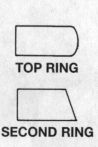

TOP RING

SECOND RING

14.9b The top and middle (second) rings can be identified by their profiles

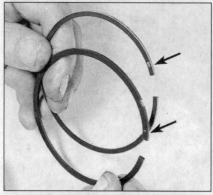

14.10 The top and middle rings have identification marks (arrows); these must be up when the rings are installed

14.12 Arrange the ring gaps like this

1 Top compression ring
2 Oil ring lower rail
3 Oil ring upper rail
4 Second compression ring

16.1 Slip the cable end out of the gap (arrow); spread the gap slightly with a screwdriver if necessary

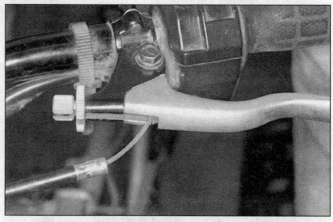

16.2 Rotate the cable and lower it away from the lever

be identified by their profiles **(see illustration)**.

10   To avoid breaking the ring, use a piston ring installation tool and make sure that the identification mark is facing up **(see illustration)**. Fit the ring into the middle groove on the piston. Do not expand the ring any more than is necessary to slide it into place.

11   Finally, install the no. 1 (top) ring in the same manner. Make sure the identifying mark is facing up. Be very careful not to confuse the top and second rings.

12   Once the rings have been properly installed, stagger the end gaps, including those of the oil ring side rails **(see illustration)**.

15   External oil pipe - removal and installation

Removal

1   Remove the union bolt and sealing washers on the right side of the engine behind the oil filter over.

2   At the other end of the pipe (at the cylinder head), remove the, union bolt and sealing washers. Detach the pipe from the engine and take it out.

Installation

3   Installation is the reverse of the removal steps, with the following additions:

a) Replace the sealing washers whenever the union bolts or hose fittings are loosened.
b) Tighten the union bolts or hose fittings to the torques listed in this Chapter's Specifications.

16   Clutch and release mechanism (all except TT-R90 models) – removal, inspection and installation

Cable and lever

Removal

Refer to illustrations 16.1, 16.2, 16.3, 16.4 and 16.5

1   Loosen the cable adjuster at the handlebar grip all the way (see Chapter 1). Rotate the cable so the inner cable aligns with the slot in the lever, then slip the cable and fitting out of the lever **(see illustration)**.

2   Slip the end of the cable through the lever slot to detach it from the lever **(see illustration)**. You may have to expand the slot very slightly by prying with a screwdriver, but don't overdo it and bend the lever.

3   Pull the cable out of the bracket and take it off the bike **(see illustration)**.

4   If necessary, detach the cable bracket from the engine **(see illustration)**.

5   To remove the lever from the handlebar, undo the clamp screws **(see illustration)**.

Inspection

6   Slide the inner cable back and forth in the housing and make sure it moves freely. If it doesn't, try lubricating it as described in Chapter 1. If that doesn't help, replace the cable.

Installation

7   Installation is the reverse of the removal steps. Refer to Chapter 1 and adjust clutch freeplay.

16.3 Pull the cable out of the bracket

16.4 Remove the cable bracket mounting screw or screws (arrows)

16.5 Remove the clamp screws (arrows) and detach the lever from the handlebar

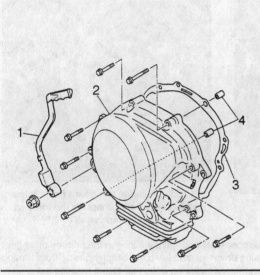

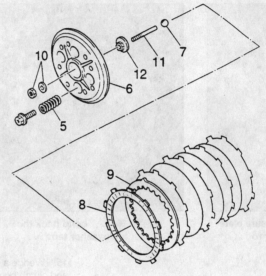

16.9a Clutch details
(TT-R125 models)

1   Kickstarter pedal
2   Right crankcase cover
3   Cover gasket
4   Cover dowels
5   Clutch springs
6   Pressure plate
7   Pushrod ball
8   Friction plates
9   Metal plates
10 Adjuster locknut and washer
11 Adjuster pushrod
12 Push plate

Right crankcase cover

Removal

Refer to illustrations 16.9a, 16.9b, 16.9c, 16.11a and 16.11b

8   Remove the oil filter (see Chapter 1). Where necessary for access, remove the right footpeg, brake pedal and kickstarter pedal (if equipped) (Chapter 7C, Chapter 6C and Section 18).

9   Remove the cover screws or bolts **(see illustrations)**. Loosen the screws evenly in a criss-cross pattern, then remove them.
10 Pull the cover off. Tap it with a rubber mallet if it won't come evenly. Don't pry the cover off or the gasket surfaces will be damaged.
11 Locate the cover dowels **(see illustration 16.9a and the accompanying illustrations)**. They may have stayed in the crankcase or come off with the cover.

16.9b Here are the right crankcase cover screws on TT-R225 and XT225 models

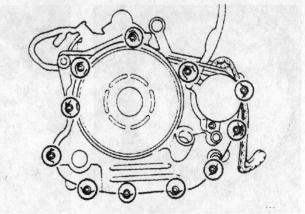

16.9c Here are the right crankcase cover screws on TT-R250 models (XT350 models similar)

16.11a Here are the right crankcase cover dowels on TT-R225 and XT225 models

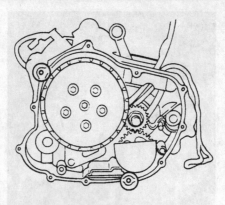

16.11b Here are the right crankcase cover dowels on TT-R250 models (XT350 models similar)

16.16a Remove the spring bolts, washers and springs . . .

16.16b . . . take off the pressure plate together with the adjuster rod . . .

16.16c . . . bend back the lockwasher tabs . . .

16.16d . . . wedge the gears from below (right arrow) and unscrew the locknut (left arrow) . . .

Installation

12   Installation is the reverse of the removal steps. Use a new gasket, coated on both sides with gasket sealer.

13   Tighten the cover screws or bolts evenly to the torque listed in this Chapter's Specifications.

Clutch

Removal

Refer to illustrations 16.16a through 16.16j

14   Remove the right crankcase cover as described above.

15   Wedge a copper washer or penny between the primary drive gear and clutch housing driven gear to keep the clutch housing from turning while you loosen the clutch spring bolts and clutch housing nut.

16   Refer to the accompanying illustrations to remove the clutch **(see illustrations)**.

Inspection

Refer to illustrations 16.17, 16.18, 16.20, 16.21 and 16.22

17   Check the bolt posts and the friction surface on the pressure plate for damaged threads, scoring or wear **(see illustration)**. Replace the pressure plate if any defects are found.

16.16e . . . pull off the lockwasher, noting how its tabs fit the slots (arrows) . . .

16.16f . . . pull the steel ball out with a magnet . . .

16.16g . . . grip the friction and metal plates . . .

16.16h . . . and slide them out; on TT-R225 and XT225 models, the colored tab (arrow) identifies the narrow friction plate

16.16i . . . pull off the clutch center and remove the thrust washer . . .

16.16j . . . and slide the clutch housing off

18   Check the edges of the slots in the clutch housing for indentations made by the friction plate tabs (see illustration 16.17). If the indentations are deep they can prevent clutch release, so the housing should be replaced with a new one. If the indentations can be removed easily with a file, the life of the housing can be prolonged to an extent. Check the bushing surface in the center of the clutch housing for score marks, scratches and excessive wear. Also, check the driven gear teeth for cracks, chips and excessive wear. If the bushing or gear is worn or damaged, the clutch housing must be replaced with a new one. On XT350 models, check the springs on the back side for breakage. If the springs are broken, replace the clutch housing. On all except XT350 models, check the primary driven gear for play (see illustration). If there is any, replace the clutch housing.

19   Check the splines of the clutch boss for indentations made by the tabs on the metal plates. Check the clutch boss friction surface for wear or scoring. Replace the clutch boss if problems are found.

20   Measure the free length of the clutch springs (see illustration) and compare the results to this Chapter's Specifications. If the springs have sagged, or if cracks are noted, replace them with new ones as a set.

21   If the lining material of the friction plates smells burnt or if it is glazed, new parts are required. If the metal clutch plates are scored or discolored, they must be replaced with new ones. Measure the thickness of the friction plates (see illustration) and replace with new parts any friction plates that are worn.

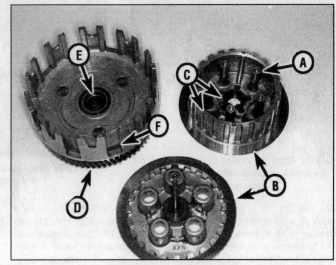

16.17 Clutch inspection points

A	Spring posts	D	Primary driven gear
B	Friction surfaces	E	Clutch housing bushing
C	Splines	F	Clutch housing slots

16.18 Grip the clutch housing and try to rotate the primary gear; if there's any play, replace the housing

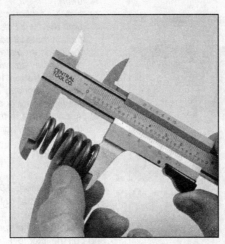

16.20 Measure the clutch spring free length

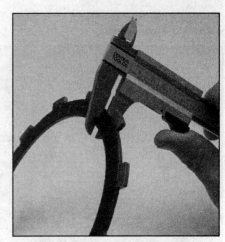

16.21 Measure the thickness of the friction plates

16.22 Check the metal plates for warpage

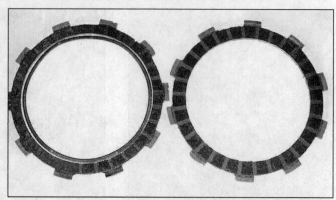

16.25a On TT-R225 and XT225 models, the narrower friction plate and damper (left) go in the third (center) position

16.25b Align the punch or arrow mark on the pressure plate with the mark on the clutch center

16.27a Note how the spring ends fit (arrows) . . .

16.27b . . . then remove the retaining screw and washer and pull the lifter lever out of the engine

22   Lay the metal plates, one at a time, on a perfectly flat surface (such as a piece of plate glass) and check for warpage by trying to slip a feeler gauge between the flat surface and the plate **(see illustration)**. The feeler gauge should be the same thickness as the maximum warp listed in this Chapter's Specifications. Do this at several places around the plate's circumference. If the feeler gauge can be slipped under the plate, it is warped and should be replaced with a new one.

23   Check the tabs on the friction plates for excessive wear and mushroomed edges. They can be cleaned up with a file if the deformation is not severe. Check the friction plates for warpage as described in Step 13.

24   Check the thrust washer for score marks, heat discoloration and evidence of excessive wear.

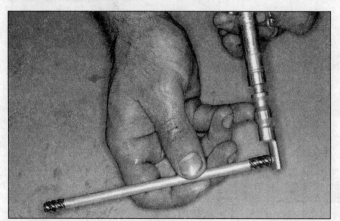

16.28 The pushrod engages the lifter lever like this when they're installed

Installation

Refer to illustrations 16.25a and 16.25b

25   Installation is the reverse of the removal steps, with the following additions:

a) *Install a new lockwasher and position its tabs between the ribs of the clutch center. Tighten the clutch nut to the torque listed in this Chapter's Specifications, then bend the lockwasher tabs against two of the flats on the nut.*

b) *Coat the friction plates with clean engine oil before you install them.*

c) *Install a friction plate, then the remaining metal and friction plates until they're all installed. Friction plates go on first and last, so the friction material contacts the metal surfaces of the clutch center and the pressure plate. On TT-R225 and XT225 models, note the location of the narrower friction plate and the damper that fits inside it* **(see illustration 16.16h and the accompanying illustration)**.

d) *If you're working on a TT-R225 or XT225, align the marks on the pressure plate and clutch center* **(see illustration)**.

e) *Apply grease to the ends of the clutch pushrod, the steel ball and the end of the adjuster rod.*

Lifter lever

Removal

Refer to illustrations 16.27a, 16.27b, 16.28 and 16.29

26   Remove the right crankcase cover and clutch adjuster as described above.

27   Note how the spring is installed, then remove the retaining bolt and pull the lifter lever out of the crankcase **(see illustrations)**.

28   Check for visible wear or damage at the contact points of the lifter lever and pushrod **(see illustration)**. Replace any parts that show problems.

16.29 Remove the snap-ring and pry out the seal

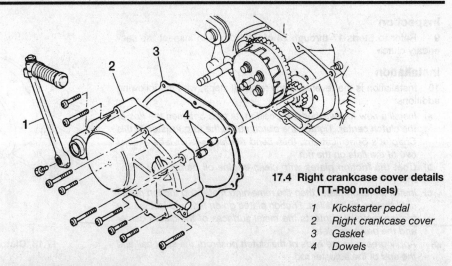

17.4 Right crankcase cover details (TT-R90 models)

1 Kickstarter pedal
2 Right crankcase cover
3 Gasket
4 Dowels

29   Remove the snap-ring and pry the lifter shaft seal out of the crankcase **(see illustration)**. If the needle bearing is worn or damaged, drive it out with a shouldered drift the same diameter as the bearing, then use the same tool to drive in a new one. Pack the needle bearing with grease and press in a new seal.
30   Installation is the reverse of the removal steps. Engage the notch in the lever shaft with the pushrod and hook the spring to the crankcase.
31   Refer to Chapter 1 and adjust clutch freeplay.

17   Primary and secondary clutches (TT-R90 models) - removal, inspection and installation

1   The secondary clutch must be removed for access to the primary clutch.

Right crankcase cover

Removal

Refer to illustration 17.4

1   Place the shift pedal in the Neutral position.
2   Drain the engine oil (see Chapter 1).
3   Remove the kickstarter pedal (Section 18).
4   Unbolt the right crankcase cover from the engine **(see illustration)**. If the cover is stuck, tap it gently with a soft hammer to free it - don't pry it loose or the gasket surfaces will be damaged.
5   Locate the cover dowels **(see illustration 17.4)**. Set them aside for safekeeping.

Installation

6   Installation is the reverse of the removal steps, with the following additions:

  a) *Make sure both dowels are installed.*
  b) *Use a new gasket, coated on both sides with gasket sealer.*
  c) *Tighten the cover bolts evenly to the torque listed in this Chapter's Specifications.*

Secondary clutch

Removal

Refer to illustration 17.8

7   Wedge a rag between the gears of the primary clutch and the secondary clutch to prevent the primary clutch from turning. **Note:** *If you plan to remove the primary clutch, wedge the gears and loosen its locknut at this time.*
8   Refer to Section 16 to remove the secondary clutch **(see illustrations 16.16a through 16.16j and the accompanying illustration)**.

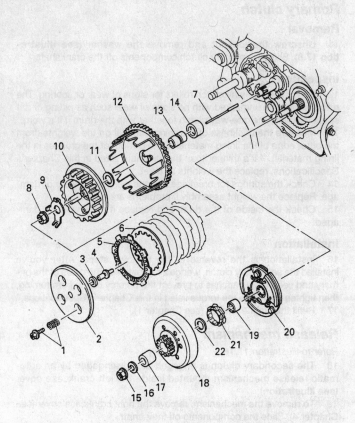

17.8 Primary and secondary clutches (TT-R90 models) - exploded view

1	Pressure plate spring and bolt	12	Clutch housing (secondary clutch)
2	Pressure plate	13	Collar
3	Washer	14	Spacer
4	Outer pushrod	15	Primary clutch locknut
5	Friction plates	16	Washer
6	Metal plates	17	Spacer
7	Inner pushrod	18	Primary clutch drum
8	Secondary clutch locknut	19	Primary clutch boss
9	Lockwasher	20	Primary clutch weight assembly
10	Clutch center (secondary clutch)	21	One-way clutch rollers
11	Thrust washer	22	Washer

Inspection

9   Refer to Steps 17 through 24 of Section 16 to inspect the secondary clutch.

Installation

10   Installation is the reverse of the removal steps, with the following additions:

a) *Install a new lockwasher and position its tabs between the ribs of the clutch center. Tighten the clutch nut to the torque listed in this Chapter's Specifications, then bend the lockwasher tabs against two of the flats on the nut.*

b) *Coat the friction plates with clean engine oil before you install them.*

c) *Install a friction plate, then the remaining metal and friction plates until they're all installed. Friction plates go on first and last, so the friction material contacts the metal surfaces of the clutch center and the pressure plate.*

d) *Apply grease to the ends of the clutch pushrod, the steel ball and the end of the adjuster rod.*

Primary clutch

Removal

11   Unscrew the locknut and remove the washer **(see illustration 17.8)**. Slide the primary clutch components off the crankshaft.

Inspection

12   Check the one-way clutch rollers for signs of wear or scoring. The rotors should be unmarked with no signs of wear such as pitting or flat spots. Replace the one-way clutch together with the drum if it's worn.

13   Measure the thickness of the lining material on the weights (from the outer edge of the lining material to the bottom of the grooves in the lining material). If it's thinner than the minimum listed in this Chapter's Specifications, replace the weights as a set.

14   Check the springs for breakage and the weights for wear or damage. Replace the weight assembly if problems are found.

15   Check the inside of the drum and replace it if it's worn or damaged.

Installation

16   Installation is the reverse of the removal steps. After you've installed the secondary clutch, wedge a rag between the gears of the primary and secondary clutches to prevent the primary clutch from turning, then tighten the nut to the torque listed in this Chapter's Specifications.

17   Refill the engine with oil (see Chapter 1).

Release mechanism

Refer to illustration 17.18

18   The secondary clutch is engaged and disengaged by an automatic release mechanism mounted inside the left crankcase cover **(see illustration)**.

19   To remove the mechanism, remove the right crankcase cover (see Chapter 4). Slide the components off their shaft.

20   Installation is the reverse of the removal steps.

---

18   Kickstarter and XT350 compression release - removal, inspection and installation

Kickstarter

Removal

Refer to illustrations 18.2a, 18.2b and 18.2c

1   Remove the right crankcase cover (Section 16 or 17).

2   Note how the kickstarter spring ends and the stopper arm on the kick axle assembly engage the crankcase, then take the kickstarter assembly out of the crankcase **(see illustrations)**.

3   On TT-R125 and XT350 models, remove the snap-ring, kick idle gear and second snap-ring.

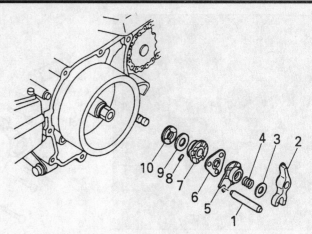

17.18 Clutch release mechanism (TT-R90 models) - exploded view

1	Shift fork	4	Spring	8	Dowel
	guide bar	5	Shift guide	9	Plate washer
2	Shift arm	6	Ball holder	10	Thrust bearing
3	Plate washer	7	Guide		

Inspection

4   Remove the components from the kickstarter shaft (except the clip on the ratchet gear on TT-R90 and TT-R125 models) **(see illustration 18.2a, 18.2b or 18.2c)**. Lay them in order so they can be reinstalled correctly.

5   Check all parts for visible wear and damage and replace any that show problems.

6   On TT-R90 and TT-R125 models, rotate the clip around the ratchet gear. It should turn when a force of about 1-1/2 to 3 pounds is applied. If it turns too easily, replace it with a new one.

7   Lubricate the parts with clean engine oil and put them back on the shaft **(see illustration 18.2a, 18.2b or 18.2c)**.

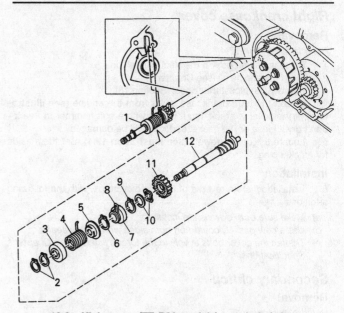

18.2a Kickstarter (TT-R90 models) - exploded view

1	Kickstarter	5	Spring guide	10	Plain washer
	assembly	6	Snap-ring		and wave
2	Snap-rigs	7	Ratchet gear		washer
3	Spring cover	8	Clip	11	Kick gear
4	Torsion spring	9	Snap-ring	12	Kickstarter shaft

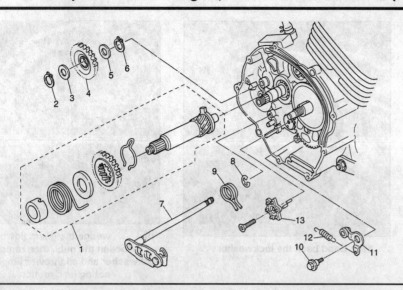

18.2b Kickstarter and external shift linkage (TT-R125 models)

1 Kickstarter assembly
2 Snap-rings
3 Washer
4 Kick idle gear
5 Washer
6 Snap-ring
7 Shift shaft
8 Circlip
9 Return spring
10 Stopper arm bolt
11 Stopper arm
12 Stopper arm spring
13 Shift cam segment

Installation

8   Installation is the reverse of the removal steps. Be sure the spring and stopper arm engage the crankcase correctly.

Compression release (XT350 models)

Removal

9   Loosen the cable locknut to provide slack in the cable. Follow the cable from the decompressor lever near the kickstarter to the cam lever at the cylinder head, removing the ties that attach it to the frame.
10   At the right crankcase cover, remove the screw that attaches the

cable bracket to the engine. At the cylinder head, remove the cable bracket Allen bolt.
11   Rotate one end of the cable to align it with its lever slot, then slip the cable end plug out of the lever. Do the same thing at the other end of the cable, then take the cable off the motorcycle.
12   At the cylinder head, remove the lockbolt directly above the decompression cam **(see illustration 18.2c)**. Slip the decompression cam and spring out of the engine.
13   Remove the right crankcase cover (see Section 16, if necessary).
14   Remove the decompression lever and its related components from the crankcase **(see illustration 18.2c)**.

18.2c Kickstarter and compression release (XT350 models)

1 Torsion spring
2 Decompression lever
3 Ratchet wheel stopper
4 Ratchet wheel guide
5 Kickstarter pedal assembly
6 Kickstarter spring
7 Spring guide
8 Decompression cam
9 Kickstarter shaft
10 Kick gear
11 Washer
12 Snap-rings
13 Ratchet wheel
14 Ratchet wheel spring
15 Kick idle gear
16 Decompression cable
17 Decompression cam

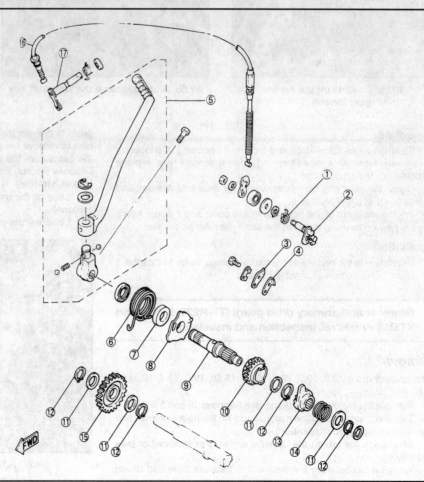

19.2 Balancer alignment marks (TT-R225, XT225 and XT350 models)

19.3 Bend back the lockwasher . . .

19.4 . . . wedge the gears (lower arrows) to loosen the nuts, then remove the lockwasher and oil thrower (upper arrow), noting its direction . . .

19.5a . . . slide off the driven gear (arrow) . . .

19.5b . . . and remove the Woodruff key

19.6 Unscrew the primary drive gear nut and remove the lockwasher . . .

Inspection

15   Slide the inner cable back and forth in its housing. If it doesn't move freely, lubricate it (see Chapter 1). If that doesn't help, replace the cable.

16   Check the lever and cam components for wear and damage and replace any that show problems.

17   Pry the seals out of the right crankcase cover and cylinder head. Press in new ones, using a socket the same diameter as the seal.

Installation

18   Installation is the reverse of the removal steps. Refer to Chapter 1 and adjust the decompressor cable freeplay.

19   Balancer and primary drive gears (TT-R225, XT225 and XT350) - removal, inspection and installation

Removal

Refer to illustrations 19.2, 19.3, 19.4, 19.5a, 19.5b, 19.6, 19.7, 19.8a, 19.8b and 19.8c

1   Remove the clutch and oil pump (see Sections 16 and 20).

2   Turn the crankshaft so the match marks on the balancer drive and driven gears align **(see illustration)**.

3   Bend back the tab on the balancer driven gear lockwasher **(see illustration)**.

4   Wedge a rag between the teeth of the balancer drive and driven

gears to prevent them from turning. Loosen the driven gear nut. If you plan to remove the primary drive gear or balancer drive gear, wedge the gears from the other side and loosen the primary drive gear nut. Unscrew the nut, remove the lockwasher and take off the oil thrower **(see illustration)**.

5   Slide off the driven gear and remove the Woodruff key **(see illustrations)**.

6   Unscrew the primary drive gear locknut and remove the lock-

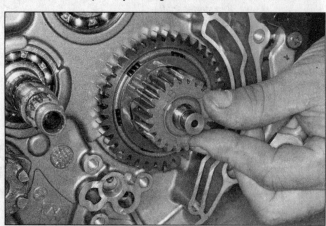

19.7 . . . then slip the gear off the crankshaft . . .

19.8a . . . remove the Woodruff key and outer holding plate . . .

19.8b . . . the balancer drive gear . . .

19.8c . . . and the inner holding plate

washer **(see illustration)**,

7   Slide the primary drive gear off the crankshaft **(see illustration)**.

8   Remove the outer holding plate, balancer drive gear and inner holding plate **(see illustrations)**.

Inspection

9   Check the gears for worn or damaged teeth and replace them as a set if problems are found.

10   Check the springs for distortion or fatigue and replace them as necessary.

11   Check the remaining components for wear and damage and replace any worn or damaged parts. Replace the lockwasher with a new one whenever it's removed.

12   Inspect the balancer and crankshaft ball bearings to the extent possible without disassembling the crankcase. If wear, looseness or roughness can be detected, the crankcase will have to be disassembled to replace the bearings.

Installation

Refer to illustration 19.13

13   Installation is the reverse of the removal steps, with the following additions:

a) *The balancer drive gear has six internal springs and three pins.*

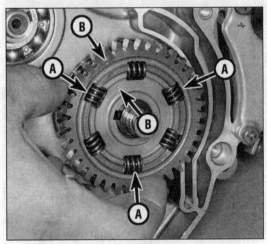

19.13 A pin fits inside every other spring (A); align the match marks on the gear boss and outer portion (B)

Assemble the gear with its three pins inside alternate springs **(see illustration)**. *Make sure the match marks on the gear boss (center) and the outer part of the gear are lined up.*

b) *Make sure the alignment marks on the drive gear and driven gear are lined up* **(see illustration 19.2)**.

c) *Use new lockwashers and make sure their tabs fit in the slots of the crankshaft and balancer shaft. Tighten the nuts to the torques listed in this Chapter's Specifications.*

20   Oil pump - removal, inspection and installation

Removal

1   Remove the right crankcase cover and clutch(es) (see Section 16 or 17).

TT-R90 and TT-R125 models

Refer to illustration 20.2

2   Remove the rotary filter and oil pump drive gear **(see illustration)**.

3   Rotate the oil pump driven gear for access to the mounting screws. Remove the mounting screws and take the pump and gasket off.

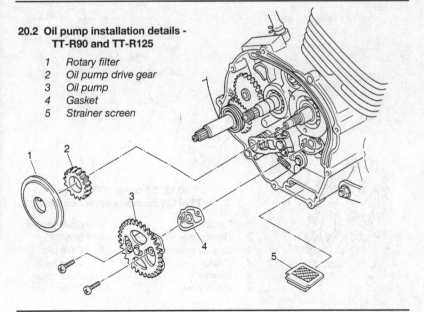

20.2 Oil pump installation details - TT-R90 and TT-R125

1   Rotary filter
2   Oil pump drive gear
3   Oil pump
4   Gasket
5   Strainer screen

20.4 Remove the gear cover . . .

20.5 Turn the driven gear to expose the mounting screws (and the assembly screw if you plan to disassemble the pump) . . .

20.6 . . . remove the mounting screws, pump and gasket

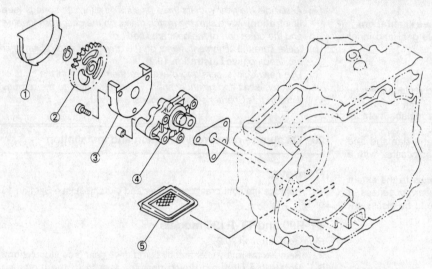

20.7 Oil pump mounting details (TT-R250 models)

1   Gear cover
2   Driven gear
3   Inner cover
4   Oil pump
5   Strainer screen

20.13a Remove the pump cover and outer rotor . . .

20.12 Oil pump (TT-R90 and TT-R125 models) - exploded view

1 Circlip	7 Cover dowels
2 Driven gear	8 Shaft
3 Conical washer	9 Drive pin
4 Circlip	10 Inner rotor
5 Washer	11 Outer rotor
6 Pump cover	12 Pump body

20.13b . . . inner rotor, drive pin and shaft; note the drive pin slots in the inner rotor

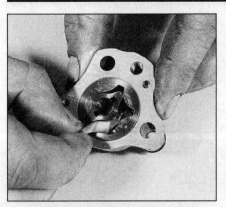

20.15a Measure the gap between the inner and outer rotors . . .

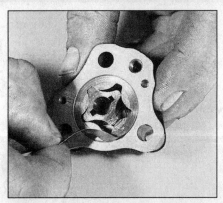

20.15b . . . and between the outer rotor and body . . .

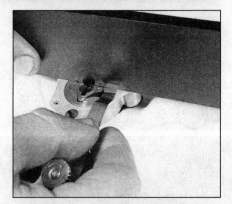

20.15c . . . and between the rotors and a straightedge

TT-R225 and XT225 models

Refer to illustrations 20.4, 20.5 and 20.6

4   Remove the oil pump gear cover **(see illustration)**.
5   Rotate the driven gear to expose the pump mounting screws **(see illustration)**. If you're planning to disassemble the pump, also loosen the assembly screw now, while the pump is secured to the engine.
6   Remove the mounting screws and take off the pump and gasket **(see illustration)**.

TT-R250 models

Refer to illustration 20.7

7   Remove the oil pump gear cover **(see illustration)**.
8   Remove the circlip and take the oil pump driven gear off its shaft.
9   Remove the three mounting screws that secure the inner cover, then remove the inner cover, oil pump and gasket.

XT350 models

10   Remove the circlip and washer from the oil pump idle gear, then slide the gear off its shaft.
11   Remove the oil pump mounting screws and take it off the engine.

Inspection

Refer to illustrations 20.12, 20.13a, 20.13b, 20.15a, 20.15b and 20.15c

12   If you need to replace the oil pump driven gear on a TT-R90 or TT-R125, remove the circlip and take it off **(see illustration)**. Remove the conical spring washer and second circlip. You can inspect the rotors and shaft without removing the gear.
13   Remove the assembly screw from the oil pump cover. Take the cover off and remove the drive pin, shaft and rotors **(see illustration 20.7a or the accompanying illustrations)**.
14   Wash all the components in solvent, then dry them off. Check the pump body, the rotors and the cover for scoring and wear. If any damage or uneven or excessive wear is evident, replace the pump. If you are rebuilding the engine, it's a good idea to install a new oil pump.
15   Place the rotors in the pump cover. Measure the clearance between the outer rotor and body, and between the inner and outer rotors, with a feeler gauge **(see illustrations)**. Place a straightedge across the pump body and rotors and measure the gap with a feeler gauge **(see illustration)**. If any of the clearances are beyond the limits listed in this Chapter's Specifications, replace the pump.
16   Reassemble the pump by reversing the disassembly steps, with the following additions:

a)   *Before installing the cover, pack the cavities between the rotors with petroleum jelly - this will ensure the pump develops suction quickly and begins oil circulation as soon as the engine is started.*
b)   *Make sure the cover dowels and drive pin are in position.*
c)   *Tighten the cover screw to the torque listed in this Chapter's Specifications.*

17   If you're working on a TT-R125 or TT-R250, this is a good time to inspect the strainer screen. Slide it out of its slot in the crankcase **(see**

illustration 20.2 or 20.7) **)**. Clean the strainer with solvent and let it dry. If it's torn or otherwise damaged, replace it.

Installation

18   Installation is the reverse of removal, with the following additions:
a)   *Install a new gasket.*
b)   *Tighten the oil pump mounting screws to the torque listed in this Chapter's Specifications.*
c)   *If you're working on a TT-R90, align the match mark on the rotary filter with the mark (small hole) in the rotary filter's mounting surface on the crankshaft.*
d)   *If you're working on a TT-R125, install the oil pump drive gear with its machined circular groove toward the engine. Position the rotary filter's drive dog away from the engine, and align the drive dog with the matching groove in the crankshaft.*

21   External shift mechanism - removal, inspection and installation

Shift pedal

Removal

Refer to illustrations 21.1 and 21.2

1   If you're working on a TT-R90, TT-R225, TT-R250 or XT350, look for alignment marks on the end of the shift pedal and shift shaft **(see illustration)**. If they aren't visible, make your own marks with a felt pen or sharp punch. Remove the shift pedal pinch bolt completely (it fits in a groove) and slide the pedal off the shaft.
2   If you're working on a TT-R125 or XT225, mark and remove the

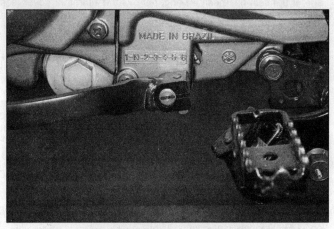

21.1 If there aren't visible alignment marks on the shift shaft and pedal, make a mark on the shaft next to the pedal gap

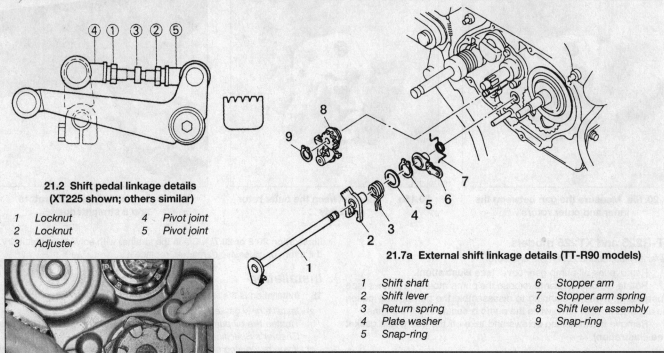

21.2 Shift pedal linkage details (XT225 shown; others similar)

1 Locknut
2 Locknut
3 Adjuster
4 Pivot joint
5 Pivot joint

21.7a External shift linkage details (TT-R90 models)

1 Shift shaft
2 Shift lever
3 Return spring
4 Plate washer
5 Snap-ring
6 Stopper arm
7 Stopper arm spring
8 Shift lever assembly
9 Snap-ring

21.7b Pull the shift shaft out of the crankcase, pulling it back from the shift cam if necessary (TT-R225 shown)

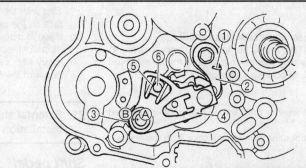

21.7c TT-R250 external shift linkage

1 Stopper arm spring
2 Stopper arm
3 Washer
4 Shift lever
5 Return spring
6 Return spring post
A Match mark
B Match mark

shift arm as described in Step 1 **(see illustration)**. Then remove the bolt that secures the shift pedal to its pivot shaft and slide the pedal off.

Inspection

3 Check the shift pedal for wear or damage such as bending. Check the splines on the shift pedal and shaft for stripping or step wear. Replace the pedal or shaft if these problems are found.

4 Check the shift shaft seal in the alternator cover for signs of leakage. If the seal has been leaking, remove the alternator cover (see Chapter 4). Pry the seal out of the cover, then tap in a new one with a seal driver or socket the same diameter as the seal.

Installation

5 Install the shift pedal or shift arm. Line up its punch marks and tighten the pinch bolt to the torque listed in this Chapter's Specifications.

6 If you're working on a TT-R125 or XT225, install the pedal pivot bolt and tighten it to the torque listed in this Chapter's Specifications. Adjust the pedal height, using the adjuster, so the center of the shift pedal is even with the top of the footpeg **(see illustration 21.2)**.

External shift linkage

Removal

Refer to illustrations 21.7a, 21.7b, 21.7c and 21.9

6 Remove the right crankcase cover and the clutch (primary clutch on TT-R90 models) (see Section 16 or 17).

7 Pull the shift shaft and its washer out of the crankcase **(see illustration 18.2b and the accompanying illustrations)**.

21.9 Take off the shift drum segment and locate its dowel

8 Remove the stopper arm snap-ring or bolt, then remove the arm and its spring.

9 Remove the Torx screw from the center of the shift drum segment (if equipped) **(see illustration)**. Remove the shift drum segment and note the location of its dowel **(see illustration)**.

Inspection

Refer to illustration 21.10

10 Check the shift shaft for bends and damage to the splines **(see**

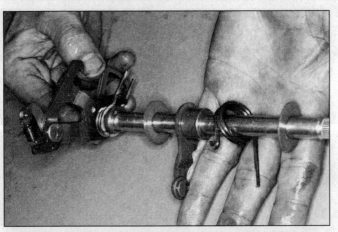

21.10 Check the shift shaft components for wear or damage (TT-R225 shown)

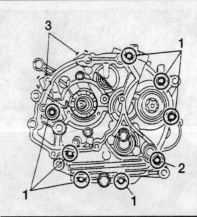

22.11a Crankcase bolts (TT-R125)

1   *45 mm bolts*
2   *55 mm bolt*
3   *30 mm bolts (on far side of crankcase)*

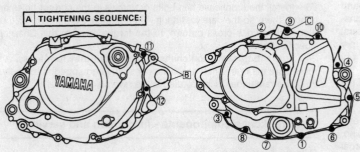

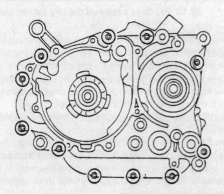

22.11c Crankcase bolts (TT-R250 models)

a) *Tighten the stopper arm bolt (if equipped) and the shift drum segment Torx screw to the torques listed in this Chapter's Specifications.*
b) *If you're working on a TT-R250, align the shift lever match marks (see illustration 21.7c).*
c) *Check the engine oil level and add some, if necessary (see Chapter 1).*

22.11b Crankcase screws (225 models)

1	*Right crankcase half*	4	*Left crankcase half*
2	*Dowels*	5	*Bracket*
3	*Crankcase ventilation*	B	*Starter motor bolts*
	hose	C	*Ground lead bolt*

illustration). If the shaft is bent, you can attempt to straighten it, but if the splines are damaged it will have to be replaced. Check the condition of the return spring, shift arm and the pawl spring. Replace the shift shaft if they're worn, cracked or distorted.

Installation

11   Installation is the reverse of the removal steps, with the following additions:

22 Crankcase - disassembly and reassembly

1   To examine and repair or replace the crankshaft, connecting rod, bearings and transmission components, the crankcase must be split into two parts.

Disassembly

Refer to illustrations 22.11a, 22.11b, 22.11c, 22.12 and 22.15

2   Remove the engine from the vehicle (see Section 5).
3   Remove the carburetor (see Chapter 3).
4   Remove the CDI magneto and the starter motor (if equipped) (see Chapter 4).
5   Remove the clutch(es) (see Sections 16 and 17).
6   Remove the external shift mechanism (see Section 21).
7   Remove the timing chain tensioner, cylinder head, cylinder and piston (see Sections 7, 8, 12 and 13).
8   Remove the timing chain and intake side guide **(see illustration 8.12b)**.
9   Remove the oil pump (see Section 20).
10   Check carefully to make sure there aren't any remaining components that attach the upper and lower halves of the crankcase together.
11   Loosen the crankcase bolts or screws in two or three stages, in a criss-cross pattern **(see illustrations)**.

22.12 Pry only between the pry points (arrow)

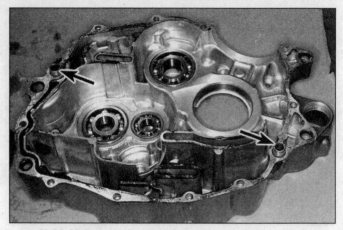

22.15 Make sure the case dowels (arrows) are in place

12   Place the engine on blocks so the transmission shafts and crankshaft can extend downward. Tap gently on the ends of the transmission shafts, balancer shaft (models with external balancer gears) and crankshaft as the case halves are being separated. Carefully pry the crankcase apart at the pry points **(see illustration)**. Don't pry against the mating surfaces or they'll develop leaks.

13   On all except TT-R250 models, lift the right crankcase half off the left half.

14   On TT-R250 models, lift the left half off the right half.

15   Locate the crankcase dowels **(see illustration)**. If they aren't secure in their holes, remove them and set them aside for safekeeping.

16   Refer to Sections 23 through 25 for information on the internal components of the crankcase.

Reassembly

Refer to illustration 22.20

17   Remove all traces of old gasket and sealant from the crankcase mating surfaces with a sharpening stone or similar tool. Be careful not to let any fall into the case as this is done and be careful not to damage the mating surfaces.

18   Check to make sure the dowel pins are in place in their holes in the mating surface of the crankcase.

19   Coat both crankcase mating surfaces with Yamaha Quick Gasket (ACC-11001-05-01) or equivalent sealant.

20   If you're working on a TT-R125 or TT-R250, make sure the timing marks on the balancer gears are aligned **(see illustration)**.

21   Pour some engine oil over the transmission gears, balancer shaft and crankshaft bearing surfaces and the shift cam. Don't get any oil on the crankcase mating surfaces.

22   Carefully place the removed crankcase half onto the other crankcase half. While doing this, make sure the transmission shafts, shift cam, crankshaft and balancer (all except TT-R90) fit into their bearings in the right crankcase half.

23   Install the crankcase half bolts or screws in the correct holes and tighten them so they are just snug. Then tighten them in two or three stages, in a criss-cross pattern, to the torque listed in this Chapter's Specifications.

24   Turn the transmission shafts to make sure they turn freely. Also make sure the crankshaft and balancer shaft (if equipped) turn freely.

25   The remainder of installation is the reverse of removal.

23   Crankcase components - inspection and servicing

Refer to illustration 23.3

1   Separate the crankcase and remove the following:

a) *Transmission shafts and gears*
b) *Balancer (if equipped)*
c) *Crankshaft and main bearings*
d) *Shift drums and forks*

2   Clean the crankcase halves thoroughly with new solvent and dry them with compressed air. All oil passages should be blown out with compressed air and all traces of old gasket sealant should be removed from the mating surfaces. **Caution:** *Be very careful not to nick or gouge the crankcase mating surfaces or leaks will result. Check both crankcase sections very carefully for cracks and other damage.*

3   Check the bearings in the case halves **(see illustration 22.15 and the accompanying illustration)**. If they don't turn smoothly, replace them. For bearings that aren't accessible from the outside, a blind hole puller will be needed for removal. Drive the remaining bearings out with a bearing driver or a socket having an outside diameter slightly smaller than that of the bearing outer race. Before installing the bearings, allow

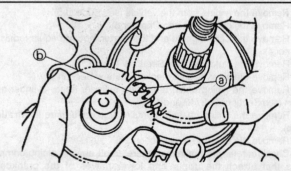

22.20 Align the balancer timing marks on the crankshaft (a) and balancer (b)

23.3 Check the case bearings for roughness, looseness or noise (TT-R225 shown)

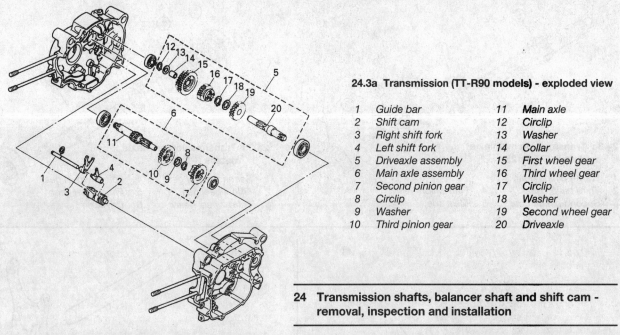

24.3a Transmission (TT-R90 models) - exploded view

1	Guide bar	11	Main axle
2	Shift cam	12	Circlip
3	Right shift fork	13	Washer
4	Left shift fork	14	Collar
5	Driveaxle assembly	15	First wheel gear
6	Main axle assembly	16	Third wheel gear
7	Second pinion gear	17	Circlip
8	Circlip	18	Washer
9	Washer	19	Second wheel gear
10	Third pinion gear	20	Driveaxle

24 Transmission shafts, balancer shaft and shift cam - removal, inspection and installation

them to sit in the freezer overnight, and about fifteen-minutes before installation, place the case half in an oven, set to about 200-degrees F, and allow it to heat up. The bearings are an interference fit, and this will ease installation. **Warning:** *Before heating the case, wash it thoroughly with soap and water so no explosive fumes are present. Also, don't use a flame to heat the case. Install the bearings with a socket or bearing driver that bears against the bearing outer race.*

4   If any damage is found that can't be repaired, replace the crankcase halves as a set.

5   Assemble the case halves (see Section 22) and check to make sure the crankshaft and the transmission shafts turn freely.

Note: *When disassembling the transmission shafts, place the parts on a long rod or thread a wire through them to keep them in order and facing the proper direction.*

Removal

Refer to illustrations 24.3a through 24.3k

1   Remove the engine, then separate the case halves (see Sections 5 and 22).

2   The balancer shaft (all except TT-R90) and transmission components (all models) remain in one case half when the case is separated.

3   Remove the shift cam, shift forks and guide bars (see illustrations).

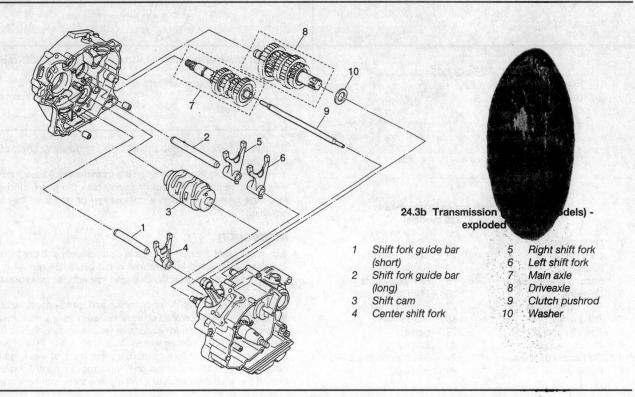

24.3b Transmission (......odels) - exploded

1	Shift fork guide bar (short)	5	Right shift fork
2	Shift fork guide bar (long)	6	Left shift fork
3	Shift cam	7	Main axle
4	Center shift fork	8	Driveaxle
		9	Clutch pushrod
		10	Washer

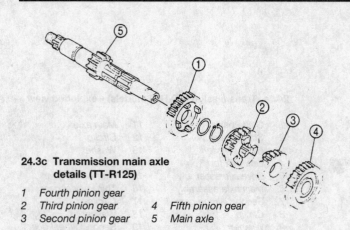

24.3c Transmission main axle details (TT-R125)

1   Fourth pinion gear
2   Third pinion gear
3   Second pinion gear
4   Fifth pinion gear
5   Main axle

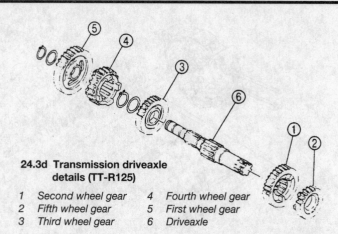

24.3d Transmission driveaxle details (TT-R125)

1   Second wheel gear
2   Fifth wheel gear
3   Third wheel gear
4   Fourth wheel gear
5   First wheel gear
6   Driveaxle

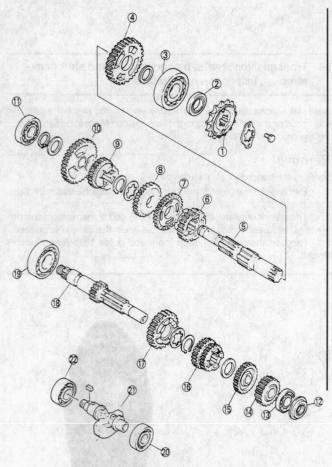

24.3e Transmission and balancer details (TT-R225 and XT225 models)

1	Drive sprocket	12	Oil seal
2	Oil seal	13	Bearing
3	Bearing	14	Second pinion gear
4	Second wheel gear	15	Fifth pinion gear
5	Driveaxle	16	Third pinion gear
6	Fifth wheel gear	17	Fourth pinion gear
7	Third wheel gear	18	Main axle
8	Fourth wheel gear	19	Bearing
9	Sixth wheel gear	20	Bearing
10	First wheel gear	21	Balancer shaft
11	Bearing	22	Bearing

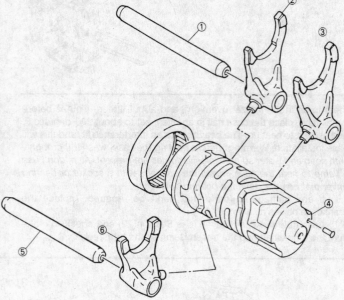

24.3f Internal shift mechanism (TT-R225 and XT225 models)

1   Shift fork guide bar (long)
2   Shift fork
3   Shift fork
4   Shift cam
5   Shift fork guide bar (short)
6   Shift fork

4   On all except TT-R90 models, lift the balancer shaft out of the crankcase.

5   Remove the transmission shafts from the crankcase. Using snapring pliers, remove the snap-rings and take the gears off the shafts. Place the gears in order on a coat hanger or dowel so they won't be mixed up.

Inspection

6   Wash all of the components in clean solvent and dry them off.

7   Inspect the shift fork grooves in the gears. If a groove is worn or scored, replace the affected part and inspect its corresponding shift fork.

8   Check the shift forks for distortion and wear, especially at the fork ears. If they are discolored or severely worn they are probably bent. Inspect the guide pins for excessive wear and distortion and replace any defective parts with new ones.

9   Check the shift fork guide bars evidence of wear, galling and other damage. Make sure the shift forks move smoothly on the guide bars. If the shafts are worn or bent, replace them with new ones.

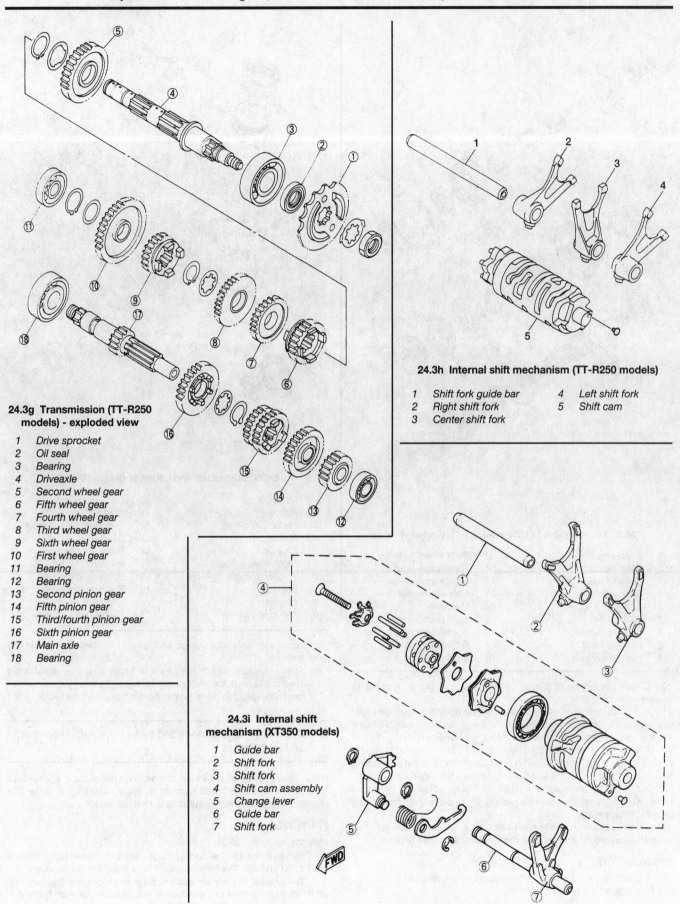

24.3g Transmission (TT-R250 models) - exploded view

1　Drive sprocket
2　Oil seal
3　Bearing
4　Driveaxle
5　Second wheel gear
6　Fifth wheel gear
7　Fourth wheel gear
8　Third wheel gear
9　Sixth wheel gear
10　First wheel gear
11　Bearing
12　Bearing
13　Second pinion gear
14　Fifth pinion gear
15　Third/fourth pinion gear
16　Sixth pinion gear
17　Main axle
18　Bearing

24.3h Internal shift mechanism (TT-R250 models)

1	Shift fork guide bar	4	Left shift fork
2	Right shift fork	5	Shift cam
3	Center shift fork		

24.3i Internal shift mechanism (XT350 models)

1　Guide bar
2　Shift fork
3　Shift fork
4　Shift cam assembly
5　Change lever
6　Guide bar
7　Shift fork

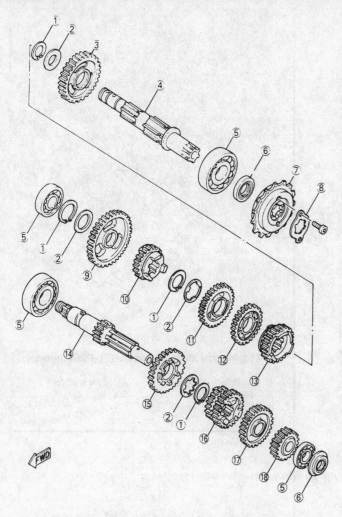

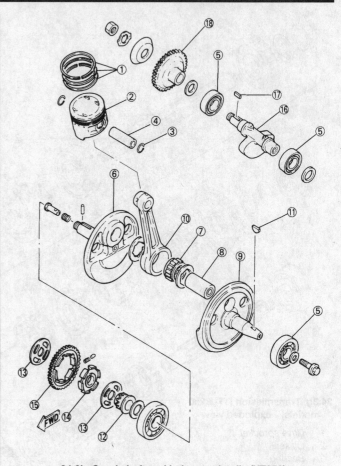

24.3j Transmission (XT350 models) - exploded view

1	Snap-ring	10	Sixth wheel gear
2	Plain washer	11	Third wheel gear
3	Second wheel gear	12	Fourth wheel gear
4	Driveaxle	13	Fifth wheel gear
5	Bearing	14	Main axle
6	Oil seal	15	Sixth pinion gear
7	Drive sprocket	16	Third/fourth pinion gear
8	Holding plate	17	Fifth pinion gear
9	First wheel gear	18	Second pinion gear

24.3k Crankshaft and balancer details (XT350)

1	Piston rings	10	Connecting rod
2	Piston	11	Woodruff key
3	Piston pin circlip	12	Timing chain sprocket
4	Piston pin	13	Washer
5	Bearing	14	Balancer gear boss
6	Right crank wheel		(center)
7	Connecting rod big-end	15	Balancer drive gear
	bearing	16	Balancer shaft
8	Crankpin	17	Woodruff key
9	Left crank wheel	18	Balancer driven gear

10   Check the edges of the grooves in the shift cams for signs of excessive wear.

11   Hold the inner race of the shift cam bearing with fingers and spin the outer race. Replace the bearing if it's rough, loose or noisy. Replace the shift cam segment if it's worn or damaged (see Section 21).

12   Check the gear teeth for cracking and other obvious damage. Check the bushing surface in the inner diameter of the freewheeling gears for scoring or heat discoloration. Replace damaged parts.

13   Inspect the engagement dogs and dog holes on gears so equipped for excessive wear or rounding off. Replace the paired gears as a set if necessary.

14   Check the transmission shaft bearings in the crankcase for wear or heat discoloration and replace them if necessary (see Section 23).

Installation

15   Installation is the basically the reverse of the removal procedure, but take note of the following points:

   a) Use new snap-rings.

   b) Lubricate the components with engine oil before assembling them.

   c) After assembly, check the gears to make sure they're installed correctly. Move the shift cams through the gear positions and rotate the gears to make sure they mesh and shift correctly.

25 Crankshaft and connecting rod - removal, inspection and installation

Note: *The procedures in this section require special tools. If you don't have the necessary equipment or suitable substitutes, have the crankshaft removed and installed by a Yamaha dealer.*

Removal

Refer to illustration 25.2

1   Remove the engine and separate the crankcase halves (Sections 5, 22 and 23). The transmission shafts need not be removed.

2   The crankshaft may be loose enough in its bearing that you can lift it out of the left crankcase half. If not, push it out with tools YU-01135 and YU-01382 or equivalent **(see illustration)**.

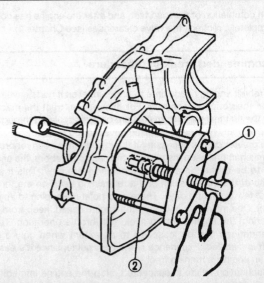

25.2 These special tools are used to push the crankshaft out of the case half

1   *Separating tool YU-01135*
2   *Puller attachment YU-01382*

25.3 Measure the gap between the connecting rod and the crankshaft with a feeler gauge

Inspection

Refer to illustrations 25.3, 25.5 and 25.6

3   Measure the side clearance between connecting rod and crankshaft with a feeler gauge **(see illustration)**. If it's more than the limit listed in this Chapter's Specifications, replace the crankshaft and connecting rod as an assembly.

4   Set up the crankshaft in V-blocks with a dial indicator contacting the big end of the connecting rod. Move the connecting rod side-to-side against the indicator pointer and compare the reading to the value listed in this Chapter's Specifications. If it's beyond the limit, the crankshaft can be disassembled and the needle roller bearing replaced. However, this is a specialized job that should be done by a Yamaha dealer or qualified machine shop.

5   Check the crankshaft splines, the cam chain sprocket, the ball bearing at the sprocket end of the crankshaft and the bearing journals for visible wear or damage **(see illustration)**. Yamaha lists the ball bearing end of the crankshaft as a separately available part, but check with your dealer first; it may be more practical to replace the entire crankshaft if the ball bearing or cam sprocket is worn or damaged. Replace the crankshaft if any of the other conditions are found.

6   Set the crankshaft in a lathe or a pair of V-blocks, with a dial indicator contacting each end **(see illustration)**. Rotate the crankshaft and

25.5 Check the cam chain sprocket and the ball bearing on the end of the crankshaft

note the runout. If the runout at either end is beyond the limit listed in this Chapter's Specifications, replace the crankshaft and connecting rod as an assembly.

7   Measure the assembly width of the crankshaft **(see illustration 25.6)**. If it exceeds the limit listed in this Chapter's Specifications, replace the crankshaft.

Installation

Refer to illustration 25.8

8   Start the crankshaft into the case half. If it doesn't go in easily,

25.6 Measure runout on each side of the crankshaft (A); if the assembly width (B) is greater than specified, replace the crankshaft

25.8 These tools are used to pull the crankshaft into the left case half

pull it in the rest of the way with Yamaha tools YU-90050, YM-01383 and YM-91044 **(see illustration)**.

9   The remainder of installation is the reverse of the removal steps.

26   Initial start-up after overhaul

1   Make sure the engine oil level is correct, then remove the spark plug from the engine. Place the engine kill switch in the Off position and unplug the primary (low tension) wires from the coil.

2   Turn on the key switch and crank the engine over with the starter several times to build up oil pressure. Reinstall the spark plug, connect the wires and turn the switch to On.

3   Make sure there is fuel in the tank, then operate the choke.

4   Start the engine and allow it to run at a moderately fast idle until it reaches operating temperature. **Caution:** *If the oil temperature light doesn't go off, or it comes on while the engine is running, stop the engine immediately.*

5   Check carefully for oil leaks and make sure the transmission and controls, especially the brakes, function properly before road testing the machine. Refer to Section 27 for the recommended break-in procedure.

6   Upon completion of the road test, and after the engine has cooled down completely, recheck the valve clearances (see Chapter 1).

27   Recommended break-in procedure

1   Any rebuilt engine needs time to break-in, even if parts have been installed in their original locations. For this reason, treat the machine gently for the first few miles to make sure oil has circulated throughout the engine and any new parts installed have started to seat.

2   Even greater care is necessary if the cylinder has been rebored or a new crankshaft has been installed. In the case of a rebore, the engine will have to be broken in as if the machine were new. This means greater use of the transmission and a restraining hand on the throttle for the first few operating days. There's no point in keeping to any set speed limit - the main idea is to vary the engine speed, keep from lugging (laboring) the engine and to avoid full-throttle operation. These recommendations can be lessened to an extent when only a new crankshaft is installed. Experience is the best guide, since it's easy to tell when an engine is running freely.

3   If a lubrication failure is suspected, stop the engine immediately and try to find the cause. If an engine is run without oil, even for a short period of time, irreparable damage will occur.

Chapter 3 Part A
Fuel and exhaust systems
(PW50 and PW80 models)

Contents

Specifications

General

Fuel type .... See Chapter 1

Carburetor

PW50

Type..	Mikuni VM12SC
I.D. mark..	4X400
Main jet..	#70
Air jet...	2.5
Jet needle..	3X1
Standard circlip position in jet needle	Second groove
Needle jet..	E-2
Throttle valve cut-away	4.0
Pilot jet...	#40
Pilot outlet size....................................	0.9
Pilot air screw setting	1-3/8 turns out from lightly-seated position
Valve seat size.....................................	1.2
Starter (choke) jet.................................	#30
Float height..	15.5 to 17.5 mm (0.61 to 0.69 inch)

PW80

Type..	Mikuni VM15SC
I.D. mark	21W00
Main jet	#125
Main air jet...	2.5
Jet needle...	3E3
Standard circlip position in jet needle	Third groove
Needle jet...	E-4
Cutaway...	2.5
Pilot jet...	#15
Pilot outlet size....................................	0.9
Pilot air screw setting	1-1/2 turns out from lightly-seated position
Valve seat size.....................................	1.2
Starter (choke) jet.................................	#30
Float height..	20.8 to 22.8 mm (0.82 to 0.90 inch)

2.2a Disconnect the tank-to-tap hose (PW50) . . .

2.2b . . . or the tap-to-carburetor hose (PW80)

1   General information

The air intake system consists of a reusable foam air filter located inside a plastic air cleaner housing. The air cleaner housing is connected to the carburetor by an intake duct. The fuel system consists of the fuel tank, the fuel tap, the filter screen, the fuel line, the carburetor and the throttle cable. All models use a piston-valve design, in which the piston acts as the throttle valve. Basic design is the same for all models. A starter plunger knob actuates a choke for cold starting. The exhaust system consists of an expansion chamber and a muffler.

Many of the fuel system service procedures are considered routine maintenance items (see Chapter 1).

2   Fuel tank, fuel tap and oil tank - removal, inspection and installation

Warning: *Gasoline is extremely flammable, so take extra precautions when you work on any part of the fuel system. Don't smoke or allow open flames or bare light bulbs near the work area, and don't work in a garage where a natural gas-type appliance (such as a water heater or clothes dryer) is present. Since gasoline is carcinogenic, wear latex gloves when there's a possibility of being exposed to fuel, and, if you spill any fuel on your skin, rinse it off immediately with soap and water. Mop up any spills immediately and do not store fuel-soaked rags where*

they could ignite. When you perform any kind of work on the fuel system, wear safety glasses and have an extinguisher suitable for a class B type fire (flammable liquids) on hand.

Fuel tank

Removal

Refer to illustrations 2.2a, 2.2b, 2.3, 2.4 and 2.5

1   Remove the seat (see Chapter 7).
2   Turn the fuel tap to OFF and disconnect the fuel line(s) from the fuel tap **(see illustrations)**.
3   Disconnect the fuel tank vent hose from the filler cap **(see illustration)**.
4   Unhook the strap from the rear of the tank **(see illustration)**.
5   Remove the fuel tank mounting through-bolt and nut **(see illustration)**.
6   Lift the fuel tank off the bike.

Inspection and installation

7   Before installing the tank, inspect the condition of the rubber mounting bushings at the front, the rubber isolators on the frame and the rubber strap at the rear. If any of these pieces are hardened, cracked, or show any other signs of deterioration, replace them.
8   When installing the tank, reverse the removal procedure. Make sure the tank does not pinch any wires. Tighten the tank mounting bolts securely, but don't overtighten them and strip the threads.

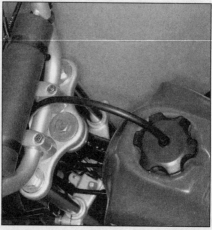

2.3 Note the routing of the tank vent hose over the handlebars, then disconnect it from the fuel filler cap

2.4 Unhook the tank hold-down strap from the rear of the tank

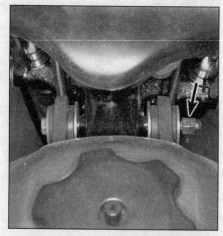

2.5 Remove the fuel tank mounting nut (arrow) and through-bolt

2.9a Remove the tap-to-frame screw (PW50) . . .

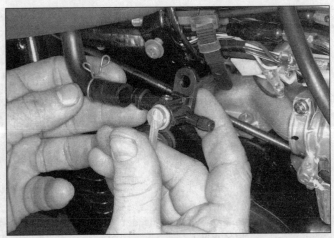

2.9b . . . take the tap off and disconnect the fuel line

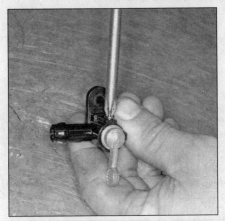

2.10a Remove the valve screw . . .

2.10b . . . then pull out the valve and inspect the O-ring

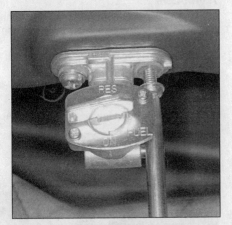

2.11a Remove the tap mounting screws (PW80) . . .

Fuel tap

PW50 models

Refer to illustrations 2.9a, 2.9b, 2.10a and 2.10b

9   The fuel tap is mounted on the frame. Disconnect the lines and remove the mounting screw to remove it **(see illustrations)**.

10   To inspect the tap O-ring, remove the screw and pull out the valve **(see illustrations)**. The O-ring isn't available separately. If it's leaking, replace the fuel tap as an assembly.

PW80 models

Refer to illustrations 2.11a, 2.11b and 2.12a through 2.12e

11   The fuel tap is mounted on the tank. To remove it, disconnect the line, remove the mounting screws and withdraw the tap from the tank **(see illustrations)**.

12   To disassemble and inspect the fuel tap, refer to the accompanying illustrations **(see illustrations)**.

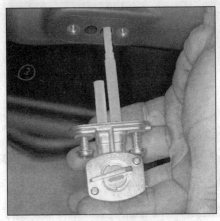

2.11b . . . then pull it off the tank and inspect the filter

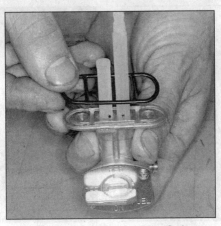

2.12a Inspect the mounting O-ring

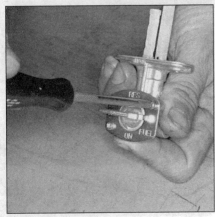

2.12b Remove the valve plate screws . . .

2.12c . . . and take off the plate to inspect its O-ring

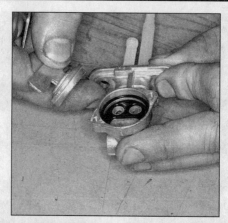

2.12d Pull the valve out of the body, remove the gasket . . .

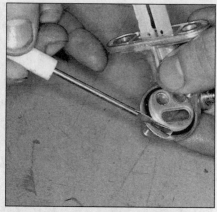

2.12e . . . and pry out the O-ring

All models

13   Assembly and installation are the reverse of disassembly and removal. Tighten the screws securely, but don't overtighten them and strip the threads.

Oil tank

PW50 models

Refer to illustrations 2.17a and 2.17b

14   Remove the front fender (see Chapter 7A).

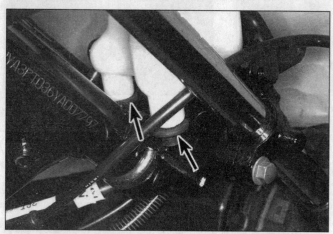

2.17a These are the PW50 oil tank mounting grommets . . .

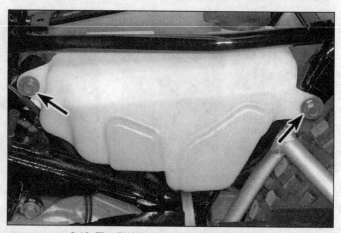

2.17b Lift the grommets out of the bracket and disconnect the oil line

15   Remove the oil tank filler cap (see Chapter 1).
16   Remove the upper triple clamp (see Chapter 5), then remove the upper tank bracket.
17   Lift the tank out of its grommets, then disconnect the oil line **(see illustrations)**. Plug the line and the line fitting on the tank so they won't leak.

PW80 models

Refer to illustration 2.19

18   Remove the seat and rear fender (see Chapter 7).
19   Remove the tank mounting bolts **(see illustration)**. Lift the tank out and disconnect the oil line from the tank. Plug the line and the line fitting on the tank so they won't leak.

All models

20   Installation is the reverse of the removal steps. Don't forget to check the oil level in the tank and add some, if necessary.

---

3   Fuel tank - cleaning and repair

---

1   Have the fuel tank repaired by a professional with experience in this critical and potentially dangerous work. Even after cleaning and flushing of the fuel system, explosive fumes can remain and ignite during repair of the tank.
2   If the fuel tank is removed from the vehicle, it should not be placed in an area where sparks or open flames could ignite the fumes coming out of the tank. Be especially careful inside garages where a natural gas-type appliance is located, because the pilot light could cause an explosion.

2.19 The PW80 oil tank is bolted in place

4.2 Slide back the clip and disconnect the oil line from the carburetor (PW50)

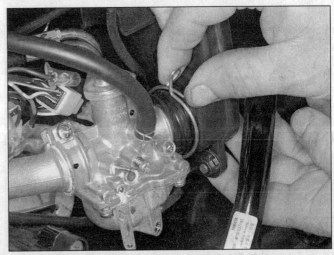

4.3 Squeeze the intake duct clamp and slide it back along the duct

4   Carburetor - removal and installation

Warning: *Gasoline is extremely flammable, so take extra precautions when you work on any part of the fuel system. See the* **Warning** *in Section 2.*

Removal

PW50 models

Refer to illustrations 4.2, 4.3, 4.4a, 4.4b, 4.5 and 4.6

1   Turn the fuel tap to the OFF position. Remove the seat (see Chapter 7) and the fuel tank (see Section 2).

2   Disconnect the oil delivery tube from the carburetor **(see illustration)**.

3   Loosen the clamping band on the air cleaner duct **(see illustration)**. Work the intake duct free of the carburetor.

4   Remove the mixing chamber top **(see illustration)** and pull out the throttle valve return spring, the throttle valve and the jet needle **(see illustration)**.

5   Loosen the clamp screw on the intake tube and disconnect the fuel hose from the carburetor **(see illustration)**.

6   Pull the carburetor off the intake tube and remove the mounting sleeve **(see illustration)**.

4.4a Remove the screw that secures the carburetor top . . .

7   After the carburetor has been removed, stuff clean rags into the intake joint and the intake duct to prevent the entry of dirt or other objects.

4.4b . . . lift the top and pull the throttle and starter (choke) valves out of their bores . . .

4.5 . . . loosen the intake tube clamp screw (left arrow) and disconnect the fuel line (right arrow) . . .

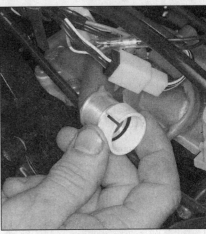

4.6 . . . then pull the carburetor off and remove the plastic sleeve from the intake tube (its rubber seal will probably stay in the carburetor bore)

4.8 Loosen the clamp screws and remove the air intake duct (PW80)

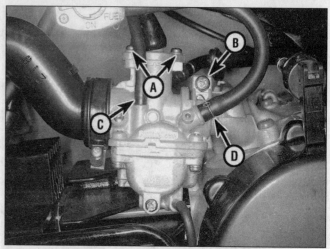

4.9a Remove the carburetor top screws (A), loosen the clamp screw (B) and disconnect the oil and fuel lines (C and D) . . .

PW80 models

Refer to illustrations 4.8, 4.9a and 4.9b

8   Loosen the clamping bands on the air intake duct and remove the duct **(see illustration)**.

9   Remove the mixing chamber top **(see illustration)** and pull out the throttle valve return spring, the throttle valve and the jet needle **(see illustration)**.

10   Disconnect the oil and fuel lines and loosen the intake joint clamp screw **(see illustration 4.9a)**. Pull the carburetor off the intake tube and remove the mounting sleeve.

Installation

11   Installation is the reverse of removal, with the following additions:

  a) *Be sure to clean and inspect the throttle valve bore, the throttle valve return spring, the throttle valve and the jet needle before reassembling the carburetor (see Section 6).*

  b) *After installing the carburetor, adjust the throttle cable freeplay and idle speed (see Chapter 1).*

5   Carburetor overhaul - general information

1   Poor engine performance, hesitation, hard starting, stalling, flooding and backfiring are all signs that major carburetor maintenance may be required.

2   Keep in mind that many so-called carburetor problems are really not carburetor problems at all, but mechanical problems within the engine or ignition system malfunctions. Try to establish for certain that the carburetor is in need of maintenance before beginning a major overhaul.

3   Before assuming that a carburetor overhaul is required, check the fuel tap and strainer screen, the fuel line, the intake joint clamp and reed valve gasket, the air filter element, cylinder compression, crankcase vacuum and compression, the spark plug and ignition timing.

4   Most carburetor problems are caused by dirt particles, varnish and other deposits that build up in and block the fuel and air passages. Also, in time, gaskets and O-rings shrink or deteriorate and cause fuel and air leaks which lead to poor performance.

5   When the carburetor is overhauled, it is generally disassembled completely and the parts are cleaned thoroughly with a carburetor cleaning solvent and dried with filtered, unlubricated compressed air. The fuel and air passages are also blown through with compressed air to force out any dirt that may have been loosened but not removed by the solvent. Once the carburetor is clean, reassemble it using the new gaskets, O-rings and other parts included in the rebuild kit. (If you're

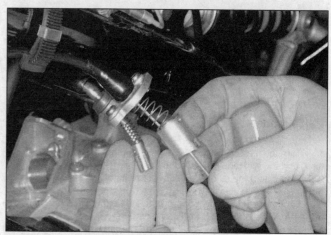

4.9b . . . then remove the carburetor top and pull the throttle and starter (choke) valves out of their bores

using individual parts instead of a rebuild kit, replace all "soft" parts - gaskets, O-rings, etc. - and any damaged or worn hard parts.)

6   Before disassembling the carburetor, make sure you have the necessary gaskets, O-rings and other parts (usually included in a carburetor rebuild kit), some carburetor cleaner, a supply of clean rags, compressed air for blowing out the carburetor passages and a clean place to work.

6   Carburetor - disassembly, cleaning and inspection

Disassembly

Warning: *Gasoline is extremely flammable, so take extra precautions when you work on any part of the fuel system. See the* **Warning** *in Section 2.*

1   Remove the carburetor from the engine (see Section 5).

2   Wipe off the outside surface of the carburetor and set it on a clean working surface.

3   Note how all vent hoses are routed, including locations of any hose retainers, then disconnect all hoses from the carburetor.

PW50 models

Refer to illustrations 6.4a through 6.4m

4   To disassemble the carburetor, refer to the accompanying illustrations **(see illustrations)**.

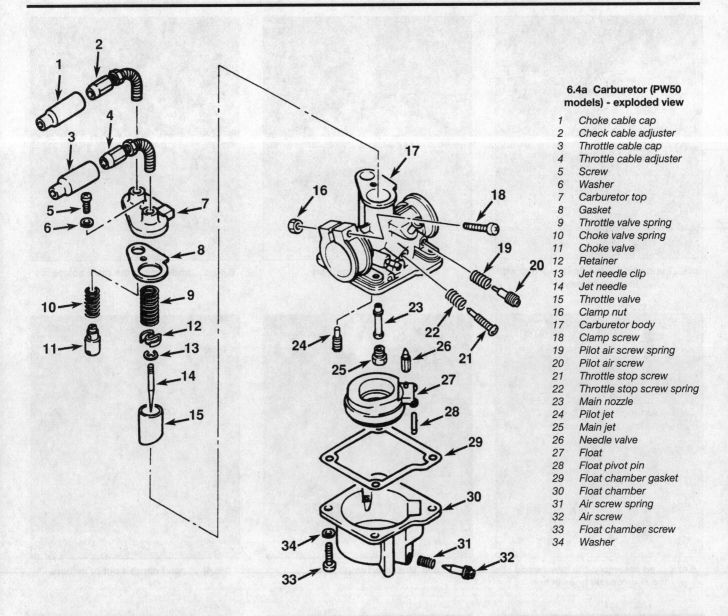

6.4a Carburetor (PW50 models) - exploded view

1   Choke cable cap
2   Check cable adjuster
3   Throttle cable cap
4   Throttle cable adjuster
5   Screw
6   Washer
7   Carburetor top
8   Gasket
9   Throttle valve spring
10 Choke valve spring
11 Choke valve
12 Retainer
13 Jet needle clip
14 Jet needle
15 Throttle valve
16 Clamp nut
17 Carburetor body
18 Clamp screw
19 Pilot air screw spring
20 Pilot air screw
21 Throttle stop screw
22 Throttle stop screw spring
23 Main nozzle
24 Pilot jet
25 Main jet
26 Needle valve
27 Float
28 Float pivot pin
29 Float chamber gasket
30 Float chamber
31 Air screw spring
32 Air screw
33 Float chamber screw
34 Washer

6.4b Remove the float chamber screws and washers . . .

6.4c . . . lift off the float chamber and remove the gasket

6.4d Push out the float pivot pin . . .

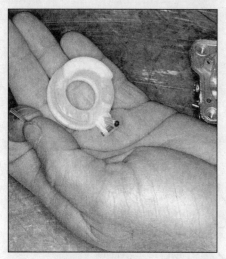

6.4e... and remove the float together with the needle valve

6.4f Unscrew the main jet ...

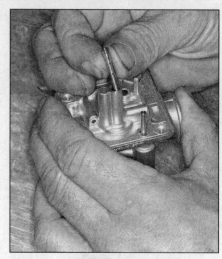

6.4g ... and remove the main nozzle ...

6.4f ... on assembly, the narrow end of the main nozzle goes in first

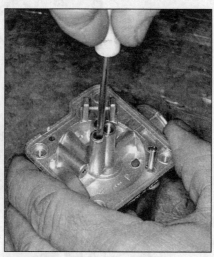

6.4i Unscrew the pilot jet ...

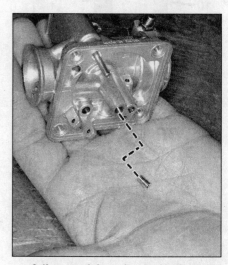

6.4j ... and dump it out of its bore

6.4k Pull the sleeve out of the carburetor if it didn't stay on the intake joint ...

6.4l ... and remove the seal, noting its installed direction

6.4m Remove the throttle stop screw and spring (left arrow) and the pilot screw and spring (right arrow)

6.5a Carburetor (PW80 models) - exploded view

1   Cap
2   Throttle cable adjuster
3   Cap
4   Screw
5   Locknut
6   Carburetor top
7   Gasket
8   Choke spring
9   Choke valve
10 Throttle valve spring
11 Retainer
12 Jet needle clip
13 Jet needle
14 Throttle valve
15 Clamp nut
16 Clamp screw
17 Carburetor body
18 Throttle stop screw spring
19 Throttle stop screw
20 Pilot screw
21 Pilot screw spring
22 Needle valve gasket
23 Needle valve
24 Pilot jet
25 Float pivot pin
26 Float chamber gasket
27 Float chamber
28 Float chamber drain screw
29 Float chamber drain screw gasket
30 Screw and washer
31 Floats
32 Main jet
33 Main nozzle

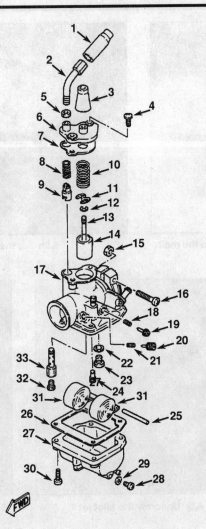

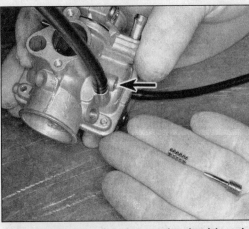

6.5b Remove the pilot screw and spring (shown) and the throttle stop screw and spring (arrow) . . .

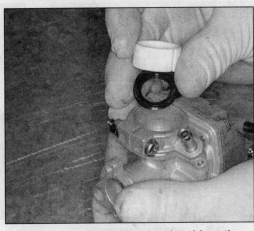

6.5c . . . remove the sleeve and seal from the carburetor bore . . .

PW80 models

Refer to illustrations 6.5a through 6.5k

5   To disassemble the carburetor, refer to the accompanying illustrations (see illustrations).

Cleaning

Caution: *Use only a carburetor cleaning solution that is safe for use with plastic parts (be sure to read the label on the container).*

6   Submerge the metal components in the carburetor cleaner for

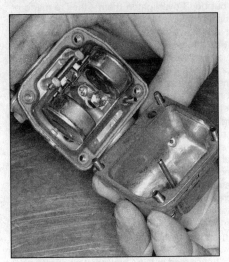

6.5d . . . remove the float chamber screws, the float chamber and gasket . . .

6.5e . . . push out the float pivot pin . . .

6.5f . . . and lift out the floats, together with the needle valve

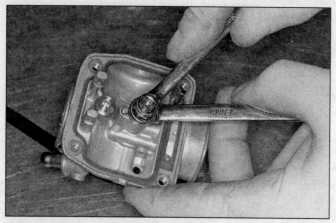

6.5g Hold the main nozzle with one wrench and loosen the main jet with another . . .

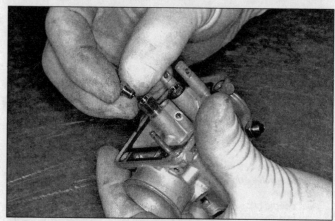

6.5h . . . then unscrew the main jet . . .

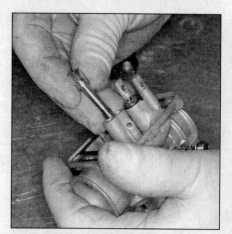

6.5i . . . and the main nozzle

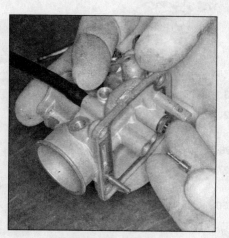

6.5j Unscrew the pilot jet

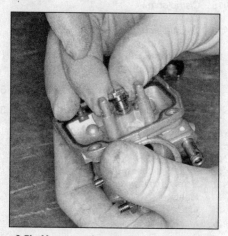

6.5k Unscrew the needle valve seat and remove the gasket

approximately thirty minutes (or longer, if the directions recommend it).

7   After the carburetor has soaked long enough for the cleaner to loosen and dissolve most of the varnish and other deposits, use a brush to remove the stubborn deposits. Rinse it again, then dry it with compressed air. Blow out all of the fuel and air passages in the carburetor body. **Caution:** *Never clean the jets or passages with a piece of wire or a drill bit, as they will be enlarged, causing the fuel and air metering rates to be upset.*

Inspection

8   Check the operation of the starter plunger. It should move smoothly in and out. If it doesn't, replace it.

9   Inspect the tapered portion of the pilot air screw for wear or damage. Replace the screw if necessary.

10   Inspect the carburetor body, float chamber and carburetor top for cracks, distorted sealing surfaces and other damage. If any defects are found, replace the carburetor.

11   Inspect the jet needle tip for excessive wear. Check the jet needle for straightness by rolling it on a flat surface (such as a piece of glass). If the jet needle is bent, or the tip is worn, replace it.

12   Inspect the tip of the needle valve. If it has grooves or scratches in it, replace it. Push in on the rod in the other end of the needle valve, and then release it; if it doesn't spring back, replace the needle valve.

13   Inspect the float assembly. If there is fuel inside either of the floats, replace the float assembly.

14   Insert the throttle valve in the carburetor body and verify that it moves up-and-down smoothly. Check the surface of the throttle valve for wear. If it's worn excessively or doesn't move smoothly in the bore, replace the carburetor.

7   Carburetor - reassembly and float height check

1   Reassembly is basically the reverse of disassembly. Invert the carburetor and install the float chamber parts first.

2   Install the needle jet and install a new O-ring and the main jet. Tighten them securely but don't overtighten them - they're made of soft material and can strip or shear easily.

3   Install the washer and valve seat and tighten the valve seat securely. Again, don't overtighten it.

4   Attach the needle valve to the float. Place the float in its installed position in the carburetor, making sure the needle valve seats correctly against the valve seat. Install the float pivot pin.

5   To check the float height, hold the carburetor upside down, so that the needle valve rests against its seat and the float arm is resting on - but not compressing - the needle valve. Using a float height gauge or a small steel pocket ruler, measure the distance between the float chamber gasket mating surface and the top of the float. Compare your measurement to the float height listed in this Chapter's Specifications. Bend the float arm as necessary to adjust the float height.

6   Install the float chamber gasket. Install the float chamber on the carburetor, install the screws and tighten them securely.

7   Place the carburetor in its upright (installed) position and install the rest of the parts.

8   Install a new O-ring on the pilot air screw, install the spring and install the pilot air screw. Turn the screw in until it seats lightly, then back it out the number of turns listed in this Chapter's Specifications.

9   If the circlip was removed from the jet needle, be sure to install it in the same groove it was in before it was removed (listed in this Chap-

8.4 Remove the air cleaner housing screw (PW50)

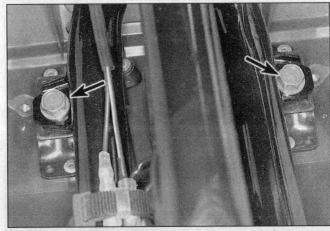

8.6 Remove the air cleaner housing bolts (PW80)

ter's Specifications). Install the jet needle and circlip in the throttle valve. If you disconnected the throttle cable, run it through the carburetor top and reattach it to the throttle valve.

10   Install the carburetor (see Section 5).

8   Air cleaner housing - removal and installation

1   Remove the seat and the side covers (see Chapter 7).
2   Remove the air filter element (see Chapter 1).

PW50 models

Refer to illustration 8.4

3   Detach the carburetor connecting tube from the carburetor and housing **(see illustration 4.3)**.
4   Remove the air cleaner housing screw and take off the housing **(see illustration)**.

PW80 models

Refer to illustration 8.6

5   Detach the carburetor connecting tube from the housing **(see illustration 4.8)**.
6   Remove the air cleaner housing bolts and take off the housing **(see illustration)**.

All models

7   Installation is the reverse of removal. If you removed the connecting tube, apply a ring of silicone sealant to the mating surface of the connecting tube and air cleaner housing.

9   Throttle cable - removal and installation

Refer to illustrations 9.4a, 9.4b, 9.4c, 9.5a, 9.5b, 9.7 and 9.10

1   Remove the fuel tank (see Section 2).
2   At the handlebar, loosen the throttle cable adjuster all the way (see Chapter 1).
3   Look for a punch mark on the handlebar next to the split in the throttle housing. If you don't see a mark, make one so the throttle housing can be installed in the correct position.
4   Remove the throttle housing screws and open up the throttle housing **(see illustrations)**.

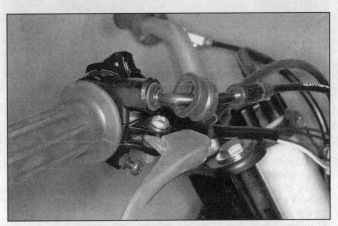

9.4a Pull back the throttle cable boot . . .

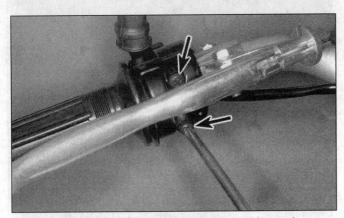

9.4b . . . remove the throttle housing screws (arrows) . . .

9.4c . . . separate the halves of the throttle housing

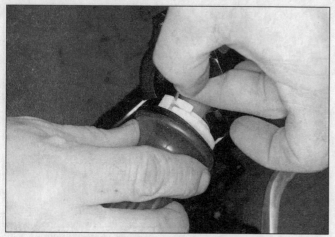

9.5a . . . unhook the cable end from the pulley . . .

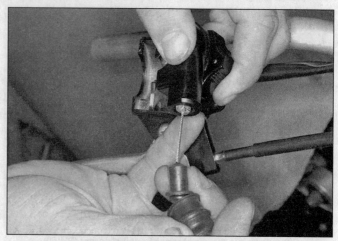

9.5b . . . then pull out the cable grommet and pull the cable through the housing

9.7 On PW80 models, open up the cable connector to separate the upper and lower throttle cables and the oil pump cable

9.10 Install the collar (if equipped)

5   Disengage the throttle cable from the throttle grip pulley and pull it out of the housing **(see illustrations)**.
6   Detach the throttle cable from the carburetor (see Section 4) and the oil pump (see Chapter 2).
7   If you're working on a PW80, the throttle cable connector can be opened up so the throttle cable, oil pump cable and carburetor cable can be replaced separately **(see illustration)**.
8   Note the routing of the old throttle cable, then remove it. Using the same routing, place the new cable in position. Make sure it doesn't interfere with any other components and isn't kinked or bent sharply.
9   Lubricate the throttle pulley end of the cable with multi-purpose grease. Reverse the disconnection steps to connect the throttle cable to the throttle grip pulley.
10   Coat the end of the handlebar with silicone grease and slide on the throttle grip. Don't forget the collar if there is one **(see illustration)**.
11   Install the throttle housing. Position the housing so that the mating line of the two halves of the housing is aligned with the punch mark on the handlebar, then install the housing screws and tighten them securely.
12   Connect the throttle cable to the carburetor and oil pump (see Section 4 and Chapter 2).
13   Operate the throttle and make sure it returns to the idle position by itself under spring pressure. **Warning:** *If the throttle doesn't return by itself, find and solve the problem before continuing with installation. A stuck throttle can lead to loss of control of the motorcycle.*
14   Adjust the cable (see *Throttle cable freeplay - check and adjustment* in Chapter 1).

15   Turn the handlebars back and forth to make sure the cable does not cause the steering to bind.
16   Once you're sure the cable operates properly, install the fuel tank.
17   With the engine idling, turn the handlebars through their full travel (full left lock to full right lock) and note whether the idle speed increases. If it does, the cable is routed incorrectly. Correct this dangerous condition before riding the bike.

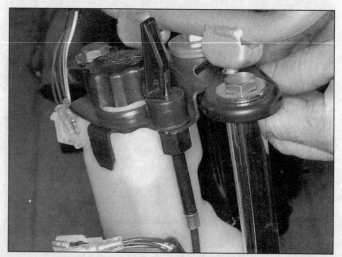

10.2a Here's the PW50 choke lever

10.2b Here's the PW80 choke lever

10.3 Unscrew the plastic nut and pull the cable
through the bracket

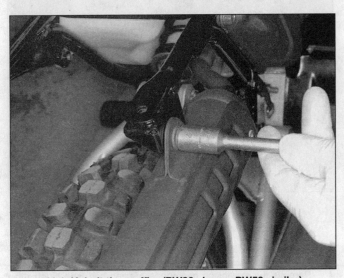

11.1 Unbolt the muffler (PW80 shown; PW50 similar)

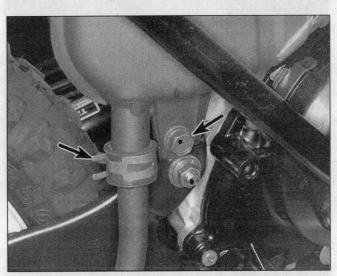

11.2a On PW50 models, loosen the clamp (left arrow) and remove
the expansion chamber bolt (right arrow); on installation, be sure
the ends of the clamp are toward the center of the bike

10 Choke cable - removal and installation

Refer to illustrations 10.2a, 10.2b and 10.3

1   Remove the carburetor top and disconnect the choke cable from the starter (choke) valve (see Section 4).

2   Locate the choke knob near the handlebars (PW50) or at the side of the bike (PW80) **(see illustrations)**.

3   Unscrew the plastic nut that secure the cable and pull it through the bracket **(see illustration)**.

4   Installation is the reverse of the removal steps.-

11 Exhaust system - removal and installation

Refer to illustrations 11.1, 11.2a, 11.2b, 11.3a, 11.3b, 11.4, 11.5a and 11.5b

1   Remove the muffler mounting bolt **(see illustration)**.

2   Loosen the clamp that attaches the expansion chamber to the muffler **(see illustrations)** and remove the muffler.

11.2b Here's the PW80 muffler-to-expansion chamber clamp

11.3a Remove the expansion chamber bolts (PW50) . . .

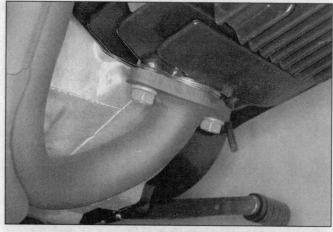

11.3b . . . or nuts (PW80)

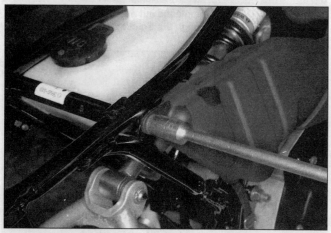

11.4 Unbolt the PW80 expansion chamber

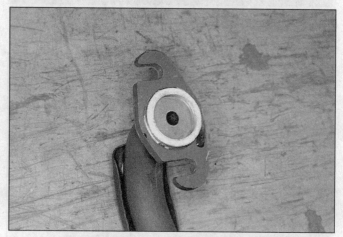

11.5a Replace the gasket with a new one . . .

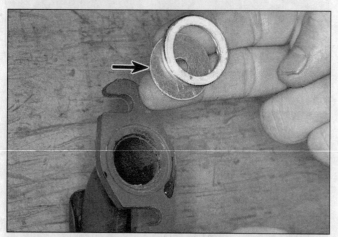

11.5b . . . the restrictor plate can be reinstalled or left out, depending on power needs

3   Remove the exhaust pipe nuts or bolts that secure the expansion chamber to the cylinder head **(see illustrations)**.
4   Remove the expansion chamber mounting bolt **(see illustration 10.3 and the accompanying illustration)**. Remove the expansion chamber and exhaust pipe.
5   Inspect the expansion chamber gasket **(see illustration)**. The restrictor plate inside the opening **(see illustration)** is meant to reduce the engine's power for inexperienced riders. It can be reinstalled or left out, depending on the riders' power needs and skill level.
6   Installation is the reverse of removal. On PW50 models, make sure that the projection on the muffler-to-expansion chamber clamp is facing in, toward the wheel **(see illustration)**. Tighten all exhaust system fasteners securely.

Chapter 3 Part B
Fuel and exhaust systems
(RT100 and RT180 models)

Contents

Specifications

General

Fuel type .... See Chapter 1

Carburetor

RT100

Main jet	140
Pilot jet	17.5
Jet needle	4L6
Standard circlip position in jet needle	Third groove
Needle jet	0-6
Throttle valve cut-away	2.0
Pilot air screw setting	1-1/2 turns out from lightly-seated position
Valve seat size	1.5
Starter jet	30
Float height	20 to 22 mm (0.79 to 0.87 inch)
Fuel level	-0.5 to +0.5 mm (-0.02 to +0.02 inch)

RT180

Main jet	130
Main air jet	0.5
Jet needle	5JP27
Standard circlip position in jet needle	Second groove
Needle jet	Px2
Pilot jet	27.5
Pilot air screw setting	1-1/2 turns out from lightly-seated position
Float height	20 to 22 mm (0.79 to 0.87 inch)
Fuel level	-0.5 to +0.5 mm (-0.02 to +0.02 inch)

Torque specifications

Exhaust pipe to cylinder nuts	
RT100	11 Nm (95 inch-lbs)
RT180	7 Nm (61 inch-lbs)
Expansion chamber bolt	
RT100	Not specified
RT180	16 Nm (132 inch-lbs)
Muffler bolt	
RT100	Not specified
RT180	23 Nm (17 ft-lbs)

2.2 Squeeze the ends of the clamp together, slide it down the hose, and disconnect the hose from the tap

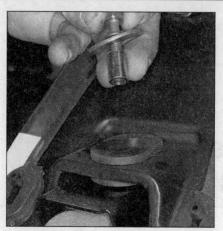

2.3 Remove the bolt or bolts at the rear of the tank . . .

2.4 . . . and one bolt at the front of the tank on each side

1   General information

The air intake system consists of a reusable foam air filter located inside a plastic air cleaner housing. The air cleaner housing is connected to the carburetor by an intake duct. The fuel system consists of the fuel tank, the fuel tap, the filter screen, the fuel line, the carburetor and the throttle cable. All RT100 and RT180 models use a piston-valve carburetor, in which the piston acts as the throttle valve. Basic design is the same for all models. A starter (choke) plunger knob actuates a fuel enrichment circuit for cold starting. The exhaust system consists of an expansion chamber and a muffler.

Many of the fuel system service procedures are considered routine maintenance items, so they're included in Chapter 1.

2   Fuel tank - removal and installation

Warning: *Gasoline is extremely flammable, so take extra precautions when you work on any part of the fuel system. Don't smoke or allow open flames or bare light bulbs near the work area, and don't work in a garage where a natural gas-type appliance (such as a water heater or clothes dryer) is present. Since gasoline is carcinogenic, wear latex gloves when there's a possibility of being exposed to fuel, and, if you spill any fuel on your skin, wash it off immediately with soap and water. Mop up any spills immediately and do not store fuel-soaked rags where they could ignite. When you perform any kind of work on the fuel system, wear safety glasses and have an extinguisher suitable for a class B type fire (flammable liquids) on hand.*

Removal

Refer to illustrations 2.2, 2.3 and 2.4

1   Remove the seat (see Chapter 7).
2   Unscrew the fuel tank cap, which conations the fuel tank vent hose, and set it aside. Turn the fuel tap to Off and disconnect the fuel line **(see illustration)**.
3   Remove the mounting bolt or bolts from the rear of the tank **(see illustration)**.
4   Remove the fuel tank front mounting bolts **(see illustration)**.
5   Lift the fuel tank off the bike together with the fuel tap.

Installation

6   Before installing the tank, check the condition of the rubber mounting bushings at the front and rear. If they're hardened, cracked, or show any other signs of deterioration, replace them.
7   When installing the tank, reverse the removal procedure. Make sure the tank does not pinch any wires. Tighten the tank mounting bolts securely, but don't overtighten them and strip the threads.

3   Fuel tank - cleaning and repair

1   Have the fuel tank repaired by a professional with experience in this critical and potentially dangerous work. Even after cleaning and flushing of the fuel system, explosive fumes can remain and ignite during repair of the tank.
2   If the fuel tank is removed from the vehicle, it should not be placed in an area where sparks or open flames could ignite the fumes coming out of the tank. Be especially careful inside garages where a natural gas-type appliance is located, because the pilot light could cause an explosion.

4   Carburetor fuel level - check and adjustment

Refer to illustration 4.3a and 4.3b

1   Adjust the float height (see Section 7).
2   Put the bike on a level surface. Then, using a floor jack, jack up the bike as necessary to put the carburetor in a perfectly vertical position. Put a wood board between the jack head and the bike to protect the engine.
3   Attach the fuel level gauge **(see illustrations)**.
4   Loosen the drain screw, start the engine and allow it to warm up for a few minutes.

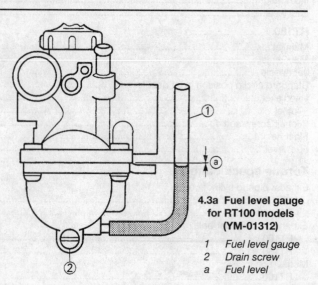

4.3a Fuel level gauge for RT100 models (YM-01312)

1 Fuel level gauge
2 Drain screw
a Fuel level

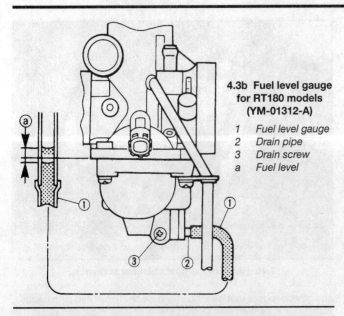

4.3b Fuel level gauge for RT180 models (YM-01312-A)

1 *Fuel level gauge*
2 *Drain pipe*
3 *Drain screw*
a *Fuel level*

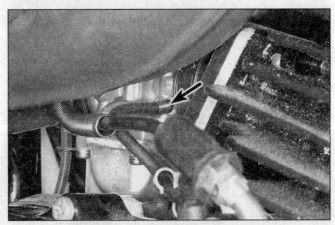

5.3a Slide back the metal fitting (arrow) . . .

5   Measure the fuel level and compare your measurement to the fuel level listed in this Chapter's Specifications.

6   If the fuel level is incorrect, remove the carburetor (see Section 5) and inspect the valve seat and needle valve (see Section 7).

7   If either the valve seat or needle valve is worn, replace both of them (see Section 7).

8   If there's nothing wrong with the valve seat and the needle valve, adjust the float height by bending the float tang (see Section 8).

9   Recheck the fuel level.

5   Carburetor - removal and installation

Warning: *Gasoline is extremely flammable, so take extra precautions when you work on any part of the fuel system. See the* **Warning** *in Section 2.*

Removal

Refer to illustrations 5.3a, 5.3b, 5.4 and 5.5

1   Turn the fuel tap to the OFF position.

2   Disconnect the fuel line from the fuel tap **(see illustration 2.2)**.

3   Disconnect the oil delivery tube **(see illustrations)**.

4   Loosen the clamping bands on the air cleaner duct and the intake joint **(see illustration)**. Work the carburetor free of the intake duct and intake joint.

5   Unscrew the top cap from the carburetor and pull out the throttle valve return spring, throttle valve and jet needle **(see illustration)**.

6   After the carburetor has been removed, stuff clean rags into the intake joint and the intake duct to prevent the entry of dirt or other objects.

Installation

7   Installation is the reverse of the removal steps, with the following additions:
a) *Adjust the throttle cable freeplay (see Chapter 1).*
b) *Adjust the idle speed (see Chapter 1).*

6   Carburetor overhaul - general information

1   Poor engine performance, hesitation, hard starting, stalling, flooding and backfiring are all signs that major carburetor maintenance may be required.

2   Keep in mind that many so-called carburetor problems are really not carburetor problems at all, but mechanical problems within the engine or ignition system malfunctions. Try to establish for certain that the carburetor is in need of maintenance before beginning a major overhaul.

3   Before assuming that a carburetor overhaul is required, check the fuel tap and strainer screen, the fuel line, the intake joint clamp and reed valve gasket, the air filter element, crankcase vacuum and compression, the spark plug and ignition timing.

4   Most carburetor problems are caused by dirt particles, varnish

5.3b . . . and disconnect the oil line from the carburetor

5.4 Loosen the hose clamps on the carburetor intake joint and the intake duct (arrows)

5.5 Unscrew the carburetor cap and pull out the jet needle, spring and throttle valve

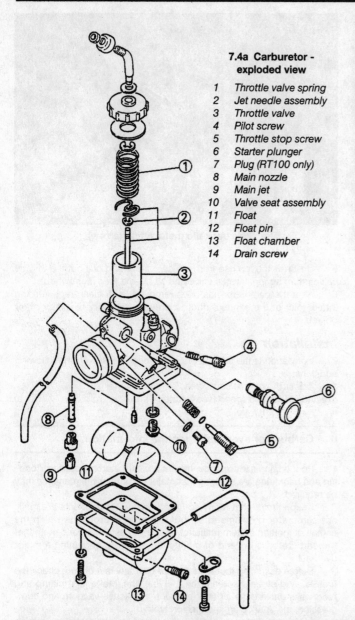

7.4a Carburetor - exploded view

1   Throttle valve spring
2   Jet needle assembly
3   Throttle valve
4   Pilot screw
5   Throttle stop screw
6   Starter plunger
7   Plug (RT100 only)
8   Main nozzle
9   Main jet
10 Valve seat assembly
11 Float
12 Float pin
13 Float chamber
14 Drain screw

7.4b Remove the float chamber screws. . .

and other deposits that build up in and block the fuel and air passages. Also, in time, gaskets and O-rings shrink or deteriorate and cause fuel and air leaks which lead to poor performance.

5   When the carburetor is overhauled, it is generally disassembled completely and the parts are cleaned thoroughly with a carburetor cleaning solvent and dried with filtered, unlubricated compressed air. The fuel and air passages are also blown through with compressed air to force out any dirt that may have been loosened but not removed by the solvent. Once the carburetor is clean, reassemble it using new gaskets, O-rings and other parts included in the rebuild kit. (If you're using individual parts instead of a rebuild kit, replace all "soft" parts - gaskets, O-rings, etc. - and any damaged or worn hard parts.)

6   Before disassembling the carburetor, make sure you have the necessary gaskets, O-rings and other parts (usually included in a carburetor rebuild kit), some carburetor cleaner, a supply of clean rags, compressed air for blowing out the carburetor passages and a clean place to work.

7   Carburetor - disassembly, cleaning and inspection

Disassembly

Refer to illustrations 7.4a through 7.4q

Warning: Gasoline is extremely flammable, so take extra precautions when you work on any part of the fuel system. See the **Warning** in

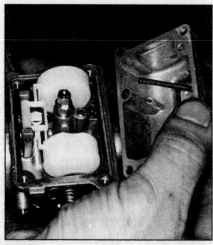

7.4c . . . remove the float chamber and gasket . . .

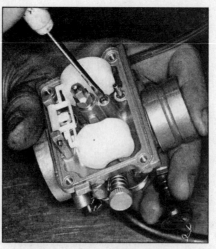

7.4d . . . unscrew the pilot jet . . .

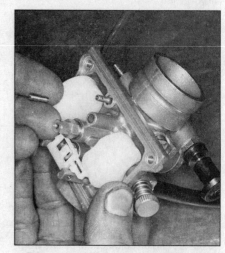

7.4e . . . and lift it out; note which end goes in first . . .

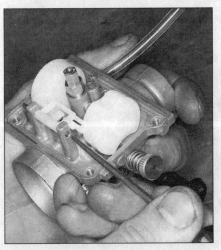

7.4f . . . push out the float pivot pin and remove the float . . .

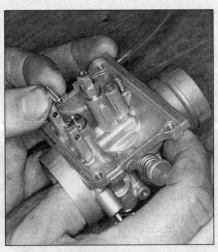

7.4g . . . remove the needle valve . . .

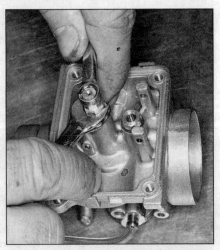

7.4h . . . hold the main jet housing with one wrench and loosen the main jet with another wrench . . .

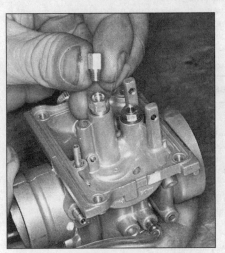

7.4i . . . then remove the main jet . . .

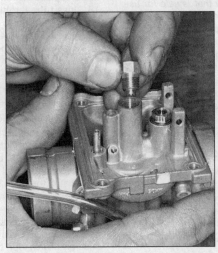

7.4j . . . unscrew the main jet housing . . .

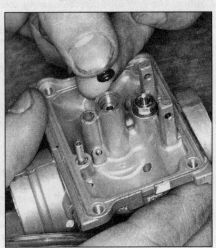

7.4k . . . and remove its O-ring . . .

Section 2.
1   Remove the carburetor from the engine (see Section 6).
2   Wipe off the outside surface of the carburetor and set it on a clean working surface.

3   Note how all vent hoses are routed, including locations of any hose retainers, then disconnect all hoses from the carburetor.
4   To disassemble the carburetor, refer to the accompanying illustrations **(see illustrations)**.

7.4l . . . remove the needle jet, noting which end goes in first . . .

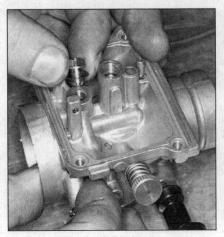

7.4m . . . unscrew the needle valve and remove its gasket . . .

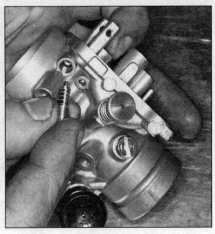

7.4n . . . unscrew the pilot screw . . .

7.4o . . . peel back the choke plunger boot . . .

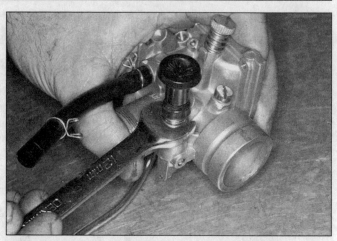

7.4p . . . and unscrew the choke plunger from the carburetor body . . .

Cleaning

Caution: *Use only a carburetor cleaning solution that is safe for use with plastic parts (be sure to read the label on the container).*

5   Submerge the metal components in the carburetor cleaner for approximately thirty minutes (or longer, if the directions recommend it).

6   After the carburetor has soaked long enough for the cleaner to loosen and dissolve most of the varnish and other deposits, use a brush to remove the stubborn deposits. Rinse it again, then dry it with compressed air. Blow out all of the fuel and air passages in the carburetor body. **Caution:** *Never clean the jets or passages with a piece of wire or a drill bit, as they will be enlarged, causing the fuel and air metering rates to be upset.*

Inspection

7   Check the operation of the starter plunger. It should move smoothly in and out. If it doesn't, replace it.

8   Inspect the tapered portion of the pilot air screw for wear or damage. Replace the screw if necessary.

9   Inspect the carburetor body, float chamber and carburetor top for cracks, distorted sealing surfaces and other damage. If any defects are found, replace the carburetor.

10   Inspect the jet needle tip for excessive wear. Check the jet needle for straightness by rolling it on a flat surface (such as a piece of glass). If the jet needle is bent, or the tip is worn, replace it.

11   Inspect the tip of the needle valve. If it has grooves or scratches in it, replace it. Push in on the rod in the other end of the needle valve, and then release it; if it doesn't spring back, replace the needle valve.

12   Inspect the float assembly. If there is fuel inside either of the floats, replace the float assembly.

13   Insert the throttle valve in the carburetor body and verify that it moves up-and-down smoothly. Check the surface of the throttle valve for wear. If it's worn excessively or doesn't move smoothly in the bore, replace the carburetor.

8   Carburetor - reassembly and float height check

Refer to illustration 8.5

Note: *When reassembling the carburetor, be sure to use all new O-rings and gaskets included in your rebuild kit.*

1   Reassembly is basically the reverse of disassembly. Invert the carburetor and install the float chamber parts first.

2   Install the main nozzle (RT100 models) or the needle jet (RT180 models), and install a new O-ring and the main jet. Tighten them securely but don't overtighten them - they're made of soft material and can strip or shear easily.

3   Install the washer and valve seat and tighten the valve seat securely. Again, don't overtighten it.

4   Attach the needle valve to the float. Place the float in its installed position in the carburetor, making sure the needle valve seats correctly against the valve seat. Install the float pivot pin.

5   To check the float height, hold the carburetor upside down, so that the needle valve rests against its seat and the float arm is resting on - but not compressing - the needle valve. Using a float height gauge or a small steel pocket ruler, measure the distance between the float

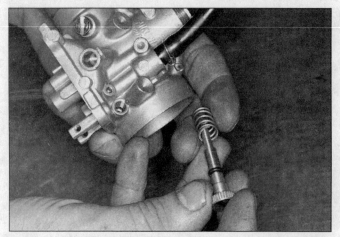

7.4q . . . unscrew the throttle stop screw and remove its spring and O-ring

8.5 Measure float height with a float height gauge or with a small steel pocket ruler

9.4 Remove the housing mounting bolts and disconnect the drain tube if necessary (arrows)

chamber gasket mating surface and the top of the float **(see illustration)**. Compare your measurement to the float height listed in this Chapter's Specifications. Bend the float arm as necessary to adjust the float height.

6 Install the float chamber gasket. Install the float chamber on the carburetor, install the screws and tighten them securely.

7 Place the carburetor in its upright (installed) position and install the rest of the parts.

8 Install a new O-ring on the pilot air screw, install the spring and install the pilot air screw. Turn the screw in until it seats lightly, then back it out the number of turns listed in this Chapter's Specifications.

9 If the circlip was removed from the jet needle, be sure to install it in the same groove it was in before it was removed (listed in this Chapter's Specifications). Install the jet needle and circlip in the throttle valve. If you disconnected the throttle cable, run it through the carburetor top and reattach it to the throttle valve. Don't forget the washer at the top of the throttle valve return spring; at the bottom of the spring there is a wire retainer (RT100 models) or another washer (RT180 models).

10 Install the carburetor (see Section 5).

---

9 Air cleaner housing - removal and installation

Refer to illustration 9.4

1 Remove the seat and the side covers (see Chapter 7).

2 Remove the air filter element (see Chapter 1).

3 Detach the carburetor connecting tube from the housing **(see illustration 5.4)**.

4 Remove the air cleaner housing bolts **(see illustration)**. Lift the housing out and disconnect the drain tube if necessary.

5 Installation is the reverse of the removal steps. If you removed the connecting tube, apply a ring of silicone sealant to the mating surface of the connecting tube and air cleaner housing.

---

10 Throttle cable - removal and installation

Refer to illustrations 10.4a, 10.4b and 10.5

1 Remove the fuel tank (see Section 2).

2 At the handlebar, loosen the throttle cable adjuster all the way (see Chapter 1).

3 Look for a punch mark on the handlebar next to the split in the throttle housing. If you don't see a mark, make one so the throttle housing can be installed in the correct position.

4 Remove the throttle housing screw, slide back the bushing and open up the throttle housing **(see illustrations)**.

5 Disengage the throttle cable from the throttle grip pulley **(see illustration)**.

6 To detach the throttle cable from the carburetor, refer to Sections 5 and 7.

7 Note the routing of the old throttle cable, then remove it. Using the same routing, place the new cable in position. Make sure it doesn't interfere with any other components and isn't kinked or bent sharply.

8 Lubricate the throttle pulley end of the cable with multi-purpose grease. Reverse the disconnection steps to connect the throttle cable to the throttle grip pulley.

9 Coat the end of the handlebar with silicone grease and slide on the throttle grip. Install the throttle housing. Position the housing so that the mating line of the two halves of the housing is aligned with the punch mark on the handlebar, then install the housing screw and tighten it securely.

10 Connect the throttle cable to the carburetor (see Sections 7 and 5).

11 Operate the throttle and make sure it returns to the idle position by itself under spring pressure. **Warning:** *If the throttle doesn't return by itself, find and solve the problem before continuing with installation. A stuck throttle can lead to loss of control of the motorcycle.*

12 Adjust the cable (see *Throttle cable freeplay - check and adjustment* in Chapter 1).

13 Turn the handlebars back and forth to make sure the cable does not cause the steering to bind.

14 Once you're sure the cable operates properly, install the fuel tank.

15 With the engine idling, turn the handlebars through their full travel (full left lock to full right lock) and note whether the idle speed increases. If it does, the cable is routed incorrectly. Correct this dangerous condition before riding the bike.

10.4a Remove the throttle housing screw . . .

10.4b . . . slide back the boot and open up the throttle housing halves

10.5 Disengage the throttle cable end plug from the throttle grip pulley

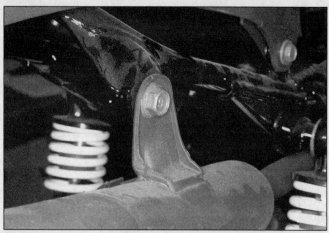

11.1 Remove the muffler mounting bolt (arrow) (RT100 shown)

11.3 Remove the expansion chamber mounting bolt (RT100 shown)

11.4 Remove the exhaust pipe nuts (arrows)

11 Exhaust system - removal and installation

Refer to illustrations 11.1, 11.3, 11.4, 11.6a and 11.6b

1   Remove the muffler mounting bolt **(see illustration)**. If you're working on an RT180, loosen the clamp at the front end of the muffler.

2   Twist the muffler to free it from the expansion chamber (RT100) or joint (RT180) and pull it free.

3   Remove the expansion chamber mounting bolt **(see illustration)**.

4   Remove the exhaust pipe nuts that secure the expansion chamber to the cylinder head **(see illustration)**. Pull the exhaust pipe forward out of the cylinder head.

5   On RT180 models, loosen the clamp that secures the muffler joint to the expansion chamber and pull the joint off. Inspect the joint for damage; if it's damaged, replace it.

6   Check the gasket in the exhaust port and the seal on the front end of the muffler pipe for damage and replace them if necessary **(see illustrations)**.

7   Installation is the reverse of removal. Tighten the exhaust pipe nuts to the torque listed in this Chapter's Specifications. Tighten all the other fasteners securely.

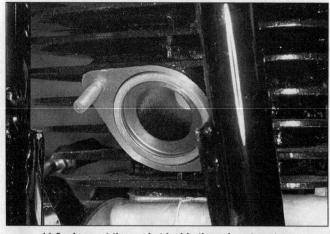

11.6a Inspect the gasket inside the exhaust port . . .

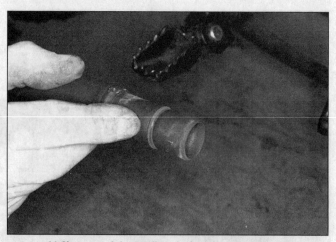

11.6b . . . and the sealing ring on the exhaust pipe

Chapter 3 Part C
Fuel and exhaust systems
(TT-R and XT models)

Contents

Specifications

General

Fuel type	Unleaded gasoline (petrol) subject to local regulations; minimum octane 91 RON (86 pump octane)

Carburetor

TT-R90 models

Main jet	90
Jet needle/clip position	4E9-2
Pilot jet	12.5
Pilot air screw setting (turns out from lightly seated position)	1-3/4
Fuel level	2 to 3 mm (0.8 to 0.1 inch)
Float height	15.5 to 16.5 mm (0.61 to 0.65 inch)

TT-R125 models

Main jet	105
Jet needle/clip position	5HGM56-2
Pilot jet	15
Pilot screw setting (turns out from lightly seated position)	2-1/2 to 3-1/2
Float height	Not specified
Fuel level	6 to 7 mm (0.24 to 0.28 inch)

TT-R225 models

Main jet	130
Jet needle/clip position	5DL27-1
Pilot jet	12.5
Pilot screw setting (turns out from lightly seated position)	2-1/8
Float height	14.1 to 15.1 mm (0.56 to 0.59 inch)
Fuel level	11 to 12 mm (0.43 to 0.47 inch)

XT225 models

Main jet	
US..	130
Canada...	122.5
Jet needle/clip position	
US 5DL27-1	
Canada...	5GN50-3/5
Pilot jet	
US..	40
Canada...	42.5
Pilot screw setting (turns out from lightly seated position)	
US..	Preset
Canada...	2
Float height...	14.1 to 15.1 mm (0.56 to 0.59 inch)
Fuel level...	11 to 12 mm (0.43 to 0.47 inch)

TT-R250 models

Main jet..	137
Jet needle/clip position...	5C9C-3/5
Pilot jet..	52
Pilot screw setting (turns out from lightly seated position).....	1-1/2
Float height...	26.5 to 27.5 mm (1.04 to 1.08 inch)
Fuel level...	7.5 to 9.5 mm (0.30 to 0.37 inch)

XT350 models

Main jet	
Primary carburetor	125
Secondary carburetor	106
Jet needle/clip position	
Primary carburetor	5C3C-1/1
Secondary carburetor	4A74-1/1
Pilot jet..	42
Pilot screw setting (turns out from lightly seated position).....	1-1/2 to 2-1/2
Float height...	Not specified
Fuel level...	5 to 7 mm (0.020 to 0.028 inch)

Tightening torques

Muffler/silencer to frame	
TT-R90	24 Nm (17 ft-lbs)
TT-R125	10 Nm (84 inch-lbs)
TT-R225, XT225, TT-R250	40 Nm (29 ft-lbs)
XT350	27 Nm (19 ft-lbs)

1   General information

The fuel system consists of the fuel tank, fuel tap, filter screen, carburetor(s) and connecting lines, hose and control cables.

A single Mikuni carburetor is used on TT-R90, TT-R125, TT-R225 and XT225 models. The TT-R90 and TT-R125 use a piston-valve design. The TT-R225 and XT225 use a CV carburetor, which has a butterfly-type throttle valve and uses engine vacuum to lift the throttle piston.

A single Teikei carburetor is used on TT-R250 models. The piston-type throttle valve is controlled by a throttle arm, which in turn is operated by the throttle cables.

XT350 models use two carburetors. The primary carburetor is a piston-valve type similar to the carburetor used on the TT-R250. The secondary carburetor is a Mikuni CV like that used on the XT225. This combination provides good low-end throttle response and high-speed power.

For cold starting, an enrichment circuit is actuated by a choke knob or lever.

The exhaust system consists of a pipe and a muffler.

Many of the fuel system service procedures are considered routine maintenance items and for that reason are included in Chapter 1.

2   Fuel tank - removal and installation

Warning: *Gasoline (petrol) is extremely flammable, so take extra precautions when you work on any part of the fuel system. Don't smoke or allow open flames or bare light bulbs near the work area, and don't work in a garage where a natural gas-type appliance (such as a water heater or clothes dryer) with a pilot light is present. Since gasoline is carcinogenic, wear latex gloves when there's a possibility of being exposed to fuel, and, if you spill any fuel on your skin, rinse it off immediately with soap and water. Mop up any spills immediately and do not store fuel-soaked rags where they could ignite. When you perform any kind of work on the fuel system, wear safety glasses and have a fire extinguisher suitable for a class B type fire (flammable liquids) on hand.*

1   The fuel tank is secured to a bracket by a bolt at the rear. At the front, the tank is supported by a bolt and rubber grommet on each side.

Removal

Refer to illustrations 2.4a and 2.4b

2   Remove the seat (see Chapter 7).

3   Unscrew the fuel tank filler cap and lay it aside. If you remove it completely, note how the vent hose on off-road models is routed over the handlebars.

2.4a Remove the mounting bolt and insulator at the rear of the fuel tank . . .

2.4b . . . and one on each side

4.3 If the pilot screw (arrow) is sealed by a plug, drill it out (see text)

4   Remove the fuel tank mounting bolts **(see illustrations)**.
5   Disconnect the fuel line from the fuel tap.
6   Pull the fuel tank backward and lift it off the motorcycle.

Installation

7   Before installing the tank, check the condition of the rubber mounting dampers - if they're hardened, cracked, or show any other signs of deterioration, replace them.
8   When installing the tank, reverse the removal procedure. Don't pinch any control cables or wires.

3   Fuel tank - cleaning and repair

1   The fuel tank is plastic and can't be repaired by traditional welding or brazing techniques. All repairs to the fuel tank should be carried out by a professional who has experience in this critical and potentially dangerous work. Even after cleaning and flushing of the fuel system, explosive fumes can remain and ignite during repair of the tank.
2   If the fuel tank is removed from the vehicle, it should not be placed in an area where sparks or open flames could ignite the fumes coming out of the tank. Be especially careful inside garages where a natural gas-type appliance is located, because the pilot light could cause an explosion.

4   Idle fuel/air mixture adjustment

Refer to illustration 4.3
1   Idle fuel/air mixture on these vehicles is preset at the factory and should not need adjustment unless the carburetor is overhauled or the pilot screw, which controls the mixture adjustment, is replaced.
2   The engine must be properly tuned up before making the adjustment (valve clearances set to specifications, spark plug in good condition and properly gapped).
3   If the mixture screw is covered by a sealing plug, drill a hole in the plug **(see illustration)**. **Caution:** *Don't drill too far or you'll damage the pilot screw.* Thread a sheet metal screw into the hole, then pull on it with pliers to remove the plug.
3   To make an initial adjustment, turn the pilot screw clockwise until it seats lightly, then back it out the number of turns listed in this Chapter's Specifications. **Caution:** *Turn the screw just far enough to seat it lightly. If it's bottomed hard, the screw or its seat may be damaged, which will make accurate mixture adjustments impossible.*
4   Warm up the engine to normal operating temperature. Shut it off and connect a tune-up tachometer, following the tachometer manufacturer's instructions.
5   Restart the engine and compare idle speed to the value listed in the Chapter 1 Specifications. Adjust it if necessary.

5   Carburetor overhaul - general information

1   Poor engine performance, hesitation, hard starting, stalling, flooding and backfiring are all signs that major carburetor maintenance may be required.
2   Keep in mind that many so-called carburetor problems are really not carburetor problems at all, but mechanical problems within the engine or ignition system malfunctions. Try to establish for certain that the carburetor is in need of maintenance before beginning a major overhaul.
3   Check the fuel tap and its strainer screen, the fuel line, the intake manifold clamps and Allen bolts, the O-ring between the intake manifold and cylinder head, the air filter element, the cylinder compression, the spark plug and the ignition timing before assuming that a carburetor overhaul is required. If the vehicle has been unused for more than a month, refer to Chapter 1, drain the float chamber and refill the tank with fresh fuel.
4   Most carburetor problems are caused by dirt particles, varnish and other deposits which build up in and block the fuel and air passages. Also, in time, gaskets and O-rings shrink or deteriorate and cause fuel and air leaks which lead to poor performance.
5   When the carburetor is overhauled, it is generally disassembled completely and the parts are cleaned thoroughly with a carburetor cleaning solvent and dried with filtered, unlubricated compressed air. The fuel and air passages are also blown through with compressed air to force out any dirt that may have been loosened but not removed by the solvent. Once the cleaning process is complete, the carburetor is reassembled using new gaskets, O-rings and, generally, a new inlet needle valve and seat.
6   Before disassembling the carburetors, make sure you have a carburetor rebuild kit (which will include all necessary O-rings and other parts), some carburetor cleaner, a supply of rags, some means of blowing out the carburetor passages and a clean place to work.

6   Carburetor - removal and installation

Warning: *Gasoline (petrol) is extremely flammable, so take extra precautions when you work on any part of the fuel system. Don't smoke or allow open flames or bare light bulbs near the work area, and don't work in a garage where a natural gas-type appliance (such as a water heater or clothes dryer) with a pilot light is present. Since gasoline is carcinogenic, wear latex gloves when there's a possibility of being exposed to fuel, and, if you spill any fuel on your skin, rinse it off immediately with soap and water. Mop up any spills immediately and do not store fuel-soaked rags where they could ignite. When you perform any kind of work on the fuel system, wear safety glasses and have a fire extinguisher suitable for a class B type fire (flammable liquids) on hand.*

6.3 Loosen the clamping band on the connecting tube at each end of the carburetor

6.4 Unbolt the manifold from the head and check its O-ring

Removal

Refer to illustrations 6.3 and 6.4

1   Remove the fuel tank (see Section 2).

2   Refer to Section 11 and remove the throttle cable housing or throttle valve cover.

3   If you're working on a TT-R90, loosen the clamping band on the air cleaner duct and unbolt the carburetor from the intake manifold. On all except TT-R90 models, loosen the clamping bands on the air cleaner duct and intake manifold **(see illustration)**.

4   Check the intake manifold and air cleaner duct for cracks, deterioration or other damage. Remove the manifold and replace its O-ring if its condition is in doubt **(see illustration)**. Since very small defects in the O-ring may affect carburetor performance, it's a good idea to replace the O-ring whenever it's removed.

5   After the carburetor has been removed, stuff clean rags into the intake port in the cylinder head to prevent the entry of dirt or other objects.

Installation

6   Installation is the reverse of the removal steps.

7   Adjust throttle lever freeplay (see Chapter 1).

7   Carburetors - disassembly, cleaning and inspection

Warning: *Gasoline (petrol) is extremely flammable, so take extra precautions when you work on any part of the fuel system. Don't smoke or allow open flames or bare light bulbs near the work area, and don't work in a garage where a natural gas-type appliance (such as a water heater or clothes dryer) with a pilot light is present. Since gasoline is carcinogenic, wear latex gloves when there's a possibility of being exposed to fuel, and, if you spill any fuel on your skin, rinse it off immediately with soap and water. Mop up any spills immediately and do not store fuel-soaked rags where they could ignite. When you perform any kind of work on the fuel system, wear safety glasses and have a fire extinguisher suitable for a class B type fire (flammable liquids) on hand.*

Disassembly

Refer to illustrations 7.2a through 7.2e and 7.5

1   Remove the carburetor from the machine as described in Section 6. Set it on a clean working surface.

2   Refer to the accompanying illustrations to disassemble the carburetor **(see illustrations)**.

3   Be sure screwdrivers fit their slots, or you may strip out the soft metal of the parts you're removing.

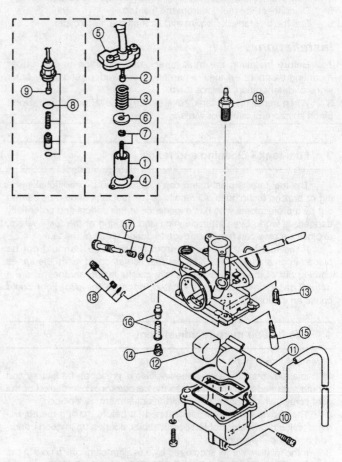

7.2a Carburetor (TT-R90 models) - exploded view

1	Throttle piston	12	Floats
2	Throttle cable end plug	13	Needle valve
3	Spring	14	Main jet
4	Gasket	15	Pilot jet
5	Top cover	16	Needle jet
6	Jet needle stopper	17	Throttle stop screw assembly
7	Clip and jet needle		
8	Choke plunger	18	Pilot screw, spring, O-ring and washer
9	Choke cable end plug		
10	Float chamber	19	Carburetor heater
11	Float pivot pin		

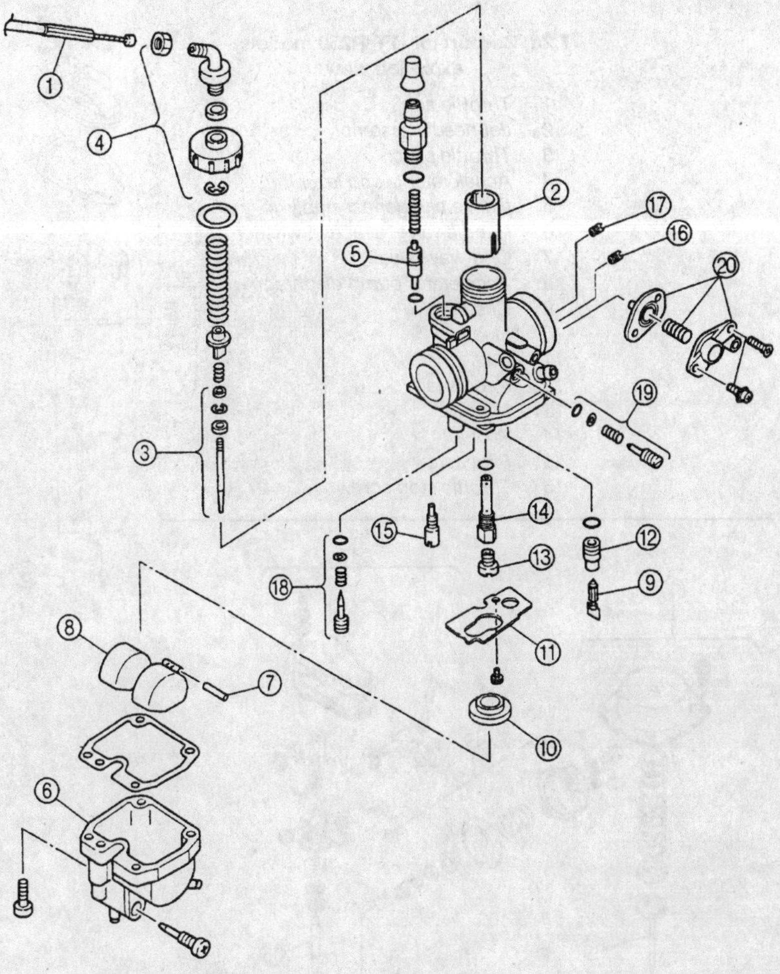

7.2b Carburetor (TT-R125 models) - exploded view

1. Throttle cable
2. Throttle piston
3. Jet needle assembly
4. Top cover assembly
5. Choke plunger
6. Float chamber
7. Float pivot pin
8. Floats
9. Needle valve
10. Main jet washer
11. Needle valve seat retainer
12. Needle valve seat
13. Main jet
14. Main nozzle
15. Pilot jet
16. Pilot air jet
17. Pilot air jet
18. Pilot air screw
19. Throttle stop screw
20. Coasting enricher assembly

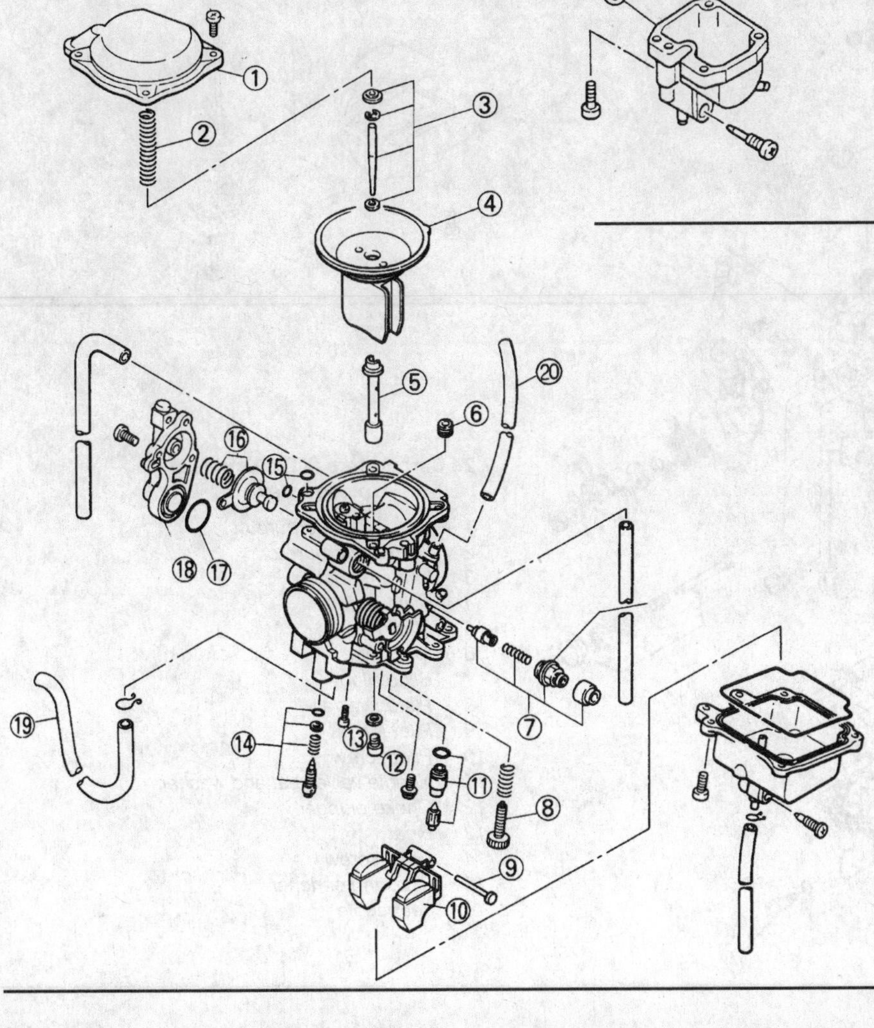

7.2c Carburetor (TT-R225 and XT225 models) – exploded view

1. Top cover
2. Diaphragm spring
3. Jet needle assembly
4. Diaphragm and throttle piston
5. Needle jet
6. Pilot air jet
7. Choke plunger assembly
8. Throttle stop screw
9. Float pivot pin
10. Float
11. Needle valve, seat and O-ring
12. Main jet
13. Pilot jet
14. Pilot screw
15. O-ring
16. Coasting enricher diaphragm and spring
17. O-ring
18. Coasting enricher diaphragm cover
19. Canister hose (California models)
20. Vent hose (except California models)

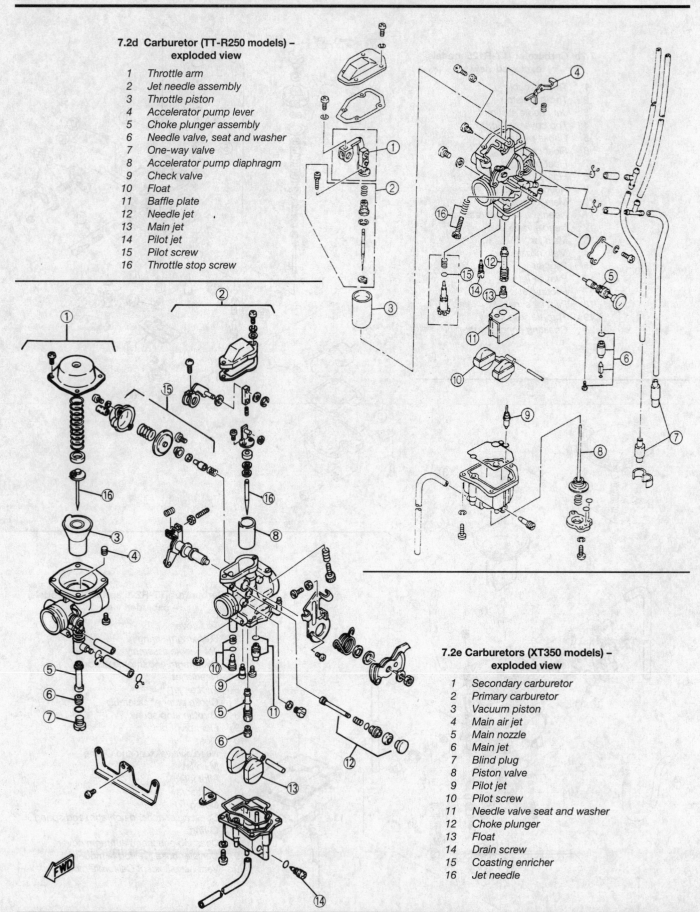

**7.2d Carburetor (TT-R250 models) –
exploded view**

1   Throttle arm
2   Jet needle assembly
3   Throttle piston
4   Accelerator pump lever
5   Choke plunger assembly
6   Needle valve, seat and washer
7   One-way valve
8   Accelerator pump diaphragm
9   Check valve
10   Float
11   Baffle plate
12   Needle jet
13   Main jet
14   Pilot jet
15   Pilot screw
16   Throttle stop screw

**7.2e Carburetors (XT350 models) –
exploded view**

1   Secondary carburetor
2   Primary carburetor
3   Vacuum piston
4   Main air jet
5   Main nozzle
6   Main jet
7   Blind plug
8   Piston valve
9   Pilot jet
10   Pilot screw
11   Needle valve seat and washer
12   Choke plunger
13   Float
14   Drain screw
15   Coasting enricher
16   Jet needle

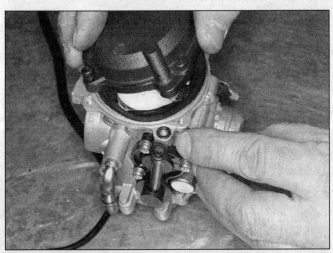

7.5 Don't forget to install this O-ring under the diaphragm cover

8.6 Hold the carburetor upside down and measure float height from the O-ring surface

4   If you're working on an XT350, most of the disassembly and cleaning procedures can be done without separating the carburetors. Don't separate them unless necessary.

5   If you're working on a Mikuni CV carburetor, be sure to reinstall the O-ring that fits under the top cover **(see illustration)**. Take care not to damage the diaphragm when you remove the top cover from the carburetor.

Cleaning

Caution: *Use only a carburetor cleaning solution that is safe for use with plastic parts (be sure to read the label on the container).*

6   Submerge the metal components in the carburetor cleaner for approximately thirty minutes (or longer, if the directions recommend it).

7   After the carburetor has soaked long enough for the cleaner to loosen and dissolve most of the varnish and other deposits, use a brush to remove the stubborn deposits. Rinse it again, then dry it with compressed air. Blow out all of the fuel and air passages in the main and upper body. **Caution:** *Never clean the jets or passages with a piece of wire or a drill bit, as they will be enlarged, causing the fuel and air metering rates to be upset.*

Inspection

8   Check the operation of the choke plunger. If it doesn't move smoothly, replace it, along with the return spring. If the plunger O-ring is deteriorated or damaged, replace it.

9   Check the tapered portion of the pilot screw for wear or damage. Replace the pilot screw if necessary.

10   Check the carburetor body, float chamber and top cover for cracks, distorted sealing surfaces and other damage. If any defects are found, replace the faulty component, although replacement of the entire carburetor will probably be necessary (check with your parts supplier for the availability of separate components).

11   Check the jet needle for straightness by rolling it on a flat surface (such as a piece of glass). Replace it if it's bent or if the tip is worn.

12   Check the tip of the fuel inlet valve needle. If it has grooves or scratches in it, it must be replaced. Push in on the rod in the other end of the needle, then release it - if it doesn't spring back, replace the valve needle.

13   Check the float chamber O-ring and the drain plug (in the float chamber). Replace them if they're damaged.

14   If you're working on a Mikuni CV carburetor, operate the throttle shaft to make sure the throttle butterfly valve opens and closes smoothly. If it doesn't, replace the carburetor.

15   Check the floats for damage. This will usually be apparent by the presence of fuel inside one of the floats. If the floats are damaged, they must be replaced.

16   If you're working on a Mikuni CV carburetor, check the coasting enricher diaphragm for splits, holes and general deterioration. Holding it up to a light will help to reveal problems of this nature. Inspect the throttle diaphragm in the same way.

17   Check the piston in the carburetor body for wear or damage. If it's worn or damaged, replace the carburetor.

8   Carburetors - reassembly and float height check

Refer to illustration 8.6

1   Reassembly is the reverse of disassembly, with the following additions. **Caution:** *When installing the jets, be careful not to over-tighten them - they're made of soft material and can strip or shear easily.* **Note:** *When reassembling the carburetor, be sure to use the new O-rings, gaskets and other parts supplied in the rebuild kit.*

2   Install the clip on the jet needle if it was removed. Place it in the needle groove listed in this Chapter's Specifications.

3   Install the pilot screw (if removed) along with its spring, washer and O-ring, turning it in until it seats lightly. Now, turn the screw out the number of turns listed in this Chapter's Specifications.

4   If you're working on a Mikuni CV carburetor, install the coasting enricher valve into the carburetor body. Seat the bead of the diaphragm into the groove in the carburetor body, making sure the diaphragm isn't distorted or kinked. Install the throttle diaphragm in the same way, making sure to reinstall the O-ring.

5   Reverse the disassembly steps to install the jets.

6   Invert the carburetor. Attach the fuel inlet valve needle to the float. Set the float into position in the carburetor, making sure the valve needle seats correctly. Install the float pivot pin. To check the float height, hold the carburetor so the float hangs down, then tilt it back until the valve needle is just seated. Measure the distance from the float chamber gasket surface to the top of the float and compare your measurement to the float height listed in this Chapter's Specifications **(see illustration)**. If it isn't as specified, bend the tang on the float to change it.

7   Install the O-ring into the groove in the float chamber. Place the float chamber on the carburetor and install the screws, tightening them securely.

Full throttle adjustment (XT350 models)

Refer to illustration 8.8

8   Loosen the locknut on the full throttle adjusting screw **(see illustration)**.

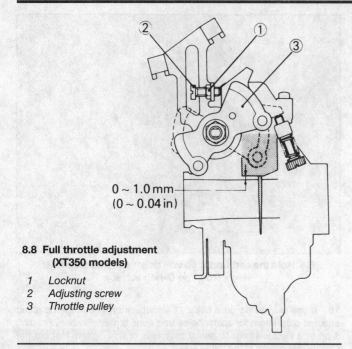

0 ~ 1.0 mm
(0 ~ 0.04 in)

**8.8 Full throttle adjustment
(XT350 models)**

1   *Locknut*
2   *Adjusting screw*
3   *Throttle pulley*

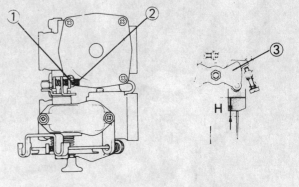

8.10 Carburetor synchronization (XT350 models)

1   *Locknut*   3   *Throttle pulley*
2   *Adjusting screw*

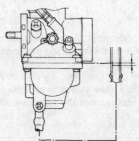

**9.2 A ruler and a clear plastic
tube like this one can be used
to measure fuel level if you
don't have the special tool**

9   Turn the throttle lever to open the throttle valve all the way. Hold it in this position and turn the full throttle adjusting screw to adjust the gap at the bottom of the throttle piston **(see illustration 8.8)**. Tighten the locknut.

Carburetor synchronization (XT350 models)

Refer to illustration 8.10

10   Loosen the locknut on the synchronizing screw **(see illustration)**.
11   Move the throttle lever so the gap at the bottom of the primary carburetor throttle piston is 2.5 mm (0.10 inch). Hold it in this position and turn the synchronizing screw so the secondary throttle piston is just beginning to open. Tighten the locknut.

9   Fuel level - check and adjustment

Refer to illustration 9.2

Warning: *Gasoline (petrol) is extremely flammable, so take extra precautions when you work on any part of the fuel system. Don't smoke or allow open flames or bare light bulbs near the work area, and don't work in a garage where a natural gas-type appliance (such as a water heater or clothes dryer) with a pilot light is present. Since gasoline is carcinogenic, wear latex gloves when there's a possibility of being exposed to fuel, and, if you spill any fuel on your skin, rinse it off immediately with soap and water. Mop up any spills immediately and do not store fuel-soaked rags where they could ignite. When you perform any kind of work on the fuel system, wear safety glasses and have a fire extinguisher suitable for a class B type fire (flammable liquids) on hand.*

1   Park the vehicle on a level surface and make sure the carburetor is level. If necessary, adjust its position slightly by placing a floor jack under the engine and raising it.
2   Attach Yamaha service tool YM-01312-A to the drain fitting on the bottom of the carburetor float bowl. This is a clear plastic tube graduated in millimeters. An alternative is to use a length of clear plastic tubing and an accurate ruler **(see illustration)**. Hold the graduated tube (or the free end of the clear plastic tube) vertically against the float chamber cover.
3   Unscrew the drain screw at the bottom of the float chamber a couple of turns, then start the engine and let it idle - fuel will flow into the tube. Wait for the fuel level to stabilize, then note how far the fuel level is below the line on the float chamber cover.
4   Measure the distance between the line and the top of the fuel in the tube or gauge. This distance is the fuel level.

5   Compare your reading to the value listed in this Chapter's Specifications. If the fuel level is not correct, remove the float chamber cover and bend the float tang up or down as necessary, then recheck the fuel level.

10   Air cleaner housing - removal and installation

Removal

1   Remove the fuel tank and carburetor (Sections 2 and 6).
2   Remove the air cleaner housing bolts. Lift the air cleaner housing out of the frame.
3   Installation is the reverse of the removal steps.

11   Throttle and choke cables - removal, installation and adjustment

Throttle cable(s)

Removal

Refer to illustration 11.6

1   If you're working on a TT-R90, remove the screws and take off the carburetor top **(see illustration 7.2a)**. Disengage the cable from the throttle piston.
2   If you're working on a TT-R125, unscrew the carburetor top and disengage the cable from the throttle piston **(see illustration 5.5 in Chapter 2B)**.
3   If you're working on a TT-R225 or XT225, loosen the cable locknuts at the carburetor and slip the cable out of the bracket on the carburetor body **(see illustration 7.5 in Chapter 1)**. Rotate the cable to align it with the slot in the pulley, then slip the cable end plug out of the pulley.
4   If you're working on a TT-R250 or XT350, loosen the throttle cable screws on the accelerator and decelerator cables **(see illustration 7.6**

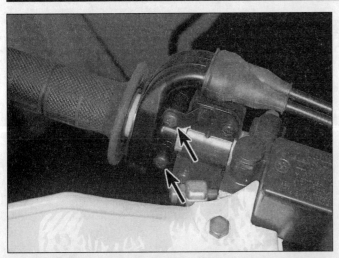

11.6 Remove the screws and separate the throttle housing halves

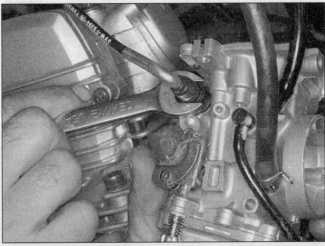

11.16 Unscrew the choke plunger from the carburetor body . . .

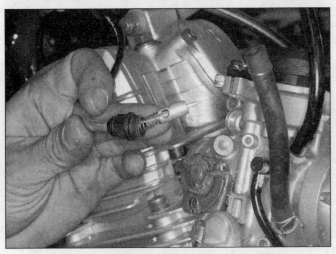

11.17 . . . and disconnect the cable from the plunger

12.1 Remove the holder bolts . . .

in Chapter 1C). Detach the cables from the throttle pulley.

5   Follow the cable(s) to the handlebar, removing any retainers and noting how the cable is routed.

6   On all models, remove the screws and separate the throttle cable housing at the handlebar **(see illustration).** Rotate the throttle grip to provide slack in the cable(s), then disengage the cable end plug(s) from the pulley.

7   If necessary, remove the throttle housing clamp screws and detach the throttle housing from the handlebar (see Chapter 5).

Installation

8   Route the cable(s) into place. Make sure it doesn't interfere with any other components and isn't kinked or bent sharply.

9   Lubricate the end(s) of the cable with multi-purpose grease and connect it to the throttle grip pulley.

10   Reverse the disconnection steps to connect the throttle cable to the carburetor.

11   Operate the throttle and make sure it returns to the idle position by itself under spring pressure. **Warning:** *If the lever doesn't return by itself, find and solve the problem before continuing with installation. A stuck lever can lead to loss of control of the vehicle.*

Adjustment

12   Follow the procedure outlined in Chapter 1, *Throttle operation/grip freeplay - check and adjustment*, to adjust the cable.

13   Turn the handlebar back and forth to make sure the cable(s) doesn't cause the steering to bind.

14   Once you're sure the cables operate properly, install the covers on the throttle lever housing and cable housing.

15   With the engine idling, turn the handlebar through its full travel (full left lock to full right lock) and note whether idle speed increases. If it does, a cable is routed incorrectly. Correct this dangerous condition before riding the motorcycle.

Choke cable (except XT350 models)

Refer to illustrations 11.16 and 11.17

16   Unscrew the choke plunger from the carburetor **(see illustration).**

17   Disengage the cable from the plunger **(see illustration).**

18   Follow the cable to the choke knob, removing any retainers and noting how the cable is routed.

19   At the choke knob, unscrew the cable retaining nut and detach the cable and knob from the bracket.

20   Installation is the reverse of the removal steps.

---

12 Exhaust system - removal and installation

Refer to illustrations 12.1 and 12.5

1   Remove the exhaust pipe holder nuts and slide the holder(s) off the mounting studs **(see illustration).**

2   If necessary, unbolt the heat shield and remove it from the exhaust pipe.

3   Remove the muffler/silencer mounting bolts.

12.5 . . . and the gasket

4   Pull the exhaust system forward, separate the pipe from the cylinder head and remove the system from the machine.

5   Installation is the reverse of removal, with the following additions:

  a) *Be sure to install a new gasket at the cylinder head* **(see illustration).**

  b) *Tighten the muffler mounting to the torques listed in this Chapter's Specifications.*

13   Evaporative emission control system (XT225 and XT350 California models) – inspection

Refer to illustration 13.1

1   This system is used on California XT225 and XT350 models to recirculate vapor emissions from the fuel tank into the engine for burn-

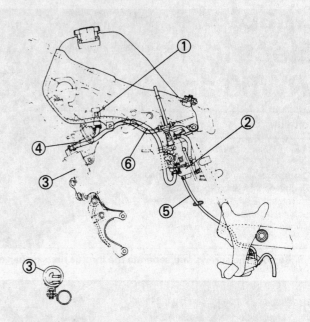

13.1 Evaporative emission control system details (XT225 California models; XT350 similar)

1	*Rollover valve*	4	*Rollover valve hose*
2	*Carburetor*	5	*Overflow hose*
3	*Canister*	6	*Carburetor hose*

ing **(see illustration).** It stores fuel vapor in a canister filled with activated charcoal while the engine is not running.

2   The system should be inspected periodically. Check for cracked or deteriorated hoses and make sure the hose connections are tight.

3   Check the canister for cracks or other visible damage. Replace it if problems are found.

Chapter 4 Part A
Electrical system
(PW50 and PW80 models)

Contents

Specifications

General

Ignition coil resistance (without spark plug cap)*	
PW50	
Primary	0.32 to 0.48 ohms
Secondary	5.68 to 8.52 k-ohms
PW80	
Primary	0.26 to 0.36 ohms
Secondary	3.5 to 4.7 k-ohms
Minimum spark plug gap	6 mm (0.24 inch)
CDI magneto resistance*	
PW50	
Charging coil	297 to 363 ohms
Pick-up coil	18 to 22 ohms
Lighting coil	0.57 to 0.69 ohm
PW80	
Charging coil	189 to 231 ohms

*At 20 degrees C (68 degrees F)

Torque specification

Magneto rotor nut	
PW50	43 Nm (31 ft-lbs)
PW80	50 Nm (36 ft-lbs)
Stator retaining screws	
PW50	9 Nm (78 in-lbs)
PW80	7 Nm (61 in-lbs)

1 General information

Because these models are strictly for offroad use, they do not have lights or turn signals, so there is no battery or charging system. There is also no electric starter. The engine is started with a kickstarter and turned off with a kill switch in a housing on the right end of the handlebar, next to the throttle twistgrip.

The ignition system on these models is a known as a capacitive discharge ignition (CDI) system. The CDI system consists of the ignition switch, a flywheel magneto (known as the "CDI magneto"), a CDI unit, a separate ignition control unit on PW50 models, an ignition coil and a spark plug. The CDI magneto consists of a flywheel rotor, a charging coil and on PW50 models, a pick-up coil and lighting coil (the lighting coil is not used). The CDI unit includes a diode, a condenser or capacitor, and a thyristor, or silicon controlled rectifier (SCR). When the engine is running, a flywheel rotor on the left end of the crankshaft generates alternating current (AC) in the CDI magneto's charging coil. This current is stored in the capacitor, which discharges its stored charge to the ignition coil primary winding each time the SCR is turned

on. The charge is then stepped up in the ignition coil secondary winding, producing the high-voltage current that fires the spark plug.

With the exception of spark plug replacement, no ignition system maintenance is necessary on these models. If a problem occurs, the sections in this chapter will show you how to locate and identify typical ignition system malfunctions. Complete wiring diagrams of each model are included at the end of this manual to help you locate a problem in the ignition circuit. **Note:** *Keep in mind that electrical parts, once purchased, can't be returned. To avoid unnecessary expense, make very sure the faulty component has been positively identified before buying a replacement part.*

2 Electrical troubleshooting

Electrical problems often stem from simple causes, such as loose or corroded connections. Prior to any electrical troubleshooting, always visually check the condition of the wires and connections in the circuit.

If testing instruments are going to be utilized, use the diagrams to plan where you will make the necessary connections in order to accurately pinpoint the trouble spot.

The basic tools needed for electrical troubleshooting include a test light or voltmeter, an ohmmeter or a continuity tester (which includes a bulb, battery and set of test leads) and a jumper wire, preferably with a circuit breaker incorporated, which can be used to bypass electrical components.

A continuity check is performed to see if a circuit, section of circuit or individual component is capable of passing electricity through it. Connect one lead of a self-powered test light or ohmmeter to one end of the circuit being tested and the other lead to the other end of the circuit. If the bulb lights (or the ohmmeter indicates little or no resistance), there is continuity, which means the circuit is passing electricity through it properly. The kill switch can be checked in the same way.

Remember that the electrical circuit on these motorcycles is designed to conduct electricity through the wires, kill switch, etc. to the electrical component (CDI unit, etc.). From there it passes to the frame (ground) through which it returns to the CDI magneto. Electrical problems are basically an interruption in the flow of electricity.

Because of their nature, the individual ignition system components can be checked but not repaired. If ignition system troubles occur, and the faulty component can be isolated, the only cure for the problem is to replace the part with a new one. Keep in mind that most electrical parts, once purchased, can't be returned. To avoid unnecessary expense, make very sure the faulty component has been positively identified before buying a replacement part.

3   Ignition system - check

Warning: *Because of the very high voltage generated by the ignition system, extreme care should be taken when these checks are performed.*

Engine starts but misfires

Refer to illustration 3.2

1   If the engine starts but misfires, check the spark at the spark plug gap before looking for a defective component in the ignition system.

2   The ignition system must be able to produce a spark across a seven millimeter (1/4-inch) gap (minimum). A simple test fixture **(see illustration)** can be constructed to make sure the minimum spark gap can be jumped. Make sure the fixture electrodes are positioned seven millimeters apart.

3   Connect the spark plug wire to the protruding test fixture electrode, then attach the fixture's alligator clip to a good engine ground.

4   Crank the engine over with the kickstarter and see if a well-defined, blue spark occurs between the test fixture electrodes. If the minimum spark gap test is positive, the ignition coil is functioning properly. If the spark will not jump the gap or if it is weak (orange colored), refer to Steps 5 through 13 and check the indicated components as follows.

3.2 A simple spark gap testing fixture can be made from a block of wood, two nails, a large alligator clip, a screw and a piece of wire

Engine will not start

5   Make sure all electrical connectors are clean and tight. Check all wires for shorts, opens and correct installation.

6   Disconnect the spark plug cap, remove the spark plug, inspect the condition of the plug and check the plug gap (see Chapter 1). If the plug looks okay, check the spark plug as described above (refer to Steps 1 through 4). Reinstall it and tighten it to the torque listed in the Chapter 1 Specifications.

7   Connect the spark plug wire to a spare spark plug and lay the plug on the engine with the threads contacting the engine. If necessary, hold the spark plug with an insulated tool. Crank the engine over and make sure a well-defined, blue spark occurs between the spark plug electrodes. **Warning:** *Don't use the spark plug installed in the engine to perform this check - atomized fuel being pumped out of the open spark plug hole could ignite, causing severe injury!*

8   If there is no spark, check the rest of the ignition system as follows.

9   Check the ignition coil primary and secondary resistance (see Section 4).

10   Check the engine kill switch (see Section 5).

11   Check the resistance of the charging coil and, on PW50 models, the resistance of the pick-up coil (see Section 6).

12   If none of the above components are defective, but there is still no spark at the plug, replace the CDI unit (see Section 7).

4   Ignition coil - check and replacement

Check

Refer to illustrations 4.4a, 4.4b and 4.4c

1   Remove the seat (see Chapter 7). Remove the fuel tank (see Chapter 3).

2   Inspect the coil for cracks and other damage. If it's obviously damaged, replace it.

3   Measure the resistance of the coil primary and secondary windings with an ohmmeter as follows.

4   Disconnect the electrical connectors from the coil primary terminals **(see illustrations)**. Pull the spark plug cap off the spark plug and unscrew the spark plug cap from the plug wire.

5   Set the ohmmeter selector switch to the Rx1 position, connect the ohmmeter positive lead to the push-on wire terminal and the negative lead to the ground wire's screw terminal. Measure the primary resistance and compare the result to the primary resistance range listed in this Chapter's Specifications.

6   Set the ohmmeter selector switch to the Rx1000 position, connect the ohmmeter between the positive primary terminal (push-on terminal) and the negative lead to the spark plug wire, measure the secondary resistance and compare the result to the secondary resistance range listed in this Chapter's Specifications.

7   If either the primary or secondary resistance is outside the specified range, the coil is defective. Replace it.

4.4a Here's the PW50 ignition coil

4.4b The PW80 ignition coil and CDI unit

1   *Coil mounting screw*
2   *Coil mounting screw and ground terminal*
3   *CDI unit*

4.4c Ignition coil test

1   *Measure primary winding resistance*
2   *Measure secondary winding resistance*
3   *Ignition coil*

Replacement

8   Remove the seat (see Chapter 7). Remove the fuel tank (see Chapter 3).
9   Disconnect the spark plug cap from the spark plug.
10   Unplug the electrical connectors to the coil primary terminals.
11   Remove the coil mounting screws or bolts **(see illustration 4.4a or 4.4b)** and remove the coil.
12   Unscrew the spark plug cap from the old spark plug lead and screw it onto the new lead.
13   Installation is the reverse of removal.

5   Kill switch - check and replacement

1   The kill switch is mounted on the right end of the handlebar. In the OFF position, it shorts the primary ignition circuit to ground, preventing the engine from starting, or shutting it off if it's already running. When the switch is turned to the RUN position, it opens the circuit to ground, closing the primary circuit. PW50 models also have a START position. This allows the engine to be started, but prevents it from being revved up by operating the throttle twistgrip.

Check

2   Follow from the switch to their connectors and disconnect them.
3   Connect an ohmmeter between the wire terminals on the *switch* side of the connectors, not the side that leads back to the wiring harness.

a) PW50: black/red and black wires
b) PW80: black/white and black wires.

With the switch in the OFF position, the ohmmeter should show continuity (little or no resistance); with the switch in the RUN position (or the START position on PW50 models), the ohmmeter should show no con-

tinuity (infinite resistance).
4   If you're working on a PW50, move the ohmmeter to the white/black and red wires. The ohmmeter should now show continuity in the RUN position. Move the ohmmeter to the red and black/yellow wires; the ohmmeter should now show continuity in the START position.
5   If the ohmmeter doesn't give the correct indication in any switch position, replace the switch.

Replacement

Refer to illustration 5.7

6   To remove the switch, remove the wiring harness retainers and disconnect the switch lead electrical connectors.
7   Remove the switch housing screws, separate the housing halves and take it off the handlebar (see Chapter 4). Remove the switch mounting screw and take it out of the throttle housing **(see illustration)**.
8   Installation is the reverse of removal. Tighten the switch housing screws securely.

6   Flywheel rotor - removal, inspection and installation

1   The flywheel rotor is mounted on the left end of the crankshaft.
Caution: *To remove the flywheel rotor, the special Yamaha puller or an aftermarket equivalent will be required. Don't try to remove the rotor without the proper puller, as it's almost sure to be damaged. Pullers are readily available from motorcycle dealers and aftermarket tool suppliers.*

PW50 models

Refer to illustrations 6.2, 6.3a, 6.3b, 6.4 and 6.7

2   Remove the left crankcase cover **(see illustration)**.
3   Hold the flywheel rotor with a universal holder or equivalent. You can also use a strap wrench. Unscrew the rotor nut, then remove the lockwasher and washer **(see illustrations)**.

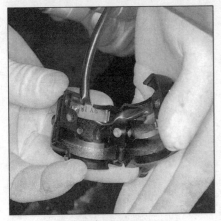

5.7 The kill switch is inside the throttle housing

6.2 Remove the left crankcase cover (PW50 models) . . .

6.3a . . . unscrew the rotor nut . . .

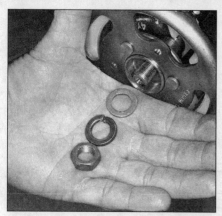

6.3b . . . and remove the nut, lockwasher and washer

6.4 Thread the puller into the rotor and hold the puller center with a wrench while you tighten the puller

6.7 Make sure the Woodruff key is in the crankshaft

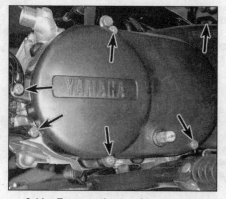

6.11a Remove the crankcase cover screws (arrows) . . .

6.11b . . . pull off the cover and locate the dowels (upper dowel shown)

6.12a Unscrew the rotor nut . . .

4   Thread a flywheel rotor puller into the center of the rotor and use it to remove the rotor (see illustration). If the rotor doesn't come off easily, tap sharply on the end of the puller to release the rotor's grip on the tapered crankshaft end. Caution: *Don't strike the rotor, as the magnets will be damaged.*

5   Once the rotor has been removed, look at the inside and inspect the magnets. If a rock or stray piece of metal has made its way inside the rotor, the magnets may be damaged, which can weaken the magneto's electrical output. Magnets can also come unglued from the rotor.

6   Degrease the center of the rotor and the end of the crankshaft.

7   Make sure the Woodruff key is positioned securely in its slot (see illustration).

8   Align the rotor slot with the Woodruff key. Place the rotor on the crankshaft.

9   Install the rotor, lockwasher, washer and nut. Hold the rotor from turning with one of the methods described in Step 6 and tighten the nut to the torque listed in this Chapter's Specifications.

10   Reinstall the left crankcase cover.

PW80 models
Refer to illustrations 6.11a, 6.11b, 6.12a, 6.12b, 6.13 and 6.16

11   Remove the left crankcase cover (see illustrations).

12   Hold the flywheel rotor with a universal holder or equivalent. You can also use a strap wrench. Unscrew the rotor nut, then remove the

6.12b . . . then remove the nut and washer

6.13 Thread the puller into the rotor and hold the puller center with a wrench while you tighten the puller

6.16 Make sure the Woodruff key is in the crankshaft

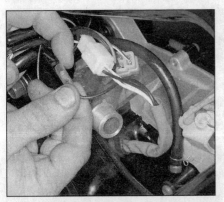

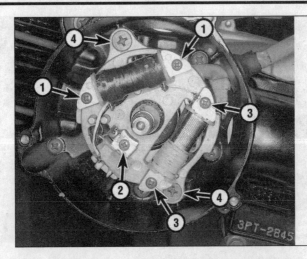

7.6a PW50 CDI magneto

1 Charging coil screws
2 Pick-up coil screw
3 Lighting coil screws
*4 Magneto base plate
    screws*

**7.1 Follow the harness to the connector
and disconnect it (PW50 models have
two connectors)**

washer (see illustrations).

13   Thread a flywheel rotor puller into the center of the rotor and use it to remove the rotor (see illustration). If the rotor doesn't come off easily, tap sharply on the end of the puller to release the rotor's grip on the tapered crankshaft end. **Caution:** *Don't strike the rotor, as the magnets will be damaged.*

14   Once the rotor has been removed, look at the inside and inspect the magnets. If a rock or stray piece of metal has made its way inside the rotor, the magnets may be damaged, which can weaken the magneto's electrical output. Magnets can also come unglued from the rotor.

15   Degrease the center of the rotor and the end of the crankshaft.

16   Make sure the Woodruff key is positioned securely in its slot (see illustration).

17   Align the rotor slot with the Woodruff key. Place the rotor on the crankshaft.

18   Install the rotor, washer and nut. Hold the rotor from turning with one of the methods described in Step 6 and tighten the nut to the torque listed in this Chapter's Specifications.

19   Reinstall the left crankcase cover.

---

7   CDI magneto - check and replacement

Check

Refer to illustration 7.1

Note: *During the next steps, connect the ohmmeter to the wires that connect to the CDI magneto, not to the CDI unit or control unit.*

1   Locate the CDI magneto harness on the left side of the engine, trace it back to the electrical connector and disconnect it (see illustration).

Charging coil (all models)

2   Connect the positive lead of an ohmmeter to the connector terminal for the black/red wire and connect the negative ohmmeter lead to the terminal for the black (ground) wire. Measure the resistance of the charging coil and compare the result to the resistance range for the charging coil listed in this Chapter's Specifications. If the readings are outside the specified resistance range, replace the charging coil as described below.

Pick-up coil and lighting coil (PW50 models only)

3   To check the pick-up coil, connect the positive lead of an ohmmeter to the connector terminal for the white/red wire and connect the negative ohmmeter lead to the terminal for the black wire. Measure the resistance of the pick-up coil and compare your measurement to the resistance range for the pick-up coil listed in this Chapter's Specifications. If the readings are outside the specified resistance range, replace the pick-up coil as described below.

4   To check the lighting coil, connect the positive lead of an ohmmeter to the connector terminal for the white wire and the negative ohmmeter lead to the terminal for the black wire. Measure the resistance of the lighting coil and compare your measurement to the resistance range for the lighting coil listed in this Chapter's Specifications. If the readings are outside the specified resistance range, replace the lighting coil as described below.

Replacement

PW50 models

Refer to illustrations 7.6a, 7.6b, 7.7a and 7.7b

5   Remove the rotor as described above.

6   Remove the magneto base mounting screws (see illustrations).

7   Push the wiring harness grommet through its mounting hole, then

**7.6b Unscrew the base plate screws (you may need an
impact driver)**

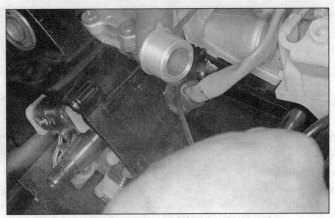

7.7a Push the grommet through the mounting hole . . .

7.7b . . . and remove the base plate together with the harness

7.11a PW80 CDI magneto
A   Base plate screws
B   Charging coil screws

remove the magneto base together with the harness **(see illustrations)**.

8   Remove the coil mounting screws **(see illustration 7.6a)**. To replace an individual coil, unsolder the old coil and solder in the new one.

9   Installation is the reverse of the removal steps. Position the wires around the stator plate center and install new tie-wraps.

PW80 models

Refer to illustrations 7.11a and 7.11b

10   Remove the rotor as described above.

11   Remove the magneto base mounting screws **(see illustration)**. Pull the grommet out of its notch, then remove the magneto base together with the harness **(see illustration)**.

12   Remove the coil mounting screws **(see illustration 7.11a)**.

13   Installation is the reverse of the removal steps.

8   CDI unit - check and replacement

Check

1   The CDI unit is tested by a process of elimination. It should be replaced only when all other possible causes of ignition problems have been checked and eliminated.

2   Inspect the condition of the spark plug and check the spark plug gap (see Chapter 1). Check the ignition coil, kill switch and charging coil. On PW50 models, check the pick-up coil.

3   Carefully inspect the wiring harnesses for breaks or bad connections.

4   If the harness and all other system components are okay, the CDI

unit is probably defective. Ideally, before buying a new CDI unit, try to substitute a known good unit and see whether the ignition system functions correctly.

Removal and installation

Refer to illustration 8.6

5   Remove the fuel tank (see Chapter 3).

6   If you're working on a PW50, locate the CDI unit **(see illustration)**. Disconnect its connector and remove the mounting screw.

7   If you're working on a PW80, locate the CDI unit **(see illustration 4.4b)**. Disconnect its connector, pull the mounting band off the frame tab and work the unit out of the mounting band.

7   Installation is the reverse of the removal Steps.

9   Control unit (PW50 models) - check and replacement

Check

1   The control unit is part of the safety system that prevents these models from being revved up when the kill switch is in the START position. If the system doesn't work properly, and the kill switch tests okay (Section 5), the control unit may be at fault. It's a good idea to check it by substituting a known good unit before replacing it.

Replacement

Refer to illustration 9.3

2   Remove the fuel tank (see Chapter 3).

3   Disconnect the control unit electrical connector and pull the unit's mounting band off the frame tab **(see illustration)**.

4   Installation is the reverse of the removal Steps.

7.11b Here's the PW80 magneto harness routing

8.6 Here's the PW50 CDI unit

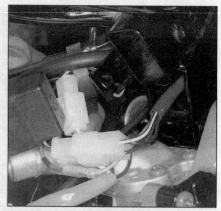

9.3 Here's the PW80 CDI unit

Chapter 4 Part B
Electrical system
(RT100 and RT180 models)

Contents

Specifications

General

Ignition coil resistance (without spark plug cap)*

RT100

Primary	0.9 to 1.1 ohms
Secondary	4.7 to 7.1 k-ohms

RT180

Primary	1.4 to 1.8 ohms
Secondary	5.1 to 7.7 k-ohms

Spark plug cap resistance* ... 4 to 6 k-ohms

CDI magneto resistance*

RT100

Source coil	270 to 330 ohms
Pick-up coil	9 to 11 ohms

RT180

Source coil	270 to 30 ohms
Pick-up coil	90 to 110 ohms

Oil level warning system (RT180)*

Resistor resistance ... 17 ohms

Lighting coil resistance

Between yellow wire and black wire	0.42 to 0.52 ohm
Between white wire and black wire	0.28 to 0.34 ohm

*At 20 degrees C (68 degrees F)

Torque specification

Magneto rotor nut

RT100	50 Nm (36 ft-lbs)
RT180	70 Nm (50 ft-lbs)

1 General information

Because these models are strictly for offroad use, they do not have headlights, taillights or turn signals. There is no battery, charging system or electric starter. The engine is started with a kickstarter and turned off with a kill switch in a housing on the right end of the handlebar, next to the throttle twist grip.

The ignition system on these models is a known as a capacitive discharge ignition (CDI) system. The CDI system consists of the ignition switch, a flywheel magneto (known as the "CDI magneto"), a CDI unit, an ignition coil and a spark plug. The CDI magneto consists of a flywheel rotor, a source coil, a pick-up coil, and on RT180 models a lighting coil. When the engine is running, a flywheel rotor on the left end of the crankshaft generates alternating current (AC) in the CDI magneto's charging coil. This current is stored in the capacitor, which

discharges its stored charge to the ignition coil primary winding each time the SCR is turned on. The charge is then stepped up in the ignition coil secondary winding, producing the high-voltage current that fires the spark plug.

RT180 models are equipped with an oil level warning system which consists of a neutral switch, an oil level gauge inside the Autolube oil tank, an OIL LEVEL indicator light on the handlebar, and the wiring connecting these three components.

With the exception of spark plug replacement, no ignition system maintenance is necessary on these models. If a problem occurs, the sections in this chapter will show you how to locate and identify typical ignition system malfunctions. Wiring diagrams are included at the end of this manual to help you locate a problem in the ignition circuit. **Note:** *Keep in mind that electrical parts, once purchased, can't be returned. To avoid unnecessary expense, make very sure the faulty component has been positively identified before buying a replacement part.*

3.2 A simple spark gap testing fixture can be made from a block of wood, two nails, a large alligator clip, a screw and a piece of wire

3.8 Unscrew the spark plug cap from the plug wire and measure its resistance with an ohmmeter

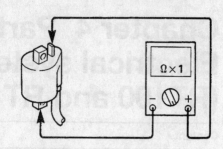

4.5 Check the coil primary resistance

2   Electrical troubleshooting

Electrical problems often stem from simple causes, such as loose or corroded connections. Prior to any electrical troubleshooting, always visually check the condition of the wires and connections in the circuit.

If testing instruments are going to be utilized, use the diagrams to plan where you will make the necessary connections in order to accurately pinpoint the trouble spot.

The basic tools needed for electrical troubleshooting include a test light or voltmeter, an ohmmeter or a continuity tester (which includes a bulb, battery and set of test leads) and a jumper wire, preferably with a circuit breaker incorporated, which can be used to bypass electrical components.

A continuity check is performed to see if a circuit, section of circuit or individual component is capable of passing electricity through it. Connect one lead of a self-powered test light or ohmmeter to one end of the circuit being tested and the other lead to the other end of the circuit. If the bulb lights (or the ohmmeter indicates little or no resistance), there is continuity, which means the circuit is passing electricity through it properly. The kill switch can be checked in the same way.

Remember that the electrical circuit on these motorcycles is designed to conduct electricity through the wires, kill switch, etc. to the electrical component (CDI unit, etc.). From there it passes to the frame (ground) through which it returns to the CDI magneto. Electrical problems are basically an interruption in the flow of electricity.

Because of their nature, the individual ignition system components can be checked but not repaired. If ignition system troubles occur, and the faulty component can be isolated, the only cure for the problem is to replace the part with a new one. Keep in mind that most electrical parts, once purchased, can't be returned. To avoid unnecessary expense, make very sure the faulty component has been positively identified before buying a replacement part.

3   Ignition system - check

Warning: *Because of the very high voltage generated by the ignition system, extreme care should be taken when these checks are performed.*

Engine starts but misfires

Refer to illustration 3.2

1   If the engine starts but misfires, check the spark at the spark plug gap before looking for a defective component in the ignition system.
2   The ignition system must be able to produce a spark across a seven millimeter (1/4-inch) gap (minimum). A simple test fixture **(see illustration)** can be constructed to make sure the minimum spark gap can be jumped. Make sure the fixture electrodes are positioned seven millimeters apart.
3   Connect the spark plug wire to the protruding test fixture electrode, then attach the fixture's alligator clip to a good engine ground.

4   Crank the engine over with the kickstarter and see if a well-defined, blue spark occurs between the test fixture electrodes. If the minimum spark gap test is positive, the ignition coil is functioning properly. If the spark will not jump the gap or if it is weak (orange colored), refer to Steps 5 through 13 and check the indicated components as follows.

Engine will not start

Refer to illustration 3.8

5   Disconnect the spark plug wire, remove the spark plug, inspect the condition of the plug and check the plug gap (see Chapter 1). If the plug is okay, reinstall it and tighten it to the torque listed in the Chapter 1 Specifications.
6   Connect the spark plug wire to a spare spark plug and lay the plug on the engine with the threads contacting the engine. If necessary, hold the spark plug with an insulated tool. Crank the engine over and make sure a well-defined, blue spark occurs between the spark plug electrodes. **Warning:** *Don't use the spark plug installed in the engine to perform this check - atomized fuel being pumped out of the open spark plug hole could ignite, causing severe injury!*
7   If there is no spark, check the rest of the ignition system as follows.
8   Unscrew the spark plug cap from the plug wire and check the cap resistance with an ohmmeter **(see illustration)**. Compare your measurement to the resistance range listed in this Chapter's Specifications. If the resistance is outside the specified range, replace the spark plug cap.
9   Check the ignition coil primary and secondary resistance (see Section 4).
10   Check the engine kill switch (see Section 5).
11   Check the resistance of the source coil and the pick-up coil (see Section 6).
12   Make sure all electrical connectors are clean and tight. Check all wires for shorts, opens and correct installation.
13   If none of the above components are defective, but there is still no spark at the plug, replace the CDI unit (see Section 7).

4   Ignition coil - check and replacement

Check

Refer to illustrations 4.5 and 4.6

1   On RT100 models, remove the fuel tank (see Chapter 3B).
2   Inspect the coil for cracks and other damage. If it's obviously damaged, replace it.
3   Measure the resistance of the coil primary and secondary windings with an ohmmeter as follows.
4   Unplug the electrical connector from the coil primary terminal, pull the spark plug cap off the spark plug and unscrew the spark plug cap from the plug lead (to check the spark plug cap resistance, see Section 3).

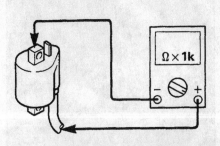

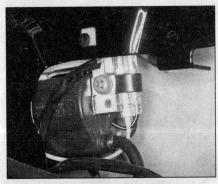

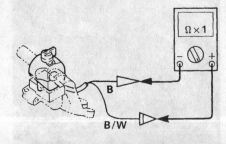

4.6 Check the coil secondary resistance

4.10 Remove the mounting screw and detach the coil (RT100 shown)

5.3 Use an ohmmeter to check the kill switch for continuity in the OFF position and no continuity in the RUN position

5   Set the ohmmeter selector switch to the Rx1 position. connect the ohmmeter between the coil primary terminal and the coil mounting flange **(see illustration)**, measure the primary resistance and compare the reading to the primary resistance range listed in this Chapter's Specifications.

6   Set the ohmmeter selector switch to the Rx1000 position. Connect the ohmmeter between the positive primary terminal and the end of the spark plug wire **(see illustration)**, measure the resistance and compare the reading to the secondary resistance range listed in this Chapter's Specifications.

7   If either the primary or secondary resistance is outside the specified range, the coil is probably defective and should be replaced.

Replacement

Refer to illustration 4.10

8   On RT100 models, remove the fuel tank (see Chapter 3B).

9   Disconnect the spark plug cap from the spark plug.

10   Disconnect the primary wire from the coil **(see illustration)**.

11   Remove the coil mounting screw and remove the coil.

12   Unscrew the spark plug cap from the old spark plug wire and screw it onto the new wire (the spark plug wire is a permanent part of the coil).

13   Installation is the reverse of removal.

---

5   Kill switch - check and replacement

1   The kill switch is mounted on the right end of the handlebar. In the OFF position, it shorts the primary ignition circuit to ground, preventing the engine from starting, or shutting it off if it's already running. When the switch is turned to the RUN position, it opens the circuit to ground, closing the primary circuit.

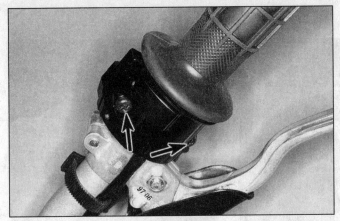

5.5 Remove the switch housing screws (arrows) and separate the housing halves

Check

Refer to illustration 5.3

2   Trace the black/white and black wires from the switch to their connectors and disconnect them.

3   Connect an ohmmeter between the wire terminals on the switch side of the connectors (not the side that leads back to the wiring harness) **(see illustration)**. With the switch in the OFF position, the ohmmeter should show continuity (little or no resistance); with the switch in the RUN position, the ohmmeter should show no continuity (infinite resistance).

4   Repeat the test several times. The ohmmeter should move from continuity to no continuity each time the switch is moved from OFF to RUN. If it continues to show continuity after it's moved to RUN, the ignition system is being shorted out constantly and won't produce a spark.

Replacement

Refer to illustration 5.5

5   To remove the switch, remove the switch housing screws, separate the housing halves and take it off the handlebar **(see illustration)**. Remove the wiring harness retainers and disconnect the switch electrical connectors.

6   Installation is the reverse of removal. Tighten the switch housing screws securely.

---

6   CDI magneto coils - check and replacement

Check

1   Locate the CDI magneto harness on the left side of the engine, trace it back to the electrical connector(s) and disconnect them.

2   Set an ohmmeter to Rx100. **Note:** *During the next two steps, connect the ohmmeter to the wires that connect to the engine, not to the wiring harness.*

3   To check the source coil, connect an ohmmeter between the terminals for the brown wire and the black wire (RT100 models) or the black/red wire and the black wire (RT180 models). Measure the resistance of the source coil and compare your measurement to the resistance range for the source coil listed in this Chapter's Specifications. If the readings are outside the specified resistance range, replace the source coil as described below.

4   To check the pick-up coil, connect an ohmmeter between the terminals for the white/red wire and the black wire. Measure the resistance of the pick-up coil and compare your measurement to the resistance range for the pick-up coil listed in this Chapter's Specifications. If the readings are outside the specified resistance range, replace the pick-up coil as described below.

Replacement

Flywheel rotor

Refer to illustrations 6.5a, 6.5b, 6.6a, 6.6b, 6.7, 6.8, 6.10 and 6.13

Caution: *To remove the flywheel rotor, the special Yamaha puller or an*

6.5a Remove the left crankcase cover screws (arrows) . . .

6.5b . . . take off the cover and remove the gasket

6.6a Hold the rotor, remove the nut and lockwasher . . .

6.6b . . . then remove the washer

6.7 Thread the puller into the rotor and hold the puller with a wrench while you tighten the puller shaft

6.8 Serious damage can occur if the engine is run with anything stuck to the rotor magnets

aftermarket equivalent will be required. *Don't try to remove the rotor without the proper puller, as it's almost sure to be damaged. Pullers are readily available from aftermarket tool suppliers.*

5   Remove the left crankcase cover **(see illustrations)**.

6   Hold the flywheel rotor with a universal holder or equivalent. You can also use a strap wrench. If you don't have one of these tools and the engine is in the frame, the rotor can be locked by placing the transmission in gear, letting out the clutch and applying the rear brake. Unscrew the rotor nut and remove the washer **(see illustrations)**.

7   Thread a flywheel rotor puller into the center of the rotor and use it to remove the rotor **(see illustration)**. If the rotor doesn't come off easily, tap sharply on the end of the puller to release the rotor's grip on the tapered crankshaft end. **Caution:** *Don't strike the rotor, as the magnets will be damaged.*

8   Once the rotor has been removed, look at the inside and inspect the magnets **(see illustration)**. If a rock or stray piece of metal has made its way inside the rotor, the magnets may be damaged, which can weaken the magneto's electrical output.

9   Degrease the center of the rotor and the end of the crankshaft.

10   Make sure the Woodruff key is positioned securely in its slot **(see illustration)**.

11   Align the rotor slot with the Woodruff key. Place the rotor on the crankshaft.

12   Install the rotor and washer and nut. Hold the rotor from turning with one of the methods described in Step 6 and tighten the nut to the torque listed in this Chapter's Specifications.

13   Reinstall the left crankcase cover, making sure the grommet and wiring harness are positioned correctly **(see illustration)**.

6.10 Make sure the Woodruff key is in the crankshaft

6.13 Note the wiring harness routing and grommet location (arrows)

6.15a Remove the stator plate mounting screws (arrows) . . .

6.15b . . . take the plate off and free the grommet from the crankcase

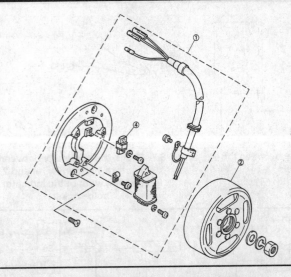

6.16a CDI magneto assembly (RT100 models) - exploded view

1   Stator assembly
2   Rotor
3   Source coil
4   Pick-up coil

Source coil and pick-up coil

Refer to illustrations 6.15a, 6.15b, 6.16a and 6.16b

14   Remove the rotor as described above.

15   Remove the stator plate mounting screws and take it off the engine **(see illustrations)**.

16   Remove the coil mounting screws **(see illustrations)**. Note how the coil wires are routed, then cut any tie-wraps and detach the coil from the stator plate.

17   Installation is the reverse of the removal steps. Position the wires around the stator plate center and install new tie-wraps (if removed).

7   CDI unit - check and replacement

Check

1   The CDI unit is tested by process of elimination. In other words, the CDI unit should be suspect only when all other possible causes of ignition problems have been checked and eliminated.

2   Inspect the condition of the spark plug and check the spark plug gap (see Chapter 1). Check the spark plug cap resistance, check the ignition coil resistance, check the kill switch and check the source coil and pick-up coil resistance as described elsewhere in this Chapter.

3   Carefully check the wiring harnesses for breaks or bad connections.

4   If the harness and all other system components are okay, the CDI unit is probably defective. Ideally, before buying a new CDI unit, try to substitute a known good unit and see whether the ignition system functions correctly.

Removal and installation

Refer to illustration 7.6

5   On RT100 models, remove the fuel tank (see Chapter 3B); on RT180 models, remove the seat and the right side cover (see Chapter 7).

6   Locate the CDI unit **(see illustration)**. Disconnect its electrical connector and detach the unit from the motorcycle.

7   Installation is the reverse of the removal steps.

8   Oil level warning system (RT180 models) - check and component replacement

Refer to illustrations 8.6, 8.7, 8.8, 8.9, 8.10, 8.11 and 8.12

1   These models are equipped with an oil level warning system which warns you when the oil level is low. The system consists of an oil level warning indicator light on the handlebar, a resistor (also located at the handlebar), an oil level gauge inside the oil tank and a Neutral switch on the left side of the engine.

2   To functionally check the oil level warning system, start the engine with the transmission in Neutral and verify that the oil warning indicator light comes on. Shift into gear and verify that the indicator light goes off.

3   If the light comes on and goes off as described, the engine oil level and the electrical circuit of the oil level warning system are okay.

4   If the light comes on but doesn't go out when you shift into gear, check the oil level in the tank and add oil if necessary (see Chapter 1).

5   If the light doesn't come on when the engine is started, trou-

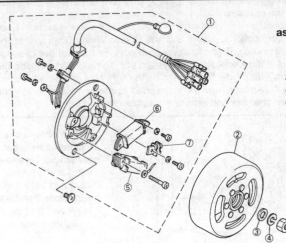

6.16b CDI magneto assembly (RT180 models) - exploded view

1   Stator assembly
2   Rotor
3   Lockwasher
4   Washer
5   Lighting coil
6   Source coil
7   Pick-up coil

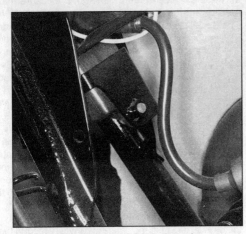

7.6 CDI unit (RT100 shown)

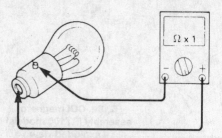

8.6 Check the continuity between the bulb terminals

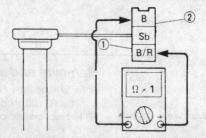

8.7 Check the continuity between connectors 1 (brown wire) and 2 (green/blue wire) of the indicator bulb socket

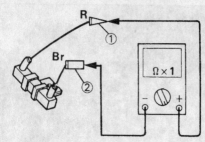

8.8 Measure the resistance between connectors 1 (red wire) and 2 (brown wire) of the resistor

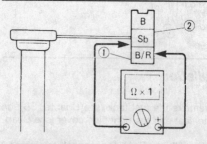

8.9 Check the continuity between connector terminals 1 (black/red wire) and 2 (sky blue wire) of the oil level gauge

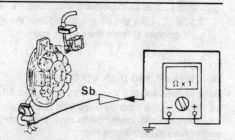

8.10 Check the continuity between connectors 1 (black/red wire) and 2 (black wire) of the oil level gauge

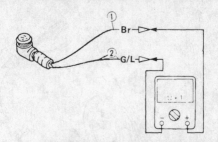

8.11 Check the continuity between the neutral switch sky blue wire connector and ground

bleshoot the system as follows.

6   Inspect the bulb filament. If it's blown, replace the bulb. If the filament looks okay, but you still suspect the bulb, set an ohmmeter to the Rx1 position and check the continuity of the bulb by touching the positive ohmmeter lead to the lower end of the bulb and the negative lead to the side post terminal **(see illustration)**.

7   Using a known good bulb, check the continuity of the bulb socket. Trace the brown and green/blue wires from the bulb socket to the electrical connectors and disconnect them. Set an ohmmeter to the Rx1 position, connect the positive ohmmeter lead to the connector for the brown wire and connect the negative lead to the connector for the green/blue wire **(see illustration)**. There should be continuity. If there isn't, either the bulb socket or the wiring is defective. If there is continuity, the bulb socket and wiring are okay. Proceed to the next Step.

8   Locate the resistor, trace the red and brown leads from the resistor to the electrical connectors and disconnect the connectors. Set an ohmmeter to the Rx10 position, connect the positive ohmmeter lead to the connector for the red lead and the negative lead to the connector for the brown lead **(see illustration)**. Measure the resistance of the resistor and compare your measurement to the value listed in this Chapter's Specifications. If the indicated resistance is incorrect, replace the resistor. If the resistance is okay, proceed to the next Step.

9   Locate the oil level gauge in the oil tank. Disconnect the electrical connector and remove the gauge from the tank. Set an ohmmeter to the Rx1 position, connect the positive ohmmeter lead to the connector terminal for the black/red wire and the negative lead to the terminal for the sky blue wire **(see illustration)**. There should be continuity. If there is no continuity, replace the oil level gauge. If there is continuity, proceed to the next Step.

10   Connect the positive ohmmeter lead to the terminal for the black/red wire and the negative lead to the terminal for the black wire **(see illustration)**. Hold the oil level gauge in its normal upright position and note whether there is continuity. With the gauge in an upright position there should be continuity. If there isn't, replace the oil level gauge. Hold the gauge upside down and note whether there is continuity. With the gauge upside down, there should be no continuity. If there is, replace the oil level gauge. If the gauge is okay, proceed to the next step.

11   Locate the Neutral switch on the left side of the engine. Trace the sky blue wire from the CDI magneto back to the electrical connector

and unplug the connector. Set an ohmmeter to the Rx1 position, connect the positive ohmmeter lead to the CDI connector terminal for the sky blue wire and the negative lead to a good frame ground **(see illustration)**. Shift the transmission into Neutral and verify that there is continuity. Shift the transmission into gear and verify that there is no continuity. If the Neutral switch fails to operate as described, replace it. If the Neutral switch is okay, proceed to the next Step.

12   Trace the yellow, white and black wires from the CDI magneto back to the electrical connectors and disconnect them. Set an ohmmeter to the Rx1 position, connect the ohmmeter positive lead to the connector for the yellow wire and the negative lead to the connector for the black wire **(see illustration)**. Measure the resistance and compare your measurement to the lighting coil resistance for the yellow wire and black wire listed in this Chapter's Specifications. Move the positive ohmmeter lead to the connector for the white wire (leave the negative ohmmeter connected to the black wire), measure the resistance and compare your measurement to the lighting coil resistance for the white wire and black wire listed in this Chapter's Specifications. If the lighting coil resistance is incorrect for either test, replace the stator assembly (see Section 6). If the lighting coil resistance is okay, proceed to the next step.

13   Inspect the electrical circuit for the oil level warning system. Look for bad connections, opens and shorts (see Wiring Diagrams at the end of this book). If you find any problems, fix them. If the circuit is okay, but the oil level warning system still isn't working, replace the rectifier/regulator, which is located on the right side of the bike, behind the right side cover, where it's strapped to the frame, just below the expansion chamber and next to the carburetor.

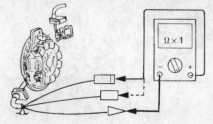

8.12 Measure the resistance between connectors 1 (yellow wire) and 3 (black wire) and between connectors 2 (yellow wire) and 3 of the lighting coil

Chapter 4 Part C
Electrical system
(TT-R and XT models)

Contents

Specifications

Battery

Voltage	12 volts
Amp-hours	
TT-R225 (fillable battery)	7
XT350 (fillable battery)	3
Sealed maintenance-free batteries	Not specified
Specific gravity	see Chapter 1
Open circuit voltage	
Fuse rating	
TT-R225, TT-R250, XT225	15 amps
XT350	10 amps
Charging system voltage	
TT-R225	14.1 to 14.9
TT-R250	13.0 to 15.0
XT225	14.3 to 15.3
XT350	14.0 to 15.0
Alternator stator coil resistance	
TT-R90, TT-R125	
Source coil resistance (brown to green)	688 to 1032 ohms
Pickup coil resistance (red to white)	248 to 372 ohms
TT-R225	
Charging coil (brown/red to green/white)	600 to 900 ohms
Charging coil (green/blue to green/white)	482 to 708 ohms
Pickup coil (white/blue to white/red	280 to 420 ohms
TT-R250	
Charging coils (white to white to white)	1.0 to 1.2 ohms
Pickup coil (yellow to blue)	190 to 230 ohms
XT225	
Charging coil (brown to green)	584 to 876 ohms
Charging coil (yellow to black)	20 to 30 ohms
Pickup coil (red to white)	656 to 984 ohms

Battery (continued)

Alternator stator coil resistance (continued)
  XT350

Charging coil (black to white)	0.46 +/- 10 per cent
Lighting coil (black to yellow)	0.29 ohms +/- 10 per cent
Pickup coil resistance (black to white/red)	221 ohms +/- 10 per cent
Source coil resistance (brown to black)	444 ohms +/- 10 per cent

Ignition coil resistance (at 20-degrees C/68-degrees F)
  TT-R90, TT-R125

Primary resistance	0.18 to 0.28 ohms
Secondary resistance	6300 to 9500 ohms

  TT-R225, XT225

Primary resistance	0.56 to 0.84 ohms
Secondary resistance	5680 to 8520 ohms

  TT-R250

Primary resistance	0.36 to 0.48 ohms
Secondary resistance	5440 to 7360 ohms

  XT350

Primary resistance	0.79 ohms +/- 15 per cent
Secondary resistance	5900 ohms +/- 15 per cent

Tightening torques
Alternator rotor bolt/nut

TT-R90	48 Nm (35 ft-lbs)
TT-R125	80 Nm (58 ft-lbs)
TT-R225, XT225	50 Nm (36 ft-lbs)
TT-R250, XT350	60 Nm (43 ft-lbs)
Stator coil Allen bolts	10 Nm (84 inch-lbs)

Right crankcase cover

Bolts	10 Nm (84 inch-lbs)
Screws	7 Nm (61 inch-lbs)
Starter one-way clutch Allen bolts	10 Nm (82 inch-lbs)*

Starter motor mounting bolts

TT-R225, XT225	7 Nm (61 inch-lbs)
TT-R250	10 Nm (84 inch-lbs)
Starter gear cover bolts (TT-R250)	10 Nm (84 inch-lbs)

*Apply non-permanent thread locking agent to the threads.

1   General information

All of the machines covered by this manual are equipped with a capacitive discharge ignition system (CDI), a headlight and a taillight. The engine on TT-R90, TT-R125 and XT350 models is started with a kickstarter. TT-R225, TT-R250 and XT225 models use electric starters.

TT-R90 and TT-R125 models do not have a battery, a fuse, turn signals or brake lights. Current generated by the alternator operates the ignition system.

TT-R225, TT-R250, XT225 and XT350 models use a 12-volt electrical system with a battery. The components include a crankshaft-mounted permanent-magnet alternator and a solid state voltage regulator/rectifier unit. The alternator consists of a multi-coil stator mounted inside the left engine cover and a permanent magnet rotor mounted on the end of the crankshaft. The regulator maintains the charging system output within the specified range to prevent overcharging. The rectifier converts the AC output of the alternator to DC current to power the lights and other components and to charge the battery. A single main fuse protects the electrical system.

Note: *Keep in mind that electrical parts, once purchased, can't be returned. To avoid unnecessary expense, make very sure the faulty component has been positively identified before buying a replacement part.*

Component locations

Refer to illustrations 1.1a through 1.1h

Electrical components are mounted in various locations around the motorcycle **(see illustrations)**.

2   Electrical troubleshooting

A typical electrical circuit consists of an electrical component, the switches, relays, etc. related to that component and the wiring and connectors that hook the component to both the battery (if equipped) and the frame. To aid in locating a problem in any electrical circuit,

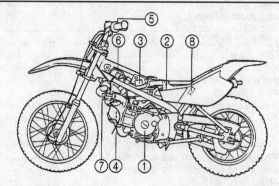

1.1a Electrical component locations (TT-R90 models)

1	CDI magneto	5	Kill switch
2	CDI unit	6	Thermo switch
3	Ignition coil	7	Carburetor heater
4	Spark plug	8	Rectifier/regulator

complete wiring diagrams of each model are included at the end of this Chapter.

Before tackling any troublesome electrical circuit, first study the appropriate diagrams thoroughly to get a complete picture of what makes up that individual circuit. Trouble spots, for instance, can often be narrowed down by noting if other components related to that circuit are operating properly or not. If several components or circuits fail at one time, chances are the fault lies in the fuse (if equipped) or ground connection, as several circuits often are routed through the same fuse and ground connections.

Electrical problems often stem from simple causes, such as loose or corroded connections or a blown fuse. Prior to any electrical troubleshooting, always visually check the condition of the fuse (if equipped), wires and connections in the problem circuit.

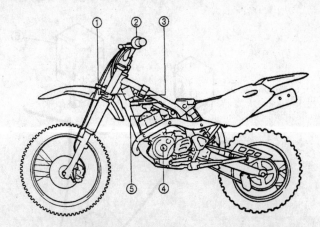

1.1b Electrical component locations (TT-R125 models)

1	CDI unit	4	CDI magneto
2	Kill switch	5	Spark plug
3	Ignition coil		

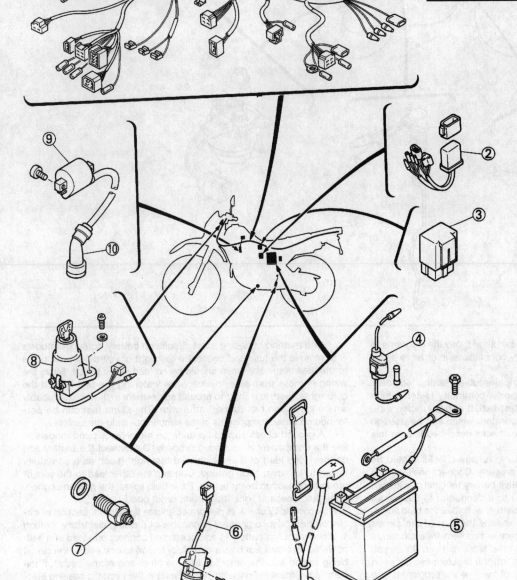

1.1c Electrical component locations (TT-R225 and XT225 models, 1 of 2)

1 Wiring harness
2 CDI unit
3 Neutral relay
4 Main fuse
5 Battery
6 Sidestand switch
7 Neutral switch
8 Ignition switch
9 Ignition coil
10 Spark plug cap

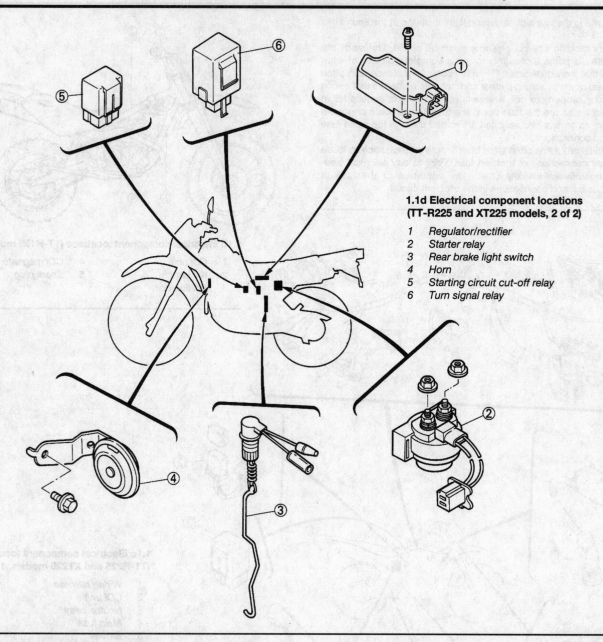

**1.1d Electrical component locations
(TT-R225 and XT225 models, 2 of 2)**

1   Regulator/rectifier
2   Starter relay
3   Rear brake light switch
4   Horn
5   Starting circuit cut-off relay
6   Turn signal relay

If testing instruments are going to be utilized, use the diagrams to plan where you will make the necessary connections in order to accurately pinpoint the trouble spot.

The basic tools needed for electrical troubleshooting include a test light or voltmeter, an ohmmeter or a continuity tester (which includes a bulb, battery and set of test leads) and a jumper wire, preferably with a circuit breaker incorporated, which can be used to bypass electrical components. Specific checks described later in this Chapter may also require an ammeter.

On models equipped with a battery, voltage checks should be performed if a circuit is not functioning properly. Connect one lead of a test light or voltmeter to either the negative battery terminal or a known good ground. Connect the other lead to a connector in the circuit being tested, preferably nearest to the battery or fuse. If the bulb lights, voltage is reaching that point, which means the part of the circuit between that connector and the battery is problem-free. Continue checking the remainder of the circuit in the same manner. When you reach a point where no voltage is present, the problem lies between there and the last good test point. Most of the time the problem is due to a loose connection. Keep in mind that some circuits only receive voltage when the ignition key is in the On position.

One method of finding short circuits on battery-equipped models is to remove the fuse and connect a test light or voltmeter in its place to the fuse terminals. There should be no load in the circuit. Move the wiring harness from side-to-side while watching the test light. If the bulb lights, there is a short to ground somewhere in that area, probably where insulation has rubbed off a wire. The same test can be performed on other components in the circuit, including the switch.

A ground check should be done on battery-equipped models to see if a component is grounded properly. Disconnect the battery and connect one lead of a self-powered test light (such as a continuity tester) to a known good ground. Connect the other lead to the wire or ground connection being tested. If the bulb lights, the ground is good. If the bulb does not light, the ground is not good.

A continuity check is performed to see if a circuit, section of circuit or individual component is capable of passing electricity through it. Disconnect the battery (if equipped) and connect one lead of a self-powered test light (such as a continuity tester) to one end of the circuit being tested and the other lead to the other end of the circuit. If the bulb lights, there is continuity, which means the circuit is passing electricity through it properly. Switches can be checked in the same way.

Remember that all electrical circuits are designed to conduct

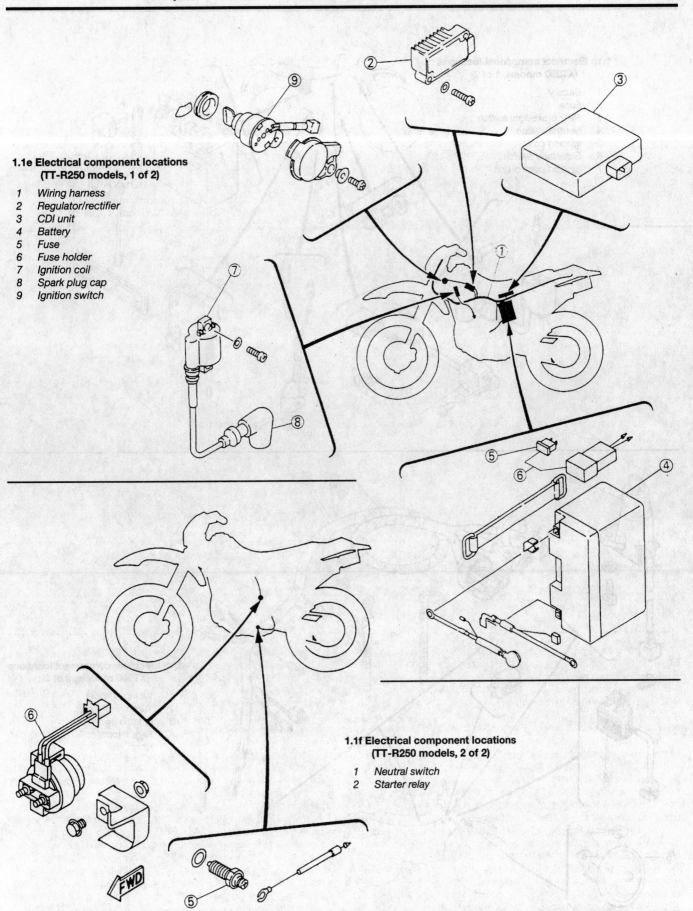

**1.1e Electrical component locations
(TT-R250 models, 1 of 2)**

1 Wiring harness
2 Regulator/rectifier
3 CDI unit
4 Battery
5 Fuse
6 Fuse holder
7 Ignition coil
8 Spark plug cap
9 Ignition switch

**1.1f Electrical component locations
(TT-R250 models, 2 of 2)**

1 Neutral switch
2 Starter relay

1.1g Electrical component locations
(XT350 models, 1 of 2)

1   Battery
2   Fuse
3   Rear brake light switch
4   Neutral switch
5   Ignition coil
6   Sidestand switch
7   Ignition control unit

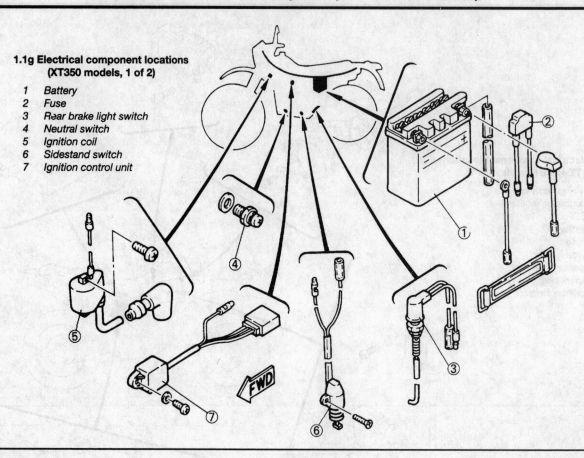

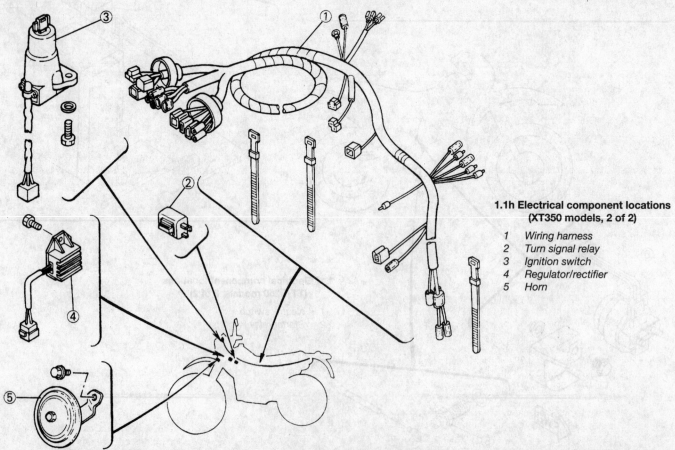

1.1h Electrical component locations
(XT350 models, 2 of 2)

1   Wiring harness
2   Turn signal relay
3   Ignition switch
4   Regulator/rectifier
5   Horn

electricity from the battery (if equipped), through the wires, switches, etc. to the electrical component (light bulb, etc.). From there it is directed to the frame (ground) where it is passed back to the battery or alternator. Electrical problems are basically an interruption in the flow of electricity from the battery or back to it.

3 Battery - inspection and maintenance

1 Most battery damage is caused by heat, vibration, and/or low electrolyte levels, so keep the battery securely mounted, check the electrolyte level frequently and make sure the charging system is functioning properly.

2 Refer to Chapter 1 for electrolyte level and specific gravity checking procedures. **Note:** *All battery-equipped models except the TT-R225 and XT350 use a sealed maintenance-free battery.*

3 Check around the base inside of the battery for sediment, which is the result of sulfation caused by low electrolyte levels. These deposits will cause internal short circuits, which can quickly discharge the battery. Look for cracks in the case and replace the battery if either of these conditions is found.

4 Check the battery terminals and cable ends for tightness and corrosion. If corrosion is evident, remove the cables from the battery and clean the terminals and cable ends with a wire brush or knife and emery paper. Reconnect the cables and apply a thin coat of petroleum jelly to the connections to slow further corrosion.

5 The battery case should be kept clean to prevent current leakage, which can discharge the battery over a period of time (especially when it sits unused). Wash the outside of the case with a solution of baking soda and water. Do not get any baking soda solution in the battery cells. Rinse the battery thoroughly, then dry it.

6 If acid has been spilled on the frame or battery box, neutralize it with the baking soda and water solution, dry it thoroughly, then touch up any damaged paint. Make sure the battery vent tube is directed away from the frame and is not kinked or pinched.

7 If the motorcycle sits unused for long periods of time, disconnect the cables from the battery terminals. Refer to Section 4 and charge the battery approximately once every month.

4 Battery - charging

1 If the machine sits idle for extended periods or if the charging system malfunctions, the battery can be charged from an external source.

Fillable batteries

2 To properly charge the battery, you will need a charger of the correct rating, a hydrometer, a clean rag and a syringe for adding distilled water to the battery cells.

3 The maximum charging rate for any battery is 1/10 of the rated amp/hour capacity. As an example, the maximum charging rate for the 14 amp/hour battery would be 1.4 amps. If the battery is charged at a higher rate, it could be damaged.

4 Do not allow the battery to be subjected to a so-called quick charge (high rate of charge over a short period of time) unless you are prepared to buy a new battery.

5 When charging the battery, always remove it from the machine and be sure to check the electrolyte level before hooking up the charger. Add distilled water to any cells that are low.

6 Loosen the cell caps, hook up the battery charger leads (red to positive, black to negative), cover the top of the battery with a clean rag, then, and only then, plug in the battery charger. **Warning:** *Remember, the gas escaping from a charging battery is explosive, so keep open flames and sparks well away from the area. Also, the electrolyte is extremely corrosive and will damage anything it comes in contact with.*

7 Allow the battery to charge until the specific gravity is as specified (refer to Chapter 1 for specific gravity checking procedures). The charger must be unplugged and disconnected from the battery when making specific gravity checks. If the battery overheats or gases

excessively, the charging rate is too high. Either disconnect the charger or lower the charging rate to prevent damage to the battery.

8 If one or more of the cells do not show an increase in specific gravity after a long slow charge, or if the battery as a whole does not seem to want to take a charge, it is time for a new battery.

9 When the battery is fully charged, unplug the charger first, then disconnect the leads from the battery. Install the cell caps and wipe any electrolyte off the outside of the battery case.

Sealed maintenance-free batteries

Refer to illustration 4.11

10 Yamaha recommends different types of charging techniques, depending on the type of battery charger. Since a hydrometer can't be used to check battery condition (there's no way to insert it into the cells), a voltmeter is used instead to measure the voltage between the positive and negative terminals (open circuit voltage). Before taking the measurement, wait at least 30 minutes after any charging has taken place (including running the engine).

11 To check open-circuit voltage, disconnect the negative cable from the battery, then the positive cable. Make sure the battery terminals are clean, then connect the positive terminal of the voltmeter to the battery positive terminal and the negative voltmeter terminal to the battery negative terminal. Compare the voltage readings to the accompanying chart **(see illustration)** to determine whether, and for how long, the battery needs to be charged.

Variable current (adjustable voltage) charger

Refer to illustration 4.12

12 Connect the charge to the battery. If the charger doesn't have an ammeter built in, connect one in series with the charger **(see illustration).**

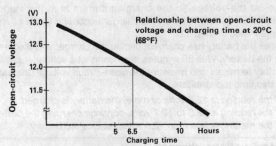

• This varies depending on the temperature, the state of charge in battery plates and the electrolyte level.

4.11 Draw a line straight across from the open circuit voltage to the bar, then straight down to find the charging time

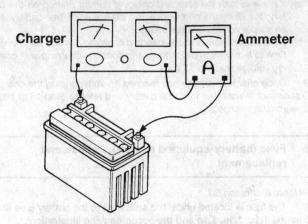

4.12 If the charger doesn't have an ammeter built in, connect one in series with the charger like this; DO NOT connect the ammeter between the battery terminals or it will be ruined

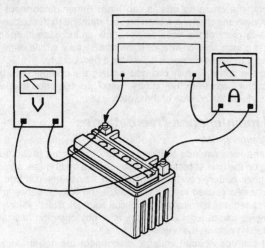

4.17 Connect the charger, ammeter and voltmeter to the battery like this; DO NOT connect the ammeter between the battery terminals or it will be ruined

13   Plug in the charger, set the voltage at 16 to 17 volts and note the charging current. If it's less than the standard charging current printed on the battery, go to Step 12. If it's more than the standard charging current, skip to Step 13.
14   Set the charging voltage at 20 to 25 volts, then watch the charging current for three to five minutes. If it reaches one amp or more, reset the voltage at 16 to 17 volts and continue charging. If the current isn't higher than the standard charging current after five minutes, replace the battery.
15   Adjust the voltage so the charging current is at the standard charging level. Set the timer on the charger according to the charging time determined in Step 11.
16   After the battery has charged, unplug the charger and disconnect it from the battery. Wait 30 minutes, then connect a voltmeter between the battery terminals and measure the open-circuit voltage (the battery needs this time top stabilize).

a) *If the reading is 12.8 volts or more, the battery is charged.*
b) *If the reading is 12.0 to 12.7 volts, continue charging the battery.*
c) *If the reading is less than 12.0 volts, replace the battery.*

Constant voltage charger

Refer to illustration 4.17
17   Connect the charger, a voltmeter and an ammeter to the battery **(see illustration)**.
18   Plug in the charger and check the ammeter reading.
a) *If it's less than the standard charging current printed on the battery, the charger won't work with a maintenance-free battery. Use a variable voltage charger instead.*
b) *If the current flow is at the standard charging current, set charging time to a maximum of 20 hours and continue charging until charging voltage reaches 15 volts.*

9   Once charging voltage has reached 15 volts, unplug the charger. Disconnect the charger from the battery and refer to Step 16 to check open-circuit voltage.

5   Fuse (battery-equipped models) - check and replacement

Refer to illustration 5.1
1   The fuse is located under the seat, next to the battery **(see illustrations 1.1c, 1.1e, 1.1g and the accompanying illustration)**.
2   The fuse can be removed and checked visually. A blown fuse is easily identified by a break in the element.
3   If the fuse blows, be sure to check the wiring harnesses very care-

5.1 Here's a typical main fuse (lower arrow) and starter relay (upper arrow)

fully for evidence of a short circuit. Look for bare wires and chafed, melted or burned insulation. If a fuse is replaced before the cause is located, the new fuse will blow immediately.
4   Never, under any circumstances, use a higher rated fuse or bridge the fuse holder terminals, as damage to the electrical system or a fire could result.
5   Occasionally a fuse will blow or cause an open circuit for no obvious reason. Corrosion of the fuse ends and fuse holder terminals may occur and cause poor fuse contact. If this happens, remove the corrosion with a wire brush or emery paper, then spray the fuse end and terminals with electrical contact cleaner.

6   Bulbs - replacement

1   Since these bikes are used off-road, it's a good idea to check the lens and bulb housing for built-up dirt and clean them thoroughly whenever a bulb is changed.

Headlight bulb

Warning: *To avoid burning your fingers, let the bulb cool before replacing it.*
Refer to illustration 6.2
2   Remove the retaining screw inside the cowling below the headlight **(see illustration)**. Pull the two cowling retainer tabs off the grommets and take the cowling off the motorcycle.
3   Unbolt the headlight case and pull it forward out of the housing.
4   Disconnect the electrical connector and pull off the rubber cover on the back of the headlight assembly.

6.2 Cowl retainer screw (lower arrow) and headlight aim adjusting screw (upper arrow)

5   Turn the bulb holder counterclockwise to free it, then lift out the bulb holder and the bulb.
6   Installation is the reverse of the removal steps.
7   Refer to Section 7 and adjust headlight aim.

Taillight bulb

Refer to illustration 6.9

8   The taillight bulb on XT225 and XT350 models also includes the brake light.
9   Remove the lens screws and take the lens off the taillight housing **(see illustration)**.
10   Press the bulb into its socket, turn it counterclockwise to align the bulb retaining pins with their grooves and pull the bulb out.
11   Installation is the reverse of the removal steps. The bulb pins are offset so the bulb can only go in one way.

Turn signal bulbs (XT225 and XT350 models)

12   Remove the lens screws from the turn signal housing and take the lens and gasket off the housing.
13   Press the bulb into its socket, turn it counterclockwise to align the bulb retaining pins with their grooves and pull the bulb out.
14   Installation is the reverse of the removal steps.

Instrument light bulbs (XL600R models)

15   Pull the bulb socket out of the underside of the instrument housing. Pull the bulb out of the socket, push in a new one and push the socket back into the housing.

---

7   Headlight aim - check and adjustment

1   An improperly adjusted headlight may cause problems for oncoming traffic or provide poor, unsafe illumination of the terrain ahead. Before adjusting the headlight, be sure to consult with local traffic laws and regulations.

XT350 models

2   Adjust the headlight vertically by loosening the headlight housing bolts, swiveling the housing and tightening the bolts.
3   Adjust the headlight horizontally by turning the screw in the underside of the headlight housing, to the left of center.

XT225 and TT-R250 models

4   These bikes don't have a horizontal adjustment. Adjust the beam vertically by turning the screw in the lower front edge of the headlight housing **(see illustration 6.2)**.

---

8   Brake light switches (XT225 and XT350) – check, replacement and adjustment

1   Before checking any electrical circuit on these models, check the fuse (see Section 5).
2   The front brake light switch is mounted under the master cylinder. The rear brake light switch is mounted in a bracket behind the brake pedal.

Test light check

3   Turn the ignition switch On. Using a test light connected to a good ground, check for voltage to the black wire at the front brake light switch or the black wire in the harness side of the connector at the rear brake light switch. Leave the connector at the rear brake light switch connected and insert the test light probe into the back of the terminal. If there's no voltage, check the wiring from the brake light switch to the ignition switch (see the wiring diagrams at the end of the book).
4   If voltage is available, connect the test light to the other terminal at the brake light switch, then pull the lever or push the pedal. If the test light comes on, the switch is good. If not, replace the switch.

6.9 Remove the lens screws (arrows) and take the lens off

Ohmmeter check

5   This test can also be made with a self-powered test light (one that has its own battery).
6   Disconnect the wires from the switch. Connect the ohmmeter or test light between the switch terminals (if you're testing a rear switch, connect the tester between the terminals in the switch side of the wiring harness).
7   Pull the lever or press the pedal. The ohmmeter should show zero or near-zero; the test light should illuminate. If not, replace the switch.

Replacement

8   To remove a front brake light switch, disconnect its wires, remove the switch mounting screw and take the switch off the master cylinder.
9   To remove a rear brake light switch, unhook the spring and disconnect the electrical connector. Loosen the adjusting nut until it comes off the switch threads, then pull the switch out of the bracket (don't turn the switch body).
10   Installation is the reverse of the removal steps.

Adjustment

11   The front switch isn't adjustable.
12   To adjust the rear brake light switch, hold the switch so it won't turn and rotate the adjusting nut. Position the switch so the brake light comes on when the brake pedal starts to move.

---

9   Ignition switch - check and replacement

Check

1   Follow the wiring harness from the ignition switch to the connector and unplug the connector.
2   Using an ohmmeter, check the continuity of the terminal pairs indicated in the wiring diagrams at the end of the book. Continuity should exist between the terminals connected by a solid line when the switch is in the indicated position.
3   If the switch fails any of the tests, replace it.

Replacement

Refer to illustration 9.7

4   Refer to Section 6 and remove the headlight housing.
5   Follow the switch wires to the connector and disconnect it.
6   Unlock the steering lock with the key and turn the handlebars so the switch can be removed.
7   Remove the switch mounting screw(s) **(see illustration 1.1e, 1.1h or the accompanying illustration)**.
8   Installation is the reverse of the removal steps.

9.7 Remove the screw(s) and take the ignition switch off

10.6 Remove the screws (arrows) and separate the switch housing halves

11.2 Unscrew the knurled nut (arrow) and pull the cable out of the drive unit (TT-R250 shown)

10 Handlebar switches - check and replacement

1   Generally speaking, the switches are reliable and trouble-free. Most troubles, when they do occur, are caused by dirty or corroded contacts, but wear and breakage of internal parts is a possibility that should not be overlooked. If breakage does occur, the entire switch and related wiring harness will have to be replaced with a new one, since individual parts are not usually available.

2   The switches can be checked for continuity with an ohmmeter or a continuity test light. If you're working on a battery-equipped model, always disconnect the battery negative cable, which will prevent the possibility of a short circuit, before making the checks.

3   Trace the wiring harness of the switch in question and unplug the electrical connectors.

4   Using the ohmmeter or test light, check for continuity between the terminals of the switch harness with the switch in the various positions. Refer to the continuity diagrams contained in the wiring diagrams at the end of the book. Continuity should exist between the terminals connected by a solid line when the switch is in the indicated position.

5   If the continuity check indicates a problem exists, disassemble the switch and spray the switch contacts with electrical contact cleaner. If they are accessible, the contacts can be scraped clean with a knife or polished with crocus cloth. If switch components are damaged or broken, it will be obvious when the switch is disassembled.

Replacement

Refer to illustration 10.6

6   The handlebar switches are composed of two halves that clamp around the bars. They are easily removed for cleaning or inspection by taking out the clamp screws **(see illustration)** and pulling the switch halves away from the handlebars.

7   To completely remove the switches, the electrical connectors in the wiring harness must be unplugged and the harness separated from the tie wraps and retainers.

8   When installing the switches, make sure the wiring harness is properly routed to avoid pinching or stretching the wires. Align the split in the switch housing or clamp with the punch mark on the handlebar.

11 Speedometer/odometer/tachometer and cable - removal and installation

Refer to illustrations 11.2 and 11.5

1   Some models use a speedometer, tachometer, odometer or a combination.

2   Unscrew the knurled nut and pull the lower end of the cable out of the gear at the front wheel **(see illustration)**.

3   Follow the cable up to the instrument cluster and remove any retainers.

4   Unscrew the knurled nut and detach the cable from the instrument housing.

5   Remove the clips and lower grommets and lift the instrument(s) out of the damper bracket **(see illustration)**.

6   Installation is the reverse of the removal steps.

12 Charging system testing (battery-equipped models) - general information and precautions

1   If the performance of the charging system is suspect, the system as a whole should be checked first, followed by testing of the individual components (the alternator and the regulator/rectifier). **Note:** *Before beginning the checks, make sure the battery is fully charged and that all system connections are clean and tight.*

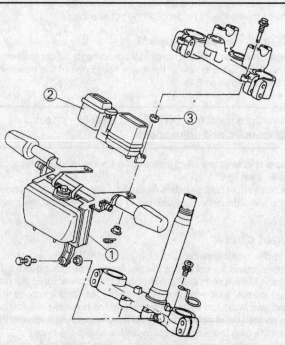

11.5 Instrument cluster and headlight assembly details (XT225 models)

2   Checking the output of the charging system and the performance of the various components within the charging system requires the use of a voltmeter, ammeter and ohmmeter or the equivalent multimeter.

3   When making the checks, follow the procedures carefully to prevent incorrect connections or short circuits, as irreparable damage to electrical system components may result if short circuits occur.

4   If the necessary test equipment is not available, it is recommended that charging system tests be left to a dealer service department or a reputable motorcycle repair shop.

13   Charging system (battery-equipped models) - leakage and output test

1   If a charging system problem is suspected, perform the following checks. Start by removing the left or right side cover for access to the battery (see Chapter 7).

Leakage test

Refer to illustration 13.3

2   Turn the ignition switch Off and disconnect the cable from the battery negative terminal.

3   Set the multimeter to the mA (milliamps) function and connect its negative probe to the battery negative terminal, and the positive probe to the disconnected negative cable **(see illustration)**. Although Yamaha doesn't specify a leakage limit for these models, it should be very low, about 0.1 milliamp or less.

4   If the reading is too high there is probably a short circuit in the wiring. Thoroughly check the wiring between the various components (see the wiring diagrams at the end of the book).

5   If the reading is satisfactory, disconnect the meter and connect the negative cable to the battery, tightening it securely. Check the alternator output as described below.

Output test

6   Start the engine and let it warm up to normal operating temperature.

7   With the engine idling, attach the positive (red) voltmeter lead to the positive (+) battery terminal and the negative (black) lead to the battery negative (-) terminal. The voltmeter selector switch (if equipped) must be in the 0-20 DC volt range.

8   Slowly increase the engine speed until voltage reaches its maximum (don't exceed 8000 rpm) and compare the voltmeter reading to the value listed in this Chapter's Specifications.

9   If the output is as specified, the alternator is functioning properly.

10   Low voltage output may be the result of damaged windings in the alternator charging coil or wiring problems between the alternator and battery. Make sure all electrical connections are clean and tight, then refer to the following Section to check the alternator charging coil. If

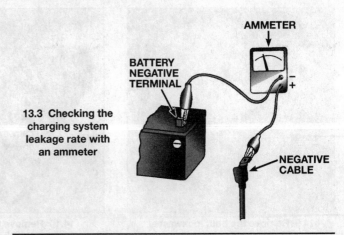

13.3 Checking the charging system leakage rate with an ammeter

the wiring and the charging coil are good, the problem may be a defective regulator/rectifier.

11   High voltage output (above the specified range) indicates a defective voltage regulator/rectifier.

14   Alternator stator coils and rotor - check and replacement

Stator coil check

1   Locate and disconnect the alternator coil connector on the left side of the vehicle frame.

2   To check the coils, connect an ohmmeter between the specified terminals in the side of the connector that runs back to the stator coils on the left side of the engine. Wire colors and resistance readings are listed in this Chapter's Specifications.

3   If the readings are much outside the value listed in this Chapter's Specifications, replace the stator coils as described below.

Stator coil replacement

Refer to illustrations 14.4 and 14.5

4   Remove the left crankcase cover **(see illustration)**.

5   On all except XT350 models, the stator coils are mounted in the left crankcase cover. To remove the coils, remove the mounting screws and take the coils out **(see illustration)**.

6   On XT350 models, the coils are mounted on the engine. Remove the stator base plate screws and take the stator assembly out.

7   Installation is the reverse of the removal steps. Tighten the stator coil bolts securely, but don't overtighten them and strip the threads.

14.4 Remove the cover Allen bolts (arrows), then remove the gasket and dowels

14.5 Remove the bolts (arrows) to detach the stator and pick-up coils

14.9 Remove the bolt, lockwasher (if equipped) and washer

14.10 Remove the rotor with a puller like this one

14.12 Look for the Woodruff key - if it isn't secure in its slot, set it aside for safekeeping

Rotor replacement

Removal

Refer to illustrations 14.9, 14.10 and 14.12

Caution: *To remove the alternator rotor, the special Yamaha puller or an aftermarket equivalent will be required. Don't try to remove the rotor without the proper puller, as it's almost sure to be damaged. Pullers are readily available from motorcycle dealers and aftermarket tool suppliers.*

8   Remove the left crankcase cover **(see illustration 14.3)**.

9   Hold the alternator rotor with a strap wrench. If you don't have one and the engine is in the frame, the rotor can be locked by placing the transmission in gear and holding the rear brake on. Unscrew the rotor bolt, remove the lockwasher (if equipped) and the washer **(see illustration)**.

10   Thread an alternator puller into the center of the rotor and use it to remove the rotor **(see illustration)**. If the rotor doesn't come off easily, tap sharply on the end of the puller to release the rotor's grip on the tapered crankshaft end.

11   Pull the rotor off.

12   Check the Woodruff key **(see illustration)**; if it's not secure in its slot, pull it out and set it aside for safekeeping. A convenient method is to stick the Woodruff key to the magnets inside the rotor, but be certain not to forget it's there, as serious damage to the rotor and stator coils will occur if the engine is run with anything stuck to the magnets.

Installation

13   Take a look to make sure there isn't anything stuck to the rotor magnets.

15.3 Here's a typical regulator/rectifier

14   Degrease the center of the rotor and the end of the crankshaft.

15   Make sure the Woodruff key is positioned securely in its slot **(see illustration 14.12)**.

16   Align the rotor slot with the Woodruff key. Place the rotor on the crankshaft.

17   Install the rotor bolt. Hold the rotor from turning with one of the methods described in Step 7 and tighten the bolt to the torque listed in this Chapter's Specifications.

18   Install the left crankcase cover **(see illustration 14.3)**. Tighten its bolts evenly, in a criss-cross pattern, to the torque listed in this Chapter's Specifications.

15   Regulator/rectifier (battery-equipped models) - replacement

Refer to illustration 15.3

1   The regulator/rectifier is tested by a process of elimination. When all other possible causes of charging system failure, including wiring problems, have been checked and eliminated, the rectifier/regulator is at fault. Since this is difficult to detect and since the new part can't be returned if it doesn't solve the problem, it's best to substitute a known good unit or have the system tested by a dealer service or other qualified motorcycle electrical shop before replacing the rectifier/regulator.

2   Follow the wiring harnesses from the regulator/rectifier to the connector and disconnect it

3   Remove the regulator/rectifier mounting screws and lift it off the bike **(see illustrations 1.1c, 1.1e, 1.1h and the accompanying illustration)**.

4   Installation is the reverse of the removal steps.

16   Ignition system - general information

These motorcycles are equipped with a breakerless (CDI) ignition system. The CDI ignition system functions on the same principle as a breaker point ignition system with the pulse generator and CDI unit performing the tasks previously associated with the breaker points and mechanical advance system. As a result, adjustment and maintenance of breakerless ignition components is eliminated (with the exception of spark plug replacement).

Because of their nature, the individual ignition system components can be checked but not repaired. If ignition system troubles occur, and the faulty component can be isolated, the only cure for the problem is to replace the part with a new one. Keep in mind that most electrical parts, once purchased, can't be returned. To avoid unnecessary expense, make very sure the faulty component has been positively identified before buying a replacement part.

17 Ignition system - check

Refer to Chapter 2 Part B for this procedure.

18 Ignition coil - check, removal and installation

Check

1 Refer to Chapter 2 Part B for this procedure.

Removal and installation

2 To remove the coil, refer to Chapter 3 and remove the fuel tank, then disconnect the spark plug wire from the plug. After labeling them with tape to aid in reinstallation, unplug the coil primary circuit electrical connector(s) .
3 Remove the coil mounting bolt, then lift the coil out **(see illustration 1.1a, 1.1b, 1.1c, 1.1e or 1.1g)**.
4 Installation is the reverse of removal.

19 Pickup coil - check, removal and installation

Check

1 Locate the pickup coil harness on the right side of the engine. Follow the harness to the connector and disconnect it.
2 Connect an ohmmeter between the wire terminals in the pickup coil side of the connector. Compare the reading to the value listed in this Chapter's Specifications. If it's outside the specified range, replace the pickup coil.

Removal and installation

3 Remove the right crankcase cover (Section 14). Disconnect the pulse generator wire at the connector above the engine.
4 On all except XT350 models, the pulse generator is replaced as part of the stator assembly (Section 14).
5 On XT350 models, remove the pulse generator mounting screws and take it off the stator baseplate.
6 Installation is the reverse of the removal steps. Tighten the bolts securely, but don't overtighten them and strip the threads.

20 CDI unit - removal and installation

1 The CDI unit is tested by process of elimination (when all other possible causes of ignition problems have been checked and eliminated, the CDI unit is at fault).
2 Remove the fuel tank if you haven't already done so (see Chapter 3).
3 Locate the CDI unit **(see illustration 1.1a, 1.1b, 1.1c, 1.1e or 1.1g)**. Unplug its connector and work the unit out of its mounting band.
4 Installation is the reverse of the removal steps.

21 Neutral switch – check and replacement

1 The neutral switch is used on TT-R225, TT-R250, XT225 and XT350 models.

Check

Refer to illustration 21.2
2 Locate the neutral switch. Loosen the screw and disconnect its wire **(see illustration 1.1c, 1.1f, 1.1g and the accompanying illustration)**.
3 Set an ohmmeter to RX1 and connect its positive terminal to the electrical terminal on the switch. Connect the ohmmeter to a good

21.2 Loosen the screw to disconnect the neutral switch wire

ground (bare metal on the engine).
4 Move the shift lever through the gear positions. The ohmmeter should show continuity when the transmission is in Neutral and no continuity in any other gear position.
5 If the switch doesn't perform properly, replace it.

Replacement

6 If you haven't already done so, disconnect the switch wire.
7 Unscrew the switch from the crankcase.
8 Installation is the reverse of the removal steps. Use a new sealing washer.

22 Sidestand switch – check and replacement

1 A sidestand switch is used on street legal models with electric start.

Check

2 Follow the wiring harness from the switch to the connector, then disconnect the connector. Connect the leads of an ohmmeter to the wire terminals. With the sidestand in the up position, there should be continuity through the switch (0 ohms).
3 With the sidestand in the down position, the meter should indicate infinite resistance.
4 If the switch fails either of these tests, replace it.

Replacement

5 With the sidestand in the up position, unscrew the two screws and remove the switch **(see illustration 1.1c)**. Disconnect the switch electrical connector.
6 Installation is the reverse of the removal steps.

23 Clutch switch – check and replacement

1 A clutch switch is used on street legal models with electric start.

Check

2 Follow the wiring harness from the switch to the connector at the clutch lever, then disconnect the connector.
3 Connect the leads of an ohmmeter to the terminals in the switch side of the wiring harness. With the clutch lever pulled in, there should be continuity through the switch (0 ohms).
4 With the clutch lever released, the meter should indicate infinite resistance.
5 If the switch fails either of these tests, replace it.

24.5 Disconnect the cable from the starter (TT-R225 shown)

24.6a The starter is secured by mounting bolts (arrows) (TT-R250 shown)

24.6b Pull the starter out and inspect the O-ring

Replacement

6   Detach the switch from the clutch lever bracket and take the switch off. Disconnect the switch electrical connector.
7   Installation is the reverse of the removal steps.

24 Starter motor – check and replacement

Check

Warning 1: *This check may cause sparks. Make sure there is no leaking gasoline or anything else flammable in the vicinity.*
Warning 2: *Make sure the transmission is in Neutral or the bike will jump forward during the next step.*
Caution: *The jumper cable used for this test must be of a gauge at least as heavy as the battery cables or it may melt.*
1   Locate the starter motor and disconnect its cable.
2   Connect a jumper cable from the battery positive terminal directly to the starter motor terminal. The starter should crank the engine.
3   If the starter doesn't crank at all, replace it. If it turns but doesn't crank the engine, remove and inspect the starter reduction gears (Section 26).

Replacement

Refer to illustrations 24.5, 24.6a and 24.6b
4   Disconnect the negative cable from the battery.
5   Disconnect the starter cable from the motor **(see illustration)**.
6   Remove the motor mounting bolts and take it out **(see illustration)**. Check the O-ring for damage and replace it if necessary **(see illustration)**.

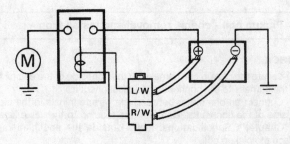

25.3 Jumper the battery to the terminals to test the relay

7   Installation is the reverse of the removal steps. Tighten the mounting bolts to the torque listed in this Chapter's Specifications.

25 Starter relay – check and replacement

Refer to illustration 25.3
1   Remove the seat and side cover for access to the starter relay (see Chapter 7).
2   Disconnect the starter relay electrical connector **(see illustration 5.1)**.
3   Connect a pair of jumper wires directly from the battery positive and negative terminals to the relay terminals **(see illustration)**.
4   If the relay doesn't click, replace it.

26.3 Remove this cover for access to the TT-R250 starter gears

26.4a Slide off the collar . . .

26.4b . . . and the gear, noting its direction, then pull out the shaft

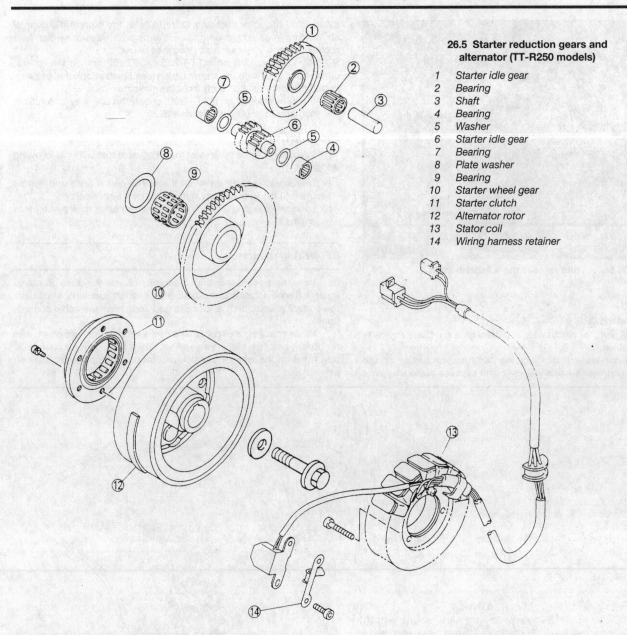

26.5 Starter reduction gears and alternator (TT-R250 models)

1   *Starter idle gear*
2   *Bearing*
3   *Shaft*
4   *Bearing*
5   *Washer*
6   *Starter idle gear*
7   *Bearing*
8   *Plate washer*
9   *Bearing*
10 *Starter wheel gear*
11 *Starter clutch*
12 *Alternator rotor*
13 *Stator coil*
14 *Wiring harness retainer*

26 Starter drive and reduction gears – removal, inspection and installation

1   The starter drive one-way clutch is bolted to the back of the alternator rotor. It engages a hub on the starter wheel gear.

Removal

Refer to illustrations 26.3, 26.4a, 26.4b, 26.5, 26.6a and 26.6b

2   Remove the right crankcase cover and alternator rotor (Section 14).
3   If you're working on a TT-R250, remove the gear cover for access to the reduction gears **(see illustration)**.
4   On TT-R225 models, pull the collar off the reduction gear shaft, then pull off the gear and pull the shaft itself out of the crankcase **(see illustrations)**.
5   On TT-R250 models, remove the large idle gear, bearing and shaft, then remove the small idle gear, thrust washers and bearings **(see illustration)**.
6   Pull the starter wheel gear off the crankshaft and remove the thrust washer behind it **(see illustrations)**. If you're working on a TT-R250 model, remove the needle roller bearing from the gear.

26.6a Slide the starter wheel gear off the crankshaft . . .

26.6b . . . and remove the washer behind it

Inspection

Refer to illustration 26.9

7   Check all parts for visible wear and damage and replace any parts that show problems.

8   Test the one-way clutch. Place the clutch friction surface on the starter wheel gear into the one-way clutch on the back of the alternator rotor. Hold the rotor steady and try to twist the starter idle gear. If should turn in one direction only. If it turns both ways or neither way, replace the one-way clutch as described below.

9   If you're working on a TT-R225 or XT225, remove the rollers, springs and pins from the starter clutch (see illustration). If necessary, unbolt the starter clutch body from the alternator rotor.

10   If you're working on a TT-R250, unbolt the one-way clutch from the alternator rotor (see illustration 26.5).

Installation

11   Installation is the reverse of the removal steps, with the following additions:

   a) Use thread locking agent on the starter clutch bolts and tighten them to the torque listed in this Chapter's Specifications.
   b) Lubricate the gears, shafts and one-way clutch rollers with clean engine oil.

27   Wiring diagrams

Prior to troubleshooting a circuit, check the fuse (battery-equipped models only) to make sure it's in good condition. Make sure the battery (if equipped) is fully charged and check the cable connections.

When checking a circuit, make sure all connectors are clean, with no broken or loose terminals or wires. When unplugging a connector, don't pull on the wires - pull only on the connector housings themselves.

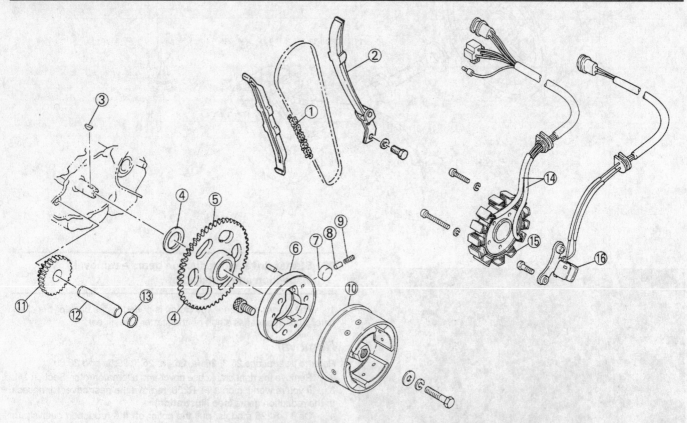

26.9 Starter reduction gears and alternator rotor (TT-R225 and XT225 models)

1	Timing chain	*7*	Dowel pin	*13*	Collar
2	Intake side timing chain guide	*8*	Starter clutch spring cap	*14*	Charge coil
3	Woodruff key	*9*	Compression spring	*15*	Stator coil
4	Washer	*10*	Rotor	*16*	Pick-up coil
5	Starter wheel gear	*11*	Starter idle gear		
6	Starter clutch	*12*	Shaft		

Chapter 5 Part A
Steering, suspension and final drive (PW50 and PW80 models)

Contents

Specifications

Front forks
Oil type (PW80)	Yamaha 15W fork oil, or equivalent
Oil capacity (PW80)	60 cc (2.0 fl oz)
Fork spring free length	
PW50	115 mm (4.53 inches)
PW80	425.1 mm (16.74 inches)

Torque specifications
Steering and front suspension
Handlebar clamp bolts	
PW50	19 Nm (156 in-lbs)
PW80	13 Nm (113 in-lbs)
Upper triple clamp/fork tube cap bolts	
PW50	32 Nm (23 ft-lbs)
PW80	40 Nm (29 ft-lbs)
Lower triple clamp pinch bolts	
PW50	32 Nm (23 ft-lbs)
PW80	33 Nm (24 ft-lbs)
Damper rod bolts (PW80)	20 Nm (14 ft-lbs)
Steering stem bolt	
PW50	32 Nm (23 ft-lbs)
PW80	40 Nm (29 ft-lbs)
Steering stem ring nut (bearing adjustment nut)	See Chapter 1

Rear suspension
Rear shock absorbers (PW50)	
Upper mounting bolts	11 Nm (8 ft-lbs)
Lower mounting bolts/nuts	23 Nm (17 ft-lbs)
Swingarm pivot bolt nut (PW80)	31 Nm (22 ft-lbs)

Torque specifications

Rear arms (PW50)

Right rear arm nuts
    Rear arm-to-bearing housing bolts .... 33 Nm (24 ft-lbs)
    Rear arm-to-engine nuts .... 29 Nm (21 ft-lbs)
Left rear arm/shaft drive housing bolts
    Arm-to-ring and pinion housing bolts .... 26 Nm (19 ft-lbs)
    Arm-to-engine bolts .... 26 Nm (19 ft-lbs)

Shaft drive assembly (PW50)

Ring nut for middle driven pinion... 58 Nm (43 ft-lbs)
Ring nut for drive pinion .... 49 Nm (36 ft-lbs)
Ring and pinion housing cover screws.. 24 Nm (18 ft-lbs)

Chain drive (PW80)

Rear wheel sprocket bolts .... 26 Nm (19 ft-lbs)

1   General information

The steering system consists of the handlebar, the upper and lower triple clamps, the steering stem and the steering head bearings. The steering stem, an integral part of the lower triple clamp, turns on ball bearings riding on races pressed into the upper and lower ends of the steering head.

The front suspension consists of telescopic forks with damper rods and rebound springs.

The rear suspension on PW50 models consists of a pair of shock absorbers and left and right rear arms. The PW50's rear arms do not pivot like a conventional swingarm; they're bolted rigidly to the engine. Instead, the entire engine/rear arm/rear wheel assembly pivots at the engine mounting bolt.

The rear suspension on PW80 models consists of a single shock absorber and a triangulated mono-shock style swingarm.

The final drive on PW50 models is a shaft-drive system housed inside the left rear arm. A bevel gear at the front end of the shaft is driven by a bevel gear on the left end of the mainshaft, while at the rear end of the shaft a pinion gear drives a ring gear, which turns the rear axle.

PW80 models are equipped with a chain final drive system.

2   Handlebar - removal, inspection and installation

PW50 models

Refer to illustrations 2.1, 2.2a and 2.2b

1   Remove the handlebar pad **(see illustration)**.

2   If you're only removing the handlebar to gain access to other components (upper/lower triple clamps, steering head bearings, etc.), simply remove the handlebar mounting nuts **(see illustration)**, lift the handlebar off the upper triple clamp and carefully lay it in front of the triple clamp **(see illustration)**. It's not necessary to disconnect the throttle cable, brake cables or kill switch wires. It is, however, a good idea to support the assembly with a piece of wire or rope to avoid unnecessary strain on the cables, hoses and wiring.

3   If you're replacing the handlebar itself, loosen the brake cable adjusters at the front and rear wheels and disconnect the cables from the levers at the handlebar (see Chapter 6).

4   Disconnect the electrical connector for the kill switch (see Chapter 4).

5   Remove the throttle housing (see Chapter 3).

6   Remove the handlebar mounting nuts and the handlebar **(see illustrations 2.2a and 2.2b)**.

7   Inspect the handlebar mounting studs. If the threads are damaged, rethread them. If the studs are loose, replace the handlebar.

8   Inspect the rear brake lever bracket. If it's cracked or damaged, replace the handlebar.

9   Inspect the handlebar grips. If they're damaged, cut off the old grips and install new ones (this is easier to do after the handlebar has been installed).

10   Inspect the front and rear brake levers. If either lever is excessively worn (especially at the hole for the pivot bolt), or if it's cracked or the end of the ball is broken off, replace the lever (see Chapter 6).

11   Installation is the reverse of removal.

PW80 models

Refer to illustrations 2.13 and 2.16

12   Remove the fuel tank (see Chapter 3) and the front fender (see

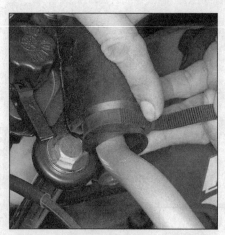
2.1 Remove the tie-wraps to detach the handlebar pad

2.2a To detach the PW50 handlebar, remove the nuts . . .

2.2b . . . and washers, then lift the handlebar off the upper triple clamp

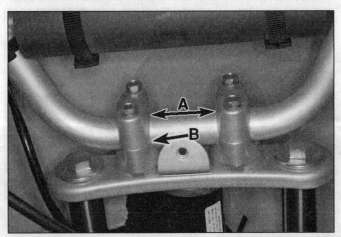

2.13 On PW80 models, mark the inside of each handlebar bracket (A) and the handlebar position relative to the bracket gap (B)

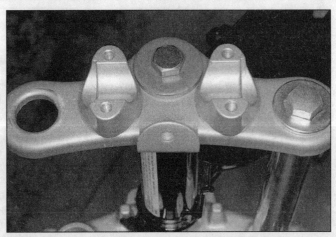

2.16 The PW80 handlebar bracket recesses face away from each other

Chapter 7).

13   Look for punch marks on the inner side of each handlebar upper clamp **(see illustration)**. If you don't see any, make your own. The handlebar clamps must be installed with these punch marks facing toward each other. If you want to make sure that the handlebar is installed in exactly the same position, put a punch mark on the bar next to the split line between the upper and lower halves of one of the handlebar clamps.

14   If you're only removing the handlebar to gain access to other components (upper/lower triple clamps, steering head bearings, etc.), simply remove the four handlebar clamp bolts **(see illustration 2.13)**, lift the handlebar off the upper triple clamp and carefully lay it in front of the triple clamp. It's not necessary to disconnect the throttle cable, brake cable or kill switch wires. It is, however, a good idea to support the assembly with a piece of wire or rope to avoid unnecessary strain on the cables, hoses and wiring.

15   If you're replacing the handlebar itself, remove the kill switch (see Chapter 4), remove the throttle housing and the throttle twist grip (see Chapter 3), and remove the brake lever bracket (see Chapter 6). Then remove the upper bracket bolts, lift off the brackets and remove the handlebars.

16   Inspect the handlebar and brackets for damage. If anything is cracked, bent or otherwise damaged, replace it. To remove the lower brackets, unscrew their mounting nuts from below. Note the directions the brackets face, then remove them **(see illustration)**.

17   Place the handlebar in the lower brackets. Line up the punch mark on the handlebar with the split between the upper and lower clamps **(see illustration 2.13)**.

18   Install the upper clamps with their punch marks facing toward each other **(see illustration 2.13)**. Tighten the front bolts, then the rear bolts, to the torque listed in this Chapter's Specifications. **Caution:** *If there's a gap between the upper and lower brackets at the rear after tightening the bolts, don't try to close it by tightening beyond the recommended torque. You'll only crack the brackets.*

3   Front forks - removal and installation

Removal

1   Support the bike securely so that it's upright, with its front wheel off the ground.

2   Remove the front wheel (see Chapter 6) and the front fender (see Chapter 7).

PW50 models
Refer to illustrations 3.3 and 3.4

3   Remove the bolts and washers from the tops of the fork tubes **(see illustration)**.

4   Loosen the lower triple clamp pinch bolts **(see illustration)**.

PW80 models
Refer to illustrations 3.6a and 3.6b

6   Remove the fork tube caps **(see illustrations)**.

3.3 Remove the PW50 fork tube bolts (arrows) and washers . . .

3.4 Loosen the lower triple clamp bolts (arrow) and lower the fork out of the triple clamps

3.6a Loosen the fork caps . . .

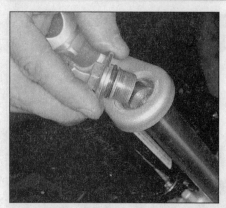

3.6b . . . then remove the caps
and O-rings

3.13a Position the fork locator in the
brake drum slot; this is the
PW50 locator . . .

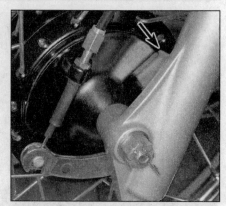

3.13b . . . and this is the PW80 locator

4.2a Remove the cap bolt and washer and
separate the fork from the triple
clamp (PW50) . . .

4.2b . . . slide the seal off the fork slider
and up the fork tube . . .

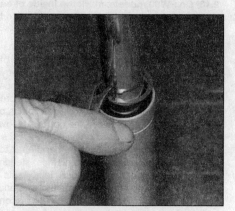

4.2c . . . remove the snap-ring from its
groove in the slider . . .

7   Remove the screw and detach the brake cable clip from the left front fork leg (see Chapter 6).
8   Loosen the lower triple clamp pinch bolts.

All models

9   Pull each fork tube down, twisting it back and forth if necessary, and slide it out of the triple clamps.

Installation

Refer to illustrations 3.13a and 3.13b

10   Insert each fork tube through the lower and upper triple clamps. Hand tighten the lower triple clamp pinch bolts enough to secure the tubes.

11   Install the bolts that secure the upper triple clamps to the fork tubes and tighten them to the torque listed in this Chapter's Specifications.
12   Tighten the lower triple clamp pinch bolts to the torque listed in this Chapter's Specifications.
13   The remainder of installation is the reverse of removal. When you reinstall the right fork leg, make sure its locating tab is in the notch of the brake drum **(see illustrations)**.

4   Forks - disassembly, inspection and assembly

1   Remove the forks (see Section 3).

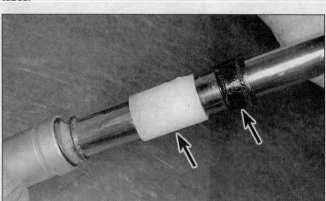

4.2d . . . pull the fork tube out of the slider, together with the
bushing (right arrow) and collar (left arrow) . . .

4.2e . . . then remove the upper spring seat, rubber bumper,
spring and lower spring seat (not shown)

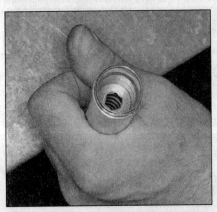

4.17a Unscrew the spring seat from the top of the fork tube . . .

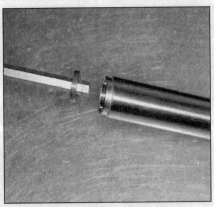

4.17b . . . using a hex bit . . .

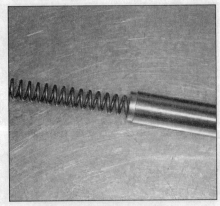

4.17c . . . remove the spring . . .

4.17d . . . pour the fork oil out of the fork into a container . . .

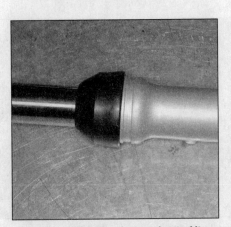

4.17e . . . slide the dust seal out of its groove in the fork slider (arrow) and up the fork tube . . .

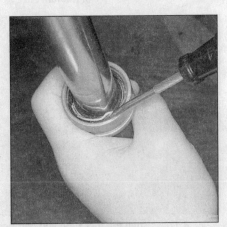

4.17f . . . pry the retaining ring out of its groove . . .

PW50 models

Disassembly

Refer to illustrations 4.2a through 4.2e

2   Refer to the accompanying illustrations **(see illustrations)**. Disassemble, inspect and reassemble one fork at a time to prevent mixing up the parts.

Inspection

4   Clean all parts in solvent and blow them dry with compressed air, if available, and then lay out the parts for inspection.

5   Inspect the fork tube mounting bolt. Make sure the threads are in good condition.

6   Inspect the dust cover for damage and wear. Unless it's in very good condition, replace it. A damaged or worn dust cover will allow water to get into the fork.

7   Inspect the dust seal circlip. Make sure it's neither weak nor bent. If it is, replace it.

8   Inspect the dust seal. Make sure that it's neither worn nor damaged. If it is, replace it.

9   Inspect the collar. Make sure that it's neither worn nor damaged. If it is, replace it.

10   Inspect the rebound spring. If it's weak or damaged, replace it.

11   Inspect the bumper stop for cracks and general deterioration. If it's damaged, replace it.

12   Inspect the fork spring for damage and fatigue. Measure the free length of the fork spring and compare your measurement to the fork spring free length listed in this Chapter's Specifications. If the spring is too short, replace both fork springs. Never replace only one spring.

13   Inspect the fork tube and damper rubber for scoring, nicks, gouges, scratches, flaking and excessive or abnormal wear. Look for

dents in the tube. Make sure the fork tube is straight by rolling it on a perfectly flat surface. If the tube is bent or damaged, replace it. **Warning:** *Don't try to straighten a bent fork tube. Straightening the tube will weaken it and cause it to fail.*

14   Inspect the bushing and collar. Make sure that neither is worn or damaged. If they are, replace them.

15   Inspect the fork slider for damage. Make sure that the slider is straight and free of gouges or nicks, particularly in the area that might cause damage to the fork tube. Make sure that the circlip groove in the slider is in good condition. If it's damaged or worn, replace the fork slider.

Reassembly

16   Reassembly is the reverse of disassembly, with the following additions:

a)   *Make sure that all components are spotlessly clean before reassembling them.*

b)   *Lubricate all the internal components of the fork assembly with grease.*

c)   *To secure the spring and spring seat, compress the spring (you can compress it by hand - no spring compressor is needed) and install the snap-ring.*

d)   *Slide the dust cover onto the fork tube and push it onto the top of the slider until it seats into the groove in the slider.*

PW80 models

Disassembly

Refer to illustrations 4.17a through 4.17k

17   Refer to the accompanying illustrations **(see illustrations)**. Disassemble, inspect and reassemble one fork at a time to prevent mixing

4.17g . . . unscrew the damper rod bolt from the bottom of the fork . . .

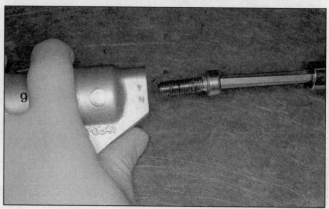

4.17h . . . with a hex bit; see the text for removal techniques . . .

4.17i . . . pull the fork tube and damper rod out of the fork slider . . .

4.17j . . . dump the damper rod and return spring out of the fork tube; don't remove the Teflon ring unless you plan to replace it . . .

up the parts. **Note:** *The damper rod bolt in the bottom of the fork tube may just spin the damper rod when you try to loosen it. There are three ways to deal with this: Use an air wrench; hold the damper rod from the top end with a special holding tool (a tapered piece of hardwood dowel will also work); or loosen the damper rod bolt while the fork is still assembled, so the pressure of the fork spring prevents the damper rod from turning.*

Inspection
Refer to illustration 4.18

18   Clean all parts in solvent and blow them dry with compressed air,

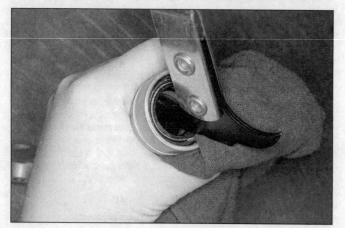

4.17k . . . and pry the oil seal out of the fork slider, using a seal remover (shown here) or a screwdriver

if available, and then lay out the parts for inspection **(see illustration)**.

19   Inspect the fork cap O-ring. Unless it's in perfect condition, replace it.

20   Inspect the fork tube for scoring, nicks, gouges, scratches, flaking and excessive or abnormal wear. Look for dents in the tube. Make sure the fork tube is straight by rolling it on a perfectly flat surface. If the tube is bent or damaged, replace it.

21   Inspect the fork slider for damage. Make sure that the slider is straight and free of gouges or nicks, particularly in the area that might cause damage to the fork tube. Make sure that the oil seal bore is free of nicks and gouges which will damage the new seal. Make sure that the circlip groove in the slider is in good condition. If it's damaged or worn, replace the fork slider.

22   Inspect the damper rod. Make sure that it's straight and the threads are in good condition. Inspect the condition of the Teflon piston ring on the damper rod. If it's worn or damaged, the piston ring can be replaced separately. Inspect the return spring. Make sure it's neither fatigued nor distorted. The spring can be replaced separately too.

23   Inspect the fork spring for damage and fatigue. Measure the free length of the fork spring and compare your measurement to the fork spring free length listed in this Chapter's Specifications. If the spring is too short, replace both fork springs. Never replace only one spring.

24   Inspect the Allen bolt. If the hex is rounded off (or is even beginning to round off), replace the Allen bolt. Replace the gasket (washer) regardless of its apparent condition.

Reassembly

25   Coat the lip of the new fork seal with lithium-soap-base grease or with clean fork oil, and then slide the seal onto the inner fork tube with the numbered side facing up. Install the new seal carefully; if the lip is damaged during installation, it will leak. Install the seal with a hydraulic press, if available. If you don't have a press, carefully drive the new

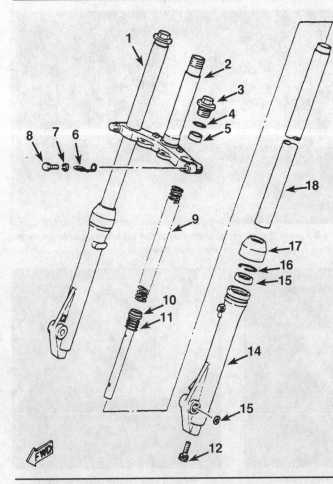

4.18 Front forks (PW80 models) - exploded view

1   Complete fork leg
2   Steering head/upper triple clamp
3   Fork cap bolt
4   O-ring
5   Spring seat
6   Brake cable retainer
7   Lockwasher
8   Upper triple clamp pinch bolt
9   Fork spring
10 Damper rod and Teflon ring
11 Rebound spring
12 Damper rod bolt and washer
13 Axle washer
14 Fork slider
15 Oil seal
16 Retaining ring
17 Dust seal
18 Fork tube

5.3 Remove the steering stem bolt and washer and the upper triple clamp

5.4a While supporting the steering stem/lower triple clamp with one hand, unscrew the bearing cover . . .

seal into place with a socket of slightly smaller diameter than the outside diameter of the seal. Don't use a socket that's too small, or you'll damage the "soft" part of the seal during installation.

26   Install the circlip. Make sure that it's fully seated in its groove.

27   Lubricate the damper rod piston ring with fork oil, slide the return spring onto the damper rod and install the damper rod into the fork tube.

28   Lubricate the lip of the new seal and the surface of the fork tube with fork oil and insert the fork tube and damper rod assembly into the slider. Be very careful not to damage the new seal lip.

29   Coat the threads of the Allen bolt with thread sealant, and then install the bolt and washer. Screw in the bolt as tightly as possible, then torque the bolt as follows:

a)   Install the fork spring and spring seat in the fork tube.
b)   Install the fork tube in the triple clamps and secure it with the pinch bolt in the lower triple clamp.
c)   Install the front axle to secure the lower ends of the fork sliders.
d)   Tighten the Allen bolt to the torque listed in this Chapter's Specifications.
e)   Remove the fork tube from the bike and remove the spring seat and fork spring from the fork tube.

30   If you're unable to tighten the Allen bolt to the specified torque without the damper rod holder (Yamaha special tool no. YM-01300-1), tighten the Allen bolt as follows with the damper rod holder (if you don't have the tool, take the assembly to a dealer and have the following step done there):

a)   Mount the special tool on a long T-handle.
b)   Mount the slider in a bench vise with soft jaws.
c)   Insert the tool through the fork tube and into the top of the damper rod.
d)   Twist the T-handle to "bite" the tool into the damper rod, then

hold the T-handle and tighten the Allen bolt to the torque listed in this Chapter's Specifications. If necessary, have an assistant hold the T-handle while you tighten the bolt. Remove the slider from the vise.

31   Add the specified fork oil to the fork as follows:

a)   Bottom out the fork tube in the slider.
b)   Add the type and amount of fork oil listed in this Chapter's Specifications.

32   Secure the slider in a bench vise with soft jaws. Pull the fork tube all the way up, then install the fork spring and spring seat.

33   Install the dust boot and seat it into the groove at the upper end of the slider.

34   Install the fork assembly in the bike (see Section 3).

5   Steering head bearings - replacement

1   If the steering head bearing check/adjustment (see *Steering and suspension - check* in Chapter 1) does not remedy excessive play or roughness in the steering head bearings, disassemble the front end and replace the bearings and races as follows.

2   Remove the handlebar (see Section 2), the front wheel (see Chapter 6), the front fender (see Chapter 7) and the forks (see Section 3).

PW50 models

Refer to illustrations 5.3, 5.4a, 5.4b and 5.5

3   Remove the steering stem bolt and lift off the upper triple clamp **(see illustration)**.

4   Unscrew the bearing top nut, lift it off and remove the ball bearings with a magnet **(see illustrations)**. Place the bearings in a con-

5.4b . . . and lift it off to expose the upper bearings

5.5 Lower the steering stem out of the steering head to expose the lower bearings

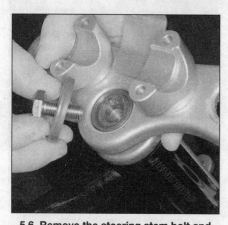

5.6 Remove the steering stem bolt and washer and the upper triple clamp . . .

5.7a . . . unscrew the ring nut . . .

5.7b . . . lift off the bearing cover and upper race . . .

tainer so they won't be lost.

5   Lower the steering stem enough to expose the lower bearings, then remove them and place them in a second container (see illustration).

PW80 models

Refer to illustrations 5.6, 5.7a, 5.7b, 5.8 and 5.9

6   Remove the steering stem flange bolt and lift off the upper triple clamp (see illustration).

7   Using a ring nut wrench of the type described in *Steering and sus-*

pension - check in Chapter 1, remove the ring nut and the bearing cover (see illustrations) while supporting the steering stem by holding the lower triple clamp.

8   Remove the upper ball race, then remove the upper bearings with a magnet (see illustration). Place the bearings in a container so they won't be lost.

9   Remove the steering stem and lower triple clamp (see illustration). If it's stuck, gently tap on the top of the steering stem with a plastic mallet or a hammer and a wood block. Remove the lower bearings and place them in a second container.

5.8 . . . and remove the upper bearings

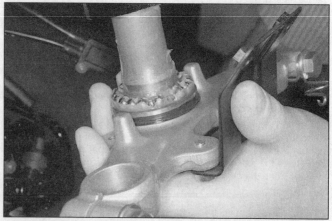

5.9 Lower the steering stem out of the steering head to expose the lower bearings

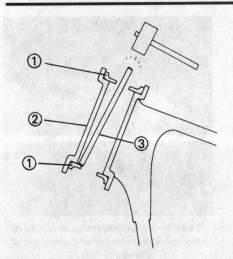

5.13a Drive out the old bearing races with a hammer and brass drift

1 *Outer races*
2 *Steering head*
3 *Brass drift*

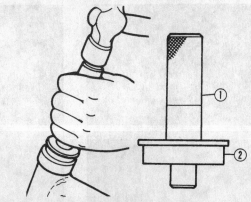

5.13b Drive in the new bearing races with a bearing driver or socket the same diameter as the bearing race

1 *Bearing driver handle*   2 *Bearing driver*

All models

Refer to illustrations 5.13a, 5.13b and 5.13c

10   Clean all the parts with solvent and dry them thoroughly, using compressed air, if available. Wipe the old grease out of the steering head and bearing races.

11   Inspect the steering stem/lower triple clamp for cracks and other damage. Do not attempt to repair any steering components. Replace them with new parts if defects are found.

12   Inspect the steering head bearings and races for cracks, dents, pits and flat spots. If the bearings and/or races are worn or damaged, replace them as a set. (Also, check with your Yamaha dealer about upgrading to tapered roller bearings.)

13   To remove the races, drive them out of the steering head with a hammer and a long drift punch **(see illustration)**. A slide hammer with the proper internal-jaw puller will also work. Since the races are an interference fit in the frame, installation will be easier if the new races are left overnight in a refrigerator. This will cause them to contract and slip into place in the frame with very little effort. When installing the races, use a bearing driver the same diameter as the outer race **(see illustration)**, or tap them gently into place with a hammer and punch or a large socket. Do not strike the bearing surface or the race will be damaged. To remove the lower bearing race from the steering stem, you may need to use a bearing puller, which can be rented. Or, pry it up with a hammer and chisel. To install the lower race on the steering stem, drive it onto the steering stem using a hollow driver or a pipe the same diameter as the race **(see illustration)**.

14   Coat the bearings and races with high-quality moly-based grease.

15   Place the lower bearings on the lower race and insert the steering stem/lower triple clamp into the steering head. Install the upper bearing, bearing cover and ring nut. Tighten the locknut (see *Steering and suspension - check* in Chapter 1) to the torque listed in the Chapter 1 Specifications.

16   Make sure the steering head turns smoothly and that there's no play in the bearings.

17   Install the upper triple clamp and steering stem bolt, but don't tighten the bolt yet.

18   Install the fork tubes and tighten the lower triple clamp bolts to the torque listed in this Chapter's Specifications.

19   Tighten the steering stem bolt to the torque listed in this Chapter's Specifications.

20   Tighten the upper triple clamp bolts to the torque listed in this Chapter's Specifications. Install the front wheel and handlebars.

21   Check the alignment of the handlebars and the front wheel. If necessary, loosen the triple clamp bolts, have an assistant hold the front wheel, then turn the handlebars to align them with the front wheel. Tighten the triple clamp bolts to the torque listed in this Chapter's Specifications.

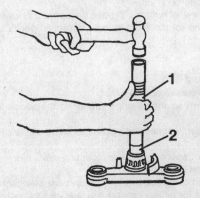

5.13c To install the new lower race on the steering stem, drive it onto the steering stem using a hollow driver or a pipe the same diameter as the race

1 *Driver*
2 *Bearing race*

6   Rear shock absorber(s) - removal and installation

1   Inspect the rear shock(s). Look for oil leaks and other obvious damage. Is the shock absorber damper rod bent? Is the spring damaged? If a shock is leaking or damaged, replace the shock(s).

2   On all models, remove the seat/side cover assembly (see Chapter 7).

3   Elevate the rear of the bike by putting a suitable jack or a milk crate under the engine. If you're using a jack, be sure to put a board between the jack head and the engine to protect the crankcase. Support the bike securely so it can't tip over.

PW50 models

Refer to illustrations 6.4a, 6.4b and 6.4c

4   Remove the upper and lower shock absorber bolts and washers **(see illustrations)**.

6.4a To detach a shock absorber from a PW50 model, remove the upper and lower shock mounting bolts (arrows) . . .

6.4b . . . lockwashers and washers . . .

6.4c . . . and at the upper end, the inner washer that fits over the mounting stud

6.9a The PW80 rear shock absorber is secured by a cotter pin and clevis pin at the upper end . . .

5   Remove the shock absorbers.

6   Installation is the reverse of removal. Tighten the upper and lower shock absorber bolts to the torque listed in this Chapter's Specifications.

PW80 models

Refer to illustrations 6.9a and 6.9b

7   Remove the fuel tank (see Chapter 3).

8   Support the swingarm so that it won't fall when the shock is unbolted.

9   Remove the cotter pin, washer and upper mounting clevis pin **(see illustrations)**.

10   Remove the cotter pin, washer and lower mounting clevis pin.

11   Remove the rear shock from the bike.

12   Even if you're only removing the shock to remove the swingarm, inspect the shock carefully for oil leaking from the seal, gas (nitrogen) leaking from the shock body or any other damage. If the shock is damaged or worn in any way, replace it.

13   Inspect the bushings at both ends of the shock. If a bushing is loose or worn, have it bearing pressed out and a new one pressed in by a dealer or motorcycle repair shop.

14   Inspect the upper and lower mounting clevis pins. If either of them is damaged or bent, replace it.

15   Installation is the reverse of removal. Be sure to use grease the clevis pins with molybdenum disulfide grease and use new cotter pins.

7   Swingarm bushings (PW80 models) - check

1   Elevate the rear of the bike by putting a suitable jack or a milk crate under the engine. If you're using a jack, be sure to put a board

between the jack head and the engine to protect the crankcase.

2   Remove the rear wheel (see Chapter 6), then remove the rear shock absorber (see Section 6).

3   Grasp the rear of the swingarm with one hand and place your other hand at the junction of the swingarm and frame, then try to move the rear of the swingarm from side-to-side. Any wear in the bushings produces play (movement) between the swingarm and the frame at the front (the swingarm will actually move back-and-forth, not side-to-side). If there's any play in the swingarm, remove the swingarm (see Section 8) and replace the swingarm bushings.

4   Move the swingarm up and down through its full travel. It should move freely, without any binding or rough spots. If it doesn't move freely, remove the swingarm (see Section 8) and lubricate the swingarm bushings with lithium soap base or moly-base grease.

8   Swingarm (PW80 models) - removal and installation

Refer to illustrations 8.6, 8.8 and 8.9

1   Elevate the rear of the bike by putting a suitable jack or a milk crate under the engine. If you're using a jack, be sure to put a board between the jack head and the engine to protect the crankcase.

2   Disconnect the drive chain (see Section 12).

3   Remove the rear wheel (see Chapter 6).

4   Disconnect the shock absorber from the swingarm (see Section 6).

5   Remove the chain guard and the chain guide from the swingarm (Section 13).

6   Remove the nut **(see illustration)** from the swingarm pivot bolt and pull out the pivot bolt, then remove the swingarm from the motorcycle.

6.9b . . . and at the lower end

8.6 Remove the PW80 swingarm pivot bolt nut

8.8 Have the bushings pressed out and new ones pressed I if they're worn or damaged

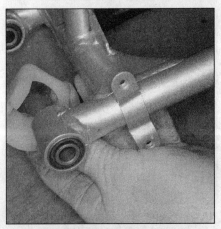

8.9 Slip the guard off the swingarm

9.5a To detach the PW50 right rear arm, remove the rear axle nut, muffler bolt and shock absorber bolt (arrows) . . .

9.5b . . . and remove these two nuts at the engine (arrows) . . .

9.5c . . . then remove the washers and separate the right rear arm from the engine

9.7a Unbolt the bearing holder from the arm . . .

9.7b . . . and pry the collar and seal out of each side . . .

7   Check the swingarm for cracks, bending or rust. If it's cracked or bent, replace it. Light rust can be sanded off and the swingarm repainted.

8   Check the swingarm bushings for wear, damage or looseness (see illustration). If problems are found, have the bushings pressed out and new ones pressed in by a machine shop.

9   If the seal guard at the front of the swingarm is worn or damaged, slip it off and slip a new one on (see illustration).

10   Installation is the reverse of removal, with the following additions:

a) Lubricate the swingarm bushings with lithium soap base or moly-base grease.

b) Tighten the swingarm pivot bolt and nut to the torque listed in this Chapter's Specifications.

c) Adjust the drive chain and rear brake pedal (see Chapter 1).

9   Right rear arm (PW50 models) - removal and installation

Refer to illustrations 9.5a, 9.5b, 9.5c, 9.7a, 9.7b, 9.7c and 9.7d

1   Elevate the rear of the bike by putting a suitable jack or a milk crate under the engine. If you're using a jack, be sure to put a board between the jack head and the engine to protect the crankcase.

2   Disconnect the right rear shock absorber from the right rear arm (see Section 6).

3   Remove the exhaust system muffler (see Chapter 3).

4   Remove the rear wheel axle nut (see "Wheels - removal, inspec-

tion and installation" in Chapter 6).

5   Remove the two nuts that attach the right rear arm to the engine (see illustrations).

6   Remove the right rear arm.

7   Unbolt the bearing carrier from the rear arm. Pry out the washers and seals and inspect the bearing (see illustrations). If the bearing is worn or damaged, have it pressed out and a new one pressed in by a machine shop. Push in new seals with a socket the same diameter as the seal (see illustration).

9.7c . . . to inspect the bearing; have the bearing pressed out and a new one pressed in if it's worn or damaged

9.7d Push the new seals in with a socket the same diameter as the seal

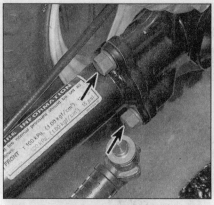

10.4a Remove the three mounting bolts (two shown, one hidden behind shaft housing) . . .

10.4b . . . and remove the ring and pinion housing from the shaft housing

10.5a Remove three mounting bolts (arrows) . . .

10.5b . . . lift the shaft housing off the crankcase . . .

10.5c . . . and remove the shaft from the middle driven pinion

8   Installation is the reverse of removal. Be sure to tighten the rear arm-to-engine nuts to the torque listed in this Chapter's Specifications.

10 Left rear arm/shaft drive assembly (PW50 models) - removal and installation

Refer to illustrations 10.4a, 10.4b, 10.5a, 10.5b and 10.5c

1   Elevate the rear of the bike by putting a suitable jack or a milk crate under the engine. If you're using a jack, be sure to put a board between the jack head and the engine to protect the crankcase.

2   Remove the right rear arm (see Section 10).

3   Remove the rear wheel (see Chapter 6).

4   If you're going to service the shaft drive assembly or the ring and pinion assembly, unbolt the ring and pinion housing from the left rear arm/shaft drive housing **(see illustrations)**. If you're only removing the left rear arm/shaft drive housing to service the engine, skip this step.

5   Remove the three bolts that attach the left rear arm/shaft drive housing to the engine crankcase **(see illustration)**. Pull the housing off and remove the driveshaft **(see illustrations)**.

6   Installation is the reverse of removal.

11 Shaft drive (PW50 models) - disassembly, inspection and reassembly

1   This procedure requires several special tools. Before starting, read through the procedure and decide whether you want to tackle it. It may be more practical to buy a used assembly from a wrecking yard or to have any needed repair work done by a dealer service department.

2   Remove the left rear arm/shaft drive housing (see Section 10).

Disassembly

Middle driven pinion (inside the engine crankcase)

Refer to illustrations 11.3a and 11.3b

3   Pry out the middle driven pinion seal from the crankcase **(see illustrations)**.

4   Using the special Yamaha hexagonal tool (no. 90890-01306 (25) or 90890-01307 (22)), remove the ring nut. Note the word "OPEN" stamped into the ring nut and the arrow next to it; turn the ring nut in the clockwise direction indicated by the arrow to unscrew the ring nut. Remove the distance collar, bearing, driven pinion and thrust shim from the crankcase **(see illustration 11.3b)**.

Shaft drive assembly (inside the left rear arm/shaft drive housing)

Refer to illustration 11.5

5   Remove the circlip, then remove the spring retainer and compression spring from the driveshaft **(see illustration 11.3b and the accompanying illustration)**.

Driven pinion and ring gear assembly (inside the ring gear housing)

Refer to illustrations 11.6, 11.8, 11.9 and 11.10

6   Using the special Yamaha hexagonal tool, remove the ring nut **(see illustration)**.

7   Remove the spacer, bearings, shim and drive pinion **(see illustration 11.3b)**.

8   Remove the ring gear housing cover screws, then remove the housing cover and the O-ring **(see illustration)**.

9   Remove the ring gear from the housing **(see illustration)**.

10   Remove the axle bearing retainer plate bolts and take off the

11.3a Unscrew the hex nut by turning it clockwise with the special tool

11.5 Compress the spring with a holding fixture and hydraulic press, then remove the snap ring and retainer; BE SURE the spring can't fly out and cause injury

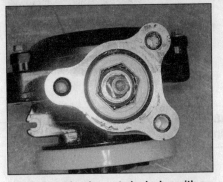

11.6 Turn the ring nut clockwise with a special tool to remove it

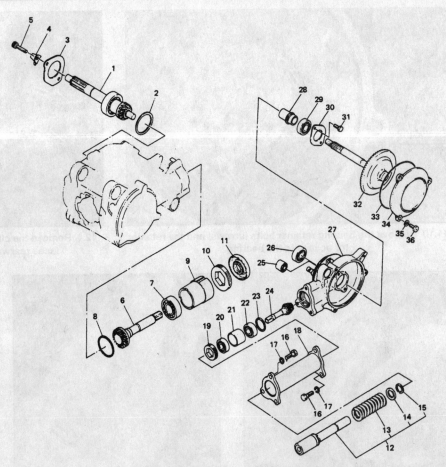

11.3b Shaft drive (PW50 models) - exploded view

1	Mainshaft and bearing	11	Oil seal	19	Ring nut	27	Ring and pinion housing
2	Pinion shim	12	Driveshaft	20	Bearing	28	Bearing spacer
3	Cover plate	13	Compression spring	21	Spacer	29	Bearing
4	Bearing retainer	14	Spring retainer	22	Bearing	30	Cover plate
5	Bolt	15	Circlip	23	Driven pinion shim	31	Bolt
6	Middle driven pinion	16	Bolt	24	Drive pinion	32	Ring gear
7	Bearing	17	Lockwasher	25	Rear cushion bushing	33	O-ring
8	Thrust shim	18	Left rear arm/shaft drive housing	26	Bearing	34	Housing cover
9	Spacer					35	Plate washer
10	Ring nut					36	Panhead screw

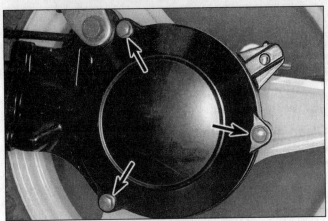

11.8 Remove the three ring gear housing bolts (arrows) and take off the cover...

11.9 ... then pull the ring gear and its shaft out of the housing

11.10 Remove the bearing retainer bolts (arrows) and the retainer for access to the bearing

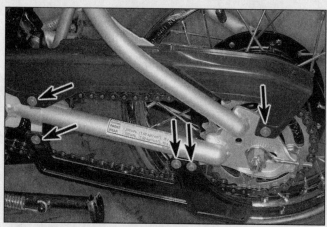

12.1 Remove the clip from the master link; its open end (arrow) faces rearward when the chain is on the top run

12.2 Place the master link (arrow) where it's accessible

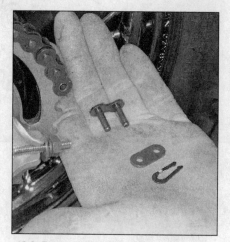

12.3 Remove the clip and plate and take the master link out of the chain

12.10a Squeeze the clip onto the master link with pliers, making sure it's secure in the grooves and that its open end faces the proper direction

retainer plate **(see illustration)**. Remove the axle bearings, bushing and spacer **(see illustration 11.3b)**.

Inspection

11   Inspect the gear teeth on the mainshaft drive gear and middle driven pinion, and on the drive pinion and ring gear, for excessive wear and damage. If the teeth on the mainshaft drive gear or the middle driven pinion are damaged or excessively worn, replace the mainshaft (see Chapter 2) and the middle driven pinion. If the teeth on the drive pinion or ring gear teeth are damaged or excessively worn, replace the drive pinion and the ring gear. (Each of these gear pairs must be replaced as a set, even if the teeth on only one gear are damaged. Do NOT replace only the damaged gear.)

12   Using a dial indicator, measure the runout of the ring gear. If ring gear runout is excessive, replace the ring gear.

13   Inspect the bearings for excessive wear and damage. If any of the bearings are damaged or worn, replace them.

Reassembly

14   Reassembly is the reverse of disassembly, with the following additions:

a) Grease the bearings with lithium base wheel bearing grease.
b) Grease the mainshaft drive gear/middle driven pinion gear and the drive pinion/ring gear with 10 grams (0.4 ounce) of lithium base wheel bearing grease.
c) Tighten the ring nuts to the torque listed in this Chapter's Specifications.

12   Drive chain (PW80 models) - removal, cleaning, inspection and installation

Removal

Refer to illustrations 12.1, 12.2 and 12.3

1   Remove the chain guards **(see illustration)**.

2   Turn the rear wheel to place the drive chain master link where it's easily accessible **(see illustration)**.

3   Remove the clip and plate and pull the master link out of the chain **(see illustration)**.

4   Remove the left crankcase cover (see Chapter 4). Lift the chain off the sprockets and remove it from the bike.

5   Check the chain guards and the guide on the swingarm for wear or damage and replace them as necessary. To replace the chain guide, you'll need to remove the swingarm (Section 8).

Cleaning and inspection

6   Soak the chain in a high flash point solvent for approximately five or six minutes. Use a brush to work the solvent into the spaces between the links and plates.

7   Wipe the chain dry, then check it carefully for worn or damaged links. Replace the chain if wear or damage is found at any point.

8   If the chain needs to be replaced, refer to Section 13 and check the sprockets. If they're worn, replace them also. If a new chain is installed on worn sprockets, it will wear out quickly.

12.10b Engage the chain guard slot with the tab on the frame

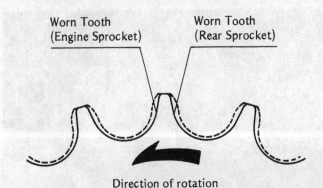

Direction of rotation

13.3 Inspect the sprockets in the areas indicated to see if they're worn excessively

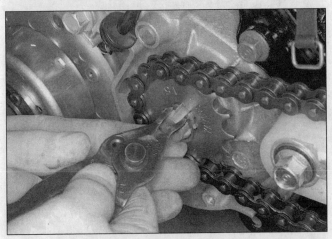

13.5 Remove the snap-ring and slide the sprocket off the countershaft

13.6a Remove the wheel spacer . . .

9   Lubricate the chain with spray chain lube compatible with O-ring chains.

Installation

Refer to illustrations 12.10a and 12.10b

10   Installation is the reverse of the removal steps, with the following additions:

a) *Install the master link clip so its opening faces the back of the motorcycle when the master link is in the upper chain run* **(see illustration)**. *Be sure to reinstall the O-rings in the master link.*

b) *Engage the upper chain guard's slot with the tab on the chain before installing the bolts* **(see illustration)**.

c) *Refer to Chapter 1 and adjust the chain.*

---

13   Sprockets and cush drive (PW80 models) - check and replacement

---

Check

Refer to illustration 13.3

1   Support the bike securely so it can't be knocked over during this procedure.

2   Whenever the sprockets are inspected, the chain should be inspected also and replaced if it's worn. Installing a worn chain on new sprockets will cause them to wear quickly.

3   Check the teeth on the engine sprocket and rear sprocket for wear **(see illustration)**.

13.6b . . . and the coupling collar; DO NOT forget to reinstall it, or you'll damage the wheel bearings when you tighten the axle

4   If the sprockets are worn, remove the drive chain (see Section 12) and the rear wheel (see Chapter 6).

Replacement

Refer to illustrations 13.5, 13.6a, 13.6b, 13.7, 13.8 and 13.9

5   To detach the engine sprocket, remove the snap-ring **(see illustration)**.

6   To detach the rear sprocket from the rear wheel hub, remove the bolts, lockwashers and nuts **(see illustrations)**. Remove the wheel spacer and the coupling sleeve.

13.7 Check the countershaft seal behind the engine sprocket

13.8 Replace the rubber dampers if they're worn or deteriorated

7   Inspect the seal behind the engine sprocket **(see illustration)**. If it has been leaking, pry it out (taking care not to scratch the seal bore) and tap in a new seal with a socket the same diameter as the seal.

8   Inspect the rubber dampers (cush drive) inside the rear hub **(see illustration)**. If the dampers are worn or deteriorated, pull them out and install new ones.

9   Installation is the reverse of the removal steps, with the following additions:

a) *Make sure the engine sprocket's snap-ring is securely seated in its groove* **(see illustration)**.

b) *Use new lockwashers to secure the rear sprocket bolts. Tighten the bolts to the torque value listed in this Chapter's Specifications.*

c) *Don't forget to reinstall the coupling sleeve or you'll damage the rear wheel bearings when you tighten the rear axle nut.*

d) *Install the master link clip so its opening faces the back of the motorcycle when the master link is in the upper chain run* **(see illustration 12.10a)**.

e) *Refer to Chapter 1 and adjust the chain.*

13.9 Make sure the snap-ring seats securely in its groove

Chapter 5 Part B
Steering, suspension and final drive (RT100 and RT180 models)

Contents

Specifications

Front forks

Oil type
RT100 .... Yamaha 10W fork oil, or equivalent
RT180 .... Yamaha 10W fork oil, or equivalent
Oil capacity
RT100 .... 110 cc (3.72 fl oz)
RT180 .... 280 cc (9.47 fl oz)
Fork spring free length
RT100
Standard .... 418.5 mm (16.5 inches)
Minimum .... 410 mm (16.1 inches)
RT180
Standard .... 535 mm (21.1 inches)
Minimum .... 524 mm (20.7 inches)

Torque specifications

Steering and front suspension

Handlebar clamp bolts
RT100 .... 20 Nm (168 in-lbs)
RT180 .... 15 Nm (132 in-lbs)
Front axle nut or bolt .... See Chapter 6
Upper triple clamp bolts
RT100 .... 26 Nm (28 ft-lbs)
RT180 .... 23 Nm (17 ft-lbs)
Lower triple clamp bolts
RT100 .... 39 Nm (28 ft-lbs)
RT180 .... 23 Nm (17 ft-lbs)
Steering stem flange bolt
RT100 .... 65 Nm (47 ft-lbs)
RT180 .... 54 Nm (39 ft-lbs)
Fork tube cap bolt
RT100 .... 20 Nm (168 in-lbs)
RT180 .... 24 Nm (18 ft-lbs)
Damper rod bolt .... 23 Nm (17 ft-lbs)*
Steering stem ring nut (bearing adjustment nut) .... See Chapter 1

Rear suspension

Rear shock absorber(s)
RT100
Upper mounting nuts .... 39 Nm (28 ft-lbs)
Lower mounting bolts .... 25 Nm (19 ft-lbs)
RT180
Upper (front) mounting nut .... 25 Nm (19 ft-lbs)
Swingarm pivot bolt nut
RT100 .... 43 Nm (31 ft-lbs)
RT180 .... 43 Nm (31 ft-lbs)

Torque specifications

Final drive

Engine sprocket retaining nut	
RT100	Not specified
RT180	60 Nm (43 ft-lbs)
Rear sprocket bolts/studs/nuts	
RT100 (bolts)	20 Nm (168 in-lbs)
RT180	
Studs	39 Nm (28 ft-lbs)
Nuts	39 Nm (28 ft-lbs)

* Apply non-permanent thread locking agent to the threads.

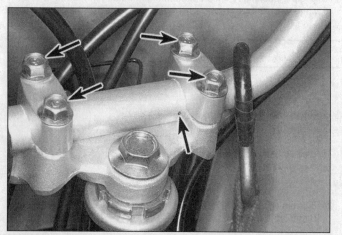

2.1 Remove the bracket bolts (upper arrows), lift off the brackets and handlebar; the punch mark (lower arrow) aligns with the bracket split line

2.3 Remove the screw (arrow) and detach the cable clip from the upper triple clamp

1 General information

The steering system consists of the handlebar, the upper and lower triple clamps, the steering stem and the steering head bearings. The steering stem, an integral part of the lower triple clamp, turns on ball bearings riding on races pressed into the upper and lower ends of the steering head.

The front suspension consists of telescopic forks with damper rods and rebound springs. The rear suspension consists of the shock absorber(s) and the swingarm. RT100 models use a pair of shocks; RT180 models have a single shock.

2 Handlebar - removal, inspection and installation

Refer to illustrations 2.1 and 2.3

1   Look for punch marks on the front part of each handlebar upper clamp. If you don't see any, make your own. The handlebar clamps must be installed with these punch marks facing toward the front. Also look for a punch mark on the bar next to the split line between the upper and lower halves of one of the handlebar clamps **(see illustration)**.

2   If you're only removing the handlebar to gain access to other components (upper/lower triple clamps, steering head bearings, etc.), simply remove the four handlebar clamp bolts, lift the handlebar off the upper triple clamp and carefully lay it in front of the triple clamp. It's not necessary to disconnect the throttle or clutch cables, brake cable or hose, or kill switch wires. It is, however, a good idea to support the assembly with a piece of wire or rope to avoid unnecessary strain on

the cables, hoses and wiring.

3   If you're replacing the handlebar itself, remove the clutch lever bracket (see Chapter 2) remove the kill switch (see Chapter 5), remove the throttle twist grip (see Chapter 3) and remove the brake lever bracket (RT100 models) or the brake master cylinder (RT180 models) (see Chapter 6). Unscrew the cable clip from the upper triple clamp **(see illustration)**. Remove the upper bracket bolts, lift off the brackets and remove the handlebar.

4   Inspect the handlebar and brackets for damage. If anything is cracked, bent or otherwise damaged, replace it.

5   Place the handlebar in the lower brackets. Line up the punch mark on the handlebar with the split between the upper and lower clamps **(see illustration 2.1)**.

6   Install the upper clamps with their punch marks facing forward. Tighten the front bolts, then the rear bolts, to the torque listed in this Chapter's Specifications. **Caution:** *If there's a gap between the upper and lower brackets at the rear after tightening the bolts, don't try to close it by tightening beyond the recommended torque. You'll only crack the brackets.*

3 Forks - removal and installation

Removal

Refer to illustrations 3.4, 3.5a and 3.5b

1   Although it's not absolutely necessary, you may want to remove the front number plate (see Chapter 7B).

2   Support the bike securely so that it's upright, with its front wheel off the ground, and remove the front wheel (see Chapter 6B).

3.4 Loosen the fork cap bolt (RT100 shown)

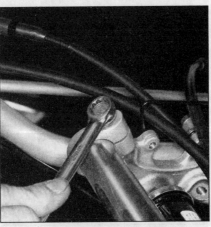

3.5a Loosen the upper pinch bolt (two bolts on RT180 models) . . .

3.5b . . . and the lower pinch bolt (two bolts on RT180 models)

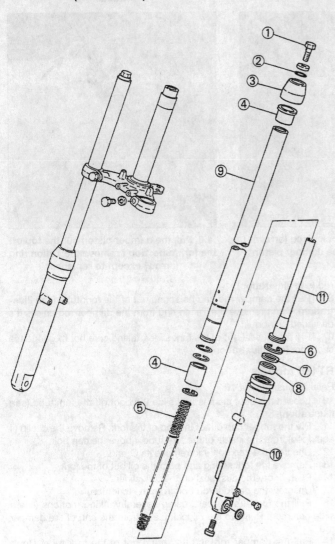

4.2 Front forks (RT100 models) - exploded view

1	Cap bolt	5	Fork spring	9	Fork tube
2	O-ring	6	Circlip	10	Fork slider
3	Dust seal	7	Plain washer	11	Damper
4	Bushing	8	Oil seal		piston

3   On RT180 models, unbolt the brake caliper and detach the brake hose clip from the left fork leg (see Chapter 6B).

4   If you plan to disassemble the forks, loosen the fork cap bolts now **(see illustration)**. (You can do this later, but the fork caps are easier to loosen while the forks are still bolted to the triple clamps).

5   Loosen the upper and lower triple clamp bolts **(see illustrations)**.

6   Pull each fork tube down, twisting it back and forth if necessary, and slide it out of the triple clamps.

Installation

7   Insert each fork tube through the lower and upper triple clamps and tighten the triple clamp pinch bolts enough to secure the tubes, but leave them loose enough so that you can slide the fork tubes up and down in the triple clamps.

8   If you're working on an RT100 models, position the fork tubes in the triple clamps so that the tops of the fork tubes are flush with the top of the upper triple clamp.

9   If you're working on an RT180, position the fork tubes in the triple clamps so that the tops of the fork tubes are 10 mm (0.4 inches) above the top of the upper triple clamp.

10   Tighten the upper and lower triple clamp pinch bolts to the torque listed in this Chapter's Specifications.

11   The remainder of installation is the reverse of removal.

4   Forks - disassembly, inspection and assembly

1   Remove the forks (see Section 3). **Note:** *The damper rod bolt may be difficult to remove because it's secured with thread locking agent to the damper piston, which may just spin inside the fork tube when you try to remove the bolt. The usual shop method is to spin the bolt out with an air wrench. If you don't have one, it may be easier to loosen the damper rod bolt now, while the pressure of the fork spring will help keep the damper piston from spinning.*

Disassembly

Note: *The damper rod bolt may be difficult to remove because it's secured with thread locking agent to the damper piston, which may just spin inside the fork tube when you try to remove the bolt. The usual shop method is to spin the bolt out with an air wrench. If you don't have one, it may be easier to loosen the damper rod bolt now, while the pressure of the fork spring will help keep the damper piston from spinning.*

RT100 models

Refer to illustrations 4.2 through 4.9

2   Unscrew the cap bolt and remove the washer and O-ring **(see illustration)**.

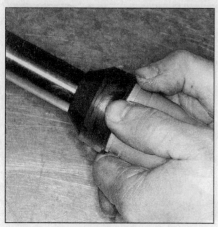

4.3 Push the dust seal off the fork slider

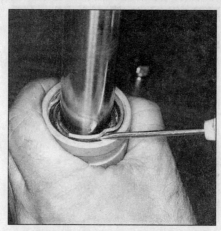

4.4 Pry the circlip out of the groove

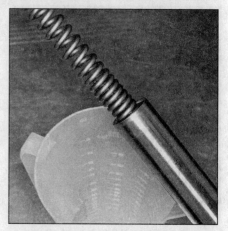

4.5 Pull out the fork spring and pour out the oil

4.6 Unscrew the damper rod bolt and remove the sealing washer

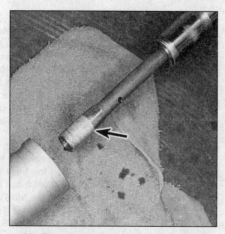

4.7 Remove the oil lock piece (arrow) from the bottom of the damper piston

4.8 Pull the damper piston out the top of the fork tube; don't remove the Teflon ring (arrow) except to replace it

3   Push the dust seal off the fork slider **(see illustration)**.

4   Pry the circlip out of its groove **(see illustration)**.

5   Remove the fork spring, noting that the closer-wound coils go into the fork tube (upward when the fork is installed on the bike) **(see illustration)**. Pour the oil out of the fork.

6   Unscrew the damper rod bolt from the fork tube **(see illustration)**.

7   Pull the fork tubes apart, using several yanking motions (like a slide hammer). Remove the oil lock piece from the end of the damper

4.9 Pry the oil seal out of the fork slider; a screwdriver will work if you don't have this special tool

rod **(see illustration)**.

8   Pull the damper rod and its spring out of the fork tube **(see illustration)**. Don't remove the Teflon ring from the damper rod unless it's damaged or worn.

9   Pry the oil seal out of the fork slider, taking care not to gouge the seal bore **(see illustration)**.

RT180 models

Refer to illustration 4.10

10   Loosen the boot clamps and slide the boot off the fork tube **(see illustration)**.

11   Pry the rubber cap out of the top of the fork. Remove the circlip (if equipped) from the inside of the fork tube, above the cap bolt.

12   Unscrew the cap bolt and remove its O-ring.

13   Remove the fork spring and pour the oil out of the fork.

14   Push or pry the dust seal off the fork slider.

15   Unscrew the damper rod bolt from the fork tube.

16   Pull the fork tubes apart, using several yanking motions (like a slide hammer). Remove the oil lock piece from the end of the damper rod.

17   Pull the damper rod and its spring out of the fork tube. Don't remove the Teflon ring from the damper rod unless it's damaged or worn.

18   Pry the oil seal out of the fork slider, taking care not to gouge the seal bore.

Inspection

19   Clean all parts in solvent and blow them dry with compressed air, if available. Check the inner and outer fork tubes and the damper rod

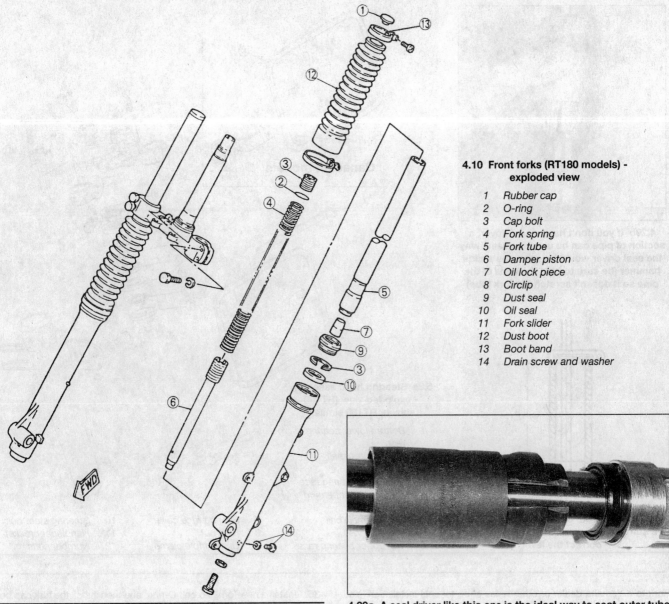

4.10 Front forks (RT180 models) - exploded view

1. Rubber cap
2. O-ring
3. Cap bolt
4. Fork spring
5. Fork tube
6. Damper piston
7. Oil lock piece
8. Circlip
9. Dust seal
10. Oil seal
11. Fork slider
12. Dust boot
13. Boot band
14. Drain screw and washer

4.29a A seal driver like this one is the ideal way to seat outer tube bushings and install fork seals

for score marks, scratches, flaking of the chrome and excessive or abnormal wear. Look for dents in the tubes and replace them if any are found. Check the fork seal seat for nicks, gouges and scratches. If damage is evident, leaks will occur around the seal-to-outer tube junction. Replace worn or defective parts with new ones.

20 Inspect the inner and outer fork tubes for nicks, gouges and scratches. Make sure the inner fork tube is straight by rolling it on a perfectly flat surface. If the tube is bent, replace it. **Warning:** Don't try to straighten a bent fork tube. Straightening the tube will weaken it and cause it to fail.

21 Inspect the fork spring for cracks or other damage. Measure the free length of the fork spring and compare the length to the minimum length listed in this Chapter's Specifications. If the spring is damaged or less than the minimum specified length, replace both fork springs. Never replace only one spring.

22 Inspect the bushing for scratches, excessive wear and other damage. If the bushing is damaged or worn, replace both bushings.

23 Inspect the damper piston for scratches, excessive wear and other damage. If it's damaged or worn, replace both damper rods. If the damper rod is okay, blow out the oil passages with compressed air. Inspect the piston ring, spring and oil lock piece. If any of them are damaged or worn, replace them.

Assembly

24 Reassembly is basically the reverse of disassembly. Make sure that all components are spotlessly clean before reassembling them.

RT100 models

Refer to illustrations 4.29a and 4.29b

25 Install the wire clip (if you removed it) on the inner fork tube.

26 Install the bushing on the inner fork tube.

27 Install the fork spring in the inner fork tube with the tightly-coiled end pointing up.

28 Coat the lip of the new fork seal with lithium-soap-base grease or with clean fork oil, and then slide the seal onto the inner fork tube with the numbered side facing up. Install the new seal carefully. If the lip is damaged during installation, it will leak.

29 Lubricate the friction surfaces of the inner fork tube with clean fork oil, and then insert the inner fork tube into the outer fork tube. Drive the seal into position with a fork seal driver (driver part no. YM-33281, weight part no. YM-33963). If you don't have access to the factory tool, use a similar aftermarket tool **(see illustration)**, or take the

4.29b If you don't have a seal driver, a section of pipe can be used the same way the seal driver would be used - as a slide hammer (be sure to tape the ends of the pipe so it doesn't scratch the fork tube)

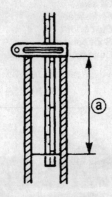

4.46 Measure the oil level in the fork with a stiff tape measure; add or drain oil to correct the level

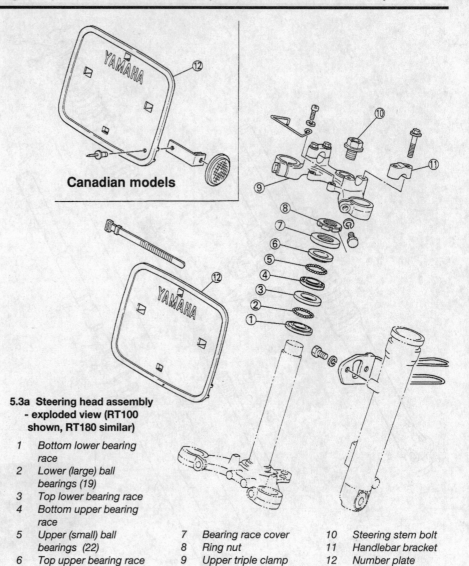

Canadian models

5.3a Steering head assembly - exploded view (RT100 shown, RT180 similar)

1. Bottom lower bearing race
2. Lower (large) ball bearings (19)
3. Top lower bearing race
4. Bottom upper bearing race
5. Upper (small) ball bearings (22)
6. Top upper bearing race
7. Bearing race cover
8. Ring nut
9. Upper triple clamp
10. Steering stem bolt
11. Handlebar bracket
12. Number plate

fork to a Yamaha dealer or other repair shop for seal installation. You can also make a substitute tool (see illustration). If you're very careful, the seal can be driven in with a hammer and drift punch. Work around the circumference of the seal, tapping gently on the outer edge of the seal until it's seated. Again, be careful not to damage the seal during this step. Be careful - if you distort the seal, you'll have to disassemble the fork and end up taking it to a dealer anyway!

30   Install the plain washer on top of the new fork seal.

31   Install the circlip on top of the plain washer. Push down on the circlip and make sure that it expands into its bore in the inner circumference of the outer fork tube.

32   Slide the dust seal down over the top of the outer fork tube. Make sure the lower end of the dust seal is fully seated on the outer fork tube.

33   Install the damper rod washer, insert the damper rod bolt through the washer and the outer fork tube, screw it into the damper rod and tighten it securely. **Note:** Apply a non-permanent thread locking agent to the threads of the bolt. Keep the two tubes fairly horizontal so the oil lock piece doesn't fall off the damper rod inside the outer fork tube. Temporarily install the fork spring and cap to place tension on the damper rod so it won't spin inside the fork tube while you tighten the Allen bolt.

34   Fill the front fork with the type and amount of fork oil listed in this Chapter's Specifications.

35   Install a new fork cap bolt O-ring, and then install the fork cap bolt and tighten it to the torque listed in this Chapter's Specifications.

36   Pump the fork up and down to distribute the new fork oil. Set the first fork aside and repeat this procedure for the other fork.

RT180 models

37   Liberally lubricate the friction surfaces of the damper rod with clean fork oil, and then insert it into the inner fork tube. Allow the rod to slide slowly down the inner fork tube until it protrudes from the lower end.

38   Install the oil lock piece on the end of the damper rod.

39   Lubricate outer surface of the inner fork tube and then insert the inner fork tube into the outer fork tube.

40   Install the damper rod bolt and washer at the lower end of the outer fork tube. Insert the damper rod bolt through the outer fork tube and thread it into the damper rod. **Note:** Apply a non-permanent thread locking agent to the threads of the bolt. Keep the two tubes fairly horizontal so the oil lock piece doesn't fall off the damper rod inside the outer fork tube. Temporarily install the fork spring and cap to place tension on the damper rod so it won't spin inside the fork tube while you tighten the Allen bolt.

41   Tighten the Allen bolt to the torque listed in this Chapter's Specifications, then remove the fork cap and spring.

42   Lubricate the lips and outer diameter of the fork seal with lithium-

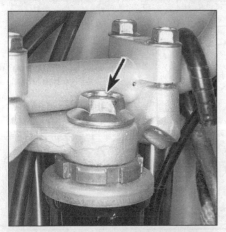

5.3b Remove the steering stem flange bolt (arrow) and lift off the upper triple clamp

5.4a While supporting the steering stem from underneath, remove the ring nut . . .

5.4b . . . and then lift off the bearing cover

5.5a Remove the upper ball race . . .

5.5b . . . and remove the upper balls

5.6 Lower the steering stem/lower triple clamp out of the steering head and catch any balls that fall out

soap-base grease or with clean fork oil. Slide the seal down the inner tube with the lips facing down. Drive the seal into position with a fork seal driver (adapter part no. YM-01369, weight part no. YM-33963). If you don't have access to the proper tool, take the fork to a Yamaha dealer or other repair shop for seal installation. You can also make a substitute tool (see illustration 4.29b). If you're very careful, the seal can be driven in with a hammer and drift punch. Work around the circumference of the seal, tapping gently on the outer edge of the seal until it's seated. Be careful - if you distort the seal, you'll have to disassemble the fork and end up taking it to a dealer anyway!

43 Install the circlip on top of the fork seal. Make sure it's completely seated in its groove in the inside of the outer fork tube.

44 Install the dust seal, making sure it seats completely.

45 Install the fork boot down into its groove on the outer fork tube and secure the upper and lower ends of the boot with the clamping bands.

All models

Refer to illustration 4.46

46 Compress the fork fully and add the recommended type and quantity of fork oil listed in this Chapter's Specifications. Measure the fork oil level from the top of the fork tube (see illustration). If necessary, add or remove oil to bring it to the proper level.

47 Install the O-ring and fork cap bolt. Tighten the fork cap bolt to the torque listed in this Chapter's Specifications.

48 Pump the fork up and down to distribute the new fork oil. Set the first fork aside and repeat this procedure for the other fork.

5 Steering head bearings - replacement

Refer to illustrations 5.3a, 5.3b, 5.4a, 5.4b, 5.5a, 5.5b, 5.6, 5.10a, 5.10b, 5.10c, 5.10d, 5.12a and 5.12b

1 If the steering head bearing check/adjustment (see *Steering and suspension - check* in Chapter 1) does not remedy excessive play or roughness in the steering head bearings, disassemble the front end and replace the bearings and races as follows.

2 Remove the front wheel (see Chapter 6B), the front fender (see Chapter 7) and the forks (see Section 3).

3 Unscrew the steering stem flange bolt and remove the upper triple clamp together with the handlebar (see illustrations).

4 Using a ring nut wrench of the type described in *Steering and suspension - check* in Chapter 1, remove the ring nut and the bearing cover (see illustrations) while supporting the steering stem by holding the lower triple clamp.

5 Remove the upper ball race and upper balls (see illustrations).

6 Lower the steering stem and lower triple clamp out of the steering head (see illustration). If it's stuck, gently tap on the top of the steering stem with a plastic mallet or a hammer and a wood block. Remove the lower balls, catching any that fall out.

7 Clean all the parts with solvent and dry them thoroughly, using compressed air, if available. Wipe the old grease out of the steering head and bearing races.

8 Inspect the steering stem/lower triple clamp for cracks and other damage. Do not attempt to repair any steering components. Replace

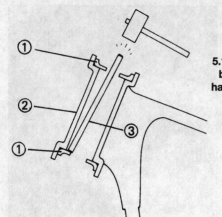

5.10a   Drive out the old bearing races with a hammer and brass drift

1   Outer races
2   Steering head
3   Brass drift

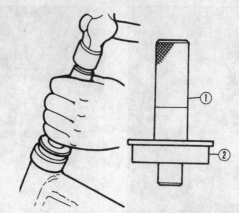

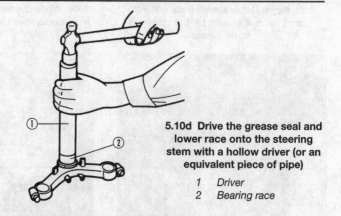

5.10b   Drive in the new bearing races with a bearing driver or socket the same diameter as the bearing race

1   Bearing driver handle
2   Bearing driver

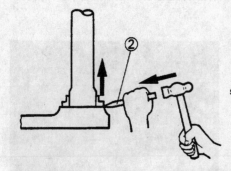

5.10c   Pry the old lower bearing race from the steering stem with a hammer and chisel

5.10d   Drive the grease seal and lower race onto the steering stem with a hollow driver (or an equivalent piece of pipe)

1   Driver
2   Bearing race

them with new parts if defects are found.

9   Inspect the steering head bearing balls and races for cracks, dents, pits and flat spots. If the bearing balls and/or races are worn or damaged, replace them as a set. (Also, check with a dealer service department about upgrading to tapered roller bearings.)

10   To remove the races, drive them out of the steering head with a hammer and a long drift punch **(see illustration)**. A slide hammer with the proper internal-jaw puller will also work. Since the races are an interference fit in the frame, installation will be easier if the new races are left overnight in a refrigerator. This will cause them to contract and slip into place in the frame with very little effort. When installing the races, use a bearing driver the same diameter as the outer race **(see illustration)**, or tap them gently into place with a hammer and punch or a large socket. Do not strike the bearing surface or the race will be damaged. To remove the lower bearing race from the steering stem, use a bearing puller, which can be rented, or pry it up with a hammer and chisel **(see illustration)**. To install the lower race on the steering stem, drive it onto the steering stem using a hollow driver or a pipe the same diameter as the race **(see illustration)**.

11   Coat the bearing balls and races with high-quality moly-based grease.

12   Stick the lower bearing balls to the lower race with grease **(see illustration)**. Insert the steering stem/lower triple clamp into the steering head. Install the upper bearing balls **(see illustration)**, then install the bearing cover and ring nut. Tighten the ring nut (see Steering and suspension - check in Chapter 1) to the torque listed in the Chapter 1 Specifications.

13   Make sure the steering head turns smoothly and that there's no play in the bearings.

14   Install the upper triple clamp and flange bolt, but don't tighten the bolt yet.

15   Install the fork tubes and tighten the lower triple clamp bolts to the torque listed in this Chapter's Specifications.

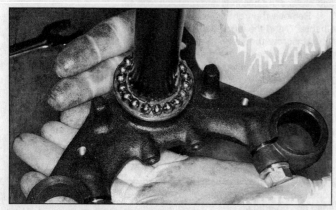

5.12a   Stick the balls to the lower race with grease

5.12b   Stick the balls to the upper bearing's lower race with grease and install the upper race

6.5 Remove the RT100 upper shock mounting bolt; there's a washer on each side of the mounting bushing . . .

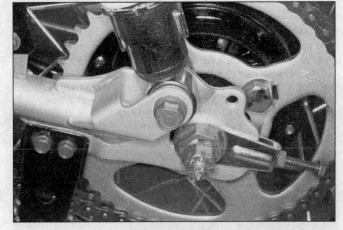

6.11 Rear shock absorber details (RT180 models)

1 *Shock absorber*   3 *Bushing*
2 *Coil spring*

16 Tighten the flange bolt to the torque listed in this Chapter's Specifications.
17 Tighten the upper triple clamp bolts to the torque listed in this Chapter's Specifications. Install the front wheel and handlebars.
18 Check the alignment of the handlebars and the front wheel. If necessary, loosen the triple clamp bolts, have an assistant hold the front wheel, then turn the handlebars to align them with the front wheel. Tighten the triple clamp bolts to the torque listed in this Chapter's Specifications.

6   Rear shock absorber(s) - removal and installation

1   Inspect the rear shock(s). Look for oil leaks and other obvious damage. Is the shock absorber damper rod bent? Is the spring damaged? If a shock is leaking or damaged, replace the shock(s).
2   Remove the seat and both side covers (see Chapter 7B).
3   Elevate the rear of the bike by putting a suitable jack or a milk crate under the engine. If you're using a jack, be sure to put a board between the jack head and the engine to protect the crankcase.

RT100 models

Refer to illustrations 6.5 and 6.6
4   If you're removing the shocks to remove the swingarm, support the swingarm before removing the shocks. If you're replacing the shock absorbers, work on one side at a time: remove one old shock and install the new unit before removing the other old shock. That way, the swingarm remains supported.
5   Remove the upper shock absorber bolts and washers **(see illustration)**.
6   Remove the lower shock absorber bolt **(see illustration)**, then remove the shock absorber.
7   Installation is the reverse of removal. Tighten the upper and lower shock absorber bolts to the torque listed in this Chapter's Specifications.
8   Remove the other shock absorber and install the new unit.

RT180 models

Refer to illustration 6.11
9   Remove the fuel tank (see Chapter 3B).
10   Support the swingarm so that it won't fall when the shock is unbolted.
11   Remove the cotter pin, washer, thrust cover and upper mounting clevis pin **(see illustration)**.
12   Remove the cotter pin, nut, washer and lower mounting bolt.
13   Remove the rear wheel (see Chapter 6B).
14   Remove the shock from the bike.
15   Even if you're only removing the shock to remove the swingarm,

6.6 . . . and remove the lower bolt to free the shock

inspect the shock carefully for oil leaking from the seal, gas (nitrogen) leaking from the shock body or any other damage. If the shock is damaged or worn in any way, replace it.
16   Inspect the bushings at both ends of the shock. If a bushing is loose or worn, have it bearing pressed out and a new one pressed in by a dealer or motorcycle repair shop.
17   Inspect the upper shock mounting bolt and the lower shock mounting clevis pin. If either of them is damaged or bent, replace it.
18   Installation is the reverse of removal. Be sure to use new cotter pins at the upper and lower ends of the shock.

7   Swingarm bushings - check

1   Elevate the rear of the bike by putting a suitable jack or a milk crate under the engine. If you're using a jack, be sure to put a board between the jack head and the engine to protect the crankcase.
2   Remove the rear wheel (see Chapter 6B), then remove the rear shock absorber(s) (see Section 6).
3   Grasp the rear of the swingarm with one hand and place your other hand at the junction of the swingarm and frame. Try to move the rear of the swingarm from side-to-side. Any wear in the bushings produces play (movement) between the swingarm and the frame at the front (the swingarm will actually move back-and-forth, not side-to-side). If there's any play in the swingarm, remove the swingarm (see Section 8) and replace the swingarm bushings (see Section 9).
4   Move the swingarm up and down through its full travel. It should move freely, without any binding or rough spots. If it doesn't move freely, remove the swingarm (see Section 8) and lubricate the swingarm bushings with lithium soap base or moly-base grease.

8.5 Unscrew the swingarm pivot bolt nut (RT100 shown) and pull out the pivot bolt

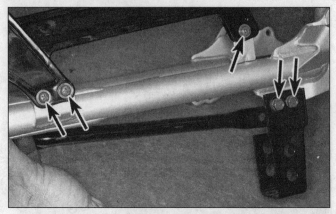

8.6a Remove the chain guard and guide screws (arrow) (RT100 shown)

8 Swingarm - removal and installation

Refer to illustrations 8.5, 8.6a, 8.6b and 8.6c

1   Elevate the rear of the bike by putting a suitable jack or a milk crate under the engine. If you're using a jack, be sure to put a board between the jack head and the engine to protect the crankcase.

2   Disconnect the drive chain (see Section 10).

3   Remove the rear wheel (see Chapter 6B).

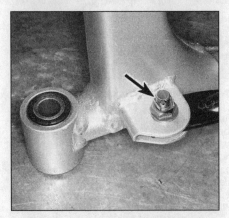

8.6b Remove the cotter pin and nut (arrow), then unbolt the brake rod from the swingarm

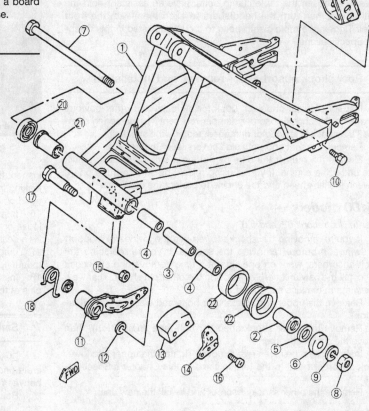

9.2 Swingarm (RT180 models) exploded view

1	Swingarm	9	Spring washer	16	Chain guide bolt
2	Bushing	10	Chain guide	17	Tensioner arm bolt
3	Bushing/spacer		bolt/washer	18	Tensioner arm torsion
4	Bushing/spacer	11	Tensioner arm		spring
5	Shim	12	Oil seal	19	Chain guide
6	Thrust cover	13	Chain tensioner	20	Thrust cover
7	Pivot bolt	14	Chain guide	21	Thrust bushing
8	Self-locking nut	15	Chain guide nut	22	Seal

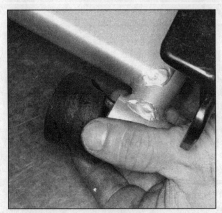

8.6c On RT100 models, remove the seal guard

9.3 Replace the bushings (arrow) if they're worn or damaged (RT100 shown)

10.1 Remove the clip from the master link (arrow); its open end faces rearward when the chain is on the top run

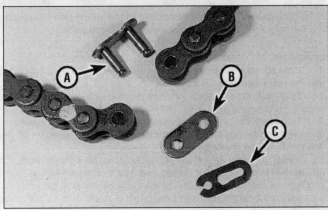

10.2 Master link details

A   *Link*   B   *Plate*   C   *Clip*

4   Disconnect the shock absorber(s) from the swingarm (see Section 6).
5   Remove the nut **(see illustration)** from the swingarm pivot bolt and pull out the pivot bolt.
6   If necessary, remove the chain guard, chain guide and brake rod from the swingarm. On RT100 models, remove the seal guard **(see illustrations)**.
7   Remove the swingarm.
8   Installation is the reverse of removal, with the following additions:
 a) *Lubricate the swingarm bushings with lithium soap base or moly-base grease.*
 b) *Tighten the swingarm pivot bolt and nut to the torque listed in this Chapter's Specifications.*
 c) *Adjust the drive chain and rear brake pedal (see Chapter 1).*

9   Swingarm bushings - replacement

Refer to illustrations 9.2 and 9.3
1   Remove the swingarm (see Section 8).
2   On RT180 models, remove the thrust covers, shims and seals **(see illustration)**.
3   Take the swingarm to a Yamaha dealer or a motorcycle machine shop and have the old bushings pressed out and the new bushings pressed in **(see illustration)**.
4   Lubricate the bushings with lithium soap base or moly-base grease.
5   On RT180 models, install the seals, shims and thrust covers.
6   Install the swingarm (see Section 8).

10   Drive chain - removal, cleaning, inspection and installation

Removal

Refer to illustrations 10.1 and 10.2
1   Turn the rear wheel to place the drive chain master link where it's easily accessible **(see illustration)**.
2   Remove the clip and plate and pull the master link out of the chain **(see illustration)**.
3   Remove the left crankcase cover (see Chapter 4B).
4   Lift the chain off the sprockets and remove it from the bike.
5   Check the chain guards and rollers on the swingarm and frame for wear or damage and replace them as necessary.

Cleaning and inspection

6   Soak the chain in a high flash point solvent for approximately five or six minutes. Use a brush to work the solvent into the spaces between the links and plates.
7   Wipe the chain dry, then check it carefully for worn or damaged links. Replace the chain if wear or damage is found at any point.
8   Stretch the chain taut and measure its length between the number of pins listed in this Chapter's Specifications. Compare the measured length to the specified value replace the chain if it's beyond the limit. If the chain needs to be replaced, refer to Section 13 and check the sprockets. If they're worn, replace them also. If a new chain is installed on worn sprockets, it will wear out quickly.
9   Lubricate the chain with spray chain lube compatible with O-ring chains.

Installation

10   Installation is the reverse of the removal steps, with the following additions:
 a) *Install the master link clip so its opening faces the back of the motorcycle when the master link is in the upper chain run. Be sure to reinstall the O-rings in the master link.*
 b) *Refer to Chapter 1 and adjust the chain.*

11   Sprockets - check and replacement

Refer to illustrations 11.3, 11.5, 11.6a, 11.6b, 11.6c and 11.7
1   Support the bike securely so it can't be knocked over during this procedure.
2   Whenever the sprockets are inspected, the chain should be inspected also and replaced if it's worn. Installing a worn chain on new

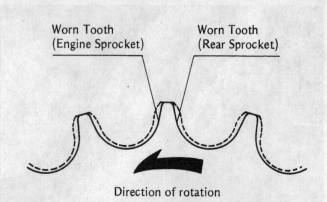

11.3 Inspect the sprockets in the areas indicated to see if they're worn excessively

Worn Tooth (Engine Sprocket)   Worn Tooth (Rear Sprocket)

Direction of rotation

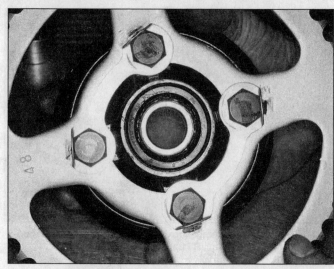

11.5   The driven sprocket is attached to the wheel hub with bolts (RT100 models) or nuts (RT180 models)

11.6a   Bend back the engine sprocket lockwasher . . .

cover slots.

4   If the sprockets are worn, remove the drive chain (see Section 10) and the rear wheel (see Chapter 6B).

5   To detach the rear sprocket from the rear wheel hub, remove the bolts (RT100 model) or nuts (RT180 models) **(see illustration)**.

6   To detach the engine sprocket, bend back the lockwasher and unscrew the retaining nut **(see illustrations)**. Slide the sprocket off the countershaft **(see illustration)**.

7   Inspect the seal behind the engine sprocket **(see illustration)**. If it has been leaking, pry it out (taking care not to scratch the seal bore) and tap in a new seal with a socket the same diameter as the seal.

8   Installation is the reverse of the removal steps, with the following additions:

a)   *Tighten the driven sprocket bolts to the torque values listed in this Chapter's Specifications. Tighten the engine sprocket bolt(s) securely, but don't overtighten them and strip the threads.*

b)   *Install the master link clip so its opening faces the back of the motorcycle when the master link is in the upper chain run.*

c)   *Refer to Chapter 1 and adjust the chain.*

sprockets will cause them to wear quickly.

3   Check the teeth on the engine sprocket and rear sprocket for wear **(see illustration)**. The engine sprocket is visible through the

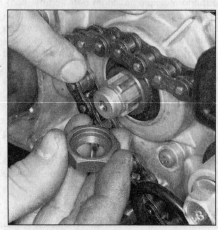

11.6b   . . . unscrew the nut (the recessed side of the nut faces the engine) . . .

11.6c   . . . remove the lockwasher and slide the sprocket off the countershaft

11.7   If the seal behind the engine sprocket is leaking, replace it

Chapter 5 Part C
Steering, suspension and final drive
(TT-R and XT models)

Contents

Specifications

Front forks

Oil type
- TT-R90 .... 15W fork oil
- TT-R125, TT-R225, XT225 .... 10W fork oil
- TT-R250 .... Yamaha fork oil "01" or equivalent
- XT350 .... 10W fork oil or SAE 10W30 grade SE motor oil

Oil capacity
- TT-R90 .... 64 cc (2.16 fl oz)
- TT-R125 .... 156 cc (5.27 fl oz)
- XT225, TT-R225 .... 355 cc (12 fl oz)
- TT-R250 .... 555cc (18.8 fl oz)
- XT350 .... 319 cc (10.8 fl oz)

Oil level (fork fully compressed and spring removed)
- TT-R90 .... 185 mm (7.28 inches)
- TT-R125, TT-R250 .... 130 mm (5.12 inches)
- XT225, TT-R225 .... 147 mm (5.8 inch)
- XT350 .... Not specified

Fork spring free length limit
- TT-R90 .... 417 mm (16.4 inches)
- TT-R125 .... 339 mm (13.35 inches)
- XT225, TT-R225 .... 5588.8 mm(23.18 inches)
- TT-R250 .... 462 mm (18.2 inches)
- XT350 .... 575 mm (22.638 inches)

Fork tube bend limit .... 0.2 mm (0.008 inch)

Tightening torques

Handlebar bracket bolts
    TT-R90 .... 13 Nm (113 inch-lbs)
    TT-R125, TT-R250 .... 23 Nm (17 ft-lbs)
    XT225, TT-R225 .... 15 Nm (123 inch-lbs)
    XT350 .... 20 Nm (168 inch-lbs)
Handlebar bracket to triple clamp nuts (TT-R90, TT-R250) ..... 40 Nm (29 ft-lbs)
Front axle nut.. see Chapter 6
Upper triple clamp bolts
    TT-R90 .... Not applicable
    TT-R125 .... 25 Nm (18 ft-lbs)
    XT225, TT-R225, TT-R250, XT350 .... 23 Nm (17 ft-lbs)
Lower triple clamp bolts
    TT-R90 .... 33 Nm (24 ft-lbs)
    TT-R125 .... 60 Nm (43 ft-lbs)
    XT225, TT-R225 .... 20 Nm (168 inch-lbs)
    TT-R250 .... 30 Nm (22 ft-lbs)
    XT350 .... 23 Nm (17 ft-lbs)
Damper rod bolt (except TT-R250)*
    TT-R90, TT-R225, XT225 .... 20 Nm (168 inch-lbs)
    TT-R125, XT350 .... 23 Nm (17 ft-lbs)
Fork base valve (TT-R250).. 55 Nm (40 ft-lbs)
Fork cap bolt
    TT-R90 .... 40 Nm (29 ft-lbs)
    TT-R125 .... 23 Nm (17 ft-lbs)
    TT-R250 .... 28 Nm (20 ft-lbs)
    XT350 .... 23 Nm (17 ft-lbs)
Steering stem bearing adjusting nut... see Chapter 1
Steering stem nut/bolt
    TT-R90 .... 40 Nm (29 ft-lbs)
    TT-R125 .... 110 Nm (80 ft-lbs)
    TT-R225, XT225 .... 70 Nm (50 ft-lbs)
    TT-R250 .... 120 Nm (85 ft-lbs)
    XT350 .... 54 Nm (39 ft-lbs)
Rear shock absorber mounting bolts
    TT-R125
        Upper bolt.. 53 Nm (38 ft-lbs)
        Lower bolt.. 35 Nm (25 ft-lbs)
    TT-R225, XT225, XT350
        Upper and lower bolts .... 32 Nm (23 ft-lbs)
    TT-R250
        Upper bolt.. 46 Nm (33 ft-lbs)
        Lower bolt.. 40 Nm (29 ft-lbs)
Connecting arm to relay arm
    TT-R125 .... 35 Nm (25 ft-lbs)
    XT225, TT-R225 .... 32 Nm (23 ft-lbs)
    TT-R250 .... 59 Nm (43 ft-lbs)
    XT350 .... 32 Nm (23 ft-lbs)
Connecting arm to frame
    TT-R125 .... 35 Nm (25 ft-lbs)
    XT225, TT-R225, XT350 .... 32 Nm (23 ft-lbs)
    TT-R250 .... 46 Nm (33 ft-lbs)
Relay arm to swingarm
    TT-R125 .... 53 Nm (38 ft-lbs)
    TT-R225, XT225 .... 55 Nm (40 ft-lbs)
    TT-R250, XT350 .... 59 Nm (43 ft-lbs)
Swingarm pivot bolt
    TT-R90 .... 55 Nm (40 ft-lbs)
    TT-R125 .... 53 Nm (38 ft-lbs)
    TT-R225, XT225 .... 80 Nm (58 ft-lbs)
    TT-R250 .... 105 Nm (75 ft-lbs)
Driven sprocket nuts/bolts
    XT350 .... 25 Nm (18 ft-lbs)
    TT-R90 .... 26 Nm (19 ft-lbs)
    TT-R225, XT226 .... 33 Nm (24 ft-lbs)
    TT-R250 .... 35 Nm (25 ft-lbs)
    XT350 .... 30 Nm (22 ft-lbs)

Apply non-permanent thread locking agent to the threads.

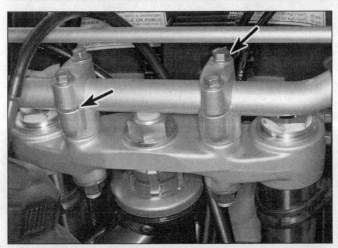

2.3 On installation, place the bracket punch marks to the front (upper arrow) and don't try to close the gap at the rear of the brackets (lower arrow)

1 General information

The steering system on these models consists of a one-piece handlebar and a steering head attached to the front portion of the frame. The front suspension consists of damper rod or cartridge forks. The rear suspension consists of a single shock absorber with concentric coil spring and a swingarm. All except TT-R90 models use a progressive rising rate suspension linkage, where the suspension stiffens as its travel increases. This allows a softer ride over small bumps in the terrain, together with firmer suspension control over large irregularities.

2 Handlebars - removal, inspection and installation

Refer to illustrations 2.3 and 2.4

1   The handlebars rest in brackets on the upper triple clamp. If the handlebars must be removed for access to other components, such as the steering head bearings, simply remove the bolts and slip the handlebars off the bracket. It's not necessary to disconnect the throttle, clutch, or decompression cables, brake hose or the kill switch wire, but it is a good idea to support the assembly with a piece of wire or rope, to avoid unnecessary strain on the cables.

2   If the handlebars are to be removed completely, refer to Chap-

ter 2 for the clutch lever removal procedure, Chapter 3 for the throttle housing removal procedure, Chapter 4 for the kill switch removal procedure and Chapter 6 for the brake master cylinder removal procedure.

3   Look for punch marks in the front end of each handlebar upper bracket **(see illustration)**. If you don't see one, make your own. There should also be a mark indicating the position of the handlebar in the brackets. Again, make your own mark if you don't see one. Remove the upper bracket bolts, lift off the brackets and remove the handlebars.

4   Check the handlebars and brackets for cracks and distortion and replace them if any problems are found. On models with integral handlebar brackets, you'll need to replace the upper triple clamp to replace the brackets. On models with separate brackets, remove the nut and washer that secure each lower bracket to the triple clamp **(see illustration)**.

5   Place the handlebars in the lower brackets. Line up the punch mark on the handlebar with the parting line of the upper and lower brackets.

6   Install the upper brackets with their punch marks facing forward. Tighten the front bolts, then the rear bolts, to the torque listed in this Chapter's Specifications. **Caution:** *If there's a gap between the upper and lower brackets at the rear after tightening the bolts, don't try to close it by tightening beyond the recommended torque* **(see illustration 2.3)**. *You'll only crack the brackets.*

3 Front forks - removal and installation

Removal

Refer to illustrations 3.3 and 3.4

1   Support the bike securely upright so it can't fall over during this procedure.

2   Remove the front wheel (see Chapter 6).

3   On all except TT-R225 models, loosen the fork cap bolts now if you plan to disassemble the forks **(see illustration)**. This can be done later, but it will be easier while the forks are securely held in the triple clamps. TT-R225 models use a spring-loaded fork cap that can be just as easily removed after the fork is off the bike.

4   Loosen the upper and lower triple clamp bolts **(see illustration 3.3 and the accompanying illustration)**.

5   Lower the fork leg out of the triple clamps, twisting it if necessary.

Installation

6   Slide each fork leg into the lower triple clamp.

7   Slide the fork legs up, installing the tops of the tubes into the

2.4 Remove the nut and washer (arrow) and pull the bracket out of the triple clamp

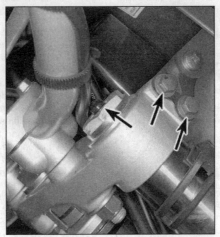

3.3 Loosen the fork cap bolt (left arrow) and the upper triple clamp bolt(s) (right arrow) (TT-R250 shown) . . .

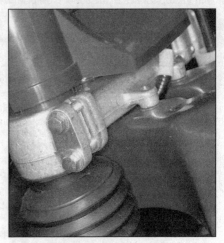

3.4 . . . and loosen the lower triple clamp bolts (TT-R250 shown)

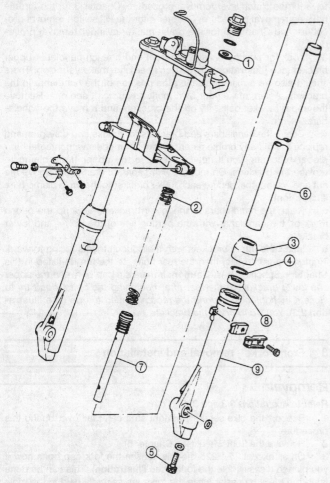

4.3a Forks (TT-R90 models) - exploded view

1	Adjuster, washer and cap bolt	5	Damper rod bolt
2	Fork spring	6	Fork tube
3	Dust seal	7	Damper rod
4	Oil seal retaining ring	8	Oil seal
		9	Outer fork tube (fork slider)

upper triple clamp. Position the forks so the top of each tube is flush with the top surface of the upper triple clamp.

8   Tighten the triple clamp bolts to the torque listed in this Chapter's Specifications.

9   The remainder of installation is the reverse of the removal steps.

---

4   Front forks - disassembly, inspection and reassembly

---

1   Remove the forks following the procedure in Section 3. Work on one fork at a time to prevent mixing up the parts.

All except TT-R250 models

Disassembly

Refer to illustrations 4.3a, 4.3b, 4.3c, 4.3d, 4.4, 4.6a through 4.6e, 4.7, 4.8, 4.9, 4.10 and 4.11

2   On all except TT-R90 models, loosen the boot clamps and remove the rubber boot from the fork.

3   On all except XT225 and TT-R225 models, unscrew the fork cap, spring seat and spring **(see illustrations)** (the cap should have been loosened before the forks were removed).

4   On TT-R225 and XT225 models, pry out or twist off the trim cap

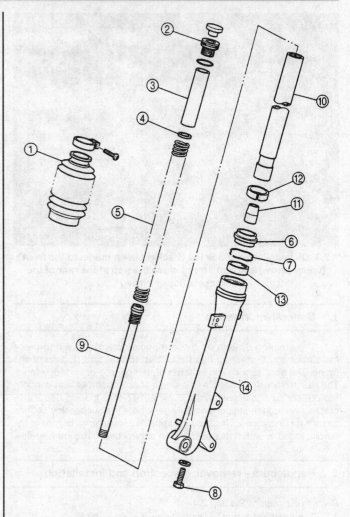

4.3b Forks (TT-R125 models) - exploded view

1	Fork boot	8	Damper rod bolt
2	Fork cap bolt	9	Damper rod
3	Spacer	10	Inner fork tube
4	Washer	11	Oil lock piece
5	Fork spring	12	Inner fork tube busing
6	Dust seal	13	Oil seal
7	Oil seal retaining ring	14	Outer fork tube (fork slider)

on top of the fork. Unscrew the air valve from the fork cap (if equipped). Press the fork cap down against the spring pressure, pry the retaining ring out of its groove, then release the spring pressure **(see illustration)**.Take out the spacer (if equipped) and the fork spring.

5   Invert the fork assembly over a graduated measuring container and allow the oil to drain out. Note how much fluid was removed.

6   Prevent the damper rod from turning using a holding handle and an adapter **(see illustration)**. Unscrew the Allen bolt at the bottom of the outer tube and retrieve the copper washer **(see illustrations)**. **Note:** *If you don't have access to these special tools, you can fabricate your own using a bolt with a head that fits inside the top of the damper rod in the fork, two nuts, a socket (to fit on the nuts), a long extension and a ratchet. Thread the two nuts onto the bolt and tighten them against each other* **(see illustration)**. *Insert the assembly into the socket and tape it into place* **(see illustration)**. *Now, insert the tool into the fork tube and engage the bolt head (or the special Yamaha tool) into the hex recess in the damper rod and remove socket head bolt. Another option is to use a piece of hardwood dowel with a taper cut in the end. Push this firmly into the end of the damper rod to keep it from turning.*

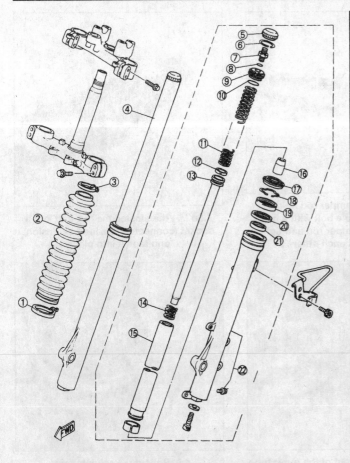

4.3c Fork (TT-R225 and XT225 models) - exploded view

1	Fork boot clamp	13	Damper rod
2	Fork boot	14	Rebound spring
3	Fork boot clamp	15	Inner fork tube
4	Fork assembly	16	Oil lock piece
5	Air valve cap	17	Dust seal
6	Retaining ring	18	Oil seal retaining ring
7	Air valve (XT225 only)	19	Oil seal
8	O-ring	20	Oil seal spacer
9	Spring seat	21	Outer fork tube (fork slider) bushing
10	O-ring	22	Outer fork tube (fork slider)
11	Fork spring		
12	Piston ring		

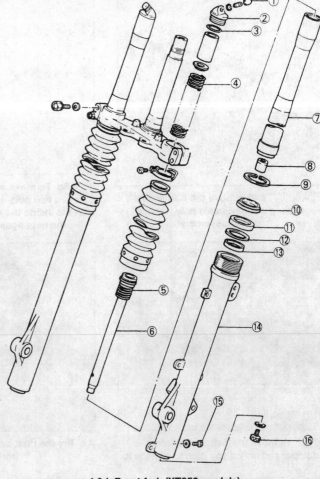

4.3d Front fork (XT350 models)

1	Air valve and cap	9	Oil seal retaining ring
2	Fork cap (early model shown)	10	Dust seal
3	O-ring	11	Oil seal
4	Fork spring	12	Oil seal washer
5	Rebound spring (on damper rod)	13	Outer fork tube (fork slider) bushing
6	Damper rod	14	Outer fork tube (fork slider)
7	Inner fork tube	15	Drain bolt
8	Oil lock piece	16	Damper rod bolt

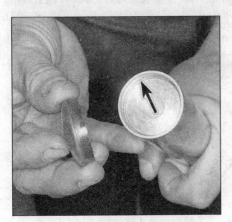

4.4 On TT-R225 models, press the retainer down against the spring and pry the retaining ring (arrow) out of its groove

4.6a This is a special tool that's used to hold the damper rod from turning

4.6b Loosen the damper rod bolt with an Allen wrench . . .

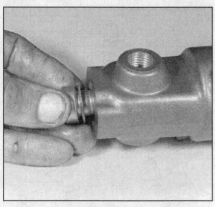

4.6c . . . and remove the bolt and its sealing washer; use a new washer during assembly

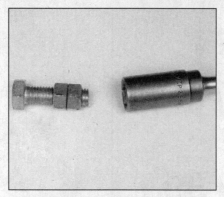

4.6d To make a damper rod holder, thread two nuts onto a bolt with a head that fits inside the damper rod and tighten the nuts against each other . . .

4.6e . . . then install the nut-end into a socket (connected to a long extension) and tape it into place

4.7 Remove the Teflon ring from the damper rod only if you plan to replace it

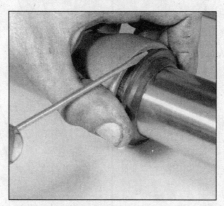

4.8 Pry the dust seal out of the outer tube (fork slider)

4.9 Pry out the retaining ring

7   Tip out the damper rod and the rebound spring **(see illustration)**. Don't remove the Teflon ring from the damper rod unless a new one will be installed.

8   Pry the dust seal from the outer tube **(see illustration)**.

9   Pry the retaining ring from its groove in the outer tube **(see illustration)**. Remove the ring.

10   Hold the outer tube and yank the inner tube away from it, repeatedly (like a slide hammer), until the seal and outer tube guide bushing pop loose **(see illustration)**.

11   Slide the seal, washer and bushing (if equipped) from the inner tube **(see illustration)**.

Inspection

12   Clean all parts in solvent and blow them dry with compressed air, if available. Check the inner and outer fork tubes and the damper rod for score marks, scratches, flaking of the chrome and excessive or abnormal wear. Look for dents in the tubes and replace them if any are found. Check the fork seal seat for nicks, gouges and scratches. If damage is evident, leaks will occur around the seal-to-outer tube junction. Replace worn or defective parts with new ones.

13   Have the inner fork tube checked for runout at a dealer service department or other repair shop. **Warning:** *If the tube is bent, it should be replaced with a new one. Don't try to straighten it.*

14   Measure the overall length of the fork spring and check it for cracks or other damage. Compare the length to the minimum length listed in this Chapter's Specifications. If it's defective or sagged, replace both fork springs with new ones. Never replace only one spring.

15   Check the Teflon ring on the damper rod for wear or damage and replace it if problems are found. **Note:** *Don't remove the ring from the damper rod unless you plan to replace it.*

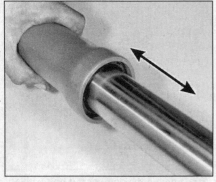

4.10 Pull the fork tubes firmly apart several times until they separate

4.11 These parts (if equipped) will come out with the inner fork tube

1   *Seal*
2   *Washer*
3   *Outer tube (fork slider) bushing*
4   *Inner fork tube bushing*

4.20a Drive the bushing into position with a tool like this one if you have it (use the tool like a slide hammer) . . .

4.20b . . . if you don't have the special tool, drive the bushing with a section of pipe, but tape the ends so it won't scratch the fork tube

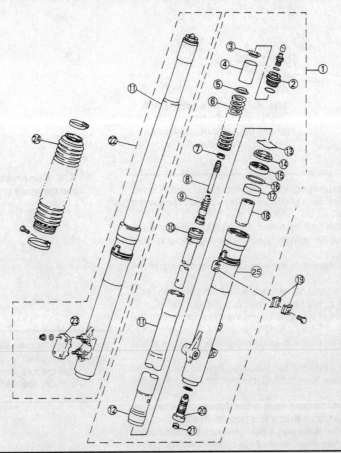

4.33 Front forks (TT-R250 models) - exploded view

1   Left fork leg
2   Cap bolt
3   Upper seat
4   Collar
5   Lower seat
6   Fork spring
7   Locknut
8   Piston rod
9   Rebound spring
10   Damper rod
11   Inner fork tube
12   Inner fork tube bushing
13   Retaining clip
14   Dust seal
15   Oil seal
16   Plain washer
17   Fork slider (outer fork tube) bushing
18   Oil lock piece
19   Brake hose retainer
20   Base valve
21   Cap
22   Right fork assembly

16   If you're working on a TT-R225, XT225 or XT350, check the fork slider bushing (the one inside the outer fork tube) for wear and replace it if its condition is in doubt.

Reassembly

Refer to illustrations 4.20a and 4.20b

17   On all except TT-R90 models, if it's necessary to replace the inner guide bushing (the one that's on the bottom of the inner tube), pry it apart at the slit and slide it off. Make sure the new one seats properly.

18   Place the rebound spring over the damper rod, then slide the rod assembly into the inner fork tube until it protrudes from the lower end of the tube. Fit the oil lock piece over the end of the damper rod.

19   Insert the inner tube/damper rod assembly into the outer tube until the Allen bolt (with a new copper washer) can be threaded into the damper rod from the lower end of the outer tube. **Note:** *Apply a non-permanent thread locking compound to the threads of the bolt. Using the tool described in Step 4, hold the damper rod and tighten the Allen bolt to the torque listed in this Chapter's Specifications. If you didn't use the tool, tighten the damper rod bolt after the fork spring and cap bolt are installed.*

20   If you're installing a new bushing in the fork slider (outer fork tube), slide the bushing down the inner tube until it seats just above its installed position in the outer fork tube. Using a special bushing driver and a used bushing placed on top of the bushing being installed, drive the bushing into place until it's fully seated **(see illustration)**. If you don't have access to one of these tools, it is highly recommended that you take the assembly to a Yamaha dealer service department or other motorcycle repair shop to have this done. It is possible, however, to drive the bushing into place using a section of pipe and an old bushing **(see illustration)**. Wrap tape around the ends of the pipe to prevent it from scratching the fork tube.

21   Slide the washer down the inner tube, into position over the guide bushing.

22   Lubricate the lips and the outer diameter of the fork seal with the recommended fork oil (see Chapter 1) and slide it down the inner tube, with the lip facing down. Drive the seal into place with the same tools used to drive in the guide bushing. If you don't have access to these, it is recommended that you take the assembly to a Yamaha dealer service department or other motorcycle repair shop to have the seal driven in. If you are very careful, the seal can be driven in with a hammer and a drift punch. Work around the circumference of the seal, tapping gently on the outer edge of the seal until it's seated. Be careful - if you distort the seal, you'll have to disassemble the fork again and end up taking it to a dealer anyway!

23   Install the retaining ring, making sure the ring is completely seated in its groove.

24   Install the dust seal, making sure it seats completely.

25   On TT-R225, XT225 and XT350 models, install the drain screw and a new gasket, if it was removed.

26   Add the recommended type and amount of fork oil (see Chapter 1).

27   Install the fork spring, with the closer-wound coils at the top.

28   Install the spring seat on top of the spring.

29   On TT-R225 models, press the fork cap down against the spring tension and secure it with the retaining ring, then install the rubber cap.

30   On all except TT-R225 models, install the fork cap bolt and tighten it slightly; it will be tightened to the specified torque after the fork is installed.

31   Install the fork by following the procedure outlined in Section 5. If you won't be installing the fork right away, store it in an upright position.

32   Tighten the fork cap bolt to the torque listed in this Chapter's Specifications.

Cartridge forks (TT-R250 models)

Disassembly

Refer to illustrations 4.33 and 4.34

33   Loosen the boot clamps and slide the boot off the fork **(see illustration)**.

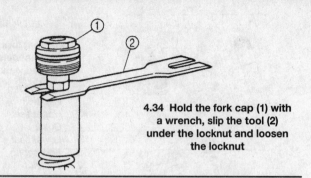

4.34 Hold the fork cap (1) with a wrench, slip the tool (2) under the locknut and loosen the locknut

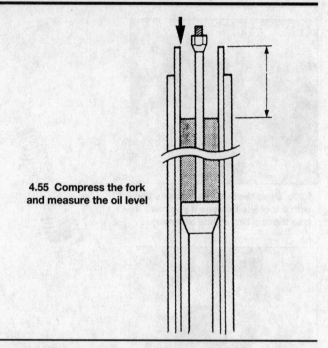

4.55 Compress the fork and measure the oil level

34   Squeeze the spacer down against the spring pressure and insert a holder tool (Yamaha part no. YM-01434) on top of it and below the locknut **(see illustration)**.

35   Hold the cap bolt with one wrench and loosen the locknut away from the cap bolt with another wrench. Unscrew the cap bolt and locknut from the damper rod.

36   Take the upper seat, spacer, lower seat and fork spring out of the fork.

37   Place the open (upper) end of the fork over a drain pan, then compress and extend the fork tubes several times to pump out the oil.

38   Pry the dust seal out of its bore, taking care not to scratch the fork tube.

39   Pry the oil seal retainer out of its groove, again taking care not to scratch the fork tube.

40   Place the outer fork tube in a padded vise. Tighten the vise just enough to keep the fork tube from rotating, but not tight enough to distort the fork tube.

41   Remove the cap from the base valve in the bottom of the fork.

42   Hold the damper rod with Yamaha tool no. YM-01418 or equivalent **(see illustrations 4.6a, 4.6d and 4.6e)**. Unscrew the base valve and remove the damper rod, together with the rebound spring, piston rod and locknut.

43   Hold one fork tube in each hand and pull the tubes apart sharply several times (like a slide hammer) to separate them. Once they're separated, remove the oil lock piece from the inner fork tube.

Inspection

44   Refer to Steps 12 through 16 above to inspect the forks.

45   Check the base valve for wear or damage and replace it if problems can be seen. If you're going to reuse it, blow out all of its passages with compressed air.

Reassembly

Refer to illustration 4.55

46   Install new bushings if necessary (see Steps 17 and 20 above).

47   Insert the piston rod into the bottom end of the damper rod, then push the rod all the way in so its other end sticks out the top of the damper rod. Thread the fork cap locknut all the way onto the piston rod. Install the oil lock piece on the bottom of the damper rod.

48   Install the damper rod assembly into the inner fork tube, then assemble the inner and outer fork tubes.

49   Install a new sealing washer on the base valve. Insert the base valve through the bottom of the fork slider (outer fork tube) into the damper rod, then tighten the base valve to the torque listed in this Chapter's Specifications, using the same special tool used for removal.

50   Seat the oil seal in its bore with a seal driver (see Step 11 above). Install the retaining ring in its groove, then seat the dust seal with the same tool used for the oil seal.

51   Pour the amount of fork oil listed in this Chapter's Specifications into the inner fork tube.

52   Slowly pump the piston rod up and down ten or more times.

53   Slowly pump the inner fork tube up and down about six inches (no more).

54   Let the fork oil settle for ten minutes so air can find its way out and the fork oil can distribute itself evenly.

55   Compress the inner fork tube all the way, then measure the oil

level in the fork **(see illustration)**. Add or remove oil as necessary to achieve the correct level.

56   Install the fork spring in the fork tube.

57   Dip a new fork cap O-ring in fork oil and place it on the fork cap.

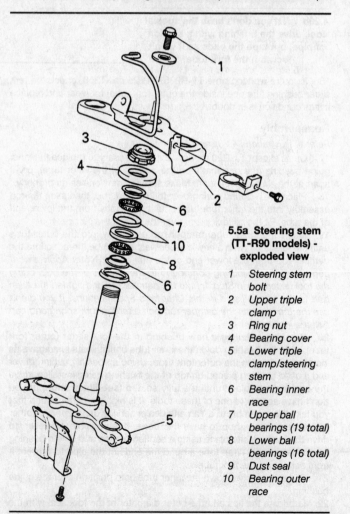

5.5a Steering stem (TT-R90 models) - exploded view

1   *Steering stem bolt*
2   *Upper triple clamp*
3   *Ring nut*
4   *Bearing cover*
5   *Lower triple clamp/steering stem*
6   *Bearing inner race*
7   *Upper ball bearings (19 total)*
8   *Lower ball bearings (16 total)*
9   *Dust seal*
10 *Bearing outer race*

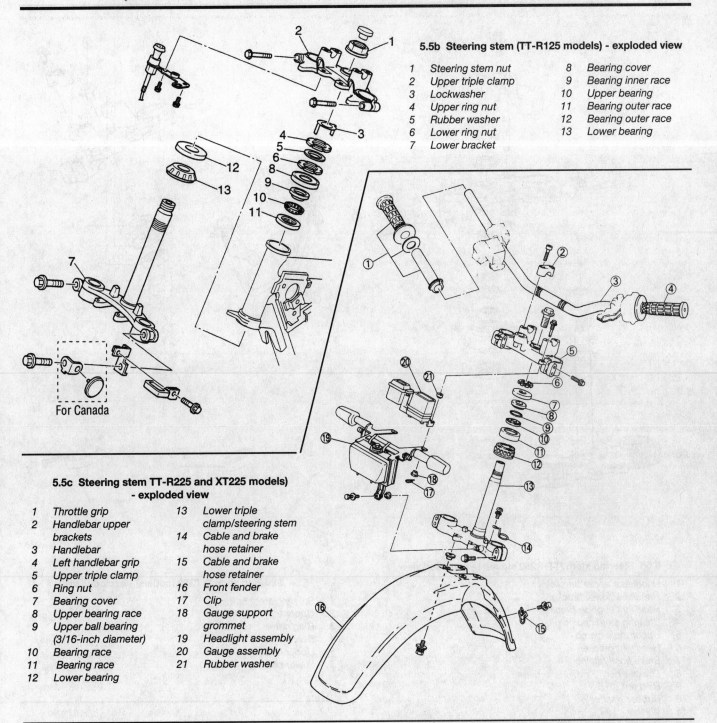

5.5b Steering stem (TT-R125 models) - exploded view

1	Steering stem nut	8	Bearing cover
2	Upper triple clamp	9	Bearing inner race
3	Lockwasher	10	Upper bearing
4	Upper ring nut	11	Bearing outer race
5	Rubber washer	12	Bearing outer race
6	Lower ring nut	13	Lower bearing
7	Lower bracket		

For Canada

5.5c Steering stem TT-R225 and XT225 models) - exploded view

1	Throttle grip	13	Lower triple clamp/steering stem
2	Handlebar upper brackets	14	Cable and brake hose retainer
3	Handlebar	15	Cable and brake hose retainer
4	Left handlebar grip	16	Front fender
5	Upper triple clamp	17	Clip
6	Ring nut	18	Gauge support grommet
7	Bearing cover	19	Headlight assembly
8	Upper bearing race	20	Gauge assembly
9	Upper ball bearing (3/16-inch diameter)	21	Rubber washer
10	Bearing race		
11	Bearing race		
12	Lower bearing		

58 Install the spring seat on top of the spring, then install the spacer and remaining spring seat.

59 Install the fork cap and thread it all the way on with fingers. Insert the tool used in Step 34 to hold the spring down, then tighten the locknut against the fork cap to the torque listed in this Chapter's Specifications.

60 Install the fork boot.

5 Steering head bearings - replacement

Refer to illustrations 5.5a through 5.5e

1 If the steering head bearing check/adjustment (see Chapter 1) does not remedy excessive play or roughness in the steering head bearings, the entire front end must be disassembled and the bearings and races replaced with new ones.

2 Remove the headlight assembly and instrument cluster (if equipped) (see Chapter 4).

3 Remove the handlebars (see Section 2), the front wheel and brake caliper (see Chapter 6), the front fender (see Chapter 7) and the forks (see Section 3).

4 If you're working on a TT-R125 or TT-R250, lift off the lockwasher, then unscrew the upper ring nut and remove the rubber washer.

5 For the bearing removal and inspection procedures, refer to Chapter 2 Part B. TT-R225 and XT225 models use a tapered roller bearing in the bottom position. TT-R250 and XT350 models use tapered roller bearings in the top and bottom positions (**see illustrations**).

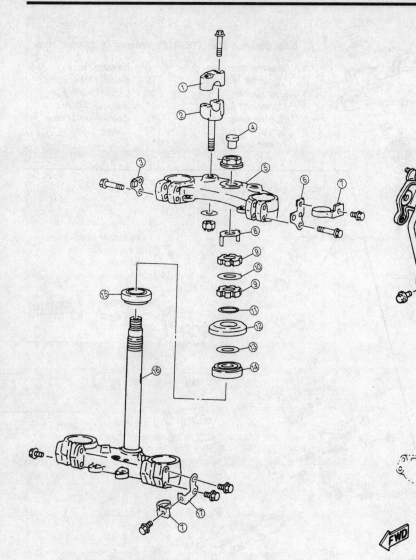

5.5d Steering stem (TT-R250 models) - exploded view

1   Handlebar upper bracket
2   Handlebar lower bracket
3   Headlight support bracket
4   Steering stem cap
5   Upper triple clamp
6   Headlight bracket
7   Brake hose retainer
8   Lockwasher
9   Ring nut
10   Rubber washer
11   Washer
12   Bearing cover
13   Washer
14   Upper bearing
15   Lower bearing
16   Lower triple clamp/steering stem

5.5e Steering stem (XT350 models) - exploded view

1   Steering stem bolt
2   Upper triple clamp
3   Ring nut
4   Bearing cover
5   Upper bearing
6   Lower bearing

6   Insert the steering stem/lower triple clamp into the frame head. Install the upper bearing, bearing cover, lockwasher and ring nut. Refer to the adjustment procedure in Chapter 1 and tighten the ring nut to the torque listed in the Chapter 1 Specifications.

7   Make sure the steering head turns smoothly and that there's no play in the bearings.

8   If you're working on a TT-R125 or TT-R250, install the rubber washer and upper ring nut as described in the steering head bearing check procedure in Chapter 1C.

9   Install the upper triple clamp and the steering stem nut or bolt, but don't tighten the nut or bolt yet.

10   Install the fork tubes and tighten the lower triple clamp bolts to the torque listed in this Chapter's Specifications.

11   Tighten the steering stem nut or bolt to the torque listed in this Chapter's Specifications.

12   Tighten the upper triple clamp bolts to the torque listed in this Chapter's Specifications. Install the front wheel and handlebars.

13   Check the alignment of the handlebars and the front wheel. If necessary, loosen the triple clamp bolts, have an assistant hold the front wheel, then turn the handlebars to align them with the front wheel. Tighten the triple clamp bolts to the torque listed in this Chapter's Specifications.

6.4 Release the clamps and detach the shock reservoir from the frame (TT-R250)

6.6a Remove the lower pivot bolt (TT-R225 shown) . . .

6.6b . . . and the upper pivot bolt (TT-R225 shown)

6 Rear shock absorber - removal, inspection and installation

Removal

Refer to illustrations 6.4, 6.6a and 6.6b

1   Support the bike securely so it can't be knocked over during this procedure. Support the swingarm with a jack so the suspension can be raised or lowered as needed for access.

2   If you're working on a TT-R90, remove the rear fender (see Chapter 7).

3   On all except TT-R90 models, remove the seat, both side covers and the fuel tank (see Chapters 7 and 3).

4   If you're working on a TT-R250, remove the rear subframe. Remove the shock reservoir's retaining bands and detach the reservoir from the bike **(see illustration)**. Remove the air cleaner housing, battery and battery case (see Chapters 3 and 4).

5   On TT-R90 models, remove the clip from the pivot at each end of the shock absorber. Pull out the pivot pins and remove the shock from the motorcycle.

6   On all except TT-R90 models, unbolt the shock arm from the linkage lever at the bottom and from the frame at the top **(see illustrations)**.

Inspection

7   Check the shock absorber for damage and oil leaks. If these can be seen, have the shock overhauled.

8   Check the bushing at the upper end of the shock for wear or damage. If any of these problems can be seen, have the bearing pressed out and a new one pressed in by a dealer or motorcycle repair shop.

9   Clean all parts thoroughly with solvent and dry them with compressed air, if available.

10   Apply a thin coat of moly-based grease to the sleeves and install them in the needle bearings.

Installation

11   The remainder of installation is the reverse of the removal steps, with the following additions:

   a) On TT-R90 models, install the upper and lower pivot pins with their heads to the left side of the motorcycle. Use new clips to secure the pivot pins.

   b) On TT-R125 models, install both pivot bolts with their heads to the left side of the motorcycle.

   c) On TT-R225 and XT225 models, install the upper bolt with its head to the left side of the bike and the lower bolt with its head to the right side.

   d) On TT-R250 models, install the upper bolt with its head to the right side of the motorcycle and the lower bolt with its head to the left.

   e) On XT350 models, install both pivot bolts with their heads to the right side of the motorcycle.

   f) On all except TT-R90 models, tighten the bolts to the torques listed in this Chapter's Specifications.

7 Swingarm bearings - check

1   Refer to Chapter 6 and remove the rear wheel, then refer to Section 6 and remove the rear shock absorber.

2   Grasp the rear of the swingarm with one hand and place your other hand at the junction of the swingarm and frame. Try to move the rear of the swingarm from side-to-side. Any wear (play) in the bushings should be felt as movement between the swingarm and the frame at the front. The swingarm will actually be felt to move forward and backward at the front (not from side-to-side). If any play is noted, the bearings should be replaced with new ones (see Section 9).

3   Next, move the swingarm up and down through its full travel. It should move freely, without any binding or rough spots. If it doesn't move freely, refer to Section 9 for servicing procedures.

8 Swingarm and rear suspension linkage - removal and installation

Refer to illustrations 8.5a through 8.5f

1   Refer to Section 10 and disconnect the drive chain.

2   Remove the rear wheel and unhook the brake pedal return spring from the swingarm (see Chapter 6). If you're working on a TT-R250, detach the brake hose from the retainers on the swingarm and support the caliper so it doesn't hang by the hose.

3   Remove the shock absorber (Section 6).

4   If you're working on a TT-R125 or TT-R225, remove the bolt that attaches the suspension linkage to the frame.

4   If you're working on an XT350, remove the shock absorber linkage bolt that passes through the swingarm.

5   Support the swingarm from below, then unscrew its pivot bolt nut and pull the bolt out **(see illustrations on following pages)**. On XT350 models, the swingarm and suspension linkage are removed together.

6   On all except TT-R90 models (which don't have a suspension linkage) and XT350 models, remove the pivot bolt that attaches the suspension linkage to the frame and take it off the motorcycle.

7   Check the chain sliders and guards for wear or damage and replace them as necessary.

8   Installation is the reverse of the removal steps, with the following additions:

   a) Tighten the pivot bolts and nuts to the torques listed in this Chapter's Specifications.

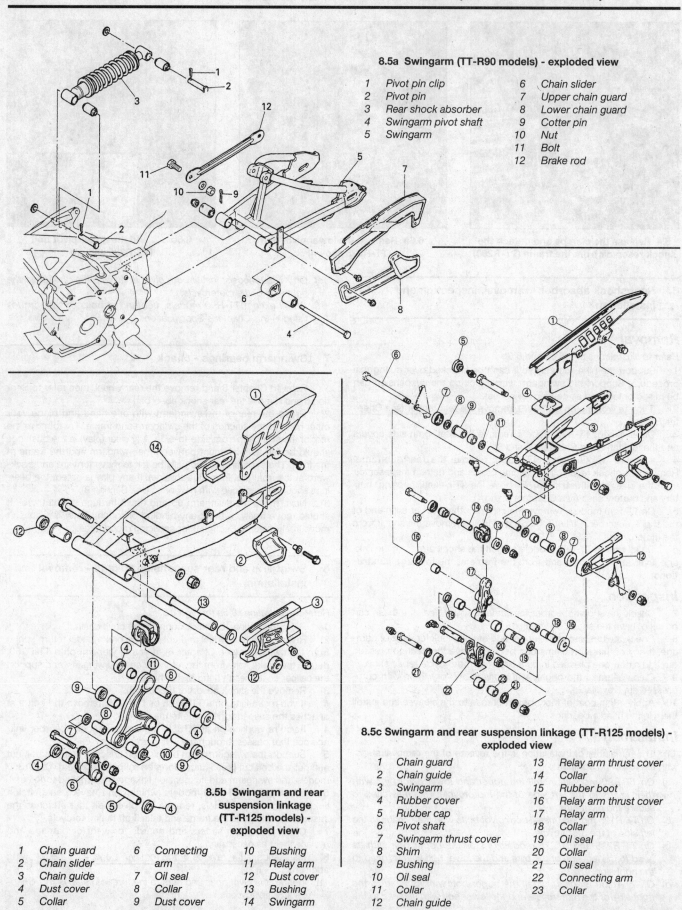

8.5a Swingarm (TT-R90 models) - exploded view

1	Pivot pin clip	6	Chain slider
2	Pivot pin	7	Upper chain guard
3	Rear shock absorber	8	Lower chain guard
4	Swingarm pivot shaft	9	Cotter pin
5	Swingarm	10	Nut
		11	Bolt
		12	Brake rod

8.5b Swingarm and rear suspension linkage (TT-R125 models) - exploded view

1	Chain guard	6	Connecting arm	10	Bushing
2	Chain slider	7	Oil seal	11	Relay arm
3	Chain guide	8	Collar	12	Dust cover
4	Dust cover	9	Dust cover	13	Bushing
5	Collar			14	Swingarm

8.5c Swingarm and rear suspension linkage (TT-R125 models) - exploded view

1	Chain guard	13	Relay arm thrust cover
2	Chain guide	14	Collar
3	Swingarm	15	Rubber boot
4	Rubber cover	16	Relay arm thrust cover
5	Rubber cap	17	Relay arm
6	Pivot shaft	18	Collar
7	Swingarm thrust cover	19	Oil seal
8	Shim	20	Collar
9	Bushing	21	Oil seal
10	Oil seal	22	Connecting arm
11	Collar	23	Collar
12	Chain guide		

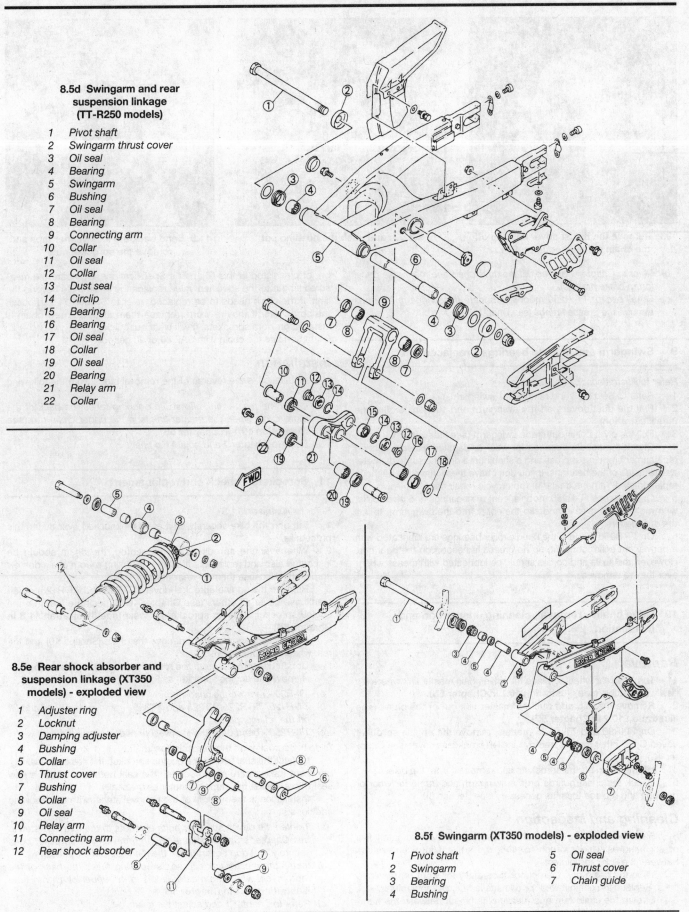

8.5d Swingarm and rear suspension linkage (TT-R250 models)

1 Pivot shaft
2 Swingarm thrust cover
3 Oil seal
4 Bearing
5 Swingarm
6 Bushing
7 Oil seal
8 Bearing
9 Connecting arm
10 Collar
11 Oil seal
12 Collar
13 Dust seal
14 Circlip
15 Bearing
16 Bearing
17 Oil seal
18 Collar
19 Oil seal
20 Bearing
21 Relay arm
22 Collar

8.5e Rear shock absorber and suspension linkage (XT350 models) - exploded view

1 Adjuster ring
2 Locknut
3 Damping adjuster
4 Bushing
5 Collar
6 Thrust cover
7 Bushing
8 Collar
9 Oil seal
10 Relay arm
11 Connecting arm
12 Rear shock absorber

8.5f Swingarm (XT350 models) - exploded view

1	Pivot shaft	5	Oil seal
2	Swingarm	6	Thrust cover
3	Bearing	7	Chain guide
4	Bushing		

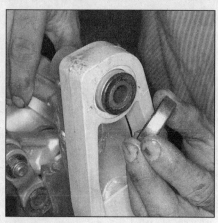

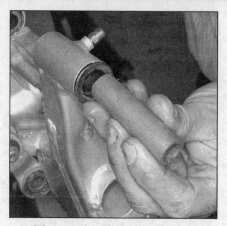

9.2 Remove the thrust cover and slip off the chain guide (if equipped) . . .

9.3 . . . and push the bushing out

11.5 Bend back the lockwasher tabs and remove the sprocket nuts

b) Refer to Chapter 1 and adjust the drive chain and rear brake pedal (drum brake models).

c) On all except TT-R250 models, lubricate the swingarm bearings through the grease fittings (see Chapter 1).

9 Swingarm and linkage bearings - replacement

Refer to illustrations 9.2 and 9.3

1   Refer to Section 8 and remove the swingarm.

2   Pull the dust covers off the swingarm and suspension linkage **(see illustration)**.

3   Pull the pivot collar out of the swingarm **(see illustration)**.

4   Check the needle bearings for wear or damage. Needle bearing replacement requires a press and a shouldered drift the same diameter as the inside of the bearings. If you don't have these, have the bearings replaced by a Yamaha dealer or motorcycle repair shop.

5   On all except TT-R250 models, coat the bearings and pivot collar with moly-based grease and slip the collar into the swingarm. Install the dust covers.

6   On TT-R250 models, the needle roller bearings are lubricated with a permanent solid lubricant, so no grease is needed on the bearings. However, the seals and collars should be lubricated with grease whenever they're removed.

10 Drive chain - removal, cleaning, inspection and installation

Removal

1   Turn the rear wheel to place the drive chain master link where it's easily accessible **(see illustration 10.1 in Chapter 5B)**.

2   Remove the clip and pull the master link out of the chain **(see illustration 10.2 in Chapter 5B)**.

3   On TT-R90 and TT-R125 models, remove the engine sprocket cover. On all other models, remove the left crankcase cover (see Chapter 4C).

4   Lift the chain off the sprockets and remove it from the bike.

5   Check the chain guards on the swingarm and frame for wear or damage and replace them as necessary (see Section 8).

Cleaning and inspection

6   Soak the chain in a high flash point solvent for approximately five or six minutes. Use a brush to work the solvent into the spaces between the links and plates.

7   Wipe the chain dry, then check it carefully for worn or damaged links. Replace the chain if wear or damage is found at any point.

8   Stretch the chain taut and measure its length between the num-
ber of pins listed in this Chapter's Specifications. Compare the measured length to the specified value replace the chain if it's beyond the limit. If the chain needs to be replaced, refer to Section 11 and check the sprockets. If they're worn, replace them also. If a new chain is installed on worn sprockets, it will wear out quickly.

9   Lubricate the chain with SAE 80 or 90 gear oil.

Installation

10   Installation is the reverse of the removal steps, with the following additions:

a) Install the master link clip so its opening faces the back of the motorcycle when the master link is in the upper chain run **(see illustration 10.1 in Chapter 5B)**.

b) Refer to Chapter 1 and adjust the chain.

11 Sprockets - check and replacement

Refer to illustration 11.5

1   Support the bike securely so it can't be knocked over during this procedure.

2   Whenever the sprockets are inspected, the chain should be inspected also and replaced if it's worn. Installing a worn chain on new sprockets will cause them to wear quickly.

3   Remove the engine sprocket cover (TT-R90 and TT-R125) or left crankcase cover all others (see Chapter 4C). Check the teeth on the engine sprocket and rear sprocket for wear **(see illustration 11.3 in Chapter 5B)**.

4   If the sprockets are worn, remove the chain (Section 10) and the rear wheel (see Chapter 6).

5   Unbolt the sprocket from the rear wheel hub **(see illustration)**.

6   Remove the engine sprocket as follows:

a) TT-R90 - remove the snap-ring.

b) TT-R125, TT-R225, XT225 and XT350 - remove two bolts and lift off the retainer plate.

c) TT-R250 - bend back the lockwasher and unscrew the nut.

Slide the sprocket off the transmission shaft.

7   Inspect the seal behind the engine sprocket. If it has been leaking, pry it out (taking care not to scratch the seal bore) and tap in a new seal with a socket the same diameter as the seal.

8   Installation is the reverse of the removal steps, with the following additions:

a) Tighten the driven sprocket bolts and nuts to the torques listed in this Chapter's Specifications. Tighten the engine sprocket bolts securely, but don't overtighten them and strip the threads.

b) Install the master link clip so its opening faces the back of the motorcycle when the master link is in the upper chain run **(see illustration 10.1 in Chapter 5B)**.

c) Refer to Chapter 1 and adjust the chain.

Chapter 6 Part A
Brakes, wheels and tires
(PW50 and PW80 models)

Contents

Specifications

Brakes

Brake shoe outside diameter
 PW50 (front and rear shoes)
  Standard .... 80 mm (3.15 inches)
  Limit .... 77 mm (3.03 inches)
 PW80
  Front
   Standard .... 95 mm (3.74 inches)
   Limit .... 92 mm (3.62 inches)
  Rear
   Standard .... 110 mm (4.33 inches)
   Limit .... 107 mm (4.21 inches)
Front brake lever freeplay .... See Chapter 1
Rear brake pedal freeplay .... See Chapter 1

Refer to marks cast into the drum (they supersede information printed here)

Wheels and tires

Tire pressures .... See Chapter 1
Minimum tire tread depth .... See Chapter 1
Wheel rim runout limit (lateral and vertical) .... 2 mm (0.08 inch)

Torque specifications

Axle nut
 PW50
  Front .... 40 Nm (29 ft-lbs)
  Rear .... 60 Nm (43 ft-lbs)
 PW80
  Front .... 35 Nm (25 ft-lbs)
  Rear .... 60 Nm (43 ft-lbs)
Brake arm bolt
 PW50
  Front .... 4 Nm (35 in-lbs)
  Rear .... 6 Nm (52 in-lbs)
 PW80 (front and rear) .... 7 Nm (61 in-lbs)
Tension bar nut and bolt (PW80) .... 16 Nm (132 in-lbs)

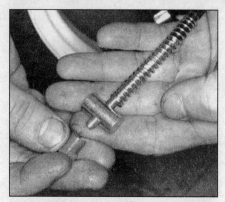

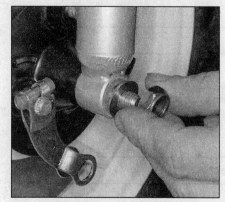

2.2 Unscrew the adjuster, pull out the clevis pin, then put them back on the cable end

2.3a Remove the axle nut and washer (PW50)

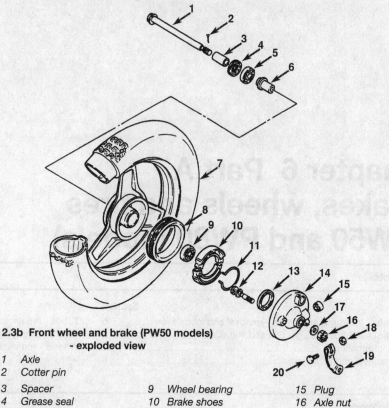

2.3b Front wheel and brake (PW50 models) - exploded view

1	Axle		
2	Cotter pin		
3	Spacer	9	Wheel bearing	15	Plug
4	Grease seal	10	Brake shoes	16	Axle nut
5	Bearing	11	Return spring	17	Washer
6	Spacer	12	Brake cam	18	Brake arm nut
7	Tire, tube and wheel	13	Grease seal	19	Brake arm
8	Sealing ring	14	Brake panel	20	Brake arm bolt

1 General information

PW50 and PW80 models are equipped with mechanical drum brakes on the front and rear wheels. A lever on the right end of the handlebar actuates the front brake. On PW50 models, a lever on the left end of the handlebar actuates the rear brake. On PW80 models, a pedal on the right side of the bike actuates the rear brake. The front brake lever is connected to the front brake by a cable. On PW50 models, the rear brake lever is connected to the rear brake by another cable. On PW80 models, the rear brake pedal is connected to the rear brake assembly by a rod.

PW50 models are equipped with steel wheels. PW80 models are equipped with spoked wheels.

2 Wheels - removal, inspection and installation

Removal

Front wheel

1   Raise the front end by placing the bike on a motorcycle stand, floor jack or milk crate. If you're using a jack, put a board between the jack head and the engine to protect the crankcase. Make sure that the bike is securely propped upright so it can't fall over when the wheel is removed.

PW50 models

Refer to illustrations 2.2, 2.3a, 2.3b and 2.4

2   Unscrew the front brake cable adjuster from the cable at the

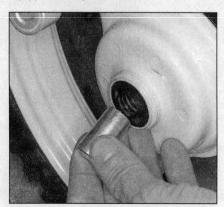

2.4 Don't forget to reinstall the wheel collar

2.6a Remove the cotter pin and axle nut . . .

2.6b . . . and the washer (A); loosen the locknut (B) and the adjuster and disconnect the brake cable (C)

2.7a Pull out the axle . . .

2.7b . . . and remove the collar (left arrow) and bearing cover (right arrow)

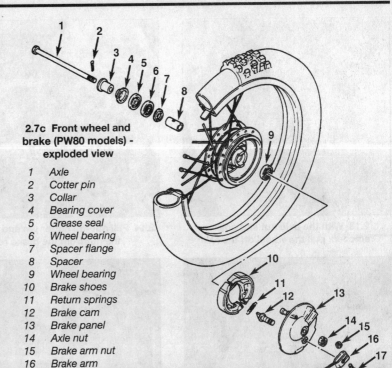

2.7c Front wheel and brake (PW80 models) - exploded view

1. Axle
2. Cotter pin
3. Collar
4. Bearing cover
5. Grease seal
6. Wheel bearing
7. Spacer flange
8. Spacer
9. Wheel bearing
10. Brake shoes
11. Return springs
12. Brake cam
13. Brake panel
14. Axle nut
15. Brake arm nut
16. Brake arm
17. Brake arm bolt

2.11a The PW50 rear axle is secured by a self-locking nut (arrow) and two collars

wheel **(see illustration)**. Disengage the cable from the clevis pin in the brake arm, then push the clevis pin out of the brake arm. Place the clevis pin and adjuster back onto the cable so they won't be lost.

3   Hold the axle with a wrench on the bolt head, then unscrew the axle nut and remove the washer **(see illustrations)**.

4   Remove the wheel spacer from the right side of the wheel **(see illustration)**. Roll the wheel out from between the front forks.

PW80 models

Refer to illustrations 2.6a, 2.6b, 2.7a, 2.7b and 2.7c

5   Disconnect the brake cable from the arm at the front wheel (see Section 5).

6   Remove the cotter pin from the axle nut **(see illustration)**. Hold the axle bolt head with a wrench and unscrew the nut, then remove the reinforcing washer that fits inside the fork leg **(see illustration)**. **Note:** *If the washer is stuck in the fork leg, you don't have to remove it; just make sure it doesn't fall out and get lost.*

7   Support the wheel and pull out the axle, then remove the seal collar and cover **(see illustrations)**. Note the sequence in which the spacers and bushings are installed **(see illustration)**. Remove the wheel.

Rear wheel

8   Raise the rear end by placing the bike on a motorcycle stand, floor jack or milk crate. If you're using a jack, put a board between the jack head and the engine to protect the crankcase. Make sure that the bike is securely propped upright so it can't fall over when the wheel is removed.

PW50 models

Refer to illustrations 2.11a, 2.11b and 2.13

9   Disconnect the right rear shock absorber from the right rear arm (see Chapter 5).

10   Remove the muffler (see Chapter 3).

11   Remove the rear axle nut **(see illustrations)**.

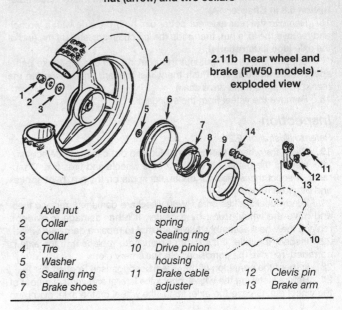

2.11b Rear wheel and brake (PW50 models) - exploded view

1	Axle nut	8	Return spring
2	Collar	9	Sealing ring
3	Collar	10	Drive pinion housing
4	Tire	11	Brake cable adjuster
5	Washer	12	Clevis pin
6	Sealing ring	13	Brake arm
7	Brake shoes		

2.13 With the axle nut and collars removed, pull the wheel off the axle

2.14 Pull out the cotter pin and unscrew the nut from the brake rod

2.16a Pull out the cotter pin and hold the axle with a wrench . . .

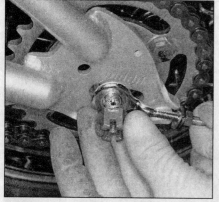

2.16b . . . unscrew the axle nut and remove the chain adjuster

2.17 Pull out the axle and remove the spacer (arrow)

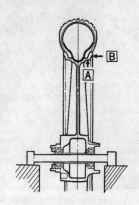

2.24 Check the wheel for out-of-round (A) and lateral movement (B)

12   Remove the right rear arm (see Chapter 5).
13   Pull the rear wheel and brake drum off the axle **(see illustration)**.

PW80 models

Refer to illustrations 2.14, 2.16a, 2.16b and 2.17
14   Remove the cotter pin and unscrew the tension bar nut from the brake panel **(see illustration)**.
15   Remove the rear brake adjuster nut from the brake rod, pull the rod out of the clevis pin and remove the spring from the rod **(see illustration 5.8 in Chapter 1A)**.
16   Remove the rear axle nut cotter pin, hold the axle with a wrench and remove the axle nut, then slide the left chain adjuster off the end of the axle **(see illustrations)**.
17   Support the wheel, pull out the axle and remove the brake panel spacer **(see illustration)**. Push the wheel forward and disengage the rear sprocket from the drive chain.
18   Remove the wheel from the swingarm.

Inspection

Refer to illustration 2.24
19   Clean the wheels thoroughly. (Mud and dirt can mask defects.)
20   Inspect the general condition of the wheels and tires (see Chapter 1). Inspect the wheels for dents, flat spots on the rim, bent spokes and other damage.
21   If individual spokes on a PW80 wheel are damaged, replace them and have the wheel trued by a dealer. If other damage is evident, replace the wheel assembly. Never attempt to repair a damaged wheel.
22   Inspect the axle. If it's bent or damaged, replace it. If the axle is corroded, remove the corrosion with fine emery cloth.
23   Inspect the condition of the wheel bearings (see Section 4).
24   Before installing the wheel, check the lateral and vertical runout of the wheel rim. Grease the axle, install the wheel on the axle, clamp up

the axle in an old swingarm or install the wheel in the swingarm and check the rim runout with a dial indicator **(see illustration)**. If the axle exceeds the maximum allowable runout limit listed in this Chapter's Specifications, it must be replaced.

Installation

25   Installation is the reverse of removal, with the following additions:
a) *Lubricate the axle and the oil seal lips with lithium soap base grease or with moly-base grease.*
b) *If you're installing the front wheel, make sure the fork locator fits into the slot in the brake panel (see illustration 3.13a or 3.13b in Chapter 5A).*
c) *If you're installing the front wheel, lubricate the barrel-shaped plug at the end of the front brake cable with multi-purpose grease before reconnecting it to the brake cam lever.*
d) *If you're installing the rear wheel on a PW80 model, make sure that the slots in the rear wheel damper are correctly engaged with the rear sprocket wheel.*
e) *Tighten the axle nut to the torque listed in this Chapter's Specifications.*
f) *Adjust the brake (see Chapter 1).*

3   Brake shoes - removal, inspection and installation

Warning: *The dust created by the brake system may contain asbestos, which is harmful to your health (Yamaha hasn't used asbestos in brake parts for a number of years, but aftermarket parts may contain it). Never blow it out with compressed air and don't inhale any of it. An approved filtering mask should be worn when working on the brakes.*

3.2 Pull the brake panel out of the wheel

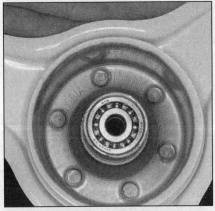

3.3 The maximum drum diameter is cast into the drum (PW50 shown)

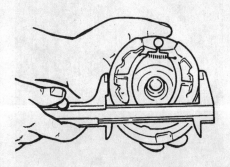

3.5 Measure the outside diameter of the brake shoes with a vernier caliper

3.6a Spread the shoes apart and pull them off the brake panel (PW50)

3.6b Spread the shoes apart and fold them into a V to release the spring tension (PW80)

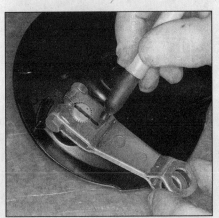

3.9 Look for alignment marks on the brake arm and cam (arrows); make your own mark, aligned with the slit in the brake cam, if you can't see any

PW50 front brake; PW80 front and rear brakes

Removal

Refer to illustration 3.2

1   Remove the wheel (see Section 2).

2   Take the brake panel out of the wheel together with the brake shoes (see illustration).

Inspection

Refer to illustrations 3.3, 3.5, 3.6a, 3.6b, 3.9 and 3.10

3   Inspect the brake drum for wear or damage. Measure the diameter at several points with a drum micrometer (or have this done by a Yamaha dealer or a qualified repair shop). If the measurements are uneven (indicating that the drum is out-of-round) or if there are scratches deep enough to snag a fingernail, replace the drum. The drum must also be replaced if the diameter is greater than the specified limit, which is cast inside the drum (see illustration). Do not try to resurface the brake drum.

4   Inspect the brake shoe linings for wear, damage and signs of contamination from road dirt or water. If the linings are damaged, replace them.

5   Measure the outside diameter of the brake shoes (see illustration) and compare your measurement with the value listed in the Chapter 1 Specifications. If the brake shoe outside diameter is at the limit, or less, replace the brake shoes.

6   To remove the shoes, spread them apart to clear the brake cam and anchor pin, then fold them toward each other slightly to release spring tension (see illustrations).

7   Inspect the ends of the shoes where they contact the brake cam

3.10 Pull the brake cam out of the brake panel

and anchor pin. Replace the shoes if there's visible wear.

8   Inspect the brake cam and anchor pin for wear and damage. If the brake cam is worn or damaged, it can be replaced separately. If the anchor pin is worn or damaged, replace the brake panel.

9   Look for alignment marks on the brake cam lever and brake cam (see illustration). If there are no alignment marks, make your own.

10   Remove the pinch bolt and nut and pull the brake cam lever off the brake cam (see illustration).

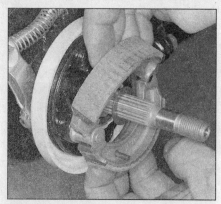

3.17a Spread the shoes apart and pull them off the return spring (PW50)

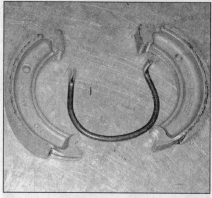

3.17b PW50 brakes use a horseshoe-shaped return spring

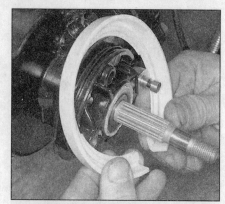

3.18 Remove the sealing ring

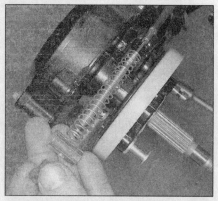

3.19 Unscrew the adjuster, pull the cable out of the clevis pin, separate the clevis pin from the brake arm, then put them back on the cable

3.20a If you don't see alignment marks on the brake arm and cam, make your own (arm and cam removed for clarity)

3.20b Remove the brake arm bolt (arrow) and slide the brake arm off the cam

Installation

11   Apply high-temperature brake grease to the brake cam, the anchor pin and the ends of the springs.
12   Install the cam through the dust seal. Align the slot in the brake cam with the projection on the wear indicator.
13   Install the brake cam lever on the cam. Make sure the punch marks are aligned. Tighten the nut and bolt to the torque listed in this Chapter's Specifications.
14   Install the brake shoes and return spring(s). Make sure the ends of the shoes fit correctly on the cam and the anchor pin.
15   The remainder of installation is the reverse of the removal steps.

3.21 The assembled PW50 rear brakes should look like this

PW50 rear brake

Refer to illustrations 3.17a, 3.17b, 3.18, 3.19, 3.20a, 3.20b and 3.21
16   Remove the wheel from the rear axle (see Section 2).
17   Inspect the shoes and remove them if necessary as described in Steps 3 through 8 above **(see illustrations)**.
18   Remove the sealing ring from the ring gear housing **(see illustration)**.
19   If you need to remove the brake cam, unscrew the adjusting nut from the end of the brake cable. Push the clevis pin out of the brake arm, then put the clevis pin and adjusting nut back on the end of the cable so they won't be lost **(see illustration)**.
20   Look for alignment marks on the brake arm and cam and make your own if you can't see any **(see illustration)**. Remove the brake arm pinch bolt and take the brake arm off the cam **(see illustration)**. Remove the cam from the brake panel.
21   Installation is the reverse of the removal Steps. Install the return spring on the inner side of the brake shoes and position its ends in the shoes **(see illustration)**.

---

4   Wheel bearing replacement

Refer to illustrations 4.4a through 4.4e and 4.7
1   Remove the wheel (see Section 2).
2   Remove any spacers or collars (see Section 2).
3   Pry the seals out of the wheel with a screwdriver. Put a shop rag between the screwdriver shaft and the wheel hub to protect the inner edge of the hub.
4   A common method of removing wheel bearings is to insert a metal rod (preferably a brass drift punch) through the center of one hub

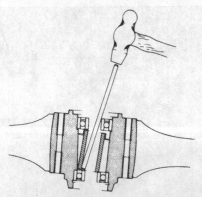

4.4a If there's room enough to tilt a metal rod so it will catch the bearing inner races, drive the bearings from the hub with a metal rod and hammer

4.4b The removal tool consists of a remover head (right) and wedged shaft (left) . . .

4.4c . . . tap the slit end of the remover head into the bearing . . .

4.4d . . . then insert the wedge through the hub into the remover head slit . . .

4.4e . . . and tap on the shaft to lock the remover head and drive the bearing out of the hub

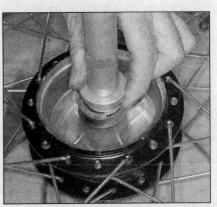

4.7 Use a bearing driver, shown here, or a socket the same diameter as the bearing outer race to tap a new bearing into the hub

bearing and tap evenly around the inner race of the opposite bearing to drive it from the hub **(see illustration)**. The bearing spacer will also come out. However, there may not be enough room to tilt the rod enough to catch the edge of the opposite bearing's inner race. In this case, use a bearing remover tool consisting of a shaft and remover head **(see illustration)**. The head fits inside the bearing **(see illustration)**, then the wedge end of the shaft is tapped into the groove in the head to expand the head and lock it inside the bearing. Once this occurs, tapping some more on the shaft will force the bearing out of

the hub **(see illustrations)**. **Note:** *Once the bearings have been removed, they must be replaced with new ones since they're almost certain to be damaged during removal.*

5   Turn the wheel over and remove the opposite bearing in the same manner.

6   If you're installing new bearings that aren't sealed on both sides, pack the open side with grease.

7   Using a socket slightly smaller in diameter than the outside diameter of the new bearing, tap a new bearing into the hub **(see illustration)**. Turn the wheel over, install the spacer and install the other bearing.

8   Tap the new seal into the hub with a seal driver or with a socket the same diameter as the seal.

9   Install the wheel (see Section 2).

5   Brake cable, lever, rod and pedal - removal and installation

Brake cable(s)

Refer to illustrations 5.3, 5.4, 5.5 and 5.6

1   If you're working on a PW50, unscrew the brake cable adjuster from the cable at the wheel **(see illustration 2.2, front brake or 3.20, rear brake)**.

2   If you're working on a PW80, loosen the brake cable adjuster at the brake arm and disengage the cable end plug from the arm **(see illustration 2.6b)**.

3   Trace the cable up to the handlebar and detach it from any clips or brackets **(see illustration)**.

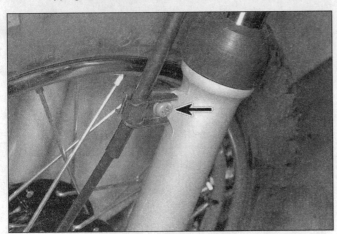

5.3 This clip (arrow) secures the PW80 front brake cable to the fork

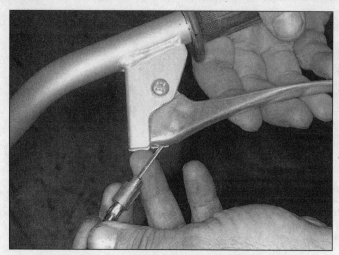

5.4 Disengage the cable housing from the lever bracket,
then rotate the cable out of the bracket and lever
(PW50 rear brake cable shown)

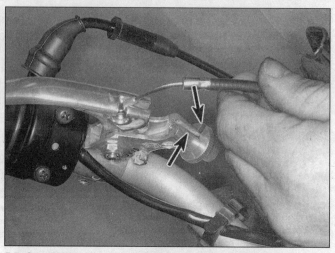

5.5 On a PW80, align the slots in the adjuster locknut (right arrow)
and adjuster (left arrow) with the lever and bracket slots,
then rotate the cable out

4   If you're working on a PW50, slide the cable housing out of the lever bracket. Rotate the cable out of the slots in the lever bracket and lever, then lower its end plug out of the lever **(see illustration)**.

5   If you're working on a PW80, loosen the handlebar adjuster all the way. Line up the slots in the adjuster and lever bracket, then rotate the cable and slip its end plug out of the lever **(see illustration)**.

6   To remove the lever, unscrew the locknut from the pivot screw or bolt and remove the pivot screw or bolt **(see illustration)**.

7   The PW50's front brake lever bracket is part of the throttle housing and its rear brake lever bracket is welded to the handlebar.

8   To remove the PW80 brake lever bracket, remove the throttle twistgrip and housing (see Chapter 3). Loosen the lever bracket clamp bolt and slide the bracket off the end of the handlebar.

9   Installation is the reverse of removal, with the following additions:

 a) Apply multi-purpose grease to the cable end plugs.
 b) Adjust the brake (see Section 5 in Chapter 1A).

Rear brake rod and pedal (PW80 models)

Refer to illustration 5.11

10   Remove the rear brake adjuster nut from the brake rod, pull the rod out of its clevis, remove the clevis from the brake cam lever and remove the spring from the rod **(see illustration 5.8 in Chapter 1)**

11   Unhook the brake pedal return spring **(see illustration)**.

12   Remove the pedal circlip and remove the pedal.

13   Remove the cotter pin and detach the rod from the pedal.

14   Installation is the reverse of removal, with the following additions:

 a) Lubricate the rod end fittings and pedal shaft with multi-purpose grease.
 b) Adjust brake pedal freeplay (see Section 5 in Chapter 1A).

6   Tires - removal and installation

1   To properly remove and install tires, you will need at least two motorcycle tire irons, some water, some talcum powder and a tire pressure gauge.

2   Begin by removing the wheel from the motorcycle. If the tire is going to be re-used, mark it next to the valve stem, wheel balance weight or rim lock.

3   Deflate the tire by removing the valve stem core. When it is fully deflated, push the bead of the tire away from the rim on both sides. In some extreme cases, this can only be accomplished with a bead-breaking tool, but most often it can be carried out with tire irons. Riding on a deflated tire to break the bead is not recommended, as damage to the rim and tire will occur.

4   Removing a tire is easier when the tire is warm, so an indoor tire change is recommended in cold climates. The rubber gets very stiff and is difficult to manipulate when cold.

5.6 Remove the lever pivot locknut (lower arrow)
and pivot screw or bolt (upper arrow)

5.11 Unhook the PW80 pedal spring (upper arrow)
and remove the circlip and washer (lower arrow)

TIRE CHANGING SEQUENCE - TUBED TIRES

 A Deflate tire. After pushing tire beads away from rim flanges push tire bead into well of rim at point opposite valve. Insert tire lever next to valve and work bead over edge of rim.

 B Use two levers to work bead over edge of rim. Note use of rim protectors

 C Remove inner tube from tire

D When first bead is clear, remove tire as shown

 E To install, partially inflate inner tube and insert in tire

F Work first bead over rim and feed valve through hole in rim. Partially screw on retaining nut to hold valve in place.

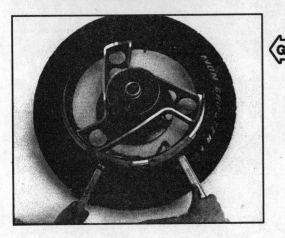

 G Check that inner tube is positioned correctly and work second bead over rim using tire levers. Start at a point opposite valve.

H Work final area of bead over rim while pushing valve inwards to ensure that inner tube is not trapped.

5   Place the wheel on a thick pad or old blanket. This will help keep the wheel and tire from slipping around.

6   Once the bead is completely free of the rim, lubricate the inside edge of the rim and the tire bead with a solution of water only. Honda recommends against the use of soap or other tire mounting lubricants, as the tire may shift on the rim. Remove the locknut and push the tire valve through the rim.

7   Insert one of the tire irons under the bead of the tire at the valve stem and lift the bead up over the rim. This should be fairly easy. Take care not to pinch the tube as this is done. If it is difficult to pry the bead up, make sure that the rest of the bead opposite the valve stem is in the dropped center section of the rim.

8   Hold the tire iron down with the bead over the rim, then move about 1 or 2 inches to either side and insert the second tire iron. Be careful not to cut or slice the bead or the tire may split when inflated. Also, take care not to catch or pinch the inner tube as the second tire iron is levered over. For this reason, tire irons are recommended over screwdrivers or other implements.

9   With a small section of the bead up over the rim, one of the levers can be removed and reinserted 1 or 2 inches farther around the rim until about 1/4 of the tire bead is above the rim edge. Make sure that the rest of the bead is in the dropped center of the rim. At this point, the bead can usually be pulled up over the rim by hand.

10   Once the entire first bead is over the rim, the inner tube can be withdrawn from the tire and rim. Push in on the valve stem, lift up on the tire next to the stem, reach inside the tire and carefully pull out the tube. It is usually not necessary to completely remove the tire from the rim to repair the inner tube. It is sometimes recommended though, because checking for foreign objects in the tire is difficult while it is still mounted on the rim.

11   To remove the tire completely, make sure the bead is broken all the way around on the remaining edge, then stand the tire and wheel up on the tread and grab the wheel with one hand. Push the tire down over the same edge of the rim while pulling the rim away from the tire. If the bead is correctly positioned in the dropped center of the rim, the tire should roll off and separate from the rim very easily. If tire irons are used to work this last bead over the rim, the outer edge of the rim may be marred. If a tire iron is necessary, be sure to pad the rim as described earlier.

12   Refer to Section 7 for inner tube repair procedures.

13   Mounting a tire is basically the reverse of removal. Some tires have a balance mark and/or directional arrows molded into the tire sidewall. Look for these marks so that the tire can be installed properly. The dot should be aligned with the valve stem.

14   If the tire was not removed completely to repair or replace the inner tube, the tube should be inflated just enough to make it round. Carefully lift up the tire edge and install the tube with the valve stem next to the hole in the rim. Once the tube is in place, push the valve stem through the rim and start the locknut on the stem.

15   Lubricate the tire bead, then push it over the rim edge and into the dropped center section opposite the inner tube valve stem. Work around each side of the rim, carefully pushing the bead over the rim. The last section may have to be levered on with tire irons. If so, take care not to pinch the inner tube as this is done.

16   Once the bead is over the rim edge, check to see that the inner tube valve stem and the rim lock are pointing to the center of the hub. If they're angled slightly in either direction, rotate the tire on the rim to straighten it out. Run the locknut the rest of the way onto the stem and rim lock but don't tighten them completely.

17   Inflate the tube to 1-1/2 times the pressure listed in the Chapter 1 Specifications. **Warning:** *Do not overinflate the tube or the tire may burst, causing serious injury.* Check to make sure the guidelines on the tire sidewalls are the same distance from the rim around the circumference of the tire.

18   After the tire bead is correctly seated on the rim, allow the tire to deflate. Replace the valve core and inflate the tube to the recommended pressure, then tighten the valve stem locknut securely and tighten the cap.

7   Tubes - repair

1   Tire tube repair requires a patching kit that's usually available from motorcycle dealers, accessory stores or auto parts stores. Be sure to follow the directions supplied with the kit to ensure a safe repair. Patching should be done only when a new tube is unavailable. Replace the tube as soon as possible. Sudden deflation can cause loss of control and an accident.

2   To repair a tube, remove it from the tire, inflate and immerse it in a sink or tub full of water to pinpoint the leak. Mark the position of the leak, then deflate the tube. Dry it off and thoroughly clean the area around the puncture.

3   Most tire patching kits have a buffer to rough up the area around the hole for proper adhesion of the patch. Roughen an area slightly larger than the patch, then apply a thin coat of the patching cement to the roughened area. Allow the cement to dry until tacky, then apply the patch.

4   It may be necessary to remove a protective covering from the top surface of the patch after it has been attached to the tube. Keep in mind that tubes made from synthetic rubber may require a special patch and adhesive if a satisfactory bond is to be achieved.

5   Before replacing the tube, check the inside of the tire to make sure the object that caused the puncture is not still inside. Also check the outside of the tire, particularly the tread area, to make sure nothing is projecting through the tire that may cause another puncture. Check the rim for sharp edges or damage. Make sure the rubber trim band is in good condition and properly installed before inserting the tube.

Chapter 6 Part B
Brakes, wheels and tires
(RT100 and RT180 models)

Contents

Specifications

Brakes

Front brake shoe lining limit (RT100)	See Chapter 1
Front brake pad lining thickness limit (RT180)	See Chapter 1
Rear brake shoe lining limit	See Chapter 1
Front brake lever freeplay	See Chapter 1
Rear brake pedal freeplay	See Chapter 1
Rear brake pedal height (RT180)	See Chapter 1
Drum inside diameter wear limit*	
RT100 (front and rear drums)	111 mm (4.37 inches)
RT180 (rear drum)	131 mm (5.16 inches)
Brake disc wear limit (RT180)	3.5 mm (0.14 inch)

*Refer to marks cast into the drum (they supersede information printed here)

Wheels and tires

Tire pressures	See Chapter 1
Tire tread depth	See Chapter 1
Wheel rim runout limit (lateral and vertical)	2 mm (0.08 inch)

Torque specifications

Axle nut	
RT100	
Front	43 Nm (31 ft-lbs)
Rear	39 Nm (28 ft-lbs)
RT180 (front and rear)	85 Nm (61 ft-lbs)
Caliper (RT180)	
Brake hose-to-caliper banjo bolt	27 Nm (19 ft-lbs)
Caliper body retaining bolt	18 Nm (156 in-lbs)
Caliper bracket-to-outer fork tube bolts	35 Nm (25 ft-lbs)
Disc retaining bolts (RT180)	20 Nm (168 in-lbs)
Master cylinder (RT180)	
Brake hose-to-master cylinder banjo bolt	27 Nm (19 ft-lbs)
Master cylinder-to-handlebar clamp bolts	9 Nm (78 in-lbs)

2.2a Unscrew the wing nut (left arrow) from the brake cable, pull the cable housing out of the bracket (right arrow) . . .

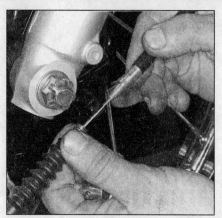

2.2b . . . slip the cable sideways to clear the bracket . . .

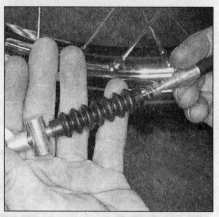

2.2c . . . remove the end plug from the brake cam lever, then put the parts back on the cable so they won't be lost

1   General information

RT100 models are equipped with mechanical drum brakes on the front and rear wheels. A lever on the right handlebar actuates the front brake. A pedal on the right side of the vehicle actuates the rear brake. The lever is connected to the front brake assembly by a cable; the pedal is connected to the rear brake assembly by a rod. RT180 models are equipped with a hydraulic disc brake on the front wheel and a mechanical drum brake at the rear wheel.

All models are equipped with spoked steel wheels. **Caution:** *Brake components rarely require disassembly. Do not disassemble the brakes unless absolutely necessary.*

2   Wheels - inspection, removal and installation

Removal

Front wheel

Refer to illustrations 2.2a, 2.2b, 2.2c, 2.2d, 2.3a, 2.3b, 2.4, 2.5a and 2.5b

1   Raise the front end by placing the bike on a motorcycle stand, floor jack or milk crate. If you're using a jack, put a board between the jack head and the engine to protect the crankcase. Make sure that the bike is securely propped upright so it can't fall over when the wheel is removed.

2   On RT100 models, loosen the brake cable adjuster at the brake cam lever and disengage the cable end plug from the lever **(see illustrations)**.

2.2d Pull the cable out of the guide

3   Remove the cotter pin from the axle. Hold the axle bolt head with a wrench, unscrew the axle nut and remove the washer **(see illustrations)**.

4   Support the wheel, pull out the axle and remove the spacer collar from between the fork leg and the wheel **(see illustration)**. Take the wheel out from between the fork legs. **Note:** *On RT180 models, do NOT squeeze the front brake lever while the wheel is removed, or the caliper piston will force the brake pads closer together, making it impossible to fit the brake disc between the pads when installing the wheel.*

2.3a Remove the cotter pin, hold the axle bolt on the other side with a wrench . . .

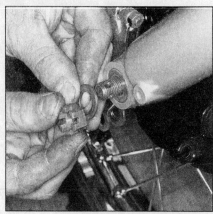

2.3b . . . unscrew the axle nut and remove the washer

2.4 Remove the axle bolt and the reinforcing washer (there's one on each fork leg)

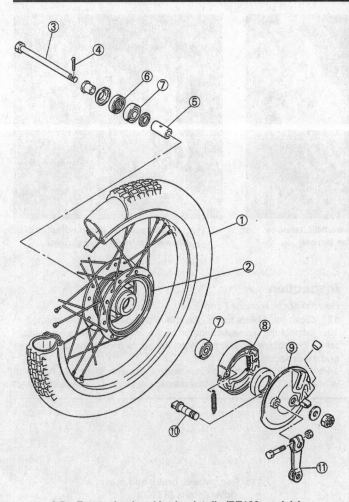

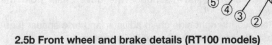

2.5b Front wheel and brake details (RT100 models)

1	Axle bolt	8	Wheel bearing
2	Collar	9	Speedometer gearbox
3	Dust cover		unit
4	Oil seal	10	Oil seal
5	Wheel bearing	11	Front wheel
6	Flanged spacer	12	Cotter pin
7	Bearing spacer		

2.5a Front wheel and brake details (RT100 models)

1	Front wheel	7	Wheel bearing
2	Hub and brake drum	8	Brake shoes
3	Front axle bolt	9	Brake panel
4	Cotter pin	10	Brake cam shaft
5	Bearing spacer	11	Brake cam lever
6	Oil seal		

5   Note the sequence in which the speedometer gearbox (models with a speedometer) and any spacer/collars are installed, and then remove them from the wheel **(see illustrations)**.

Rear wheel

Refer to illustrations 2.7, 2.8a, 2.8b, 2.9, 2.11a, 2.11b and 2.11c

6   Raise the rear end by placing the bike on a motorcycle stand, floor jack or milk crate. If you're using a jack, put a board between the jack head and the engine to protect the crankcase. Make sure that the bike is securely propped upright so it can't fall over when the wheel is removed.

7   On RT100 models, remove the cotter pin from the rear end of the tension bar, remove the tension bar-to-brake shoe plate nut **(see illustration)** and detach the tensioner bar from the brake shoe plate.

8   Remove the rear brake adjuster nut from the brake rod, pull the rod out of the clevis pin and remove the spring from the rod **(see illustrations)**.

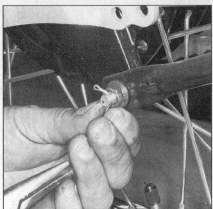

2.7 Remove the cotter pin, unscrew the nut and slip the tension bar off the stud

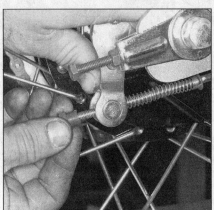

2.8a Unscrew the brake adjuster nut from the brake rod, pull the rod out of the clevis pin . . .

2.8b . . . push the clevis pin out of the brake cam lever and put the parts back on the brake rod so they won't be lost

2.9 Remove the cotter pin, unscrew the axle nut (left arrow) and on RT100 models, unscrew the coupling nut (right arrow)

2.10 Pull out the axle bolt, remove the spacer collar (arrow) . . .

2.11a . . . and pull the chain adjuster off the swingarm (RT100 shown)

9   Remove the axle cotter pin (if equipped) **(see illustration)**. Hold the axle with a wrench and remove the axle nut. If you're working on an RT100, remove the cush drive spacer nut.

10   Support the wheel and pull out the axle **(see illustration)**. Push the wheel forward and disengage the drive chain from the rear sprocket.

11   Remove the right side chain adjuster and axle spacer **(see illustrations)**. Remove the wheel from the swingarm.

Inspection

Refer to illustrations 2.17 and 2.18

12   Clean the wheels thoroughly. (Mud and dirt can mask defects.)

13   Inspect the general condition of the wheels and tires (see Chapter 1). Inspect the wheels for dents, flat spots on the rim, bent spokes and other damage.

14   If individual spokes are damaged, replace them and have the wheel trued by a dealer. If other damage is evident, replace the wheel

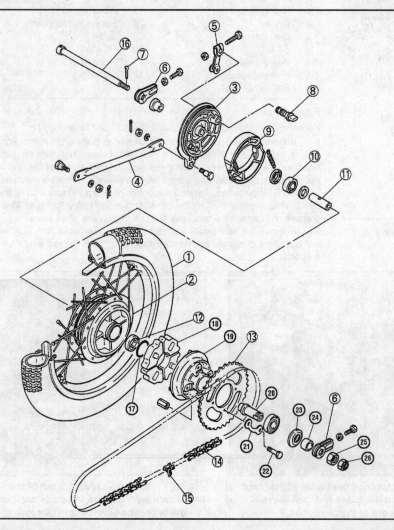

2.11b Rear wheel, brake and cush drive details (RT100)

1   Rear wheel
2   Hub and brake drum
3   Brake panel
4   Tension bar
5   Brake cam lever
6   Drive chain adjuster
7   Cotter pin
8   Brake cam shaft
9   Brake shoes
10   Wheel bearing
11   Bearing spacer
12   Wheel bearing
13   Driven sprocket
14   Drive chain
15   Master link
16   Axle bolt
17   Coupling O-ring
18   Cush drive dampers
19   S[rocket hub
20   Coupling shaft
21   Sprocket lockwasher
22   Sprocket bolt
23   Coupling oil seal
24   Coupling collar
25   Coupling shaft nut
26   Axle nut

2.11c Rear wheel and brake details (RT100)

1　Drive chain adjuster
2　Collar
3　Brake cam lever
4　Wear indicator
5　Brake panel
6　Brake cam shaft
7　Brake shoes
8　Seal
9　Wheel bearing
10　Bearing spacer
11　Collar
12　Wheel bearing
13　Seal
14　Collar
15　Drive chain
16　Driven sprocket
17　Hub and brake drum
18　Rear wheel
19　Washer
20　Axle nut

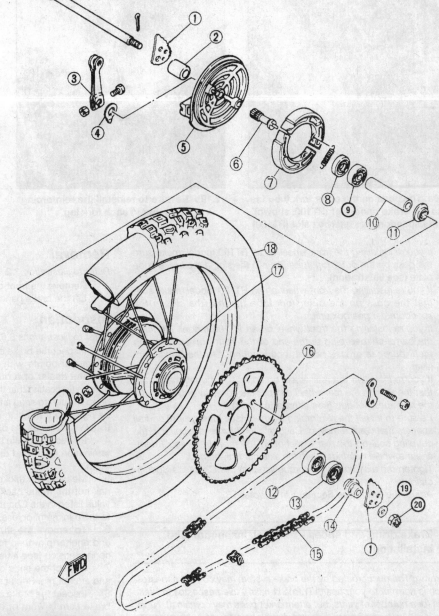

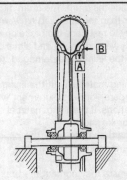

2.17 Check the wheel for out-of-round (A) and lateral runout (B)

2.18 Be sure the slots in the cush drive dampers align with the coupling tabs

assembly. Never attempt to repair a damaged wheel.

15　Inspect the axle. If it's bent or damaged, replace it. If the axle is corroded, remove the corrosion with fine emery cloth.

16　Inspect the condition of the wheel bearings (see Section 9).

17　Before installing the wheel, check the lateral and vertical runout of the wheel rim. Grease the axle, install the wheel on the axle, clamp up the axle in an old swingarm or install the wheel in the swingarm and check the rim runout with a dial indicator **(see illustration)**. If the axle exceeds the maximum allowable runout limit listed in this Chapter's Specifications, it must be replaced.

18　If you're working on an RT100, lift the socket hub out of the wheel and inspect the cush drive dampers **(see illustration)**. If any of the segments are worn, crushed or deteriorated, replace them all as a set.

Installation

Refer to illustrations 2.19a and 2.19b

19　Installation is the reverse of removal, with the following additions:

a) Lubricate the axle and the oil seal lips with multi-purpose lithium grease or with moly-base grease.

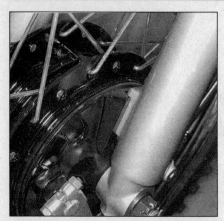

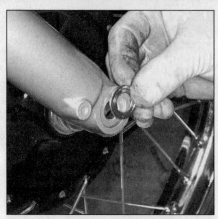

2.19a The boss on the outer fork tube fits into the brake panel slot (RT100, shown) or the speedometer gearbox slot (RT180)

2.19b Be sure to reinstall the reinforcing washer in each fork leg

3.2 Lift the brake panel out of the drum

b) *If you're installing the front wheel on an RT100 model, make sure the boss on the outer fork tube fits into the slot in the brake shoe plate* **(see illustration)**.

c) *If you're installing the front wheel on an RT180 model, make sure that the boss on the outer fork tube fits into the slot in the speedometer gearbox unit.*

d) *If you're installing the front wheel on an RT100 model, lubricate the barrel-shaped plug at the end of the front brake cable with multi-purpose grease before reconnecting it to the brake cam lever.*

e) *If you're installing the rear wheel on an RT100 model, make sure that the slots in the rear wheel damper are correctly engaged with the rear sprocket hub* **(see illustration 2.18)**.

f) *Be sure to install the reinforcing washers* **(see illustration)** *and all spacers that were removed. Caution: Don't forget the collar in the coupling seal on the rear wheel of RT100 models, or you'll damage the wheel bearings when the axle nut is tightened.*

g) *Tighten the axle nut to the torque listed in this Chapter's Specifications.*

h) *Adjust the brake (see Section 5 in Chapter 1B).*

---

3   Brake drum and shoes - removal, inspection and installation

Warning: *The dust created by the brake system may contain asbestos, which is harmful to your health (Yamaha hasn't used asbestos in brake parts for a number of years, but aftermarket parts may contain it). Never blow it out with compressed air and don't inhale any of it. An approved filtering mask should be worn when working on the brakes.*

Removal

Refer to illustration 3.2

1   Remove the front or rear wheel (see Section 2).

2   Lift the brake panel out of the wheel **(see illustration)**.

Inspection

Refer to illustrations 3.6, 3.8, 3.9, 3.10a and 3.10b

3   Inspect the brake drum for wear or damage. Measure the diameter at several points with a drum micrometer (or have this done by a Yamaha dealer or a qualified repair shop). If the measurements are uneven (indicating that the drum is out-of-round) or if there are scratches deep enough to snag a fingernail, replace the drum. The drum must also be replaced if the diameter is greater than the specified limit, which is usually cast inside the drum. Do not try to resurface the brake drum.

4   Inspect the brake shoe linings for wear, damage and signs of contamination from road dirt or water. If the linings are damaged, replace them.

5   Measure the thickness of the lining material (just the lining material, not the metal backing) and compare your measurement with the value listed in the Chapter 1 Specifications. If the lining material is worn to the minimum, or less, replace the brake shoes.

6   To remove the shoes, spread them apart to clear the brake cam and anchor pin, then fold them toward each other slightly to release spring tension **(see illustration)**.

7   Inspect the ends of the shoes where they contact the brake cam and anchor pin. Replace the shoes if there's visible wear.

8   Inspect the brake cam and anchor pin for wear and damage. If the brake cam is worn or damaged, it can be replaced separately. If the anchor pin is worn or damaged, replace the brake panel. Inspect the brake panel seal (if equipped) and replace it if it's worn or damaged

3.6 Spread the shoes apart and fold them into a V to release the spring tension

3.8 Inspect the brake panel seal

3.9 Make alignment marks on the brake cam lever and cam if you can't see any

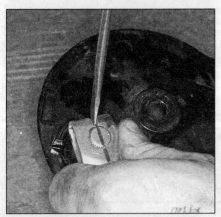

3.10a Remove the pinch bolt and nut, spread the lever and take it off the cam shaft . . .

3.10b . . . and twist and pull the cam shaft out of the brake panel

3.15 The assembled brakes should look like this

(see illustration).

9   Look for alignment marks on the brake cam lever and brake cam. If there are no alignment marks, make your own **(see illustration).**

10   Remove the pinch bolt and nut and pull the brake cam lever off the brake cam **(see illustration)**, then pull the cam out of the brake panel **(see illustration).**

11   If you're servicing the rear brake on an RT180 model, remove the wear indicator. Pull the brake cam out of the brake panel.

Installation

Refer to illustration 3.15

12   Apply high-temperature brake grease to the brake cam, the anchor pin and the ends of the springs.

13   Install the cam through the dust seal. If you're servicing the rear brake on an RT180 model, install the wear indicator. Align the slot in the brake cam with the projection on the wear indicator.

14   Install the brake cam lever on the cam. Make sure the alignment marks are aligned. If you're working on an RT100, there should be 73 mm (2-7/8 inch) between the center of the cable hook on the brake cam lever and the nearest edge of the cable housing bracket on the brake panel. Tighten the nut and bolt to the torque listed in this Chapter's Specifications.

15   Hook the ends of the springs to the shoes. Position the shoes in a V on the brake panel, and then fold them down into position **(see illustration 3.6)**. Make sure the ends of the shoes fit correctly on the cam and the anchor pin **(see illustration).**

16   The remainder of installation is the reverse of the removal steps.

4   Brake pads (RT180 models) - replacement

Refer to illustration 4.1

1   Remove the caliper body retaining bolt **(see illustration)**, pivot the caliper in a counterclockwise direction to expose the brake pads and support it so the hose won't be strained. (It's not necessary to disconnect the brake hose to change the brake pads.)

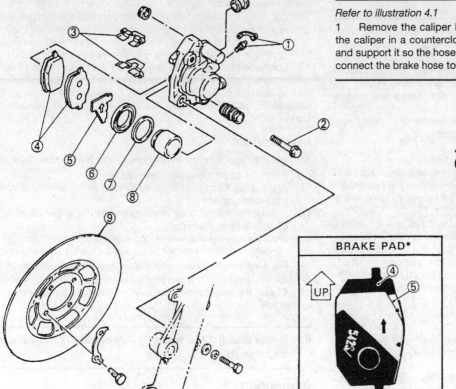

4.1 Front brake caliper and disc (RT180 models) - exploded view

1   *Bleed valve and cap*
2   *Caliper mounting bolt*
3   *Pad springs*
4   *Brake pads*
5   *Pad shim*
6   *Dust seal*
7   *Piston seal*
8   *Piston*
9   *Brake disc*

BRAKE PAD*
UP

2   Remove the pads. Remove the shim from the pad that's adjacent to the caliper piston.

3   Note exactly how the pad springs are installed, then remove them.

4   Note whether either of the brake pads is worn down to the wear indicator (see Chapter 1B). If either of the pads is worn down to the indicator, replace the pads as a set. (If you're replacing the brake pads, replace the pad springs too.)

5   Inspect the condition of the caliper (see Section 5). If the caliper piston seal is leaking, overhaul the caliper.

6   Inspect the condition of the brake disc (see Section 6). If it must be machined or replaced, remove it (see Section 6). If it's okay, deglaze it with sandpaper or emery cloth, using a swirling motion.

7   Install the shim on the pad that goes next to the piston. The arrow on the shim must face up **(see illustration 4.1)**.

8   Remove the cover from the master cylinder reservoir (see Section 7) and siphon out some fluid. Push the piston into the caliper as far as it will go, while keeping an eye on the master cylinder reservoir to ensure that it doesn't overflow. If you can't depress the piston with thumb pressure, try using a C-clamp. If the piston sticks, remove the caliper and overhaul it (see Section 5).

9   Install the pad springs. Make sure that they're installed correctly.

10   Install the brake pads. Make sure that that the rounded edges of the pads face to the rear **(see illustration 4.1)** and that the arrow on the pad shim faces up.

11   Lubricate the caliper body retaining bolt with multi-purpose lithium grease or silicone grease. Swing the caliper back into position, install the caliper body retaining bolt and tighten it to the torque listed in this Chapter's Specifications.

12   Operate the brake lever or pedal several times to bring the pads into contact with the disc.

13   Check the brake fluid level in the master cylinder and add fluid as necessary (see Chapter 1B).

14   Check the operation of the brake carefully before riding the motorcycle.

---

5   Brake caliper (RT180 models) - removal, overhaul and installation

Warning: *When a caliper is overhauled, all old brake fluid must be flushed from the system. Also, the dust created by the brake system may contain asbestos, which is harmful to your health. Don't blow out asbestos dust with compressed air and don't inhale it. An approved filtering mask should be worn when working on the brakes. Do not use petroleum-based solvents to clean brake parts. Use brake system cleaner or denatured alcohol.*

Note: *If you are removing the caliper only to remove the front or rear wheel, don't disconnect the hose from the caliper.*

Removal

1   Remove the master cylinder reservoir cover and diaphragm and siphon out the brake fluid inside the reservoir. Install the diaphragm and cover. **Note:** *If you're just removing the caliper to remove the wheel, ignore this step and the next step.*

2   Remove the brake hose-to-caliper banjo bolt and sealing washers **(see illustration 7.4)** and disconnect the brake hose from the caliper. Discard the sealing washers. Plug the end of the hose or wrap a plastic bag tightly around it to prevent excessive fluid loss and contamination.

3   Remove the caliper body retaining bolt and the caliper bracket-to-outer fork tube bolts **(see illustration 4.1)** and remove the caliper assembly.

Overhaul

Note: *If you're planning to disassemble the caliper, read through the overhaul procedure, paying particular attention to the steps involved in removing the pistons with compressed air.*

4   Remove the brake pads and spring from the caliper (see Section 4).

5   Remove the old retaining bolt dust boot **(see illustration 4.1)**.

6   Clean the exterior of the caliper with denatured alcohol or brake

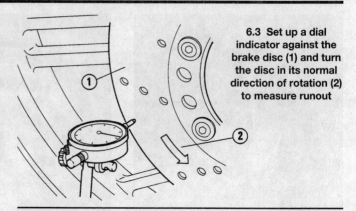

6.3 Set up a dial indicator against the brake disc (1) and turn the disc in its normal direction of rotation (2) to measure runout

system cleaner.

7   Put a block of wood or pack a shop rag into the space for the brake pads. Using small, quick bursts of compressed air directed through the caliper fluid inlet, gently dislodge the piston from the caliper. Use air pressure sparingly, just enough to pop the piston out of the bore. If the piston is blown out with too much force, even with the rag in place, it could be damaged. **Warning:** *Never put your fingers in front of the piston in an attempt to catch or protect it when applying compressed air. If the piston pops out with too much force, you could be seriously injured.*

8   Remove the piston dust seal **(see illustration 4.1)** (it might be stuck to the piston or to the caliper bore).

9   Using a wood or plastic tool, such as a toothpick, remove the piston seal **(see illustration 4.1)**. (Metal tools can damage the bore.)

10   Remove the bleeder screw **(see illustration 4.1)**.

11   Clean the pistons and the bores with denatured alcohol, brake fluid or brake system cleaner and blow them off with filtered, unlubricated compressed air.

12   Inspect the surfaces of the piston and the piston bore for nicks, scratches, rust and plating loss. If you see any surface defects in the piston or bore, replace the caliper. If the caliper is in bad shape, inspect the master cylinder too.

13   Lubricate the piston seal with clean brake fluid and install it in its groove in the caliper bore. Make sure it's fully seated and isn't twisted.

14   Lubricate the piston dust seal with clean brake fluid and install it in its groove in the piston, making sure it seats correctly.

15   Lubricate the piston with clean brake fluid and install it into the caliper bore. Using your thumbs, push the piston all the way in, making sure it doesn't get cocked in the bore. Once the piston is fully depressed, make sure the piston dust seal is correctly seated in the bore.

Installation

16   Installation is the reverse of removal, with the following additions:

a) *Install the springs and pads (see Section 4).*

b) *Apply lithium soap base grease or silicone grease to the caliper body retaining bolt.*

c) *Tighten the caliper body retaining bolt to the torque listed in this Chapter's Specifications.*

d) *Use new sealing washers on the brake hose banjo bolt. Tighten the banjo bolt to the torque listed in this Chapter's Specifications.*

17   Fill the master cylinder with the recommended brake fluid (see Chapter 1B) and bleed the system (see Section 8). Check for leaks.

18   Check the operation of the brakes carefully before riding the motorcycle.

---

6   Brake disc (RT180 models) - inspection, removal and installation

Inspection

Refer to illustration 6.3

1   Support the bike securely upright. Place a jack beneath the bike

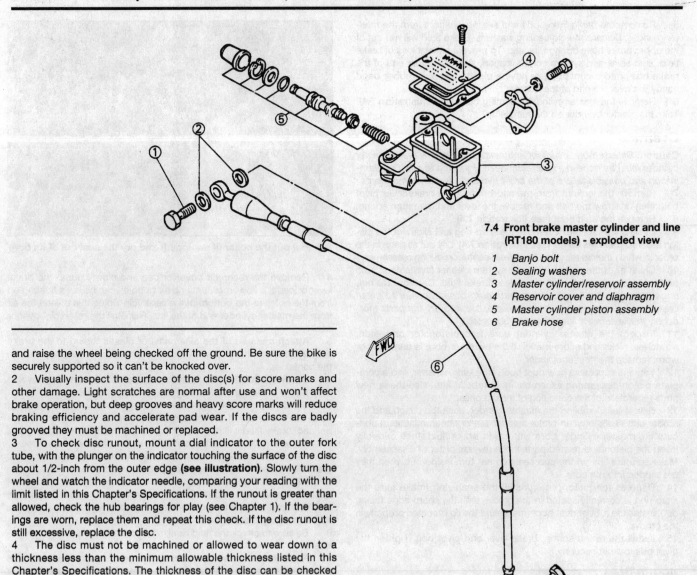

7.4 Front brake master cylinder and line (RT180 models) - exploded view

1 *Banjo bolt*
2 *Sealing washers*
3 *Master cylinder/reservoir assembly*
4 *Reservoir cover and diaphragm*
5 *Master cylinder piston assembly*
6 *Brake hose*

and raise the wheel being checked off the ground. Be sure the bike is securely supported so it can't be knocked over.

2   Visually inspect the surface of the disc(s) for score marks and other damage. Light scratches are normal after use and won't affect brake operation, but deep grooves and heavy score marks will reduce braking efficiency and accelerate pad wear. If the discs are badly grooved they must be machined or replaced.

3   To check disc runout, mount a dial indicator to the outer fork tube, with the plunger on the indicator touching the surface of the disc about 1/2-inch from the outer edge **(see illustration)**. Slowly turn the wheel and watch the indicator needle, comparing your reading with the limit listed in this Chapter's Specifications. If the runout is greater than allowed, check the hub bearings for play (see Chapter 1). If the bearings are worn, replace them and repeat this check. If the disc runout is still excessive, replace the disc.

4   The disc must not be machined or allowed to wear down to a thickness less than the minimum allowable thickness listed in this Chapter's Specifications. The thickness of the disc can be checked with a micrometer. If the thickness of the disc is less than the minimum allowable, it must be replaced. The minimum thickness is also stamped into the disc.

Removal

5   Remove the wheel (see Section 2). **Caution:** *Don't lay the wheel down and allow it to rest on the disc - the disc could become warped. Set the wheel on wood blocks so the disc doesn't support the weight of the wheel.*

6   Mark the relationship of the disc to the wheel, so it can be installed in the same position. Remove the disc retaining bolts **(see illustration 4.1)**. Loosen the bolts a little at a time, in a criss-cross pattern, to avoid warping the disc. Discard the old washers.

Installation

7   Position the disc on the wheel, aligning the previously applied matchmarks (if you're reinstalling the original disc).

8   Apply a non-hardening thread-locking compound to the threads of the disc retaining bolts. Using new washers, install the bolts, tightening them a little at a time in a criss-cross pattern, to the torque listed in this Chapter's Specifications. Using acetone or brake system cleaner, clean off all grease from the brake disc.

9   Install the wheel.

10   Operate the brake lever or pedal several times to bring the pads into contact with the disc. Check the operation of the brakes carefully before riding the motorcycle.

7   Master cylinder (RT180 models) - removal, overhaul and installation

1   If brake fluid is leaking from the master cylinder, or if the lever doesn't produce a firm feel when the brake is applied, and bleeding the brakes doesn't help, overhaul the master cylinder. Before disassembling the master cylinder, read through the entire procedure and make sure that you have the correct rebuild kit. Also, you will need some new, clean brake fluid of the recommended type, some clean rags and internal snap-ring pliers. **Note:** *To protect the paint from spilled brake fluid, always cover the gas tank when working on the master cylinder.*

Removal

Refer to illustration 7.4

2   Place rags beneath the master cylinder to protect the paint in case of brake fluid spills.

3   Loosen the brake lever pivot bolt locknut.

4   Remove the master cylinder reservoir cover and diaphragm **(see illustration)** and siphon the brake fluid from the reservoir.

5   Remove the banjo fitting bolt and sealing washers from the master cylinder. Discard the old sealing washers. Brake fluid will run out of the upper brake hose during this step. To prevent excess loss of brake fluid, fluid spills and system contamination, stick the upper end of the brake hose into a container, or have a plastic bag and rubber band handy to cover the end of the hose.

6   Remove the master cylinder mounting bolts **(see illustration 7.4)**. Take the master cylinder off the handlebar.

Overhaul

Caution: *Disassembly, overhaul and reassembly of the brake master cylinder must be done in a spotlessly clean work area to avoid contamination and possible failure of the brake hydraulic system components.*

7   Remove the locknut from the underside of the brake lever pivot bolt, then unscrew the bolt and remove the lever and the return spring.

8   Remove the dust boot **(see illustration 7.4)**.

9   Using snap-ring pliers, remove the snap-ring and slide out the piston assembly and the spring **(see illustration 7.4)**. Lay out all parts in the order in which they're removed to prevent confusion during reassembly.

10   Clean all of the parts with brake system cleaner (available at auto parts stores), isopropyl alcohol or clean brake fluid. **Caution:** *Do not, under any circumstances, use a petroleum-based solvent to clean brake parts. If compressed air is available, use it to dry the parts thoroughly (make sure it's filtered and unlubricated).*

11   Inspect the master cylinder bore and piston for corrosion, scratches, nicks and score marks. If the piston or bore is damaged or worn, replace the master cylinder.

12   Yamaha supplies a new dust boot, snap-ring, washer, and a complete piston/seal/spring assembly in its rebuild kits. Use these new parts regardless of the condition of the old ones.

13   Before reassembling the master cylinder, soak the piston and the rubber cup seals in clean brake fluid for ten or fifteen minutes. Lubricate the master cylinder bore with clean brake fluid, then carefully insert the piston and related parts in the reverse order of disassembly. Make sure the lips on the cup seals do not turn inside out when they are slipped into the bore.

14   Depress the piston, then install the snap-ring (make sure the snap-ring is correctly seated in the groove with the sharp edge facing out). Install the rubber dust boot (make sure the lip is seated properly in the groove).

15   Install the return spring, brake lever and pivot bolt. Tighten the pivot bolt locknut securely.

Installation

16   Installation is the reverse of removal, with the following additions:

a)   *Make sure the arrow and the word UP on the master cylinder clamp are pointing up, then tighten the bolts to the torque listed in this Chapter's Specifications.*

b)   *Using new sealing washers, install the brake hose banjo bolt and tighten it to the torque listed in this Chapter's Specifications.*

17   Add the recommended brake fluid to the reservoir (see Chapter 1B) and bleed the air from the system (see Section 8).

---

8   Brake system bleeding (RT180 models)

---

1   Bleeding the brakes is the process of removing all the air bubbles from the brake fluid reservoir, the lines and the brake caliper. Bleeding is necessary whenever a brake system hydraulic connection is loosened, when a component or hose is replaced, or when the master cylinder or caliper is overhauled. Leaks in the system may also allow air to enter, but leaking brake fluid will reveal their presence and warn you of the need for repair.

2   To bleed the brakes, you will need some new, clean brake fluid of the recommended type (see Chapter 1), a length of clear vinyl or plastic tubing, a small container partially filled with clean brake fluid, some rags and a wrench to fit the brake caliper bleeder valve.

3   Cover the fuel tank and other painted components to prevent damage in the event that brake fluid is spilled.

9.3 Pull out the collar (if equipped) and pry the seal out of its bore

4   Remove the reservoir cover or cap and slowly pump the brake lever or pedal a few times, until no air bubbles can be seen floating up from the holes at the bottom of the reservoir. Doing this bleeds the air from the master cylinder end of the line. Reinstall the reservoir cover or cap.

5   Attach one end of the clear vinyl or plastic tubing to the brake caliper bleeder valve and submerge the other end in the brake fluid in the container.

6   Check the fluid level in the reservoir. Do not allow the fluid level to drop below the lower mark during the bleeding process.

7   Carefully pump the brake lever or pedal three or four times and hold it while opening the caliper bleeder valve. When the valve is opened, brake fluid will flow out of the caliper into the clear tubing and the lever will move toward the handlebar or the pedal will move down.

8   Retighten the bleeder valve, then release the brake lever or pedal gradually. Repeat the process until no air bubbles are visible in the brake fluid leaving the caliper and the lever or pedal is firm when applied. Remember to add fluid to the reservoir as the level drops. Use only new, clean brake fluid of the recommended type. Never reuse the fluid lost during bleeding.

9   Be sure to check the fluid level in the master cylinder reservoir frequently.

10   Replace the reservoir cover or cap, wipe up any spilled brake fluid and check the entire system for leaks. **Note:** *If bleeding is difficult, it may be necessary to let the brake fluid in the system stabilize for a few hours (it may be aerated). Repeat the bleeding procedure when the tiny bubbles in the system have settled out.*

---

9   Wheel and coupling bearing replacement

Wheel bearings

Refer to illustrations 9.3, 9.4a, 9.4b, 9.4c and 9.5

1   Remove the wheel (see Section 2). If you're working on a drum brake model, remove the brake panel (see Section 3).

2   Remove the speedometer gearbox (if equipped) and any spacer/collars (see Section 2).

3   Pry the seals out of the wheel with a seal remover or screwdriver **(see illustration)**. Put a shop rag between the screwdriver shaft and the wheel hub to protect the inner edge of the hub.

4   Remove the bearings with a suitable bearing remover **(see illustrations)**. Or, take the wheel to a dealer or motorcycle machine shop and have the old bearings removed and the new bearings pressed in. (Because the wheel hub openings are small, it's difficult to insert a drift through one bearing and tap out the opposite bearing.) **Note:** *Once the bearings have been removed, they must be replaced with new ones since they're almost certain to be damaged during removal.*

5   Using a bearing driver or a socket slightly smaller in diameter than the outside diameter of the new bearing, tap a new bearing into the

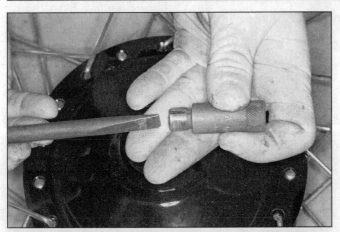

9.4a Remove the bearings with a bearing remover like this one . . .

9.4b . . . tap the split end of the remover head into the bearing . . .

9.4c . . . then tap the wedge into the split; this will lock the
remover to the bearing and drive them both out

9.5 Using a bearing driver or socket slightly smaller in diameter
than the outside diameter of the new bearing, tap
a new bearing into the hub

hub **(see illustration)**. Turn the wheel over, install the spacer and
install the other bearing.
6   Tap the new seals into the hub with a seal driver or with a socket
the same diameter as the seal.
7   Install the wheel (see Section 2).

Rear coupling bearing

Refer to illustrations 9.10 and 9.11
8   RT100 models use a cush drive rear coupling. Its bearing is simi-

lar to the rear wheel bearings, but is mounted in the sprocket hub.
9   Remove the rear wheel and lift the sprocket hub out of the wheel.
10   Pull out the seal collar (if you haven't already done so **(see illustration)**. Pad the sprocket hub with a shop rag and pry the seal out
with a seal remover or screwdriver.
11   Pull the coupling shaft out of the bearing **(see illustration)**.
12   Drive the bearing out of the coupling, using a bearing driver or a
socket the same diameter as the bearing.

9.10 DO NOT forget to reinstall the coupling collar on
RT100 models, or the wheel bearings will be
damaged when the axle is tightened

9.11 Remove the coupling shaft from the bearing

13   Drive in the new bearing, then drive in the new seal, using the same tool used for removal.

14   The remainder of installation is the reverse of the removal steps. **Caution:** *Don't forget to reinstall the collar in the coupling seal, or the wheel bearings will be damaged when the axle nut is tightened.*

10   Brake cable, lever, rod and pedal - removal and installation

Front brake cable and lever (RT100 models)

Refer to illustration 10.4

1   Loosen the brake cable adjuster at the brake cam lever and disengage the cable end plug from the lever **(see illustrations 2.2a and 2.2b)**.

2   Trace the cable up to the handlebar and detach it from any clips or brackets **(see illustration 2.2d)**.

3   Loosen the handlebar adjuster all the way **(see illustration 5.1b in Chapter 1B)**, then rotate the cable and slip its end plug out of the lever.

4   Remove the throttle twist grip and throttle cable housing (see Chapter 4B). Remove the lever pivot bolt and nut and the lever bracket clamp bolt **(see illustration)**. Slide the lever off the handlebar.

5   Installation is the reverse of removal, with the following additions:

a) *Apply multi-purpose grease to the cable end plugs.*
b) *Adjust the front brake and throttle cable (see Chapter 1).*

Rear brake rod and pedal

Refer to illustration 10.8

6   Remove the rear brake adjuster nut from the brake rod, pull the rod out of its clevis pin, remove the clevis pin from the brake cam lever and remove the spring from the rod **(see illustrations 2.8a and 2.8b)**

7   Unhook the brake pedal return spring.

8   Remove the pedal snap-ring **(see illustration)** and remove the pedal.

9   Detach the rod from the pedal.

10   Installation is the reverse of removal, with the following additions:

a) *Lubricate the rod end fittings and pedal shaft with multi-purpose grease.*
b) *Adjust brake pedal freeplay (see Section 5 in Chapter 1B).*

11   Tires - removal and installation

1   To properly remove and install tires, you will need at least two motorcycle tire irons, some water, some talcum powder and a tire pressure gauge.

2   Begin by removing the wheel from the motorcycle. If the tire is going to be re-used, mark it next to the valve stem, wheel balance weight or rim lock.

3   Deflate the tire by removing the valve stem core. When it is fully deflated, push the bead of the tire away from the rim on both sides. In some extreme cases, this can only be accomplished with a bead-breaking tool, but most often it can be carried out with tire irons. Riding on a deflated tire to break the bead is not recommended, as damage to the rim and tire will occur.

4   Removing a tire is easier when the tire is warm, so an indoor tire change is recommended in cold climates. The rubber gets very stiff and is difficult to manipulate when cold.

5   Place the wheel on a thick pad or old blanket. This will help keep the wheel and tire from slipping around.

6   Once the bead is completely free of the rim, lubricate the inside edge of the rim and the tire bead with a solution of water only. Honda recommends against the use of soap or other tire mounting lubricants, as the tire may shift on the rim. Remove the locknut and push the tire valve through the rim.

7   Insert one of the tire irons under the bead of the tire at the valve

10.4 Remove the lever pivot bolt and the bracket clamp bolt (arrows) and slide the bracket off the handlebar

10.8 Remove the pedal snap-ring (arrow) and remove the pedal

stem and lift the bead up over the rim. This should be fairly easy. Take care not to pinch the tube as this is done. If it is difficult to pry the bead up, make sure that the rest of the bead opposite the valve stem is in the dropped center section of the rim.

8   Hold the tire iron down with the bead over the rim, then move about 1 or 2 inches to either side and insert the second tire iron. Be careful not to cut or slice the bead or the tire may split when inflated. Also, take care not to catch or pinch the inner tube as the second tire iron is levered over. For this reason, tire irons are recommended over screwdrivers or other implements.

9   With a small section of the bead up over the rim, one of the levers can be removed and reinserted 1 or 2 inches farther around the rim until about 1/4 of the tire bead is above the rim edge. Make sure that the rest of the bead is in the dropped center of the rim. At this point, the bead can usually be pulled up over the rim by hand.

10   Once the entire first bead is over the rim, the inner tube can be withdrawn from the tire and rim. Push in on the valve stem, lift up on the tire next to the stem, reach inside the tire and carefully pull out the tube. It is usually not necessary to completely remove the tire from the rim to repair the inner tube. It is sometimes recommended though, because checking for foreign objects in the tire is difficult while it is still mounted on the rim.

11   To remove the tire completely, make sure the bead is broken all the way around on the remaining edge, then stand the tire and wheel up on the tread and grab the wheel with one hand. Push the tire down over the same edge of the rim while pulling the rim away from the tire.

TIRE CHANGING SEQUENCE - TUBED TIRES

 A Deflate tire. After pushing tire beads away from rim flanges push tire bead into well of rim at point opposite valve. Insert tire lever next to valve and work bead over edge of rim.

B Use two levers to work bead over edge of rim. Note use of rim protectors

 C Remove inner tube from tire

When first bead is clear, remove tire as shown **D**

E To install, partially inflate inner tube and insert in tire

 Work first bead over rim and feed valve through hole in rim. Partially screw on retaining nut to hold valve in place. **F**

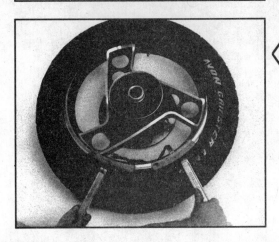

G Check that inner tube is positioned correctly and work second bead over rim using tire levers. Start at a point opposite valve.

Work final area of bead over rim while pushing valve inwards to ensure that inner tube is not trapped. **H**

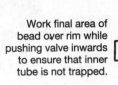

If the bead is correctly positioned in the dropped center of the rim, the tire should roll off and separate from the rim very easily. If tire irons are used to work this last bead over the rim, the outer edge of the rim may be marred. If a tire iron is necessary, be sure to pad the rim as described earlier.

12   Refer to Section 7 for inner tube repair procedures.

13   Mounting a tire is basically the reverse of removal. Some tires have a balance mark and/or directional arrows molded into the tire sidewall. Look for these marks so that the tire can be installed properly. The dot should be aligned with the valve stem.

14   If the tire was not removed completely to repair or replace the inner tube, the tube should be inflated just enough to make it round. Carefully lift up the tire edge and install the tube with the valve stem next to the hole in the rim. Once the tube is in place, push the valve stem through the rim and start the locknut on the stem.

15   Lubricate the tire bead, then push it over the rim edge and into the dropped center section opposite the inner tube valve stem. Work around each side of the rim, carefully pushing the bead over the rim. The last section may have to be levered on with tire irons. If so, take care not to pinch the inner tube as this is done.

16   Once the bead is over the rim edge, check to see that the inner tube valve stem and the rim lock are pointing to the center of the hub. If they're angled slightly in either direction, rotate the tire on the rim to straighten it out. Run the locknut the rest of the way onto the stem and rim lock but don't tighten them completely.

17   Inflate the tube to 1-1/2 times the pressure listed in the Chapter 1 Specifications. **Warning:** *Do not overinflate the tube or the tire may burst, causing serious injury.* Check to make sure the guidelines on the tire sidewalls are the same distance from the rim around the circumference of the tire.

18   After the tire bead is correctly seated on the rim, allow the tire to deflate. Replace the valve core and inflate the tube to the recom-mended pressure, then tighten the valve stem locknut securely and tighten the cap. Tighten the locknut on the rim locknut to the torque listed in the Chapter 1 Specifications.

12 Tubes - repair

1   Tire tube repair requires a patching kit that's usually available from motorcycle dealers, accessory stores or auto parts stores. Be sure to follow the directions supplied with the kit to ensure a safe repair. Patching should be done only when a new tube is unavailable. Replace the tube as soon as possible. Sudden deflation can cause loss of control and an accident.

2   To repair a tube, remove it from the tire, inflate and immerse it in a sink or tub full of water to pinpoint the leak. Mark the position of the leak, then deflate the tube. Dry it off and thoroughly clean the area around the puncture.

3   Most tire patching kits have a buffer to rough up the area around the hole for proper adhesion of the patch. Roughen an area slightly larger than the patch, then apply a thin coat of the patching cement to the roughened area. Allow the cement to dry until tacky, then apply the patch.

4   It may be necessary to remove a protective covering from the top surface of the patch after it has been attached to the tube. Keep in mind that tubes made from synthetic rubber may require a special patch and adhesive if a satisfactory bond is to be achieved.

5   Before replacing the tube, check the inside of the tire to make sure the object that caused the puncture is not still inside. Also check the outside of the tire, particularly the tread area, to make sure nothing is projecting through the tire that may cause another puncture. Check the rim for sharp edges or damage. Make sure the rubber trim band is in good condition and properly installed before inserting the tube.

Chapter 6 Part C
Brakes, wheels and tires
(TT-R and XT models)

Contents

Specifications

Brakes

Front brake shoe lining limit (TT-R90)	See Chapter 1
Rear brake shoe lining limit	See Chapter 1
Brake pad lining thickness limit	See Chapter 1
Front brake lever freeplay	See Chapter 1
Rear brake pedal freeplay	See Chapter 1
Rear brake pedal height	See Chapter 1
Drum inside diameter wear limit*	
TT-R90	
Front drum (TT-R90)	96 mm (3.78 inches)
Rear drum	
TT-R90, TT-R125, TT-R225, XT225)	111 mm (4.37 inches)
XT350	131 mm (5.16 inches)
Brake disc wear limit	
TT-R125	2.5 mm (0.10 inch)
TT-R225, XT225, XT350	3.0 mm (0.118 inch)
TT-R250	
Front	3.0 mm (0.118 inch)
Rear	4.0 mm (0.157 inch)

*Refer to marks cast into the drum (they supersede information printed here)

Wheels and tires

Tire pressures	See Chapter 1
Tire tread depth	See Chapter 1
Wheel rim runout limit (lateral and vertical)	2 mm (0.08 inch)

Torque specifications

Axle nut
  TT-R90
    Front.. 35 Nm (25 ft-lbs)
    Rear... 60 Nm (43 ft-lbs)
  TT-R125
    Front.. 45 Nm (32 ft-lbs)
    Rear... 60 Nm (43 ft-lbs)
  TT-R225, XT225 (front and rear)... 85 Nm (61 ft-lbs)
  TT-R250
    Front.. 58 Nm (42 ft-lbs)
    Rear... 105 Nm (75 ft-lbs)
  XT350
    Front.. 85 Nm (61 ft-lbs)
    Rear... 107 Nm (77 ft-lbs)
Caliper
  TT-R125
    Caliper bracket to fork bolts .... 30 Nm (22 ft-lbs)
    Caliper to bracket bolt .... 22 Nm (16 ft-lbs)
    Brake hose-to-caliper banjo bolt .... 27 Nm (19 ft-lbs)
  TT-R225, XT225
    Caliper bracket to fork bolt .... 35 Nm (25 ft-lbs)
    Caliper to bracket bolt .... 23 Nm (17 ft-lbs)
    Brake hose-to-caliper banjo bolt .... 27 Nm (19 ft-lbs)
  TT-R250
    Front caliper bracket to fork bolts .... 23 Nm (17 ft-lbs)
    Rear caliper shield bolts .... 10 Nm (84 inch-lbs)
    Front and rear pad pins .... 23 Nm (17 ft-lbs)
    Front and rear brake hose-to-caliper banjo bolt.......................... 30 Nm (22 ft-lbs)
  XT350
    Caliper bracket to fork bolts .... 35 Nm (25 ft-lbs)
    Caliper to bracket bolt .... 18 Nm (13 ft-lbs)
    Brake hose-to-caliper banjo bolt .... 27 Nm (19 ft-lbs)
Disc retaining bolts
  TT-R125, TT-R250 (front and rear)...................................... 12 Nm (104 inch-lbs)
  TT-R225, XT225 .... 10 Nm (84 inch-lbs)
  XT350 .... Not specified
Master cylinder
  Brake hose-to-master cylinder banjo bolt.......................... 27 Nm (19 ft-lbs)
  Brake hose to master cylinder fitting (TT-R125)................. 14 Nm (120 inch-lbs)
  Master cylinder fitting to master cylinder (TT-R125) .... 27 Nm (19 ft-lbs)
  Master cylinder-to-handlebar clamp bolts
    TT-R125, XT350 .... 9 Nm (78 inch-lbs)
    TT-R225, TT-R250, XT225 .... 7 Nm (61 inch-lbs)

1 General information

TT-R90 models are equipped with mechanical drum brakes on the front and rear wheels. A lever on the right handlebar actuates the front brake. A pedal on the right side of the vehicle actuates the rear brake. The lever is connected to the front brake assembly by a cable; the pedal is connected to the rear brake assembly by a rod.

TT-R125, TT-R225, XT225 and XT350 models are equipped with a hydraulic disc brake on the front wheel and a mechanical drum brake at the rear wheel. TT-R250 models are equipped with hydraulic disc brakes at front and rear.

All models are equipped with spoked steel wheels. **Caution:** *Brake components rarely require disassembly. Do not disassemble the brakes unless absolutely necessary.*

2 Wheels - inspection, removal and installation

Removal

Front wheel

Refer to illustrations 2.3a through 2.3e

1   Raise the front end by placing the bike on a motorcycle stand, floor jack or milk crate. If you're using a jack, put a board between the jack head and the engine to protect the crankcase. Make sure that the bike is securely propped upright so it can't fall over when the wheel is removed.

2   On TT-R90 models, loosen the brake cable adjuster at the brake cam lever and disengage the cable end plug from the lever **(see illustration 2.2a through 2.2d in Chapter 6B)**.

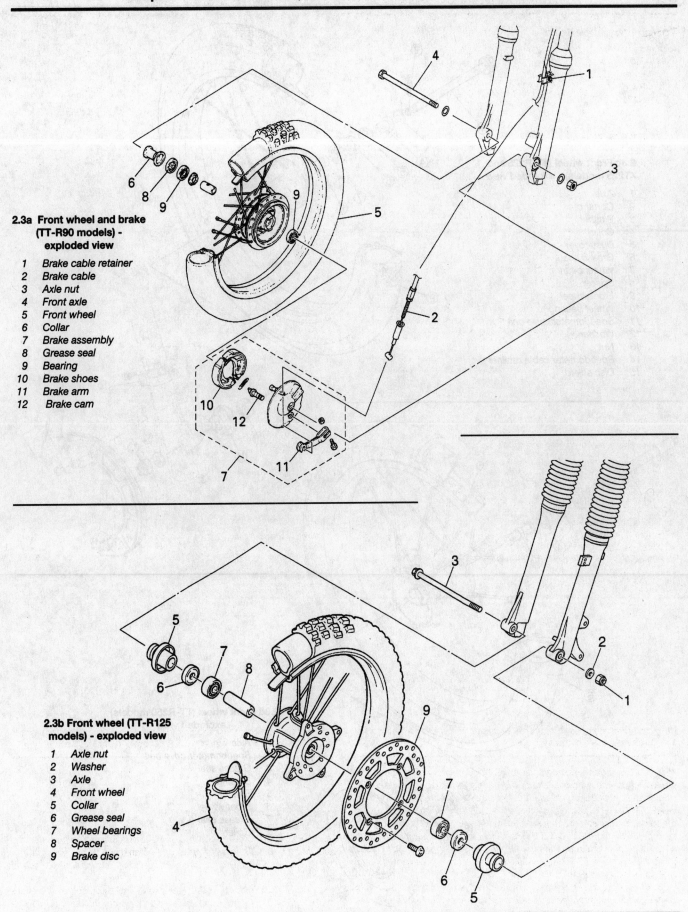

2.3a Front wheel and brake (TT-R90 models) - exploded view

1   Brake cable retainer
2   Brake cable
3   Axle nut
4   Front axle
5   Front wheel
6   Collar
7   Brake assembly
8   Grease seal
9   Bearing
10 Brake shoes
11 Brake arm
12   Brake cam

2.3b Front wheel (TT-R125 models) - exploded view

1   Axle nut
2   Washer
3   Axle
4   Front wheel
5   Collar
6   Grease seal
7   Wheel bearings
8   Spacer
9   Brake disc

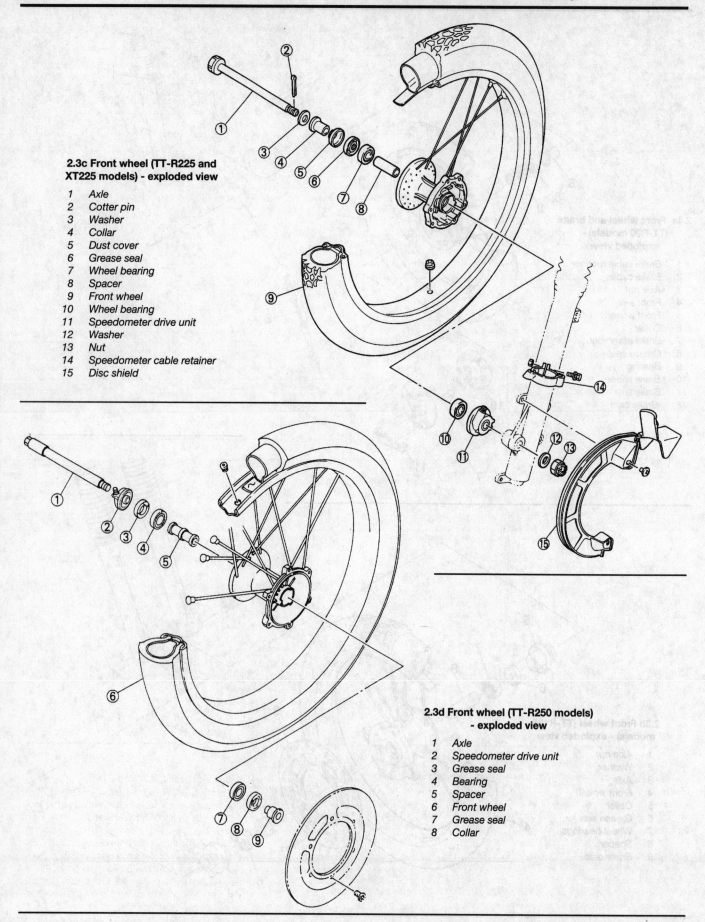

2.3c Front wheel (TT-R225 and XT225 models) - exploded view

1   Axle
2   Cotter pin
3   Washer
4   Collar
5   Dust cover
6   Grease seal
7   Wheel bearing
8   Spacer
9   Front wheel
10   Wheel bearing
11   Speedometer drive unit
12   Washer
13   Nut
14   Speedometer cable retainer
15   Disc shield

2.3d Front wheel (TT-R250 models) - exploded view

1   Axle
2   Speedometer drive unit
3   Grease seal
4   Bearing
5   Spacer
6   Front wheel
7   Grease seal
8   Collar

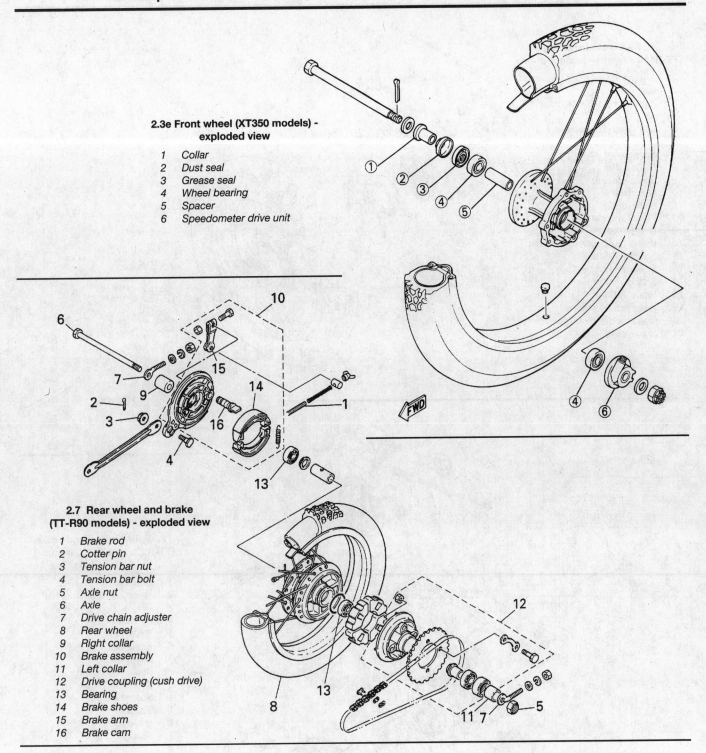

2.3e Front wheel (XT350 models) - exploded view

1   Collar
2   Dust seal
3   Grease seal
4   Wheel bearing
5   Spacer
6   Speedometer drive unit

2.7 Rear wheel and brake (TT-R90 models) - exploded view

1   Brake rod
2   Cotter pin
3   Tension bar nut
4   Tension bar bolt
5   Axle nut
6   Axle
7   Drive chain adjuster
8   Rear wheel
9   Right collar
10 Brake assembly
11 Left collar
12 Drive coupling (cush drive)
13 Bearing
14 Brake shoes
15 Brake arm
16 Brake cam

3   Remove the cotter pin from the axle. Hold the axle bolt head with a wrench, unscrew the axle nut and remove the washer **(see illustrations)**.

4   Support the wheel, pull out the axle and remove the spacer collar from between the fork leg and the wheel. Take the wheel out from between the fork legs. **Note:** *On disc brake models, do NOT squeeze the front brake lever while the wheel is removed, or the caliper piston will force the brake pads closer together, making it impossible to fit the brake disc between the pads when installing the wheel.*

5   Note the sequence in which the speedometer gearbox (models with a speedometer) and any spacer/collars are installed, and then remove them from the wheel.

Rear wheel

Refer to illustrations 2.7, 2.8a, 2.8b, 2.8c, 2.8d and 2.9

6   Raise the rear end by placing the bike on a motorcycle stand, floor jack or milk crate. If you're using a jack, put a board between the jack head and the engine to protect the crankcase. Make sure that the bike is securely propped upright so it can't fall over when the wheel is removed.

7   On TT-R90 models, remove the cotter pin from the rear end of the tension bar, remove the tension bar-to-brake shoe plate nut **(see illustration)** and detach the tensioner bar from the brake shoe plate.

8   Remove the rear brake adjuster nut from the brake rod, pull the rod out of the clevis pin and remove the spring from the rod **(see illustration 2.7 and the accompanying illustrations)**.

**2.8a Rear wheel and brake
(TT-R125 models) - exploded view**

1   Brake rod
2   Axle nut
3   Right drive chain adjuster
4   Axle
5   Left drive chain adjuster
6   Drive chain
7   Rear wheel
8   Right collar
9   Brake assembly
10   Left collar
11   Lockwasher
12   Wheel sprocket
13   Grease seal
14   Wheel bearing
15   Spacer
16   Brake shoes
17   Spring
18   Brake arm
19   Wear indicator plate
20   Brake cam
21   Brake panel

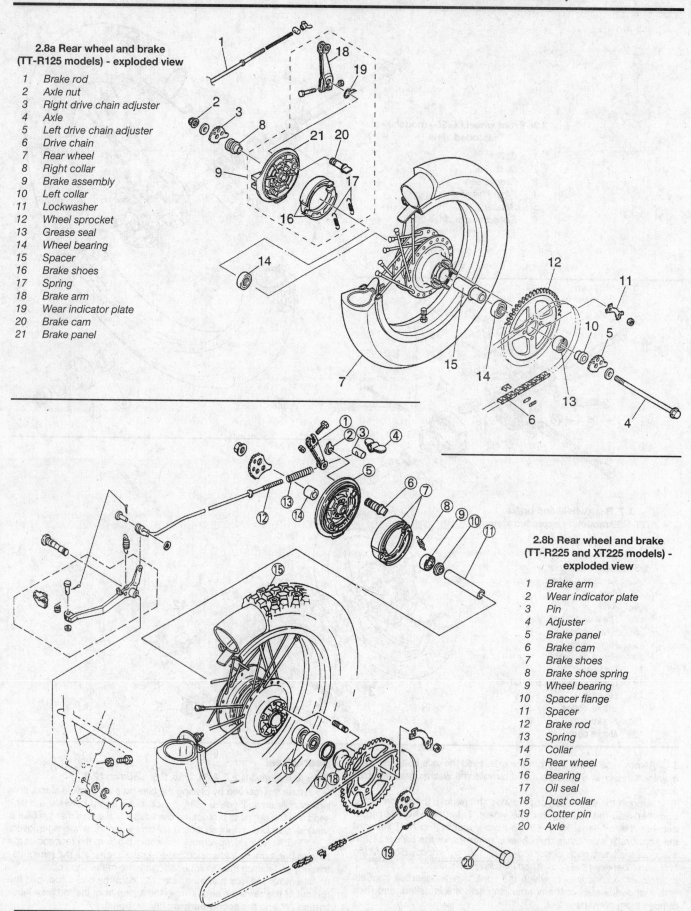

**2.8b Rear wheel and brake
(TT-R225 and XT225 models) -
exploded view**

1   Brake arm
2   Wear indicator plate
3   Pin
4   Adjuster
5   Brake panel
6   Brake cam
7   Brake shoes
8   Brake shoe spring
9   Wheel bearing
10   Spacer flange
11   Spacer
12   Brake rod
13   Spring
14   Collar
15   Rear wheel
16   Bearing
17   Oil seal
18   Dust collar
19   Cotter pin
20   Axle

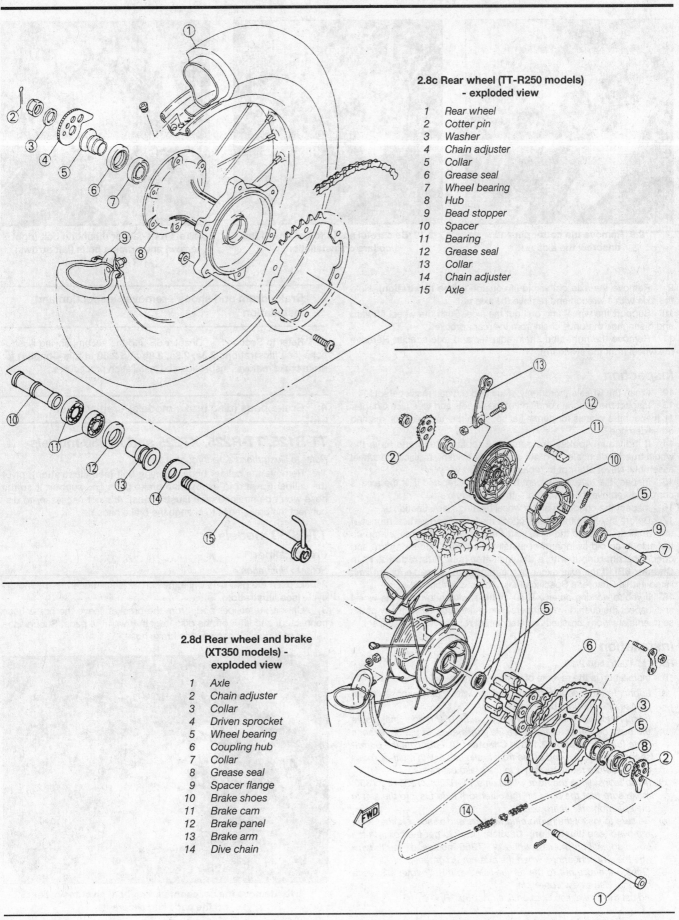

2.8c Rear wheel (TT-R250 models) - exploded view

1 Rear wheel
2 Cotter pin
3 Washer
4 Chain adjuster
5 Collar
6 Grease seal
7 Wheel bearing
8 Hub
9 Bead stopper
10 Spacer
11 Bearing
12 Grease seal
13 Collar
14 Chain adjuster
15 Axle

2.8d Rear wheel and brake (XT350 models) - exploded view

1 Axle
2 Chain adjuster
3 Collar
4 Driven sprocket
5 Wheel bearing
6 Coupling hub
7 Collar
8 Grease seal
9 Spacer flange
10 Brake shoes
11 Brake cam
12 Brake panel
13 Brake arm
14 Dive chain

2.9 Remove the cotter pin and unscrew the axle nut

2.19 Be careful not to forget any of the collars on installation

4.1a Front caliper mounting bolt (right arrow) and bracket bolts (left arrows) (TT-R225 shown)

9   Remove the axle cotter pin (if equipped) **(see illustration)**. Hold the axle with a wrench and remove the axle nut.
10   Support the wheel and pull out the axle. Push the wheel forward and disengage the drive chain from the rear sprocket.
11   Remove the right side chain adjuster and axle spacer. Remove the wheel from the swingarm.

Inspection

12   Clean the wheels thoroughly. (Mud and dirt can mask defects.)
13   Inspect the general condition of the wheels and tires (see Chapter 1). Inspect the wheels for dents, flat spots on the rim, bent spokes and other damage.
14   If individual spokes are damaged, replace them and have the wheel trued by a dealer. If other damage is evident, replace the wheel assembly. Never attempt to repair a damaged wheel.
15   Inspect the axle. If it's bent or damaged, replace it. If the axle is corroded, remove the corrosion with fine emery cloth.
16   Inspect the condition of the wheel bearings (see Section 9).
17   Before installing the wheel, check the lateral and vertical runout of the wheel rim. Grease the axle, install the wheel on the axle, clamp up the axle in an old swingarm or install the wheel in the swingarm and check the rim runout with a dial indicator **(see illustration 2.17 in Chapter 6B)**. If the axle exceeds the maximum allowable runout limit listed in this Chapter's Specifications, it must be replaced.
18   If you're working on an XT350, lift the socket hub out of the wheel and inspect the cush drive dampers **(see illustration 2.8d)**. If any of the segments are worn, crushed or deteriorated, replace them all as a set.

Installation

Refer to illustration 2.19

19   Installation is the reverse of removal, with the following additions:
   a) *Lubricate the axle and the oil seal lips with multi-purpose lithium grease or with moly-base grease.*
   b) *If you're installing the front wheel on a TT-R90 model, make sure the boss on the outer fork tube fits into the slot in the brake shoe plate* **(see illustration 2.19a in Chapter 6B)**. *Lubricate the barrel-shaped plug at the end of the front brake cable with multi-purpose grease before reconnecting it to the brake cam lever.*
   c) *If you're installing the front wheel on a TT-R225, XT225 or XT350, make sure that the boss on the outer fork tube fits into the slot in the speedometer gearbox unit.*
   d) *Be sure to install the reinforcing washers and all spacers that were removed* **(see illustration)**. *Caution: Don't forget the collar in the coupling seal on the rear wheel of XT350 models, or you'll damage the wheel bearings when the axle nut is tightened.*
   e) *Tighten the axle nut to the torque listed in this Chapter's Specifications. Use a new cotter pin.*
   f) *Adjust the brake (see Section 5 in Chapter 1B).*

3   Brake drum and shoes - removal, inspection and installation

Refer to Section 3 in Chapter 6B and the accompanying illustrations **(see illustrations 2.3a, 2.8a, 2.8b and 2.8d in this Chapter)** for drum brake removal, inspection and installation procedures.

4   Brake pads (disc brake models) - replacement

TT-R125, TT-R225, XT225 and XT350 models

Refer to illustrations 4.1a through 4.1e

1   Remove the caliper body retaining bolt **(see illustration)**, pivot the caliper upward to expose the brake pads and support it so the hose won't be strained **(see illustrations)**. (It's not necessary to disconnect the brake hose to change the brake pads.)

TT-R250 models

Front caliper

Refer to illustration 4.2

2   Loosen the pad pins while the caliper is still bolted to the motorcycle **(see illustration)**.
3   Unbolt the caliper body from the bracket (leave the brake hose connected) and lift it off the disc, together with the pads. Support the caliper so it doesn't hang by the brake hose.

4.1b Remove the caliper mounting bolt, pivot the caliper off the pads and secure it

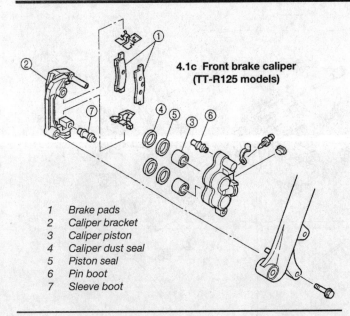

4.1c Front brake caliper (TT-R125 models)

1   Brake pads
2   Caliper bracket
3   Caliper piston
4   Caliper dust seal
5   Piston seal
6   Pin boot
7   Sleeve boot

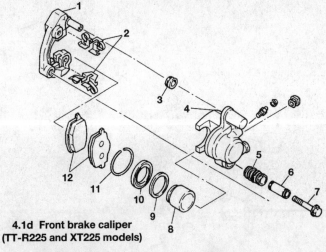

4.1d Front brake caliper (TT-R225 and XT225 models)

1   Caliper bracket | | 7   Bolt
2   Pad clips | | 8   Piston
3   Pin boot | | 9   Piston seal
4   Caliper body | | 10   Dust seal
5   Boot | | 11   Retaining ring
6   Bushing | | 12   Brake pads

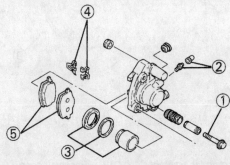

4.1e Front brake caliper (XT350 models)

1   Bolt   4   Pad clips
2   Bleed valve and dust cap   5   Pads
3   Piston and seals

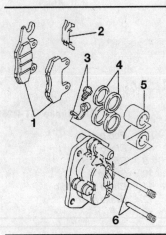

4.2 Front brake caliper (TT-R250 models)

1   Pads
2   Pad spring
3   Bleed valve and dust cap
4   Piston seals
5   Pistons
6   Pad pins

Rear caliper

Refer to illustration 4.4

4   Remove the caliper shield **(see illustration)**.

4.4 TT-R250 rear caliper mounting details

1   Shield bolts (rear bolt hidden)
2   Bleed valve
3   Brake hose union bolt

All models

Refer to illustrations 4.5 and 4.6

5   If you're working on a front caliper, remove the pads from the bracket **(see illustration)**.

4.5 Take off the pads, note how the clips fit in the bracket, then remove them

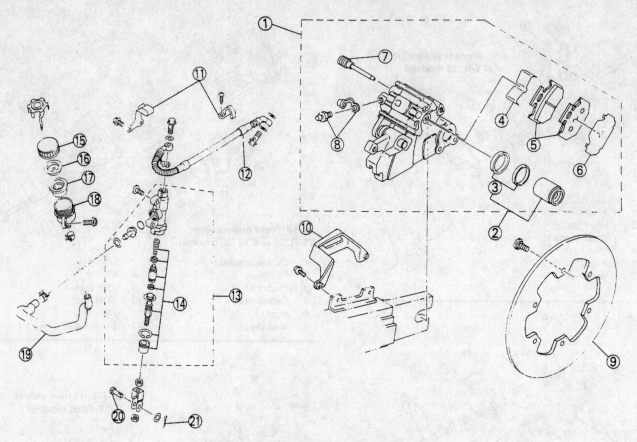

4.6 Rear brake (TT-R250 models) - exploded view

1	Caliper assembly	7	Pad pin	13	Master cylinder assembly	19	Reservoir hose
2	Piston and seals	8	Bleed valve	14	Master cylinder kit	20	Pushrod clevis pin
3	Seals	9	Brake disc	15	Reservoir cap	21	Cotter pin
4	Pad spring	10	Shield	16	Diaphragm bushing		
5	Brake pads	11	Brake hose holder	17	Diaphragm		
6	Shim	12	Brake hose	18	Reservoir		

6   If you're working on a rear caliper, unscrew the pad pins and pull the pads out from the rear of the caliper **(see illustration)**. The pad closest to the caliper piston has a shim.

6   Note exactly how the pad springs are installed, then remove them.

7   Note whether either of the brake pads is worn down to the wear indicator (see Chapter 1C). If either of the pads is worn down to the indicator, replace the pads as a set. (If you're replacing the brake pads, replace the pad springs too.)

8   Inspect the condition of the caliper (see Section 5). If the caliper piston seal is leaking, overhaul the caliper.

9   Inspect the condition of the brake disc (see Section 6). If it must be machined or replaced, remove it (see Section 6). If it's okay, deglaze it with sandpaper or emery cloth, using a swirling motion.

10   Remove the cover from the master cylinder reservoir (see Section 7) and siphon out some fluid. Push the piston into the caliper as far as it will go, while keeping an eye on the master cylinder reservoir to ensure that it doesn't overflow. If you can't depress the piston with thumb pressure, try using a C-clamp. If the piston sticks, remove the caliper and overhaul it (see Section 5).

11   If you're working on a front caliper, install the pad springs. Make sure that they're installed correctly.

12   Install the brake pads. On XT350 models, make sure that that the rounded edges of the pads face to the rear. On TT-R250 rear calipers, make sure the shim is installed on the pad closest to the caliper piston.

13   Lubricate the caliper body retaining bolt with multi-purpose lithium grease or silicone grease. Swing the caliper back into position, install the caliper body retaining bolt and tighten it to the torque listed in this Chapter's Specifications.

14   Operate the brake lever or pedal several times to bring the pads into contact with the disc.

15   Check the brake fluid level in the master cylinder and add fluid as necessary (see Chapter 1B).

16   Check the operation of the brake carefully before riding the motorcycle.

5   Brake caliper (disc brake models) - removal, overhaul and installation

Warning: *When a caliper is overhauled, all old brake fluid must be flushed from the system. Also, the dust created by the brake system may contain asbestos, which is harmful to your health. Don't blow out asbestos dust with compressed air and don't inhale it. An approved filtering mask should be worn when working on the brakes. Do not use petroleum-based solvents to clean brake parts. Use brake system cleaner or denatured alcohol.*

Note: *If you are removing the caliper only to remove the front or rear wheel, don't disconnect the hose from the caliper.*

Removal

Front caliper

1   Remove the master cylinder reservoir cover and diaphragm and siphon out the brake fluid inside the reservoir. Install the diaphragm and cover. **Note:** *If you're just removing the caliper to remove the wheel, ignore this step and the next step.*

2   Remove the brake hose-to-caliper banjo bolt and sealing washers **(see illustration 4.1a)** and disconnect the brake hose from the caliper. Discard the sealing washers. Plug the end of the hose or wrap a plastic bag tightly around it to prevent excessive fluid loss and contamination.

3   Remove the caliper mounting bolts and remove the caliper assembly.

Rear caliper

4   Remove the brake pads (Section 4).

5   Disconnect the brake line from the caliper **(see illustration 4.4)**. Remove the caliper mounting bolts and lift the caliper off.

Overhaul

6   Refer to Chapter 6B for this procedure.

Installation

7   Installation is the reverse of removal, with the following additions:
   a) *Install the springs and pads (see Section 4).*
   b) *Apply lithium soap base grease or silicone grease to the caliper body retaining bolt.*
   c) *Tighten the caliper mounting bolt(s) to the torque listed in this Chapter's Specifications.*
   d) *Use new sealing washers on the brake hose banjo bolt. Tighten the banjo bolt to the torque listed in this Chapter's Specifications.*

8   Fill the master cylinder with the recommended brake fluid (see Chapter 1C) and bleed the system (see Section 8). Check for leaks.

9   Check the operation of the brakes carefully before riding the motorcycle.

---

6   Brake disc (disc brake models) - inspection, removal and installation

Inspection

1   Inspection, which is done before the disc is removed, is the same as for RT180 models. Refer to Chapter 6B for inspection procedures.

Removal

Refer to illustration 6.3

2   Remove the wheel (see Section 2). **Caution:** *Don't lay the wheel down and allow it to rest on the disc - the disc could become warped. Set the wheel on wood blocks so the disc doesn't support the weight of the wheel.*

3   Mark the relationship of the disc to the wheel, so it can be installed in the same position. Remove the disc retaining bolts **(see illustration 4.6 (TT-R250 rear brake) or the accompanying illustration (all others)**. Loosen the bolts a little at a time, in a criss-cross pattern, to avoid warping the disc. Discard the old washers.

Installation

4   Position the disc on the heel, aligning the previously applied matchmarks (if you're reinstalling the original disc).

5   Apply a non-hardening thread-locking compound to the threads of the disc retaining bolts. Using new washers (if equipped), install the bolts, tightening them a little at a time in a criss-cross pattern, to the torque listed in this Chapter's Specifications. Using acetone or brake system cleaner, clean off all grease from the brake disc.

6   Install the wheel.

10   Operate the brake lever or pedal several times to bring the pads into contact with the disc. Check the operation of the brakes carefully before riding the motorcycle.

6.3 Unscrew the mounting bolts (arrows) and remove the disc

7   Master cylinder (disc brake models) - removal, overhaul and installation

1   If brake fluid is leaking from the master cylinder, or if the lever or pedal doesn't produce a firm feel when the brake is applied, and bleeding the brakes doesn't help, overhaul the master cylinder. Before disassembling the master cylinder, read through the entire procedure and make sure that you have the correct rebuild kit. Also, you will need some new, clean brake fluid of the recommended type, some clean rags and internal snap-ring pliers. **Note:** *To protect the paint from spilled brake fluid, always cover the gas tank when working on the master cylinder.*

Removal

Front master cylinder

2   This procedure is the same as for RT180 models, described in Chapter 6B.

Rear master cylinder (TT-R250 models)

Refer to illustrations 7.3 and 7.4

3   Remove the clip and clevis pin and disconnect the master cylinder from the pedal **(see illustration)**.

4   Unscrew the brake hose banjo bolt and disconnect the hose from

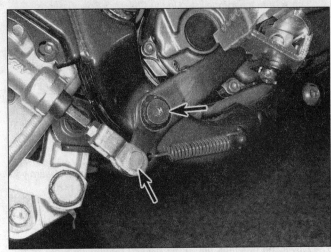

7.3 Here are the TT-R250 pushrod clevis pin (lower arrow) and brake pedal pivot bolt (upper arrow)

the master cylinder **(see illustration)**. Wrap the end of the hose in a plastic bag, secured with a rubber band.

5   Disconnect the reservoir hose from the master cylinder and wrap it with a plastic bag.

6   Unscrew the master cylinder mounting bolts and take it off the motorcycle.

Overhaul

Caution: *Disassembly, overhaul and reassembly of the brake master cylinder must be done in a spotlessly clean work area to avoid contamination and possible failure of the brake hydraulic system components.*

Front master cylinder

7   This procedure is the same as for RT180 models, described in Chapter 6B.

Rear master cylinder (TT-R250 models)

8   Using snap-ring pliers, remove the snap-ring and slide out the piston assembly and the spring **(see illustration 4.6)**. Lay out all parts in the order in which they're removed to prevent confusion during reassembly.

9   Clean all of the parts with brake system cleaner (available at auto parts stores), isopropyl alcohol or clean brake fluid. **Caution:** *Do not, under any circumstances, use a petroleum-based solvent to clean brake parts. If compressed air is available, use it to dry the parts thoroughly (make sure it's filtered and unlubricated).*

10   Inspect the master cylinder bore and piston for corrosion, scratches, nicks and score marks. If the piston or bore is damaged or worn, replace the master cylinder.

11   If you're installing a rebuild kit, use all of the new parts, regardless of the condition of the old ones.

12   Before reassembling the master cylinder, soak the piston and the rubber cup seals in clean brake fluid for ten or fifteen minutes. Lubricate the master cylinder bore with clean brake fluid, then carefully insert the piston and related parts in the reverse order of disassembly. Make sure the lips on the cup seals do not turn inside out when they are slipped into the bore.

13   Depress the piston, then install the snap-ring (make sure the snap-ring is correctly seated in the groove with the sharp edge facing out). Install the rubber dust boot (make sure the lip is seated properly in the groove).

Installation

14   Installation is the reverse of removal, with the following additions:

a) Tighten the mounting bolts to the torque listed in this Chapter's Specifications.

b) Using new sealing washers, install the brake hose banjo bolt and tighten it to the torque listed in this Chapter's Specifications.

15   Add the recommended brake fluid to the reservoir (see Chapter 1C) and bleed the air from the system (see Section 8).

7.4 Remove the mounting bolts (lower arrows); on installation, place the neck of the hose against the stop (upper arrow)

lever or pedal a few times, until no air bubbles can be seen floating up from the holes at the bottom of the reservoir. Doing this bleeds the air from the master cylinder end of the line. Reinstall the reservoir cover or cap.

5   Attach one end of the clear vinyl or plastic tubing to the brake caliper bleeder valve and submerge the other end in the brake fluid in the container **(see illustration 4.4 for the TT-R250 rear brake or the accompanying illustration for all others)**.

6   Check the fluid level in the reservoir. Do not allow the fluid level to drop below the lower mark during the bleeding process.

7   Carefully pump the brake lever or pedal three or four times and hold it while opening the caliper bleeder valve. When the valve is opened, brake fluid will flow out of the caliper into the clear tubing and the lever will move toward the handlebar or the pedal will move down.

8   Retighten the bleeder valve, then release the brake lever or pedal gradually. Repeat the process until no air bubbles are visible in the brake fluid leaving the caliper and the lever or pedal is firm when applied. Remember to add fluid to the reservoir as the level drops. Use only new, clean brake fluid of the recommended type. Never reuse the fluid lost during bleeding.

9   Be sure to check the fluid level in the master cylinder reservoir frequently.

10   Replace the reservoir cover or cap, wipe up any spilled brake fluid and check the entire system for leaks. **Note:** *If bleeding is difficult, it may be necessary to let the brake fluid in the system stabilize for a few hours (it may be aerated). Repeat the bleeding procedure when the tiny bubbles in the system have settled out.*

8   Brake system bleeding (disc brake models)

1   Bleeding the brakes is the process of removing all the air bubbles from the brake fluid reservoir, the lines and the brake caliper. Bleeding is necessary whenever a brake system hydraulic connection is loosened, when a component or hose is replaced, or when the master cylinder or caliper is overhauled. Leaks in the system may also allow air to enter, but leaking brake fluid will reveal their presence and warn you of the need for repair.

2   To bleed the brakes, you will need some new, clean brake fluid of the recommended type (see Chapter 1), a length of clear vinyl or plastic tubing, a small container partially filled with clean brake fluid, some rags and a wrench to fit the brake caliper bleeder valve.

3   Cover the fuel tank and other painted components to prevent damage in the event that brake fluid is spilled.

4   Remove the reservoir cover or cap and slowly pump the brake

9   Wheel and coupling bearing replacement

Wheel bearings

1   Wheel bearing replacement is the same as for RT100 and RT180 models, described in Chapter 6B **(see illustrations 2.3a through 2.3e, 2.7 or 2.8a through 2.8d)**. Be sure not to leave out any spacers when you install the wheel.

Rear coupling bearing

2   TT-R90 and XT350 models use a cush drive rear coupling. Its bearing is similar to the rear wheel bearings, but is mounted in the sprocket hub. Replacement is the same as for wheel bearings, described in Chapter 6B. Be sure not to forget the coupling collar when you reassemble and install the wheel, or the rear wheel bearings will be damaged when you tighten the axle nut.

TIRE CHANGING SEQUENCE - TUBED TIRES

 Deflate tire. After pushing tire beads away from rim flanges push tire bead into well of rim at point opposite valve. Insert tire lever next to valve and work bead over edge of rim.

Use two levers to work bead over edge of rim. Note use of rim protectors

 Remove inner tube from tire

When first bead is clear, remove tire as shown

 To install, partially inflate inner tube and insert in tire

Work first bead over rim and feed valve through hole in rim. Partially screw on retaining nut to hold valve in place.

 Check that inner tube is positioned correctly and work second bead over rim using tire levers. Start at a point opposite valve.

Work final area of bead over rim while pushing valve inwards to ensure that inner tube is not trapped.

10.8 Disconnect the return spring and remove the pedal snap-ring (arrow)

10 Brake cable, lever, rod and pedal - removal and installation

Front brake cable and lever (TT-R90 models)

1   Loosen the brake cable adjuster at the brake cam lever and disengage the cable end plug from the lever **(see illustrations 2.2a and 2.2b in Chapter 6B)**.

2   Trace the cable up to the handlebar and detach it from any clips or brackets **(see illustration 2.2d in Chapter 6B)**.

3   Loosen the handlebar adjuster all the way **(see illustration 5.1b in Chapter 1B)**, then rotate the cable and slip its end plug out of the lever.

4   Remove the throttle twist grip and throttle cable housing (see Chapter 4B). Remove the lever pivot bolt and nut and the lever bracket clamp bolt **(see illustration 10.4 in Chapter 6B)**. Slide the lever off the handlebar.

5   Installation is the reverse of removal, with the following additions:

 a) *Apply multi-purpose grease to the cable end plugs.*
 b) *Adjust the front brake and throttle cable (see Chapter 1).*

Rear brake rod and pedal

Refer to illustration 10.8

6   If you're working on a drum brake model, remove the rear brake adjuster nut from the brake rod, pull the rod out of its clevis pin,

remove the clevis pin from the brake cam lever and remove the spring from the rod **(see illustrations 2.7, 2.8a, 2.8b or 2.8d)**

7   If you're working on a disc brake model, disconnect the master cylinder pushrod from the pedal **(see illustration 7.3)**.

7   Unhook the brake pedal return spring.

8   Remove the pedal snap-ring or pivot **(see illustration 7.3 or the accompanying illustration)** and remove the pedal.

9   If you're working on a drum brake model, detach the rod from the pedal.

10   Installation is the reverse of removal, with the following additions:

 a) *Lubricate the rod end fittings and pedal shaft with multi-purpose grease.*
 b) *Adjust brake pedal freeplay (see Section 5 in Chapter 1B).*

11 Tires - removal and installation

To replace tubeless tires, refer to Chapter 6B. To replace tube-type tires, refer to the illustrations at the end of this chapter.

12 Tubes - repair

1   Tire tube repair requires a patching kit that's usually available from motorcycle dealers, accessory stores or auto parts stores. Be sure to follow the directions supplied with the kit to ensure a safe repair. Patching should be done only when a new tube is unavailable. Replace the tube as soon as possible. Sudden deflation can cause loss of control and an accident.

2   To repair a tube, remove it from the tire, inflate and immerse it in a sink or tub full of water to pinpoint the leak. Mark the position of the leak, then deflate the tube. Dry it off and thoroughly clean the area around the puncture.

3   Most tire patching kits have a buffer to rough up the area around the hole for proper adhesion of the patch. Roughen an area slightly larger than the patch, then apply a thin coat of the patching cement to the roughened area. Allow the cement to dry until tacky, then apply the patch.

4   It may be necessary to remove a protective covering from the top surface of the patch after it has been attached to the tube. Keep in mind that tubes made from synthetic rubber may require a special patch and adhesive if a satisfactory bond is to be achieved.

5   Before replacing the tube, check the inside of the tire to make sure the object that caused the puncture is not still inside. Also check the outside of the tire, particularly the tread area, to make sure nothing is projecting through the tire that may cause another puncture. Check the rim for sharp edges or damage. Make sure the rubber trim band is in good condition and properly installed before inserting the tube.

Chapter 7 Part A
Frame and bodywork
(PW50 and PW80 models)

Contents

1 General information

This Chapter covers the procedures necessary to remove and install the fenders and other body parts. Since many service and repair operations on these motorcycles require removal of the fenders and/or other body parts, the procedures are grouped here and referred to from other Chapters.

In the case of damage to plastic body parts, it is usually necessary to remove the broken component and replace it with a new (or used) one. The material that the fenders and other plastic body parts are composed of doesn't lend itself to conventional repair techniques. There are, however, some shops that specialize in "plastic welding", so it would be advantageous to check around before throwing the damaged part away.

Note: *When attempting to remove any body panel, first study the panel closely, noting any fasteners and associated fittings, to be sure of returning everything to its correct place on installation. In some cases, the aid of an assistant may be required when removing panels, to help avoid damaging the paint. Once the visible fasteners have been removed, try to lift off the panel as described but DO NOT FORCE the panel - if it will not release, check that all fasteners have been removed and try again. Where a panel engages another by means of lugs and grommets, be careful not to break the lugs or damage the bodywork. Remember that a few moments of patience at this stage will save you a lot of money in replacing broken panels!*

2 Seat/rear fender/side covers - removal and installation

PW50 models

Refer to illustrations 2.1a, 2.1b and 2.2

1   To detach the seat/rear fender/side cover assembly from PW50 models, remove the two retaining bolts and detach the inner rear fender **(see illustrations)**. Lift the seat and disengage its tab from the boss on the frame.

2.1a The PW50 seat/rear fender bolts are accessible from below (arrows) . . .

2.1b . . . undo the bolts and separate the seat from the rear fender . . .

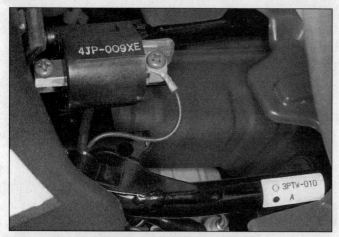

2.2 . . . then pull the seat back to disengage its tab from the frame boss

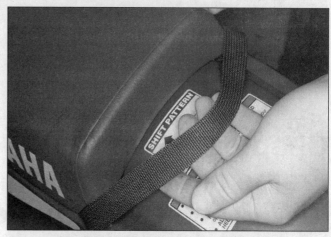

2.3a Pull the PW80 seat strap off the seat . . .

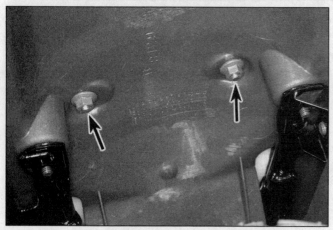

2.3b . . . remove the seat nuts from below (arrows) . . .

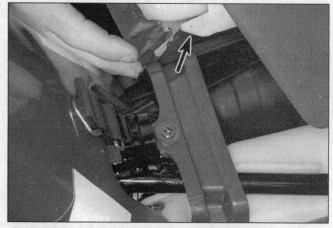

2.4 . . . then pull the seat back to disengage its tab (arrow) from the frame boss

2   Installation is the reverse of removal. Tighten the bolts securely, but don't overtighten them and strip the threads **(see illustration)**.

PW80 models

Refer to illustrations 2.3a, 2.3b, 2.4, 2.5, 2.6a and 2.6b

3   Pull back the strap, then remove the seat mounting nuts from beneath the rear fender **(see illustrations)**.

4   Lift the seat up and back to disengage its front tab from the frame mount **(see illustration)**.
5   To detach the inner fender from the rear fender, remove the three push pins **(see illustration)**.
6   To remove the fender and side covers, remove the seat strap bolts and the front mounting bolt **(see illustrations)**. Lift the fender/side cover assembly off the bike.
7   Installation is the reverse of the removal steps.

2.5 Remove the three push pins (arrows) to detach the PW80 rear fender from the inner fender

2.6a Unbolt the seat strap . . .

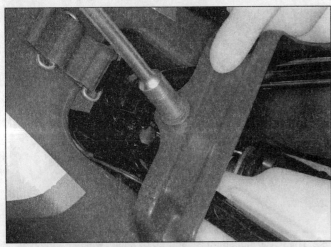

2.6b . . . and remove the front mounting bolt to free the rear fender

3.1a Here are the PW50 front fender brackets (lower arrows) and inner fender screws (upper arrows)

3.1b Remove the screws and lower the fender slot clear of the tab on the oil tank bracket

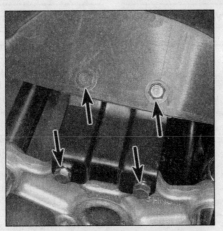

3.4a Here are the PW80 front fender bolts (upper arrows) and bracket bolts (lower arrows)

3.4b Remove the bolts and this screw to detach the front fender

3 Front fender - removal and installation

PW50 models

Refer to illustrations 3.1a and 3.1b

1   Remove the fender screws and washers to detach it from the fender stays **(see illustration)**. Pull the fender down to disengage its slot from the tang on the oil tank mounting bracket **(see illustration)**.
2   Remove the mounting screws to detach the inner fender **(see illustration 3.1a)**.
3   Installation is the reverse of the removal steps.

PW80 models

Refer to illustrations 3.4a and 3.4b

4   To detach the front fender from PW80 models, remove the two retaining bolts and the retaining screw **(see illustrations)**.
5   Installation is the reverse of removal. Tighten all bolts and screws securely, but don't overtighten them and strip the threads.

4 Footpegs - removal and installation

Refer to illustration 4.2

1   Support the bike securely so it can't be knocked over during this procedure.

2   To detach the footpeg from the pivot pin, note how the spring is installed, then remove the cotter pin, washer and pivot pin **(see illustration)**. Separate the footpeg from the motorcycle.
3   Installation is the reverse of removal, with the following addition: Use a new cotter pin and wrap its ends around the pivot pin.

4.2 Remove the cotter pin and washer and pull out the pivot pin (arrow) to free the footpeg

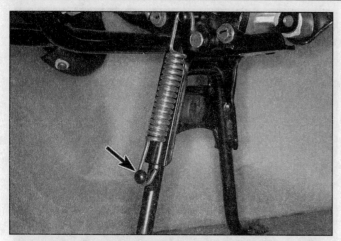

5.1 Unhook the spring from its pegs (PW50 lower peg shown)

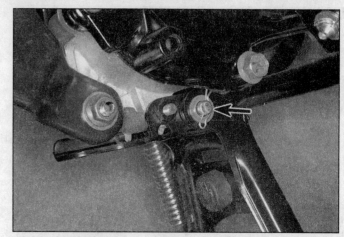

5.2 The PW50 sidestand is secured by a clip, washer and pivot pin (arrow)

5 Centerstand (PW50) and sidestand (PW80) – removal and installation

Refer to illustrations 5.1, 5.2 and 5.3
1   Support the bike securely. Unhook the centerstand or sidestand spring from its pegs **(see illustration)**.
2   If you're working on a PW50, remove the cotter pin and washer, then remove the pivot pin and take off the centerstand **(see illustration)**.
3   If you're working on a PW80, remove the sidestand pivot bolt **(see illustration)**.
4   Installation is the reverse of the removal steps.

6 Engine protector (PW80) – removal and installation

Refer to illustration 6.1
1   To remove the engine protector, undo its mounting screws and take it off the bike **(see illustration)**.
2   Installation is the reverse of the removal steps.

7 Frame - general information, inspection and repair

1   All models use a semi-double cradle frame made of round-section steel tubing.
2   The frame shouldn't require attention unless accident damage has occurred. In most cases, frame replacement is the only satisfactory remedy for such damage. A few frame specialists have the jigs and other equipment necessary for straightening the frame to the required standard of accuracy, but even then there is no simple way of assessing to what extent the frame may have been overstressed.
3   After the motorcycle has accumulated a lot of running time, the frame should be examined closely for signs of cracking or splitting at the welded joints. Corrosion can also cause weakness at these joints. Loose engine mount bolts can cause ovaling or fracturing to the mounting bolt holes. Minor damage can often be repaired by welding, depending on the nature and extent of the damage.
4   Remember that a frame that is out of alignment will cause handling problems. If misalignment is suspected as the result of an accident, it will be necessary to strip the machine completely so the frame can be thoroughly checked.

5.3 The PW80 sidestand is secured by a bolt (arrow)

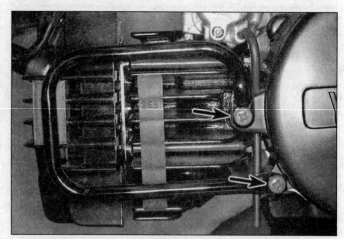

6.1 The PW80 engine protector is secured by these screws (arrows)

Chapter 7 Part B
Frame and bodywork
(RT100 and RT180 models)

Contents

1 General information

This Chapter covers the procedures necessary to remove and install the fenders and other body parts. Since many service and repair operations on these motorcycles require removal of the fenders and/or other body parts, the procedures are grouped here and referred to from other Chapters.

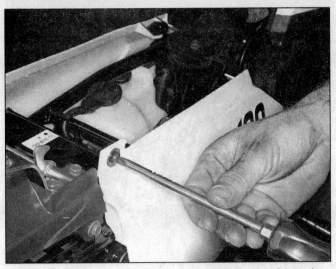

2.2 RT100 side covers are secured by a Phillips screw (shown) as well as pins and grommets

In the case of damage to plastic body parts, it is usually necessary to remove the broken component and replace it with a new (or used) one. The material that the fenders and other plastic body parts are composed of doesn't lend itself to conventional repair techniques. There are, however, some shops that specialize in "plastic welding", so it would be advantageous to check around before throwing the damaged part away.

Note: *When attempting to remove any body panel, first study the panel closely, noting any fasteners and associated fittings, to be sure of returning everything to its correct place on installation. In some cases, the aid of an assistant may be required when removing panels, to help avoid damaging the paint. Once the visible fasteners have been removed, try to lift off the panel as described but DO NOT FORCE the panel - if it will not release, check that all fasteners have been removed and try again. Where a panel engages another by means of lugs and grommets, be careful not to break the lugs or damage the bodywork. Remember that a few moments of patience at this stage will save you a lot of money in replacing broken panels!*

2 Side covers - removal and installation

Refer to illustration 2.2

1   The side covers are attached to the frame by pins on the inside of each side cover, which are pushed into grommets in the frame. RT100 models also use a Phillips screw in each cover. The right side cover on RT180 models is also secured by a lock knob.

2   If you're working on an RT100, remove the screw from the corner of the side cover **(see illustration)**.

3   If you're working on an RT180 right side cover, turn the lock knob

3.1 Push the latch levers (RT100, shown) or remove the bolt from each side (RT180) . . .

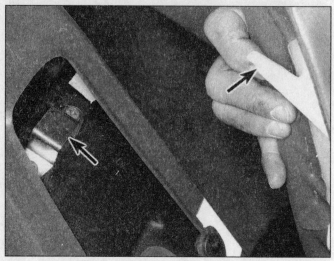

3.2 . . . and pull the seat backward and up; engage the hook with the bracket (arrows) on installation

clockwise a quarter-turn to release it.
4　Carefully pull the cover pins free of the grommets and lift the cover off.
5　Installation is the reverse of removal.

3　Seat - removal and installation

RT100 models

Refer to illustrations 3.1, 3.2 and 3.3
1　Push the latch lever to unhook the seat latches **(see illustration)**.
2　Lift the rear end of the seat and pull it backward to disengage the seat hook from the bracket on the frame **(see illustration)**.
3　If necessary, unbolt the seat latch bracket from the frame and rear fender **(see illustration)**.

RT180 models

4　Remove the side covers (see Section 2).
5　Remove the seat bolts.
6　Lift up the rear end of the seat and pull it backward to detach the front hook from the bracket in the frame.

All models

7　Installation is basically the reverse of removal. Push down on the front of the seat and slide the seat forward, making sure that the front hook is inserted into the frame bracket. If the seat is installed with the hook above the bracket and the bike is ridden like this, the hook will be damaged or broken off by the rider's weight.

4　Footpegs - removal and installation

Refer to illustrations 4.2a, 4.2b and 4.3
1　Support the bike securely so it can't be knocked over during this procedure.
2　On RT100 models, the footpegs and sidestand are a single assembly. To detach the footpeg/sidestand assembly, remove the two mounting bolts from each side **(see illustrations)**.
3　To detach a footpeg from an RT180 model, note how the spring is installed, then remove the cotter pin, washer and pivot pin **(see illustration)**.
4　Installation is the reverse of removal. On RT180 models, be sure to use a new cotter pin and wrap its ends around the pivot pin.

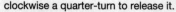

3.3 Unbolt the latch mechanism (RT100) from the frame and rear fender

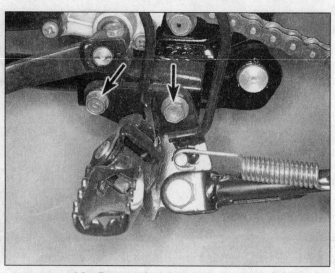

4.2a Remove the left bolts (arrows) . . .

4.2b . . . and the right bolts (arrows) and lower the
sidestand/footpeg bracket away from the bike

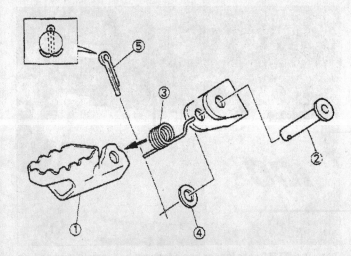

4.3 Footpeg assembly details (RT180 models)

1	*Footpeg*	3	*Spring*	5	*Cotter pin*
2	*Clevis pin*	4	*Washer*		

5   Number plate - removal and installation

Refer to illustration 5.1

1   To detach the number plate from an RT100, undo or cut the cable
ties **(see illustration)**.
2   To detach the number plate from an RT180 model, undo the integral tie, unscrew the retaining bolt and remove the washer.
3   Installation is the reverse of removal.

6   Front fender - removal and installation

Refer to illustrations 6.1a and 6.1b

1   Remove the four fender bolts **(see illustration)**. Lower the fender
away from the bike and remove the washers. If necessary, remove the
fender bracket on RT100 models **(see illustration)**.
2   Installation is the reverse of removal. Be sure to reinstall the
grommets in their correct locations. Tighten the bolts securely, but
don't overtighten them and strip the threads.

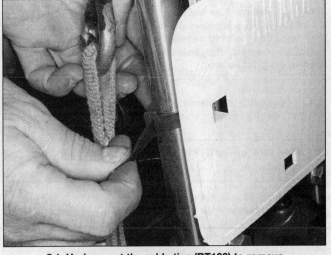

5.1 Undo or cut the cable ties (RT100) to remove
the number plate

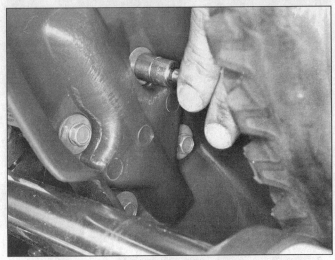

6.1a Remove the fender bolts from beneath the fender
(RT100 shown) . . .

6.1b . . . on RT100 models, unbolt the fender bracket from the
lower triple clamp if necessary

7.3a The RT100 rear fender has a forward bolt (arrow) and one on each side . . .

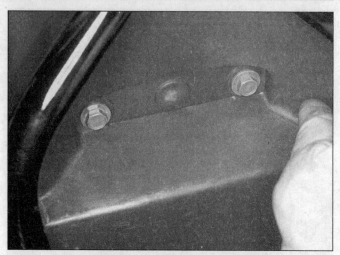

7.3b . . . and all models have two bolts accessible from beneath the fender (RT100 shown; RT180 similar)

7   Rear fender - removal and installation

Refer to illustrations 7.3a and 7.3b
1   Remove the side covers and the seat (see Sections 2 and 3).
2   Unbolt the forward section of the fender and take it out. The bolt(s) are accessible from below, so you may find it easier to remove the rear wheel for access.
3   Remove the main fender mounting bolts and take off the fender **(see illustrations)**.
4   Installation is the reverse of removal. Tighten the bolts securely, but don't overtighten them and strip the threads.

8   Fuel tank cover (RT100 models) - removal and installation

Refer to illustrations 8.2a and 8.2b
1   Remove the seat (see Section 3).
2   Remove one bolt and two screws from each side of the cover **(see illustrations)**, then take the cover off.
3   Installation is the reverse of the removal steps.

9   Frame - general information, inspection and repair

1   All models use a semi-double cradle frame made of round-section steel tubing.
2   The frame shouldn't require attention unless accident damage has occurred. In most cases, frame replacement is the only satisfactory remedy for such damage. A few frame specialists have the jigs and other equipment necessary for straightening the frame to the required standard of accuracy, but even then there is no simple way of assessing to what extent the frame may have been overstressed.
3   After the motorcycle has accumulated a lot of running time, the frame should be examined closely for signs of cracking or splitting at the welded joints. Corrosion can also cause weakness at these joints. Loose engine mount bolts can cause ovaling or fracturing to the mounting bolt holes. Minor damage can often be repaired by welding, depending on the nature and extent of the damage.
4   Remember that a frame that is out of alignment will cause handling problems. If misalignment is suspected as the result of an accident, it will be necessary to strip the machine completely so the frame can be thoroughly checked.

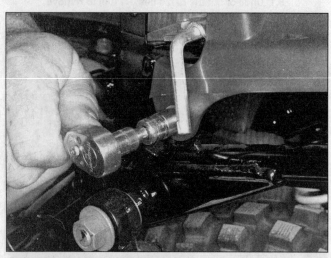

8.2a Remove the bolt from each side . . .

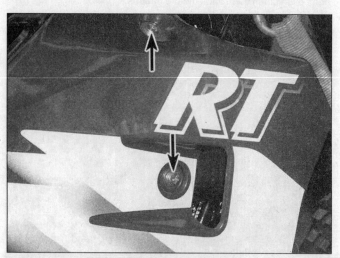

8.2b . . . and the screws (arrows)

Chapter 7 Part C
Frame and bodywork
(TT-R and XT models)

Contents

1 General information

This Chapter covers the procedures necessary to remove and install the fenders and other body parts. Since many service and repair operations on these motorcycles require removal of the fenders and/or other body parts, the procedures are grouped here and referred to from other Chapters.

In the case of damage to plastic body parts, it is usually necessary to remove the broken component and replace it with a new (or used) one. The material that the fenders and other plastic body parts are composed of doesn't lend itself to conventional repair techniques. There are, however, some shops that specialize in "plastic welding", so it would be advantageous to check around before throwing the damaged part away.

Note: *When attempting to remove any body panel, first study the panel closely, noting any fasteners and associated fittings, to be sure of returning everything to its correct place on installation. In some cases,* *the aid of an assistant may be required when removing panels, to help avoid damaging the paint. Once the visible fasteners have been removed, try to lift off the panel as described but DO NOT FORCE the panel - if it will not release, check that all fasteners have been removed and try again. Where a panel engages another by means of lugs and grommets, be careful not to break the lugs or damage the bodywork. Remember that a few moments of patience at this stage will save you a lot of money in replacing broken panels!*

2 Seat - removal and installation

TT-R90 models

1 Remove two nuts from under the seat.
2 Lift the rear end of the seat and pull it backward to disengage the seat hook from the bracket on the frame.
3 Installation is the reverse of the removal steps.

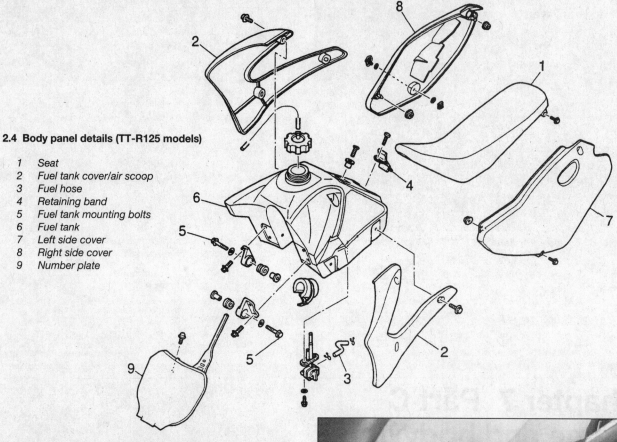

2.4 Body panel details (TT-R125 models)

1	Seat
2	Fuel tank cover/air scoop
3	Fuel hose
4	Retaining band
5	Fuel tank mounting bolts
6	Fuel tank
7	Left side cover
8	Right side cover
9	Number plate

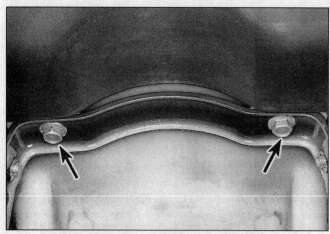

2.8 Unscrew the mounting bolts (arrows) . . .

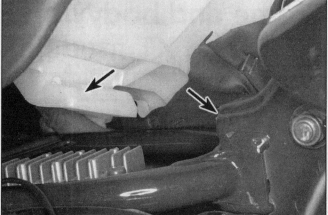

**2.9 . . . and pull the seat rearward to disengage its tab
from the bracket (arrows)**

TT-R125 and XT350 models

Refer to illustration 2.4

4   Remove the side covers (Section 3).
5   Remove one bolt from each side of the seat **(see illustration)**.
6   Lift the rear end of the seat and pull it backward to disengage the seat hook from the bracket on the frame.
7   Installation is the reverse of the removal steps.

TT-R225, TT-R250 and XT225 models

Refer to illustrations 2.8 and 2.9

8   Remove two bolts from under the seat **(see illustration)**.
9   Lift the rear end of the seat and pull it backward to disengage the

seat hook from the bracket on the frame **(see illustration)**.
10   Installation is the reverse of the removal steps.

---

3   Side covers - removal and installation

TT-R90 models

1   The side covers are part of an assembly the includes the rear fender.
2   Remove the seat (Section 2).
3   Remove one screw at the center front of the side cover/fender unit. Carefully pull the retaining pin on each side loose from its grommet, then lift the unit off the bike.
4   Installation is the reverse of the removal steps.

4.3 Footpeg assembly details (TT-R250 shown; others similar)

A   Footpeg cotter pin, washer and pivot pin
B   Footpeg bracket mounting bolts
C   Engine guard mounting bolt

TT-R125, TT-R225, XT225, TT-R250 models

5   Remove one screw at the bottom center of the side cover, then carefully pull the retaining pins (one at the front and one at the rear of the cover) loose from their grommets.
6   Remove the other cover in the same way.
7   Installation is the reverse of the removal steps.

XT350 models

8   Carefully pull the three retaining pins (one at the front and one at the rear of the cover) loose from their grommets.
9   Remove the other cover in the same way.
10   Installation is the reverse of the removal steps.

4   Footpegs and sidestand - removal and installation

Refer to illustrations 4.3 and 4.4

1   Support the bike securely so it can't be knocked over during this procedure.
2   To detach a footpeg, note how the spring is installed, then remove the cotter pin, washer and pivot pin.
3   To remove the footpeg bracket, unscrew its bolts and take it off **(see illustration)**.
4   To remove the sidestand, support the bike securely. Unhook the sidestand spring, remove the pivot bolt and take the sidestand off **(see illustration)**.
5   Installation is the reverse of removal. If you removed a footpeg, be sure to use a new cotter pin and wrap its ends around the pivot pin.

5   Number plate - removal and installation

1   To detach the number plate, undo the integral tie, unscrew the retaining bolt and remove the washer.
2   Installation is the reverse of removal.

6   Front fender - removal and installation

Refer to illustration 6.1

1   Remove the four fender bolts **(see illustration)**. Lower the fender away from the bike and remove the washers.

4.4 Support the bike, then unhook the spring and remove the sidestand pivot bolt

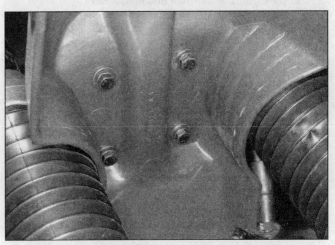

6.1 Remove the fender bolts from beneath the fender (TT-R225 shown) . . .

2   Installation is the reverse of removal. Be sure to reinstall the grommets in their correct locations. Tighten the bolts securely, but don't overtighten them and strip the threads.

7   Rear fender (except TT-R90 models) - removal and installation

1   Remove the seat and side covers (see Sections 2 and 3).
2   Unbolt the fender and take it out. The bolt(s) are accessible from below, so you may find it easier to remove the rear wheel for access.
3   Remove the main fender mounting bolts and take off the fender.
4   Installation is the reverse of removal. Tighten the bolts securely, but don't overtighten them and strip the threads.

8   Fuel tank cover (TT-R90 and TT-R125 models) – removal and installation

1   Remove the seat (see Section 3).
2   Remove one bolt from each cover **(see illustration 2.4)**. Carefully pull the retaining pins loose from their grommets, then take the cover off.
3   Installation is the reverse of the removal steps.

9.1a Remove the skid plate mounting bolt . . .

9.1b . . . and pull the mounting grommets out of their brackets (arrow)

9   Engine guard – removal and installation

Refer to illustrations 9.1a and 9.1b

1   Some models use a skid plate under the engine. To remove this, unscrew the bolt at the front, then pull the mounting grommets forward out of their brackets **(see illustrations)**.

2   Other models use a guard bar to protect the engine. To remove this, simply unbolt it and take it off **(see illustration 4.3)**.

3   Installation is the reverse of the removal steps.

10   Frame - general information, inspection and repair

1   All models use a semi-double cradle frame made of round-section steel tubing.

2   The frame shouldn't require attention unless accident damage has occurred. In most cases, frame replacement is the only satisfactory remedy for such damage. A few frame specialists have the jigs and other equipment necessary for straightening the frame to the required standard of accuracy, but even then there is no simple way of assessing to what extent the frame may have been overstressed.

3   After the motorcycle has accumulated a lot of running time, the frame should be examined closely for signs of cracking or splitting at the welded joints. Corrosion can also cause weakness at these joints. Loose engine mount bolts can cause ovaling or fracturing to the mounting bolt holes. Minor damage can often be repaired by welding, depending on the nature and extent of the damage.

4   Remember that a frame that is out of alignment will cause handling problems. If misalignment is suspected as the result of an accident, it will be necessary to strip the machine completely so the frame can be thoroughly checked.

Color code

B: Black	**G**: Green	**Br**: Brown
R: Red	**W**: White	**O**: Orange
L: Blue	**Ch**: Chocolate	**Br**: Brown
P: Pink	**Dg**: Dark green	
Y: Yellow	**Sb**: Sky blue	

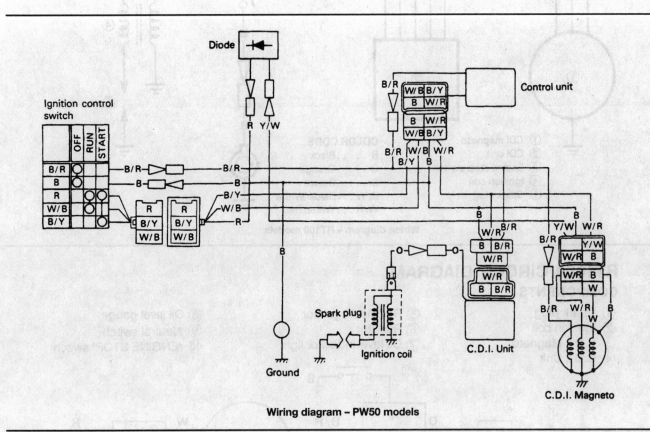

Wiring diagram – PW50 models

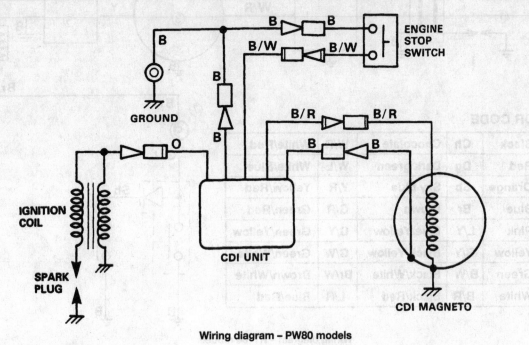

Wiring diagram – PW80 models

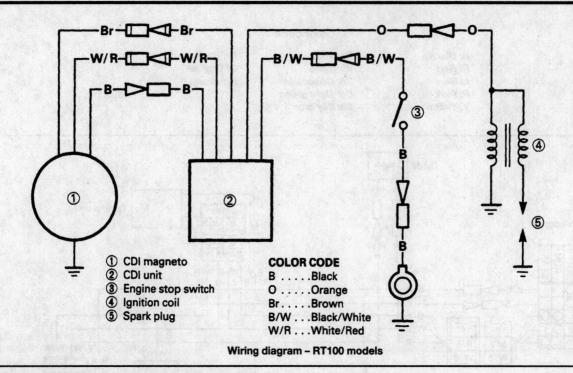

① CDI magneto
② CDI unit
③ Engine stop switch
④ Ignition coil
⑤ Spark plug

COLOR CODE
B . . . . .Black
O . . . . .Orange
Br . . . . Brown
B/W . . .Black/White
W/R . . .White/Red

Wiring diagram – RT100 models

RT180A CIRCUIT DIAGRAM
COMPONENTS

① Spark plug
② Ignition coil
③ C.D.I. Magneto
④ C.D.I. Unit

⑤ Rectifier/regulator
⑥ Resistor
⑦ Oil level indicator light

⑧ Oil level gauge
⑨ Neutral switch
⑩ "ENGINE STOP" switch

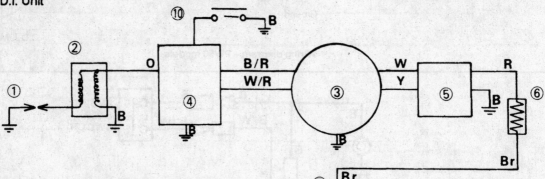

COLOR CODE

B	Black	Ch	Chocolate	W/R	White/Red
R	Red	Dg	Dark green	W/L	White/Blue
O	Orange	Sb	Sky blue	Y/R	Yellow/Red
L	Blue	Br	Brown	G/R	Green/Red
P	Pink	L/Y	Blue/Yellow	G/Y	Green/Yellow
Y	Yellow	B/Y	Black/Yellow	G/W	Green/White
G	Green	B/W	Black/White	Br/W	Brown/White
W	White	B/R	Black/Red	L/R	Blue/Red

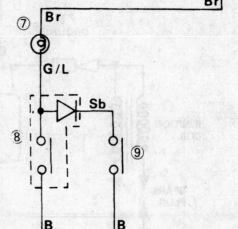

Wiring diagram – RT180 models

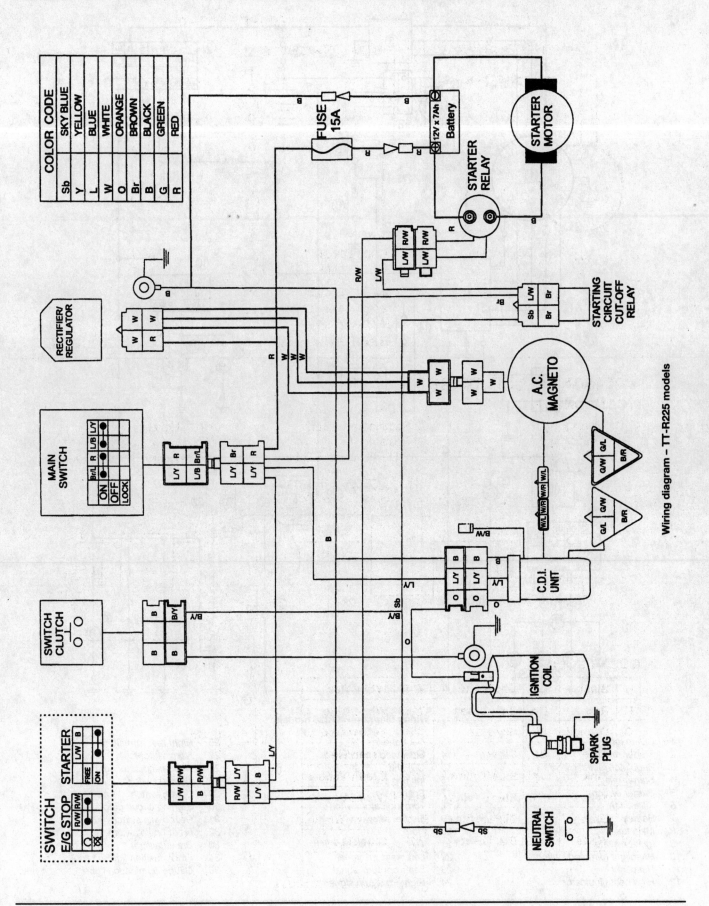

Wiring diagram – TT-R225 models

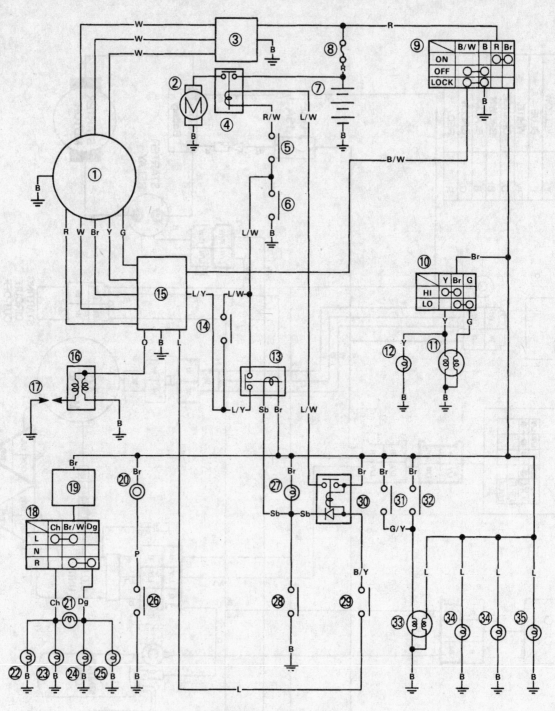

Wiring diagram – XT225 models

1 CDI magneto	13 Neutral relay	25 Right rear turn signal
2 Starter motor	14 Sidestand switch	26 Horn switch
3 Regulator/rectifier	15 CDI unit	27 Neutral indicator light
4 Starter relay	16 Ignition coil	28 Neutral switch
5 Starter switch	17 Spark plug	29 Clutch switch
6 Kill switch	18 Turn indicator switch	30 Starting circuit cutoff relay
7 Battery	19 Flasher relay	31 Rear brake switch
8 Main fuse	20 Horn	32 Front brake switch
9 Ignition switch	21 Turn signal indicator light	33 Brake/taillight
10 Headlight (dimmer) switch	22 Left rear turn signal	34 Front position light
11 Headlight	23 Left front turn signal	35 Gauge illumination light
12 High beam indicator	24 Right front turn signal	

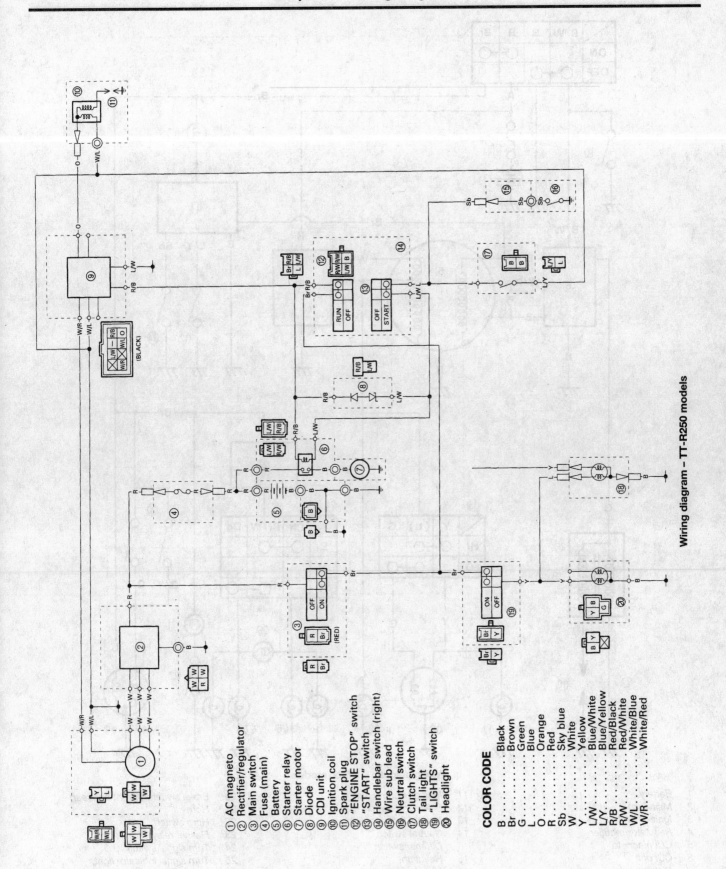

Wiring diagram – TT-R250 models

1 AC magneto
2 Rectifier/regulator
3 Main switch
4 Fuse (main)
5 Battery
6 Starter relay
7 Starter motor
8 Diode
9 CDI unit
10 Ignition coil
11 Spark plug
12 "ENGINE STOP" switch
13 "START" switch
14 Handlebar switch (right)
15 Wire sub lead
16 Neutral switch
17 Clutch switch
18 Tail light
19 "LIGHTS" switch
20 Headlight

COLOR CODE

B	Black
Br	Brown
G	Green
L	Blue
O	Orange
R	Red
Sb	Sky blue
W	White
Y	Yellow
L/W	Blue/White
L/Y	Blue/Yellow
R/B	Red/Black
R/W	Red/White
W/L	White/Blue
W/R	White/Red

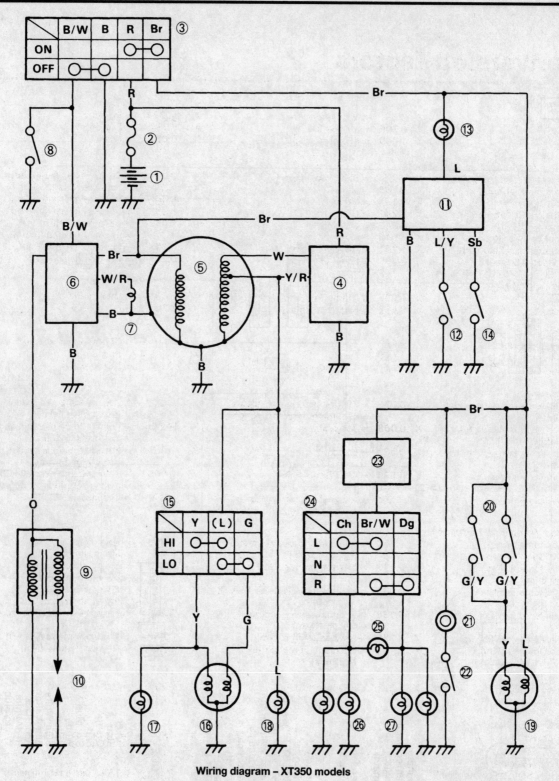

Wiring diagram – XT350 models

1 Battery	11 Ignition control unit	20 Brake switches (front and rear)
2 Main fuse	12 Sidestand switch	21 Horn
3 Ignition switch	13 Neutral indicator light	22 Horn switch
4 Regulator/rectifier	14 Neutral switch	23 Flasher relay
5 CDI magneto	15 Dimmer switch	24 Turn signal switch
6 CDI unit	16 Headlight	25 Turn signal indicator light
7 Pick-up coil	17 High beam indicator	26 Left turn signals
8 Kill switch	18 Gauge illumination lights	27 Right turn signals
9 Spark plug	19 Brake/taillight	

Conversion factors

Length (distance)

Inches (in)	X 25.4 = Millimetres (mm)	X 0.0394 = Inches (in)
Feet (ft)	X 0.305 = Metres (m)	X 3.281 = Feet (ft)
Miles	X 1.609 = Kilometres (km)	X 0.621 = Miles

Volume (capacity)

Cubic inches (cu in; in³)	X 16.387 = Cubic centimetres (cc; cm³)	X 0.061 = Cubic inches (cu in; in³)
Imperial pints (Imp pt)	X 0.568 = Litres (l)	X 1.76 = Imperial pints (Imp pt)
Imperial quarts (Imp qt)	X 1.137 = Litres (l)	X 0.88 = Imperial quarts (Imp qt)
Imperial quarts (Imp qt)	X 1.201 = US quarts (US qt)	X 0.833 = Imperial quarts (Imp qt)
US quarts (US qt)	X 0.946 = Litres (l)	X 1.057 = US quarts (US qt)
Imperial gallons (Imp gal)	X 4.546 = Litres (l)	X 0.22 = Imperial gallons (Imp gal)
Imperial gallons (Imp gal)	X 1.201 = US gallons (US gal)	X 0.833 = Imperial gallons (Imp gal)
US gallons (US gal)	X 3.785 = Litres (l)	X 0.264 = US gallons (US gal)

Mass (weight)

Ounces (oz)	X 28.35 = Grams (g)	X 0.035 = Ounces (oz)
Pounds (lb)	X 0.454 = Kilograms (kg)	X 2.205 = Pounds (lb)

Force

Ounces-force (ozf; oz)	X 0.278 = Newtons (N)	X 3.6 = Ounces-force (ozf; oz)
Pounds-force (lbf; lb)	X 4.448 = Newtons (N)	X 0.225 = Pounds-force (lbf; lb)
Newtons (N)	X 0.1 = Kilograms-force (kgf; kg)	X 9.81 = Newtons (N)

Pressure

Pounds-force per square inch (psi; lbf/in²; lb/in²)	X 0.070 = Kilograms-force per square centimetre (kgf/cm²; kg/cm²)	X 14.223 = Pounds-force per square inch (psi; lbf/in²; lb/in²)
Pounds-force per square inch (psi; lbf/in²; lb/in²)	X 0.068 = Atmospheres (atm)	X 14.696 = Pounds-force per square inch (psi; lbf/in²; lb/in²)
Pounds-force per square inch (psi; lbf/in²; lb/in²)	X 0.069 = Bars	X 14.5 = Pounds-force per square inch (psi; lbf/in²; lb/in²)
Pounds-force per square inch (psi; lbf/in²; lb/in²)	X 6.895 = Kilopascals (kPa)	X 0.145 = Pounds-force per square inch (psi; lbf/in²; lb/in²)
Kilopascals (kPa)	X 0.01 = Kilograms-force per square centimetre (kgf/cm²; kg/cm²)	X 98.1 = Kilopascals (kPa)

Torque (moment of force)

Pounds-force inches (lbf in; lb in)	X 1.152 = Kilograms-force centimetre (kgf cm; kg cm)	X 0.868 = Pounds-force inches (lbf in; lb in)
Pounds-force inches (lbf in; lb in)	X 0.113 = Newton metres (Nm)	X 8.85 = Pounds-force inches (lbf in; lb in)
Pounds-force inches (lbf in; lb in)	X 0.083 = Pounds-force feet (lbf ft; lb ft)	X 12 = Pounds-force inches (lbf in; lb in)
Pounds-force feet (lbf ft; lb ft)	X 0.138 = Kilograms-force metres (kgf m; kg m)	X 7.233 = Pounds-force feet (lbf ft; lb ft)
Pounds-force feet (lbf ft; lb ft)	X 1.356 = Newton metres (Nm)	X 0.738 = Pounds-force feet (lbf ft; lb ft)
Newton metres (Nm)	X 0.102 = Kilograms-force metres (kgf m; kg m)	X 9.804 = Newton metres (Nm)

Vacuum

Inches mercury (in. Hg)	X 3.377 = Kilopascals (kPa)	X 0.2961 = Inches mercury
Inches mercury (in. Hg)	X 25.4 = Millimeters mercury (mm Hg)	X 0.0394 = Inches mercury

Power

Horsepower (hp)	X 745.7 = Watts (W)	X 0.0013 = Horsepower (hp)

Velocity (speed)

Miles per hour (miles/hr; mph)	X 1.609 = Kilometres per hour (km/hr; kph)	X 0.621 = Miles per hour (miles/hr; mph)

Fuel consumption*

Miles per gallon, Imperial (mpg)	X 0.354 = Kilometres per litre (km/l)	X 2.825 = Miles per gallon, Imperial (mpg)
Miles per gallon, US (mpg)	X 0.425 = Kilometres per litre (km/l)	X 2.352 = Miles per gallon, US (mpg)

Temperature

Degrees Fahrenheit = (°C x 1.8) + 32   Degrees Celsius (Degrees Centigrade; °C) = (°F - 32) x 0.56

*It is common practice to convert from miles per gallon (mpg) to litres/100 kilometres (l/100km), where mpg (Imperial) x l/100 km = 282 and mpg (US) x l/100 km = 235

Fraction/Decimal/Millimeter Equivalents

DECIMALS TO MILLIMETERS

Decimal	mm	Decimal	mm
0.001	0.0254	0.500	12.7000
0.002	0.0508	0.510	12.9540
0.003	0.0762	0.520	13.2080
0.004	0.1016	0.530	13.4620
0.005	0.1270	0.540	13.7160
0.006	0.1524	0.550	13.9700
0.007	0.1778	0.560	14.2240
0.008	0.2032	0.570	14.4780
0.009	0.2286	0.580	14.7320
0.010	0.2540	0.590	14.9860
0.020	0.5080	0.600	15.2400
0.030	0.7620	0.610	15.4940
0.040	1.0160	0.620	15.7480
0.050	1.2700	0.630	16.0020
0.060	1.5240	0.640	16.2560
0.070	1.7780	0.650	16.5100
0.080	2.0320	0.660	16.7640
0.090	2.2860	0.670	17.0180
0.100	2.5400	0.680	17.2720
0.110	2.7940	0.690	17.5260
0.120	3.0480	0.700	17.7800
0.130	3.3020	0.710	18.0340
0.140	3.5560	0.720	18.2880
0.150	3.8100	0.730	18.5420
0.160	4.0640	0.740	18.7960
0.170	4.3180	0.750	19.0500
0.180	4.5720	0.760	19.3040
0.190	4.8260	0.770	19.5580
0.200	5.0800	0.780	19.8120
0.210	5.3340	0.790	20.0660
0.220	5.5880	0.800	20.3200
0.230	5.8420	0.810	20.5740
0.240	6.0960	0.820	21.8280
0.250	6.3500	0.830	21.0820
0.260	6.6040	0.840	21.3360
0.270	6.8580	0.850	21.5900
0.280	7.1120	0.860	21.8440
0.290	7.3660	0.870	22.0980
0.300	7.6200	0.880	22.3520
0.310	7.8740	0.890	22.6060
0.320	8.1280	0.900	22.8600
0.330	8.3820	0.910	23.1140
0.340	8.6360	0.920	23.3680
0.350	8.8900	0.930	23.6220
0.360	9.1440	0.940	23.8760
0.370	9.3980	0.950	24.1300
0.380	9.6520	0.960	24.3840
0.390	9.9060	0.970	24.6380
0.400	10.1600	0.980	24.8920
0.410	10.4140	0.990	25.1460
0.420	10.6680	1.000	25.4000
0.430	10.9220		
0.440	11.1760		
0.450	11.4300		
0.460	11.6840		
0.470	11.9380		
0.480	12.1920		
0.490	12.4460		

FRACTIONS TO DECIMALS TO MILLIMETERS

Fraction	Decimal	mm	Fraction	Decimal	mm
1/64	0.0156	0.3969	33/64	0.5156	13.0969
1/32	0.0312	0.7938	17/32	0.5312	13.4938
3/64	0.0469	1.1906	35/64	0.5469	13.8906
1/16	0.0625	1.5875	9/16	0.5625	14.2875
5/64	0.0781	1.9844	37/64	0.5781	14.6844
3/32	0.0938	2.3812	19/32	0.5938	15.0812
7/64	0.1094	2.7781	39/64	0.6094	15.4781
1/8	0.1250	3.1750	5/8	0.6250	15.8750
9/64	0.1406	3.5719	41/64	0.6406	16.2719
5/32	0.1562	3.9688	21/32	0.6562	16.6688
11/64	0.1719	4.3656	43/64	0.6719	17.0656
3/16	0.1875	4.7625	11/16	0.6875	17.4625
13/64	0.2031	5.1594	45/64	0.7031	17.8594
7/32	0.2188	5.5562	23/32	0.7188	18.2562
15/64	0.2344	5.9531	47/64	0.7344	18.6531
1/4	0.2500	6.3500	3/4	0.7500	19.0500
17/64	0.2656	6.7469	49/64	0.7656	19.4469
9/32	0.2812	7.1438	25/32	0.7812	19.8438
19/64	0.2969	7.5406	51/64	0.7969	20.2406
5/16	0.3125	7.9375	13/16	0.8125	20.6375
21/64	0.3281	8.3344	53/64	0.8281	21.0344
11/32	0.3438	8.7312	27/32	0.8438	21.4312
23/64	0.3594	9.1281	55/64	0.8594	21.8281
3/8	0.3750	9.5250	7/8	0.8750	22.2250
25/64	0.3906	9.9219	57/64	0.8906	22.6219
13/32	0.4062	10.3188	29/32	0.9062	23.0188
27/64	0.4219	10.7156	59/64	0.9219	23.4156
7/16	0.4375	11.1125	15/16	0.9375	23.8125
29/64	0.4531	11.5094	61/64	0.9531	24.2094
15/32	0.4688	11.9062	31/32	0.9688	24.6062
31/64	0.4844	12.3031	63/64	0.9844	25.0031
1/2	0.5000	12.7000	1	1.0000	25.4000

Index